Learning
Microsoft® Office
Professional Version
Word ▪ Excel ▪ PowerPoint ▪ Access

Blanc/Vento/Singleton/Toliver

ACKNOWLEDGEMENTS

TO OUR FAMILIES: Alan, Pamela and Jaime
Jim, Jimmy and Mindi, Chris and Dirk

We would like to thank the following authors for their contributions to this book:
Pam Toliver of Soft Spec, Inc. in Monclaire, VA; Michael Singleton of East Williston, NY; and Harriet Goldstein of Albuquerque, NM.

Acknowledgments

Managing Editor	*Editors*	*Technical Editors*	*Assistant Editors*
Kathy Berkemeyer,	Jennifer Harris,	Carol Havlisek	Rebecca Fiala
Willowbook, IL	New York, NY	Long Beach, NY	Boston, MA
	Rosemary O'Connell,	Glenn Davis	Stephanie Finucane
	New York, NY	Maplewood, NJ	New York, NY

Layout and Design
Jeff Kurek
New York, NY

TABLE OF CONTENTS

TABLE OF CONTENTS

Continued...

WORD FILES

Exercise	Filename	On Disk As	Solution File
1	TRY	-	-
2	TRYAGAIN	-	-
3	LETTER	-	-
4	BLOCK	-	-
5	PERSONAL	-	-
SUMMARY	OPEN	-	WOPEN.1AS
6 (1)	TRY	WTRY.6	WTRY.6S
7 (2)	TRYAGAIN	WTRYAGAI.7	WTRYIT.7S
8	DIVE	WDIVE.8	WDIVE.8S
9 (3)	LETTER	WLETTER.9	WLETTER.9S
10 (4)	BLOCK	WBLOCK.10	WBLOCK.10S
11	OPEN/TRIT/	WOPEN.11	WOPEN.11S
(SUMMARY 1)	PERSONAL		
SUMMARY	REGRETS	WREGRET.2A	WREGRET.2AS
12	COMPANY	-	-
13	ESTATE	WESTATE.13	WESTATE.13S
14	GLOBAL	WGLOBAL.14	WGLOBAL.14S
15	CAFÉ	WCAFE.15	WCAFE.15S
16	DESIGN	WDESIGN.16	WDESIGN.16S
SUMMARY	COLOR	WCOLOR.3A	WCOLOR.3AS
17	DIVE	WDIVE.17	WDIVE.17S
18	BULLETIN	WBULLETI.28	WBULLETI.18S
19	TIPS	WTIPS.19	WTIPS.19S
20 (18)	BULLETIN	WBULLETI.20	WBULLETI.20S
21 (19)	TIPS	WTIPS.21	WTIPS.21S
SUMMARY		-	WDIVE.4AS
(17, 18)	DIVE	-	-
22	SOD	WSOD.22	WSOD.22S
23	BRANCH	WBRANCH.23	WBRANCH.23S
24 (20, 18)	BULLETIN	WBULLETI.24	WBULLETI.24S
25	CARS	WCARS.25	-
26	GREEN	WGREEN.26	-
SUMMARY		-	TRENDS.5AS
27	NYC	WNYC.27	WNYC.27S
28	PREVIEW	WPREVIEW.28	WPREVIEW.28S
29	VOYAGE	WVOYAGE.29	WVOYAGE.29S
30	USA	WUSA.30	WUSA.30S
31	PREVIE/USA	WPREVIEW.31	WPREVIEW.28S
		WUSA.31	WUSA.31S
SUMMARY		WBRAZIL.6A	WBRAZIL.6AS
32	HOTELS/DIVE/	WHOTELS.32	HOTELS.32S
	GLOBAL		-
		-	WDIVE.32S
		WGLOBAL.32	WGLOBAL.32S
33	HOMES	WHOMES.33	WHOMES.33S
34	WILL	WWILL.34	WWILL.34S
35	CLOSING/	-	-
	BEGIN/LINE	-	-
36	SETTLE	-	WSETTLE.36S
SUMMARY	WORKOUT	-	WWORKOUT.7AS
37	COCOA	WCOCOA.37	WCOCOA.37S
38	GOODBYE	WGOODBYE.38	WGOODBYE.38S
39	PHONE	-	WPHONE.39S
40	AGELESS/	-	-
	CRUISE	-	WAGELESS.40S
41	AGELESS/	-	-
	CRUISE	WAGELESS.41	WAGELESS.41S
		WCRUISE.41	WCRUISE.41S
42	MICRO	-	WMICRO.43S
		-	WMICRO.43S
SUMMARY	BALI	WBALI.8A	WBALI.8AS
43	HUG	-	WHUGMN.43S
		-	WHUGDAT.43S
44	DUE	-	WDUEMN.43S
		-	WDUEDAT.43S
45	ERRORMN	-	WERRORMN.45S
	ERRORDAT	-	-
46	COASTAL	-	WCOASTAL.46S
47	JOURNEY	-	WJOURNEY.47S
48	ANNOUNCE	-	-
49	FAX	-	WFAX.49S
50		-	-
SUMMARY	ALUMNI	-	ALUMNI10.AS

EXCEL FILES

Exercise	Filename	On Disk As	Solution File
1		-	-
2	DAILY	-	EDAILY.2S
3	SALARY	-	ESALARY.3S
4	PARTS	-	EPARTS.4S
5	PRICE	-	EPRICE.5S
6	PRICE	EPRICE06.XLS	EPRICE.6S
7	SALARY	ESALAR07.XLS	ESALARY.7S
8	DAILY	EDAILY8.XLS	ESALARY.8S
9	UNIV	EUNIV09.XLS	EUNIX.9S
10	PRICE	EPRICE10.XLS	EPRICE.10S
11	WOOD	EWOOD11.XLS	EWOOD.11S
12	SALARY	ESALAR12.XLS	ESALARY.12S
13	WOOD	EWOOD13.XLS	EWOOD.13S
14	TRIPS	ETRIPS14.XLS	ETRIPS.14S
15	IS	EIS15.XLS	EIS.15S
16	TEST	-	ETEST.16S
17	SALARY	ESALAR17.XLS	ESALRY.17S
18	IS	EIS18.XLS	EIS.18S
19	IS	EIS19.XLS	EIS.19S
			EANA.19S
20	SALARY	ESALAR20.XLS	ESALNEW.20S
21	WOOD	EWOOD21.XLS	EWOOD.21S
22	WOOD	EWOOD22.XLS	
	WOODSUM	-	EWOODSUM.22S
23	IS	EIS23.XLS	EIS.23S
	ISQTRS	-	-
24	SALETMP	ESALTM.XLS	ESALETMP.24S
	SUM	ESUM24.XLS	ESAM.24S
	CAROL	-	ECAROL.24S
	JOHN	-	EJOHN.24S
	SUMM	-	ESAMU.24S
			ESUMU.24S
25	SALNEW	ESALNW25.XLS	ESALNEW.25S
26	TEST	ETEST26.XLS	ETEST.26S
	TESTSUM	-	ETESTSUM.26S

Continued...

Exercise	Filename	On Disk As	Solution File
27	TESTSUM	ETESTSUM.27.XLS	ETESTSUM.27S
28	INCR	EINCR28.XLS	EINCR.28S
29	MARKET	EMARK29.XLS	EMARKET.29S
30	AGE	EAGE30.XLS	EAGE.30S
31	TABLE	ETABLE31.XLS	ETABLE.31S
32	TABLE	ETABLE32.XLS	ETABLE.32S
			EHOME.32S
33	AGE	EAGE33.XLS	EAGE.33
34	REWARD	EREWAR34.XLS	EREWARD.34S
35	HS	EHS35.XLS	EHS.35S
36	HS	EHS36.XLS	EHS.36S
37	HS	EHS37.XLS	EHS.37
38	NJDATA	ENJDATA.38	EJNDATA.38S

ACCESS FILES

Exercise	Filename	On Disk As	Solution File
1	COMPANY	-	ACOMPANY.1S
2	COMPANY	ACOMPANY.2	ACOMPANY.2S
3	HUGCLUB	-	AHUGCLUB.3S
4	COMPANY	ACOMPANY.4	ACOPMANY.4S
5	CLUBS	-	ACLUBS.5S
6	COMPANY	ACOMPANY.6	ACOMPANY.65
7	CLUBS	ACLUBS.7	ACLUBS.7S
8	COMPANY	ACOMPANY.8	ACOMPANY.8S
9	HUGCLUB	AHUGCLUB.9	AHUGCLUB.9S
10	CLUBS	ACLUBS.10	ACLUBS.10S
11	COMPANY	ACOMPANY.11	ACOMPANY.11S
12	COMPANY	ACOMPANY.12	ACOMPAN1.12S
		ACOMPAN2.12	ACOMPAN2.12S
13	HUGCLUB	AHUGCLUB.13	AHUGCLUB.13S
14	COMPANY	ACOMPANY.14	ACOMPANY.14S
15	HUGCLUB	AHUGCLUB.15	AHUGCLUB.15S
16	CLUBS	ACLUBS.16	ACLUB.16S
17	JANESHOP	AJANSHP2.17	AJANSHP1.17S
		-	AJANSHP2.17S
18	HUGCLUB	AHUGCLUB.18	AHUGCLUB.18S
19	COMPANY	ACOMPANY.19	ACOMPANY.19S
20	COMPANY	ACOMPANY.20	ACOMPANY.20S
21	COMPANY	ACOMPANY.21	ACOMPANY.21S
22	COMPANY	ACOMPANY.22	ACOMPANY.22S
23	COMPANY	ACOMPANY.23	ACOMPANY.23S
24	COMPANY	ACOMPANY.24	ACOMPANY.24S
25	JANESHOP	AJANSHOP.25	AJANSHOP.25S
26	COMPANY	ACOMPANY.26	ACOMPANY.26S
27	COMPANY	ACOMPANY.27	ACOMPANY.27S
28	COLLEGE	-	ACOLLEGE.28S

POWERPOINT FILES

Exercise	Filename	On Disk As	Solution File
1	KIT	-	PKIT.IS
	FLAGSHIP	-	PFLAGSHI.1S
2	KIT	PKIT.2	PKIT.2S
	FLAGSHIP	PFLAGSHI.2	PFLAGSHI.2S
3	FLAGSHIP	PFLAGSHI.3	PFLAGSHI.3S
	KIT	PKIT.3	PKIT.3S
4	KIT	PKIT.4	PKIT.4S
	FLAGSHIP	PFLAGSHI.4	PFLAGSHI.4S

Exercise	Filename	On Disk As	Solution File
5	FOOD	-	PFOOD.5S
SUM1	BRAZIL	-	PBRAZIL.1AS
6	KIT	PKIT.6	PKIT.6S
7	BRAZIL	PBRAZIL.7	PBRAZIL.7S
8	FLAGSHIP	PFLAGSHI.8	PFLAGSHI.8S
9	FOOD	PFOOD.9	PFOOD.9S
10	FLAGSHIP	PFLAGSHI.10	PFLAGSHI.10S
11	KIT	PKIT.11	PKIT.11S
SUM2	INVEST	-	PINVEST.2AS
12	BRAZIL	PBRAZIL.12	PRBAZIL.12S
13	FOOD	PFOOD.13	PFOOD.13S
14	FLAGSHIP	PFLAGSHI.14	PFLAGSHI.14S
15	FOOD	PFOOD.15	PFOOD.15S
SUM3	INVEST	PINVEST.3a	PINVEST.3AS

INTEGRATION FILES

Exercise	Filename	On Disk As	Solution File
1	DAILY	IDAILY.XLS	-
	UNIV	IUNIV.XLS	-
	INCR	IINCR.XLS	-
	REWARD	IREWARD.XLS	-
	BULLETIN	IBULLETN.DOC	-
2	BRANCH	IBRANCH.DOC	IBRSUM.2S
			(WORD)
	WOODSUM	IWOODSUM.XLS	-
3	SOD	ISOD.DOC	ISODQTR.3S
	ISQTRS	IISQTRS.XLS	(WORD)
4	SODQTR	ISODQTR.DOC	ISODQTR.4S
	ISQTRS	IISQTR3S.XLS	(WORD)
5	JANESHOP	IJANSHOP.MDB	ISTOCKE.5S
		-	(EXCEL)
6	HUGMN	IHUGMN.DOC	IHUGLETS.6S
	HUGCLUB	IHUGCLUB.MDB	(WORD)
7	GREEN	IGREEN.DOC	IGREENPP.7S
		ISQTRCHT.XLS	(POWERPOINT)
8	GREENPP.PPT	ILANMEM.DOC	ILANDMEM.8S
		IGREENPP.PPT	(WORD)
		IREVMEM.DOC	ICONTACT.8S
		-	(WORD)
		-	IREVMEM.8S
			(WORD)
9 SUMMARY	COLLEGE.MDB	IPRESENT.DOC	IPRESENT.9S
		IBRAZIL.PPT	IREPLY.9S
		IREPLY.DOC	INVITMER.9S
		IINFLAT.XLS	(ALL WORD)
		IINVITE.DOC	-
		ICOLLEGE.MDB	-

INTRODUCTION

ABOUT MICROSOFT® OFFICE

Microsoft® Office Professional version combines Word, Excel, Access®, PowerPoint® and Mail, five popular software packages into one office suite. Each of these tools can be used separately or they can be used together to produce professional looking documents.

> ✓ Note: If you have the standard version of Microsoft Office, you will not get Microsoft Access. Microsoft Mail is not covered in this book.

In Microsoft® Office Professional version, you get the following programs:

Microsoft Word, a word processing program, used for creating and editing documents.

Microsoft Excel, a spreadsheet program, used for analysis and graphing of numerical data.

Microsoft Access, a database program, used for organizing and sorting information.

Microsoft PowerPoint, a presentation graphics program, used for creating visual presentations.

Microsoft Mail, an electronic mail program, used for sending and receiving mail over a network.

The information created in one tool can be shared with the other tools. For instance, a spreadsheet created in Excel, or a database created in Access, can be easily incorporated into a memo or letter which was created in Word. Data created in Word, Excel or Access can be incorporated into PowerPoint. Files created in any one tool can be transmitted using Mail.

ABOUT THIS BOOK

Learning Microsoft Office will teach you to use four tools in the Microsoft Office Suite on an IBM PC or compatible computer. In addition, you will learn to integrate applications from one tool into another.

Each lesson in this book explains concepts, provides numerous exercises to apply those concepts and illustrates the necessary keystrokes or mouse actions to complete the exercises Lesson summary exercises are provided to challenge and reinforce the concepts learned.

After completing the exercises in this book, you will be able to use the basic features of each tool in the Microsoft Office suite with ease.

HOW TO USE THIS BOOK

Each exercise contains four parts:

- **Notes** explain the Microsoft® Office concept and application being introduced.

- **Exercise Directions** tell how to complete the exercise.

- **Exercise** lets you apply the new concept.

- **Keystroke and Mouse Procedures** outline the keystrokes or mouse actions necessary to complete the exercise.

> ✓ Note: Keystrokes and mouse actions are provided only when a new concept is being introduced. Therefore, if you forget the keystroke/mouse procedures necessary to complete a task, you can use the the Help feature (explained in the Introductory Basics section) or the book's index to find the procedures.

Before you begin working on the exercises in any Office application, you will need to read the first chapter on Office Basics. This chapter will explain the screens, the Help feature, working in Windows, Toolbars, menus and other necessary preliminary information.

INTRODUCTION

Universal Functions

Toolbars, commands, keystrokes, and menus are similar in each application. Some functions operate the same way in Word, Excel, Access, and PowerPoint. We have chosen to call these operations Universal Functions. They will be noted by a globe graphic 🌐 when they are introduced in each section.

The Data and Solutions Disks

Data and solutions disks may be purchased separately from DDC Publishing. You may use the data files on the data disk to complete an exercise without keyboarding lengthy text or data. However, exercise directions are given for both data disk and non-data disk users. Exercise directions will include a keyboard icon to direct non-data disk users as well as a disk icon to direct data disk users. For example, a typical direction might read: Open ⌨ **TRY** or 💾 **WTRY.3**.

The data disk contains Word, Excel, Access, and PowerPoint files. Each filename is prefaced with the letter of the tool in which it was created and contains the exercise number as the filename extension. Thus, **WTRY.3** indicates a Word file, exercise 3; **ETRY.3** indicates an Excel file, exercise 3.

In order to maintain the integrity of the data disk, make a backup copy of the data disk, open data files as Read Only, and use the Save As feature to save the file under a new name *(see explanation of Read Only and Save As in the Word Section, Lesson 7).*

The solutions disk may be used for you to compare your work with the final version or solution on disk.

A directory of data disk and solutions disk files are listed in the Log of Exercises.

The Instructor's Guide

While this text can be used as a self-paced learning book, a comprehensive instructor's guide is available. The instructor's guide contains the following:

- Lesson objectives
- Exercise objectives
- Related vocabulary
- Points to emphasize
- Exercise settings

Features of This Text

- Lesson Objectives

- Exercise Objectives

- Application concepts and vocabulary

- A Log of Exercises, which lists filenames in exercise number order

- A Directory of Files, which lists filenames alphabetically and the exercise numbers in which they were used

- Exercises to apply each concept

- End of lesson summary exercises to review and test your knowledge of lesson concepts

- Keystrokes/mouse actions necessary to complete each application

CHAPTER 1

MICROSOFT OFFICE

Exercises 1-3

- Starting Office

- Microsoft Office Manager

- Learning Office

- The Mouse and the Keyboard

- Office Windows

- Menus, Toolbars, and Commands

- Select Menu Items

- Options in a Dialog Box

- The Zoom Option

- Change Window Display

- Get Help

EXERCISE

- STARTING OFFICE - MICROSOFT OFFICE MANAGER
- LEARNING OFFICE - THE MOUSE AND THE KEYBOARD
- WORKING WITH OFFICE MANAGER

NOTES:

Starting Office

■ Microsoft® Office provides a full range of powerful tools that may be used independently or in an integrated fashion to efficiently complete all your office applications. Microsoft® Office includes Microsoft Word (word processor tool), Microsoft Excel® (spreadsheet tool), Microsoft PowerPoint® (presentation tool), and Microsoft Access® (database tool).

■ After the software is installed, a program group for Microsoft Office and a toolbar, called the **Microsoft Office Manager** or MOM, will appear on your window display.

Microsoft Office Manager

■ The Microsoft Office Manager Toolbar displays icons (symbols) that represent each tool or office application. The MOM toolbar is displayed at all times so that you can access any tool from within windows or switch to another tool from any Office application. The toolbar contains icons for Word, Excel®, PowerPoint®, Access®, Find File, and Microsoft® Office.

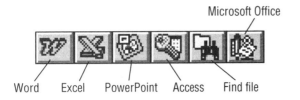

Microsoft Office

Word   Excel   PowerPoint   Access   Find file

■ The Microsoft Office Manager Toolbar may be customized to add other applications you may have installed.

Learning Office

■ All the Microsoft Office applications have similar toolbars, menus, commands, and dialog boxes. The skills learned in one tool, such as accessing the toolbars, moving around the screen, using the menus and dialog boxes, and utilizing the online help features, are used consistently in all Office applications.

Mouse and Keyboard

■ You may use the mouse or the keyboard to choose commands and perform tasks.

Using the Mouse

■ When the mouse is moved on the tabletop, a corresponding movement of the mouse pointer occurs on the screen. The mouse pointer changes shape depending on the tool being used, the object it is pointing to, and the action it will be performing. The mouse pointer will not move if the mouse is lifted up and placed back on the tabletop.

■ The mouse terminology and the corresponding actions described below will be used throughout the book:

Point to	Move the mouse (on the tabletop) so the pointer touches a specific item.
Click	Point to item and quickly press and release the left mouse button.
Right-click	Point to item and press and release the right mouse button.

Double-click Point to item and press the left mouse button twice in rapid succession.

Drag Point to item and press and hold down the left mouse button while moving the mouse. When the item is in the desired position, release the mouse button to place the item.

Right-Drag Point to item and press and hold down the right mouse button while moving the mouse. When the item is in the desired position, release the mouse button to place the item.

- All references to the use of mouse buttons in this book refer to the left mouse button unless otherwise directed.

- Specific mouse shapes will be discussed within each application as they are activated.

Using the Keyboard

- In addition to the alphanumeric keys found on most typewriters, computers contain additional keys:

  - **Function keys** (F1 through F10 or F12) perform special functions and are located across the top of an enhanced keyboard (12 function keys) or on the side (10 function keys).

  - **Modifier keys** (Shift, Alt, Ctrl) are used in conjunction with other keys to select certain commands or perform actions. To use a modifier key with another key, you must hold down the modifier key while tapping the other key.

  - **Numeric keys**, found on keyboards with a number pad, allow you to enter numbers quickly. When Num Lock is ON, the number keys on the pad are operational, as is the decimal point. When Num Lock is OFF, the cursor control keys (Home, PgUp, End, PgDn) are active. The numbers on the top row of the keyboard are always active.

  - **Escape key** (Esc) is used to cancel some actions, commands, menus, or an entry.

- **Enter keys** (there are two on most keyboards) are used to complete an entry of data in some applications.

- **Directional arrow keys** are used to move the active screen insertion point as determined by the tool being used.

- Keyboard templates that apply to each tool will be presented within the appropriate section of the text.

Working with Microsoft Office Manager

- **To identify each icon on the MOM toolbar**, place the mouse pointer on the icon. A ToolTips bubble will appear with the name or function of the button.

- **To start an application with Office Manager**, click on the application button.

- **To start a second application**, hold down Ctrl and click the application button.

- **To arrange or tile two applications on the screen**, hold down Shift and click the application button you want to place next to the current application.

- **To exit an application**, hold down Alt and click the application button.

- **To exit Microsoft Office Manager**, click the Microsoft Office icon, and choose Exit from the Office menu.

✓ *Note:*   *The MOM toolbar buttons are accessed using the mouse. However, when the Microsoft Office icon is clicked, a drop-down menu appears.*

There are numerous ways to access commands. Menus, Toolbars, and Commands will be detailed in Exercise 2.

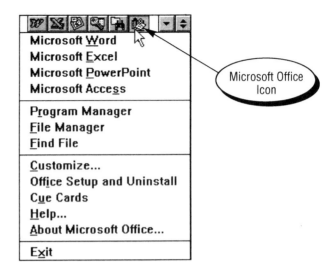

EXERCISE DIRECTIONS:

1. Roll the mouse up, down, left, and right on the tabletop or the mousepad.

2. Place the mouse pointer on each tool icon in the Office Manager Toolbar to read the ToolTips notation for each button.

3. Click on the Word icon.

    ✓ *Note the screen, menus, toolbars, and the Tip of the Day.*

4. Hold down the Alt key and click on the Word button to close the application.

5. Click on the Excel icon.

    ✓ *Note the screen, menus, and toolbars.*

6. Hold down the Alt key and click on the Excel button to close the application.

7. Click on the PowerPoint icon.

    ✓ *Note the screen, menus, and toolbars.*

8. Hold down the Alt key and click on the PowerPoint button to close the application.

9. Click on the Access icon.

    ✓ *Note the screen, menus, and toolbars.*

10. Hold down the Alt key and click on the Access button to close the application.

11. Click on the Microsoft Office icon. Click on the Microsoft Word command.

12. To open and view the Excel tool at the same time, hold down the Shift key and click on the Excel button.

13. Quit both tools using the Alt key and the appropriate buttons.

14. Exit Microsoft Office.

NEXT EXERCISE

EXERCISE 2

- **OFFICE WINDOWS** ▪ **MENUS, TOOLBARS, AND COMMANDS**
- **SELECT MENU ITEMS** ▪ **OPTIONS IN A DIALOG BOX**
- **THE ZOOM OPTION**

NOTES:

Office Windows

■ When you access each Office application, you will see its opening screen. The common parts of all the Office application windows will be discussed using the Word screen. The specific screen parts for each Office tool will be detailed in the appropriate section of this book.

- The **(3) application window minimize button, maximize,** and **restore buttons** are located on the right side of the application window title bar. Clicking the minimize button shrinks the window to an icon. Clicking the maximize button enlarges the window to a full screen. Once the window has been maximized, the maximize button changes to the restore button. Clicking the restore button restores the window to its previous size.

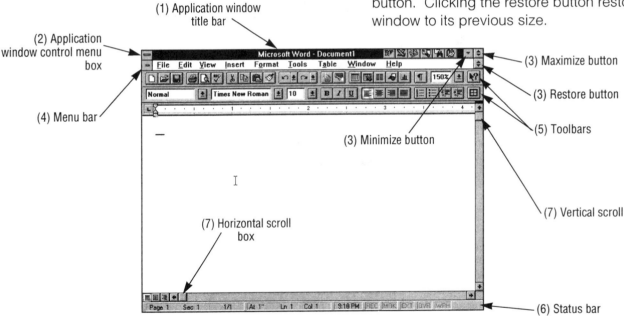

(1) Application window title bar
(2) Application window control menu box
(4) Menu bar
(3) Maximize button
(3) Restore button
(5) Toolbars
(3) Minimize button
(7) Vertical scroll
(7) Horizontal scroll box
(6) Status bar

✓ *Note the following universal window parts:*

- The **(1) application window title bar**, located at the top of the application window, displays the program name (Microsoft Word, Excel, etc.,) and may also display the name of an opened file if the window is maximized. You can drag the title bar to move the window, or double-click it to maximize the window.

- The **(2) application window control menu box**, located to the left of the application window title bar, can be opened to access a drop-down menu from which you can choose commands that control the window.

- The **(4) menu bar**, located below the title bar, displays menu names from which drop-down menus may be accessed.

- The **(5) toolbars**, located below the menu bar, contain buttons, each of which has a small picture or icon displayed on it that can be used to select commands quickly.

- Pointing to and resting the pointer on a toolbar button displays the tool's name, while an explanation of the button is displayed on the status bar.

- The **(6) status bar**, located at the bottom of the window, displays information about the current mode or operation.

- The **(7) horizontal** and **vertical scroll bars** are used to move the screen view horizontally or vertically. The **scroll box** on the vertical scroll bar can be dragged up or down to move more quickly toward the beginning or end of the document.

Menus, Toolbars, and Commands

- The menu bar and toolbars may be used to access commands. Each application contains two toolbars. The **standard toolbar**, located below the main menu bar, contains icons that accomplish many common tasks easily, like saving and printing a file.

WORD STANDARD TOOLBAR

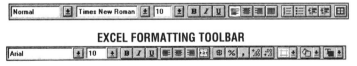

EXCEL STANDARD TOOLBAR

- The **formatting toolbar**, located below the standard toolbar, contains icons that easily change the appearance of data. While each application contains both toolbars with many of the same icons, the toolbars also contain buttons unique to that tool.

WORD FORMATTING TOOLBAR

EXCEL FORMATTING TOOLBAR

- You may display the Toolbars at the top of your screen, or you may hide one or both of them to make room on your screen for text or data.

■ **To select a command from a toolbar:**

- Use the mouse to point to a toolbar button and click once.

■ **To access menu bar items:**

- Use the mouse to point to a menu item on the menu bar and click once, or
- Press Alt + *underlined letter* in the menu name.

✓ Note the drop-down that appears when *View* is selected in Word.

✓ Note the drop-down menu that appears when *Insert* is selected in Excel.

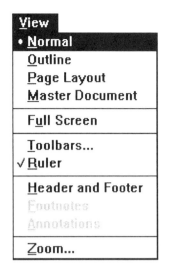

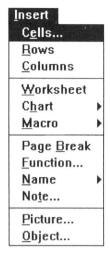

■ **To select a command from the drop-down menu:**

- Use the mouse to point to the command on the drop-down menu and click once, or

- Press the underlined letter in the command name, or

- Use the up or down arrow key to highlight the command, then press Enter.

- Some menu options are dimmed, while others appear black. **Dimmed options** are not available for selection at this time, while black options are.

- A **check mark** next to a drop-down menu item means the option is currently selected.

- A menu item followed by an **arrow** ▶ opens a **submenu** with additional choices.

- A menu item followed by an **ellipsis** (...) indicates that a **dialog box** (which requires you to provide additional information to complete a task) will be forthcoming.

■ Procedures for completing a task will be illustrated as follows throughout this book. Mouse actions are illustrated on the left, while keystroke procedures are illustrated on the right and keyboard shortcut keys are illustrated below the heading. Use whichever method you find most convenient.

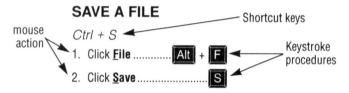

SAVE A FILE

Options in a Dialog Box

■ A **dialog box** contains different ways to ask you for information:

- The **title bar** identifies the title of the dialog box.

- The **text box** is a location where you type information.

- **Command buttons** carry out actions described on the button. When command names have an ellipsis following them, they will access another dialog box.

- The **drop-down list** is marked with a down arrow. Clicking the drop-down list arrow accesses a short list of options from which a choice should be made.

- An **increment box** provides a space for typing a value. An up or down arrow (usually to the right of the box) gives you a way to select a value with the mouse.

- A **named tab** is used to display options related to the tab's name in the same dialog box.

- **Option buttons** are small circular buttons marking options appearing as a set. You may choose only one option from the set. A selected option button contains a dark circle.

- A **check box** is the small square box where options may be selected or deselected. An "X" in the box indicates the option is selected. If several check boxes are offered, you may select more than one.

- A **list box** displays a list of items from which selections can be made. A list box may have a scroll bar that can be used to show hidden items in the list.

- A **scroll bar** is a horizontal or vertical bar providing scroll arrows and a scroll box that can be dragged up or down to move more quickly through the file.

  ✓ Note the labeled parts in the dialog boxes below:

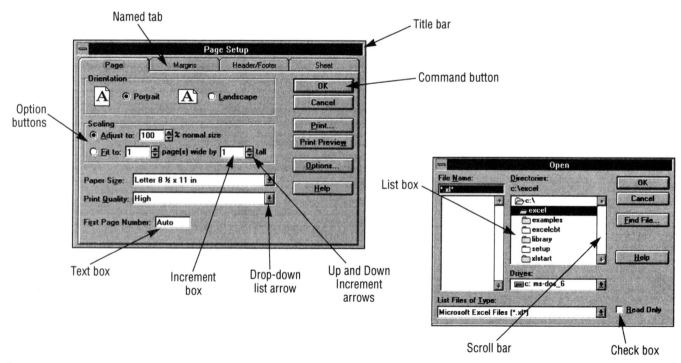

The Zoom Option

- The **View** menu contains a **Zoom** option that allows you to set the magnification of the data on the screen. When **Zoom** is selected, the following dialog box appears:

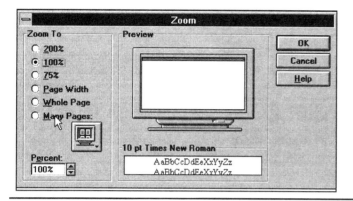

- By clicking an option button, you can display the text at **200%**, **100%**, **75%**, or fill the **Page Width**. However, the zoom control box |100% ▼| located on the Standard Toolbar, lets you easily set the magnification of text in a document without opening the menu or dialog box.

✓ Note: To work through the exercises in this text, the Standard and Formatting Toolbars as well as the Ruler must be displayed on your screen. If these items are not displayed, follow the keystrokes below.

EXERCISE DIRECTIONS:

1. Access the **Word** application.
2. Select **View** from the menu bar.
3. Deselect **Ruler**.
   ✓ Note the change in the screen.
4. Select **View**; select **Toolbars**.
5. Deselect Standard.
   ✓ Note the change in the screen.
6. Select **View** and re-select **Ruler** to return the ruler to the screen.
7. Select **View**; select **Toolbars**. Re-select Standard to return toolbar to the screen.
8. Make the following changes:
   - Deselect **Ruler**.
   - Select **Full** Screen.
   ✓ Note the changes.
9. Restore the screen to the default view by clicking on the Full Screen icon in the lower right corner and by selecting the **Ruler** option.
10. Type your name on the screen.
11. Select **View** from the menu bar.
12. Select **Zoom**.

13. Select the **200%** magnification option.
14. Select **OK**.
    ✓ Note the change.
15. Repeat steps 8-11 using the 75% option.
16. Repeat steps 8-9 and use the increment box to set the magnification at 150%.
17. Return to 100% magnification.
18. Click on the Zoom control box arrow on the toolbar and change to 25%.
19. Return to 100% magnification.
20. Select **Page Setup** from the **File** menu.
21. Select the **Paper Size** tab.
22. Use the **Paper Size** drop-down list to select Legal 8 1/2 x 14 in.
    ✓ Note the change in the illustration.
23. Return the paper size to the Letter 8 1/2 x 11 in. default setting.
24. Click on each tab to note the available print options.
25. Click on Cancel.
26. Exit Word.

ZOOM

To specify a custom zoom:

1. Click in on Standard toolbar, where 100% is the current setting.
2. Type zoom percentage (10-400) ...*number*
3. Press Enter.

To select a zoom:

1. Click drop-down arrow in ..... |100% ▼| on Standard Toolbar, where 100% is the current setting.
2. Select zoom percentage.

HIDE/DISPLAY TOOLBARS

1. Click **View** menu .... |Alt|+|V|
2. Click **Toolbars** .... |T|

   The Toolbars dialog box will display.

3. Click **Toolbars** list box .... |Alt|+|T|
4. Select toolbars .... |↑↓| then Space to display
5. Choose from the following toolbar options:
   - **Color buttons** .... |Alt|+|O|
   - **Large buttons** .... |Alt|+|L|

   - **Show Tooltips** .... |Alt|+|S|
6. Select **OK** .... |Enter|

HIDE/DISPLAY RULERS (WORD)

Toggles display of horizontal and vertical rulers

1. Click **View** .... |Alt|+|V|
2. Click **Ruler** .... |R|

EXERCISE

■ CHANGE WINDOW DISPLAYS ■ GET HELP

NOTES:

Change Window Displays

■ The **minimize** and **maximize** buttons on the application window title bar may be used to shrink and enlarge the application window on the desktop.

■ Once the application window has been maximized, the maximize button is replaced with a restore button. Use the restore button to return the window to its previous size.

Get Help

■ Help may be accessed by clicking **Help** on the menu bar or by pressing F1. Each application's Help menu has some commands in common; in addition, each application has tool-specific help commands.

> ✓ Note: If you are in a Help window, F1 will close the window and open the How to Use Help screen.

> ✓ Note the following Help menu from Microsoft Word and Microsoft Excel and the discussion of the standard commands.

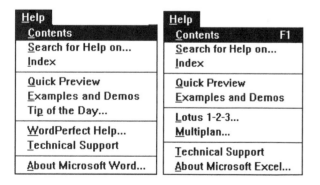

- **Contents** provides the overall contents of the Help system. Green text items with a solid underline may be clicked on to access a submenu of further information on the topic. Green text items with a dotted underline may be clicked on to obtain definitions of terms.

- **Search for Help on...** provides a Search dialog box whereby a topic or word is entered to search the Help system for information on the task. This feature will show you Help system titles and information related to your search item.

- **Index** provides an alphabetical listing of all Help topics.

- **Quick Preview** displays a menu from which you can select interactive introductory lessons.

- **Examples and Demos** displays a menu from which you can select examples of topics and practice lessons with feedback.

- **WordPerfect Help...\Lotus 1-2-3...\ Multiplan...** provides information about the Word or Excel equivalents to WordPerfect, Lotus 1-2-3, or Multiplan.

- **Technical Support** provides information on common questions and tells you where you can get technical support.

- **About Microsoft Word.../About Microsoft Excel...** provides system status information.

To Exit Help:

✓ *Note:* *It may be necessary to click Cancel or Close or press Escape to close a dialog box before exiting help.*

■ Double-click the Help window control menu box.

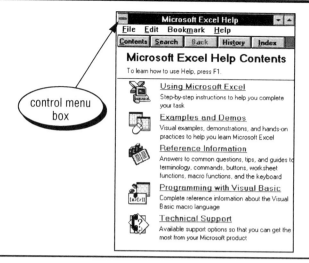

control menu box

EXERCISE DIRECTIONS:

1. Access the Excel application.

2. Select **Help** from the menu bar.

3. Select the **Contents** option. Do the following:
   - Click Using Microsoft Excel from the list.
   - Click **Back** button to return to the Contents menu.
   - Double-click the Help window control menu box to exit Help.

4. Select **Help** from the menu bar.

5. Select the **Search for Help on** option. Do the following:
   - Type *maximize.*
   - Select the topic **Maximize** button in the list.
   - Select **Show Topics** button.
   - Select **Go To** button.

   ✓ *Note definitions.*

   - Double-click the Help window control menu box to exit Help.

6. Select the **Help** menu.
   - Select **Index**.

   ✓ *Note the list of Help topics.*

   - Click the M button.

   ✓ *Note the list of Help topics beginning with the letter M.*

   - Double-click the Help window control menu box to Exit Help.

7. Select the **Help** menu.
   - Select the **Quick Preview** option.

   ✓ *Note the contents.*

   - Click **Return** to Microsoft Excel button.

8. Select the **Help** menu.
   - Select the **Examples and Demos** option.

   ✓ *Note the options.*

   - Click the **Close** button.

9. Click the minimize button on the title bar (which contains the software name).

   ✓ *Note the Microsoft Excel icon on the Program Manager desktop.*

10. Double-click the Microsoft Excel icon to return to the program.

11. If the window is not maximized, click the maximize button on the title bar (which contains the software name).

   ✓ *Note the Excel window fills the screen.*

12. Click the restore button on the title bar (which contains the software name).

   ✓ *Note the Excel window returns to its previous size.*

13. If the window is not maximized, click the maximize button on the workbook window title bar.

14. Click the restore button on the menu bar to return the workbook window to its previous size.

15. Click the minimize button on the workbook window title bar.

   ✓ *Note the workbook icon in the Excel window.*

16. Double-click the icon to return the workbook to a window.

17. Exit Excel.

GET HELP

F1

1. Click **Help** menu..................... **Alt** + **H**

2. Click desired option:

   - **Contents** .... **C**
   - **Search for Help on** .... **S**
   - **Index** .... **I**
   - **Quick Preview** .... **Q**
   - **Examples and Demos** .... **E**
   - **Lotus 1-2-3** .... **L**
   - **Multiplan** .... **M**
   - **Technical Support** .... **T**
   - **About Microsoft Excel** .... **A**

To exit Help:

✓ *It may be necessary to click Cancel or Close, or press Escape to close a dialog box before exiting Help.*

Double-click Help window .... ⊟

   OR

   Press **Alt + F** .... **Alt** + **F4**

MAXIMIZE A WINDOW

Click **Maximize** button .... ▲

OR

1. Click **Application Window** .... ⊟
   Control Menu box

2. Click **Maximize** .... **X**

✓ *After a window is maximized, the maximize button is replaced with the restore button.*

RESTORE A MAXIMIZED WINDOW

Click **Maximize** button .... ◆

✓ *The restore button of a maximized workbook window is located to the right of the menu bar.*

OR

Click **Document Control box** .... ⊟

✓ *The control menu box of a maximized workbook window is located to the left of the menu bar.*

OR

1. Click **Application Window** .... ⊟
   Control Menu box

2. Click **Restore** .... **R**

✓ *After a window is restored, the restore button is replaced with the maximize button.*

MINIMIZE A WINDOW

Click **Minimize** button .... ▼

   OR

Click **Document Control** box .... ⊟

✓ *The control menu box of a maximized workbook window is located to the left of the menu bar.*

   OR

1. Click **Application Window** .... ⊟
   Control Menu box

2. Click **Minimize** .... **N**

RESTORE A MINIMIZED WINDOW

Double-click desired window icon.

   OR

1. Click **Application** ..... **Alt** + **Space**
   icon to open its
   control menu.

2. Click **Restore** .... **R**

CHAPTER 2

LESSON 1

CREATING AND PRINTING DOCUMENTS

Exercises 1-5

- The Word Window

- Default Settings

- If You Make an Error

- Creating a New Document

- Saving a New Document

- Closing a Document

- Using the Tab Key

- AutoCorrect

- Spelling

- Insertion Point Movements

- Creating a Business Letter

- Creating a Personal Business Letter

- The Date Feature

- Uppercase Mode

- Previewing a Document

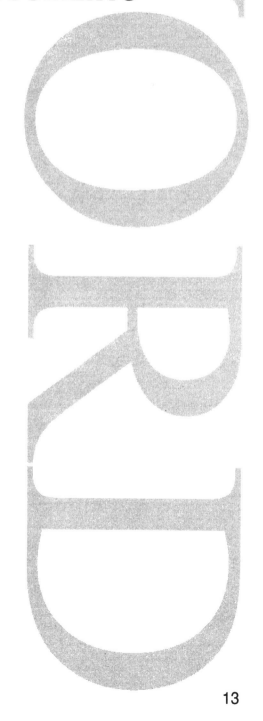

EXERCISE

- **THE WORD WINDOW** ■ **DEFAULT SETTINGS** ■ **IF YOU MAKE AN ERROR**
- **CREATING A NEW DOCUMENT** ■ **SAVING A NEW DOCUMENT**
- **CLOSING A DOCUMENT**

NOTES:

The Word Window

- Shown below is the Microsoft Word for Windows default window. It appears when the program is first accessed.

- The numbered key below and on the next page explains each window area specific to MS Word.

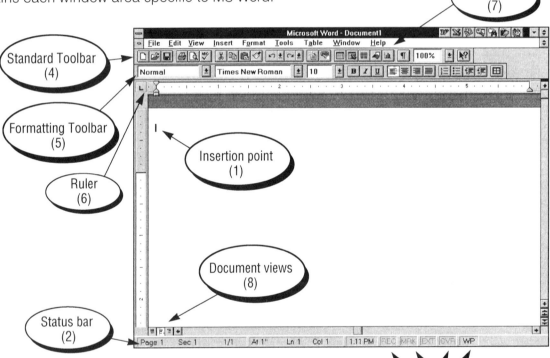

Insertion point (1)

- The blinking vertical line that appears in the upper left-hand corner when Word for Windows is started. It indicates where the next character to be keyed will appear and blinks *between* characters rather than below them.

- The insertion point does not always appear on the document screen. It may be made visible by clicking the left mouse button at the desired location or by tapping any one of the arrow keys.

Status bar (2)

- Appears at the bottom of the screen. It displays:

Page 1	The page number.
Sec 1	The section.
1/1	The current page and total number of pages in the document (1/1 meaning page one of a one-page document).

At 1"	The measurement in inches from the top edge of the page to the current location of the insertion point.
Ln 1	The line number at which the insertion point is currently located.
Col 1	The distance of the insertion point from the left margin in number of characters.
1:11 PM	The current time.

Mode buttons (3)

- Located on the right of the Status bar. They may be activated by double-clicking them. They place Word in various **modes**. Modes will be explained in related exercises.

Standard Toolbar (4)

- A collection of icons (pictures) that enables you to accomplish many common word processing tasks easily, like saving and printing a file.

Formatting Toolbar (5)

- A collection of icons that lets you easily change the appearance of your document.

Ruler (6)

- Measures the horizontal distance from the left margin of a page. You will learn to use this ruler and other ruler settings to change tabs, indents, and margins quickly.

Menu bar (7)

- Displays items that you can select when executing commands. When an item is selected using either the keyboard or the mouse, a group of subitems appears in a **drop-down submenu**.

Document Views (8)

- Word provides various ways to view documents on the screen. The view buttons allow you to quickly switch between views. You may also change document views by selecting the particular view from the <u>V</u>iew main menu.

  - **Normal view** ▤ is the default. It is used for most typing, editing, and formatting.
  - **Page Layout view** ▤ is used to see a document just as it will look when printed. This view allows you to see headers and footers, footnotes and endnotes, columns, etc.
  - **Outline view** ▤ allows you to collapse a document to see only the main headings or expand it to see the entire document.

Default Settings

- **Default settings** are preset conditions created by the manufacturer of the software. For example, when you begin work in Word for Windows, left and right margins have been set at 1.25", and top and bottom margins have been set at 1". Word assumes you are working on a standard 8.5" x 11" sheet of paper. The **At indicator** in the Status bar is defaulted to show the insertion point position as measured in inches from the top of the paper. Tab stops are set every .5". Type style (the design of your characters) is defaulted to Times Roman (or Times New Roman, depending on your version of Windows and the printer you are using).

*IMPORTANT: Type size is measured in **points**. One point is 1/72 of an inch. The default font size in Word is 10 point. The exercises in this book have been created using a larger and more readable 12 point font. **Therefore, it is important to change the default font size from 10 point to 12 point so your work will appear like the book exercises. Because printers vary, your line endings may not appear exactly as in the exercises shown in this text. Change the default font size to 12 point by executing the following procedure:***

1. Click **F**o**rmat**... Alt + O
2. Click **S**tyle .... S
3. Click **Modify** .... Alt + M
4. Click **Add to Template** .... Alt + A
   check box if necessary.

continued...

5. Click **F<u>o</u>rmat**... `Alt` + `O`

6. Click **<u>F</u>ont** .... `F`

7. Click **<u>S</u>ize** .... `Alt` + `S`

8. Type 12 .... `1` `2`

9. Press **Enter**........................... `Enter` , `Enter` , `Enter`
   three times

Changing font style and size will be covered in detail in Lesson 3, Exercise 13.

If You Make an Error...

■ The following keys will get you out of trouble:

- **Backspace**   Will erase characters to the immediate left of the insertion point.

- **Escape**   Or clicking a **Cancel** button, will back you out of most commands without executing them.

Mouse Shapes and Their Meanings

■ When the mouse is moved on the tabletop, a corresponding movement of the mouse pointer occurs on the screen. The mouse pointer changes shape depending on the tool being used, the object it is pointing to, and the action it will be performing. Basic mouse pointer shapes and their meanings are outlined below.

MOUSE POINTER SHAPE	MEANING
I	Appears when mouse pointer is placed within document text. Use the I-beam pointer to indicate where you will begin typing.
⇖	Appears in menus, toolbars, scroll bars, and the ruler. Use to select a menu item, click a button, scroll, place or remove tabs, or drag tabs to new positions. Also used for dragging margins or indent symbols to new locations or resizing graphic images in documents.
⧗	Appears when you are requested to wait for an operation to be completed before issuing additional commands.
⇗	Appears when you move the pointer into the selection bar along the left edge of the screen or the left edge of a table. Use it to select (highlight) a line, paragraph, or the whole document.
⇖?	Appears when you press Shift + F1 to get Help. Position the pointer on a menu item or on a screen region for which you desire help; click once.
←‖→	Appears when the pointer is placed on the line separating columns in a table. Use it to change the width of table columns by dragging.
⇕ ⤡ ⟷ ⤢	One of these four shapes appear when the pointer is on a window border. Change the size of the window by dragging.
⇖⁺	Appears when the mouse pointer is placed on selected text and the left mouse button is held down. Use to drag the selection to a new location.
⇖⁺	Appears when mouse pointer is placed on the border of a frame. Use it to drag the frame to a new position.

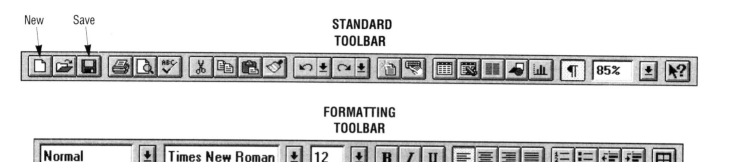

New   Save

STANDARD TOOLBAR

FORMATTING TOOLBAR

Click to change font size

Creating a New Document

■ When you start MS Word, a New dialog box appears. After clicking OK, a blank screen appears, ready for you to begin keyboarding text.

■ However, because of different installation settings, some software may bypass this dialog box and provide you with a blank screen immediately.

■ As you type, the **Col** (Column) **indicator** in the status bar changes. As text advances to another line, the **Ln** (Line) **indicator** also changes. If you move the insertion point, the **Col** and **Ln** indicators display the new location of the insertion point.

■ The **At** indicator displays the vertical position of the insertion point as measured in inches from the top edge of the page.

■ As text is typed, the insertion point automatically advances to the next line. This is called **word wrap** or **wraparound**. It is only necessary to use the Enter key at the end of a short line or to begin a new paragraph.

Saving a Document

■ Documents may be saved on a removable disk or on an internal hard drive for future recall.

■ Documents must be given a name for identification. A **filename** may contain a maximum of eight characters and is automatically assigned the file extension **.doc**. If desired, a filename extension other than .doc can be assigned when the file is saved. Filenames and extensions are separated by a period.

EXAMPLE: travel.doc

filename.extension

■ Filenames are not case sensitive; they may be typed in either upper- or lowercase.

Closing a Document

■ When saving a file, you must preface the filename with the drive letter where the disk is located. A drive letter is usually A or B; the hard drive letter is usually C. Thus, if you were saving a document named "tryagain" to a disk located in a disk drive, the filename would appear as:

   a:tryagain (A colon separates drives from filenames.)

   or

   b:tryagain

■ If you save to the hard drive, you may indicate a specific location or directory on the drive where you want your document saved. Think of a hard drive as a file cabinet; think of a drawer in the file cabinet as the directory; think of a folder in the drawer as a subdirectory. Thus, if you were saving a document named "tryagain" to the hard drive, it would automatically be saved to c:\msoffice\winword. The filename would appear as follows:

c:\msoffice\winword\tryagain.doc

- A colon (:) separates drives from directories and filenames; a backslash (\) separates directories from subdirectories and filenames.

- To save a document for the first time, select <u>S</u>ave from the <u>F</u>ile main menu, or click the Save icon 💾 on the Standard Toolbar.

- When you save a document for the first time, the following Save As dialog box appears:

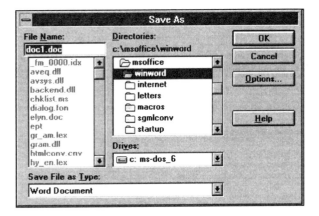

- Note the open folders in the Directories box. These tell you that you are currently working in "winword" which is a subdirectory of "msoffice," all of which are on the C drive (hard drive). Your saved file will actually reside in the subdirectory "winword." To save a file in this directory/subdirectory, type the name of your file in the File <u>N</u>ame text box.

- Once your document is named, the filename appears in the title bar.

- After saving your document for the first time, you can save the document again and continue working (update it) by selecting <u>S</u>ave from the <u>F</u>ile main menu or by clicking the Save icon on the Standard Toolbar 💾. The Save As dialog box does not reappear; it simply saves any changes you have made to your file. *Save often to prevent losing data.*

- Documents may also be saved by selecting Save <u>A</u>s from the <u>F</u>ile main menu. Use this command when you want to save your document under a different filename or in a different drive/directory.

- When a document has been saved, it remains on your screen. If you wish to clear the screen, you may close the document window (see keystrokes on next page).

- If you attempt to close a document before saving it, Word will prompt you to save it before exiting. You may respond **Y** for Yes or **N** for No.

- If you make a mistake and would like to begin again, close the document window without saving it.

- To begin a new document after closing the document window, you must select <u>N</u>ew from the <u>F</u>ile main menu or click the New icon on the Standard Toolbar 🗋. This will give you a new document window.

EXERCISE DIRECTIONS:

1. Create a NEW document.
   - ✓ *Note:* Be sure point size is set to 12 points. (See page 15.)

2. Keyboard the paragraphs on the right, allowing the text to word wrap to the next line.

3. Begin the exercise at the top of your screen. Press the Enter key twice to start a new paragraph.

4. Correct only immediately detected errors using the Backspace key.

5. Save the document; name it **TRY**.

6. Hide and then display each Toolbar.

7. Close the document window.

As you type, notice the Col indicator on your status bar change as the position of your insertion point changes.

The wraparound feature allows the operator to decide on line endings, making the use of Enter unnecessary except at the end of a paragraph or short line. Each file is saved on a disk or hard drive for recall. Documents must be given a name for identification.

🌐 OPEN A NEW DOCUMENT

Ctrl + N

Click **New Document** icon .... 🗋

OR

1. Click **File** .... `Alt` + `F`
2. Click **New** .... `N`
3. Click **OK** .... `Enter`

🌐 SAVE A DOCUMENT FOR THE FIRST TIME

Ctrl + S

1. Click **Save** icon .... 💾
2. Type document name .... *name*
3. Click **OK** .... `Enter`

OR

1. Click **File** .... `Alt` + `F`
2. Click **Save** .... `S`
3. Type document name .... *name*
4. Click **OK** .... `Enter`

🌐 CLOSE DOCUMENT WINDOW

1. Double-click **document control box** .. ⊟

2. Click **Yes** .... `Alt` + `Y`
   to save changes.

OR

Click **No** .... `N`
to abandon changes.

OR

1. Click **File** .... `Alt` + `F`
2. Click **Close** .... `C`
3. Click **Yes** .... `Alt` + `Y`
   to save changes.

OR

Click **No** .... `Alt` + `N`
to abandon changes.

🌐 EXIT WORD FOR WINDOWS PROGRAM

1. Double-click **program control box** .... ⊟
2. Click **Yes** .... `Y`
   to save changes.

OR

Click **No** .... `N`
to abandon changes.

OR

1. Click **File** .... `Alt` + `F`

2. Click **Exit** .... `X`
3. Click **Yes** to save changes .... `Y`

OR

Click **No** .... `N`
to abandon changes.

🌐 HIDE OR DISPLAY STANDARD AND FORMATTING TOOLBARS

1. Click **View** .... `Alt` + `V`
2. Click **Toolbars** .... `T`
   to display Toolbars dialog box.
3. Select **Standard** .... `↓` , `Space`
   to display or hide.

OR

Select **Formatting** .... `↓` , `Space`
to display or hide.

4. Select remaining .... `↓` , `Space`
   to turn off, if necessary.
5. Click **OK** .... `Enter`

HIDE OR DISPLAY RULER

1. Click **View** .... `Alt` + `V`
2. Click **Ruler** .... `R`

EXERCISE

■ USING THE TAB KEY ■ AUTOCORRECT ■ SPELLING

2

Spelling

STANDARD TOOLBAR

NOTES:

Using the Tab Key

■ Tab stops are preset (the default) .5" apart. Each time the Tab key is pressed, the insertion point advances half an inch.

■ Defaults may be changed at any time and as often as desired throughout a document. For example, the default tab settings could be set to .8" rather than .5". Defaults may be changed to affect all documents or individual documents. (Changing defaults will be covered in a later lesson.)

AutoCorrect

■ The AutoCorrect feature automatically replaces common spelling errors and mistyped words with the correct text as soon as you press the spacebar.

■ There are numerous words already in the AutoCorrect dictionary. However, you can enter words that you commonly misspell into the AutoCorrect dictionary by selecting AutoCorrect from the Tools main menu.

■ If you find this feature annoying, you can deselect the Replace Text as You Type option in the AutoCorrect dialog box.

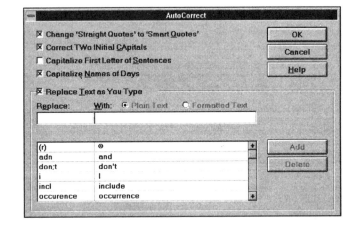

■ You can specify other types of corrections in the AutoCorrect dialog box:

- **Change 'Straight Quotes' to 'Smart Quotes'** allows you to change straight quotation marks to curly (typesetter) quotation marks.

- **Correct TWo INitial CApitals** automatically converts two initial capital letters of a word to an initial capital letter and a lowercase second letter.

- **Capitalize First Letter of Sentences** automatically capitalizes the first letter of a sentence.

- **Capitalize Names of Days** automatically capitalizes names of days of the week.

Spelling

- Word's Spelling feature checks the spelling of a word, a block of text, or an entire document. Occurrences of double words will also be flagged.·

- The Speller compares the words in your document with the words in the Word for Windows dictionary. Proper names and words not in Word's dictionary will be identified as errors. When an error is detected, Word will supply a list of suggested spellings. You may accept Word's suggestions or ignore them.

- Spelling may be accessed by selecting Spelling from the Tools main menu or by clicking the Spelling button on the Standard Toolbar. The following dialog box will appear:

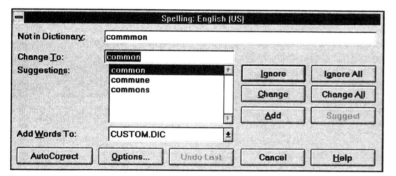

- Words may be added to the custom dictionary before, after, or during the spell check session.

- To avoid having proper names flagged as incorrect spellings during the spell check session, add them to the custom dictionary.

In this exercise, you will type two short paragraphs using word wrap and purposely misspell several words. After typing the word incorrectly and pressing the Spacebar, you will note the correct spelling appears for several words. You will then use Spelling to correct the other misspellings.

EXERCISE DIRECTIONS:

1. Create a NEW document.

2. Begin the exercise at the top of your screen.

3. Access the AutoCorrect feature. Be sure Replace Text as You Type has been selected.

4. Keyboard the paragraphs on the next page exactly as shown, including the circled, misspelled words. Allow the text to word wrap to the next line.

5. Press the Enter key twice to begin a new paragraph, and press the Tab key once to indent the paragraph.

6. Spell check the document.

7. Save the exercise using the Save button on the Toolbar; name it **TRYAGAIN**.

8. Close the document window.

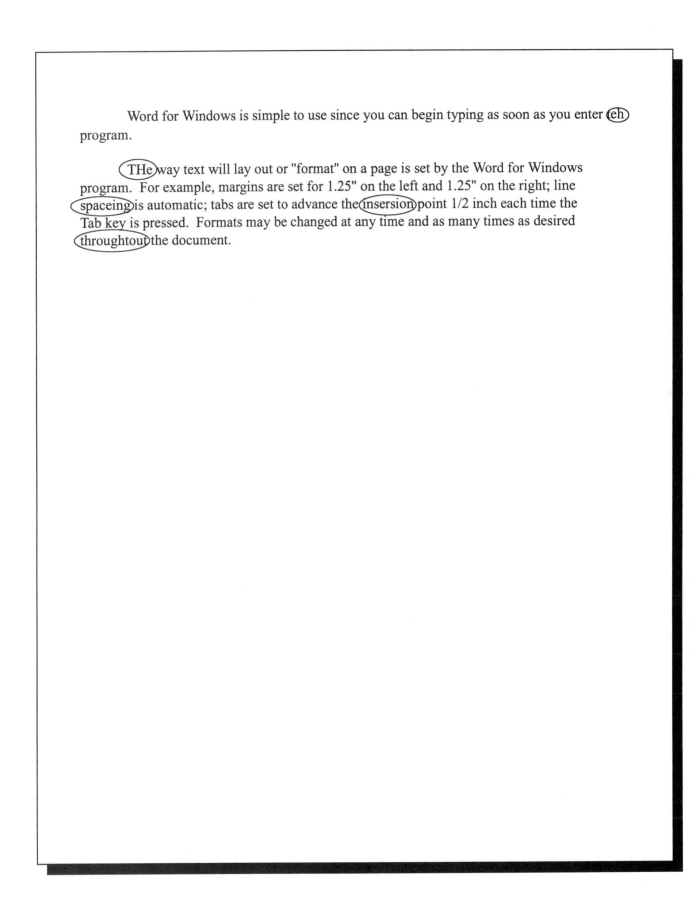

Word for Windows is simple to use since you can begin typing as soon as you enter the program.

THe way text will lay out or "format" on a page is set by the Word for Windows program. For example, margins are set for 1.25" on the left and 1.25" on the right; line spaceing is automatic; tabs are set to advance the insersion point 1/2 inch each time the Tab key is pressed. Formats may be changed at any time and as many times as desired throughtout the document.

TAB

Press **Tab** .... `Tab`

AUTOCORRECT

1. Click **Tools** .... `Alt`+`T`

2. Click **AutoCorrect** .... `A`

3. Select **Replace Text as You Type** option.

   To add words to AutoCorrect Dictionary:

   • Click **Replace** text box .... `Alt`+`E`

   • Type commonly misspelled word to be included.

   • Click **With** text box .... `Alt`+`W`

   • Type correct version of word.

4. Click **Add** .... `Alt`+`A`

5. Click **OK** .... `Enter`

🌐 SPELLING

F7

1. Place insertion point where spell check should begin.

   OR

   Select a word or block of text to spell check.

2. Click **Spelling** icon ....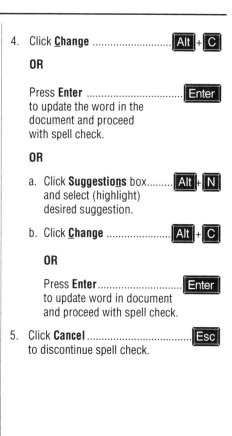

   OR

   a. Click **Tools** .... `Alt`+`T`

   b. Click **Spelling** .... `S`

✓ *When the system encounters a word not found in its dictionary, the word is displayed in the **Not in Dictionary** box and the insertion point will appear in the **Change To** box.*

3. Click **Ignore** .... `Alt`+`I` to proceed without changing the word.

   OR

   Edit the word in the **Change To** box.

4. Click **Change** .... `Alt`+`C`

   OR

   Press **Enter** .... `Enter` to update the word in the document and proceed with spell check.

   OR

   a. Click **Suggestions** box......... `Alt`+`N` and select (highlight) desired suggestion.

   b. Click **Change** .... `Alt`+`C`

   OR

   Press **Enter**........................... `Enter` to update word in document and proceed with spell check.

5. Click **Cancel** .... `Esc` to discontinue spell check.

EXERCISE

■ INSERTION POINT MOVEMENTS ■ CREATING A BUSINESS LETTER

NOTES:

Insertion Point Movements

■ The arrow keys on the numeric keypad, or the separate arrow keys located to the left of the keypad, are used to move the insertion point in the direction indicated by the arrow. The insertion point will only move through text, spaces, or codes. The insertion point cannot be moved past the beginning or the end of your document.

■ To move the insertion point quickly from one point in the document to another, you may use **express insertion point movements**. Note the keystroke procedures on page 27 carefully.

Creating a Business Letter

■ There are a variety of letter styles for business and personal use.

■ The parts of a **business letter** and the vertical spacing of letter parts are the same regardless of the style used.

■ A business letter is comprised of eight parts: 1. **date**, 2. **inside address** (to whom and where the letter is going), 3. **salutation**, 4. **body**, 5. **closing**, 6. **signature line**, 7. **title line**, and 8. **reference initials** (the first set of initials belongs to the person who wrote the letter; the second set belongs to the person who typed the letter). Whenever you see "yo" as part of the reference initials in an exercise, substitute *your* *own* initials.

■ The letter style illustrated in this exercise is a **modified-block business letter** since the date, closing, signature, and title lines begin at the center point of the paper. Because a standard page is 8.5" X 11" and Word uses 1.25" for the left margin and 1.25" for the right margin, there are 6" between the margins available for text.

Note that the ruler measures only the 6" work area. Therefore, the middle of your work area (and page) on this ruler is 3". To place the date, closing, signature, and title lines in the center of the page, you must tab six times to bring the insertion point to the 3" mark.

RULER

■ A letter generally begins 15 lines, or 2.5", from the top of a page. If the letter is long, it may begin 12 lines, or 2", from the top of the paper. If the letter is short, it may begin three or more inches from the top.

■ Margins and the size of the characters may also be adjusted to make correspondence fit more appropriately on the page.

> ✓ *Note:* *Changing margins and font size will be covered in a later lesson.*

> *In this exercise, you will create a modified-block letter and practice moving the insertion point through the document.*

EXERCISE DIRECTIONS:

✓ *Note:* *Directions are given for a 12 point font setting. Be sure your default font is set to 12 point; otherwise, there will be discrepancies between your document and the one shown in the exercise.*

1. Create a NEW document.

2. Keyboard the letter on the following page exactly as shown.

3. Use the default margins and tabs.

4. Access the AutoCorrect feature. Be sure Replace Text as You Type has been selected.

5. With your insertion point at the top of the screen, press the Enter key eight times to begin the date on Ln 9 (At 2.5" down from the top of the paper).

   ✓ *Note:* *Your line count and inch measurement may vary from this direction depending on the printer, printer driver, and font style you are using.*

6. Press the Enter key between parts of the letter as directed in the exercise.

7. Press the Tab key six times to begin the date and closing at the center point of the page.

   ✓ *Note:* *It is more efficient to set one tab stop at 3" and press the Tab key once to type the date and closing.*

8. Spell check.

9. After completing the exercise, move the insertion point to the top of the screen (Ctrl+Home) and back to the end of the document.

10. Save the document; name it **LETTER**.

11. Close the document window.

8x

= 2.5"

TAB → TAB → TAB → TAB → TAB → TAB → October 1, 199-

↓ 4x

Ms. Renee S. Brown
54 Williams Street
Omaha, NE 68101

↓ 2x

Dear Ms. Brown:

↓ 2x

Thank you for your $150 contribution to the American Art Institution. This contribution automatically makes you a member in our arts program.

As an active member, you can participate in our many educational activities.

For example, you can take part in our monthly art lectures, our semi-annual auctions and our frequent art exhibits. Admission to all these events is free.

We look forward to seeing you at our next meeting. We know you will enjoy speaking with our other members and participating in very stimulating conversation.

TAB → TAB → TAB → TAB → TAB → TAB → Sincerely,

↓ 4x

TAB → TAB → TAB → TAB → TAB → TAB → Alan Barry
President

↓ 2x

ab/yo

EXPRESS INSERTION POINT MOVEMENTS

TO MOVE: **PRESS:**

- *One character left* .... [◄]
- *One character right* .... [►]
- *One line up* .... [▲]
- *One line down* .... [▼]
- *Previous word* .... [Ctrl]+[◄]

- *Next word* .... [Ctrl]+[►]
- *Top of screen* .... [Ctrl]+[PgUp]
- *Bottom of screen* .... [Ctrl]+[PgDn]
- *Beginning of document* ...... [Ctrl]+[Home]
- *End of document* .... [Ctrl]+[End]
- *Top of pg.* [F5], *number,* [Enter], [Esc]

- *Beginning of line* .... [Home]
- *End of line* .... [End]
- *Top of previous pg.* .... [Alt]+[Ctrl]+[PgUp]
- *Top of next pg.* .... [Alt]+[Ctrl]+[PgDn]
- *To last revision* .... [Shift]+[F5]

EXERCISE

■ **CREATING A BUSINESS LETTER** ■ **THE DATE FEATURE** ■ **PRINTING**
■ **UPPERCASE MODE** ■ **PREVIEWING A DOCUMENT**

Print   Preview

STANDARD TOOLBAR

NOTES:

Creating a Business Letter

■ The letter style in this exercise is called **full-block**. This style is very popular because all parts of the letter begin at the left margin, so there is no need to tab the date and closing. The spacing between parts of a block letter is the same as the modified-block letter.

■ When you type the date in this exercise, you will use Word's Date feature.

The Date Feature

■ The **Date** feature enables you to insert the current date into your document automatically.

■ When using the Date feature to insert the date into a document, a dialog box will appear requiring you to provide additional information. Select the desired date format from the list of available formats.

DATE AND TIME FORMAT DIALOG BOX

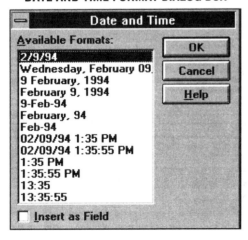

Printing

■ Word allows you to print *part* or *all* of a document that is on your screen. You can print a page of the document, selected pages of the document, one or more blocks of text within the document, or the entire document. You may also print a single document or multiple documents from a disk without retrieving them to the screen. In this exercise, you will print a complete document from a window on your screen.

■ Check to see that your printer is turned on and that paper is loaded.

■ There are three ways to print an entire document in Word.

• Click the **Print icon** 🖨, or

• Select File, **Print** from the menu bar, or

• Click the **Print icon** 🖨 in Print Preview mode.

Previewing a Document

- The **Print Preview** feature allows you to see how a document will look on paper before printing it. To preview a document, select Print Preview from the File menu, or click the Print Preview icon [image] on the Standard Toolbar.

Uppercase Mode

- Pressing the Caps Lock key once will allow you to type all capital letters without holding down the Shift key. Only *letters* are changed by Caps Lock. To end uppercase mode, press the Caps Lock key again.

PRINT PREVIEW SCREEN

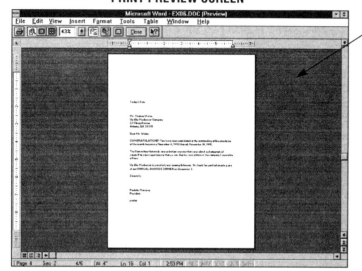

Print Preview

Print   Multiple pages   View Ruler

PRINT PREVIEW TOOLBAR

- Note the Print Preview Toolbar above.

  Clicking the **Multiple Pages icon** [image] allows you to view either one page at a time or several pages.

  Clicking the **View Ruler icon** [image] allows you to display or hide the vertical and horizontal rulers. It is suggested that you keep both rulers visible because they are very useful in viewing and adjusting margin settings. In later lessons, you will learn how to adjust margin settings and page breaks easily in Print Preview mode using the mouse.

- You may scroll backward or forward through your document in Print Preview mode by pressing the Page Up or the Page Down key on the keyboard or by clicking on the scroll bar using the mouse. Exit Print Preview by pressing the Escape key or by clicking Close.

In this exercise, you will create a full-block letter using the Date feature and print one copy of the full document.

EXERCISE DIRECTIONS:

1. Create a NEW document.

2. Keyboard the letter on the following page using the default margins.

3. Access the AutoCorrect feature. Be sure Replace Text as You Type has been selected.

4. With the insertion point at the top of the screen, press the Enter key eight times. Use the automatic Date feature to insert the date 2.5" from the top edge of the page.

5. Press the Enter key between parts of the letter as directed in the exercise.

6. Spell check.

7. Preview your work.

8. Print one copy either:
    *   From the Print Preview screen, or
    *   Using the Print icon on the Toolbar, or
    *   By selecting File, Print on the menu bar.

9. Save the document; name it **BLOCK**.

10. Close the document window.

INSERT CURRENT DATE

1. Click **Insert** .... `Alt` + `I`

2. Click **Date and Time** .... `T`

3. Click desired format .... `↑` , `↓`

4. Click **OK** .... `Enter`

UPPERCASE MODE

1. Press **Caps Lock** .... `CapsLock`

2. Type text...*text*

3. Press **Caps Lock** .... `CapsLock` to end uppercase mode.

PRINT A DOCUMENT

Ctrl + P

Click **Print** icon....................................... 🖨

OR

1. Click **File** .... `Alt` + `F`

2. Click **Print** .... `P`

3. Click **OK** .... `Enter`

🌐 PRINT PREVIEW

1. Click **Print Preview** icon.................. 🔍

    OR

    a. Click **File**........................... `Alt` + `F`

    b. Click **Print Preview** .... `V`

2. Press **Page Up**............................. `PgUp`

    OR

    Press **Page Down** .... `PgDn` to page through the document.

3. Click **Close**.................................... `Esc` to exit Print Preview mode.

PRINT A DOCUMENT FROM THE PRINT PREVIEW SCREEN

1. Click **File**................................. `Alt` + `F`

2. Click **Print Preview** .... `P`

3. Click **Print** icon.............................. 🖨

SET NUMBER OF PAGES TO DISPLAY IN PRINT PREVIEW

1. Click **Print Preview** icon .... 🔍 to enter Print Preview mode.

2. Click **Multiple Pages** icon .... ⊞

3. Drag to indicate desired number of pages to view.

$8x = 2.5''$

Today's Date

↓ 4X

Mr. Thomas Walen
Updike Mechanics Company
23 Clogg Avenue
Atlanta, GA 30315

↓ 2X

Dear Mr. Walen:

↓ 2X

CONGRATULATIONS! You have been nominated as the outstanding office employee
of the month beginning November 4, 1996 through November 30, 1996.

↓ 2X

The Committee that made your selection requires that you submit a photograph of
yourself to your supervisor so that we can display your picture in the company's
executive offices.

↓ 2X

Updike Mechanics is proud of your accomplishments. We look forward to honoring
you at our ANNUAL AWARDS DINNER on December 3.

↓ 2X

Sincerely,

↓ 4X

Paulette Manning
President

↓ 2X

pm/yo

EXERCISE

■ **CREATING A PERSONAL BUSINESS LETTER**

NOTES:

■ A **personal business letter** is written by an individual representing him/herself, not a business firm.

■ A personal business letter begins 2.5" down from the top of the page (same as the other letter styles) and includes the writer's return address (address, city, state, and zip code) which precedes the date. However, if personalized letterhead is used, keying the return address is unnecessary. Personal business letters may be formatted in full-block or modified-block style. Operator's initials are not included. Depending on the style used, the writer's return address will appear in a different location on the letter. A full-block format appears below left. Note that the return address is typed below the writer's name.

FULL-BLOCK

March 7, 199-

Mr. John Smith
54 Astor Place
New York, NY 10078

Dear Mr. Smith:

xxxxxxxxxxxxxxxxxxxxxxxxxxxxxxxxxxxxxxxx
xxxxx.

xxxxxxxxxxxxxxxxxxxxxxxxxxxxxxxxxxxxxxxx
xxxxxxxxxxxxxxxxxxxxxxxxxxxxxxxxxxxx.

Sincerely,

Paula Zahn
765 Nehring Street
Staten Island, NY 10324

MODIFIED-BLOCK

657 Nehring Street
Staten Island, NY 10324
March 7, 199-

Mr. John Smith
54 Astor Place
New York, NY 10078

Dear Mr. Smith:

xxxxxxxxxxxxxxxxxxxxxxxxxxxxxxxxxxxxxxxx
xxxxxx.

xxxxxxxxxxxxxx xxxxxxxxxxxxxxxxxxxxxxxxx
xxxxxxxxx.

Sincerely,

Paula Zahn

In this exercise, you will create a modified block personal business letter using the automatic date feature.

EXERCISE DIRECTIONS:

1. Create a NEW document.

2. Keyboard the personal business letter below in modified-block style as shown.

3. Use the default margins and tabs.

4. Access the AutoCorrect feature. Be sure Replace Text as You Type has been selected.

5. Begin the exercise At 2.5".

6. Press the Tab key 6 times to begin the return address and closing at the center point on the page.

   ✓ Note: It is more efficient to set one tab stop at 3" and press the Tab key once to type

the return address and closing. After learning to set tabs in Lesson 5, you will format subsequent exercises using a single tab setting for the inside address, date, and closing of a modified-block letter.

7. Spell check.

8. After completing the exercise, scroll your page up.

9. Preview your work.

10. Print one copy.

11. Save the exercise; name it **PERSONAL**.

12. Close the document window.

---

765 Robeling Street
Teaneck, NJ 07666
[Date Feature]

Ms. Gina Palmisaro, Associate
PRC Securities, Inc.
50 Wall Street
New York, NY 10260

Dear Ms. Palmisaro:

It was a pleasure meeting you last week and discussing my summer internship prospect in Global Markets at PRC Securities.

I found our talk to be insightful, and it has given me a new focus on a possible career in sales. The chance to work on a trading floor for the summer, therefore, would be invaluable.

Once again, thank you for your time and the opportunity to meet with you. I look forward to hearing from you soon.

Sincerely,

Karen Winn

EXERCISE DIRECTIONS:

1. Keyboard the letter below in modified-block style.

2. Use the default margins and tabs.

3. Access the <u>A</u>utoCorrect feature. Be sure Replace <u>T</u>ext as You Type has been selected.

4. Use the automatic Date feature to insert the current date.

5. Spell check.

6. Preview your document.

7. Print one copy.

8. Save the file; name it **OPEN**.

9. Close the document window.

Today's date Mr. Martin Quincy 641 Lexington Avenue New York, NY 10022
Dear Mr. Quincy: We are pleased to announce the opening of a new subsidiary of our company. We specialize in selling, training and service of portable personal computers.¶This may be hard to believe, but we carry portable personal computers that can do everything a conventional desktop can. Our portables can run all of the same applications as your company's conventional PCs. With the purchase of a computer, we will train two employees in your firm on how to use an application of your choice.¶For a free demonstration, call us at 212-555-9876 any day from 9:00 a.m. to 5:00 p.m. Sincerely, Theresa Mann President tm:yo

LESSON 2

OPENING AND EDITING DOCUMENTS

Exercises 6-11

- Opening a Document File

- Insert and Overtype Mode

- Save As

- Undo

- Redo

- Selecting and Deleting Text

- Show/Hide Codes

- Non-breaking Spaces

- Inserting and Deleting Text

- Find File

- Printing Multiple Files

EXERCISE

■ OPENING A DOCUMENT FILE ■ INSERT AND OVERTYPE MODE

Open

STANDARD TOOLBAR

NOTES:

Opening a Document File

■ A document is revised when corrections or adjustments need to be made. **Proofreaders' marks** are symbols on a printed copy of a document that indicate changes to be made. As each proofreaders' mark is introduced in an exercise in this text, it is explained and illustrated.

■ A document containing proofreaders' symbols is often referred to as a **rough draft**. After all revisions are made, the completed document is referred to as a **final copy**.

■ Before a file can be revised or edited, it must be retrieved or opened from the disk to the screen.

Opening a Recently Saved File

■ Word lists the four most recently opened files at the bottom of the File menu. To open a recently opened file, select the desired filename on the list of recently opened files.

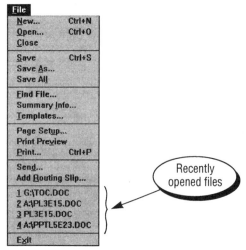

Recently opened files

Opening a File Not Recently Saved

■ After you select Open from the File main menu or click the Open icon on the Standard Toolbar, a dialog box appears which requires you to provide the drive, directory, type of file, and file name information. You must then click the OK button to open the selected file. Note the Open dialog box below:

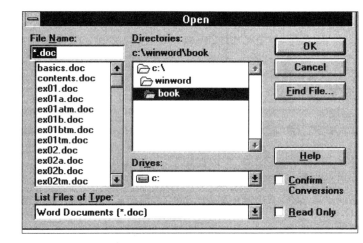

Insert and Overtype Mode

■ To make corrections, you must move through the document to the point of correction using the insertion point movement keys. These keys include End, Home, Page Up, Page Down, and the arrow keys. You have already had some practice moving the insertion point through your document in previous exercises.

- To insert text, place the insertion point to the left of the character that will follow the inserted material. When typing inserted text, the existing text moves to the right. When inserting a word, the space following the word must also be inserted.

- Another way to edit text is to put Word into **Overtype mode** so you can typeover the existing text with new text. In Overtype mode, existing text does not move to the right; it is typed over. By default, Word is in Insert mode. You may switch to Overtype mode by pressing the Insert key. When in Overtype mode, the **OVR** mode indicator is highlighted in the status bar.

  To switch back to Insert mode, press the Insert key again. For most editing, it is recommended that you work in Insert mode.

- To create a new paragraph in existing text, place the insertion point immediately to the left of the first character in the new paragraph and press the Enter key twice.

- When a file is retrieved and revisions are made, the revised or updated version must be resaved or replaced. When a document is resaved, the old version is replaced with the new version.

- The proofreaders' mark for insertion is:

- The proofreaders' mark for a new paragraph is:

In this exercise, you will open a previously saved document and insert new text.

EXERCISE DIRECTIONS:

1. Open ⌨ **TRY**, or open 💾 **WTRY.6**.

2. Make the insertions indicated in the exercise on the next page.

3. Use the Overtype mode to insert the word "determine" in the second paragraph; return to Insert mode immediately following this step.

4. Print one copy.

5. Spell check.

6. Close the file; save the changes.

As you type, [you will] notice the Col indicator on your status bar change as the position of your insertion point changes.

The "wraparound" feature allows the [computer] operator to ~~decide on~~ [determine] line endings, making the use of [the] Enter unnecessary except at the end of a paragraph or short line. Each file is saved on a [Key] [data] disk or hard drive for recall. Documents must be given a name [or number] for identification.

🌐 OPEN A DOCUMENT

Ctrl + O

1. Click **Open File** icon ....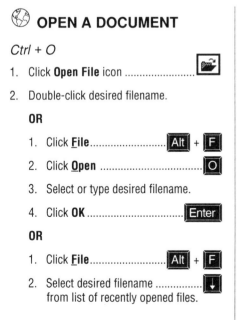

2. Double-click desired filename.

   OR

   1. Click **File**......................... `Alt` + `F`

   2. Click **Open** .... `O`

   3. Select or type desired filename.

   4. Click **OK** .... `Enter`

   OR

   1. Click **File**......................... `Alt` + `F`

   2. Select desired filename .... `↓`
      from list of recently opened files.

USE OVERTYPE

1. Press **Insert** .... `Ins`
   to enter Overtype mode.

2. Type text...*text*

3. Press **Insert** .... `Ins`
   again to return to Insert mode.

🌐 RESAVE A DOCUMENT

Click **Save** icon..................................... `💾`

   OR

   1. Click **File** .... `Alt` + `F`

   2. Click **Save** .... `S`

   OR

   1. Click **File** .... `Alt` + `F`

   2. Click **Close** .... `C`

3. Click **Yes** .... `Y`
   When prompted to save changes.

INSERT TEXT

1. Place insertion point to left of character
   that will immediately follow inserted text.

2. Type text...*text*

EXERCISE

■ **OPENING A DOCUMENT (READ ONLY)** ■ **SAVE AS** ■ **UNDO** ■ **REDO**

STANDARD TOOLBAR

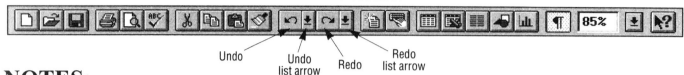

Undo   Undo list arrow   Redo   Redo list arrow

NOTES:

Opening a Copy of a File (Read Only)

■ If you wish to open a file but not make changes to it, click the **Read Only** option in the Open dialog box. This will make the document a read-only copy and will require you to save it with a different filename. Selecting this option prevents you from accidentally affecting the file.

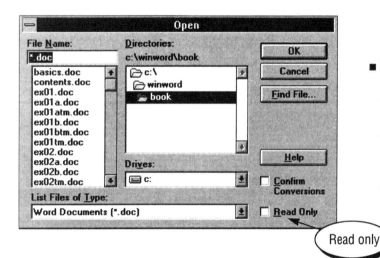

Read only

■ If you save, close, or exit a document that you opened using the Read Only option, Word automatically displays the Save As dialog box for you to give the file another name, thus leaving the original document intact.

Save As

■ If you wish to save any document under a different filename or in a different location, you may select **Save As** from the File menu. When any document is saved under a new filename, the original document remains intact.

Undo and Redo

■ The **Undo** feature lets you undo the last change you made to the document. Word remembers up to 300 actions in a document and allows you to undo any or all of them. You can undo all your recent actions by repeatedly clicking the Undo icon on the Standard Toolbar, or you can undo a selected action by clicking the **Undo list arrow** next to the Undo icon and choosing the action to undo from the list presented.

■ The **Redo** feature allows you to reverse the last undo. Like Undo, Redo allows you to reverse up to 300 actions in a document. You can redo an action by repeatedly clicking the Redo icon on the Standard Toolbar, or you can redo a selected action by clicking the **Redo list arrow** next to the Redo icon and choosing the action to redo.

> *In this exercise, you will insert text at the top of the page and create a modified-block letter. To insert the date, press the Enter key nine times to bring the At indicator to 2.5"; then press the Tab key six times to begin the date at the middle of the page. Remember to use the automatic Date feature.*
>
> *After inserting the date, you will continue inserting the inside address and salutation. Text will adjust as you continue creating the letter.*

EXERCISE DIRECTIONS:

1. Open 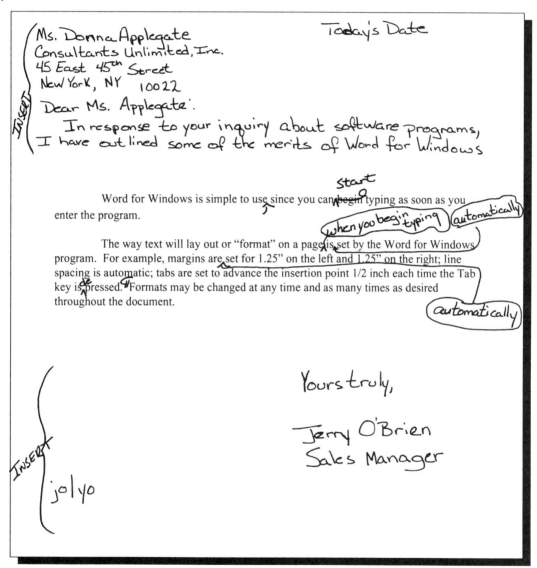**TRYAGAIN** as a Read Only file, or ⊟Open **TRYAGAIN.7** from the data disk as a Read Only file.

2. Make the indicated insertions. Follow the spacing for a modified-block letter illustrated in Exercise 3.

3. Use the automatic Date feature to insert today's date.

4. Use Overtype mode to insert the word "start" in the second paragraph; return to Insert mode immediately.

5. After typing the initials (jo/yo), use Undo. Retype them in all caps.

6. After typing the initials in all caps, use Undo.

7. Use Redo to return the initials to all capitals.

8. Print one copy.

9. Use Undo to return the initials to lowercase.

10. Close the file; save as **TRYIT**.

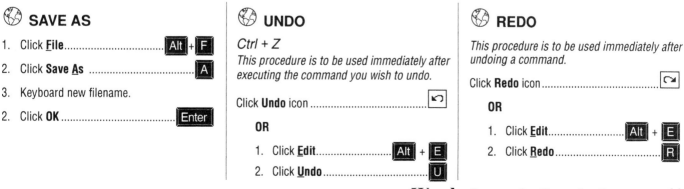

SAVE AS

1. Click **File** .... `Alt` + `F`

2. Click **Save As** .... `A`

3. Keyboard new filename.

2. Click **OK** .... `Enter`

UNDO

Ctrl + Z
This procedure is to be used immediately after executing the command you wish to undo.

Click **Undo** icon .... `↜`

   OR

1. Click **Edit** .... `Alt` + `E`

2. Click **Undo** .... `U`

REDO

This procedure is to be used immediately after undoing a command.

Click **Redo** icon .... `↝`

   OR

1. Click **Edit** .... `Alt` + `E`

2. Click **Redo** .... `R`

EXERCISE

■ SELECTING AND DELETING TEXT ■ SHOW/HIDE CODES

Cut   Paste   Show/Hide

STANDARD TOOLBAR

NOTES:

Deleting Text

■ The **Delete** feature allows you to remove text, graphics, or codes from a document.

■ Procedures for deleting text vary depending upon what is being deleted: a character, previous character, a word, line, paragraph, page, remainder of page, or a blank line.

■ The Backspace key may be used to delete characters and close up spaces to the left of the insertion point.

■ To delete a character or a space, place the insertion point immediately to the left of the character or space to delete, then press the Delete (Del) key (located on the right side of your keyboard).

■ Note the **Cut icon** ✂ on the Toolbar above. Blocks of text (words, sentences, or paragraphs) may be deleted by highlighting or selecting them, and then either pressing the Delete key or clicking the Cut icon on the Toolbar.

Selecting Text

■ Text may be highlighted or selected in several ways:

• **Using the keyboard** by holding down the Shift key while pressing insertion point movement keys, or

• **Using the keyboard in combination with the mouse** by clicking where the selection should begin, holding down the Shift key, and clicking where the selection will end, or

• **Using the mouse** by dragging the mouse pointer over desired text, or

• **Using the F8 selection extender key** by pressing F8 which places Word in Extend Selection mode (the letters EXT appear in the status bar).

Pressing F8 anchors the insertion point and allows you to use the insertion point movement keys to highlight or select text in any direction from the position of the insertion point. When in Extend mode, you may extend the selection to any character or symbol by pressing that character or symbol on the keyboard. Word will instantly highlight from the insertion point to the next occurrence of that character or symbol. Hit Esc to cancel the Extend Mode.

• **Using the mouse with the selection bar** by clicking in the selection bar. The *selection bar* is a vertical space alongside the left edge of the Word screen. Note the illustration of the selection bar below.

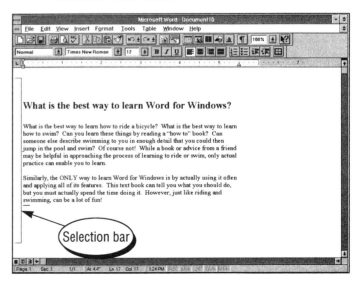

- When you move the mouse pointer into the selection bar, the mouse pointer changes to the shape of an arrow pointing upward toward the top right of the screen.

- Clicking the left mouse button while the pointer is in the selection bar will highlight the entire line of text opposite the pointer. Holding the left mouse button and dragging the mouse pointer up or down in the selection bar will allow you to highlight or select as many lines of text as you wish. To abandon the selection process, release the mouse button and click once anywhere on the Word screen.

Show/Hide Codes

- As a document is created in Word, codes are inserted.

- When the **Show/Hide icon** ¶ on the Standard Toolbar is selected, codes for paragraph marks (¶), tabs (→), and spaces (•) are visible in your document. These symbols will *not* appear, however, when printed.

- To combine two paragraphs into one, it is necessary to delete the returns that separate the paragraphs. Returns are represented on the screen by paragraph symbols (¶). Therefore, deleting the symbol will delete the return.

- To delete a tab, place the insertion point to the left of the tab symbol (→), and press the Delete key.

- It is recommended that you keep paragraph marks visible when editing a document because:

  - It is easier to combine and separate paragraphs by deleting and inserting the actual paragraph symbols, and

  - Each paragraph symbol contains important information about the format of the paragraph preceding it (type size and style, indentation, borders, etc.).

    ✓ Note: You will learn more about this feature in a later lesson.

- The proofreader's mark for:

  deletion is ℓ

  closing up space is ⌒

  moving text to the left is [or ↤

In this exercise, you will use various deletion methods to edit a document. Use block highlighting procedures to delete sentences, words, or blocks of text.

EXERCISE DIRECTIONS:

1. Create a NEW document.

2. Create the exercise as shown in Part I, or open 💾 **WDIVE.8**.

3. Click the Show/Hide icon on the Standard Toolbar to display codes.

4. Using the selection and deletion procedures indicated in Part II of the exercise, make the revisions.

5. After deleting the last paragraph, undelete it.

6. Using another deletion method, delete the last paragraph again.

7. Spell check.

8. Print one copy.

9. Close the file; *save as* **DIVE**.

DIVING VACATIONS
DIVING IN THE CAYMAN ISLANDS

Do you want to see sharks, barracudas and huge stingrays? Do you want to see gentle angels, too?

The Cayman Islands were discovered by Christopher Columbus in late 1503. The Cayman Islands are located just south of Cuba. The Caymans are the home to only about 125,000 year-around residents. However, they welcome approximately 200,000 visitors each year. Each year, more and more visitors arrive. Most visitors come with colorful masks and flippers in their luggage ready to go scuba diving.

Because of the magnificence of the coral reef, scuba diving has become to the Cayman Islands what safaris are to Kenya. If you go into a bookstore, you can buy diving gear.

Now, you are ready to jump in.

Recommendations for Hotel/Diving Accommodations:

Sunset House, Post Office Box 4791, George Towne, Grand Cayman; (800) 555-4767.

Coconut Harbour, Post Office Box 2086, George Towne, Grand Cayman; (809) 555-7468.

Seeing a shark is frightening at first; they seem to come out of nowhere and then return to nowhere. But as soon as the creature disappears, you will swim after it. You will just want to keep this beautiful, graceful fish in view as long as you can.

PART II

DIVING VACATIONS
DIVING IN THE CAYMAN ISLANDS

REMAINDER OF LINE

CHARACTER/WORD

Do you want to see sharks, barracudas and ~~huge~~ stingrays? Do you want to see ~~gentle~~ angels, too?

CHARACTER/WORD

The Cayman Islands were discovered by Christopher Columbus in ~~late~~ 1503. The Cayman Islands are located ~~just~~ south of Cuba. The Caymans are ~~the~~ home to only about 125,000 year-around residents. However, they welcome ~~approximately~~ 200,000 visitors each year.

SENTENCE

~~Each year, more and more visitors arrive.~~ Most visitors come with ~~colorful~~ masks and flippers in their luggage ~~ready to go scuba diving.~~

REMAINDER OF LINE

PARAGRAPH

~~Because of the magnificence of the coral reef, scuba diving has become to the Cayman Islands what safaris are to Kenya. If you go into a bookstore, you can buy diving gear.~~

Now, you are ready to jump in.

WORD

~~Recommendations for~~ Hotel/Diving Accommodations:

PART OF WORD/ CHARACTER

Sunset House, ~~Post Office~~ Box 4791, George Towne, Grand Cayman; (800) 555-4767.

Coconut Harbour, ~~Post Office~~ Box 2086, George Towne, Grand Cayman; (809) 555-7468.

REMAINDER OF PAGE

~~Seeing a shark is frightening at first; they seem to come out of nowhere and then return to nowhere. But as soon as the creature disappears, you will swim after it. You will just want to keep this beautiful, graceful fish in view as long as you can.~~

DELETE

Character:

1. Place insertion point to the left of character to delete.
2. Press **Delete** .... Del

OR

1. Place insertion point to the right of character to delete.
2. Press **Backspace** .... Backspace

Word:

1. Double-click desired word.
2. Press **Delete** .... Del

OR

1. Place insertion point to the left of word to delete.
2. Press **Ctrl + Delete** .... Ctrl + Del

OR

1. Place insertion point to the right of word to delete.
2. Press .... Ctrl + Backspace
   Ctrl + Backspace

🌐 Block of Text:

1. Select (highlight) block to delete using procedures described on the right.
2. Click **Cut** icon .... ✂

   to place text on clipboard.

   OR

   Press **Delete** .... Del

   OR

   Press **Shift + Delete** ... Shift + Del
   to move block to clipboard.

✓ *The **clipboard** is a temporary storage area in computer memory. The text most recently sent to the clipboard may be retrieved by pressing **Shift + Insert** or by clicking the **Paste** icon on the Toolbar.*

REPLACE DELETED TEXT WITH TYPED TEXT

1. Select text to replace using procedures described below.
2. Type new text .... *text*

SELECT (HIGHLIGHT) BLOCKS OF TEXT

– USING THE KEYBOARD –

Place insertion point where highlight is to begin.

TO HIGHLIGHT:	PRESS:
One character to the left	Shift + ←
One character to the right	Shift + →
One line up	Shift + ↑
One line down	Shift + ↓
To the end of a line	Shift + End
To the beginning of a line	Shift + Home
To the end of a word	Shift + Ctrl + →
To the beginning of a word	Shift + Ctrl + ←
Top of screen	Shift + Ctrl + PgUp
Bottom of screen	Shift + Ctrl + PgDn
To the end of a paragraph	Shift + Ctrl + ↓
To the beginning of a paragraph	Shift + Ctrl + ↑
To the end of the document	Shift + Ctrl + End
To the beginning of the document	Shift + Ctrl + Home
Entire document	Ctrl + A

🌐 – USING THE HIGHLIGHT EXTENDER KEY (F8) –

1. Place insertion point where block highlighting is to begin.
2. Press **F8** F8

EXT appears on the status bar.

3. Press any character, punctuation, or symbol to highlight to the next occurrence of that key.

   OR

   Press any of the insertion movement keys to extend the highlighting.

   OR

   Press **F8** F8
   repeatedly until desired block is selected.

4. Press **Escape** .... Esc
   to cancel Extend mode.

– USING THE MOUSE –

1. Place insertion point where block highlighting is to begin.
2. Hold down the left mouse button and drag the insertion point to desired location.
3. Release the mouse button.

OR

1. Place insertion point where block highlighting is to begin.
2. Point to where selection should end.
3. Press **Shift** .... Shift
   and click left mouse button.

Mouse Selection Shortcuts

To select a word:

1. Place insertion point anywhere in word.
2. Double-click left mouse button.

To select a sentence:

1. Place insertion point anywhere in sentence.
2. Hold down **Ctrl** .... Ctrl
   and click left mouse button.

To select a paragraph:

1. Place insertion point anywhere in paragraph.
2. Triple-click left mouse button.

To select a line of text:

1. Place mouse pointer in **selection bar** opposite desired line.

   Mouse pointer will point to the right when you're in the selection bar area.

2. Click left mouse button once.

To select an entire document:

1. Place mouse pointer anywhere in selection bar.
2. Hold down **Ctrl** .... Ctrl
   and double-click with left mouse button.

To cancel a selection:

Click anywhere in text.

EXERCISE

▪ OPENING A DOCUMENT ▪ DELETING TEXT

NOTES:

- Remember, to combine paragraphs or lines or eliminate skipped lines, it is necessary to delete the paragraph marks.

  ✓ *Note:*　*Paragraph marks will be visible only when you have set the Show/Hide icon to Show mode.*

- To delete a paragraph mark, place the insertion point immediately to the left of the paragraph mark and press the Delete key.

- After deleting paragraph marks between lines, it is sometimes necessary to adjust the text by inserting spaces between the last word of the first line and the first word of the second line.

- The proofreaders' mark for changing uppercase to lowercase is　/　or　*l.c.* ·

In this exercise, you will edit a previously created letter.

EXERCISE DIRECTIONS:

1. Open ⌨ **LETTER** or 💾 **WLETTER.9**.

2. Make the indicated deletions.

   ✓ *Note:*　*To bring the date and closing to the left margin (making this letter block style), place the insertion point at the left margin on the same line as the date. Press the Delete key several times until the date is aligned at the margin. Do the same to bring the closing to the left margin.*

3. Print one copy.

4. Close the file; s*ave as* **LETTER**.

October 1, 199-

Ms. Renee B. Brown
54 Williams Street
Omaha, NE 68101

Dear Ms. Brown:

Thank you for your $ 150 contribution to the American Art Institution. This contribution automatically makes you a member in our arts program.

As an active member, you can participate in our many educational activities.

For example, you can take part in our monthly art lectures, our semi-annual auctions and our frequent art exhibits. Admission to all these events is free.

We look forward to seeing you at our next meeting. We know you will enjoy speaking with our other members and participating in very stimulating conversation.

Sincerely,

Alan Barry
President

ab/yo

EXERCISE

■ NON-BREAKING SPACES ■ INSERTING AND DELETING TEXT

10

NOTES:

■ To prevent two or more words from splitting during word wrap, a **non-breaking space** can be inserted between the words. This is a particularly useful function when keying first and last names, names with titles, dates, equations, and time. When inserting a non-breaking space, it is necessary to delete the original space, or the non-breaking space will have no effect.

■ The proofreaders' mark for moving text right is **]→** or **→]** .

■ The proofreaders' mark for capitalization is ≣ .

■ The proofreaders' mark for non-breaking space is **△** .

EXERCISE DIRECTIONS:

1. Open ⌨ **BLOCK**, or 💾 open **WBLOCK.10**.

2. Make the indicated revisions, inserting a non-breaking space where you see the triangular symbol (△).

3. After all revisions are made, undo the last deleted sentence.

4. Spell check.

5. Print one copy.

6. Close the file; *save as* **BLOCK**.

Today's Date

Mr. Thomas T. Walen
Updike Mechanics Company
23 Clogg Avenue
Atlanta, GA 30315

Dear Mr. Walen:

CONGRATULATIONS! , Mr. Walen You have been nominated as the outstanding office employee
of the month beginning November△4,△1996 through November△30,△1996. ¶ We made
your selection based on the recommendations of your supervisors.
The Committee that made your selection requires that you to submit a photograph of
yourself to your supervisor so that we can display your picture in the company's
executive offices.

Selection   immediate   , Mr. Quinn   throughout

Updike Mechanics is proud of your accomplishments. We look forward to honoring
you at our ANNUAL AWARDS DINNER on December△3.

Sincerely,

Paulette Manning
President

pm/yo

Undo the last deletion.

NON-BREAKING SPACE

1. Type the first word.

2. Press
   **Ctrl + Shift
   + Spacebar** .... `Ctrl` + `Shift` + `Space`

3. Type next word.....................................*word*

OR

1. Delete the normal space between words.

2. Press
   **Ctrl + Shift
   + Spacebar** .... `Ctrl` + `Shift` + `Space`
   to insert a non-breaking space.

EXERCISE

■ **FIND FILE** ■ **PRINTING MULTIPLE FILES**

NOTES:

Find File

■ The **Find File** feature lets you preview or print a file without retrieving it to the screen.

■ Find File is an important feature for locating and organizing files, particularly when you do not remember the name of a file or the nature of its contents.

■ Select Find File from the File main menu.

■ In the Search dialog box which follows, you provide additional information about how you want a file search carried out.

FIND FILE SEARCH DIALOG BOX

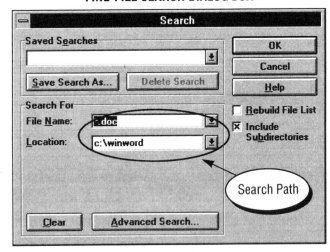

■ When using the Find File feature, the drives and directories to search must be properly set by filling in the Location text box in the Search dialog box.

■ This **search path** tells the computer which drives and directories to search. It is possible to change the search path so you can look for a document on the hard or the floppy drive or on all drives. In the example above, Word will list all

the document (*.doc) files in the directory WINWORD on the C: drive and in any subdirectories under the WINWORD directory because the Include Subdirectories check box has been set to on.

■ Find File lists all files in alphabetical order. The search criteria indicated in the Search Path resulted in the listing of files shown below:

FIND FILE LIST AND PREVIEW SCREEN

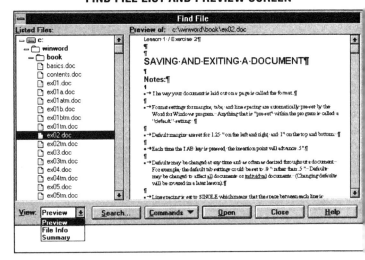

■ In the Find File Preview screen illustration above, the file ex02.doc is highlighted and appears in the Preview area.

■ You can scan a previewed file by clicking the scroll bar or the scroll arrow to the right of the Preview screen.

- Find File may also be used to obtain detailed information about a file or group of files. The File Info option with the View list displays the file size and the date last saved. The Summary option displays other relevant information about the file:

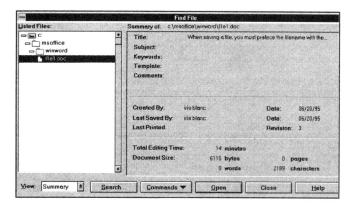

- Find File may also be used for printing, copying, deleting, or sorting a group of files. To print more than one file without opening each to the screen, for example, click (select) the desired file(s) in the file list, click the Commands button, and choose the desired option. Note the options on the drop-down Commands menu below:

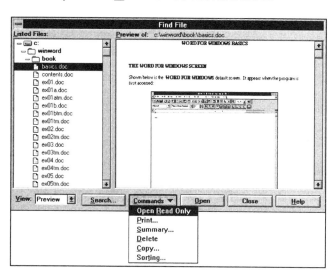

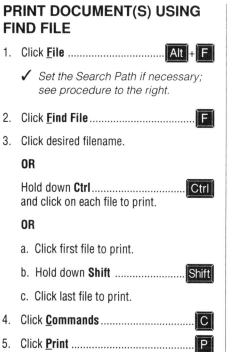

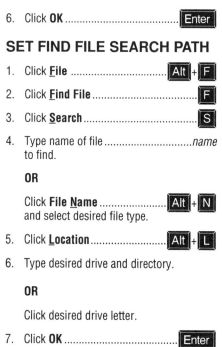

PRINT DOCUMENT(S) USING FIND FILE

1. Click **File** .... Alt + F

   ✓ Set the Search Path if necessary; see procedure to the right.

2. Click **Find File** .... F

3. Click desired filename.

   OR

   Hold down **Ctrl** .... Ctrl
   and click on each file to print.

   OR

   a. Click first file to print.

   b. Hold down **Shift** .... Shift

   c. Click last file to print.

4. Click **Commands** C

5. Click **Print** .... P

6. Click **OK** .... Enter

SET FIND FILE SEARCH PATH

1. Click **File** .... Alt + F

2. Click **Find File** .... F

3. Click **Search** .... S

4. Type name of file ....*name*
   to find.

   OR

   Click **File Name** .... Alt + N
   and select desired file type.

5. Click **Location** .... Alt + L

6. Type desired drive and directory.

   OR

   Click desired drive letter.

7. Click **OK** .... Enter

PREVIEW A DOCUMENT BEFORE OPENING OR PRINTING

1. Click **File** .... Alt + F

2. Click **Find File** .... F

3. Set desired search path if necessary. *(See **SET FIND FILE SEARCH PATH**, left.)*

4. Click **View** .... Alt + V

5. Click **Preview** .... ↓ , Enter

6. Click desired filename.

7. Use scroll bar to preview document as desired.

8. Select **Close** .... Esc
   to return to document window.

In this exercise, you will insert text into a letter created previously.

EXERCISE DIRECTIONS:

1. Use Find File to view ⌨ **PERSONAL**, ⌨ **TRYIT**, and ⌨ **OPEN** or view 💾 **WPERSONAL.5**, 💾 **WTRYIT.7**, and 💾 **WOPEN.11**.

2. Open the file (your own or from the data disk) containing the text illustrated in the exercise.

3. Make the indicated revisions.
4. Spell check.
5. Close the file; *save as* **OPEN**.
6. Use Find File to print one copy of OPEN and PERSONAL.

Arnco Industries

January 22, 199-

Mr. Martin Quincy, ^President
641 Lexington Avenue
New York, NY 10022

Dear Mr. Quincy:

We are very pleased to announce the opening of a new subsidiary of our company. COMPUSELLTRAIN We specialize in service, training and sales of portable personal computers.

This may be hard to believe, but we carry a full line of portable personal computers that can do everything your conventional desktop can. Our portables can run all of the same All of applications as your company's conventional PCs. With the purchase of a computer, we will train two employees on your firm on how to use the an application of your choice.

For a free demonstration, call us at 212-555-9876 any day from 9:00 a.m. to 5:00 p.m.

Very Truly Yours
Sincerely,

The rep for your area is Ms. Sally Hansen. She will phone you to discuss your possible needs.

The graphic capabilities are outstanding

Theresa Mann
President

tm:yo

Restore the deleted paragraph.

LESSON 2
SUMMARY EXERCISE

EXERCISE DIRECTIONS:

1. Create a NEW document.

2. Keyboard the exercise as shown in Part I, or open 💾 **WREGRETS.2A**.

3. Begin the exercise at 2.5".

4. Click the Show/Hide icon on the Standard Toolbar to display codes.

5. Make the revisions as shown in Part II.

6. Spell check.

7. Preview your document.

8. Print one copy.

9. Save the file; name it **REGRETS**.

10. Close the document window.

PART I

Today's date Ms. Kristin Paulo 765 Rand Road Palatine, IL 60074 Dear Ms. Paulo: Thank you for your inquiry regarding employment with our firm. ¶We have reviewed your qualifications with several members of our firm. We regret to report that we do not have an appropriate vacancy at this time. ¶We will retain your resume in our files in the event that an opening occurs in your field. ¶Your interest in our organization is very much appreciated. We hope to be able to offer you a position at another time. Very truly yours, Carol B. Giles PERSONNEL MANAGER cbg/yo

PART II

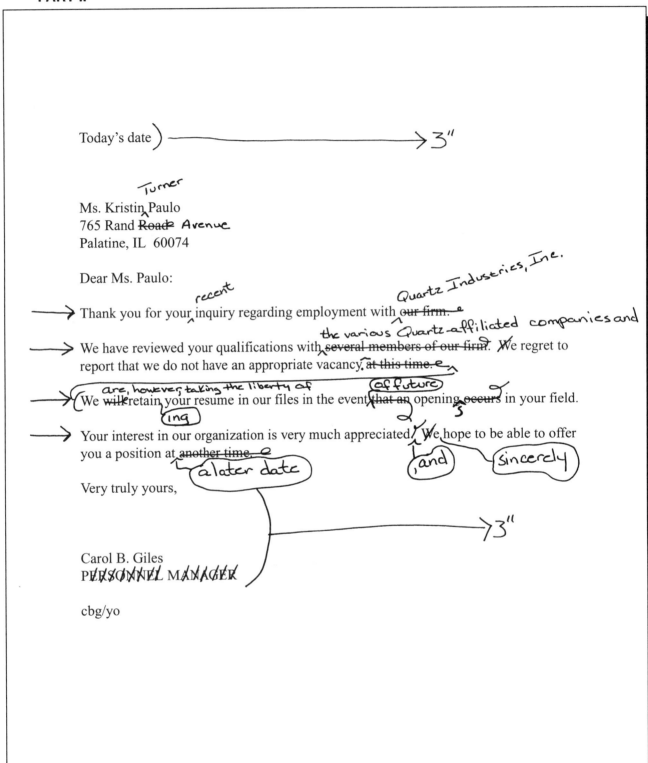

Today's date) ————————————→ 3"

Turner

Ms. Kristin Paulo
765 Rand ~~Road~~ Avenue
Palatine, IL 60074

Dear Ms. Paulo:

recent

→ Thank you for your inquiry regarding employment with ~~our firm.~~ Quartz Industries, Inc.

→ We have reviewed your qualifications with the various Quartz-affiliated companies and ~~several members of our firm~~. We regret to report that we do not have an appropriate vacancy ~~at this time.~~

are, however, taking the liberty of

→ We ~~will~~retain(ing) your resume in our files in the event that an opening ~~occurs~~ of future in your field.

→ Your interest in our organization is very much appreciated, and We hope to be able to offer you a position at ~~another time.~~ a later date. sincerely

Very truly yours, ————————————→ 3"

Carol B. Giles
~~PERSONNEL MANAGER~~

cbg/yo

LESSON 3

TEXT ALIGNMENTS AND ENHANCEMENTS

Exercises 12-16

- Text Alignment

- Vertical Centering

- Changing Font Face, Style, and Size

- Bold, Underline, Italics, Strikethrough, and Small Caps

- Remove Character Formatting

- Using Symbols and Special Characters

- Bullets and Numbering

EXERCISE 12

■ TEXT ALIGNMENT ■ VERTICAL CENTERING

NOTES:

Text Alignments

■ Word lets you align all text that follows the alignment code until another justification code is entered. Word provides four alignment options:

xxxxxxxxxx
xxxxxxxx
xxxxx
xxxxxx

- **Left** - all lines are even at the left margin but are ragged at the right margin (the default).

xxxxxx
xxxxxxxx
xxxx

- **Center** - all lines are centered between the margins.

xxxxxxxxxx
xxxxxxxx
xxxxx
xxxxx

- **Right** - all lines are ragged at the left margin and are even at the right margin.

xxxxxxxxxxxx
xxxxxxxxxxxx
xxxxxxxxxxxx
xxxx.

- **Justify** - all lines are even at the left and right margins, except for the last line of the paragraph.

■ Alignments may affect blocks of text as well as individual lines.

■ Alignments may be changed before or after typing text.

■ Word applies left justification to your text by default.

■ Text may be aligned by selecting the text to be affected, then clicking the appropriate alignment icon on the Formatting Toolbar. Or, to affect the alignment of a paragraph, position the insertion point anywhere within the paragraph and click an alignment icon.

■ The proofreaders' mark for centering is: ⌐⌐ .

Vertical Centering

■ Text may be centered vertically between the top and bottom margins or between the top and bottom edges of the page.

■ To vertically center text, select File, Page Setup, Layout from the menu bar. The following dialog box will appear:

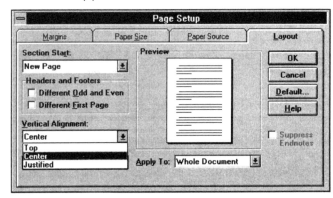

■ Click the Vertical Alignment list arrow, choose Center from the choices, and select OK. *(Note illustration above.)*

■ In order to see the position of the vertically centered material on the page, switch to Page Layout view by selecting View, Page Layout on the menu bar.

In this exercise, you will use various text alignments to create an announcement.

EXERCISE DIRECTIONS:

1. Create a NEW document.
2. Use the default margins and tabs.
3. Center the page from top to bottom.
4. Type each section of text shown in the exercise, changing the alignment appropriately.
5. Preview your document.
6. Print one copy.
7. Save the exercise; name it **COMPANY**.
8. Close the document window.

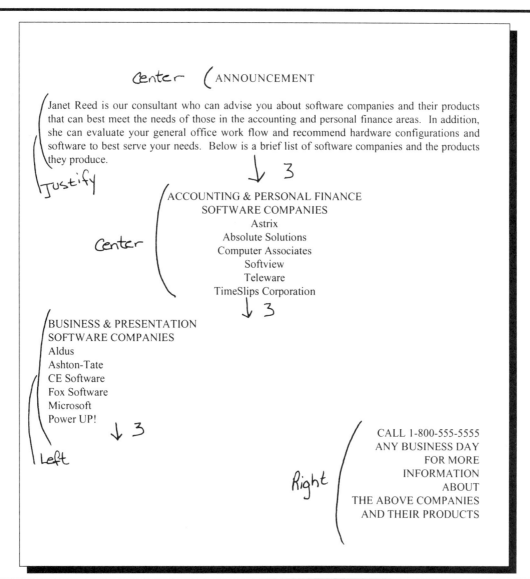

Center (ANNOUNCEMENT

Justify Janet Reed is our consultant who can advise you about software companies and their products that can best meet the needs of those in the accounting and personal finance areas. In addition, she can evaluate your general office work flow and recommend hardware configurations and software to best serve your needs. Below is a brief list of software companies and the products they produce.

↓ 3

Center
ACCOUNTING & PERSONAL FINANCE
SOFTWARE COMPANIES
Astrix
Absolute Solutions
Computer Associates
Softview
Teleware
TimeSlips Corporation

↓ 3

BUSINESS & PRESENTATION
SOFTWARE COMPANIES
Aldus
Ashton-Tate
CE Software
Fox Software
Microsoft
Power UP!

↓ 3

Left

Right
CALL 1-800-555-5555
ANY BUSINESS DAY
FOR MORE
INFORMATION
ABOUT
THE ABOVE COMPANIES
AND THEIR PRODUCTS

ALIGN TEXT CENTER

– BEFORE TYPING TEXT –

CTRL + E

1. Place insertion point anywhere in line or paragraph to center.

2. Click **Center** icon ....

3. Type text...*text*

4. Press **Enter** .... `Enter`

– EXISTING TEXT –

1. Place insertion point in paragraph to center.

   OR

   Select (highlight) block of text to center.

2. Click **Center** icon............................

   OR

   Press **Ctrl + E** .... `Ctrl` + `E`

✓ If you are centering a single line, there must be a paragraph mark (¶) at the end of the line.

To return to flush left:

Ctrl + L

Click **Flush Left** icon .... to return to flush left mode.

JUSTIFY

Ctrl + J

1. Select paragraphs to justify.

   OR

   Place insertion point in desired paragraph.

2. Click **Justify** icon ....

FLUSH RIGHT

– BEFORE TYPING TEXT –

Ctrl + R

1. Place insertion point where text will be typed.

2. Click **Align Right** icon ....

3. Type text...*text* as necessary.

To return to flush left mode:

Ctrl + L

Click **Align Left** icon .... to return to flush left mode.

To align existing text flush right:

1. Select (highlight) text to right align.

2. Click **Align Right** icon ....

   OR

   Press **Ctrl + R** .... `Ctrl` + `R`

VERTICALLY CENTER TEXT

1. Click **File**................................... `Alt` + `F`

2. Click **Page Setup**.......................... `U`

3. Click **Layout**.......................... `Alt` + `L`

4. Click **Vertical Alignment** .... `Alt` + `V` list arrow.

5. Select **Center**.................................... `↓`

6. Click **OK** .... `Enter`

EXERCISE

13

■ **CHANGING FONT FACE, STYLE, AND SIZE**

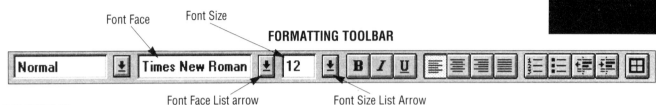

Font Face — Font Size

FORMATTING TOOLBAR

Font Face List arrow — Font Size List Arrow

NOTES:

- A **font** is a complete set of characters in a specific face, style, and size. Each set includes upper- and lowercase letters, numerals, and punctuation. A font that might be available to you in Word is Arial.

- A **font face** (often called **typeface** or just **font**) is the design of a character. Each design has a name and is intended to convey a specific feeling.

- You should select typefaces that will make your document attractive and communicate its particular message. As a rule, use no more than two or three font faces in any one document.

Font Faces

- There are basically three types of font faces: serif, sans serif, and script. A **serif** face has lines, curves, or edges extending from the ends of the letter (**T**), while a **sans serif** face is straight-edged (**T**) and **script** looks like handwriting (𝒯).

Serif Font Face:

> Times New Roman

Sans Serif Font Face:

> Helvetica

Script Font Face:

> *Freestyle Script*

- A serif font face is typically used for document text because it is more readable. Sans serif is often used for headlines or technical material. Script typefaces are used for formal invitations and announcements.

- Font faces may be changed by selecting Font from the Format menu, then selecting the desired font listed in the Font dialog box.

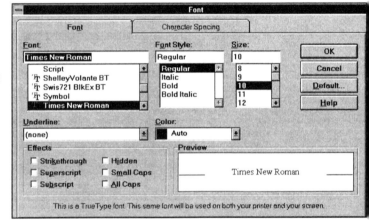

- It may also be changed by clicking the Font Face list arrow button on the Formatting Toolbar (which drops down a list of font choices).

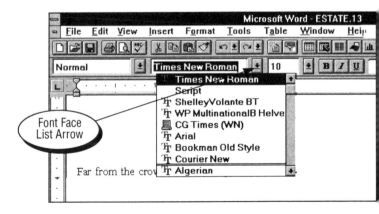

- The Font dialog box may also be accessed by clicking the *right* mouse button anywhere in the document window and selecting Font.

- The typefaces that are available to you depend on the printer you are using. While there are hundreds of varieties of typefaces, Word includes some that will work with most printers. Those that will work with your printer will have a small 🖳 next to the typeface name in the list of typefaces.

- Windows version 3.1 supports the use of **True Type fonts**. Using True Type fonts permits your screen to display text the way it will appear when you print it. True Type fonts are identified by a double ᵀᵣ in front of the font name.

Font Style

- **Font style** refers to the slant and weight of letters, such as bold and italic.

> Times New Roman Regular
> *Times New Roman Italic*
> **Times New Roman Bold**
> ***Times New Roman Bold Italic***

- Note the Font dialog box illustrated on the previous page. The Font Style box lists the styles or weights specially designed and available for the selected font.

Font Size

- **Font size** generally refers to the height of the font, usually measured in points.

> Bookman 8 point
>
> Bookman 12 point
>
> Bookman 18 point

- There are 72 points to an inch. Use 10 to 12 point type size for document text and larger sizes for headings and headlines.

- Font size may be changed in the Font dialog box or by clicking the Font Size list arrow on the Formatting Toolbar (which drops down a list of font sizes).

- The currently selected font, style, and size is displayed in the Preview window and described at the bottom of the Font dialog box.

- You can change fonts *before* or *after* typing text.

In this exercise, you will create an advertisement and apply text alignments and enhancements to the document.

EXERCISE DIRECTIONS:

1. Create a NEW document.

2. Keyboard the exercise exactly as shown in Part I using proper text alignments, or open 💾 **WESTATE.13**.

3. Change the font face, font size, and font style as shown in Part II.

4. Vertically center the exercise.

5. Spell check.

6. Preview your document.

7. Print one copy.

8. Close the file; *save as* **ESTATE**.

PART I

PINEVIEW ESTATES

The country home
that's more like a country club.

Far from the crowds, on the unspoiled North Fork of Long Island, you'll find a unique country home. PineView Estates. A condominium community perfectly situated between Peconic Bay and Long Island Sound on a lovely wooded landscape. And like the finest country club, it offers a community club house, tennis court, pool and a golf course.

Models Open Daily 11 to 4
PineView Estates
Southhold, New York
(516) 555-5555

The complete terms are in an offering plan available from the sponsor.

PART II

PINEVIEW ESTATES

) Sans Serif
(Braggadocio)
18 point

*The country home
that's more like a country club.*

) Script
(Shelly Volante BT)
22 point

Far from the crowds, on the unspoiled North Fork of Long Island, you'll find a unique country home. PineView Estates. A condominium community perfectly situated between Peconic Bay and Long Island Sound on a lovely wooded landscape. And like the finest country club, it offers a community club house, tennis court, pool and a golf course.

) Sans Serif
10 point

Models Open Daily 11 to 4
PineView Estates
Southhold, New York
(516) 555-5555

) Sans Serif 10pt
) 9 point

The complete terms are in an offering plan available from the sponsor.

) Sans Serif
6 point

CHANGE FONT FACE

✓ *If all text in a paragraph will be in the same font, it is recommended that you include the paragraph mark at the end of the paragraph in your selection (highlighting) before changing font.*

1. Select text for which font is to be changed.

    OR

    Place insertion point where new font is to begin.

2. Click **font list arrow** on the Formatting Toolbar and click desired font.

    OR

a. Click **Format**........................ `Alt`+`O`

b. Click **Font** .... `F`

c. Select **Font** .... `Alt`+`F`

d. Click desired font.............. `↓`or `↑`

e. Click **OK**.............................. `Enter`

CHANGE FONT SIZE

1. Select text for which font size is to be changed.

    OR

    Place insertion point where new font size is to begin.

2. Click **point size list arrow** on the Formatting Toolbar and click desired point size.

    OR

a. Click **Format** .... `Alt`+`O`

b. Click **Font**.................................. `F`

c. Select **Size** .... `Alt`+`S`

d. Click desired point size. ....`↓`or `↑`

e. Click **OK** .... `Enter`

EXERCISE

- **BOLD, UNDERLINE, DOUBLE UNDERLINE, ITALICS, STRIKETHROUGH, AND SMALL CAPS** - **REMOVE CHARACTER FORMATTING**

FORMATTING TOOLBAR

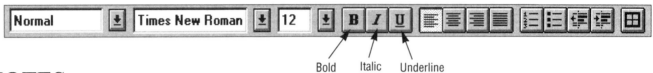

Bold   Italic   Underline

NOTES:

- **Bold**, <u>underline</u>, <u>double underline,</u> and *italic* are features used to emphasize or enhance text. These features work as on/off toggle switches. You must choose the command to turn on the feature; then choose the command to turn off the feature.

- The appearance of a font face is changed by using the style buttons shown above (there is no double underline button in the Toolbar).

- Double underline must be accessed by pressing CTRL+SHIFT+D.

- As indicated in the previous exercise, font styles also adds bold and italics to a font face, but not all font faces have these styles added.

- In addition to bold, underline, and double underline, Word provides other effects. These include small caps, all caps and strikeout. The **strikeout** effect is used to indicate text has been added, deleted or moved, and is useful when comparing the current document with a different version of a document. Note examples below:

> SMALL CAPS
> ALL CAPS
> ~~strikeout~~

- Like the other appearance changes, these may be applied *before* or *after* typing text. They may be accessed by selecting one of the Effects in the Font dialog box.

- If your printer does not support italics, the printed copy will appear underlined.

- Text may be emphasized before or after typing text.

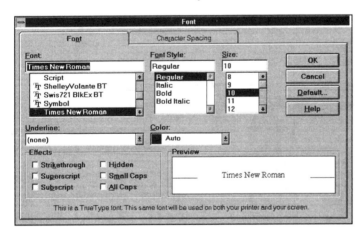

- Bolding, italicizing, underlining, and double underlining may be removed using the same procedure used when applying these special character formats.

- You may remove character formatting individually, or you may remove *all* character formatting from a selected (highlighted) block of text by pressing the Ctrl key and the Spacebar. This is a useful feature when you wish to remove two or more formats in one step, such as bolding *and* underlining *and* italicizing.

- The proofreaders' mark for each style is:

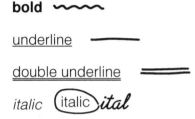

bold

underline

double underline

italic

In this exercise, you will create and enhance a letter using bold, double underline, italics, and small caps.

EXERCISE DIRECTIONS:

1. Create a NEW document.

2. Keyboard the exercise as shown, using the appropriate alignments and enhancements indicated, or open 💾 **WGLOBAL.14** and format and enhance the text as shown in the exercise.

3. Begin the letterhead At 1"; begin the date At 2.5". Use the date feature to insert the date.

4. Use the default margins.

5. Spell check.

6. Justify paragraph text.

7. Preview your document.

8. Print one copy.

9. Close the file; *save as* **GLOBAL**.

THE GLOBAL TRAVEL GROUP *[Sans Serif 16pt bold]*

485 Madison Avenue
New York, NY 10034 *[Sans Serif 10pt italics]*

PHONE: (212) 234-4566
FAX: (212) 345-9877 *[Sans Serif 10pt italics]*

[Serif 12pt]

Today' Date

Mr. Astrit Ibrosi
45 Lake View Drive
Huntington, NY 11543

Dear Mr. Ibrosi:

Ms. Packer in our office has referred your letter to me. You had asked her to provide you with a list of hotels in the San Francisco area that have a business center which offers laptop rentals, fax services, and teleconferencing capabilities.

Since I am the representative for the San Francisco area, I have compiled a list of hotels that offer the services you requested. They appear below:

[Small Caps 12pt]

REGENCY CENTRAL
SURRY HOTEL
FAIRMONT HOTEL
RENAISSANCE CENTER
MARRIOTT MARK
GRAND HYATT

When you are ready to make your reservations, please call our office. If you have any other travel needs, call <u>GLOBAL</u>. Our experienced staff will give you prompt and courteous service and will answer all your travel questions. *[double underline]*

[Serif 12pt]

Sincerely,

Marietta Dunn
Travel Representative

md/yo

BOLD

Ctrl + B

– BEFORE TYPING TEXT –

1. Place insertion point where bold is to begin.

2. Click **Bold** icon.............................. **B**

   OR

   Press **Ctrl + B** .... **Ctrl** + **B**

3. Type text..*text*

4. Click **Bold** icon .... **B**
   to discontinue bolding.

   OR

   Press **Ctrl + B** .... **Ctrl** + **B**
   to discontinue bolding.

– EXISTING TEXT –

1. Select (highlight) text to bold.

2. Click **Bold** icon.................................... **B**

   OR

   Press **Ctrl + B** .... **Ctrl** + **B**

UNDERLINE

Ctrl + U

– BEFORE TYPING TEXT –

1. Place insertion point where underline is to begin.

2. Click **Underline** icon .... **U**

   OR

   Press **Ctrl + U** .... **Ctrl** + **U**

3. Type text..*text*

4. Click **Underline** icon .... **U**
   to discontinue underlining.

   OR

   Press **Ctrl + U** .... **Ctrl** + **U**
   to discontinue underlining.

– EXISTING TEXT –

1. Select (highlight) text to underline.

2. Click **Underline** icon .... **U**

   OR

   Press **Ctrl + U** .... **Ctrl** + **U**

✓ Remove underlining by repeating the steps above.

ITALICS

Ctrl + I

– BEFORE TYPING TEXT –

1. Place insertion point where italicizing is to begin.

2. Click **Italic** icon .... **I**

   OR

   a. Click **Format** .... **Alt** + **O**

   b. Click **Font** .... **F**

   c. Click **Font Style**.................. **Alt** + **O**

   d. Click **Italic** .... **↓** , **↑**

   e. Click **OK** .... **Enter**

3. Type text..*text*

4. Click **Italic** icon .... **I**
   to discontinue italicizing.

   OR

   Press **Ctrl + I** .... **Ctrl** + **I**
   to discontinue italicizing.

– EXISTING TEXT –

1. Select (highlight) text to italicize.

2. Click **Italic** icon .... **I**

   OR

   Press **Ctrl + I** .... **Ctrl** + **I**

   OR

   a. Click **Format** .... **Alt** + **O**

   b. Click **Font** .... **F**

   c. Click **Font Style**.................. **Alt** + **O**

   d. Click **Italic** .... **↓** , **↑**

   e. Click **OK** .... **Enter**

✓ Remove italics by repeating the steps above.

DOUBLE UNDERLINE

Ctrl + Shift + D

– BEFORE TYPING TEXT –

1. Place insertion point where double underlining is to begin.

2. Press
   Ctrl + Shift + D .... **Ctrl** + **Shift** + **D**

3. Type text..text

4. Press
   Ctrl + Shift + D .... **Ctrl** + **Shift** + **D**
   to discontinue
   double underlining.

– EXISTING TEXT –

1. Select (highlight) text to double underline.

2. Press
   Ctrl + Shift + D .... **Ctrl** + **Shift** + **D**

✓ To remove double underlining, repeat the steps above.

REMOVE CHARACTER FORMATTING

Ctrl + B, Ctrl + D, Ctrl + I, Ctrl + Space

1. Select (highlight) text containing the formatting to remove.

2. Click **Bold** icon .... **B**
   to remove bolding.

   OR

   Click **Underline** icon......................... **U**
   to remove underlining.

   OR

   Press **Ctrl + U** .... **Ctrl** + **U**
   to remove double underlining.

   OR

   Click **Italics** icon .... **I**
   to remove italics.

   OR

   Press **Ctrl + I** .... **Ctrl** + **I**
   to remove italics.

   OR

   Press **Ctrl + Space** .... **Ctrl** + **Space**
   to remove *all* character
   formatting.

EFFECTS (Strikethrough, Small Caps, All Caps)

1. Click **Format** .... **Alt** + **O**

2. Click **Font** .... **F**

3. Click desired Effects.

   • **Strikethrough** .... **K**

   • **Small Caps**.................................. **M**

   • **All Caps** .... **A**

4. Click **OK** .... **Enter**

EXERCISE

USING SYMBOLS AND SPECIAL CHARACTERS

NOTES:

- **Wingdings** is an ornamental symbol font face collection that is used to enhance a document. Illustrated below is the Wingdings font collection.

- A symbol font face must be available with your printer.

Click to select other symbols and special characters

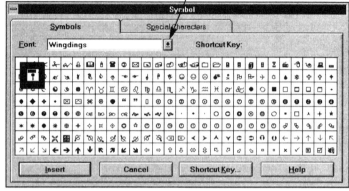

WINGDINGS FONT COLLECTION

- The upper- and lowercase of the letter and character key provide different Wingdings. To create a Wingding, press and then highlight the corresponding keyboard letter or character shown in the chart, and select Wingdings from the Font Face list. Or, select Symbol from the Insert menu and select a Wingding from the Symbol dialog box.

- There are other ornamental fonts and special characters which may be accessed by clicking on the list arrow next to the Font text box in the Symbols dialog box.

- Ornamental fonts and special character sets are also found as fonts. They can be accessed through the Font dialog box. Some names begin with WP.

- You may change the size of a symbol font face as you would any other character, by changing the point size.

- Ornamental fonts can be used to:

  - Separate items on a page:

    Wingdings
    ❖❖◆❖❖
    Graphics

  - Emphasize items on a list:

    ✎dresses
    ✎coats
    ✎suits

  - Enhance a page:

    BOOK SALE

In this exercise, you will create a menu and add a symbol face to separate portions of it.

EXERCISE DIRECTIONS:

1. Create a NEW document.
2. Keyboard the exercise as shown, using the appropriate alignments and enhancements indicated, or open 💾 **WCAFE.15**, format and enhance the text as shown in the exercise.
3. Use the default margins.
4. Enhance the document with symbols from the Wingdings and WP Iconic SymbolsA font collections. Use any desired symbol.

5. Spell check.
6. Preview your document.
7. Vertically center the exercise.
8. Print one copy.
9. Close the file; *save as* **CAFE**.

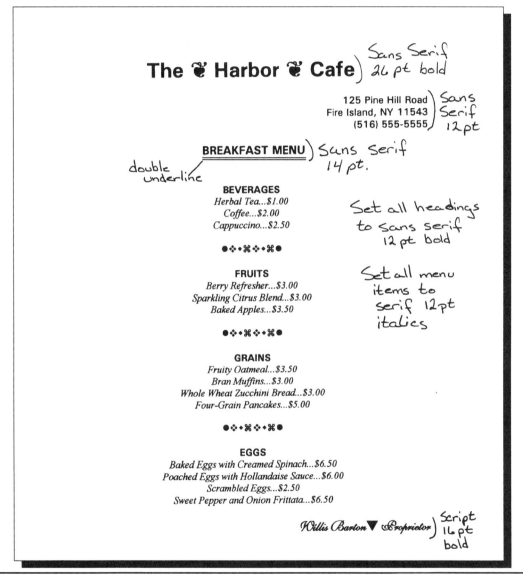

The ❦ Harbor ❦ Cafe) Sans Serif 26 pt bold

125 Pine Hill Road
Fire Island, NY 11543
(516) 555-5555) Sans Serif 12pt

BREAKFAST MENU) Sans serif 14 pt.

double underline

BEVERAGES
Herbal Tea...$1.00
Coffee...$2.00
Cappuccino...$2.50

Set all headings to sans serif 12 pt bold

●❖✦✳❖✳❖✦●

FRUITS
Berry Refresher...$3.00
Sparkling Citrus Blend...$3.00
Baked Apples...$3.50

Set all menu items to serif 12pt italics

●❖✦✳❖✳❖✦●

GRAINS
Fruity Oatmeal...$3.50
Bran Muffins...$3.00
Whole Wheat Zucchini Bread...$3.00
Four-Grain Pancakes...$5.00

●❖✦✳❖✳❖✦●

EGGS
Baked Eggs with Creamed Spinach...$6.50
Poached Eggs with Hollandaise Sauce...$6.00
Scrambled Eggs...$2.50
Sweet Pepper and Onion Frittata...$6.50

Willis Barton ▼ *Proprietor*) Script 16 pt bold

INSERT A SYMBOL OR SPECIAL CHARACTER

1. Place insertion point where special character will be inserted.
2. Click **Insert** .... [Alt] + [I]
3. Click **Symbol** .... [S]
4. Click **Symbols** tab .... [Alt] + [S]
5. Click **Font** list arrow .... [Alt] + [F]

6. Select desired font ....
7. Click and hold left mouse button down to enlarge desired special character for viewing.
8. Double-click desired special character to insert it into document.

OR

a. Click .... [Alt] + [P]
   Special Characters tab.

b. Select desired character ...
c. Double-click desired special character to insert it into document.

OR

a. Type the corresponding letter or symbol shown on the chart
b. Highlight the symbol.
c. Click Font list arrow on toolbar.
d. Select Wingdings.

EXERCISE

BULLETS AND NUMBERING

16

Numbering   Bullets

FORMATTING TOOLBAR

NOTES:

■ A **bullet** is a dot or symbol used to highlight points of information or to itemize a list that does not need to be in any particular order.

• red	• apple
• blue	• pear
• green	• orange

■ Using the **Bullets and Numbering** feature, you can insert bullets automatically to create a bulleted list for each paragraph or item you type.

■ The Bullets and Numbering feature also allows you to create numbered paragraphs for items that need to be in a particular order. The numbers you insert increment automatically.

The Bullets and Numbering feature allows you to:
1.   Create numbered paragraphs.
2.   Create bulleted paragraphs.
3.   Use symbols instead of the traditional round dot or square bullet.

■ The Bullets and Numbering feature is accessed by selecting Bullets & Numbering from the Format main menu.

■ In the Bullets and Numbering dialog box which follows, you may click the Bulleted tab and select the bullet style you desire. Or, you may click the Numbered tab and select the number style you desire.

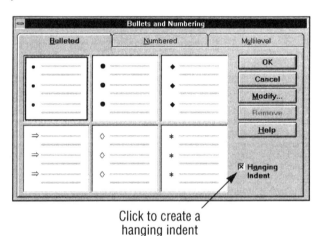

Click to create a
hanging indent

■ Once the bullet or number style is chosen, you may type your text. The bullet or number is entered automatically each time the Enter key is pressed. If the hanging indent option is selected, the bullet or number begins at the left margin, and the text automatically advances to the first tab stop. To return the second line of text to the left margin, deselect the Hanging Indent option in the dialog box.

■ Bullets and Numbering may also be accessed by clicking the Bullets ▤ or Numbering ▤ icon on the Formatting Toolbar.

- You can add bullets and numbers to existing text by selecting/highlighting the text and then choosing Bullets and Numbering from the Format main menu or clicking the appropriate icon on the Formatting Toolbar.

- Symbols may also be used as bullets.

- When using the Bullets and Numbering feature for numbered paragraphs, adding or deleting paragraphs will result in all paragraphs being automatically renumbered.

- To change the bullet style to a symbol, select Modify in the Bullets and Numbering dialog box. Then click the Bullet button. The Symbol dialog box appears, allowing you to select a desired symbol.

Remove Bullets or Numbers

- Bullets may be removed from a bulleted list by selecting the part of the list from which bullets are to be removed. You must place the mouse pointer to the right of the selected lines and click the *right* mouse button. A shortcut menu will appear. Choose **Stop Numbering** to remove the bullets from the selected text and discontinue the indenting that accompanies bulleted items. Choose **Skip Numbering** to remove bullets from the selected text but continue the indenting of subsequent lines.

In this exercise, you will create a flyer and add a symbol face to separate portions of it.

EXERCISE DIRECTIONS:

1. Create a NEW document.

2. Keyboard the exercise as shown, using the appropriate alignments and enhancements. Use any desired bullet style, or open 💾 **WDESIGN.16**, then format and enhance the text as shown in the exercise.

3. Use the default margins.

4. Enhance the document with symbols from the Wingdings and WP Iconic SymbolsA font collections. Use any desired symbols in those collections

5. Spell check.

6. Preview your document.

7. Vertically center the exercise.

8. Print one copy.

9. Close the file; *save as* **DESIGN**.

Create a) Script 40 pt bold

Design with Color) Serif 30 point bold

4 Reasons Why) sans serif 24 pt

The world is a colorful place.
So, why not include color in all your) serif 14 pt italic
processing?

⇒ *Color increases the visual impact of the message and makes*) Sans Serif 14 pt
it more memorable.   Don't you want your ads to have impact and be) Serif 12pt
noticed?

⇒ *Color creates a feeling and helps explain the subject.* Greens   use same
and blues are cool, relaxing tones, while reds and oranges scream with← font face
emphasis. Pastels communicate a gentle tone.   and size as
first item

⇒ *Color creates a personality.* You can make your corporate forms and
brochures have their own identity and personality with color.

⇒ *Color highlights information.* An advertisement or manual might have
warnings in red, explanations in black and instructions in blue.

◆ ◆ ◆) 12 pt wingdings

Our color processing labs will take care of *all* your color processing needs.) Sans
Just call *1-800-555-6666* for information. Our courteous staff is ready to) serif
assist you with any technical question.   12 pt.

L ◆A◆ B◆ P◆ R ◆O
FOR
COLOR PROCESSING) Sans Serif 12 pt

BULLETS

1. Place insertion point where text will be typed.

   OR

   Select text to convert to a bulleted list.

2. Click **Bullet List** icon.......................... ▤

   OR

   a. Click **F<u>o</u>rmat**...................... Alt + O
   b. Click **Bullets and <u>N</u>umbering** .... N
   c. Click **<u>B</u>ulleted**.................... Alt + B
   d. Click desired bullet style ...... ⤶ ⇅
   e. Click **OK**............................... Enter

REMOVE BULLETS

1. Select the part of the list from which bullets are to be removed.

2. Place mouse pointer to right of selected text.

3. Click *right* mouse button.

4. Choose **Stop Numbering** to remove bullets and end the list.

   OR

   Choose **Skip Numbering** to remove bullets and continue list.

NUMBERING

1. Select (highlight) block of paragraphs to convert to a numbered list.

2. Click **Numbered List** icon .... ▤

   OR

   a. Click **F<u>o</u>rmat** .... Alt + O
   b. Click **Bullets and <u>N</u>umbering** ...... N
   c. Click **<u>N</u>umbered** .... Alt + N
   d. Click........................ Tab , ⤶ ⇅
      desired
      numbering style.
   e. Click **OK** .... Enter

REMOVE NUMBERING

1. Select the part of the list from which numbering is to be removed.

2. Place mouse pointer to the right of the selected text.

3. Click *right* mouse button.

4. Click **Stop Numbering** to remove numbering and terminate the list.

   OR

   Choose **Skip Numbering** to remove numbering and continue list with adjusted numbering.

In this exercise, you will create a flyer using text alignments, enhancements, bullets, and numbers.

EXERCISE DIRECTIONS:

1. Create a NEW document.

2. Keyboard the exercise as shown, using the appropriate alignments and enhancements. Use any desired bullet style for the bulleted items, or open 💾 **WCOLOR.3A**, then format and enhance the text as shown in the exercise.

3. Use the default margins.

4. Enhance the document with any desired symbols from the Wingdings and WP Iconic SymbolsA font collections.

5. Spell check.

6. Preview your document.

7. Vertically center the exercise.

8. Print one copy.

9. Close the file; save as **COLOR**.

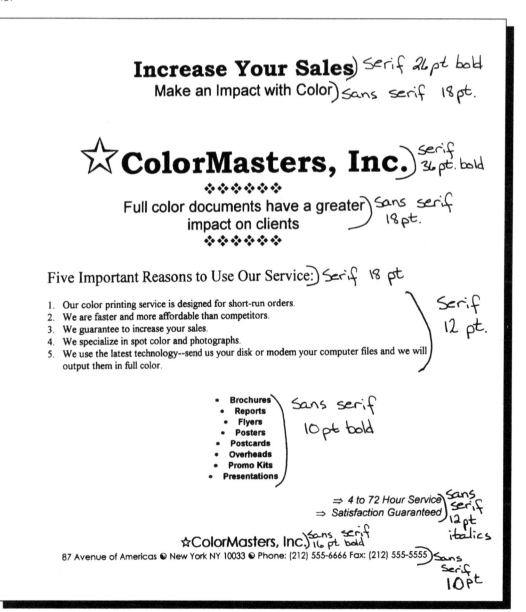

LESSON 4

FORMATTING AND EDITING DOCUMENTS

Exercises 17-21

- Line Spacing

- Indenting Text

- Hanging Indents

- Format a One-Page Report

- Set Margins

- Cut and Paste

- Drag and Drop

- Format Painter

- Moving Text

- Copy and Paste

EXERCISE

■ LINE SPACING ■ INDENTING TEXT ■ HANGING INDENTS

FORMATTING TOOLBAR

Decrease Indent   Indent

NOTES:

Line Spacing

■ Use **line spacing** to specify the spacing between lines of text. A line spacing change affects text in the paragraph that contains the insertion point. Line spacing may also be applied to selected text. If your line spacing is set for double, two hard returns will result in four blank lines.

■ The quickest way to change line spacing is to press Ctrl + 2 for double space, Ctrl + 3 for triple space, etc. Other methods for changing line spacing are outlined in the keystrokes.

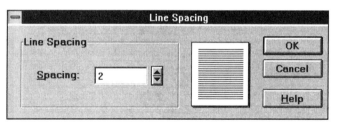

Indenting Text

■ The **indent** feature moves a complete paragraph one tab stop to the right and sets a temporary left margin for the paragraph or indents paragraph text one tab stop from the right margin or both margins.

ILLUSTRATION OF INDENTED PARAGRAPHS

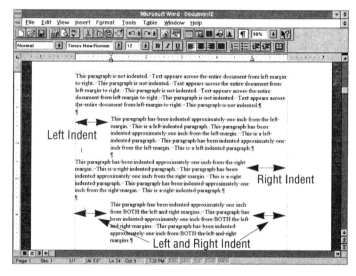

■ Paragraphs may be indented before or after text is typed.

■ Since text is indented to a tab setting, accessing the Indent feature once will indent text .5" to the right (or left and right); accessing it twice will indent text 1", etc.

■ The Indent mode is ended by a hard return.

■ Before accessing the Indent feature, be sure to position the insertion point to the left of the first word in the paragraph to be indented or within the paragraph.

■ There are numerous ways to indent text.

- Each method of indenting text has its own advantage:

  - **Dragging the indent markers on the ruler** is the most convenient way of setting left *and* right indents.

  - **Clicking the indent icon on the Toolbar** is the most convenient method if you wish to set *only* the left indent.

  - **Selecting the F̲ormat, P̲aragraph, I̲ndents and Spacing** command on the menu bar allows greater precision for setting left *and* right indents.

    ✓ *Note:* *These methods are described in detail below.*

Dragging the Indent Markers on the Ruler

PAGE LAYOUT VIEW RULER

✓ *Note:* *Indent markers are shown 1" from left and right margins.*

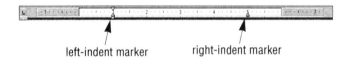

left-indent marker   right-indent marker

NORMAL VIEW RULER

✓ *Note:* *Indent markers are shown 1" from left and right margins.*

left-indent marker   right-indent marker

- Note the illustrations of the rulers above. The ruler in both Page Layout view and Normal view is the same except that in Normal view the area outside of the left margin is not visible on screen. Observe that the same indent markers appear in each ruler. These rulers show the indent settings for the last paragraph in the illustration of indented paragraphs above.

- To change indents, the left- and right-indent markers may be *dragged* to the desired indent positions. Note that the left-indent marker consists of three parts:

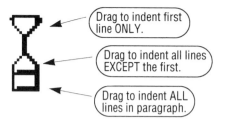

Drag to indent first line ONLY.

Drag to indent all lines EXCEPT the first.

Drag to indent ALL lines in paragraph.

Clicking the Indent Icon on the Toolbar

Indent

FORMATTING TOOLBAR

Decrease Indent

- Text may be indented only from the *left* margin using Toolbar icons.

- To change indents using the Indent icons, select the desired block of text and click the **Indent** icon, or place insertion point in the paragraph to indent and click the Indent icon.

- Left indents may be removed by selecting the desired text and clicking the **Decrease** indent icon.

Selecting the F̲ormat, P̲aragraph, I̲ndents and Spacing Command

PARAGRAPH INDENTS AND SPACING DIALOG BOX

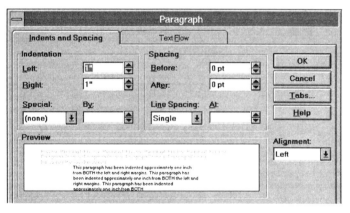

- Note the I̲ndents and Spacing dialog box above. It contains the same settings as those displayed on the two ruler illustrations on the previous page; one inch indents from both left and right margins.

- To set left and right indents, click the increase or decrease arrows in the Indentation area until the desired indent positions appear, or place the insertion point in the L̲eft or R̲ight indent text box and key the desired indent setting.

Word ▪ Lesson 4 ▪ Exercise 17   75

- Use the Format, Paragraph, Indents and Spacing dialog box to set indents when maximum precision is required.

Hanging Indents

- It is possible to indent all of the lines in a paragraph *except* the first line. This creates a **hanging indent**.

- A hanging indented paragraph appears below. Note the effect in which the paragraph appears to be hanging from the first line:

> The way text will lay out or format on a page is set by the Word for Windows program. For example, margins are set for 1.25" on the left and 1.25" on the right; line spacing is automatic; tabs are set to advance the cursor .5" inch each time the Tab key is pressed. Formats may be changed at any time and as many times as desired throughout the document.

- Each of the three methods of creating (or removing) a hanging indent has its own advantage:

  - **Dragging the left-indent marker and the first-line indent marker on the ruler** is the most convenient method and lets you see the indents change as you adjust them.

  - **Pressing Ctrl + T, a keyboard shortcut,** for the quickest way to indent to a previously set tab stop.

  - **Selecting the Format, Paragraph, Indents and Spacing command on the menu bar** to set left and first line indents to allow greater precision.

    ✓ Note: *These methods are described in detail to the right.*

Dragging the Left-Indent Marker and the First-Line Indent Marker on the Ruler
FIRST-LINE INDENT AND LEFT-INDENT MARKERS ON RULER

First-line indent marker

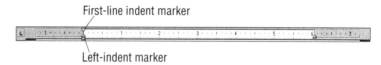

Left-indent marker

- Note the illustration of the **first-line indent marker** and the **left-indent marker** on the ruler above. The first-line indent marker sets the indent for the first line of the paragraph, the left-indent marker sets the indent for all remaining lines in the paragraph *except* the first line.

- To set a hanging indent, drag the left-indent marker to a position anywhere to the right of the first-line indent marker. Note the ruler position of the first-line and left-indent markers in the illustrations below before and after creating a hanging indent.

PARAGRAPH BEFORE ADDITION OF HANGING INDENT

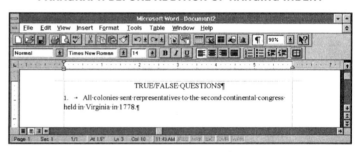

PARAGRAPH WITH A HANGING INDENT

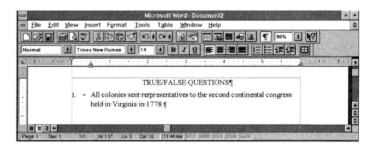

- Dragging the first-line and left-indent markers has the advantage of allowing you to create the hanging indent visually. The small box below the left-indent marker may be used to drag *both* the first-line *and* the left-indent markers simultaneously, if you should wish to indent the first line in a paragraph as well as all remaining lines.

Pressing Ctrl + T, a Keyboard Shortcut

■ Place the insertion point in the desired paragraph and press Ctrl + T to set the left indent at the next tab stop. The first-line indent will remain unchanged, while all paragraph text *except* the first line will be indented to the next tab stop. Ctrl + T may be repeated as necessary to achieve the desired hanging indent.

■ Pressing Ctrl + Shift + T will *undo* indents created with Ctrl + T.

Selecting the Format, Paragraph, Indents and Spacing Command on the Menu Bar to Set Left and First-Line Indents

■ With the insertion point in the desired paragraph, select Format, Paragraph, Indents and Spacing from the menu bar. Key the desired left indent in the Left box. Select Special and choose Hanging, then select By and key the desired measurement for the hanging indent. Press the Enter key when settings are complete.

■ Note the illustration below of a hanging indent which begins at the left margin. The left margin is at zero. The first-line marker of the paragraph is set at the margin; the remaining lines of the paragraph are left indented .25" from the margin.

> a. Take the Cross County Expressway three miles to the exit for Grand Avenue Overpass. (Watch for the tall building with three flags just before you reach the Grand Avenue exit.)

■ It is also possible to create a hanging indent in which *all* lines in the paragraph are indented from the left margin, but the first line is not indented as much as the remaining lines.

■ Note the illustration on the top right of a hanging indent in which *all* lines in the second paragraph are indented from the left margin, but the first line is not indented as much as the remaining lines. The left margin is at zero. The first line of the paragraph is indented .5" from the margin; the remaining lines of the paragraph are left indented .75" from the margin.

> Because of the construction work being done on the Memorial Highway, employees driving to the Regional Sales Convention this weekend may wish to consider the following alternate route:
>
> > a. Take the Cross County Expressway three miles to the exit for Grand Avenue Overpass. (Watch for the tall building with three flags just before you reach the Grand Avenue exit.)

✓ *Note:* *To create the second paragraph in the illustration above, the ruler was set as follows:*

first-line indent set at .5"
left-indent set at .75"

> *In this exercise, you will change line spacing, indent text, and change fonts to create a flyer.*

EXERCISE DIRECTIONS:

1. Create a NEW document.

2. Open 📟 **DIVE** or 🖫 **WDIVE.17**.

3. Make the indicated revisions.

4. Use any desired method to indent hotel listings paragraphs.

5. Set all document text to 14 point.

6. Justify hotel text.

7. Double space paragraph text.

8. Spell check.

9. Preview your document.

10. Print one copy.

11. Reformat the indented paragraphs to hanging indented paragraphs. Leave the first line of each paragraph where it is; set an additional .5" indent for the remaining lines. *(See Desired Result II.)*

12. Print one copy.

13. Close the file; *save as* **DIVE**.

LINE SPACING

1. Place insertion point where new line spacing is to begin.

   OR

   Select the paragraphs in which line spacing is to be changed.

2. Select desired line spacing option:

   - Press **Ctrl + 2** .... `Ctrl` + `2` to change to double space lines.

   - Press **Ctrl + 1** .... `Ctrl` + `1` to change to single space lines.

   - Press **Ctrl + 5** .... `Ctrl` + `5` to change to 1.5 space lines.

   OR

1. Place insertion point where new line spacing is to begin.

   OR

   Select the paragraphs in which line spacing is to be changed.

2. Click **Format** .... `Alt` + `O`
3. Click **Paragraph** .... `P`
4. Click **Indents and Spacing**. `Alt` + `I`
5. Click **Line Spacing** .... `Alt` + `N`
6. Click desired option .... `↓` , `↑`
7. Click **OK** .... `Enter`

INDENT TEXT FROM THE LEFT MARGIN

1. Place insertion point in paragraph to block indent.

   OR

   Place insertion point where block indenting will begin.

   OR

   Select paragraphs to block indent.

2. Click **Increase Indent** icon .... `⯮`
   on Toolbar to indent text to desired tab stop.

Click **Decrease indent** icon .... `⯬`
on Toolbar to move text back to left.

OR

Drag left-indent marker box .... `⌛`
to desired position on ruler.

✓ *Dragging the left-indent marker* **box** *will change* **both** *the first line indent* **and** *the left indent simultaneously.*

INDENT PARAGRAPHS FROM LEFT AND RIGHT MARGINS

1. Place insertion point in paragraph to block indent.

   OR

   Place insertion point where block indent will begin.

   OR

   Select paragraphs to block indent.

2. Drag left-indent marker box .... `⌛`
   to desired position on ruler.

   ✓ *Dragging the left-indent marker* **box** *will change* **both** *the first line indent* **and** *the left indent simultaneously.*

3. Drag right indent marker .... `△`
   to desired position on ruler.

   OR

   a. Select **Format** .... `Alt` + `O`
   b. Select **Paragraph** .... `P`
   c. Select **Indents and Spacing** .... `Alt` + `I`
   d. Select **Left** .... `Alt` + `L`
   e. Key distance from .... *number* **Left** margin.
   f. Select **Right** .... `Alt` + `R`
   g. Key distance from .... *number* **Right** margin.

4. Select **OK** .... `Enter`

HANGING INDENTS

Place the insertion point in paragraph to be affected.

   OR

   Select (highlight) the desired paragraphs.

– *USING INDENT MARKERS ON RULER* –

   a. Drag **left-indent marker** .... `⌛` to desired position.

   b. Drag **first-line indent marker** .... `▽` to desired position.

– *USING KEYBOARD SHORTCUTS* –

   a. Press **Ctrl + T** .... `Ctrl` + `T` as necessary to left indent all paragraph text except first line to the desired tab stop.

   b. Press **Ctrl + Shift + T** .... `Ctrl` + `Shift` + `T` as necessary to *undo* any left indents created with Ctrl + T.

– *USING THE FORMAT PARAGRAPH COMMAND ON THE MENU BAR* –

   a. Click **Format** .... `Alt` + `O`
   b. Click **Paragraph** .... `P`
   c. Click **Indents and Spacing**. `Alt` + `I`
   d. Type .... `Alt` + `L` desired paragraph left indent in **Left** box.
   e. Click **Special** .... `Alt` + `S`
   f. Click **Hanging** .... `↓`
   g. Click **By** .... `Alt` + `Y`
   h. Type distance that all lines, except the first, will be indented.
   i. Click **OK** .... `Enter`

DIVING IN THE CAYMAN ISLANDS   *)Center and set to 18pt*
Sans serif bold

andangelfish

Do you want to see sharks, barracudas ~~and~~ stingrays? Do you want to see angels,
too?

The Cayman Islands were discovered by Christopher Columbus in 1503. ~~The~~   *(and)*
~~Cayman Islands~~ are located south of Cuba. The Caymans are home to ~~only~~ about 25,000
year-round residents. However, they welcome 200,000 visitors each year. Most visitors
come with masks and flippers in their luggage. ~~Now, you are ready to jump in.~~

Hotel/Diving Accommodations: *)set to sans serif 14 pt bold*

Single space; indent .5" from left and right margins.

PO
(Sunset House) Box 479, George Town, Grand Cayman; (800) 555-4767.
            ^

PO
(Coconut Harbour,) Box 2086, George Town, Grand Cayman; (809) 555-7468.

(Red Sail Sports,) PO Box 1588, George Town, Grand Cayman; (809) 555-7965

(Cayman Diving Lodge,) PO Box 11, East End, Grand Cayman; (809) 555-7555

(Anchorage View,) PO Box 2123, Grand Cayman, (809) 555-4209

Double-space between hotel names.

Set hotel names to italic.

DESIRED RESULT I

DIVING IN THE CAYMAN ISLANDS

Do you want to see sharks, barracudas, stingrays and angelfish?
The Cayman Islands were discovered by Christopher Columbus in
1503 and are located south of Cuba. The Caymans are home to about 25,000
year-around residents. However, they welcome 200,000 visitors each year.
Most visitors come with masks and flippers in their luggage.

Hotel/Diving Accommodations:

Sunset House, PO Box 479, George Town, Grand Cayman;
   (800) 555-4767.

Coconut Harbour, PO Box 2086, George Town, Grand
   Cayman; (809) 555-7468.

Red Sail Sports, PO Box 1588, George Town, Grand Cayman;
   (809) 555-7965.

Cayman Diving Lodge, PO Box 11, East End, Grand Cayman;
   (809) 555-7555.

Anchorage View, PO Box 2123, Grand Cayman; (809) 555-
   4209.

DESIRED RESULT II

DIVING IN THE CAYMAN ISLANDS

Do you want to see sharks, barracudas, stingrays and angelfish?
The Cayman Islands were discovered by Christopher Columbus in
1503 and are located south of Cuba. The Caymans are home to about 25,000
year-around residents. However, they welcome 200,000 visitors each year.
Most visitors come with masks and flippers in their luggage.

Hotel/Diving Accommodations:

Sunset House, PO Box 479, George Town, Grand Cayman;
   (800) 555-4767.

Coconut Harbour, PO Box 2086, George Town, Grand
   Cayman; (809) 555-7468.

Red Sail Sports, PO Box 1588, George Town, Grand Cayman;
   (809) 555-7965.

Cayman Diving Lodge, PO Box 11, East End, Grand Cayman;
   (809) 555-7555.

Anchorage View, PO Box 2123, Grand Cayman; (809) 555-
   4209.

EXERCISE

■ FORMAT A ONE-PAGE REPORT ■ SET MARGINS

NOTES:

- A **report** or manuscript generally begins 2" from the top of the page and is prepared in double space. Each new paragraph begins .5" from the left margin (tab once). The title of a report is centered and keyed in all caps. A quadruple space follows the title.

- Margins vary depending on how the report is bound. For an unbound report, use margins of 1" on the left and right (the default).

Set Margins

- Word measures margins in inches.

- The default margins are 1.25" on the left and right and 1" margins on the top and bottom of the page.

- There are three ways to change left and right margins, each having its own advantage:

  - **Dragging margin boundaries on the ruler in Page Layout view** is usually the most convenient way to adjust margins for the *entire document*.

  - **Dragging margin boundaries in Print Preview mode** enables you to see the effects of margin changes on the *entire document* as you make them.

  - **Using the File, Page Setup command** allows greater precision and permits you to limit margin changes to *sections* of your document.

    - ✓ *Note:* *These methods are described in detail on the right and on the next page.*

Dragging Margin Boundaries on the Ruler in Page Layout View

RULER IN PAGE LAYOUT VIEW

Left and Right Margin Boundaries

- Note the **ruler** illustration above. To change margins, place the mouse pointer over the left or right **margin boundary**. When the pointer assumes the shape of a left and right pointing arrow, drag the left or right margin boundary to the desired position. If you hold down the Alt key as you drag, you will see the margin measurements on the ruler.

- The numbers in the **white area** of the ruler represent the measurement of the *text area* in the document (six inches in the example to the left, zero through six). The **gray areas** at the left and right sides of the ruler represent the *margins* between text and the edges of the page.

  To set appropriate margins for an unbound report on 8.5" x 11" paper, the left margin marker would be set at 1" and the right margin marker would be set at 7.5".

- The advantage of changing margins in Page Layout view is convenience; because you can adjust margins as you are working, you can immediately see the effect on text, and if you have set the Tools, Options, View, Text Boundaries check box to on, you can see both margins simultaneously.

Dragging Margin Boundaries in Print Preview Mode

Left and Right margin markers

PRINT PREVIEW SCREEN

Top and bottom margin markers

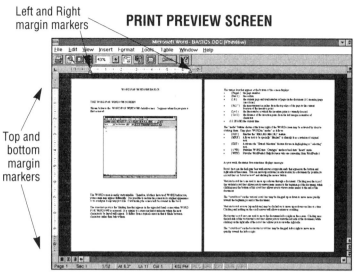

Using the File, Page Setup Command

PAGE SETUP MARGINS DIALOG BOX

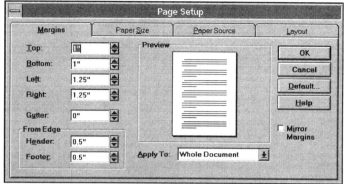

■ Note the illustration of the Print Preview screen above is set to display two pages. It is possible to reset left and right margins by dragging **margin boundaries** on the horizontal Print Preview ruler. This has the advantage of allowing you to see the immediate effect of a margin change on two pages of your document. Of course you could set your Print Preview screen to display many pages and see the effect of margin changes on all of them at once.

■ Note also that in addition to the horizontal ruler, there is also a vertical ruler which may be used for changing top and bottom margins. You will have an opportunity to change top and bottom margins in a future exercise.

■ Note the Page Setup dialog box above. When changing margins using the File, Page Setup, **Margins** command, you may apply margin changes to sections of the document, the Whole Document, or This Point Forward. If you choose This Point Forward, the margin changes begin at the top of a new page.

■ The Page Setup, **Margins** dialog box measures the left margin from the left edge of the page and the right margin from the right edge of the page. Therefore, to set 1" left and right margins, you must click the increase or decrease arrows until the desired margin setting appears, or place the insertion point in the appropriate margin box, and key the desired margin setting.

> *In this exercise, you will create a one-page report, setting new margins and tabs. You will also review line spacing and indent procedures.*

EXERCISE DIRECTIONS:

1. Create a NEW document.

2. Set 1" left and right margins.

3. Keyboard the report on the right:
   - Begin the title At 2". Use any desired Wingdings before and after the heading as shown.
   - Center and set the title to sans serif 14 point bold.
   - Set the subheadings to sans serif 12 point bold.
   - Set the body text to serif 12 point.

4. Double space the first and last two paragraphs; single space and indent the middle paragraphs 1" from the left and right margins. Use the telephone as the bullet symbol before each middle paragraph.

5. Justify paragraph text.

6. Spell check.

7. Preview your document.

8. Print one copy.

9. Save the file; name it **BULLETIN**.

10. Close the document window.

SET MARGINS IN PAGE LAYOUT VIEW

1. Place mouse pointer over the desired margin boundary on the horizontal ruler.

2. Hold down **Alt** .... `Alt`
   and drag boundary to desired position.

SET MARGINS IN PRINT PREVIEW MODE

1. Place mouse pointer over the desired margin boundary on the horizontal ruler.

2. Hold down **Alt** .... `Alt`
   and drag boundary to desired position.

SET MARGINS USING PAGE SETUP DIALOG BOX

1. Click **File** .... `Alt`+`F`

2. Click **Page Setup** .... `U`

3. Click **Margins** .... `Alt`+`M`

---

4. Click **increase** or **decrease** arrows to set left margin.

   OR

   Click **Left** .... `Alt`+`F`, *number*
   and type distance from left edge of paper.

5. Click **increase** or **decrease** arrows to set desired right margin.

   OR

   Click **Right** .... `Alt`+`G`, *number*
   and type distance from right edge of paper.

6. Click **Apply to** .... `Alt`+`A`

7. Click **This Point Forward** .... `↓`, `↑`

   OR

   Click **Whole Document**. .... `↓`, `↑`

8. Click **OK** .... `Enter`

SHOW TEXT BOUNDARIES IN PAGE LAYOUT VIEW

1. Click **View** .... `Alt`+`V`

2. Click **Page Layout** .... `P`

3. Click **Tools** .... `Alt`+`T`

4. Click **Options** .... `O`

5. Click **View** .... `V`

6. Click **Text Boundaries** .... `Alt`+`X`
   to on.

♦□♦□♦□♦ ELECTRONIC BULLETIN BOARDS ♦□♦□♦□♦

Thousands of people across the nation are using computer bulletin boards. Through their computer, they spend hours on line "talking" with other users, "discussing" topics from zoology, finding information about taxes or taxis, completing graduate courses to even exchanging wedding vows.

PRODUCTIVE USES INCLUDE:

☎ A system created by a car expert in Las Vegas lists thousands of collectors' cars.

☎ A system developed by a retired guidance counselor in Atlanta provides current information on scholarships and loans.

☎ A system set up by a hospital in West Virginia offers detailed answers to medical questions for people who do not want to travel long distances necessary to see a doctor.

BASIC NEEDS:

All you need to connect a bulletin board is a computer and a modem connected to a telephone line.

BASIC COSTS:

Besides the basic fee of subscribing to a bulletin board, the cost of "talking" on your computer is the same as talking on your phone, since phone lines are used for data transmission. While most bulletin boards are free, some of the largest are professional operations that charge a fee.

EXERCISE 19

■ CUT AND PASTE ■ DRAG AND DROP ■ FORMAT PAINTER

Cut Format Painter

STANDARDTOOLBAR

Paste Undo Show/Hide

NOTES:

- **Cut and Paste** and **Drag and Drop** are features that let you move a block of text, a sentence, paragraph, page, or column to another location in the same document or to another document.

Cut and Paste

- The **Cut** procedure allows you to cut or delete selected text from the screen and temporarily place it on the Clipboard (temporary storage buffer). The **Paste** procedure allows you to retrieve text from the Clipboard and place it in a desired location in the document.

- There are several procedures to cut and paste text. *(See keystrokes on page 87.)*

- Information remains on the Clipboard until you cut or copy another selection (or until you exit Windows). Therefore, you can paste the same selection into many different locations, if desired.

Drag and Drop

- The **Drag and Drop** method of moving text allows you to move selected text using your mouse. This method is convenient for moving a word(s) or a block of text from one location to another.

- Once text to be moved is selected, place the mouse pointer anywhere on the selected text and click and hold the *left* mouse button as you **drag** the highlighted text to the new location. The mouse pointer changes to a box with a dotted shadow to indicate that you are dragging text.

- When you reach the new location, release the mouse button to **drop** the text into place. Be sure to remove the selection highlight before pressing any key, so that you do not delete your newly moved text.

- When moving a word or sentence, be sure to move the space following the word or sentence. Before pasting the moved text, the insertion point should always be placed immediately to the left of where the text will be reinserted.

- If text was not reinserted at the correct point, you can undo it (Edit, Undo). It is sometimes necessary to insert or delete spaces, returns, or tabs after completing a move.

- If you wish to move an indented or tabbed paragraph, be sure the indent or tab code to the left of the text is moved along with the paragraph. To insure this, reveal codes and check that the insertion point is to the left of the code to be moved before selecting text.

- In Word, a paragraph is the amount of text followed by a **paragraph mark** (¶). Since all paragraph formatting instructions, such as indents and tabs, are stored in the paragraph mark, it is essential that you move the paragraph mark along with the paragraph; otherwise, you will lose the formatting.

- To insure that you include the paragraph mark when moving (or copying) text, click the Show/Hide icon ¶ so the paragraph marks are visible in your document.

Format Painter

- The **Format Painter** feature allows you to copy formatting, such as font face, style and size, from one part of text to another.

- To copy formatting from one location to another, select the text that contains the format you wish to copy. Then click the **Format Painter** icon 🖌 on the Standard Toolbar (the I-beam displays a paintbrush) and select the text to receive the format. To copy formatting from one location to several locations, select the text that contains the format you wish to copy, then *double-click* the Format Painter icon 🖌. Select the text to receive the format, release the mouse button and select additional text anywhere in the document. To turn off this feature and return the mouse pointer to an I-beam, click the Format Painter icon.

- The proofreaders' mark for moving text is: ↵ or ↶.

In this exercise, you will move paragraphs, then format them using the Format Painter feature.

EXERCISE DIRECTIONS:

1. Create a NEW document.

2. Keyboard the exercise as shown in Part I, or open 💾 **WTIPS.19**.

3. Use the default margins.

4. Begin the exercise At 1".

   To create Desired Result:

5. Center the heading and set text to sans serif 20 point bold. Press Enter twice after the heading.

6. Move the paragraphs in alphabetical order (according to the first word in each tip). Use any desired move procedure.

7. Use the numbering feature to number each item.

8. Set the left margin to 2" and the right margin to 1".

9. Press the Enter key once after each tip. Indent 1" from the left and right margins for the text below each tip.

   ✓ Note: After pressing the Enter key, a new number will appear. To remove the number, position insertion point in the sentence containing the number to be removed and click the numbering icon on the Formatting Toolbar 📋.

10. Set the text for the first tip CARE FOR YOURSELF to sans serif 14-point bold.

11. Using Format Painter, copy the character formatting (font size and bolding) to the remaining tips.

12. Set the text below the first tip to italics.

13. Using Format Painter, copy the character formatting to the remaining text below each tip.

14. Spell check.

15. Center the page top to bottom.

16. Preview your document.

17. Print one copy.

18. Close the file; *save as* **TIPS**.

PART I

SIX TIPS FOR THE WORKAHOLIC

SLOW DOWN. Make a conscious effort to eat, talk, walk and drive more slowly. Give yourself extra time to get to appointments so you are not always rushing.

DRAW THE LINE. When you are already overloaded and need more personal time, do not take on any other projects. You will be just causing yourself more stress.

LEARN TO DELEGATE. Let others share the load--you don't have to do everything yourself. You will have more energy and the end result will be better for everyone.

TAKE BREAKS. Take frequent work breaks: short walks or meditating for a few minutes can help you unwind and clear your head.

CARE FOR YOURSELF. Eat properly, get enough sleep and exercise regularly. Do what you can so that you are healthy, both mentally and physically.

CUT YOUR HOURS. Be organized, but do not let your schedule run your life. Also, try to limit yourself to working eight hours a day--and not a minute more.

DESIRED RESULT

SIX TIPS FOR THE WORKAHOLIC

1. **CARE FOR YOURSELF.**
   Eat properly, get enough sleep and exercise regularly. Do what you can so that you are healthy, both mentally and physically.

2. **CUT YOUR HOURS.**
   Be organized, but do not let your schedule run your life. Also, try to limit yourself to working eight hours a day--and not a minute more.

3. **DRAW THE LINE.**
   When you are already overloaded and need more personal time, do not take on any other projects. You will be just causing yourself more stress.

4. **LEARN TO DELEGATE.**
   Let others share the load--you don't have to do everything yourself. You will have more energy and the end result will be better for everyone.

5. **SLOW DOWN.**
   Make a conscious effort to eat, talk, walk and drive more slowly. Give yourself extra time to get to appointments so you are not always rushing.

6. **TAKE BREAKS.**
   Take frequent work breaks: short walks or meditating for a few minutes can help you unwind and clear your head.

MOVE

Cut and Paste:

1. Select text to move.

2. Click **Cut** icon .... ✂

   OR

   Press **Shift + Delete** .... Shift + Del

3. Place insertion point where text will be inserted.

4. Click **Paste** icon .... 📋

   OR

   Press **Shift + Insert** .... Shift + Ins

Using the Keyboard:

1. Select text to move.

2. Press **F2** F2

3. Click to position insertion point where text will be inserted.

4. Press **Enter** .... Enter

   OR

   1. Press **Shift + Delete** ..... Shift + Del

   2. Click to position insertion point where text will be inserted.

   3. Press **Shift + Insert** ...... Shift + Ins

Drag and Drop:

1. Select text to move.

2. Point to selected text.

3. Hold down left mouse button, and drag text to new location.

4. Release mouse button.

✓ *Clicking the **Undo** icon immediately after a move operation will restore moved text to its original location.*

FORMAT PAINTER

1. Select (highlight) paragraph mark containing the formatting you wish to copy.

2. Click **Format Painter** icon ....

3. When mouse pointer assumes shape of I-beam with paint brush, select paragraphs *to receive* the new formatting.

4. Click **Format Painter** icon ....

EXERCISE

MOVE TEXT

20

NOTES:

- Word provides a shortcut key combination for moving entire paragraphs up or down in a document. To move a paragraph up, press and hold the Alt + Shift keys and tap the Up Arrow key. To move an entire paragraph down, press and hold the Alt + Shift keys and tap the Down Arrow key. Repeat the keystrokes as necessary to move the paragraph to the desired location.

- The proofreaders' mark for inserting a space is: #

- In this exercise you will move indented paragraphs. When you select the paragraph to move, be sure to include the paragraph mark.

In this exercise, you will gain more practice moving text. You will also use the Format Painter feature to format side headings.

EXERCISE DIRECTIONS:

1. Open ⌨ **BULLETIN**, or open 💾 **WBULLETI.20**.

2. Set 1.5" left and right margins.

3. Move the paragraphs as indicated. Use any procedure you desire to move the paragraphs.

4. Change the first side heading to serif 14 point italic.

5. Using Format Painter, change the remaining side headings to serif 14 point italic.

6. Make the remaining revisions.

7. Preview your document.

   ✓ *Note: If your document runs on to a second page, begin the document at 1.5" from the top of the page.*

8. Print one copy.

9. Close the file; *save as* **BULLETIN**.

◆□◆□◆□◆ ELECTRONIC BULLETIN BOARDS ◆□◆□◆□◆

Thousands of people across the nation are using computer bulletin boards.

Through their computer, they spend hours on line "talking" with other users, "discussing"

topics from zoology, finding information about taxes or taxis, completing graduate courses
ranging

to even exchanging wedding vows.

PRODUCTIVE USES INCLUDE:

Change side headings to serif 14pt italic

☎ A system created by a car expert in Las Vegas lists thousands of collectors' cars.

☎ A system developed by a retired guidance counselor in Atlanta provides current information on scholarships and loans.

☎ A system set up by a hospital in West Virginia offers detailed answers to medical questions for people who do not want to travel ~~long~~ distances necessary to see a doctor. *great*

BASIC NEEDS:

All you need to connect a bulletin board is a computer and a modem connected to a telephone line.

BASIC COSTS:

Besides the basic fee of subscribing to a bulletin board, the cost of "talking" on your computer is the same as talking on your phone, since phone lines are used for data transmission. While most bulletin boards are free, some of the largest are professional operations that charge a fee.

MOVE

MOVE AN ENTIRE
PARAGRAPH UP OR DOWN

1. Place insertion point in desired paragraph.

2. Press
   Alt + Shift + Up .... Alt + Shift + ↑

   OR

   Press
   Alt + Shift + Down .... Alt + Shift + ↓

3. Repeat steps above, as necessary, to move paragraph to desired location.

EXERCISE

■ COPY AND PASTE ■ DRAG AND DROP

Copy

STANDARD TOOLBAR

Paste

Show/Hide

NOTES:

■ **Copy and Paste** and **Drag and Drop** are features that let you copy text from one location to another.

■ Copying leaves text in its original location while placing a duplicate in a different location in the same document or another document. (Copying text to another document will be covered in a later lesson.) In contrast, moving removes text from its original location and places it elsewhere.

Copy and Paste

The procedure for copying text is similar to the procedure for moving text. (See keystrokes on page 93.)

■ Text may be copied by either:

- Highlighting it, clicking the **Copy icon** 📋 on the Toolbar (which temporarily copies the highlighted text to the clipboard), placing the insertion point in the desired location, and clicking the **Paste icon** 📋 on the Toolbar, or

- Using the mouse in combination with the keyboard.

■ When text is copied, it remains on the screen while a copy of it is placed on the Clipboard.

■ Text remains on the Clipboard until you copy another selection (or until you exit Windows). Therefore, you can paste the same selection into many different locations, if desired.

■ Text is reinserted or retrieved from the Clipboard at the insertion point. Therefore, place the insertion point to the immediate left of where the text is to be reinserted before following the paste procedures outlined in the keystrokes.

Drag and Drop

■ Use the drag and drop method to copy selected text using your mouse.

■ Once text to be copied is selected, place the mouse pointer anywhere on the selected text, press the Ctrl key while **dragging** text to the new location (a box with a plus sign appears). Then, **drop** a copy of the text into its new location by releasing the mouse button. Be sure to release the mouse button before releasing the Ctrl key.

■ As with the Move feature, if text was not copied properly, you can undo it.

■ When moving or copying paragraphs with indent formatting, be sure to include the paragraph mark along with the moved or copied text. To ensure that you do, click the Show/Hide icon ¶ so the paragraph marks are visible in your document.

In this exercise, you will enhance a flyer created earlier using the copy procedure. In addition, you will gain practice using the Format Painter feature.

EXERCISE DIRECTIONS:

1. Open 🖳 **TIPS**, or open 💾 **WTIPS.21**.

2. Set top and bottom margins to .5".

3. Change the first side heading and number to serif 14 point italics.

4. Using Format Painter, change the remaining headings to serif 14 point italics.

5. Using the letter "s" and the Wingdings font, create a line of diamonds to the right of the first tip. Press the Tab key once before the line of diamonds.

6. Copy the line of diamonds from the first tip, and paste it next to the remaining tips. Press the Tab key once before pasting each line of diamonds.

7. Type and center **To Summarize**: in serif 14 point bold as shown.

8. Copy each tip as shown.
   - Center align all tips.
   - Set font to serif 12 point.
   - Add bullets preceding each tip (use any desired bullet symbol).

9. Set the title to 25 point bold.

10. Spell check.

11. Preview your document.

12. Print one copy.

13. Close the file; *save as* **TIPS**.

PART I

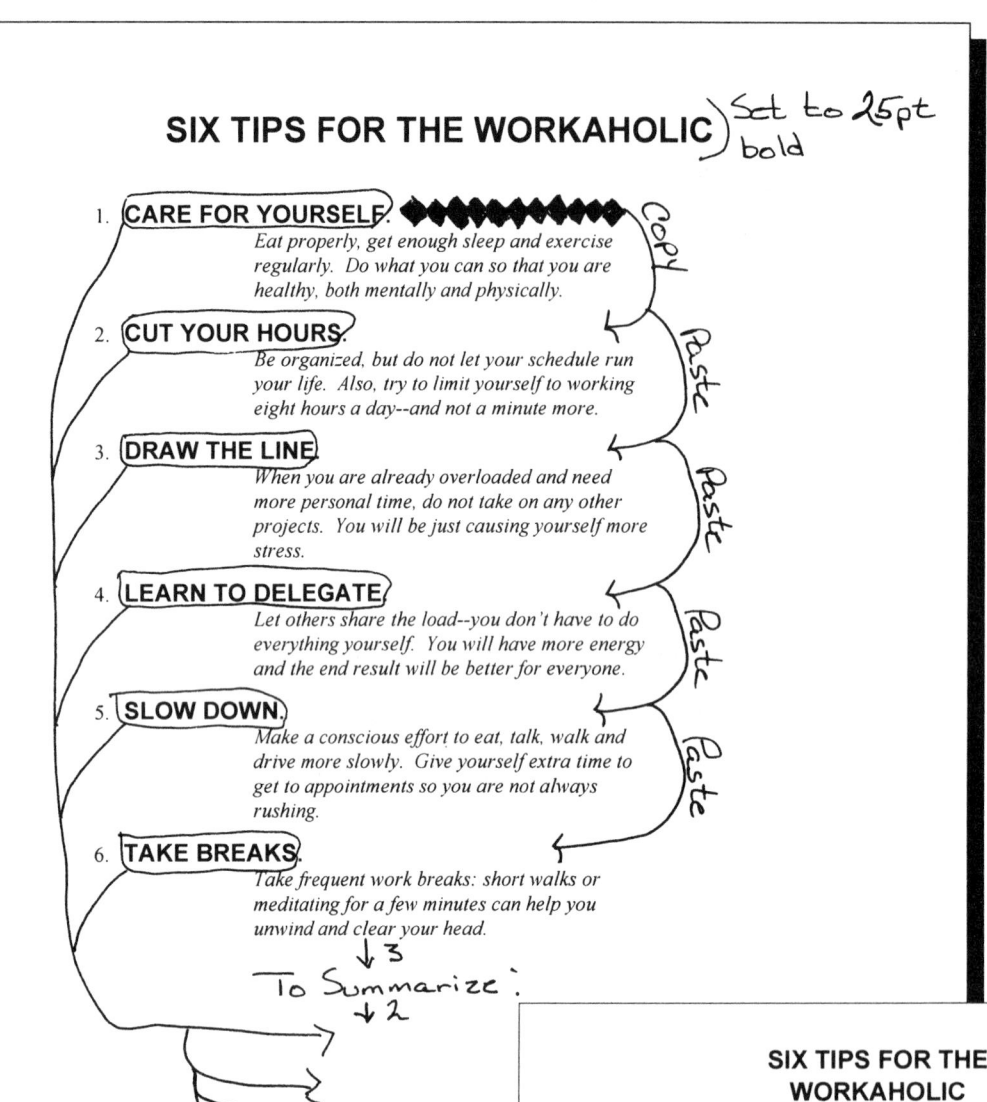

SIX TIPS FOR THE WORKAHOLIC) *Set to 25pt bold*

1. **CARE FOR YOURSELF.** ◆◆◆◆◆◆◆◆◆ *Copy*
   Eat properly, get enough sleep and exercise regularly. Do what you can so that you are healthy, both mentally and physically. *Paste*

2. **CUT YOUR HOURS.**
   Be organized, but do not let your schedule run your life. Also, try to limit yourself to working eight hours a day--and not a minute more. *Paste*

3. **DRAW THE LINE.**
   When you are already overloaded and need more personal time, do not take on any other projects. You will be just causing yourself more stress. *Paste*

4. **LEARN TO DELEGATE.**
   Let others share the load--you don't have to do everything yourself. You will have more energy and the end result will be better for everyone. *Paste*

5. **SLOW DOWN.**
   Make a conscious effort to eat, talk, walk and drive more slowly. Give yourself extra time to get to appointments so you are not always rushing. *Paste*

6. **TAKE BREAKS.**
   Take frequent work breaks: short walks or meditating for a few minutes can help you unwind and clear your head.
   ↓ 3
   To Summarize:
   ↓ 2

DESIRED RESULT

SIX TIPS FOR THE WORKAHOLIC

1. *CARE FOR YOURSELF.* ◆◆◆◆◆◆◆◆◆◆◆◆◆◆◆
   Eat properly, get enough sleep and exercise regularly. Do what you can so that you are healthy, both mentally and physically.

2. *CUT YOUR HOURS.* ◆◆◆◆◆◆◆◆◆◆◆◆◆◆◆
   Be organized, but do not let your schedule run your life. Also, try to limit yourself to working eight hours a day--and not a minute more.

3. *DRAW THE LINE.* ◆◆◆◆◆◆◆◆◆◆◆◆◆◆◆
   When you are already overloaded and need more personal time, do not take on any other projects. You will be just causing yourself more stress.

4. *LEARN TO DELEGATE.* ◆◆◆◆◆◆◆◆◆◆◆◆◆◆
   Let others share the load--you don't have to do everything yourself. You will have more energy and the end result will be better for everyone.

5. *SLOW DOWN.* ◆◆◆◆◆◆◆◆◆◆◆◆◆◆◆
   Make a conscious effort to eat, talk, walk and drive more slowly. Give yourself extra time to get to appointments so you are not always rushing.

6. *TAKE BREAKS.* ◆◆◆◆◆◆◆◆◆◆◆◆◆◆◆
   Take frequent work breaks: short walks or meditating for a few minutes can help you unwind and clear your head.

To summarize:

➢ CARE FOR YOUR SELF
➢ CUT YOUR HOURS
➢ DRAW THE LINE
➢ LEARN TO DELEGATE
➢ SLOW DOWN
➢ TAKE BREAKS

COPY TEXT USING TOOLBAR

1. Select text to copy.

2. Click **Copy** icon..................................

3. Place insertion point where text will be inserted.

4. Click **Paste** icon ....

   OR

   Press **Shift + Insert** ....

COPY TEXT USING THE KEYBOARD

1. Select text to copy.

2. Press **Shift + F2**...................

3. Position insertion point where text will be inserted.

4. Press **Enter** ....

DRAG AND DROP

1. Select text to copy.

2. Hold down **Ctrl**..............................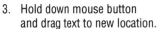
   and point to selected text.

3. Hold down mouse button and drag text to new location.

4. Release mouse button.

   ✓ *Clicking the **Undo** icon immediately after a copy operation will restore copied text to its original location.*

LESSON 4
SUMMARY EXERCISE

In this exercise, you will gain more practice moving and copying text. When moving/copying the hotel information, be sure that the paragraph mark is moved/copied along with the hotel information.

EXERCISE DIRECTIONS:

1. Open ⌨ **DIVE**, or open 💾 **WDIVE.4A**
2. Insert the paragraphs indicated.
3. Single space paragraph text (double space between paragraphs).
4. Copy and move hotel information as indicated.
5. Set all paragraph text to serif 12 point.
6. Using Format Painter, bold each hotel name.
7. Using Format Painter, apply the same font and size format to the second side heading (Hotels Offering Free Diving Instruction) as used in the first side heading.
8. Spell check.
9. Preview your document.
10. Print one copy.
11. Close the file; *save as* **DIVE**.

DIVING IN THE CAYMAN ISLANDS

Single Space {

Do you want to see sharks, barracudas, stingrays and angelfish?

The Cayman Islands were discovered by Christopher Columbus in 1503 and are located south of Cuba. The Caymans are home to about 25,000 year-around residents. However, they welcome 200,000 visitors each year. Most visitors come with masks and flippers in their luggage.

Hotel/Diving Accommodations:

Move Hotels in alphabetical order {

Sunset House, PO Box 479, George Town, Grand Cayman; (800) 555-4767.

Coconut Harbour, PO Box 2086, George Town, Grand Cayman; (809) 555-7468.

Red Sail Sports, PO Box 1588, George Town, Grand Cayman; (809) 555-7965.

Cayman Diving Lodge, PO Box 11, East End, Grand Cayman; (809) 555-7555.

Anchorage View, PO Box 2123, Grand Cayman; (809) 555-4209.

Single Space {

¶→ Before you descend the depths of the ocean, it is important that you have a few lessons on the don'ts of diving. Don't touch the coral. Don't come up to the surface too fast holding your breath. If you do, your lungs will explode.

¶→ Now, you are ready to jump in!

¶→ Here are some hotel suggestions

Hotels Offering Free Diving Instruction.

Copy   *Copy*   *Copy*

94

LESSON 5

ADDITIONAL FORMATTING AND EDITING

Exercises 22-26

- Thesaurus

- Grammar Check

- Creating a Memorandum

- Find and Replace Text

- Hyphenating Text

- Creating an Outline

- Editing an Outline

EXERCISE 22

THESAURUS

NOTES:

Thesaurus

- The **Thesaurus** feature lists the meanings, synonyms, and antonyms (if any) of a desired word and also indicates the part of speech of each meaning.

THESAURUS DIALOG BOX

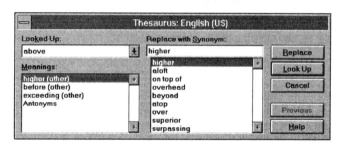

- Note the Thesaurus dialog box in which the word "above" was looked up. You may replace a word in your document with a word listed in the thesaurus by clicking the desired meaning then selecting the desired synonym (or antonym) and clicking the Replace button. It is sometimes necessary to edit the new word so it fits properly in the sentence *(EXAMPLE: Singular/Plural endings)*.

- If you are using the Thesaurus to look up a plural word and it does not produce sufficient synonyms, try looking up the singular form of the word.

- The Thesaurus feature may be accessed by selecting Thesaurus from the Tools main menu or selecting the word to look up and pressing Shift+F7.

In this exercise, you will format a report and use the Thesaurus feature to substitute words marked in brackets.

EXERCISE DIRECTIONS:

1. Create a NEW document.

2. Keyboard the exercise on the right, or open 🖫 **WSOD.22**.

3. Set 1" left and right margins.

4. Set a 1" first line indent.

5. Begin the exercise At 2".

6. Set line spacing to 2 after typing the title.

7. Center and bold the main title in serif 12 point bold. Set the body text to serif 10 point.

8. Use Format Painter to bold and italicize text throughout the document.

9. Use the Thesaurus feature to substitute the words marked in brackets.

10. Spell check.

11. Preview your document.

12. Print one copy.

13. Close the file; *save as* **SOD**.

GREENTHUMB LANDSCAPE SERVICE
OPERATING EXPENSE ANALYSIS
199-

We have seen many changes at Greenthumb Landscape Service this year. An explanation of the Quarterly Income Statement for 199- is worthwhile. After much analysis, we have decided to place our *advertising* with our local radio station, WDOV. We have developed a comprehensive advertising program that runs year-round in an effort to develop business during our lighter winter months.

The *lower expense and income figures for the first quarter* reflect the *closing of our service center* during the month of February. The policy to close in February is under review for this winter, since we have developed and sold additional contracts for snow removal. The executive committee will be meeting to develop a vacation system for full-time employees so that the center is staffed at all times. For *winter services*, we are contemplating the purchase of another snow removal vehicle to increase our capability. We are aware that our snow handling equipment must be kept in good repair to avoid the breakdowns we experienced last winter. These factors will cause increases in repair and depreciation expenses for next year which should be offset by our increased revenues.

Our *salaries expenses* vary with the season. We are continuing the practice of maintaining a core full-time staff while hiring additional part-time staff for the peak service periods of the year. This has worked well in the past; however, we are being pressured to increase benefits for our full-time employees.

The high expenses for *supplies* in the third quarter reflects the increase in our full landscaping service.

We are always striving to improve our service to our customers and community and continue to monitor our expenditures while increasing our client base.

THESAURUS

1. Place insertion point on word to look up.

   OR

   Select desired word.

2. Press **Shift + F7** .... `Shift`+`F7`

   OR

   a. Click **Tools** .... `Alt`+`T`

   b. Click **Thesaurus** .... `T`

3. Select .... `Alt`+`M`, `↓`
   desired meaning.

4. Select .... `Alt`+`S`, `↓`
   desired synonym.

   OR

   Click **Look Up**........................... `Alt`+`L`
   to list synonyms for
   selected meaning.

   OR

   Select Antonyms.

5. Select desired synonym or antonym.

6. Click **Replace** .... `Alt`+`R`

EXERCISE

■ GRAMMAR CHECK ■ CREATING A MEMORANDUM

23

NOTES:

Grammar Check

■ Word's **Grammar Check** feature will scan through your document for proper word usage and style. If you use the Grammar Check feature, Word simultaneously checks spelling. You may accept Word's suggestions or ignore them.

■ The Grammar Check feature will not detect all grammatical errors; therefore, documents must still be proofread.

Creating a Memorandum

■ The **memo** is a written communication within a company. Some companies create memos on blank paper, while others use letterhead or preprinted forms. Memos may also be created using Word's Template feature *(see Lesson 10)*.

■ A memo should begin 1" from the top of the page, which is the top of your screen. The word MEMORANDUM may be centered at the top of the page or it may be omitted.

■ Memorandums are usually prepared with all parts beginning at the left margin.

■ Re (in reference to) is often used in place of the word Subject in the memorandum heading.

■ Memorandums are generally not centered vertically.

■ Double space between each part of the memorandum heading. The body of the memo begins a double or triple space below the subject line.

■ If copies are to be sent to others, a copy notation may be indicated as the last item on the page.

In this exercise, you will create a memorandum and use Grammar Check to check the grammar and spelling.

EXERCISE DIRECTIONS:

1. Create a NEW document.

2. Use the default margins.

3. Begin the exercise At 1".

4. Use the date feature to insert today's date.

5. Keyboard the memo on the right exactly as shown, including the circled, misspelled words and usage errors, or open 💾 **WBRANCH.23**.

6. Using the Thesaurus feature, substitute the words marked in brackets.

7. Use the Grammar Check feature to grammar and spell check the document. Make the necessary corrections.

8. Insert a hard space between Jim Thompson.

9. Use Format Painter to bold the side headings (TO, FROM, DATE, SUBJECT).

10. Print one copy.

11. Close the file; *save as* **BRANCH**.

TO:　　　　Dennis Jones, Corporate Financial Manager

FROM:　　　Harriet Cardoza

DATE:　　　Today's

SUBJECT:　Quarterly Salary Summary

↓ 3

I have compiled the quarterly salary summary for the first three quarters of this year for the Oxford branch. As you can see, last quarter we added a new employee, Jim Thompson.

Insert a non-breaking Space

I know you are in the process of compiling expense data from all the Woodworks Furniture Company's stores to aid you in long-term planning for our organization. The addition of our new employee increase our expenses at a difficult economic juncture for our company. However, Jim has vital community contacts that we expect will increase our level of sales.

Early indications shows that we have made the right decision. Our sales has picked up and there is an increase in sales to corporate cleints. We will be sending a detailed data analyses report next week.

↓ 2

hc/

↓ 2

copy to: Andrea Zoren

GRAMMAR AND STYLE CHECK

1. Place insertion point where grammar check will begin.

   OR

   Select block of text to check.

2. Select **Tools** .... Alt + T

3. Select **Grammar** .... G

4. Select **Ignore** .... Alt + I
   to reject suggested change and continue grammar check.

   OR

a. Select (highlight) desired suggestion if more than one suggestion appears.

b. Select **Change** .... Alt + C
   to accept highlighted suggestion and make suggested correction in document.

✓ *If grammatical corrections cannot be made by Word, the **Change** button will be dimmed. You must edit the document to make these changes.*

   OR

Select **Cancel** .... Esc
to return to document window.

5. Edit document as desired.

6. Select **Tools** .... Alt + T

7. Select **Grammar** .... G
   to resume grammar checking.

8. Select **Cancel** .... Esc
   to return to document window.

EXERCISE

■ FIND AND REPLACE TEXT ■ HYPHENATING TEXT

24

NOTES:

Find Text

■ The **Find** feature will scan your document and search for occurrences of specified text, symbols, or formatting. Once the desired text or formatting is found, it can be edited or replaced. Word searches in either a forward direction (from the insertion point to the end of the document) or reverse direction (from the insertion point to the beginning of the document).

FIND DIALOG BOX

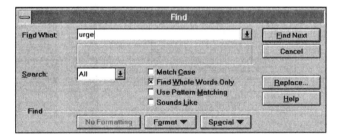

■ Find may be accessed by selecting Find from the Edit menu. In the Find dialog box which follows, you may instruct Word to find all occurrences of the specified search text or only those occurrences that match the capitalization pattern of the search text. Note the Find dialog box above. In this illustration, all occurrences of the word "urge" will be found, regardless of the capitalization, since Match Case was not selected.

■ Word can be instructed to find separate, whole words rather than characters embedded in other words by selecting the Find Whole Words Only option. For example, if this option is *not* selected, a search for the word "and" would find not only "and" but also *sand, candy, Sandusky, android*, etc. It can be helpful to select the Find Whole Words Only option, particularly when searching for short words.

Replace Text

■ When you wish to locate all occurrences of certain text and *replace* it with different text, use the Edit, **Replace** feature. In addition to text, you may also search for and replace occurrences of special characters, such as tab symbols or paragraph marks.

REPLACE DIALOG BOX

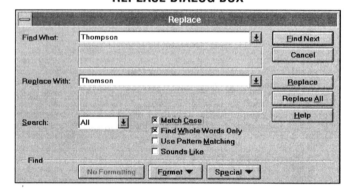

■ Replace may be accessed by selecting Replace from the Edit menu. In the Replace dialog box which follows, you indicate what you wish to find and what you wish to replace.

■ In the illustration above, the Replace command is used to change an incorrect spelling of a client's last name throughout a document.

■ To search for and replace special characters, click the Special button in the Replace dialog box and select the desired character from the pop-up list *(see below)*.

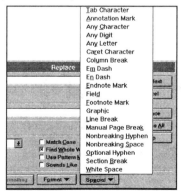

- Turn on the Show/Hide icon ¶ to assist you when searching for and replacing special characters.

- Word gives you the option of replacing all occurrences of text or special characters (Replace All – global search and replace) or confirming each replacement (Replace – selective search and replace).

Hyphenating Text

- **Hyphenating** text produces a tighter right margin. If text is justified and hyphenated, the sentences will have smaller gaps between words.

- Because text is frequently inserted or deleted in word processed documents, words that once had to be hyphenated at the end of a line may be repositioned in the middle of a line, eliminating the need for the hyphen. Still other words should retain their hyphenation regardless of where they fall in a line. Word provides for each of these circumstances by allowing you to place regular hyphens, optional hyphens, or non-breaking hyphens.

- If you choose to place hyphens manually, Word gives you three hyphenation options:

- **Regular hyphen** — Inserted with the Hyphen key. Use for words in which the hyphen should *always* appear in the word. A compound word like "sister-in-law" should always retain the hyphen.

- **Optional hyphen** — Inserted by pressing Ctrl+Hyphen. Use for words that should be hyphenated *only* when they must be divided at the end of a line.

- **Non-breaking hyphen** — Inserted by pressing Ctrl+Shift+Hyphen. Use when parts of the word connected by the hyphen are *never* to be *separated* at the end of a line. Examples of this kind of word include hyphenated surnames (Alice Harris-Gomez) and negative numbers.

- Although all three types of hyphens will look the same when printed, they appear different on your screen. Turn the Show/Hide icon ¶ to on to make the different hyphens visible in your document.

HYPHENATION COMMAND DIALOG BOX

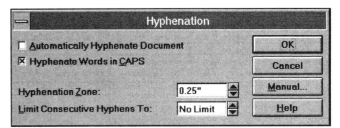

- In addition to manual placement, Word also allows you to place hyphens automatically. To hyphenate, select Tools, Hyphenation from the main menu. In the Hyphenation dialog box which appears, check to see if the Manual button is selected. If it is, Word suggests hyphen placement. You may accept or reject the suggestion.

- If the Automatically Hyphenate Document check box is clicked, hyphenation is fully automatic. In automatic hyphenation, Word adds hyphens according to its rules without asking for confirmation from the user.

- All hyphens added in automatic or manual mode are entered as *optional hyphens (see above)*. They will be used only if a word must be divided at the end of a line.

> *In this exercise, you will search for the words shown in brackets. The Search feature will quickly place the insertion point on those words so you can substitute them using the Thesaurus feature. In addition, you will use the Replace feature to find and replace words in the document and hyphenate to produce a tighter right margin.*

EXERCISE DIRECTIONS:

1. Open ⌨ **BULLETIN**, or open 💾 **WBULLETI.24**.

2. Use the Find feature to place your insertion point on each word marked in brackets. Then, use the Thesaurus feature to replace each word.

3. Search for each occurrence of the word "bulletin" and replace with BULLETIN.

4. Search for the word "talking" and replace with *talking*.

5. Hyphenate the document.

6. Print one copy.

7. Close the file; *save as* **BULLETIN**.

FIND TEXT

Ctrl + F

1. Click **Edit** .... `Alt`+`E`

2. Click **Find** .... `F`

3. Click **Find What** .... `Alt`+`N`

4. Type desired search text .... *text*

5. Do one of the following:

   - Click **No Formatting** .... `Alt`+`T` if necessary, so Word does not search for formatting.

   - Click .... `Alt`+`W` **Find Whole Words Only**, if desired.

   - Click **Match Case** .... `Alt`+`C` if desired.

   - Click **Search** .... `Alt`+`S`

   Click **Up** .... `U` to search from insertion point to beginning of document.

   OR

   Click **Down** .... `D` to search from insertion point to end of document.

   OR

   Click **All** .... `A` to search entire document.

6. Click **Find Next** .... `Alt`+`F`

   OR

   Press **Enter** .... `Enter` to find next occurrence of search text.

7. Press **Cancel** .... `Esc` to return to document at point where most recently located search text appears.

REPLACE TEXT OR SPECIAL CHARACTERS

1. Click **Edit** .... `Alt`+`E`

2. Click **Replace** .... `E`

3. Click **Find What** .... `Alt`+`N`

4. Type desired search text .... *text*

   OR

   Click **Special** .... `Alt`+`E`

   Select special character .... `↓`, `↑`, `←`

5. Select **No Formatting** .... `Alt`+`T` if necessary, so Word does not search for formatting.

6. Click **Replace With** .... `Alt`+`R`

7. Type replacement text .... *text*

   OR

   a. Click **Special** .... `Alt`+`E`

   b. Select special character .... `↓`, `↑`

8. Click one of the following, if desired.

   a. **Find Whole Word Only** .... `Alt`+`W`

   b. **Match Case** .... `Alt`+`C`

   c. Click **Find Next** .... `Alt`+`F` to find next occurrence of search text.

   d. Click **Replace** .... `Alt`+`R` to replace this occurrence of search text.

   OR

   Click **Replace All** .... `Alt`+`A` to replace **All** occurrences of search text.

9. Repeat **Find Next** .... `Alt`+`F` as necessary to search through entire document.

   ✓ *If search began anywhere other than the beginning of the document, Word will ask if you wish to resume the search at the beginning of the document. Select **Yes** or **No** as desired.*

10. Press **Cancel** .... `Esc` to return to document at point where most recently located search text appears.

HYPHENATE USING THE KEYBOARD

1. Place insertion point where hyphen will appear.

2. Press **Hyphen** .... `-` to insert regular hyphen.

   OR

continued...

◆□◆□◆□◆ ELECTRONIC BULLETIN BOARDS ◆□◆□◆□◆

Thousands of people across the nation are using computer bulletin boards. Through their computer, they spend hours on line "talking" with other users, "discussing" topics from zoology, finding information about taxes or taxis, completing graduate courses to even exchanging wedding vows. While most bulletin boards are free, some of the largest are professional operations that charge a fee.

PRODUCTIVE USES INCLUDE:

☎ A system set up by a hospital in West Virginia offers detailed answers to medical questions for people who do not want to travel great distances necessary to see a doctor.

☎ A system developed by a retired guidance counselor in Atlanta provides current information on scholarships and loans.

☎ A system created by a car expert in Las Vegas lists thousands of collectors' cars.

BASIC COSTS:

Besides the fee of subscribing to a bulletin board, the cost of "talking" on your computer is the same as talking on your phone, since phone lines are used for data transmission.

BASIC NEEDS:

All you need to connect a bulletin board is a computer and a modem connected to a telephone line.

Press **Ctrl + Hyphen** .... `Ctrl` + `-`
to insert optional hyphen.

OR

Press .... `Ctrl` + `Shift` + `-`
Ctrl + Shift + Hyphen
to insert non-breaking hyphen.

HYPHENATE
(Automatically or Manually)

1. Select text to hyphenate.

   OR

   Place insertion point where hyphenation will begin.

2. Click **Tools** .... `Alt` + `T`

3. Click **Hyphenation** .... `H`

4. Do one of the following:

   a. Click .... `Alt` + `A`
      Automatically Hyphenate Document check box to allow Word to hyphenate independently.

   b. Click **OK** .... `Enter`

   OR

   a. Click **Manual** .... `Alt` + `M`
      to have Word prompt you to approve or disapprove each hyphenation.

   b. Click **Yes** .... `Alt` + `Y`
      to accept suggested hyphen placement.

   OR

   Click **No** .... `Alt` + `N`
   to reject suggested hyphen placement.

OR

   a. Click to place the insertion point where you want hyphen inserted.

   b. Click **Yes** .... `Alt` + `Y`

5. Press **Cancel** .... `Esc`
   to end hyphenation process.

   OR

   Click **OK** .... `Enter`
   when hyphenation is complete.

   ✓ *If hyphenation began anywhere other than the beginning of the document, Word will ask if you wish to resume hyphenation at the beginning of the document. Select Yes or No as desired.*

EXERCISE 25

- CREATING AN OUTLINE - EDITING AN OUTLINE

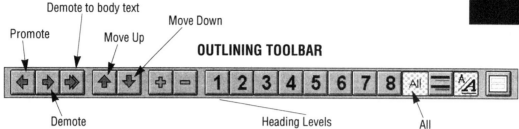

OUTLINING TOOLBAR

Promote — Demote to body text — Move Up — Move Down — Demote — Heading Levels — All

NOTES:

Creating an Outline

- A **traditional outline** is used to organize information about a subject before you begin writing a report or delivering a speech. The **Outline** feature will automatically number, letter, and indent each section of your outline.

- An outline contains many topics and subtopics, or **levels**, which are indicated by different number and letter sequences. Some levels have a higher **rank** than others. Word allows up to nine levels of number and letter sequencing.

- After you create the outline, you must use a separate procedure to number and format it.

- After executing the automatic numbering procedure, it is possible to remove numbering from the entire outline. If you wish to remove numbering from one item in the outline, demote it to body text by selecting it and clicking the Demote to Body Text icon ⬚. You may wish to do this if Word assigns a number to the major document heading at the top of your outline.

- You may change the rank or level of text by **promoting** or **demoting** it. To create a lower level subheading (for example from level II. to level B.), you must *demote*. To return the heading to a higher level (for example from level B. to level II.), you must *promote*.

- A heading is promoted or demoted by selecting it and clicking the Promote icon ⬚ or the Demote icon ⬚ on the Outlining Toolbar. Note the demote and promote icons illustrated above.

- To see your document in Outline view, click the Outline View icon ⬚ (located at the left side of the horizontal scroll bar), or select Y_iew, O_utline from the menu bar.

- Word automatically formats each level of heading differently. Some levels are bolded, some are underlined, and some appear in a different type size. As headings are promoted or demoted, the formatting will change.

- You may hide or display as many levels of headings as desired by clicking the appropriate heading level button in the Outlining Toolbar. Clicking the All icon displays all heading levels, the default in Word. Note the Heading Level icons below:

- An outline generally begins 2" from the top of the page and has a centered heading. A triple space follows the title.

- A **topic outline** summarizes the main topics and subtopics of a longer document in short phrases, while a sentence outline uses complete sentences for each.

Editing an Outline

■ You may move headings in an outline without affecting the level or rank by using the Move Up ⬆ or Move Down ⬇ icon located on the Outline Bar. It is important to note that when you move headings in this way, *only* the heading itself moves up or down; any subheadings or subtext under that heading will remain in their original positions. If you want to move all information under a heading (subheadings and subtext), first select the heading and all desired subheadings, then click the Move Up or Move Down icons.

■ Another easy way to move a heading with all its information under it (subheadings and subtext), is to drag its **heading symbol** (♦ or ▭) up or down to the desired location. If you simply want to change the position of the heading on the outline, there are two rules to follow:

• When moving a heading **up**, move it to a location just *above* a heading of equal rank.

• When moving a heading **down**, move it to a location just *below* a heading of equal rank.

In this exercise, you will create a topic outline. The outline you create will contain five levels. The keystroke procedures are provided in the exercise directions for this first outline exercise.

EXERCISE DIRECTIONS:

1. Open a NEW document.

2. Set the left margin to 1.75". Center the title 2" from the top in serif 14 point bold.

3. Press Enter three times.

4. Click the Outline View icon ▤, or select <u>V</u>iew, <u>O</u>utline to change to Outline view.

5. Create the topic outline on the following page.

6. Key first level heading, *Reasons for Purchasing a Car*.

   ✓ Note: Do not type the numerals or letters that precede the headings; you will use the automatic Numbering feature to add them after completing the outline.

7. Click the Promote icon .

8. Press the Enter key.

9. Key the second level heading, *Convenience*.

10. Click the Demote icon .

11. Press the Enter key.

12. Key the next second level heading, *Prestige*.

13. Press the Enter key.

   ✓ Note: There is no need to promote or demote since this heading has the same rank as the preceding heading.

14. Key the next level heading, *Reasons for Not Purchasing a Car*. Since this is a first level heading, promote it to the first level rank; press the Enter key.

15. Key the remaining headings, promoting or demoting as necessary, to achieve the proper indentation for each level of text; *do not* press the Enter key after the last heading, *Timing*.

   To insert numbers and letters in the outline:

   • Select F<u>o</u>rmat, <u>H</u>eading Numbering from the menu bar.

   • Select desired numbering style.

   • Select OK.

16. Click the Heading Level icon **2** that will display only two levels of headings. Click each Heading Level icon from 3 through 5 to see the effect on your outline. Click the All icon All to reset the default to display all headings.

17. Spell check.

18. Preview your document.

19. Move B. Hazards and the numbered items below it after the items in D. Continuing Costs.

20. Print one copy from Outline view.

21. Save the file; name it **CARS**.

22. Close the document window.

PURCHASING VS. NOT PURCHASING A CAR

I.   **Reasons for Purchasing a Car**
    A.   *Convenience*
    B.   *Prestige*
II.   **Reasons for Not Purchasing a Car**
    A.   *Inconvenience*
        1.   Expense of gasoline
        2.   Parking problems
            a)   *Expensive parking garages*
            b)   *Increasing tows*
    B.   *Hazards*
        1.   Possibility of accidents
        2.   Unpredictable weather
    C.   *Bad Financial Investment*
        1.   High taxes
        2.   High interest rates
    D.   *Continuing Costs*
        1.   Fuel
        2.   Maintenance
            a)   *Brakes*
            b)   *Oil*
            c)   *Filter*
            d)   *Tune-up*
                (1)   Points
                (2)   Plugs
                (3)   Timing

CREATE AN OUTLINE

To switch to Outline view:

a. Click **View** .... `Alt`+`V`

b. Click **Outline** .... `O`

1. Type topic or sentence heading.

2. Press **Enter** .... `Enter`

3. Type next heading.

4. Press **Enter** .... `Enter`
   to keep new heading at same
   level as previous heading.

   OR

   Click **Demote** icon .... `➡`
   to create a lower level heading.

   OR

   Click **Promote** icon .... `⬅`
   to create a higher level heading.

PROMOTE OR DEMOTE A HEADING

1. Switch to Outline view, if necessary. *(See procedure above.)*

2. Place insertion point anywhere in desired heading.

3. Click **Promote** icon .... `⬅`

   OR

   Click **Demote** icon........................... `➡`

4. Repeat steps above, as necessary, to achieve desired heading level.

AUTOMATICALLY NUMBER AND FORMAT AN OUTLINE

1. Switch to **Outline view** ... `Alt`+`V`, `O`
   if necessary.

2. Click **Format** .... `Alt`+`O`

3. Click **Heading Numbering**................. `H`

4. Click desired format.

5. Click **OK** .... `Enter`

REMOVE NUMBERING FROM HEADINGS IN AN OUTLINE

1. Switch to Outline view, if necessary. *(See CREATE AN OUTLINE, left.)*

2. Place insertion point in section from which numbering will be removed.

3. Click **Format** .... `Alt`+`O`

4. Click **Heading Numbering**................. `H`

5. Click **Remove** .... `Alt`+`R`

REMOVE NUMBERING FROM A SINGLE HEADING

1. Select the heading.

2. Click **Demote to Body Text** icon .... `⮕`
   on Outlining Toolbar.

HIDE OR DISPLAY HEADING LEVELS

1. Switch to **Outline view** ... `Alt`+`V`, `O`
   if necessary.

2. Click appropriate **Heading Level** icon to display desired number of levels.

   OR

   Click **All** icon.................................. `All`
   to display all heading levels.

MOVE HEADINGS AND TEXT

1. Switch to **Outline view** ... `Alt`+`V`, `O`

2. Drag heading symbol .... `✛` or `▭`
   to desired location.

   OR

   Select heading, subheadings and text to move.

3. Click **Move Up** icon .... `⬆`

   OR

   Click **Move Down** icon .... `⬇`
   as often as necessary to move heading to desired location.

EXERCISE

26

■ **CREATING AN OUTLINE** ■ **EDITING AN OUTLINE**

NOTES:

■ Remember to type the title and then press Enter three times before turning on Outline view.

In this exercise, you will gain more practice creating a topic outline. This outline will eventually be used to create a presentation in PowerPoint (See Integration Chapter, Exercise 7).

EXERCISE DIRECTIONS:

1. Create a NEW document

2. Set the left margin to 1.5".

3. Center the title beginning At 2" in serif 14 point bold. Press Enter three times.

4. Switch to Outline view.

5. Create the topic outline illustrated on the next page.

   ✓ Note: Do not type the numerals or letters that precede the headings; you will use the automatic Numbering feature to add them after completing the outline.

6. Use the Heading Numbering feature to insert numbers and letters in the outline. Use the default numbering style.

7. Spell check.

8. Move V. information (Company Mission) to become IV. Move IV. information (Greenthumb Landscaping Service) to become V.

9. Preview your document.

10. Print one copy.

11. Save the file; name it **GREEN**.

12. Close the document window.

GREENTHUMB LANDSCAPING SERVICE, INC.

I. **Welcome**
II. **Overview**
    A. *Company history*
    B. *Organizational structure*
    C. *Company mission*
    D. *Sales trends*
    E. *Employee benefits*
    F. *Questions and answers*
III. **Company History**
    A. *Started by Peter Moss in 1965*
    B. *Began as a snow removal company*
    C. *Diversifying into a full landscaping service with a year round advertising program*
IV. **Greenthumb Landscaping Service**
    A. *John Moss, President*
    B. *Wendy Hynes, Vice President*
    C. *Pamela Leigh, Finance*
    D. *Matt Chasin, Customer Service*
V. **Company Mission**
    A. *To design quality landscapes in this city*
    B. *To maintain quality landscapes of all customers*
VI. **Sales Trends**
VII. **Employee Benefits**
    A. *Health Benefits*
        1. Life Insurance
        2. Medical, dental, optical
            a) *GHI*
            b) *Major Medical*
    B. *Commissions and Bonus*
    C. *Vacation and Sick Leave*
        1. Vacation: 2 weeks after 12 months
        2. Sick leave: 2.5 days earned each month
        3. Extra provisions for employees who work winters
VIII. **Questions and Answers**

LESSON 5
SUMMARY EXERCISE

In this exercise, you will create and edit an outline.

EXERCISE DIRECTIONS:

1. Create a NEW document.
2. Use the default margins.
3. Switch to Outline view.
4. Create the outline illustrated in Part I below. Use the British pound symbol found in the WP Typographic Symbols in item Ib1.

5. Spell check.
6. Move the information as shown in Part II.
7. Preview your document.
8. Print one copy.
9. Save the file; name it **TRENDS**.
10. Close the document window.

PART I

I. **Performance of Auto Retailing Stocks in the UK**
 A. *Only major market of auto retailing stocks in world*
 B. *Size and length of existence*
  1. range from £8 million to £3 million
  2. privately held for over 20 years
  3. went public in 1980s
II. **Characteristics of US Automotive Retailers**
 A. *Increased efficiency*
 B. *Improved profitability*
 C. *Higher used car sales*
 D. *Lower new car sales*
III. **Recent Trends and Automotive Industry Outlook**
 A. *Increased industry sales*
  1. light vehicle unit sales
  2. dealership service and parts sales
  3. total dealership sales
   a) **Ford -$3 million**
   b) **GM - $8 million**
 B. *Automotive sales mirror the performance of the economy*
IV. **Consolidation of US Automotive Retailing Industry**
 A. *Dealerships decreased in number between 1950 and 1993*
  1. recession of 1990s
  2. aging dealer principal population
 B. *Lower new car sales/Higher used car sales*

PART II

I. **Performance of Auto Retailing Stocks in the UK**
 A. *Only major market of auto retailing stocks in world*
 B. *Size and length of existence*
  1. range from £8 million to £3 million
  2. privately held for over 20 years
  3. went public in 1980s
II. **Characteristics of US Automotive Retailers**
 A. *Increased efficiency*
 B. *Improved profitability*
 C. *Higher used car sales*
 D. *Lower new car sales*
III. **Recent Trends and Automotive Industry Outlook**
 A. *Increased industry sales*
  1. light vehicle unit sales
  2. dealership service and parts sales
  3. total dealership sales
   a) **Ford -$3 million**
   b) **GM - $8 million**
 B. *Automotive sales mirror the performance of the economy*
IV. **Consolidation of US Automotive Retailing Industry**
 A.B *Dealerships decreased in number between 1950 and 1993*
  1. recession of 1990s
  2. aging dealer principal population
 B. *Lower new car sales/Higher used car sales*

Move

110

LESSON 6

MULTIPLE-PAGE DOCUMENTS

Exercises 27-31

- Hard vs. Soft Page Breaks

- Creating a Two-Page Letter

- Headers/Footers

- Page Numbers

- Letters with Special Notations

- Printing Multiple Pages

- Footnotes/Endnotes

- Widow/Orphan Lines

- Page Numbering Placement and Formats

- Moving Text from One Page to Another

- Change Case

EXERCISE 27

■ HARD VS. SOFT PAGE BREAKS ■ CREATING A TWO-PAGE LETTER ■ HEADERS/FOOTERS ■ PAGE NUMBERS

NOTES:

Hard vs. Soft Page Breaks

■ Word assumes you are working on a standard sheet of paper measuring 8.5" wide x 11" long. Remember, Word is defaulted to leave a 1" top and 1" bottom margin. Therefore, there are 9" of vertical space on a standard sheet of paper for entering text.

■ The At indicator indicates how far you are from the top of the page. When you are working *At 9.8"*, you are working on the last line of the page (one inch top margin plus 9" of text). Therefore, when you enter text beyond 9.8" (the last line of the 9" text page), Word will automatically end one page and start another.

■ When Word ends the page automatically, it is referred to as a **soft page break**. To end the page before 9.8", you can enter a **hard page break** by pressing Ctrl+Enter. A hard page break is indicated by a closely dotted horizontal line across the screen. When you insert a hard page break, Word automatically adjusts the soft page breaks that follow.

■ A hard page break may be deleted, which will allow text below the hard page break to flow into the previous page, as room allows. You may also select a hard page break and drag it to a new position.

■ In Normal view, Word inserts a thinly dotted horizontal line across the screen to indicate a soft page break and adds the words *Page Break* to indicate a hard page break. In Page Layout view, the pages appear as they will be printed. Once the insertion point is below the page break line, you will note that the Page indicator on the status line displays *Page 2* and the **At indicator** displays *At 1"*.

■ A multiple-page letter requires a heading on the second and succeeding pages. The heading should include the name of the addressee (to whom the letter is going), the page number, and the date. To include the heading on the second and succeeding pages, a header may be created.

Headers and Footers

■ A **header** is the same text appearing at the top of every page or every other page, while a **footer** is the same text appearing at the bottom of every page or every other page.

■ After typing a desired header or footer once, the Header/Footer feature will automatically insert it on every page or on specific pages of your document. Word also provides an automatic Page Numbering feature.

■ To see headers, footers, or page numbers on your screen, you must be in either Page Layout view or Print Preview. Although they will not appear on screen in Normal view, they will still print.

■ The header is defaulted to print .5" from the top of the page; the footer is defaulted to print .5" from the bottom of the page. However, the header/footer printing position may be changed, if desired.

> header with
> page number
> and date

Mr. Brendon Basler
Page 2
June 29, 1995

staying at while you are visiting. I have included those that would be in walking distance to your meeting locations. And, while you are attending your meetings, your family can take advantage of some of the sights and shopping near your hotel. I have called the hotels to be certain they can accommodate you and

---

✓ Note: Headers, footers, and page numbers usually appear on the second and succeeding pages of a letter or report; they generally do not appear on the first page. This is the default setting in Word.

■ To add headers or footers, the Header and Footer Toolbar must be displayed by selecting **Header and Footer** from the View menu.

HEADER AND FOOTER TOOLBAR

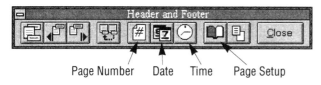

Page Number   Date   Time   Page Setup

■ If you wish to include a date or the time as header/footer text, use the **Date icon** and/or **Time icon** on the Header and Footer Toolbar to insert these items. The Time icon causes the time of printing to appear in the header or footer.

■ Page numbers may be added to headers or footers by clicking the **Page Number icon** on the Header and Footer Toolbar. Page numbers may be positioned in the header or footer by inserting tabs or spaces, or by adding formatting such as center or right alignment.

■ To suppress the header, footer, or page number on the first page, select the Page Setup icon on the Header and Footer Toolbar and be sure the Different First Page check box is set to on.

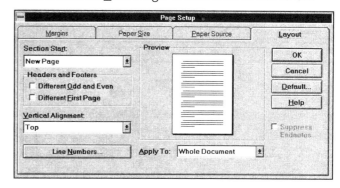

Page Numbers

■ The **Page Numbering** feature will allow you to insert page numbers independent of Headers and footers and indicate where on the printed page the page number should appear: upper or lower corners (left or right) or centered at the top or bottom of the page. (See Page Numbering Placement, Exercise 30.)

■ If you plan to use only page numbers (not headers or footers), use the separate Page Numbering feature. If you plan to insert a header and page numbering or a footer and page numbering, it is easier to use the Header and Footer feature to enter the header/footer along with the page numbers.

■ Headers, footers, and page numbers may be inserted before or after the document is typed.

In this exercise, you will create a two-page letter and insert a header as the second-page heading. Allow Word to insert the page break for you.

EXERCISE DIRECTIONS:

1. Open a NEW document.

2. Keyboard the exercise on the right, or open 💾 **WNYC.27**.

3. Use the default margins.

4. Begin the exercise At 2.5".

5. Create a header which includes the name of the addressee (Mr. Brendon Basler), the page number, and today's date. Be sure to suppress the header on the first page.

6. Use the Bullet feature to create the bullets on the first page.

7. Create hanging indented paragraphs with a left margin indent of .5" for the hotels listed on the second page.

8. Use Format Painter to bold the hotel names.

9. Spell check.

10. Preview your document.

11. Close the file; *save as* **NYC**.

DELETE A HARD PAGE BREAK

1. Position insertion point on hard page break.

2. Press **Delete**.......................**Del**

MOVE A HARD PAGE BREAK

1. Select hard page break.

2. Drag it to the desired position.

CREATE HEADERS/FOOTERS

1. Click **View**.......................**Alt** + **V**

2. Click **Header/Footer**.......................**H**
   to display the Header and Footer Toolbar.

3. Click **Header/Footer** icon ....
   to set header or footer as desired.

4. Type and format header or footer text as desired.

   ✓ *Header/footer text may be bolded, italicized, centered, right aligned, etc., just as you would normal text.*

5. Click **Close**.......................**Close**

VIEW HEADERS/FOOTERS

1. Click **View**.......................**Alt** + **V**

2. Click **Page Layout**.......................**P**

3. Scroll to header/footer location.

ADD PAGE NUMBERS, DATE, OR TIME TO A HEADER/FOOTER

1. Click **View**.......................**Alt** + **V**

2. Click **Header/Footer**.......................**H**
   to display the Header and Footer Toolbar.

3. Click **Header/Footer** icon ....
   to view header or footer as desired.

4. Click **Page Number** icon ....
   to add page numbering to header/footer.

   OR

   Click **Date** icon.................................
   to add date to header/footer.

   OR

   Click **Time** icon ....
   to add time to header/footer.

5. Click **Close**.......................**Close**

SUPPRESS HEADER/FOOTER ON FIRST PAGE

1. Click **View**.......................**Alt** + **V**

2. Click **Header/Footer**.......................**H**
   to display the Header and Footer Toolbar.

3. Click **Page Setup** icon.......................

4. Click **Different First Page** ....**Alt** + **F**

5. Click **OK**.......................**Enter**

DELETE HEADERS/FOOTERS

1. Click **View**.......................**Alt** + **V**

2. Click **Header/Footer**.......................**H**

3. Click **Header/Footer** icon ....
   to view header or footer as desired.

4. Select header or footer text to delete.

5. Press **Delete**.......................**Del**

6. Click **Close**.......................**Close**

INSERT PAGE NUMBERS ONLY

1. Click **Insert** ....**Alt** + **I**

2. Click **Page Numbers** ....**U**

   PAGE NUMBERS DIALOG BOX

3. Click **Position** ....**Alt** + **P**

4. Click **Bottom of Page (Footer)** .. ↓ , ↑

   OR

   Click **Top of Page (Header)**....... ↓ , ↑

5. Click **Alignment**.......................**A**

6. Select desired location:

   • **Right**.......................↑ , ↓
   • **Left** ....↑ , ↓
   • **Center**.......................↑ , ↓
   • **Inside** ....↑ , ↓
   • **Outside**.......................↑ , ↓

7. Click **OK** ....**Enter**

Today's date

Mr. Brendon Basler
54 West Brook Lane
Fort Worth, TX 76102-1349

Dear Mr. Basler:

I am so glad to hear that you might be moving to Manhattan. You asked me to write to tell you what it is like living in Manhattan. Since I have been a New Yorker for most of my life and love every minute of it, I will describe to you what it might be like for you to live here.

- If you move to an apartment in Manhattan with a view, you might see the Empire State Building, the Metropolitan Life Tower, the Chrysler Building or even the Citicorp Center. Depending on where your apartment is located, you might even see the twin towers of the World Trade Center. The Brooklyn and Manhattan Bridges are off to the east, and on a clear day you can see the Hudson River.

- Traffic in New York, as well as waiting in long lines at the post office and the movie theaters, can be very frustrating. However, after you have lived here for a short while, you will know the best times to avoid long lines.

- It is absolutely unnecessary and *very* expensive to own a car in Manhattan. The bus and subway systems are excellent means to travel within the city.

- There is always something to do here. If you love the opera, ballet, theater, museums, art galleries, and eating foods from all over the world, then New York is the place for you.

Before you actually make the move, I suggest that you come here for an extended visit. Not everyone loves it here.

You mentioned that you would be visiting some time next month. I have listed on the next page some of the hotels (and their phone numbers) you might want to consider

Mr. Brendon Basler
Page 2
Today's date

3

staying at while you are visiting. I have included those that would be in walking distance to your meeting locations. And, while you are attending your meetings, your family can take advantage of some of the sights and shopping near your hotel. I have called the hotels to be certain they can accommodate you and your family. They all seem to have availability at the time you are planning to visit.

Plaza Hotel - located at 59th Street and Central Park South at the foot of Central Park. 1 (800) 555-5555.

Pierre Hotel - located at 61st Street and Fifth Avenue across the street from Central Park 1 (800) 555-6666.

Drake Hotel - located at 56th Street and Park Avenue. (212) 555-7777.

Of course, you realize that there are many other hotel options available to you. If these are not satisfactory, let me know and I will call you with other recommendations.

Good luck with your decision. When you get to New York, I will show you some of the sights and sounds of the City. Hopefully, you will then be able to decide whether or not New York City is the place for you.

Sincerely,

Pamela Davis

pd/yo

EXERCISE

■ **LETTERS WITH SPECIAL NOTATIONS**
■ **PRINTING MULTIPLE PAGES**

NOTES:

Letters with Special Notations

■ Letters may include special parts in addition to those learned thus far. The letter in this exercise contains a mailing notation, a subject line, and an enclosure and copy notations.

■ When a letter is sent by a **special mail service** such as Express mail, Registered mail, Federal Express, Certified mail, or by hand (via a messenger service), it is customary to include an appropriate notation on the letter. This notation is placed a double space below the date and typed in all caps.

■ The **subject** identifies or summarizes the body of the letter. It is typed a double space below the salutation. A double space follows it. It may be typed at the left margin or centered in modified-block style. *Subject* may be typed in all caps or in upper- and lowercase. *Re* (in reference to) is often used instead of *Subject*.

■ An **enclosure** (or attachment notation) is used to indicate that something else besides the letter is included in the envelope. The enclosure or attachment notation is typed a double space below the reference initials and may be typed in several ways (the number indicates how many items are enclosed in the envelope):

ENC.	Enclosure	Enclosures (2)
Enc.	Encls.	Attachment
Encl.	Encls (2)	Attachments (2)

■ If copies of the document are sent to others, a **copy notation** is typed a double space below the enclosure/attachment notation (or the reference initials if there is no enclosure/ attachment). A copy notation may be typed in several ways:

| Copy to: | c: |
| CC: | pc: (photocopy) |

Printing Multiple Pages

■ You may choose to print the entire document, a specific page, several pages, selected (highlighted) text, or the current page. You may also specify the number of copies you wish to print.

✓ Note: It is possible to edit text and change page breaks in Print Preview mode. When working with multiple-page documents, it is convenient and helpful to use Print Preview to edit text and page breaks because you can see the effect on several pages at once as you change a page break or insert or delete text.

In this exercise, you will create a two-page letter and insert a header as the second-page heading. You will insert a hard page break to create the second page.

EXERCISE DIRECTIONS:

1. Open a NEW document.
2. Keyboard the exercise on the right, or open 💾 **WPREVIEW.28**.
3. Use the default margins.
4. Begin the exercise At 2.5".
5. Create a header which includes the name of the addressee, the page number, and today's date. Be sure to suppress the header on the first page.
6. Hyphenate the document. Limit the consecutive hyphens to 1.
   - ✓ *Note:* *Limiting the number of consecutive hyphens is an option within the Hyphenation dialog box.*

7. In Print Preview mode, set the display for two pages, and insert a hard page break to end the first page where indicated.
   - ✓ *Note:* *You may have to change the location of the hard page break from that shown in the illustration depending upon the printer you are using.*
8. Spell check.
9. Preview your document.
10. Print one copy of the entire document and two copies of page 2.
11. Close the file; *save as* **PREVIEW**.

Today's date
↓2
REGISTERED MAIL
↓2
Ms. Michelle Ryan
Broward College
765 Southfield Road
Marietta, GA 30068
↓2
Dear Ms. Ryan:
↓2
Subject: **Educational Films for High Schools and Colleges**

Thank you for your interest in the films that we have available for high school and college students. We are pleased to send you the enclosed flyer which describes the films in detail. Also enclosed is a summary of those films that have recently been added to our collection since the publication of the flyer.

There have been many positive reactions to our films. Just three weeks ago, a group of educators, editors and vocational experts were invited to view the films at the annual EDUCATORS' CONFERENCE. Here are some of their comments:

We will be sure to send the films in time for you to preview them. Please be sure to list the date on which you wish to preview the film.

Mr. William R. Bondlow, Jr., president of the National Vocational Center in Washington, D.C. and editor-in-chief of *Science Careers*, said,

> I like the films very much. They are innovative and a great benefit to all those interested in the earth sciences as a professional career. Furthermore, they have captured the objects on film so true to life that anyone watching them is captivated.

Ms. Andra Burke, a leading expert presently assigned to the United States Interior Department, praised the films by saying that,

Ms. Michelle Ryan
Page 2
Today's date

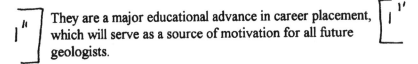

They are a major educational advance in career placement, which will serve as a source of motivation for all future geologists.

A member of the National Education Center, Dr. Lawrence Pilgrim, also liked the films and said,

I will institute a program which will make schools throughout the country aware of their vocational potential.

These are just some of the reactions we have had to our films. We know you will have a similar reaction.

We would very much like to send you the films that you would like during the summer session. You can use the summer to review them. It is important that your request be received quickly since the demand for the films is great, particularly during the summer sessions at the colleges and universities throughout the country.

Cordially,

William Devane
Executive Vice President
Marketing Department
↓2
wd/yo
Enclosures (2)
↓2
Copy to: Robert Williams
              Nancy Jackson

PRINT A DOCUMENT

Ctrl + P

Print Entire Document:

Click **Print** icon .... 🖨️

Print Multiple Copies:

1. Click **File**................................. `Alt`+`F`
2. Click **Print** .... `P`
3. Type desired number ....*number* of copies.
4. Click **OK** .... `Enter`

Print Specific Pages:

1. Click **File**................................. `Alt`+`F`
2. Click **Print** .... `P`
3. Click **Pages**............................... `Alt`+`G`
4. Do one of the following:
   - Type non-sequential page numbers separated by commas.

     EXAMPLE: 3,7,9
   - Type range of pages separated by a hyphen

     EXAMPLE: 3-9

   - Type a combination of non-sequential pages and a range of pages.

     EXAMPLE: 2,5,7-10

5. Click **OK** .... `Enter`

Print Selected Text:

1. Select (highlight) text to print.
2. Click **File**................................. `Alt`+`F`
3. Click **Print** .... `P`
4. Click **Selection** .... `Alt`+`N`
5. Click **OK** .... `Enter`

Print Current Page:

1. Click **File**................................. `Alt`+`F`
2. Click **Print** .... `P`
3. Click **Current Page**................. `Alt`+`E`
4. Click **OK** .... `Enter`

INSERT A HARD PAGE BREAK

1. Place insertion point where you would like to place page break.
2. Press **Ctrl + Enter** .... `Ctrl`+`Enter`

   OR

---

1. Click **Insert** .... `Alt`+`I`
2. Click **Break**....................................... `B`
3. Click **Page Break** .... `Alt`+`P`
4. Click **OK**...................................... `Enter`

EDIT TEXT IN PRINT PREVIEW MODE

1. Click **Print Preview** icon .... 🔍 on the Standard Toolbar.

   OR

   a. Click **File**.......................... `Alt`+`F`

   b. Click **Print Preview** .... `V`

2. Select and drag the **Multiple Pages** icon 🔲 to set display for the number of pages desired.

3. Click **Magnifier** icon .... 🔍 to enter Edit mode.

4. Edit text and page breaks as usual.

✓ *Observe the differences between the* **Print Preview** *icon* 🔍 *and the* **Magnifier** *icon* 🔍 *.*

EXERCISE

■ FOOTNOTES ■ ENDNOTES ■ WIDOW/ORPHAN LINES

29

NOTES:

■ A **footnote** is used in a document to give information about the source of quoted material. The information includes the author's name, the publication, the publication date, and the page number from which the quote was taken.

■ There are several footnoting styles. Traditional footnotes are printed at the bottom of a page. A **separator line** separates footnote text from the text on the page.

■ A **reference number** appears immediately after the quote in the text, and a corresponding footnote number or symbol appears at the bottom of the page.

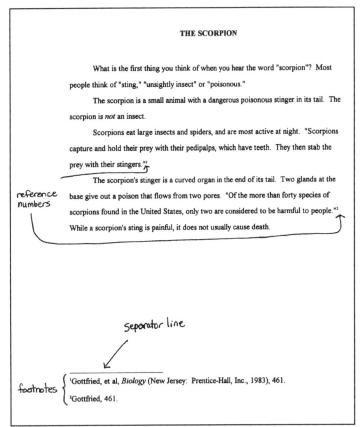

■ An **endnote** contains the same information as a footnote but is typed on the last page of a report.

■ The Footnote feature automatically inserts the reference number after the quote, inserts the separator line, numbers the footnote, and formats your page so that the footnote appears on the same page as the reference number. If you desire endnotes instead of footnotes, Word will compile the endnote information on the last page of your document.

■ The actual note may be viewed in Page Layout view if you scroll to the bottom of the page. In Normal view, you must double-click the footnote number or reference mark to view the footnote in a pane at the bottom of the screen.

■ Footnotes may be inserted by selecting Foot<u>n</u>ote from the <u>I</u>nsert main menu.

■ After selecting Footnote or Endnote in the Footnote/Endnote dialog box which follows, a footnote screen displays, ready for you to type the text of the first footnote.

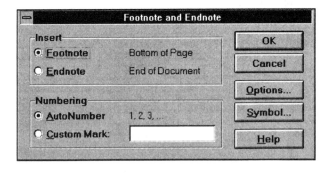

■ It is possible to have both footnotes and endnotes in the same document. In this exercise, however, you will create just footnotes.

■ When a footnote or endnote is inserted or deleted, Word automatically renumbers all existing footnotes or endnotes as necessary.

Widow and Orphan Lines

- A **widow** line occurs when the last line of a paragraph is printed by itself at the top of a page. An **orphan** line occurs when the first line of a paragraph appears by itself on the last line of the page. Widow and orphan lines should be avoided.

- The Widow/Orphan Control feature eliminates widows and orphans in a document and may be accessed by selecting Paragraph, Text Flow, Widow/Orphan Control from the Format main menu.

FOOTNOTES/ENDNOTES

1. Place insertion point where footnote reference number will appear.

2. Click **Insert** .... `Alt` + `I`

3. Click **Footnote** .... `N`

4. Click **Footnote** .... `Alt` + `F`

   OR

   Click **Endnote** .... `Alt` + `E`

5. Click **OK** .... `Enter`

6. Type footnote/endnote information.

   – IN NORMAL VIEW –

7. Press **Shift + F6** .... `Shift` + `F6`
   to leave footnote pane open and return to where you were working in the document.

   OR

   Click **Close** to close footnote pane and return to where you were working in the document.

   – IN PAGE LAYOUT VIEW –

   Press **Shift + F5** .... `Shift` + `F5`
   as often as necessary to return to where you were working in the document.

VIEW FOOTNOTES/ENDNOTES

– IN NORMAL VIEW –

Double-click the footnote reference mark.

   OR

   a. Click **View** .... `Alt` + `V`

   b. Click **Footnotes** .... `F`

   – IN PAGE LAYOUT VIEW –

   Double-click the footnote reference mark.

   OR

   Scroll to footnote location.

DELETE FOOTNOTES/ENDNOTES

1. Select the footnote reference mark.

2. Press **Delete** .... `Del`

   OR

   a. Click **Edit** .... `Alt` + `E`

   b. Click **Cut** .... `T`

WIDOW AND ORPHAN CONTROL

1. Click **Format** .... `Alt` + `O`

2. Click **Paragraph** .... `P`

3. Click **Text Flow** .... `Alt` + `F`

4. Click **Widow/Orphan Control** .... `W`
   check box to turn Widow/Orphan Control off or on.

> *In this exercise, you will create a report with footnotes, a header, and page numbers.*
>
> ✓ *While the exercise is shown in single space, you are to use double space. Your printed document will result in two or three pages, depending on the selected font, and footnotes will appear on the same page as reference numbers.*

EXERCISE DIRECTIONS:

1. Create a NEW document.

2. Create the report shown on the following page, or open 💾 **WVOYAGE.29**.

3. Begin the exercise At 2".

4. Use the default margins. Set line spacing to double.

5. Create the header: DIFFICULTIES COMING TO AMERICA. Include a right-aligned page number as part of the header. Suppress the header and page number on the first page.

6. Use widow and orphan control.

7. Spell check.

8. Preview your document.

9. Edit the header. Delete DIFFICULTIES from the title.

10. Print one copy.

11. Close the file; *save as* **VOYAGE**.

IMMIGRATION TO THE UNITED STATES
IN THE NINETEENTH CENTURY

The United States is sometimes called the "Nation of Immigrants" because it has received more immigrants than any other country in history. During the first one hundred years of US history, the nation had no immigration laws. Immigration began to climb during the 1830s. "Between 1830-1840, 44% of the immigrants came from Ireland, 30% came from Germany, 15% came from Great Britain, and the remainder came from other European countries."[1]

The movement to America of millions of immigrants in the century after the 1820s was not simply a flight of impoverished peasants abandoning underdeveloped, backward regions for the riches and unlimited opportunities offered by the American economy. People did not move randomly to America but emanated from very specific regions at specific times in the nineteenth and twentieth centuries. "It is impossible to understand even the nature of American immigrant communities without appreciating the nature of the world these newcomers left."[2]

The rate of people leaving Ireland was extremely high in the late 1840s and early 1850s due to overpopulation and to the potato famine of 1846. "By 1850, there were almost one million Irish Catholics in the United States, especially clustered in New York and Massachusetts."[3]

Germans left their homeland due to severe depression, unemployment, political unrest, and the failure of the liberal revolutionary movement. It was not only the poor people who left their countries, but those in the middle and lower-middle levels of their social structures also left. "Those too poor could seldom afford to go, and the very wealthy had too much of a stake in the homelands to depart."[4]

Many immigrants came to America as a result of the lure of new land, in part, the result of the attraction of the frontier. America was in a very real sense the last frontier--a land of diverse peoples that, even under the worst conditions, maintained a way of life that permitted more freedom of belief and action than was held abroad. "While this perception was not entirely based in reality, it was the conviction that was often held in Europe and that became part of the ever-present American Dream."[5]

---

[1]Lewis Paul Todd and Merle Curti, *Rise of the American Nation* (New York: Harcourt Brace Jovanovich, Inc., 1972), 297.

[2]John Bodner, *The Transplanted* (Bloomington: Indiana University Press, 1985), 54.

[3]E. Allen Richardson, *Strangers in This Land* (New York: The Pilgrim Press, 1988), 6.

[4]Richardson, 13.

[5]Richardson, 72.

EXERCISE

PAGE NUMBERING PLACEMENT AND FORMATS

30

NOTES:

Page Numbering Placement

- As indicated in Exercise 27, page numbers may be included independent of the header/footer text by selecting Page Numbers from the Insert main menu.

- Word provides numerous page numbering position options. Numbers may be positioned at the top or bottom left, center or right of the page and aligned left, center, right, inside, or outside. The Page Numbers dialog box (which appears after Insert, Page Numbers are selected) displays the page numbering position you select in the preview window.

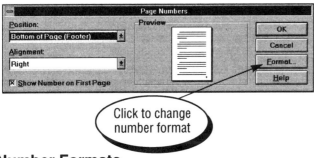

Click to change number format

Number Formats

- Word provides five different number formats. Numbering formats may be selected by clicking Format on the Page Numbers dialog box shown above.

Numbers	1, 2, 3, 4, 5, etc.
Lowercase Letter	a, b, c, d, e, f, etc.
Uppercase Letter	A, B, C, D, E, F, etc.
Lowercase Roman	i, ii, iii, iv, v, etc.
Uppercase Roman	I, II, III, IV, V, etc.

- Once selected, the numbering position displays in the Page Numbers dialog box in the preview window.

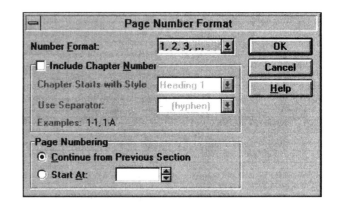

In this exercise, you will create a report with footnotes, a header, and bottom centered page numbers. Remember to suppress headers and page numbers on the first page.

✓ When a quotation is longer than two sentences, it is single spaced and indented. In this exercise, you will indent the quoted material, as directed.

✓ While the exercise is shown in single space, you are to use double space. Your printed document will result in two or three pages, depending on the selected font, and footnotes will appear on the same page as reference numbers.

EXERCISE DIRECTIONS:

1. Create a NEW document.
2. 🖮 Create the report on the right, or open 💾 **WUSA.30**.
3. Begin the exercise At 2".
4. Set line spacing to 2.
5. Use a serif 13 point font for the document.
6. Set 1.5" left and right document margins.
7. Set the title to 14 point bold.
8. Use widow and orphan protection.
9. Indent and single space the quoted text, as indicated.

Continued...

10. Create the following header:
    BUILDING THE UNITED STATES
    OF AMERICA
11. Include an Uppercase Roman page number on the bottom center of the second and succeeding pages.
12. Spell check.

13. Edit the header to read:
    BUILDING THE U. S. A.
14. Preview your document.
15. Print one copy.
16. Save the file; name it **USA**.
17. Close the document window.

IMMIGRATION'S IMPACT IN THE UNITED STATES

The opportunity to directly transfer a skill into the American economy was great for newcomers prior to the 1880s. "Coal-mining and steel-producing companies in the East, railroads, gold- and silver-mining interests in the West, and textile mills in New England all sought a variety of ethnic groups as potential sources of inexpensive labor."[1] Because immigrants were eager to work, they contributed to the wealth of the growing nation. During the 1830s, American textile mills welcomed hand-loom weavers from England and North Ireland whose jobs had been displaced by power looms. It was this migration that established the fine-cotton-goods trade of Philadelphia. "Nearly the entire English silk industry migrated to America after the Civil War, when high American tariffs allowed the industry to prosper on this side of the Atlantic."[2]

Whether immigrants were recruited directly for their abilities or followed existing networks into unskilled jobs, they inevitably moved within groups of friends and relatives and worked and lived in clusters.

As the Industrial Revolution progressed, immigrants were enticed to come to the United States through the mills and factories who sent representatives overseas to secure cheap labor. An example was the Amoskeag Manufacturing Company, located along the banks of the Merrimack River in Manchester, New Hampshire. In the 1870s, the Amoskeag Company recruited women from Scotland who were expert gingham weavers. Agreements were set specifying a fixed period of time during which employees would guarantee to work for the company.[3]

In the 1820s, Irish immigrants did most of the hard work in building the canals in the United States. In fact, Irish immigrants played a large role in building the Erie Canal. American contractors encouraged Irish immigrants to come to the United States to work on the roads, canals, and railroads, and manufacturers lured them into the new mills and factories.

"Most German immigrants settled in the middle western states of Ohio, Indiana, Illinois, Wisconsin and Missouri."[4] With encouragement to move west from the Homestead Act of 1862, which offered public land free to immigrants who intended to become citizens, German immigrants comprised a large portion of the pioneers moving west. "They were masterful farmers and they built prosperous farms."[5]

---

[1]E. Allen Richardson, *Strangers in This Land* (New York: The Pilgrim Press, 1988), 67.

[2]John Bodnar, *The Transplanted* (Bloomington: Indiana University Press, 1985), 54.

[3]Bodnar, 72.

[4]David A. Gerber, *The Making of An American Pluralism* (Chicago: University of Illinois, 1989), 124.

[5]Bodnar, 86.

INSERT PAGE NUMBERS

1. Click **Insert** .... Alt + I
2. Click **Page Numbers** .... U
3. Click **Position** .... Alt + P
4. Click **Bottom of Page (Footer)** .. ⬇ , ⬆

OR

Click **Top of Page (Header)** .... ⬇ , ⬆

5. Click **Alignment** .... A
6. Select desired location:
   - **Right** .... ⬆ , ⬇

- **Left** .... ⬆ , ⬇
- **Center** .... ⬆ , ⬇
- **Inside** .... ⬆ , ⬇
- **Outside** .... ⬆ , ⬇

7. Click **OK** .... Enter

EXERCISE

■ **MOVING TEXT FROM ONE PAGE TO ANOTHER** ■ **CHANGE CASE**

NOTES:

Moving Text From One Page to Another

■ The procedure for moving blocks of text from one page to another is the same as moving blocks of text on the same page. However, if text is to be moved from page one to another, the **Go To** key (F5) may be used to quickly advance to the page where the text is to be reinserted.

■ When moving text from one page to another, if the pages are within two or three pages of each other, it is helpful to work in Print Preview mode using the drag and drop technique.

■ If a hard page break was inserted, delete the break, then move the text. Word will then insert a soft page break. If the soft page break is not in a satisfactory location, insert a hard page break in the desired location.

Change Case

■ It is possible to change the case of a letter, a word, or a group of words by highlighting them and selecting Change Case from the Format main menu. In the Change Case dialog box which follows, you may select from five case options:

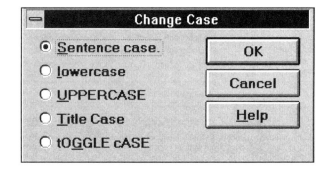

In this exercise, you will edit two different documents and gain practice moving text from one page to another, using the Thesaurus and other editing features.

EXERCISE DIRECTIONS:

PART I:

1. Open ⌨ **PREVIEW**, or open 🖫 **WPREVIEW.31**.

2. Set Widow/Orphan Control to off.

3. Using the Thesaurus, replace words marked in brackets. Be sure replacement words maintain the same tense/endings as the original words.

4. Access Print Preview mode and set the display for two pages; make the indicated revisions in Print Preview or Page Layout mode.

5. Return to Page Layout view.

6. Change EDUCATORS' CONFERENCE to lowercase with initial capitals.

7. Preview your document.

8. Print one copy.

9. Close the file; save the changes.

PART II:

✓ Note: Moving paragraphs in this exercise will not affect footnote placement. Word automatically readjusts footnote placement.

1. Open ⌨ **USA**, or 🖫 **WUSA.31**.

2. Using the Thesaurus, replace words marked in brackets. Be sure replacement words maintain the same tense/endings as the original words.

3. Access Print Preview mode and set the display for two (or three) pages; make the indicated revisions in this mode.

4. Return to Page Layout view.

5. Justify and hyphenate the document.

6. Preview your document.

7. Print one copy.

8. Close the file; save the changes.

Today's date

REGISTERED MAIL

Ms. Michelle Ryan
Broward College
765 Southfield Road
Marietta, GA 30068

Dear Ms. Ryan:

Subject: **Educational Films for High Schools and Colleges**

Thank you for your interest in the films that we have available for high school and college students. We are pleased to send you the enclosed flyer which describes the films in detail. Also enclosed is a summary of those films that have recently been added to our collection since the publication of the flyer.

There have been many positive reactions to our films. Just three weeks ago, a group of educators, editors and vocational experts were invited to view the films at the annual EDUCATORS' CONFERENCE. Here are some of their comments:

(A) move to next page

We will be sure to send the films in time for you to preview them. Please be sure to list the date on which you wish to preview the film.

insert (B)

Mr. William R. Bondlow, Jr., president of the National Vocational Center in Washington, D.C. and editor-in-chief of *Science Careers*, said,

> I like the films very much. They are innovative and a great benefit to all those interested in the earth sciences as a professional career. Furthermore, they have captured the objects on film so true to life that anyone watching them is captivated.

(C) Ms. Andra Burke, a leading expert presently assigned to the United States Interior Department, praised the films by saying that,

move to next page

Ms. Michelle Ryan
Page 2
Today's date

Insert (C)

> They are a major educational advance in career placement, which will serve as a source of motivation for all future geologists.

(B) move to page 1

A member of the National Education Center, Dr. Lawrence Pilgrim, also liked the films and said,

> I will institute a program which will make schools throughout the country aware of their vocational potential.

These are just some of the reactions we have had to our films. We know you will have a similar reaction.

Insert (A)

We would very much like to send you the films that you would like during the summer session. You can use the summer to review them. It is important that your request be received quickly since the demand for the films is great, particularly during the summer sessions at the colleges and universities throughout the country.

Cordially,

William Devane
Executive Vice President
Marketing Department

wd/yo
Enclosures (2)

Copy to: Robert Williams
             Nancy Jackson

PART II

IMMIGRATION'S IMPACT IN THE UNITED STATES

The opportunity to directly transfer a skill into the American economy was great for newcomers prior to the 1880s. Coal-mining and steel-producing companies in the East, railroads, gold- and silver-mining interests in the West, and textile mills in New England all sought a variety of ethnic groups as potential sources of inexpensive labor.[1] Because immigrants were eager to work, they contributed to the wealth of the growing nation. During the 1830s, American textile mills welcomed hand-loom weavers from England and North Ireland whose jobs had been displaced by power looms. It was this migration that established the fine-cotton-goods trade of Philadelphia. "Nearly the entire English silk industry migrated to America after the Civil War, when high American tariffs allowed the industry to prosper on this side of the Atlantic."[2]

Whether immigrants were recruited directly for their abilities or followed existing networks into unskilled jobs, they inevitably moved within groups of friends and relatives and worked and lived in clusters.

Single space and indent quote

Insert (A)

---

[1]E. Allen Richardson, *Strangers in This Land* (New York: The Pilgrim Press, 1988), 67.

[2]John Bodnar, *The Transplanted* (Bloomington: Indiana University Press, 1985), 54.

BUILDING THE U. S. A.

As the Industrial Revolution progressed, immigrants were enticed to come to the United States through the mills and factories who sent representatives overseas to secure cheap labor. An example was the Amoskeag Manufacturing Company, located along the banks of the Merrimack River in Manchester, New Hampshire. In the 1870s, the Amoskeag Company recruited women from Scotland who were expert gingham weavers. Agreements were set specifying a fixed period of time during which employees would guarantee to work for the company.[3]

(A)

Move to page 1

In the 1820s, Irish immigrants did most of the hard work in building the canals in the United States. In fact, Irish immigrants played a large role in building the Erie Canal. American contractors encouraged Irish immigrants to come to the United States to work on the roads, canals, and railroads, and manufacturers lured them into the new mills and factories.

"Most German immigrants settled in the middle western states of Ohio, Indiana, Illinois, Wisconsin and Missouri."[4] With encouragement to move west from the Homestead Act of 1862, which offered public land free to immigrants who intended to become citizens, German immigrants comprised a large portion of the pioneers moving west. "They were masterful farmers and they built prosperous farms."[5]

---

[3]Bodnar, 72.

[4]David A. Gerber, *The Making of An American Pluralism* (Chicago: University of Illinois, 1989), 124.

[5]Bodnar, 86.

II

CHANGE CASE

1. Select text to change.

2. Press **Shift + F3**..............[Shift] + [F3]

3. Repeat step two until desired case appears.

   OR

1. Click **Format**...................[Alt] + [O]

2. Click **Change Case** ....[E]

3. Select desired option.

4. Click **OK** ....[Enter]

LESSON 6
SUMMARY EXERCISE

> *In this exercise, you will create a report with footnotes. This report will be bound on the left. Therefore, you will need to place the footer and page number accordingly.*

EXERCISE DIRECTIONS:

1. Format the exercise below, or open
   💾 **WBRAZIL.6A.**
2. Set a 2" left margin and a 1.5" right margin.
3. Begin the exercise At 2.5" down from the top of the page.
4. Create a footer in a sans serif 12 point bold font which reads, BRAZIL; Investment Opportunities.
5. Include a page number in the top right corner of the page.
6. Set line spacing for 2.

7. Use a serif 13 point font for the document; center and set the title to 16 point bold.
8. Use widow and orphan control.
9. Edit the footer to read, BRAZIL.
10. Justify and hyphenate the document. Limit hyphenation to two consecutive lines.
11. Spell check.
12. Preview your document.
13. Print one copy.
14. Save the file; name it **BRAZIL**.

BRAZIL

Brazil is often viewed as the economic giant of the Third World. It's economy and territory are larger than the rest of South America's and its industry is the most advanced in the developing world. Brazilian foreign debt is also the Third World's largest. The problem of foreign debt has plagued the Latin American economies since the 1960s when foreign borrowing was the only way for Latin American nations to sustain economic growth. However, when international interest rates began to rise in the 1980s, the debt these nations accumulated became unmanageable. In Brazil, the debt crisis of the 1980s marked the decline of an economy that had flourished since 1967 when foreign borrowing enabled the nation to develop its own productive industries and lessen its dependence on foreign manufactured goods. "Similar to other Latin American nations, Brazilian overseas borrowing between 1967 and 1981 became a drain on the economy when international interest rates rose; by 1985, its excessive borrowing resulted in economic disaster, political dissension and protest, and the rise of an opposition government in Brazil."[1]

Throughout the beginning of the twentieth century, growth of the Brazilian economy remained dependent upon agricultural exports. The twentieth century witnessed a decline in the export of sugar from the northeast of Brazil and a rise in the export of coffee from the southeast of Brazil. This concentrated economic growth and political power in the developed southeast part of the nation, particularly in the states of Rio de Janeiro and Sao Paulo. Industrial growth in this region progressed gradually and by 1919, domestic firms supplied over 70% of the local demand for industrial products and employed over 14% of the labor force."[2]

However, by the 1980s, Brazil accumulated massive foreign debt which ultimately caused the government to cut foreign spending and investment, drove interest rates so high that businesses could not borrow money for investment and expansion, and precipitated the bankruptcy of numerous companies, the unemployment of wage laborers, and growing social unrest. Between 1979 and 1982, the debt amassed by Brazilian banks increased from $7.7 billion to $16.1 billion. "By 1982, debt-service payments were equivalent to 91% of Brazil's merchandise exports, up from 51% in 1977."[3] In mid-1988, inflation in Brazil ran above 500% and the value of the foreign debt Brazil has to repay remains the largest in the Third World.

Brazil's financial situation is improving. Currently, Brazil has been able to sustain a 5% economic growth rate and is encouraging expanded foreign investment. Inflation in Brazil has fallen to 1.5% a month while United States exports to Brazil jumped by 35% last year."[4]

Rising international trade which may culminate in a South African free trade zone has enabled the Brazilian economy to flourish once again. Brazil's huge foreign debt, however, remains outstanding and continues to loom over its recent economic success.

---

[1] Jeffrey A. Frieden, *Debt, Development and Democracy: Modern Political Economy and Latin America, 1965-1985* (Princeton: Princeton University Press, 1991), 98.
[2] Frieden, 118.
[3] Frieden, 128.
[4] Barry Eichgreen and Peter H. Lindert, *The International Debt Crisis in Historical Perspective* (Cambridge, MA: The MIT Press, 1989), 130.

LESSON 7

WINDOWING, MULTIPLE DOCUMENTS, AND MACROS

Exercises 32-36

- Windowing

- Copying Text from One Document to Another

- Inserting a File

- AutoText

- Shrink to Fit

- Record a Macro

- Run a Macro

EXERCISE

■ WINDOWING ■ COPYING TEXT FROM ONE DOCUMENT TO ANOTHER

NOTES:

- It is often convenient to work with more than one document at once. Word allows you to have as many documents as you wish open at the same time. You can view one document at a time, or you can **tile** your screen so two or more documents are visible at the same time. Documents may be tiled by selecting Arrange All from the Window menu. The document that contains the insertion point is known as the **active document**. You can switch from one document to another by pressing Ctrl + F6 until the desired document is active, clicking in the desired document, or selecting the document name from the Window menu.

TILED DOCUMENTS

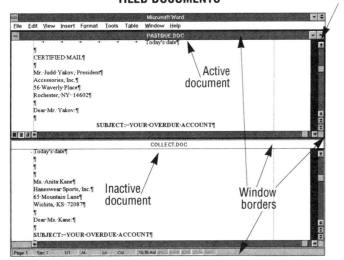

- **Windowing** (viewing two or more documents simultaneously) provides a convenient way to copy or move text from one document to another since you can see where the text is coming from and where it is going. When tiling documents, it is helpful to clear the Toolbars and Ruler from the screen to make more screen space available for the documents.

- **Sizing** a document window may be achieved by dragging any one of the four **Window borders** until the desired shape and size is achieved. Tiled documents can be viewed side-by-side by dragging them into the desired position and size. Note the illustration below.

TILED DOCUMENTS DRAGGED TO SIDE-BY-SIDE POSITION

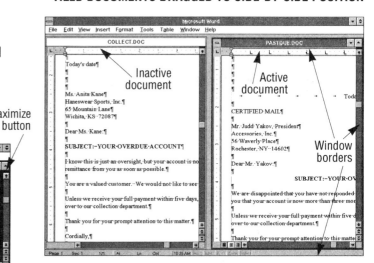

- After viewing multiple documents simultaneously, you may return to viewing a single document by making that document active and then clicking the maximize button.

- It is possible to save each open document individually or to save all open documents at once using the File, Save All command. However, each document must be closed individually.

- After closing one of your open documents, you may rearrange the remaining documents on the screen by selecting Window, Arrange All.

In this exercise, you will open several documents, tile them, and copy some text from each to a create a new document. This procedure may also be used for moving text from one document to another.

Reminder: *Copying text leaves text in its original location and pastes a copy of it in its new location.*

EXERCISE DIRECTIONS:

1. Create a NEW document.

2. Keyboard the letter exactly as shown on the following page, or open 🖫 **WHOTELS.32**.

3. Use the default margins; begin the date At 3".

4. Open **GLOBAL** and **DIVE** if you completed them in a previous exercise, or open 🖫 **WGLOBAL.32** and **WDIVE.32**.

5. Tile the documents.

6. Copy the letterhead from **GLOBAL** to the top of the NEW document. Copy the remaining indicated text in each document into the NEW document. Leave a double space before and after each insert.

   ✓ Note: The document to be copied from must be the active document. When you are ready to place the text, the new document must become the active document. Follow keystrokes carefully.

7. Close all documents except the NEW document.

8. Maximize the NEW document window.

9. Change text in small caps to normal.

10. Insert an appropriate page 2 heading as a header in the NEW document.

11. Set a .5" bottom margin on the second page.

12. Make any necessary adjustments to the text. Avoid awkward paragraph breaks.

13. Spell check the NEW document.

14. Print one copy of the NEW document.

15. Close and save the NEW document; name it **HOTELS**.

HOTELS (New Document)

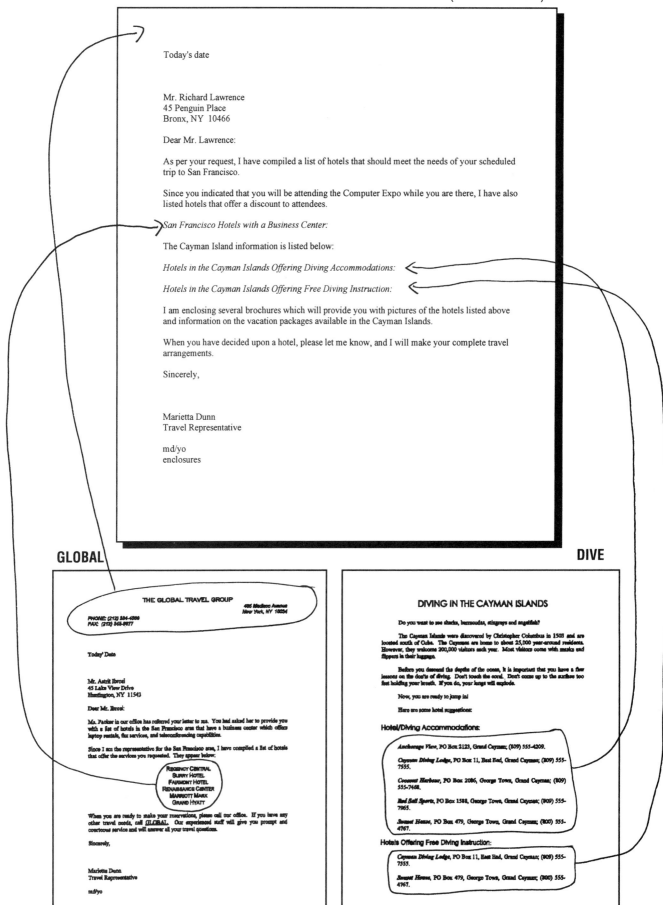

Today's date

Mr. Richard Lawrence
45 Penguin Place
Bronx, NY 10466

Dear Mr. Lawrence:

As per your request, I have compiled a list of hotels that should meet the needs of your scheduled trip to San Francisco.

Since you indicated that you will be attending the Computer Expo while you are there, I have also listed hotels that offer a discount to attendees.

San Francisco Hotels with a Business Center:

The Cayman Island information is listed below:

Hotels in the Cayman Islands Offering Diving Accommodations:

Hotels in the Cayman Islands Offering Free Diving Instruction:

I am enclosing several brochures which will provide you with pictures of the hotels listed above and information on the vacation packages available in the Cayman Islands.

When you have decided upon a hotel, please let me know, and I will make your complete travel arrangements.

Sincerely,

Marietta Dunn
Travel Representative

md/yo
enclosures

GLOBAL

DIVE

THE GLOBAL TRAVEL GROUP

496 Madison Avenue
New York, NY 10054

PHONE: (212) 394-4566
FAX: (212) 345-9977

Today' Date

Mr. Astrit Ibrosi
45 Lake View Drive
Huntington, NY 11543

Dear Mr. Ibrosi:

Ms. Packer in our office has referred your letter to me. You had asked her to provide you with a list of hotels in the San Francisco area that have a business center which offers laptop rentals, fax services, and teleconferencing capabilities.

Since I am the representative for the San Francisco area, I have compiled a list of hotels that offer the services you requested. They appear below:

REGENCY CENTRAL
SURRY HOTEL
FAIRMONT HOTEL
RENAISSANCE CENTER
MARRIOTT MARK
GRAND HYATT

When you are ready to make your reservations, please call our office. If you have any other travel needs, call GLOBAL. Our experienced staff will give you prompt and courteous service and will answer all your travel questions.

Sincerely,

Marietta Dunn
Travel Representative

md/yo

DIVING IN THE CAYMAN ISLANDS

Do you want to see sharks, barracudas, stingrays and angelfish?

The Cayman Islands were discovered by Christopher Columbus in 1503 and are located south of Cuba. The Caymans are home to about 25,000 year-around residents. However, they welcome 200,000 visitors each year. Most visitors come with masks and flippers in their luggage.

Before you descend the depths of the ocean, it is important that you have a few lessons on the don'ts of diving. Don't touch the coral. Don't come up to the surface too fast holding your breath. If you do, your lungs will explode.

Now, you are ready to jump in!

Here are some hotel suggestions:

Hotel/Diving Accommodations:

Anchorage View, PO Box 2123, Grand Cayman; (809) 555-4209.

Cayman Diving Lodge, PO Box 11, East End, Grand Cayman; (809) 555-7555.

Coconut Harbour, PO Box 2086, George Town, Grand Cayman; (809) 555-7468.

Red Sail Sports, PO Box 1588, George Town, Grand Cayman; (809) 555-7965.

Sunset House, PO Box 479, George Town, Grand Cayman; (800) 555-4767.

Hotels Offering Free Diving Instruction:

Cayman Diving Lodge, PO Box 11, East End, Grand Cayman; (809) 555-7555.

Sunset House, PO Box 479, George Town, Grand Cayman; (800) 555-4767.

OPEN MULTIPLE DOCUMENTS

1. Click **File** .... `Alt` + `F`
2. Click **Open** .... `O`
3. Hold down **Ctrl** .... `Ctrl`
   and click each file to open.

   OR

   a. Hold down **Shift** .... `Shift`
   b. Click first file to open.
   c. Click last file to open.
4. Click **OK** .... `Enter`

MAKE A DOCUMENT ACTIVE

Press **Ctrl + F6** .... `Ctrl` + `F6`
until desired document
is active.

   OR

   a. Click **Window** .... `Alt` + `W`
   b. Click document ..... `↓`, `↑`, `Enter`
      number to switch
      to desired document.

CLEAR TOOLBARS AND RULER FROM SCREEN

1. Click **View** .... `Alt` + `V`
2. Click **Toolbars** .... `T`
3. Click Toolbar check .... `↓`, `↑`, `Space`
   boxes with X to clear
   Toolbars.
4. Click **OK** .... `Enter`
5. Click **View** .... `Alt` + `V`
6. Click **Ruler** .... `R`
   to clear ruler.
7. Repeat steps 1-4 and set desired Toolbar
   check boxes to on to restore Toolbars.
8. Repeat step 5-6 to restore ruler.

TILE DOCUMENTS

1. Open desired documents.
2. Click **Window** .... `Alt` + `W`
3. Click **Arrange All** .... `A`

REMOVE TILING AND RETURN TO SINGLE DOCUMENT DISPLAY

1. Make desired document active.
2. Click **Maximize** button .... `Ctrl` + `F10`

COPY TEXT FROM ONE DOCUMENT TO ANOTHER

1. Open both documents.
2. Make source document the active file.
3. Select (highlight) text to copy.

   – USING TOOLBAR –

   a. Click **Copy** icon ....
   b. Make the destination document active.
   c. Place insertion point where text will be
      inserted.
   d. Click **Paste** icon ....

   OR

   Press **Shift + Insert** .... `Shift` + `Ins`

   – USING KEYBOARD –

   a. Press **Shift + F2** .... `Shift` + `F2`
   b. Position insertion point in destination
      document where text will be inserted.
   c. Press **Enter** .... `Enter`

   – USING MOUSE –

   a. Hold down **Ctrl** .... `Ctrl`
      and point to selected text.
   b. Hold down left mouse button
      and drag text to new location.
   c. Release left mouse button.

✓ *Clicking the **Undo** icon immediately
after a copy operation will restore
copied text to its original location.*

MOVE TEXT FROM ONE DOCUMENT TO ANOTHER

1. Open both documents.
2. Make the source document the active file.
3. Select (highlight) text to be moved.
4. Do one of the following:

   a. Click **Cut** icon ....

   b. Press **Ctrl + F6** .... `Ctrl` + `F6`

   OR

   a. Click **Window** .... `Alt` + `W`
   b. Select desired document name
      to make the destination document
      active.
5. Place insertion point where copied
   text will be inserted.
6. Click **Paste** icon ....

   OR

   Press **Shift + Insert** .... `Shift` + `Ins`

   OR

   a. Click **Edit** .... `Alt` + `E`
   b. Click **Paste** .... `P`

SAVE ALL OPEN DOCUMENTS USING ONE COMMAND

1. Click **File** .... `Alt` + `F`
2. Click **Save All** .... `L`
3. Close each document individually.

SIZE DOCUMENT WINDOWS

1. Place mouse pointer on any window
   border.

   Pointer assumes double arrow shape.

2. Drag border to desired position.

EXERCISE

INSERTING A FILE

33

NOTES:

- When you insert a file into a document, the inserted file is made part of the current document window. This is quite different from opening a document. When you open a document, each new, opened document is layered over the previous one.

- The file which has been inserted will remain intact. You may insert it into another documen when needed.

- A file may be inserted by selecting File from th Insert main menu.

In this exercise, you will create a memo and insert a previously created file into it.

EXERCISE DIRECTIONS:

1. Create a NEW document.

2. Keyboard the memo shown on the right, or open 🖫 **WHOMES.33**.

3. Use the default margins.

4. Begin the letterhead At 1".

5. Set the letterhead title to sans serif 14 point bold; set the address and phone number information to sans serif 10 point italics. Use a Wingdings flag symbol where shown in 14 point bold.

6. Begin the memo heading At 2.5".

7. Set memo side headings to sans serif 12 point bold. Type memo text in serif 12 point.

8. Insert **ESTATE** or 🖫 **WESTATE.33** where indicated. Leave a double space before and af the insert.

9. Spell check.

10. Print one copy.

11. Close the file; name it **HOMES**.

INSERT A FILE

1. Place insertion point where you want file inserted.

2. Click **Insert** .... Alt + I

3. Click **File** L

4. Type or select name of document to insert.

5. Click **OK** .... Enter

ꚛ ꚛ **FLAGSHIP REALTY** ꚛ ꚛ

111 Center Street
Southhold, NY 11555

Phone: (516) 555-5555
Fax: (516) 666-6666

TO: All Branch Managers

FROM: Jawanza Hughes

RE: Pineview Estates Listing

DATE: Today's

We just received notice that we have been given the exclusive listing for Pineview Estates, the country condominium residences located on the North Fork.   The builder placed an advertisement for this new development in several local newspapers.   The ad ran last Sunday and will run again next Sunday; a copy appears below:

As a result of this local exposure, you should have considerable activity on these properties.   Keep me apprised of all activity.

Insert Estate File

EXERCISE
34

■ AUTOTEXT ■ SHRINK TO FIT

Shrink to fit

PRINT PREVIEW TOOLBAR

NOTES:

AutoText

■ When preparing certain types of documents, the same wording is often used for many of the paragraphs in those documents. For example, in a Last Will and Testament, many of the paragraphs are standard and are used for all clients. Only those paragraphs that relate to specific items or names are changed; sometimes, relevant information is inserted after the document is created.

■ Standard or repetitive text may be saved under its own filename and inserted into a document when needed. You may use the **AutoText** feature to save repetitive text. Repetitive text may also be inserted into a document as a macro. (Macros will be covered in Exercise 35.)

■ An unlimited amount of text or graphics may be stored in an AutoText entry. You may use up to 31 characters in naming AutoText entries, and you may include spaces, but it is recommended to use names that are easy to remember and key.

■ AutoText may be created by keyboarding or highlighting the text to become the AutoText entry, then selecting AutoText from the Edit main menu.

■ An AutoText entry can be edited by inserting it into a document, making the desired changes, and resaving it.

Shrink to Fit

■ The **Shrink to Fit** feature lets you shrink a document to fill a desired number of pages.

■ If, for example, your document fills 1 1/4 pages, but you would like it to fit on one page, Shrink to Fit automatically adjusts margins, font size, or line spacing so that the text will shrink to one page.

■ You may return your document to the original number of pages by selecting Undo from the Edit menu.

■ Shrink to Fit may be accessed by selecting Print Preview from the File menu and clicking the Shrink to Fit button on the Toolbar ▦.

EXERCISE DIRECTIONS:

Part I:

1. Create a NEW document.

2. Keyboard the first standardized paragraph as shown in Part I on the next page, including the asterisks (*). (Do not include the AutoText name in the paragraph.)

3. Spell check.

4. Create an AutoText entry using the AutoText name indicated above the paragraph.

   ✓ Note: To create the lines, press the underline key several times and select *Edit, Repeat Typing (Ctrl + Y)*.

5. Keyboard the remaining paragraphs.

6. Spell check.

7. Highlight each paragraph and create an AutoText entry using the name indicated above it.

8. Close the document window without saving.

Part II:

1. Create a NEW document.

2. Keyboard the Last Will and Testament as shown in Part II on page 141, or open 🖫 **WWILL.34**.

3. Use the default margins.

4. Begin the exercise At 2".

5. Set the title to serif 14 point bold; set the body text to serif 12 point.

6. Set a left paragraph indent of 2" for the first, second, and third paragraphs (Alt + O, P, Alt + S, First Line, Alt + Y).

7. Insert the AutoText entries indicated.

8. Using the Find feature, locate each asterisk and insert the appropriate information indicated.

9. Spell check.

10. Preview your document.

11. Use the Shrink to Fit feature to shrink text to one page.

12. Print one copy.

13. Close the file; *save as* **WILL**.

PART I

AutoText Name: **Will1**

I, *, of *, do make, publish and declare this to be my Last Will and Testament, hereby revoking all wills and codicils heretofore made by me.

AutoText Name: **Will2**

IN TESTIMONY WHEREOF, I have to this my Last Will and Testament, subscribed my name and affixed my seal, this * day of *, 199*.

_____
   *

Signed, sealed, published and declared by the above-named testator, as and for his Last Will and Testament, in our presence, and we at his request, in his presence and in the presence of each other, do hereunto, sign our names and set down our addresses as attesting witnesses, all on this * day of * 199*.

_____ residing at _____

_____ residing at _____

_____ residing at _____

AutoText Name: **PSA**

PsA Micro**Computer** Systems, Inc.

AutoText Name: **CO**

Computer Technology Group, Inc.

CREATE AN AUTOTEXT ENTRY

1. Select (highlight) text/graphics to store as a AutoText entry.
2. Click **Edit** .... `Alt` + `E`
3. Click **AutoText** .... `X`
4. Type name for AutoText entry.
5. Click **Add** .... `Alt` + `A`

DELETE AN AUTOTEXT ENTRY

1. Click **Edit** .... `Alt` + `E`
2. Click **AutoText** .... `X`
3. Select AutoText name to delete.
4. Click **Delete** .... `Alt` + `D`
5. Click **Close** .... `Esc`

INSERT AN AUTOTEXT ENTRY

– USING KEYBOARD SHORTCUT –

1. Place insertion point where AutoText entry will be inserted.
2. Type name of AutoText entry.
3. Press **F3** .... `F3`

– USING THE EDIT MENU –

1. Place insertion point where AutoText entry will be inserted.
2. Click **Edit** .... `Alt` + `E`
3. Click **AutoText** .... `X`
4. Select or type desired AutoText name.
5. Click **Insert** .... `I`

EDIT AN AUTOTEXT ENTRY

1. Insert AutoText into document.

2. Edit as desired.
3. Select (highlight) the edited text.
4. Click **Edit** .... `E`
5. Click **AutoText** .... `X`
6. Select or type the AutoText name.
7. Click **Add** .... `Alt` + `A`
8. Select **Yes** .... `Y`
   when asked if you want to redefine the AutoText entry.

SHRINK TO FIT

1. Click **File** .... `Alt` + `F`
2. Click **Print Preview** .... `V`
3. Click **Shrink to Fit** button .... 🔲
   on Toolbar.
4. Click **Close** .... `C`

LAST WILL AND TESTAMENT
OF
JOHN RICHARD ADAMS

 # Insert WILL 1

* *John Richard Adams*

4 ↓

* *105 Oakwood Lane
Goshen, NY*

FIRST: I direct that all my just debts, the expenses of my last illness and funeral and the expenses of administering my estate be paid as soon as convenient.

SECOND: I give all my articles of personal, household or domestic use or adornment, including automobile and boats, to my wife, Mary Adams, or, if she does not survive me, to my children, Thomas Adams and Betsy Adams, as shall survive me, in shares substantially equal as to value.

THIRD: I give and devise all my residential real property, and all my interest in any policies of insurance thereon, to my wife, Mary Adams, if she survives me or if she does not survive me, to my surviving children, to be held by them jointly.

 # Insert WILL 2

* *third*

* *January*

* *1995*

* *John Richard Adams*

EXERCISE

RECORD A MACRO

NOTES:

- A **macro** is a saved series of commands and keystrokes which may be played with a single keystroke or mouse click. It is different from an AutoText entry in that it may contain commands and mouse actions in addition to text.

- Macros may be used to record repetitive phrases like the complimentary closing of a letter. When the phrase is needed, it is played with a single keystroke.

- A macro may also be used to automate a particular task, like changing margins and/or line spacing. Rather than press many keys to access a task, it is possible to record the process and play it with one keystroke.

- The macro exercises in this text will not cover programming commands. *(See your Word documentation for macro programming command information.)*

- To record a macro, select <u>M</u>acro from the <u>T</u>ools main menu.

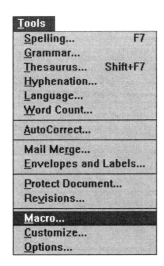

- In the Macro dialog box which follows, keyboard the name of your macro in the Macro <u>N</u>ame text box. Then, select Rec<u>o</u>rd.

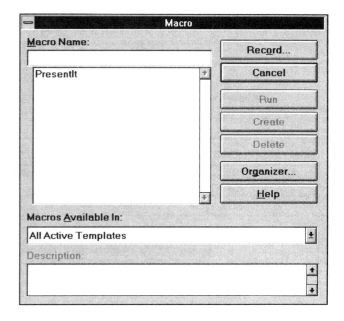

- Macro names may be up to 36 characters in length. Macro names may include letters and numbers, but they may not contain any spaces or special characters.

- As macros are created, it is important to type a description of what each macro accomplishes. This will enable others to use them. Also, because macro names are easy to forget, you will always be reminded as to what each macro does by its description.

- Macro keystrokes must be recorded very carefully. When the **Record Macro** signal, REC, is highlighted in the status bar and the macro control box appears in the document screen, any key you press will be captured into the macro.

- To stop recording, click the Stop button on the Macro control box.

In this exercise, you will create three macros to automate tasks. One of the macros will contain a closing in addition to task automation. In the next exercise, you will run the macros.

EXERCISE DIRECTIONS:

1. Create a NEW document.

2. Create macro #1 (a closing, spell check, and print preview); name it **CLOSING** and use **Alt + Shift + S** as the shortcut keys.

3. Create macro #2 (font size and margin change); name it **BEGIN** and use **Alt + C** as the shortcut keys.

4. Create macro #3 (line spacing change); name it **LINE** and use **Alt + Shift + L** as the shortcut keys.

5. Close the document window.

Macro # 2:
Macro Name: **BEGIN**
Shortcut keys: **Alt + C**

1. Click Font size button on Toolbar.
2. Select 12 point.
3. Click File.
4. Click Page Setup.
5. Click Margins.
6. Change left and right margins to 1".
7. Click OK.

Macro # 1:
Name: **CLOSING**
Shortcut keys: **Alt + Shift + S**

Sincerely,

David Altmann, Esq.

da/yo

1. Click Spelling button on Toolbar.
2. Respond to all prompts.
3. Click File.
4. Click Print Preview.

Macro # 3:
Macro Name: **LINE**
Shortcut keys: **Alt + Shift + L**

1. Click Format.
2. Click Paragraph.
3. Click in At text box (line spacing).
4. Enter 1.3" as line spacing amount.
5. Click OK.

RECORD A MACRO

1. Click **Tools** .... Alt + T
2. Click **Macro** .... M
3. Type a name for the macro.
4. Click **Record** .... Alt + O
5. Click **Description** .... Alt + D
6. Type a description of the macro's function.
7. Click **Keyboard** .... Alt + K
8. Press Alt plus a desired shortcut key.

   ✓ *Do not use a key that is assigned to another function. Word will indicate whether each key you propose is unassigned.*

9. Click **Assign** .... A
10. Click **Close** .... Enter
11. Type keystrokes to store in the macro.
12. Click **Tools** .... Alt + T
13. Click **Macro** .... M
14. Click **Stop Recording** .... Alt + O
15. Click **Close** .... Enter

   OR

   Click **Stop** button .... ▪
   on **Macro Control box**
   to stop recording keystrokes.

✓ *Mouse actions in menus and dialog boxes may be used in a macro, but mouse actions that select text or position the insertion point may not be stored in a macro.*

DELETE A MACRO

1. Click **Tools** .... Alt + T
2. Click **Macro** .... M
3. Select desired macro name .... ↓ , ↑
4. Click **Delete** .... Alt + D
5. Click **Yes** .... Y
6. Click **Close** .... Esc

Word

EXERCISE

RUN A MACRO

36

NOTES:

- Once a macro has been recorded and saved, it can be *run* (or played) into your document whenever desired.

- To run a macro, select Macro from the Tools main menu.

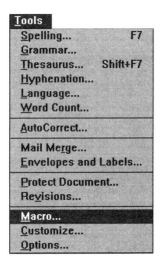

- In the Macro dialog box which follows, keyboard the macro name to play in the Macro Name text box. Or, select a macro from the filenames listed in the window and click Run. Or, simply use the shortcut keys to run the macro.

- If you select Word Commands from the Macros Available In list box, numerous macros will be listed in the macro window that you did not create. Word has provided you with numerous macros to automate a variety of tasks. To determine what each macro does, click the macro and note the description at the bottom of the dialog box.

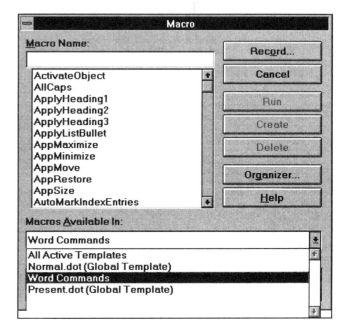

In this exercise, you will create a legal letter, and, where indicated, play two AutoText entries as well as two macros you created earlier. You will note that this document contains a Re line, which is commonly used in legal correspondence. "Re" means "in reference to" or "subject." Press the Enter key twice before and after typing the "re" line.

EXERCISE DIRECTIONS:

1. Create a NEW document.

2. Run the BEGIN macro (Alt + C) to change font size and margins.

3. Keyboard the letter shown on the right.

4. Begin the exercise At 2.5".

5. Justify paragraph text.

6. Play the PSA and CO AutoText entries wherever they appear in the text.

7. Run the CLOSING macro (Alt + Shift + S) to close, spell check, and print preview the letter.

8. Print one copy.

9. Close the file; *save as* **SETTLE**.

Today's date

Thomas Wolfe, Esq.
Wolfe, Escada & Yates
803 Park Avenue
New York, NY 10023

Dear Mr. Wolfe:

Re: [AutoText PSA] vs.
         ABC Manufacturing Company

I am enclosing a copy of the Bill of Sale that transfers all Gordon's assets to [AutoText PSA].

In addition, you asked us to represent [AutoText PSA] in their $200,000 payment to [AutoText PSA]. Because of this payment, [AutoText Co] became subrogated to the claim made by [AutoText PSA], and [AutoText PSA] cannot settle this matter without the approval of [AutoText Co].

[AutoText Co] would also be entitled to recover some portion of any judgment recovered by [AutoText PSA] in the above action. In order to get a settlement in this matter, we will need to obtain a release of ABC Manufacturing Company by [AutoText Co].

Let's discuss this so that we can quickly settle this matter.

enclosure

Run closing macro

RUN A MACRO

1. Click **Tools** .... Alt + T
2. Click **Macro** .... M
3. Select desired macro name .... ↓ , ↑
4. Click **Run** .... Alt + R
   OR
   Press shortcut keys for desired macro.

LESSON 7
SUMMARY EXERCISE

EXERCISE DIRECTIONS:

1. Create the following AutoText entry in italics; name it **AD**.

   RideTheTrack Exerciser

2. Close the document window.

3. Keyboard the advertisement below.

4. Begin At 2".

5. Play the macros and AutoText entries indicated.

6. Spell check.

7. Preview your document.

8. Print one copy.

9. Save the file; name it **WORKOUT.**

10. Close the document window.

[Begin (Alt+C)]
DISCOVER AN EXCITING NEW WAY TO
ACHIEVE WELLNESS OF BODY AND MIND
[Line]

According to medical fitness experts, regular aerobic exercise is essential for achieving all-around wellness. Aerobic exercise helps you prevent illness, feel better physically and mentally, boost your energy level, and increase the years on your life. That's why you need **[AutoText AD]**. **[AutoText AD]** will provide you with the following benefits:

[Return to Single Space and format paragraph to 1" left indent. Use bullet feature.]

- you can burn more fat than on other exercisers and burn up to 1,100 calories per hour!
- you can improve your cardiovascular fitness and lower your overall cholesterol level.
- you'll feel more mentally alert, relaxed, positive and self-confident.

[Line]

With regular workouts on a **[AutoText AD]**, you'll feel wonderful because you're doing something positive for yourself.

Seven out of ten **[AutoText AD]** owners use their machines an average of three times per week.

Call your **[AutoText AD]** representative today at 1-800-555-4444 to receive a FREE video and brochure.

[AutoText AD]

LESSON 8

COLUMNS AND TABLES; CALCULATE AND SORT

Exercises 37-42

- Newspaper Columns

- Newspaper Columns with Custom Widths

- Tabular Columns

- Setting Custom Tabs

- Tabular Columns with Leaders

- Create a Table

- Move Within a Table

- Entering Text in a Table

- Creating a Table From an Excel Worksheet

- Alignment within Table Cells

- Inserting and Deleting Columns and Rows

- Change Columns Width

- Horizontal Positioning of a Table

- AutoFormat

- Calculating in Tables

- Sort Within a Table

EXERCISE

NEWSPAPER COLUMNS

37

Columns

STANDARD TOOLBAR

NOTES:

- The **Newspaper Column** feature allows text to flow from one column to another. When the first column is filled with text, additional text automatically continues to flow into the next column. These are called **snaking columns** of text.

- Newspaper-style columns are particularly useful when creating newsletters, pamphlets, brochures, lists, or articles.

- The Column feature is accessed by selecting Columns from the Format main menu.

- To create newspaper columns quickly without accessing the dialog box, click the Columns icon on the Toolbar and drag to highlight the desired number of columns.

Drag to indicate number of columns

- In the Columns dialog which appears, you may select the number of columns you desire for a document or particular parts of a document. (You may vary the number of columns used in different sections of a document by selecting From This Point Forward in the Apply To list box.) You can also set the distance between columns (often called the **gutter space**), or you may let Word set it automatically. You also have the option of having vertical lines placed between the columns.

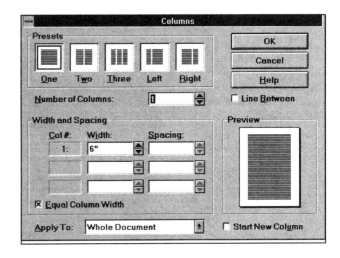

- The insertion point may be moved from column to column quickly by clicking the desired column.

- In order to see columns side-by-side as they will print, you must switch to Page Layout view.

In this exercise, you will create a two-column report using newspaper columns.

EXERCISE DIRECTIONS:

1. Create a NEW document.
2. Set left and right margins to 1".
3. Begin the exercise At 1", or open 💾 **WCOCOA.37**.
4. Center the title in sans serif 18 point bold as shown; press Enter twice.
5. Create the article on the right using a two-column, newspaper-style format. Use the default gutter space between columns. Select From This Point Forward from the Apply To list box.
6. Set column text to serif 14 point.
7. Set line spacing to 2.
8. Insert a vertical line between columns.
9. Justify document text.
10. Spell check.
11. If necessary, use Shrink to Fit to keep all text on one page.
12. Preview your document.
13. Print one copy.
14. Close the file; *save as* **COCOA**.

CHOCOLATE

CHOCOLATE is probably the world's favorite food. You can drink it hot or cold, or eat it as a snack or as part of a meal. It is made into pies, cakes, cookies, candy, ice cream and even breakfast cereal. It is nourishing, energy-giving and satisfying.

Chocolate came to us from Mexico, by way of Europe. When the Spanish explorer Cortez arrived at the court of Montezuma, the Aztec Emperor, he found him drinking a cold, bitter drink called Chocolatl. It was made from seeds of the cacao tree, ground in water and mixed with spices. Montezuma gave Cortez the recipe and some cacao and vanilla beans. Cortez took them back to Spain, where the Spanish king and queen quickly improved the drink by adding sugar and having it served hot. For about a hundred years, chocolate was exclusively a royal Spanish treat. But once the secret leaked out, the upper classes in most of the European capitals were soon sipping hot chocolate. The Dutch settlers brought chocolate to the American colonies, and in 1765 a man named Baker started a chocolate mill near Boston.

A hundred years later a man in Switzerland found a way to make solid sweet milk chocolate, and a great candy business was born. Chocolate companies like Nestle and Hershey need a lot of cacao beans. About one-third of the supply, over 350 thousand tons, is imported each year from the African country of Ghana. Ghana is the world's largest supplier of cacao beans. For many years, chocolate was made by hand. Now, machines do most of the work.

THE CHOCOLATE FACTORY has been specializing in the finest chocolate products for over 50 years. Stop in and sample some of our outstanding chocolate delights.

CREATE COLUMNS

— USING MOUSE AND TOOLBAR —

1. Select section you wish to format.

   OR

   Highlight text to format for columns.

2. Click **View** .... `Alt` + `V`

3. Click **Page Layout** .... `P`
   to switch to Page Layout view.

   `▦`

4. Click **Column** icon ....
   on Standard Toolbar.

5. Drag to right to select desired number of columns.

— USING DIALOG BOX—

1. Click **Format** .... `Alt` + `O`

2. Click **Columns** .... `C`

3. Click **Number of Columns** ...... `Alt` + `N`

4. Click up or down arrow to set desired number of columns

   OR

   Click **One**, **Two**, or **Three**.

   OR

   Click **Left** or **Right**.

5. Click **Apply To** list arrow .... `Alt` + `A`

6. Select **This Point Forward**.

7. Click **OK** .... `Enter`

MOVE INSERTION POINT FROM COLUMN TO COLUMN

Click desired column.

Word

EXERCISE

NEWSPAPER COLUMNS WITH CUSTOM WIDTHS

NOTES:

Drag column markers on ruler to reset column widths.

- Word allows you to create columns with custom widths. As indicated in the Columns dialog box, the default width of a two-column table using default margins is 2.75"; the gutter space is .5". To change the column width, click the Equal Column Width option to OFF. Then click the Column 1 and/or Column 2 text box and type the desired width.

- Column widths may also be changed by dragging the left and right column width markers on the Ruler bar.

- If you wish to create only two unequal columns, one wide and one narrow, you can choose the Right or Left options in the Columns dialog box.

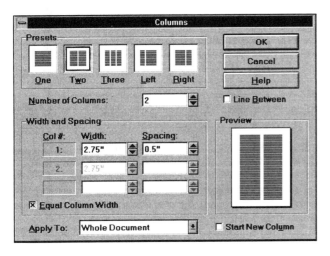

In this exercise, you will create an article using a two-column, newspaper-style format in which the second column is narrower than the first. The text does not fill up the first column and requires that you force the insertion point to the top of the second column. This is done by inserting a column break (pressing Ctrl+Shift+Enter) when you are ready to move to the top of the second column. You will also change your line spacing back to single space when you begin the second column.

EXERCISE DIRECTIONS:

1. Create a NEW document.
2. ⌨ Keyboard the exercise as shown, or open 💾 **WGOODBYE.38**.
3. Begin the exercise At 2".
4. Set left and right margins to 1".
   To create the heading:
5. Type the heading in sans serif 24 point bold italic; set the "V" to 56 points.
   To make the ampersand (&):
6. Select the ampersand from the Wingdings symbols: set the size to 72 points.
7. Right align GUIDEBOOKS; set the size to 24 point bold.

To create the remaining exercise:

8. Begin the column text At 4.4". Select This Point Forward from the Apply To list box.

9. Create a two-column, newspaper-style format.
10. Change the width of column one to 5.5"; change the width of column two to 1.5". Use the default gutter space between columns (.5").
11. Set column one text to sans serif 12 point; set column two text to sans serif 10 point bold.
12. Justify and hyphenate column one text. Hyphenate column two text.
13. Set line spacing to 2 for the first column; set line spacing to 1 for the second column.
14. Spell check.
15. Preview your document.
16. Print one copy.
17. Close the file; *save as* **GOODBYE**.

VACATION PLANNING & GUIDEBOOKS

It can be very exciting to plan a vacation. There are a number of ways to go about it. Of course, you could have a travel agent make all the arrangements. But it is more exciting to investigate all the possibilities of travel.

First, you can check the hundreds of guidebooks which can be purchased at bookstores. Then, you can send away to the government tourist offices in the country you are planning to visit. They will send you lots of free literature about the country -- places to visit and a list of accommodations. The travel advertisements in your newspaper will tell you where the bargains are. After you have planned your trip by looking through the guidebooks listed to the right, ask your travel agent to do the actual booking.

Enjoy!

OFFICIAL AIRLINE GUIDE

RUSSELL'S NATIONAL MOTOR COACH GUIDE

STEAMSHIP GUIDE

HOTEL AND RESORT GUIDE

RESTAURANT, INN AND MUSEUM GUIDE

SIGHTSEEING GUIDE

FARM VACATIONS AND ADVENTURE TRAVEL GUIDE

CREATE COLUMNS WITH CUSTOM WIDTHS

1. Click **Format** .... `Alt` + `O`
2. Click **Columns** .... `C`
3. Select **Number of Columns** .... `Alt` + `N`
4. Click up or down arrow to set desired number of columns.

   OR

   Click **One**, **Two**, or **Three**.
5. Click **Apply To** list arrow .... `Alt` + `A`
6. Select **This Point Forward**.
7. Click **OK** .... `Enter`

CREATE TWO UNEQUAL COLUMNS WITH CUSTOM WIDTHS

1. Click **Format** .... `Alt` + `O`

2. Click **Columns** .... `C`
3. Click **Left** .... `Alt` + `L`

   OR

   Click **Right** .... `Alt` + `R`
4. Click **OK** .... `Enter`
5. Drag column markers as desired to adjust column width.

INSERT A COLUMN BREAK TO FORCE TEXT TO NEXT COLUMN

Ctrl + Shift + Enter

1. Place insertion point where you want column break to occur.
2. Click **Insert** .... `Alt` + `I`
3. Click **Break** .... `B`

4. Click **Column Break** .... `C`
5. Click **OK** .... `Enter`

Column markers on ruler

CHANGE COLUMN WIDTH

1. Place mouse pointer over a column marker on the ruler until it assumes the shape of a two-headed arrow.
2. Drag the column marker to size the column as desired.

   ✓ *Equal columns will all change as you drag the column marker for one column, but when columns are unequal, only the column you are adjusting will change.*

EXERCISE 39

■ TABULAR COLUMNS ■ SETTING CUSTOM TABS
■ TABULAR COLUMNS WITH LEADERS

NOTES:

- Tabs may be used to align columns of information. However, since Word does have a Table feature which will organize information into columns and rows without using tabs or tab settings, using tab settings to align columns is not the most efficient way to tackle this task.
- Nonetheless, it is important for you to understand how tabs are used for tabular columns and the tab types available in Word (other than left aligned). (*Tables will be introduced in Exercise 40.)*
- When you change tab settings in a document, changes take effect from that point forward.
- When you open a document, there are left-aligned tabs set every half inch. This is the default setting. Whenever you press the Tab key, the insertion point jumps to the next tab stop and the space is filled with a tab character (→). This character does not print and will display on screen *only* if you have chosen to display special characters.
- It is possible to change the location and type of tab settings. Custom tabs are set in Word in two steps:
  - Click the **Tab Type** icon at the left side of the ruler to set the desired type of tab.
  - Click the ruler at the position where a custom tab is desired.

  ✓ *Note:* *Custom tabs are represented by a different symbol than the default tabs.*

RULER IN PAGE LAYOUT VIEW

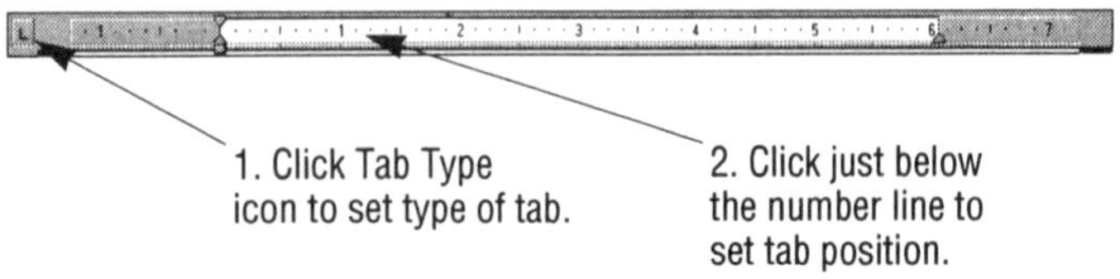
1. Click Tab Type icon to set type of tab.
2. Click just below the number line to set tab position.

- When a custom tab has been set, default tabs to the left of it are deleted.
- There are four different tab types. Each tab type is represented on the Ruler by a different symbol.

└	**Left**
┴	**Center**
┘	**Right**
┴.	**Decimal**

- Note the effect each tab type has on text:

Left Tab
Text moves to the right of the tab as you type.

```
XXXXXXXXX
XXXXX
XXXXXX
```

Centered Tab
Text centers at the tab stop.

```
XXXXXXXXX
  XXXX
 XXXXXX
```

Right Tab
Text moves to the left or backwards from the tab as you type.

```
XXXXXXXXX
     XXXX
   XXXXXX
```

Decimal Tab

Text before the decimal point moves to the left of the tab. Text you type after the decimal point moves to the right of the tab. The decimals stay aligned.

```
123.65
 56.77
  4.66
```

- Tab settings become part of paragraph formatting, and all paragraph formatting is stored in the **paragraph mark** (¶) at the end of the paragraph. If this mark is deleted, or if you move the insertion point to another paragraph, you may not have the tab settings you expect.

  ✓ *Note:* *Columns of text are generally horizontally centered between existing margins. To determine where to set tabs so they appear horizontally centered, it is necessary to create a **set-up line**. The set-up line is a blueprint for setting tab stops.*

  To create a set-up line:

  - *Center the longest line of each column and the space between the columns.*

  - *Scroll the text so it is below the ruler.*

  - *Move the insertion point to the first character in each column of the set-up line and click the ruler at these positions.*

  - *Delete the set-up line.*

- Tabs may be set on the Ruler or by selecting Tabs from the Format main menu.

Setting Tabs on the Ruler Bar

- Tab settings are displayed on the bottom of the Ruler as gray dots which are set .5" apart.

- **To set a new left-aligned tab**, click anywhere on the Ruler where a new tab is desired; a new tab marker is inserted. To delete a tab setting, drag the tab marker off the Ruler.

- **To set right-aligned centered or decimal tabs**, you must first change the tab type by clicking the tab type icon at the left end of the ruler. After the tab type is selected, each click on the Ruler will insert the tab type you have chosen. *(See keystrokes on next page.)*

Setting Tabs in the Dialog Box

- Tabs may also be set using the Tabs dialog box (Format, Tabs or double-click the ruler). This method lets you set and clear tab positions and tab types in one operation. You cannot, however, see the result of your changes on text until all settings have been made.

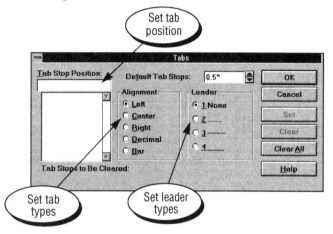

Tabular Columns with Dot Leaders

- A **dot leader** is a series of dots that connect one column to another to keep the reader's eye focused.

- To create dot leaders, select a dot leader tab type when you set your tabs.

- After all tab settings are made, use the Tab key to advance to each column. The dot leaders will automatically appear preceding those columns which contain a dot leader tab setting.

In this exercise, you will create a four column tabular document in which the first and second columns are left aligned, the third is right aligned, and the fourth is decimal aligned.

EXERCISE DIRECTIONS:

1. Create a NEW document.

2. Use the default margins.

3. Center the title lines; press Enter three times.

4. To determine where tab stops should be set, create the set-up line:

   a. Center the longest line in each column, including the intercolumn space (leave 10 spaces between columns).

   b. Scroll the page so the text is below the ruler.

   c. Using the directional keys or clicking the mouse, move the insertion point to the left of the first character in the first and second columns and set a left tab on the ruler. Move the insertion point to the right of the last character in the third column, and set a right tab on the ruler. Move the insertion point to the decimal in the fourth column, and set a decimal tab on the ruler.

   d. Delete the set-up line. Change text alignment to left, if necessary.

5. Type the remainder of the exercise.

6. Vertically center the exercise (Alt+F, U, Alt+L, Alt+V).

7. Preview your document.

8. Print one copy.

9. Save the exercise; name it **PHONE**.

10. Close the document window.

CHANGE DEFAULT TAB SETTINGS

1. Click **Format** .... Alt + O

2. Click **Tabs**.. T

3. Click **Default Tab Stops**.......... Alt + F

4. Type desired distance ....*number* between tabs.

   OR

   Select **Increase/Decrease** icons ↑ , ↓ to set desired distance.

5. Click **OK**.. Esc

SET A CUSTOM TAB

1. Place insertion point in paragraph in which tabs are to be set.

   OR

   Select (highlight) paragraphs in which tabs are to be set.

2. Click one of the following Tab Type icons to set desired tab type:

   • **Left-aligned** tab............................ L

   • **Center-aligned** tab .... ⊥

   • **Right-aligned** tab .... ⅃

   • **Decimal-aligned** tab.................... ⊥

3. Click below number line in ruler where tab is to be set.

REMOVE A CUSTOM TAB

1. Place insertion point in paragraph in which tab is to be removed.

   OR

   Select (highlight) paragraphs in which tab is to be removed.

2. Drag desired tab symbol *down* out of the ruler.

MOVE A TAB

1. Place insertion point in paragraph in which tabs are to be moved.

   OR

   Select (highlight) paragraphs in which tabs are to be moved.

2. Drag tab symbol to desired location.

CLEAR CUSTOM TABS

1. Place insertion point in paragraph containing tabs to clear.

   OR

   Select (highlight) paragraphs which contain tabs to clear.

2. Double-click desired custom tab symbol in the ruler to open the **Tabs** dialog box.

   OR

   a. Click **Format**.................... Alt + O

   b. Click **Tabs** .... T
   to open Tabs dialog box.

3. Click **Clear All** .... Alt + A

4. Click **OK** .... Enter

✓ *Default tab settings will remain after clearing all custom tabs.*

LONG DISTANCE CALLS from BETHLEHEM, PA
Destination, Number Called, Minutes and Charges
June 1995

left tab	*left tab*	*right tab*	*decimal tab*
Washington, DC	202-444-5555	28	$3.83
New Haven, CT	203-436-5555	1	.19
New York, NY	212-628-5555	52	4.94
New Haven, CT	203-436-5555	10	1.04

EXERCISE

■ **CREATE A TABLE** ■ **MOVE WITHIN A TABLE** ■ **ENTERING TEXT IN A TABLE**
■ **CREATE A TABLE FROM AN EXCEL WORKSHEET**

Table icon

STANDARD TOOLBAR

NOTES:

■ The **Table** feature allows you to organize information into columns and rows without using tabs or tab settings.

■ A table consists of **rows**, which run horizontally, and columns, which run vertically. The rows and columns intersect to form empty boxes, called **cells**. Note the example below of a table with three rows and four columns:

■ Text, graphics, numbers, or formulas are entered into cells after you have defined the structure of your table—that is, how many columns and rows you require for your table. (Formulas will not be covered in this text.)

Create a Table

■ Select Insert Table from the Table main menu. In the Insert Table dialog box which follows, indicate the desired number of Columns and Rows.

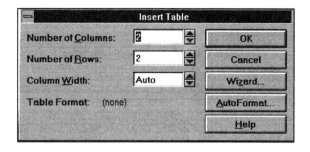

■ You can also create tables quickly by clicking the Table icon on the Standard Toolbar and dragging the mouse to select the desired number of rows and columns.

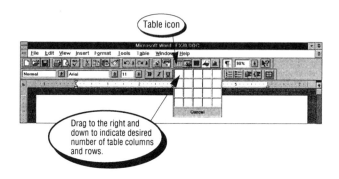

Drag to the right and down to indicate desired number of table columns and rows.

■ The columns adjust automatically to fit between the left and right margins.

■ You can create a table with up to 31 columns.

■ After the table is created, the ruler displays table markers that indicate the left and right boundaries of the table columns.

Note table column markers on the Ruler

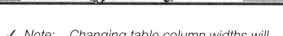

✓ *Note:* *Changing table column widths will be covered in Exercise 41.*

Move Within a Table

■ The insertion point moves in a table the same way it moves in a document. You may use the mouse to click in the desired cell, or you may use the tab key to move to the next column. When the insertion point is in the last cell of the right-most column of a table, pressing the Tab key creates a new row.

Entering Text in a Table

- As you enter text in a table cell, the cell expands downward to accommodate the text.

- Pressing Enter in a cell extends the cell vertically. It will not advance you to the next cell.

Creating a Table from an Excel Worksheet

- If you created a table in Excel that you wish to use in Word, it is not necessary to recreate the data in Word. You can import the table that was previously created in Excel into a Word document.

In Part I of this exercise, you will create minutes of a meeting using 2 columns and 11 rows. Skip one row after each entry. Note: You will learn to adjust column widths in the next exercise.

EXERCISE DIRECTIONS:

PART I:

1. Create a NEW document.

2. Use the default margins.

3. Begin the exercise At 1.7".

4. Center the main heading in sans serif 18 point bold italics. Use any desired special character before and after the heading as shown. Center the minor headings in sans serif 12 point italics. Enter twice after the date.

5. Center four special characters to separate the date from the body text. Enter three times after the special characters.

6. Create a table using 2 columns and 11 rows.

7. Set the side headings to sans serif 12 point italics; set the body text to serif 12 point.

8. Spell check.

9. Preview your document.

10. Print one copy.

11. Save the exercise; name it **AGELESS**.

12. Close the document window.

ஒ-ஒ*PERFECTION PLUS, INCORPORATED*ஒ-ஒ
MINUTES OF MEETING

March 29, 199-

ஒ-ஒ-ஒ-ஒ

Present	Robin Jones, Quincy Garin, Zachary Malvo, Wendy Carley, Bill McKinley, Andrew Yang, Shirley DeChan.
Research	Mr. Malvo announced the development of a new product line. Several new chemical formulas were developed for a cream which will reduce skin wrinkling. The cream will be called **Ageless**.
Publicity	To launch this new product, Ms. Carley announced that promotions would be made at all the high-end New York department stores. Samples of the products will be given away at demonstration counters. Press releases will be sent to members of the press.
Advertising	The advertising budget was estimated at $5,223,000. Several advertising agencies were asked to submit presentations, and a decision will be made by the Advertising Committee as to which agency will represent this new line.
Sales	Mr. Garin, National Sales Manager, projected that sales could reach $10,000,000 the first year.
Adjournment	The meeting was adjourned at 4:00 p.m. Another meeting has been scheduled for Tuesday of next week to discuss future research and marketing of this new product.

EXERCISE DIRECTIONS:

PART II:

1. Create a NEW document.

2. Use the default margins.

3. Center the page from top to bottom.

4. Center the title as shown. Set the main title to sans serif 14 point bold; set the second and third lines of the title to 12 point; set the third line to italics. Press the Enter key 3 times.

5. Create the table shown below using 4 columns and 5 rows.

6. Enter the table text as shown. Bold the column headings. Use serif 12 point for table text.

7. Preview your document.

8. Print one copy.

9. Save the exercise; name it **CRUISE**.

10. Close the document window.

FESTIVAL TRAVEL ASSOCIATES

WORLD CRUISE SEGMENTS
SPRING 1995

DESTINATION	**DEPARTS**	**NO. OF DAYS**	**COST**
Panama Canal	March 6	13	$2,529
Trans Pacific	March 19	11	$4,399
Israel to New York	March 19	18	$5,299
Naples to New York	March 19	11	$3,499

CREATE A TABLE

1. Click **Table** icon .... 🖼️
   on the Toolbar.

2. Drag to the right and down to indicate desired number of columns and rows.

   OR

   1. Click **Table** .... `Alt` + `A`

   2. Click **Insert Table** .... `I`

   3. Click .... `Alt` + `C`
      Number of Columns

4. Type number .... *number*
   of columns.

5. Click **Number of Rows** ..... `Alt` + `R`

6. Type number of rows .... *number*

7. Click **Column Width** .... `Alt` + `W`

8. Type desired width .... *number*

9. Click **OK** .... `Enter`

MOVE FROM COLUMN TO COLUMN IN A TABLE

Press **Tab** to move .... `Tab`
one column to the right.

   OR

Press **Shift + Tab** .... `Shift` + `Tab`
to move one column
to the left.

EXERCISE 41

■ **ALIGNMENT WITHIN TABLE CELLS** ■ **INSERTING AND DELETING COLUMNS AND ROWS** ■ **CHANGING COLUMN WIDTHS** ■ **HORIZONTAL POSITIONING OF A TABLE**

NOTES:

Alignment Within Table Cells

■ Word allows you to change the alignment of data for a cell, column, or the entire table.

■ You may left, center, right, or decimal align data either during the table creation process or afterward.

Left	Decimal Align: .1 10.0 1000.00
Center	**Full justify** needs more than one line to show its effect.
Right	

■ To align data in a table, place the insertion point in any cell or select (highlight) several cells or columns in which you wish to align data and click the alignment icon on the Toolbar, or you may set a tab type (center, right, or decimal). However, it is recommended that you use the alignment icons on the Toolbar to center or right align data and that you use the tab type to set decimal alignments with a table.

■ To decimal align data in a table, click the decimal tab type, then click the Ruler where the decimal alignment is desired. You must then press Ctrl + Tab to advance the insertion point to decimal align the data.

Inserting and Deleting Columns and Rows

■ One row and/or column may be inserted or deleted in a table.

■ To insert a row, select Insert Rows from the Table main menu. A new row will be inserted above the insertion point position.

■ To insert a column, highlight the column to the right of the column to be inserted. Then select Insert Columns from the Table main menu.

■ The text in the inserted column or row takes on the same formatting as the row or column of the insertion point.

■ To delete a column, highlight the column to be deleted and select Delete Columns from the Table main menu.

■ To delete a row, position the insertion point in the row to be deleted and select Delete Cells from the Table main menu. Or, highlight the row to be deleted and select Delete Rows from the Table main menu.

Deleting a Table

■ The entire table may also be deleted by selecting the entire table, then selecting Delete Rows from the Table main menu.

■ When a column or row is deleted, the contents of that column or row are also deleted.

Change Column Widths

■ **Column widths** may be changed using a specific measurement or by dragging the vertical lines between columns to the desired width.

■ To adjust column widths and see the immediate effect of the change on the table as it is being made, place the mouse pointer on a vertical line between a column to be sized. (To adjust table size, place mouse pointer on the far left or right vertical line.) The pointer's shape changes to a table sizing arrow ╬. Press and hold the mouse as you drag the dotted line left or right to the desired width or table size.

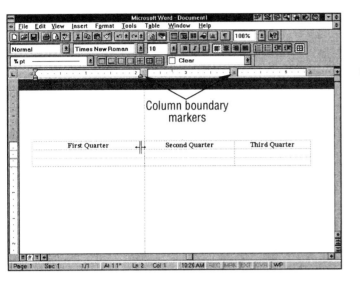

- You can also adjust column widths and margins and see the immediate effect by dragging the column boundary markers on the Ruler.

- You can also adjust column widths and margins and see the immediate effect by dragging the column on the Ruler boundary markers.

- The **AutoFit** feature allows you to adjust the width of a cell or column automatically to fit the width of the text by selecting Cell Height and Width from the Table main menu. In the Cell Height and Width dialog box which follows, select the Column Tab, then choose AutoFit.

- You may also adjust column widths and margins using a specific measurement in the Cell Height and Width dialog box.

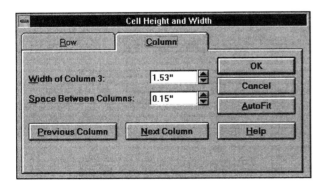

Horizontal Positioning of a Table

- Word sets column widths in a table to spread out evenly between the margins whether your table contains two or ten columns. When you change column width, Word keeps the same left margin. This means the table is no longer centered across the page.

- To center the table horizontally, select Cell Height and Width from the Table main menu. In the Cell Height and Width dialog box which follows, select the Row tab and click Center.

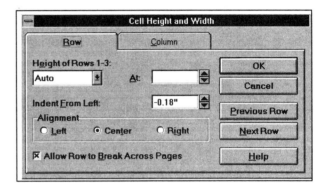

- You may also position the table to the left or right of the page or a specific amount from the left edge of the page.

- To enhance the appearance of table columns, the following guidelines should be followed regarding the distance between text in one column and the beginning of the next column:

Two column table	Approximately one inch
Three column table	Approximately three quarters of an inch
Four column table	Approximately one half inch
Five column table	Approximately one quarter inch

- Note the illustration of a two-column table below. Refer to the ruler to assist you in approximating one inch, a half inch, etc.

In Part I of this exercise, you will insert one column and one row, adjust column widths using specific amounts and AutoFit, and reposition the table horizontally in a previously created table. In Part II of this exercise, you will adjust column widths by dragging column boundary markers.

EXERCISE DIRECTIONS:

Part I:

1. Open ⌨ **CRUISE** or 💾 **WCRUISE.41**.

2. Insert one column after DESTINATION and enter the text as shown.

3. Insert one row after the column headings and after each destination, and two rows at the end of the table; enter the text as shown.

4. Set the first column width to 1.5"; set the second column width to 1.31"; leave .25" between columns.

5. Use the AutoFit feature to size the third, fourth, and fifth columns.

6. Center all headings and the text in the fourth column.

7. Horizontally reposition the table to center on the page.

8. Preview your document.

9. Print one copy.

10. Close the file; *save as* **CRUISE**.

Part II: (Page 164)

1. Open ⌨ **AGELESS** or 💾 **WAGELESS.41**.

2. Select the second column.

3. Drag column boundary markers to change the second column to 4".

4. Justify text in column 2.

5. Horizontally reposition the table to center on the page.

6. Preview your document.

7. Print one copy.

8. Close the file; *save as* **AGELESS**.

PART I

FESTIVAL TRAVEL ASSOCIATES

WORLD CRUISE SEGMENTS
SPRING 1995

Insert Column

Insert Row

Insert Row

DESTINATION	PORTS	DEPARTS	NO. OF DAYS	COST
Panama Canal	New York, Cartegena, Panama Canal, Acapulco	March 6	13	$2,529
Trans Pacific	Los Angeles, Ensenada, Kona, Honolulu, Fiji, Auckland	March 19	11	$4,399
Israel to New York	Haifa, Kusadasi, Istanbul, Athens, Naples, Cannes, New York	March 19	18	$5,299
Naples to New York	Naples, Cannes, Lisbon, Southhampton, New York	March 19	11	$3,499
Trans-Atlantic	Fort Lauderdale, Madiera, Lisbon, Gibralter, Genoa	April 16	15	$2,599

PART II

❧❧PERFECTION PLUS, INCORPORATED❧❧
MINUTES OF MEETING

March 29, 199-

❧❧❧❧

Present	Robin Jones, Quincy Garin, Zachary Malvo, Wendy Carley, Bill McKinley, Andrew Yang, Shirley DeChan.
Research	Mr. Malvo announced the development of a new product line. Several new chemical formulas were developed for a cream which will reduce skin wrinkling. The cream will be called **Ageless**.
Publicity	To launch this new product, Ms. Carley announced that promotions would be made at all the high-end New York department stores. Samples of the products will be given away at demonstration counters. Press releases will be sent to members of the press.
Advertising	The advertising budget was estimated at $5,223,000. Several advertising agencies were asked to submit presentations, and a decision will be made by the Advertising Committee as to which agency will represent this new line.
Sales	Mr. Garin, National Sales Manager, projected that sales could reach $10,000,000 the first year.
Adjournment	The meeting was adjourned at 4:00 p.m. Another meeting has been scheduled for Tuesday of next week to discuss future research and marketing of this new product.

ALIGN TEXT WITHIN CELLS, COLUMNS, OR TABLE (Center, Right, Left)

1. Place insertion point in desired cell.

   OR

   Select a cell, several cells or columns to receive alignment change.

2. Click desired alignment icon on toolbar:

   • **Left**...▤

   • **Right**...▤

   • **Center**..▤

SELECT (HIGHLIGHT) A ROW, COLUMN OR TABLE

To highlight a row:

1. Position insertion point to the left of the row to be selected until the insertion point changes to a white upward pointing arrow.

2. Click the left mouse button once.

   OR

   1. Click **Table**........................▊Alt▊+▊A▊

   2. Click **Select Row**..........................▊R▊

To highlight a column:

1. Position insertion point above the column to be selected until the insertion point changes to a black downward pointing arrow.

2. Click the left mouse button once to select the column or drag to select multiple columns.

   OR

   1. Click **Table**........................▊Alt▊+▊A▊

   2. Click **Select Column**...................▊C▊

To highlight the table:

1. Position insertion point above the column to be selected until the insertion point changes to a black downward pointing arrow.

2. Drag the arrow right to highlight all columns in the table.

   OR

   1. Click **Table**........................▊Alt▊+▊A▊

   2. Click **Select Table**......................▊A▊

SET TABS IN A TABLE COLUMN (Preferably for decimal alignments)

1. Place insertion point in desired cell.

   OR

   Select desired columns.

2. Click **Tab Type** icon.............................▊⊥▊ to set desired type of tab.

3. Click desired position in the ruler.

4. Drag tab symbol to adjust position if necessary.

5. Press Ctrl + Tab to advance insertion point to tab alignment position.

INSERT ROW/COLUMN

– ROWS –

1. Place insertion point inside table, before desired insertion is to occur.

2. Click **Table**..........................▊Alt▊+▊A▊

3. Click **Insert Rows**..............................▊I▊

– COLUMNS –

1. Highlight column to the right of desired insert.

2. Click **Table**..........................▊Alt▊+▊A▊

3. Click **Insert Columns**.........................▊I▊

DELETE ROWS/COLUMNS

1. Select columns or rows to delete.

2. Click **Table**..........................▊Alt▊+▊A▊

3. Click **Delete Rows**.............................▊D▊

   OR

   Click **Delete Columns**.......................▊D▊

DELETE TABLE

1. Select entire table.

2. Click **Table**..........................▊Alt▊+▊A▊

3. Click **Delete Rows**.............................▊D▊

CHANGE COLUMN WIDTH/MARGINS

To see immediate changes:

1. Place mouse pointer on a vertical line separating the column until it changes to a table sizing arrow ┉┠┉.

2. Drag sizing arrow left or right to desired width.

   OR

   1. Place insertion point in the table.

   2. Drag column boundary markers to change the table.

   OR

   1. Place insertion point in cell containing longest text.

   2. Click **Table**.......................▊Alt▊+▊A▊

   3. Click **Cell Height and Width**........▊W▊

   4. Click **Column**....................▊Alt▊+▊C▊

   5. Click **AutoFit**....................▊Alt▊+▊A▊

To set specific settings:

1. Place insertion point in column to format.

   OR

   Select several columns to format.

2. Click **Table**...........................▊Alt▊+▊A▊

3. Click **Cell Height and Width**.............▊W▊

4. Click **Column**.......................▊Alt▊+▊C▊

   To set column width:

   a. Click in................................▊Alt▊+▊W▊
      Width of Column

   b. Type column width amount.....*number*

HORIZONTALLY CENTER A TABLE

1. Select table.

2. Click **Table**...........................▊Alt▊+▊A▊

3. Click **Cell Height and Width**.............▊W▊

4. Click **Row**............................▊Alt▊+▊R▊

5. Click **Center**........................▊Alt▊+▊T▊

6. Click **OK**...................................▊Enter▊

EXERCISE
42

■ AUTOFORMAT ■ CALCULATING IN TABLES ■ SORT WITHIN A TABLE

NOTES:

AutoFormat

■ Word provides a quick way to enhance the appearance of tables through its Table **AutoFormat**. Word provides 34 predefined formatting styles from which you can select to apply to your table. AutoFormat may be accessed by selecting Table AutoFormat from the Table main menu. In the Table AutoFormat dialog box which follows, available styles are listed on the left, and a preview window displays the selected style.

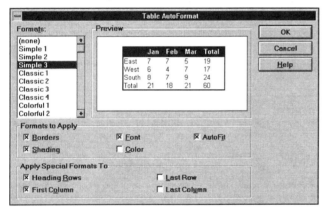

Calculating in Tables

■ Word can add consecutive numbers in table columns or rows. You can also perform calculations for subtraction, multiplication, and division within a table cell. This exercise will focus on performing addition calculations. If your data requires subtraction, multiplication, division, averaging, finding the highest or lowest value, or more extensive calculations, use Excel to perform these calculations. Remember, the worksheets created in Excel can be imported into Word, if needed.

■ To add numbers in a table cell, place the insertion point in the cell where the answer should appear. Then select Formula from the Table main menu.

■ The correct formula for computing the sum of a column of figures above the insertion point cell is:

=SUM(ABOVE)

■ The correct formula for adding a row of figures to the left of the insertion point cell is:

=SUM(LEFT)

■ If one of the numbers in a calculation includes a dollar sign ($), the answer will include a dollar sign and will appear with two places after the decimal.

Sort Within a Table

■ Word's **Sort** feature lets you arrange text alphabetically or numerically in ascending order (from A to Z or 1 to 25) or descending order (Z to A or 25 to 1).

■ To begin the sort, place your insertion point in the first column to be sorted and select Sort from the Table main menu. In the Sort dialog box which follows, you are required to indicate which column is to be sorted and which item in the column to sort.

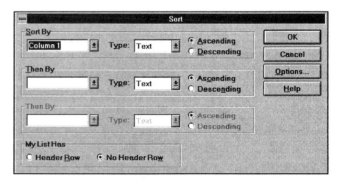

✓ Note: *It is important to save your document before you begin a sort. If your sort produces unexpected results, you can close your file without saving it, open the file again, and repeat the sort process.*

- It is possible to sort one column and then subsort another column within the first column. Note the illustration below of records sorted on one column and subsorted on another.

- Word allows you to sort up to 3 columns of data.

- This exercise will focus on simple sorts. If you require extensive sorting and/or selective sorting of data, use Access, the database tool. *(See Chapter 4, Exercise 14.)*

Subsort by CITY

TITLE	FIRST	LAST	ADDRESS	CITY	ST	ZIP
Ms.	Barbara	Center	43 Beverly Road	Beverly Hills	CA	90210
Ms.	Donna	Brown	76 York Avenue	Santa Monica	CA	90087
Ms.	Rose	Casen	500 Carlin Way	Venice	CA	90122
Mr.	Paul	Rivlin	14 Hidden Hills	Stone Mountain	GA	30088
Ms.	Sharon	Walker	34 Prince Street	Bronx	NY	10456
Mr.	Nick	Batos	43 Wilmer Street	Brooklyn	NY	11230
Mr.	Roy	Porter	235 Belmill Road	Brooklyn	NY	11244
Ms.	Jaime	Leigh	111 John Street	New York	NY	10033
Ms.	Pamela	Jones	66 West 66 Street	New York	NY	10056
Mr.	Richard	Zarin	12 Circle Drive	Dallas	TX	78666
Mr.	Miles	Brown	1640 Ocean Avenue	Lubbock	TX	79410
Ms.	Natasha	Alesi	77 Midi Drive	San Marcos	TX	78666
Mr.	Jay	Stanis	9 Times Road	Orem	UT	84057

Sort by ST

In this exercise, you will create a monthly sales table and use the Calculate feature to find quarter totals.

EXERCISE DIRECTIONS:

Part I:

1. Create a NEW document.

2. Set the left and right margins to .5".

3. Center the main heading in serif 14 point bold and the minor headings in 12 point and italics where shown. Press Enter three times.

4. Create a table using 5 columns and 11 rows.

5. Set body text to 12 point.

6. Enter the data as shown on the next page. Center and bold the column headings; bold and italicize TOTALS.

7. Save the file; name it **MICRO**.

Part II:

1. Set width of columns 2-5 to 1.25". Use AutoFit to adjust column 1 width.

2. Highlight the columns which contain numerical data. Set a decimal tab in the second column so the data centers within the column (at 2").

   ✓ Note: Setting a decimal tab in the second column affects all the columns that were highlighted.

3. Find the totals for JANUARY, FEBRUARY, and MARCH and QTR TOTALS. *(Use =SUM(ABOVE) for JANUARY, FEBRUARY, and MARCH and =SUM(LEFT) for QTR TOTALS.)*

4. Sort the first column to arrange the names alphabetically. (Select only the names before sorting or totals will be sorted also.)

5. Insert a dollar sign ($) where shown.

6. Horizontally and vertically center the exercise.

7. Apply any desired Table AutoFormat to the exercise.

8. Preview your document.

9. Print one copy.

10. Save the file; name it **MICRO1**.

11. Close the document window.

   ✓ Note: If you made an error in any of the steps in Part II, you may close this file, open MICRO, and begin again.

PART I

MICRO ELECTRONICS

MONTHLY SALES BY SALESPERSON
First Quarter 199-

	JANUARY	FEBRUARY	MARCH	QTR TOTALS
Mauro, John	3456.99	3456.88	2345.99	
Singh, Chandra	8634.88	3466.88	2356.66	
Doyle, Ebony	7643.99	5558.99	4765.00	
Dunn, Brad	7777.00	7776.55	6668.00	
Ho, Bruce	7745.00	3456.99	5666.95	
Kennedy, Sharon	5987.00	6575.85	4556.88	
Yerman, Jonathan	6432.25	6554.00	5090.00	

TOTALS

PART II

MICRO ELECTRONICS

MONTHLY SALES BY SALESPERSON
First Quarter 199-

	JANUARY	FEBRUARY	MARCH	QTR TOTALS
Doyle, Ebony	$7643.99	$5558.99	$4765.00	$17967.98
Dunn, Brad	7777.00	7776.55	6668.00	22221.55
Ho, Bruce	7745.00	3456.99	5666.95	16868.94
Kennedy, Sharon	5987.00	6575.85	4556.88	17119.73
Mauro, John	3456.99	3456.88	2345.99	9259.86
Singh, Chandra	8634.88	3466.88	2356.66	14458.42
Yerman, Jonathan	6432.25	6554.00	5090.00	18076.25
TOTALS	$47676.86	$36846.14	$31449.48	$115972.73

TABLE AUTOFORMAT

1. Pace insertion point anywhere in table to format.

2. Click **Table**............................ Alt + A

3. Click **Table AutoFormat** .... F

4. Select desired style .... Alt + T from list of **Formats**.

5. Click any or all of following **Formats to Apply** to turn check boxes on or off as desired:

   • **Borders** .... Alt + B

   • **Shading** .... Alt + S

   • **Font** .... Alt + F

   • **Color** .... Alt + C

   • **Autofit** .... Alt + I

6. Click any or all of the following to **Apply Special Formats To** specified parts of table:

   • **Heading Rows** .... Alt + R

   • **First Column** .... Alt + O

   • **Last Row** .... Alt + L

   • **Last Column** .... Alt + U

7. Click **OK** .... Enter

USING FORMULAS

1. Place insertion point where answer will appear.

2. Click **Table** .... Alt + A

3. Click **Formula** .... O

4. Click **OK** .... Enter if Word proposes the correct formula.

   OR

   Edit expression in parentheses as necessary.

5. Click **OK** .... Enter

SORT

1. Place insertion in column to be sorted.

2. Click **Table** .... Alt + A

   OR

   Highlight data to be sorted.

3. Click **Sort** .... T

4. Click **Sort By** .... Alt + S

5. Select column to sort.

6. Click **Type** .... Alt + Y

7. Select data type to be sorted.

8. Click:

   Ascending .... Alt + A

   OR

   Descending .... Alt + D

9. Repeat steps 4-8 for 2nd and 3rd column to sort.

10. Click **OK** .... Enter

LESSON 8
SUMMARY EXERCISE

In this exercise, you will create a table, size the columns, calculate the columns, and format the table using the Table AutoFormat feature.

EXERCISE DIRECTIONS:

1. Create a NEW document.
2. Use the default margins.
3. Create the table as shown below, or open WBALI.8A.
4. Enter and align the text in serif 10 point as shown.
5. Use AutoFit to size the columns.
6. Total the STAFF and SALES columns.
7. Center all column headings; right align STAFF data.
8. Set a decimal tab in the SALES column to align data.
9. Horizontally and vertically center the exercise.
10. Apply any desired Table AutoFormat to the exercise.
11. Preview your document.
12. Save the file; name it **BALI**.
13. Print one copy.
14. Sort the data in descending order by SALES.
15. Print one copy.
16. Sort the data alphabetically by STATE, and subsort alphabetically by BRANCH. (Select both columns before sorting.)
17. Print one copy.
18. Close the document window; do not save the changes.

BALIWANE SPORTSWEAR
New Branches/Locations/Gross Sales

As of January 31, 199-

BRANCH	CITY	STATE	STAFF	SALES
Paramount	New York	NY	18	350,000.25
Sunview	Hollywood	CA	12	125,000.00
Seaview	Portland	ME	8	100,000.00
Cornielle	Providence	RI	20	450,000.00
Astro Center	Houston	TX	19	99,000.00
Mountainaire	Troy	NY	6	95,000.99
Sunnyvale	New York	NY	16	150,000.00
Downtown Center	Dallas	TX	16	183,000.00
Beverly Road	Beverly Hills	CA	8	259,865.00
TOTALS				

170

LESSON 9

MERGING

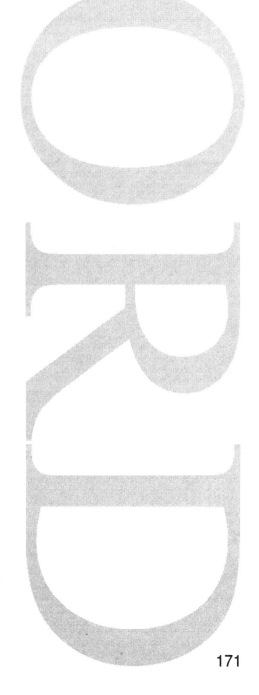

Exercises 43-45

- Merging Main and Data Source Documents

- Preparing Envelopes and Labels While Merging

EXERCISE

CREATING THE MAIN AND DATA SOURCE DOCUMENTS

43

NOTES:

The Main Document

■ The **Merge** feature allows you to mass produce letters, envelopes, mailing labels, and other documents so they appear to be personalized.

■ The main document (the form letter) is combined with a data source document (the names and addresses of those who will receive the letters) to produce a **merged** document.

■ The same data file may then be used to produce the envelopes and/or labels, thus making it unnecessary to type the name and address list a second time.

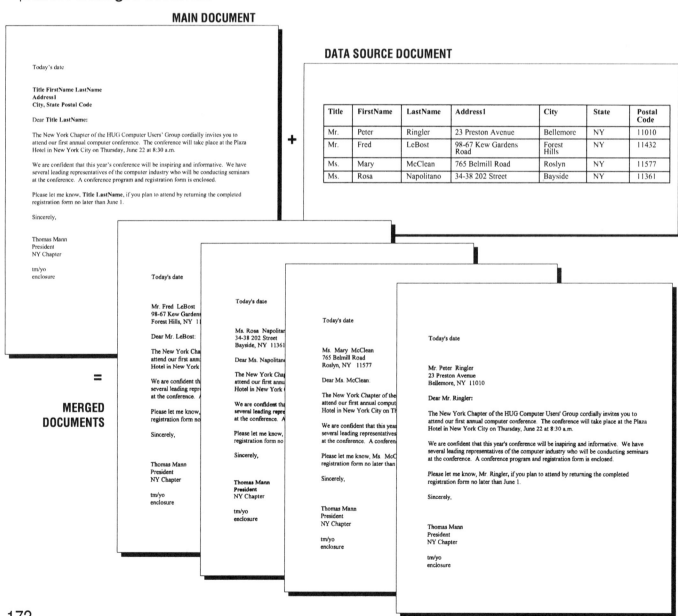

MAIN DOCUMENT

DATA SOURCE DOCUMENT

Title	FirstName	LastName	Address1	City	State	Postal Code
Mr.	Peter	Ringler	23 Preston Avenue	Bellemore	NY	11010
Mr.	Fred	LeBost	98-67 Kew Gardens Road	Forest Hills	NY	11432
Ms.	Mary	McClean	765 Belmill Road	Roslyn	NY	11577
Ms.	Rosa	Napolitano	34-38 202 Street	Bayside	NY	11361

MERGED DOCUMENTS

- There are three steps in a mail merge operation:

  1. Create a **main document** containing the body text that will be common to every form letter.

  2. Create a data document (**data source document**) that contains the personalized Information about each person to receive the form letter (name, address, etc.).

  3. Merge the main document and the data source document to create individual form letters that are personalized for each recipient.

- The main document contains information that does not change. All formatting, margins, spacing, etc., as well as graphics and paper size information, should be included in the main document.

- Each piece of variable information is called a **field**.

- Each field is named for what will eventually be inserted into that location. These names are called **merge field names**.

- At each location in the main document where variable information will be placed, we will set a temporary *placeholder* that will be replaced by personalized information from the data document. These placeholders can be simply asterisks (***), but we will use merge field names that describe the kind of data that will be merged from the data source document. For example, we will use *FirstName* as a placeholder in the location where we want each letter recipient's first name to appear.

- Although you may make up your own merge field names, Word provides a list of the most commonly used merge fields. In this exercise, we will choose the merge field names from the list provided by Word.

- In a typical letter, the variable information would include the person's title (Miss, Ms., Mrs., Mr., Dr.), first name, last name, house number and street, city, state, and zip code. In this exercise,

each piece of information will be named as follows:

INFORMATION	MERGE FIELD NAME
Title	Title
First name	FirstName
Last name	LastName
House number and street	Address1
City	City
State	State
Zip	PostalCode

- As you type each merge field into your main document, space between each merge field and the surrounding text as you would want the spacing to appear when text is substituted for the merge field in the letter. Punctuation must also be added before or after merge fields in the main document when appropriate.

- The same merge field can be inserted in the letter as many times as desired. Note that Title, LastName and City are each used more than once in the form letter you will create in this exercise. There are three occurrences of someone's title and last name, and two references to the person's home city.

- Any document, new or existing, can become a main document if you take steps to define it as a main document. It must then be saved (or resaved) in the usual way.

- When a document has been defined as a main document, the Merge Toolbar appears at the top of the screen (see below, right).

MERGE TOOLBAR

The Data Source Document

- The **data source document** contains the variable information (Title, FirstName, LastName, etc.) for those people who will be receiving the letter created as the main document.

- A data source document may contain many **records**. A record is a collection of related information. A record might consist of all the variable information for one person. The information in each record is divided into

fields. The field names used in the main document must match the field names used in the data document.

■ Note the data source document below. The top row is the header record because it contains all the merge field names. Each column represents a merge field and each row is a record.

Title	FirstName	LastName	Address1	City	State	Postal Code
Mr.	Peter	Ringler	23 Preston Avenue	Bellemore	NY	11010
Mr.	Fred	LeBost	98-67 Kew Gardens Road	Forest Hills	NY	11432
Ms.	Mary	McClean	765 Belmill Road	Roslyn	NY	11577
Ms.	Rosa	Napolitano	34-38 202 Street	Bayside	NY	11361

■ To create a data source document, select Mail Merge from the Tools main menu. In the Mail Merge Helper dialog box which follows, select Get Data, Create Data Source. In the Create Data Source dialog box which follows, Word presents you with a list of commonly used merge field names. You indicate which field names your document contains by deleting from the list those field names you do not wish to use and adding others that might not appear on the list.

CREATE DATA SOURCE DIALOG BOX

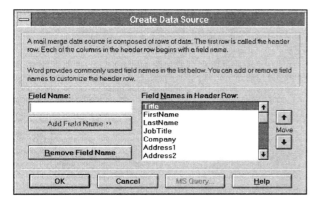

■ After selecting the merge field names that are contained in your document and selecting OK, you will be presented with the Save Data Source dialog box so that you can save your data document. After saving your document, a Data Form dialog box appears, allowing you to enter the actual data for each person receiving your form letter.

DATA FORM DIALOG BOX

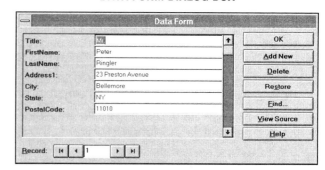

■ When you have finished, you may view the data source document. It will appear as a table of columns and rows with the merge field names at the top of each column (in the header row).

Insert Merge Field Names into Main Document

■ After completing the data source document, switch to or open the main document. Select (highlight) each placeholder, click the Insert Merge Field button on the Mail Merge Toolbar, and select a merge field name from the drop-down list that will replace the placeholder.

Merge Main and Data Source Documents

■ The main document and the data document may be merged to a new, third document. When the main and data documents are merged, the new merged file may be saved on disk, or the merged letters may be printed without saving them. Note the result of the merge shown in the illustration on page 172.

■ Note that the comma used after the city name was part of the main document. When replacing the placeholders with merge field names, be sure to insert proper spacing between merge fields and to add punctuation as needed.

■ If the main and data documents do not merge properly, check to make sure the text in the data document has been entered under the proper merge field names and that merge field names have been properly placed in the main document.

■ When working with mail merge, you may have as many as three documents open at the same time: the main document, the data source document, and the merged form letters document. To switch from one document to the other, press Ctrl + F6 or Shift + Ctrl + F6 to switch back.

In Part I of this exercise, you will create a main document. In Part II of this exercise, you will create a data source document, merge the two documents to a third document and print them.

EXERCISE DIRECTIONS:

Part I:

1. Create a NEW document.

2. Begin the exercise At 2.6".

3. Create the main document illustrated on the right; type the merge field names as placeholders as shown.

    ✓ *Note: The merge field names are shown in bold to make them easy for you to recognize. Do not use bold for the merge fields when creating your main document.*

4. Define the file as a main document.

5. Spell check.

    ✓ *Note: Ignore misspelled merge field names.*

6. Preview your document.

7. Print one copy.

8. Save the file; name it **HUGMN**.

9. Do not close the document window.

Part II:

1. Create the data source document shown on the following page using merge field names and data indicated.

2. Save the file; name it **HUGDAT**.

3. View the source document.

4. Preview your document.

5. Switch to the main document.

6. Check main and data documents for errors (to see if merge field names in both documents are the same).

7. Insert merge field names into main document.

8. Merge the main document, **HUGMN**, with the data document, **HUGDAT**, using the merge to *document* option.

9. Scroll through the new merged document; check the form letters for errors.

10. Save the merged letters under a new filename, **HUGFI**.

11. Merge the main document, **HUGMN**, with the data document, **HUGDAT**, using the merge to *printer* option.

12. Close the **HUGMN** and **HUGDAT** files.

MAIN DOCUMENT   **PART I**

Today's date

Title FirstName LastName
Address1
City, State Postal Code

Dear **Title LastName:**

The New York Chapter of the HUG Computer Users' Group cordially invites you to attend our first annual computer conference. The conference will take place at the Plaza Hotel in New York City on Thursday, June 22 at 8:30 a.m.

We are confident that this year's conference will be inspiring and informative. We have several leading representatives of the computer industry who will be conducting seminars at the conference. A conference program and registration form is enclosed.

Please let me know, **Title LastName**, if you plan to attend by returning the completed registration form no later than June 1.

Sincerely,

Thomas Mann
President
NY Chapter

tm/yo
enclosure

DATA SOURCE DOCUMENT   **PART II**

Title	FirstName	LastName	Address1	City	State	Postal Code
Mr.	Peter	Ringler	23 Preston Avenue	Bellemore	NY	11010
Mr.	Fred	LeBost	98-67 Kew Gardens Road	Forest Hills	NY	11432
Ms.	Mary	McClean	765 Belmill Road	Roslyn	NY	11577
Ms.	Rosa	Napolitano	34-38 202 Street	Bayside	NY	11361

CREATE A MAIN DOCUMENT

1. Type the document you wish to use as a main document.

   OR

   Open an existing document you wish to use as a main document.

2. At locations in the document where variable information will be inserted, type the **merge field name** of that information.

   OR

   Type an asterisk (*) as a placeholder for the variable information.

   ✓ *You may make up your own merge field names, use those on the list provided by Word, or use a combination of both your own names and Word's. It is also okay to type an asterisk (*) as a placeholder instead of a merge field name.*

3. Click **Tools**............................... Alt + T
4. Click **Mail Merge** .... R
5. Click **Create** .... Alt + C
   to define document as a main document.
6. Click **Form Letters** L
7. Click **Active Window** .... A
8. Click **Close** .... Esc
9. Click **File** .... Alt + F
10. Click **Save** .... S

CREATE A DATA SOURCE DOCUMENT

1. Open the **main document**.
2. Click **Tools** .... Alt + T
3. Click **Mail Merge** .... R
4. Click **Get Data** .... Alt + G
5. Click **Create Data Source** C
6. Click .... Alt + N
   Field Names in Header Row

   ✓ *Word suggests a list of commonly used field names. You may add new field names, delete suggested names, or use the suggested fields in their entirety.*

7. Do one of the following:

   a. Select field name ....
      to delete.

b. Click .... Alt + R
   Remove Field Name.

c. Repeat steps a-b for each field name not wanted.

AND/OR

a. Click **Field name** .... Alt + F

b. Type name of new merge field to add to list.

c. Click **Add Field Name** .... Alt + A

d. Repeat steps a-c for each new field name you wish to add.

8. Repeat steps 6 and 7 for each merge field name.

9. Click **OK** .... Enter

10. Key a name for the ....*name* data source document in the File **N**ame box.

11. Click **OK** .... Enter

   ✓ *A message will appear indicating that there are no records in the data source file. By selecting **Edit Data Source**, you cause the **Data Form** dialog box to appear.*

12. Click **Edit Data Source** .... Alt + E
    to open Data Form dialog box.

13. Key information for the first field.

14. Press **Enter** .... Enter
    to move to next field.

15. Repeat for each field.

   ✓ *Press **Shift+Tab** to go back to edit a field.*

16. Click **Add New** .... Alt + A
    after entering information for last field.

   ✓ *See illustration of filled in **Data Form** dialog box in the **Notes** section of this exercise, page 174.*

17. Repeat steps 14 and 16 for each person who will receive the form letter.

18. Click **View Source** .... Alt + V
    to see data source document.

19. Save and close data source document in the usual way.

20. Save and close main document in the usual way.

SWITCH FROM DATA DOCUMENT TO MAIN DOCUMENT

Click **Main Document** icon ....

SWITCH FROM MAIN DOCUMENT TO DATA DOCUMENT

1. Click **Edit Data Source** icon ....

2. Click **View Source** .... Alt + V

INSERT MERGE FIELD NAMES INTO MAIN DOCUMENT

1. Open the main document.

2. Select (highlight) the first placeholder in the **main document**.

3. Click **Insert Merge Field** button..........
   on Mail Merge Toolbar.

4. Click the merge field name that will replace the placeholder.

5. Add spacing or punctuation before or after the merge field name, if needed.

6. Repeat steps 2-5 at each location where a merge field name is to be inserted.

7. Resave the main document.

MERGE MAIN AND DATA SOURCE DOCUMENTS

1. Open the main document.

2. Click **View Merged Data** icon..........
   on Mail Merge Toolbar.

3. Click **Next Record** icon ....

   OR

   Click **Previous Record** icon..............
   to view additional records.

4. Click **Check for Errors** icon ....

5. Click **OK** .... Enter
   to merge to a new document while checking for errors.

6. Click **Merge to Printer** icon ....
   to print merged form letters.

7. Save and close the main document and the merge document.

CHECK MAIN DOCUMENT AND DATA DOCUMENT FOR ERRORS

1. Click **Main Document** icon ....
   to switch to main document, if necessary.

2. Click **Error Check** icon.....................

EXERCISE

44

CREATING AND MERGING MAIN AND DATA SOURCE DOCUMENTS

NOTES:

- In the previous exercise, each of the records in the merged file contained the same number of variables. However, this is not always the case. Not all inside addresses are three lines. Some people receiving a form letter may have inside addresses that contain a company name.

- When creating the main document, include a placeholder for every possible variable. When filling out the data form, you will not fill in any information in a field if it is not relevant for that record. For example, if some records contain a company name while others do not, you must include a placeholder for a company name in the main document. When filling out the data form, you will leave blank the company name for those records that do not contain one. During the merge process Word will insert a company name if it was included in the data form; otherwise, Word eliminates that line from the address.

In this exercise, you will create a main document and a data source document and merge the two files. The main document will contain more variables than the previous exercise.

EXERCISE DIRECTIONS:

1. Create a NEW document.
2. Use the default margins.
3. Begin the exercise At 2.5".
4. Create a main document from the letter shown on the next page. Insert the following merge field names as placeholders where appropriate:

   Title
   FirstName
   LastName
   Company
   Address1
   City
   State
   PostalCode
   Amount
   Date

5. Define the document as a main document.
6. Spell check.
7. Preview your document.
8. Print one copy.
9. Save the file; name it **DUEMN**. Do not exit the document window.
10. Create a data source document using the merge field names and data shown on the next page.
11. Save the file; name it **DUEDAT**.
12. View the data source document.
13. Preview your document.
14. Switch to the main document; insert merge field names in placeholder locations.
15. Check main and data documents for errors (to see if merge field names in both documents are the same).
16. Switch back to the data document.
17. Close the data document (DUEDAT); save the changes.
18. Merge the main document, DUEMN, with the data document, DUEDAT, using the merge to document option.
19. Print one copy of the merged documents.
20. Close all files; save the changes.

Today's date

☐ ☐ ☐

☐

☐

☐ , ☐ ☐

Dear ☐ ☐ :

Just a brief reminder, ☐ ☐ , that your account is now past due. As you can see from the enclosed statement, you still have an outstanding balance of $ ☐ which was due on ☐ .

We need your cooperation so that we can continue to give you the service we have provided you for many years.

Please mail your remittance for $ ☐ today, so we are not forced to send your account to our collection agency.

Cordially,

Brenda Nadia
Collection Manager

bn/yo

DATA SOURCE DOCUMENT

Title	FirstName	LastName	Company	Address1	City	State	PostalCode	Amount	Date
Ms.	Vanessa	Jackson	Ace Chemical Co.	48 Endor Avenue	Brooklyn	NY	11221	256.98	March 1
Mr.	Kenneth	Hall		5 Windsor Drive	West Long Branch	NJ	07764	450.50	March 15
Mr.	Glenn	Babbin		187 Beach 147 Street	Queens	NY	11694	128.86	February 28
Ms.	Stefanie	Eaton	XYZ Broadcasting Company	137 Brighton Avenue	Perth Amboy	NJ	08861	612.75	February 15

✓ Note: In the above letter, boxes have been used to indicate each place where a placeholder for a merge field name should be inserted. In place of the boxes, use the appropriate merge field names from the list provided on the previous page.

EXERCISE

45

- **CREATING AND MERGING MAIN AND DATA SOURCE DOCUMENTS**
- **PREPARING ENVELOPES AND LABELS WHILE MERGING**

NOTES:

Envelopes

- Rather than typing an envelope for each merged form letter, Word can automatically print an envelope for each merged letter using the same data source document that was used to prepare the merged letters.

Labels

- Word can prepare mailing labels for each merged letter using a method similar to preparing envelopes. (See keystrokes below.)

- **Label paper** contains removable labels that may be placed on envelopes. Word provides a list of product numbers for Avery brand label paper. If you are using a different brand, you may be able to find an equivalent product number. Otherwise, you can experiment to find product equivalence.

In this exercise, you will create a main document and a data source document and merge the two files. In addition, you will create a label file and merge it with the data source document to create labels.

EXERCISE DIRECTIONS:

1. Create a NEW document.
2. Use the default margins.
3. Begin the exercise At 2.5".
4. Create a main document from the letter shown on the next page. Refer to the following information next to the letter, and insert placeholders where necessary (you are to determine the placeholder names).
5. Define the document as a main document.
6. Spell check
7. Preview your document.
8. Print one copy.
9. Save the file; name it **ERRORMN**. Do not exit the document window.
10. Click the Mail Merge Helper Icon 🖳 and create a data document using the variable information shown to the right of the letter.
11. Save the file; name it **ERRORDAT**.
12. View the data document.
13. Switch to the main document; insert merge field names in placeholder locations.
14. Check main and data documents for errors (to see if merge field names in both documents are the same).
15. Switch back to the data document.
16. Save the changes.
17. Merge the main document, ERRORMN, with the data document, ERRORDAT.
18. Print one copy of the merged letters.
19. Create and save a mailing label main document; name it **ERORLABL**.
20. Merge the mailing label main document with the data document.
21. Print one copy. (Use plain paper to see how labels will print on page.)
22. Close all files; save the changes.

CREATING MAILING LABELS WHILE MERGING

1. Open a new document.
2. Click **Tools** .... Alt + T
3. Click **Mail Merge** .... R
4. Click **Create** .... Alt + C
5. Click **Mailing Labels** .... M
6. Click **Active Window** .... A
7. Click **Get Data** .... Alt + G
8. Click **Open Data Source** .... O
9. Select document containing address data.
10. Click **OK** .... Enter
11. Click **Set Up Main Document** .... S
12. Click **Laser** .... Alt + L

   OR

   Click **Dot Matrix** .... Alt + M

Today's date

____ ____ _____
_____
_____
_____, ___ ____

Dear _____:

Thank you for your check No. _____, in the amount of $_____. We notice that you erroneously deducted a discount, even though the discount period has expired.

We know this is an oversight. We are returning your check No. _____, and we would appreciate your sending us another check for $_____ to cover the correct amount.

Thank you for your attention to this matter.

Sincerely,

Arnold Zahn
Credit Manager

az/yo

Mr. Harold Dembo
Holistic, Inc.
654 Sanborn Street
Denver, CO 80202
Check no. 8768
Incorrect amount 654.86
New amount 682.75

Ms. Jennifer Downing
7659 Utica Avenue
San Antonio, TX 78202
Check no. 6543
Incorrect amount 76.99
New amount 109.10

Mr. Daniel Davis
Acme Plumbing Supply
90 Plaza Z
Milwaukee, WI 53212
Check no. 7888
Incorrect amount 333.33
New amount 386.86

✓ *Word provides a list of product numbers for Avery brand label paper.*

If you are using a different brand, you may be able to find an equivalent product number. Otherwise, you can experiment to determine product equivalence.

*If unsure, use **Custom Laser** or **Custom Dot Matrix** for this exercise.*

Print labels on plain paper to see how they align with your label paper. It may be advisable to use plain paper until you have determined the kind of label paper to use.

13. Click **OK** .... `Enter`

14. Click **In**s**ert Merge Field** .... `Alt` + `S`

15. Click desired merge fields to include in first line of envelope address.

16. Type any necessary spaces or punctuation between fields.

17. Press **Enter** .... `Enter`
    at the end of each line.

18. Repeat steps 15 through 17 for each line of the envelope address.

19. Click **OK** .... `OK`

    – *MERGE THE DATA WITH THE DOCUMENT* –

20. Click **Merge** .... `Alt` + `M`

21. Close the label documents without saving.

CREATE ENVELOPES WHILE MERGING

1. Open a new document.

2. Click **Tools** .... `Alt` + `T`

3. Click **Mail Merge** .... `R`

4. Click **Create** .... `Alt` + `C`

5. Click **Envelopes** .... `E`

6. Click **Active Window** .... `A`

7. Click **Get Data** .... `Alt` + `G`

8. Click **Open Data Source** .... `O`

9. Select document containing address data.

10. Click **OK** .... `Enter`

11. Click **Set Up Main Document** .... `S`

12. Click **Printing Options** .... `P`

13. Click **OK** .... `Enter`

14. Click **In**s**ert Merge Field** .... `Alt` + `S`

15. Click desired merge fields to include in first line of envelope address.

16. Type any necessary spaces or punctuation between fields.

17. Press **Enter** .... `Enter`
    at the end of each line.

18. Repeat 15-17 for each line of the envelope address.

19. Click **OK** .... `OK`

20. Click **Main Document**, **Edit** ..... `Alt` + `E`

21. Select envelope .... `↑`, `↓`
    document name.

22. Edit return address as desired.

23. Click **Merge to Printer** icon ....
    on the Mail Merge Toolbar.

24. Close the envelope document without saving.

EXERCISE DIRECTIONS:

1. Create a main document and a data document from the information below.

2. Format the main document in any letter style.

3. Use the default margins; begin At 2.5".

4. Save the main document; name it **TRVLMAIN**.

5. Save the data document; name it **TRVLDATA**.

6. Preview your document.

7. Spell check.

8. Merge the main and data documents to the printer; print an envelope for each merged form letter.

9. Close the document window.

Today's date _____ Thank you for your inquiry about a cruise to _____. We are enclosing a brochure on _____ which might be of interest to you if you should decide to sail to _____. There are two sailings scheduled in the next season: _____. The cost varies depending upon your accommodations. If you would like more information about the vacation of a lifetime, call _____, who is one of the representatives in our office who will be delighted to help you. Sincerely, Susan Crawford Travel Agent sc:yo enclosure

Customer:	Mrs. Beverly Oberlin 65 Court Street Portland, ME 04141	Mr. Wayne Viscosa ABC, Incorporated 690 Eldridge Drive Richmond, VA 23808	Ms. Edna Hamilton 76 Rider Avenue Baltimore, MD 21201
Cruise to:	Spain	The Bahamas	Trinidad
Brochure on:	*Hidden Treasures*	*Caribbean Coral*	*Breathtaking Voyages*
Sailings:	December 15 and February 12	June 29 and August 1	December 15 and February 12
Representative:	Sarah	Patricia	Michael

LESSON 10

GRAPHICS AND TEMPLATES; ENVELOPES AND LABELS

Exercises 46-50

- Working with Graphics

- Framing and Positioning Text

- Anchoring Framed Boxes

- Wrapping Text

- Drop Caps

- Drawing Lines

- Creating a Newsletter

- Creating a Memo Using a Template

- Using a Wizard to Create a Fax Cover Sheet

- Envelopes and Labels

EXERCISE

- **WORKING WITH GRAPHICS** - **FRAMING AND POSITIONING TEXT**
- **ANCHORING FRAMED BOXES**

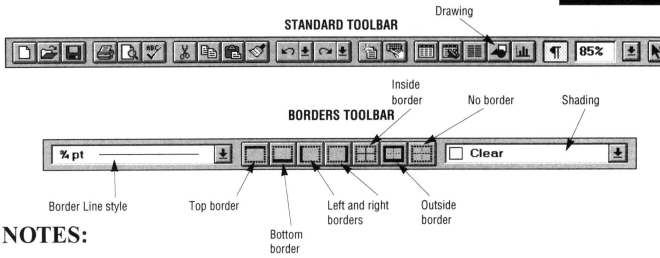

STANDARD TOOLBAR — Drawing

Inside border / No border / Shading
BORDERS TOOLBAR

Border Line style / Top border / Bottom border / Left and right borders / Outside border

NOTES:

Working with Graphics

- The **Graphics** features allow you to include pictures and images in a document. The ability to combine graphics and text will enable you to create newsletters, brochures, flyers, letterheads, and other documents where pictures contribute to the effectiveness of the message.

- Word 6 contains 94 predesigned graphic image files which are often referred to as **clip art**. Each file has its own name and is saved in the \WINWORD\CLIPART subdirectory of Word. The filenames each contain the extension .WMF which identifies them as a Windows Metafile Format. You may purchase disks with many additional graphic files in several different formats to import into Word.

- A graphic is imported into Word by selecting Picture from the Insert main menu.

- When a graphic is imported into Word, it is aligned at the left margin by default. However, the horizontal alignment may be changed so the graphic is left aligned or centered by clicking the alignment icons on the ruler just as you would align text. In addition, a graphic image may be positioned anywhere on the page, even in the margins, by inserting a **frame** around it and dragging it with the mouse. A frame is placed

around a graphic by selecting it and choosing Frame from the Insert menu or by clicking on the Insert Frame icon on the Drawing toolbar.

- The Drawing toolbar may be selected by clicking the Drawing icon on the Standard toolbar.

DRAWING TOOLBAR

Insert Frame Icon

- When framing a graphic, or when working with framed items, change to Page Layout view so you can see actual placement on the page. If you are in Normal view, Word will prompt you to change to Page Layout view.

- When a graphic is imported, its size is determined by Word. However, after a graphic is imported, you may make it smaller, larger, stretch it into exaggerated shapes, move it, or delete it.

- To change the size of a graphic, move it, or delete it, it must first be **selected** by clicking the image. A selected image appears on the following page. Note the **sizing handles** that appear once the graphic is selected. When the mouse pointer is placed on one of the sizing handles, it changes to a double-headed arrow. You may then change the size or shape of the image by simply dragging the sizing handle.

SELECTED GRAPHIC
Note sizing handles.

- When any of the four corner handles are dragged, the size of the entire image changes (smaller or larger) and the picture retains its proportions. When any of the four side handles are dragged, only the height or the width changes, thus changing the proportions or **scale** of the image and giving it a different appearance and a different shape as in the set of stars below. Changing the proportions of an image by dragging the side handles is called scaling.

ORIGINAL SIZE

PROPORTIONALLY SMALLER

PROPORTIONALLY LARGER

DRAGGED TO A TALLER AND NARROWER SCALE

DRAGGED TO A SHORTER AND WIDER SCALE

- Note that as you resize the image by dragging corner handles, the percent of original size (height and width) appears in the status line at the lower left corner of your screen. When dragging side handles, the percent of original height or width appears.

- You may return the graphic to its original size by holding down Ctrl while double-clicking anywhere in the image.

- To delete a graphic, select it and press Delete.

Framing and Positioning Text

- Text within a box is typically used for setting off special text such as tables, charts, sidebars, and callouts.

- It is possible to create a frame around text as you did with a graphic. When text is framed, it can be sized, moved, and positioned anywhere in a document in the same way as the framed graphic. It can be placed in the margins, between columns, or in the middle of a column.

- Word automatically places a border around framed text. You may use the Borders Toolbar to remove a border, change its style, add shading to the contents of the frame, or leave it as is. To make the Borders toolbar visible, select Toolbars from the View main menu and click Borders. Note the framed text boxes below.

This is an **example** of text which has been framed. Note the default 3/4 point line Word places around the text. You may change frame style or the font face or size of the text within the frame.

This is an **example** of framed text in which the frame style has been changed and shading has been added. Note, too, that the text has been *centered* within the frame.

- To frame text, highlight the text to be framed and select Frame from the Insert main menu.

- You may create the frame first and place text or a graphic in it later. To create the frame first, select Frame from the Insert main menu. The mouse pointer changes to a crosshair [+]. Drag the crosshair to the desired size of the frame and type the text into it.

- While you may change the size of the framed text box, the text characters inside the frame will not be sized. Font size and style may be changed as you learned previously.

Anchoring Framed Boxes

- After a framed object has been positioned on a page, you can set the graphic to remain in the position it was placed, or you can have it move with text as the text changes. To anchor text, select the graphic, then select Frame from the Format main menu. In the Frame dialog box which appears, click the Move with Text check box. If you turn this on (the default), the graphic will move as you edit text. If you turn this check box off, the graphic will stay in a fixed position.

FRAME DIALOG BOX

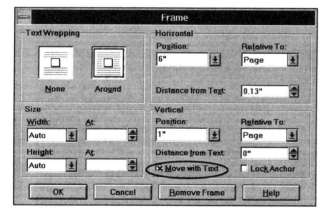

- You may remove a frame by selecting Remove Frame in the Frame dialog box.

In this exercise, you will create an advertisement in which you frame and position a text box and anchor framed graphics.

EXERCISE DIRECTIONS:

1. Create a NEW document.
2. Set .5" top and bottom margins.
3. Begin the exercise at the top of the screen.
4. Insert the COMPUTER.WMF graphic at the top of the page.
   - Scale it to 565% high by 550% wide.
   - Frame the graphic and move it in the center of the page as shown.
   - Anchor the graphic to stay in this position (turn off the Move with Text check box in the Frame dialog box).
5. Center and bold the headline text in any desired font in 28 point.
6. Create a frame below the headline and insert the text as shown in sans serif 10 point.
   - ✓ Note: It does not matter how large you create the frame since you can adjust the frame size at any time to suit your needs.
   - Bold the heading.
   - Use any bullet other than the round dot.
   - Use a dotted border.
   - Shade the framed text 20%.
   - Position the text box in the middle of the page as shown.

7. Enter the text in serif 12 point. Set the line spacing to 1.5".
8. Insert the COMPASS.WMF graphic.
   - Scale it to 16%.
   - Frame the graphic and move it as shown.
   - Anchor the graphic to stay in this position (turn off the Move with Text check box in the Frame dialog box).
9. Set Coastal Electronics and the phone number to the same font style used in the headline text in 10 point bold.
10. Spell check.
11. Preview your document.
12. Print one copy.
13. Save the file; name it **COASTAL**.
14. Close the document window.

Send and Receive Computer Data and Faxes
From Wherever You Happen to Be.

With Phone/Data Link, you constraints of your office, but The Phone/Data Link is a Coastal Electronics that gives and communicate anytime or allows you to connect your or fax machine to a portable the ability to send and receive virtually anywhere that **Coastal Electronics. 1-800-555-5555**

Phone/Data Link
Advantages

☑ Connects any modem-equipped computer or fax machine to a portable cellular telephone.
☑ Enables you to send and receive computer data or faxes via your cellular phone.
☑ Compatible with your existing software.
☑ Compact design.
☑ Features simple two-cable connection.

can leave behind the physical never really lose touch. new business tool from you the freedom to compute anywhere. Phone/Data Link modem-equipped computer cellular telephone and have data and faxes from cellular service is available.

INSERT AN EMPTY FRAME INTO A DOCUMENT

1. Click **Frame** icon .... on Drawing Toolbar.

   OR

   a. Click **Insert** .... Alt + I

   b. Click **Frame** .... F

   Mouse pointer assumes shape of crosshairs.

2. Position crosshairs pointer where you want top left corner of frame to appear.

3. Hold down left mouse button and drag down and to the right until desired frame size is created.

4. Release left mouse button.

5. Size, scale, or reposition frame as desired.

ENTER TEXT IN AN EMPTY FRAME

1. Click at position in frame where text will be inserted.

2. Type text; format as usual.

continued...

FRAME EXISTING TEXT

1. Select (highlight) text to frame.
2. Click **Insert Frame** icon ....
   on Drawing Toolbar

   OR

   a. Click **Insert** .... `Alt` + `I`

   b. Click **Frame** .... `Alt` + `F`

3. Position frame as desired by dragging entire frame.
4. Size frame as desired by dragging sizing handles.

ALIGN TEXT WITHIN A FRAME

1. Place insertion point in desired paragraph.

   OR

   Select desired text.

2. Click **Left Align** icon ....

   OR

   Click **Right Align** icon ....

   OR

   Click **Center** icon ....

DISPLAY BORDER TOOLBAR

1. Click **View** .... `Alt` + `V`
2. Click **Toolbars** .... `T`
3. Click **Borders** check box.
4. Click **OK** .... `Enter`

ADD A BORDER TO SIDES OF TEXT OR A GRAPHIC

1. Place insertion point in paragraph to receive border.

   OR

   Select paragraphs to receive border.

   OR

   Press **Ctrl + 5** .... `Ctrl` + `5`
   on numeric keypad
   to place border around
   entire document.

2. Click desired partial or full border icons on Borders Toolbar:

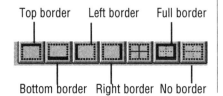

Top border   Left border   Full border

Bottom border   Right border   No border

CHANGE BORDER LINE STYLE

1. Click **Line Style** icon....
   on Borders Toolbar.
2. Click desired line style.

INSERT A GRAPHIC

1. Place insertion point where graphic is to be inserted.
2. Click **Insert** .... `Alt` + `I`
3. Click **Picture** .... `P`
4. Click **Directories** .... `Alt` + `D`
5. Click directory (C:\WINWORD\CLIPART) containing the graphic.

   ✓ *The WINWORD\CLIPART subdirectory is the default directory for pictures in Word. However, you may save or retrieve graphic images to or from any directory you choose.*

6. Click **OK** .... `Enter`
7. Select **File Name** .... `Alt` + `N`
8. Select desired file name .... `↓` , `↑`
9. Double-click desired file name ..... `Enter`

   OR

   Click **OK** .... `Enter`

SELECT A GRAPHIC

Click anywhere in the graphic.

DESELECT A GRAPHIC

Click anywhere outside the graphic to deselect.

SIZE OR SCALE A GRAPHIC

1. Select the graphic.
2. Drag any of the four side handles to scale the height or width of the graphic.

   OR

   Drag any of the four corner handles to change the size of the entire graphic proportionally (height and width change at the same time).

MAKE DRAWING TOOLBAR VISIBLE ON SCREEN

Click **Drawing** icon ....
on Standard Toolbar

   ✓ *Click **Drawing** icon again to hide Drawing Toolbar.*

   OR

1. Click *right* mouse button anywhere on existing Toolbars.
2. Click Drawing choice on drop-down menu.

   OR

1. Click **View** .... `Alt` + `V`
2. Click **Toolbars** .... `T`
3. Click **Drawing** check box to select, if necessary.
4. Click **OK** .... `Enter`

INSERT A FRAME AROUND A GRAPHIC

1. Select graphic.
2. Click **Insert Frame** icon ....
   on Drawing Toolbar.

   OR

   a. Click **Insert** .... `Alt` + `I`

   b. Click **Frame** .... `F`

MOVE/POSITION A FRAMED GRAPHIC

1. Place mouse pointer on any side of framed image until four-arrow shape appears at end of mouse pointer.
2. Drag framed image to desired location

REMOVE A FRAME FROM A GRAPHIC

1. Select framed graphic.
2. Click **Format** .... `Alt` + `O`
3. Click **Frame** .... `M`
4. Click **Remove Frame** .... `Alt` + `R`

RETURN A GRAPHIC TO ITS ORIGINAL SIZE

1. Place mouse pointer anywhere in graphic.
2. Hold down **Ctrl** and double-click.

DELETE A GRAPHIC

1. Select graphic.
2. Press **Delete** .... `Del`

   OR

   Click **Cut** icon ....

EXERCISE

- WRAPPING TEXT - DROP CAPS - DRAWING LINES - CAPTIONS
- CREATING A NEWSLETTER

DRAWING TOOLBAR

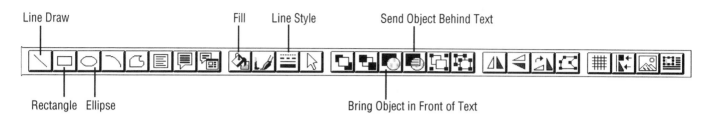

NOTES:

Wrapping Text

- Word provides two options for wrapping text around a graphic (image or text box).

- To wrap text around a graphic, select the framed graphic. Then select Frame from the Format main menu. Select a wrap option from the two displayed in the dialog box.

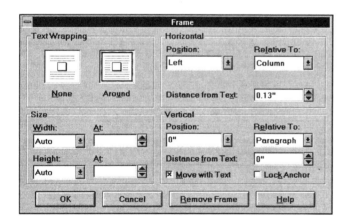

- When using text wrapping, carefully proofread the text that flows around the graphic. You may need to adjust the graphic position to avoid awkward word breaks.

Drop Caps

- A **drop capital** is an enlarged capital letter that drops below the first line of body text. It is usually the first letter of a paragraph. It is often used to draw the reader's attention to chapter beginnings, section headings, and main body text.

Drop capitals are large decorative letters often used to mark the beginning of a document, section or chapter. Drop caps are set to a much larger font than the text, and often span the height of three or four lines.

- To create a drop capital, place the insertion point in the paragraph where the drop cap will appear. Then select Drop Cap from the Format main menu.

Drawing Lines

- You can create horizontal and vertical lines in your document, in headers, or in footers.

- Lines are used to create designs, to separate parts of a document, or to draw attention to a particular place.

- You may adjust the position, length, and thickness of the lines. You may select decorative line styles such as dotted or dashed lines. You can also create lines with arrowheads.

- Lines may be created by clicking the **Line Style** icon on the Drawing Toolbar and selecting a line style. Once a line style is selected, click on the **Line Draw** icon to draw your line. (The insertion point changes to a crosshair. Drag the crosshair to create the desired horizontal or vertical line.)

- To create a line of a particular thickness, size, or style, you can create a custom line in the Drawing Defaults dialog box, which may be accessed by selecting Drawing Object from the Format main menu or by clicking More from the pop-up list of line styles on the Drawing Toolbar.

DRAWING DEFAULTS DIALOG BOX

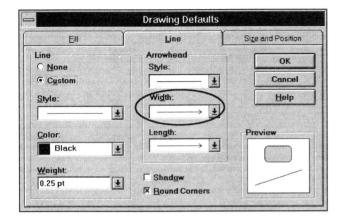

- Lines may be repositioned by dragging the whole object just as you did with a framed object, or they may be reshaped and sized by dragging the handle.

- Line thickness is measured in point size.

Adding a Caption to a Graphic

- A caption is a brief comment or explanation of the graphic to which the caption relates. It is possible to insert a caption below a graphic by framing the graphic, pressing Enter, and typing the caption. The caption should be created in a font that contrasts with regular parapraph text. Once created, the caption stays with the graphic. When the graphic is moved, the caption moves with it.

Creating a Newsletter

- A newsletter is a document used by an organization to communicate information about an event, news of general interest, or information regarding new products.

- Newsletters consist of several parts:
  - Nameplate - may include name of the newsletter, the organization publishing the newsletter, or the logo (a symbol or distinctive type style used to represent the organization).
  - Dateline - may include the volume number, issue number, and the date.
  - Headline - title preceding each article.
  - Body Text - the text of the article.

- Newsletters may also be created using a template. *(See Exercise 48.)*

In this exercise, you will create a newsletter and include graphics, text boxes, and drop caps.

EXERCISE DIRECTIONS:

1. Create a NEW document.
2. Set left and right margins to 1". Set top and bottom margins to .5".
3. Type the nameplate as shown using serif 30 point bold for "American" and 48 point for "Traveler."
4. Move the insertion point to the end of the Traveler and change font to sans serif 10 point.
5. Press Enter three times.
6. Enter dateline information as shown. Left align Volume 3, Number 3, use a center tab to center A Publication of Carl's Travel Network, and use a right tab to right align Summer 1995.
7. Draw a 2 point horizontal line before and after nameplate and dateline information.
8. Position insertion point after Summer 1995 and press Enter three times.
9. Format the remainder of the document for 3 columns (Format, Columns) and include a line between each column as shown.
10. Keyboard the newsletter as shown; note the following:
    - Center the headlines; set them to sans serif 14 point bold.
    - Create drop caps as shown.
    - Set all paragraph text to serif 12 point.
    - Insert an empty frame and type TRAVEL TRIVIA text in sans serif 12 point as shown. Use the Around Text Wrapping option. Set the Move with Text check box to on.
    - Insert an empty frame and type TRAVEL HIGHLIGHT OF THE SEASON text. Use sans serif 10 point for the text and 12 point bold for the title. Shade the framed text 20%, and use no border.
    - Hyphenate the document. Limit consecutive hyphens to 1.
        - ✓ Note: Adjust the size of the framed text box as appropriate.
11. Insert the SUMMER.WMF graphic as shown. Insert a frame around it, and size it proportionally to 60% of its original size. Position it between columns and add a centered caption in sans serif 10 point bold. Use the Around text wrapping option.
12. Insert CONTINEN.WMF graphic as shown. Insert a frame around it, size it to 40% of its original size, and position it where shown.
13. Spell check.
14. Preview your document.
15. Save the file; name it **JOURNEY**.
16. Close the document window.

FORMAT A FRAMED OBJECT TO PREVENT OR ALLOW TEXT WRAPPING

1. Click framed object.
2. Click **Format** .... Alt + O
3. Click **Fra**m**e** .... M
4. Click **None** .... Alt + N
   to force text above
   and below framed item.

   OR

   Click **Aro**u**nd** .... Alt + U
   to allow text to wrap around
   framed object.
5. Click **OK** .... Enter

PLACE CAPTION BELOW GRAPHIC

1. Select graphic.
2. Insert frame around graphic.
3. Press **Enter** .... Enter

4. Type caption ....*text*
5. Format caption as desired.
6. Click outside the graphic when finished.

CREATE A DROP CAP

1. Place insertion point in paragraph where drop cap will appear.
2. Click **Format** .... Alt + O
3. Click **Drop Cap** .... D
4. Click desired position:

   None .... N
   Dropped .... D
   In Margin .... M
5. Click **Lines to Drop** .... Alt + L
6. Select increase or decrease ...... ⬆, ⬇
   arrows to set desired
   number of lines.
7. Click **Distance from Te**x**t** .... Alt + X

8. Select increase or decrease .... ⬆, ⬇
   arrows to set desired
   distance from text.
9. Click **OK** .... Enter

✓ *Drawing Toolbar must be visible on your screen for all of the following procedures. Click the Draw icon  on the Formatting Toolbar to bring the Drawing Toolbar to the screen.*

SET LINE STYLE

1. Select desired line if line style of existing line is to change.
2. Click **Line Style** icon..........................
   on Drawing Toolbar.
3. Click desired line style.

DRAW A LINE

1. Set line style as desired.
2. Click **Line Draw** icon ....

Continued...

AMERICAN
TRAVELER

Volume 3, Number 3   A Publication of Carl's Travel Network   Summer 1995

SMOKERS MEET NEW RESTRICTIONS DURING TRAVEL

Travelers should be aware of increased constraints on the ability to smoke in public places. About five years ago, smoking was prohibited on all domestic airline flights.

Travel Trivia:

Q: *What city is said to take its name from a Huron word meaning "Meeting Place of the Waters?"*

A: *Toronto*

Now, the Dallas-Fort Worth Airport recently declared the entire passenger terminal off limits to smokers. Those wishing to smoke will now have to leave the airport premises to do so. Perhaps more far

reaching is the law passed in Los Angeles and New York which makes cigarette smoking illegal in restaurants. Violators face a $50 fine for the first offense, $100 fine for the second offense within a year, and $250 fine for every offense after that. Be cautious when traveling not to violate unexpected smoking laws!

CRUISING ON THE RHINE

Strasbourg, the capital of French Alsace, is a wonderful city to begin or end a cruise. Its pink sandstone Cathedral and a well-preserved old town are enchanting attractions for vacationing tourists. The cost of a three-day cruise including two evening meals, two breakfasts, two luncheons and coffee and cakes will cost approximately $567 a person. The view from the middle of

Fly-cruise vacations are quite popular

the river is more dramatic than the glimpses of the same scenery that a passenger sees on the train ride along the river bank from Cologne to Frankfurt. For further information, contact your local travel agent and request the "RIVER CRUISES TO EUROPE PACKAGE" or the "SILLIA TOURS PACKAGE"

TRAVEL HIGHLIGHT OF THE SEASON

The Greek Islands

There are over 3,000 islands which comprise what are commonly referred to as "The Greek Islands." However, only 170 of these islands are inhabited, each with its own character and terrain. This summer, Sunshine Travel Network is offering special fares on cruises to many of these charming islands. A four-day cruise to Rhodes, Heraklion, Santorini, and Piraeus costs $799 per person.

Since the prices include fabulous meals and breathtaking land tours, this package is definitely the buy of the season! Call today. (201) 555-5555

---

3. Place crosshairs where line will begin.

4. Hold down **Alt** while dragging to point where line will end.

REPOSITION A LINE

1. Place mouse pointer on edge of line until a four-headed arrow figure is added to the end of the mouse pointer.

2. Drag object to desired position.

RESIZE A LINE

1. Select the line.

2. Drag side handles to the desired length.

EXERCISE 48

CREATING A MEMO USING A TEMPLATE

New

STANDARD TOOLBAR

NOTES:

- A **template** is a skeleton document that may contain formatting, graphics, and/or text. It may be used to create documents that are used over and over again.

- Using Word's predesigned templates, you can create documents such as memos, faxes, letters, and résumés (as well as other documents).

- To create a template, select New from the File main menu and select the Template you desire in the New dialog box. For each template, there are usually several styles from which to choose. The memo group provides three styles: Classic, Contemporary, and Typewriter. Each template style is designed to communicate a different feeling, as indicated by its name.

- Many templates also offer a Wizard option *(note Memo Wizard option below, left). (Wizards will be covered in Exercise 49.)*

- If you select Memo1 as your desired template, a predesigned memo form displays. The date is pulled from the computer's memory and automatically inserted in the proper location. Highlight the bracketed information and enter the relevant information for your memo.

- Pressing Enter will automatically double return at the end of a paragraph.

> *In this exercise, you will use a template to create a memorandum.*

EXERCISE DIRECTIONS:

1. Create a NEW document.

2. Use the Memo1 template to create the memo illustrated on the following page.

3. Highlight the bracketed prompts, and enter the following relevant information:

To:	Janice Smith
RE:	New Product Announcement
FROM:	Your name
cc:	Latifa Jones

4. Type the memo text as shown.

5. Print one copy.

6. Save the file; name it **ANNOUNCE**.

7. Close the document window.

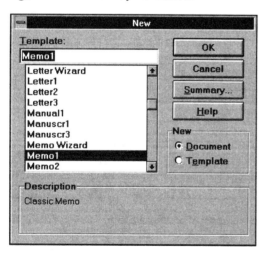

Memorandum

DATE: July 18, 1995

TO: Janice Smith

FROM: Your name

RE: New Product Announcement

CC: Latifa Jones

The new Product Development Committee will meet on Thursday at 10 a.m. to discuss the details of the MicroForm announcement.

We will need to prepare a press release later this month and plan for promotion. Please bring development files with you.

ACCESS TEMPLATES

1. Click **File**................................. `Alt` + `F`
2. Click **New** .... `N`
3. Click **Template** style .... `Alt` + `T`
4. Click **OK** .... `Enter`
5. Highlight and replace bracketed prompts.

EXERCISE

USING A WIZARD TO CREATE A FAX COVER SHEET

49

NOTES:

Using Wizards

■ Some templates contain a Wizard option (such as Memo Wizard, Letter Wizard, Fax Wizard, etc.) as one of the template styles listed in the New dialog box.

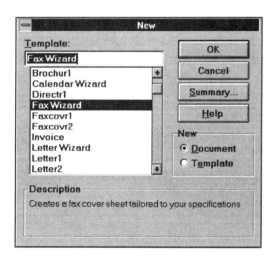

■ **Wizards** walk you through the steps for creating and sending a document.

■ A **fax cover sheet** is used as the first page of several to be faxed. Its purpose is to identify the recipient and the sender of the faxed pages. You can also use the fax cover sheet to type a message.

■ When you access Fax Wizard, for example, the following dialog box appears in which you must choose the direction you want to print your fax cover sheet.

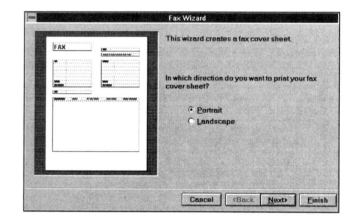

■ After clicking the Next> button, follow the prompts to complete your fax cover sheet.

■ After completing the prompted information and clicking Finish, the fax cover sheet will appear, ready for you to enter the recipient's name, phone, fax, copies to, and remarks information.

In this exercise, you will create a fax cover sheet using the Fax Wizard.

EXERCISE DIRECTIONS:

1. Create a NEW document.

2. Use the traditional Fax Wizard to create the fax cover sheet illustrated on the following page.

3. Use portrait orientation and any desired cover sheet style.

4. Use the information shown in the exercise to fill in the prompted information as well as recipient's name and comment information.

5. Print one copy.

6. Save the file; name it **FAX**.

7. Close the document window.

Video Conferencing Centers   2323 Image Street,   Baldwin, NY 11543

FAX

Date: **07/18/95**

Number of pages including cover sheet: **1**

To:

Brittany Williams

Phone: **(516) 777-7777**

Fax phone: **(516) 888-8888**

CC: Xaviar Quinn

From:

Your name

Phone: **(516) 555-5555**

Fax phone: **(516) 666-6666**

REMARKS: ☐ Urgent   ☒ For your review   ☐ Reply ASAP   ☐ Please comment

Please make note that the June 5 meeting, scheduled in my office, has been cancelled until further notice.

EXERCISE

ENVELOPES AND LABELS

50

NOTES:

- In Exercise 45, you learned to create envelopes and labels as part of the merge process.

- Envelopes and labels can also be created independent of merging or templates.

- To create envelopes and labels independent of templates or merging, select Envelopes and Labels from the Tools main menu.

- In the Envelopes and Labels dialog box which follows, select the Envelopes or Labels tab as desired.

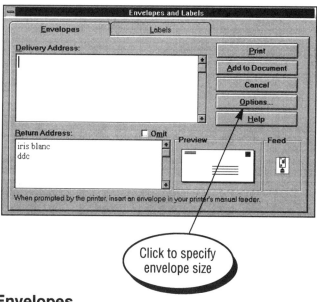

Click to specify envelope size

Envelopes

- If a document is on screen (in the current document window), Word automatically retrieves its mailing address into the Delivery Address window.

- You may also type a return address in the Return Address window. To insure that the return address is printed, the Omit check box must *not* be selected.

- Clicking the Add to Document button appends the envelope file to the beginning of the document so you can print it with the document at any time (providing you name and save the document). The Print button allows you to print your envelope without appending it to the document.

- To specify an envelope size, select the Options button in the Envelope and Labels dialog box and then the Envelope Options tab in the Envelope Options dialog box.

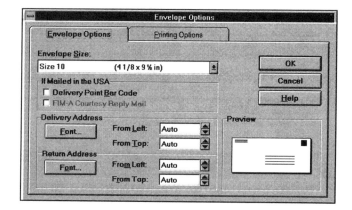

- To change the appearance of the return or mailing address text, you may select a desired font face and font size by selecting one of the Font buttons in this dialog box.

- The Printing Options tab provides envelope feed methods. You must select the feed method that is compatible with your printer.

Labels

- The Label feature allows you to create mailing labels, file folder labels, or diskette labels.

- To create labels, you must select the Labels tab in the Envelopes and Labels dialog box. In the dialog which follows, you set label specifications.

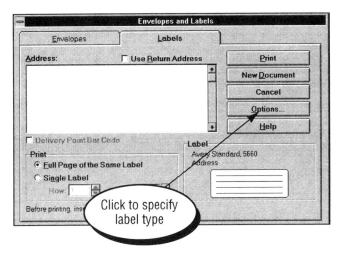

- To specify the label type you will be using, click the Options button. In the Label Options dialog box which follows, you may select the type of label on which you will be working from the predefined Label Products and Product Number list.

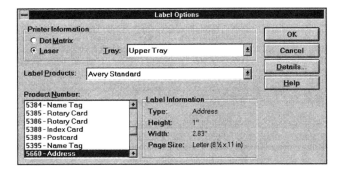

- For each label type you highlight, information about the label and sheet size is displayed in the Label Information area of the dialog box.

- Once the label format has been specified and you click OK, you will be brought back to the previous dialog box. Click New Document and blank labels will display, ready for you to start keyboarding text onto the labels. Press the Tab key to advance from label to label.

- To see the labels as they will be arranged when printed, use Print Preview.

- When you are ready to print, load your printer with the proper size and type of label paper you specified, and then print. When you print a single page, the entire physical page is printed.

- If you desire to print a sheet of labels with the same information, enter the information in the Address window and select the Full Page of the Same Label radio button in the Envelope and Labels dialog box.

In Part I of this exercise, you will create an envelope for a previously created letter. In Part II of this exercise, you will create labels for three addresses.

EXERCISE DIRECTIONS:

Part I:

1. Open **REGRETS**.

2. Create an envelope for this letter (the inside address will automatically display in the Address window).

3. Use the default envelope size.

4. Append the envelope file to the document.

5. Print one copy of the letter and the envelope.

6. Close the file; save the changes.

Part II:

1. Create a NEW document

2. Create three labels using the addresses below.

Ms. Margie Zana
2399 Santiago Lane
Denver, CO 80333

Mr. Michael Chen
Acme Design Studio, Inc.
80 Plaza A
Milwaukee, WI 53212

Ms. Tom Polanski
Holistic, Inc.
777 Westgate Road
San Antonio, TX 76888

3. Use Avery Standard 5660 Address as your label type.

4. Print one copy of the page.

   ✓ Note: If you have the label type specified, insert a sheet of labels and print. Otherwise, print on letter size paper.

5. Save the file; name it **LABEL**.

CREATE AN ENVELOPE

1. Click **Tools**............................ `Alt` + `T`

2. Click **Envelopes and Labels**.............. `E`

3. Click **Envelopes tab** .... `Alt` + `E`

4. Type mailing address............. `Alt` + `D`
   in **Delivery Address** window.

✓ *If a document containing an inside
   address is on screen, the mailing address
   will automatically be retrieved into the
   Delivery Address window.*

5. Type return address............... `Alt` + `R`
   in **Return Address** window.

6. Select a print option:

   • **Add to Document** .... `Alt` + `A`

   • **Print** .... `Alt` + `P`

CREATE A LABEL

1. Click **Tools**............................ `Alt` + `T`

2. Click **Envelopes and Labels**............... `E`

3. Click **Labels tab** .... `Alt` + `L`

4. Click **Options** .... `Alt` + `O`

5. Select a label type.

6. Click **OK** .... `Enter`

7. Click **New Document** .... `Alt` + `D`

8. Keyboard address for first label.

9. Press **Tab** to advance to the next
   label tab.

10. Repeat steps 8-9 for each additional
    address.

11. Load labels into printer.

12. Print as a normal document.

EXERCISE DIRECTIONS:

1. Create the Alumni newsletter shown below.

2. Set left and right margins to .5".

3. Use the fonts faces (serif, sans serif) and type styles (bold, italic) exactly as shown in the exercise.

4. There were six type sizes used in creating the exercise: 36, 24, 18, 14, 12, and 10 point. Determine where they should be used.

   ✓ Note: *It may not be possible to make your newsletter appear exactly as that in the illustration since available fonts and printers vary.*

5. Use 10% shading in the framed text box.

6. Spell check.

7. Preview your document.

8. Print one copy.

9. Save the document; name it **ALUMNI**.

10. Close the document window.

THOMAS JEFFERSON HIGH SCHOOL

ALUMNI NEWS

Newsletter No. 27

Winter 1994

Happy New Year from the Association!

We wish to remind you to check your dues status for '94 on your mailing label and, if you have not paid, send your dues in now. We cannot continue mailings to those who are deliquent in their dues. Don't risk being dropped from our mailing list...Pay up now!!!

In Search Of...

'34 Gladstone, Jack:
"If there is anyone still around from the Class of '34, I would sure like to hear from them." Reach me at:
888 North 6th Street
Burbank, CA 91344

'52 Edwards, Phyllis:
"I am searching for any alumni from the class of '48 and/or any grads who remember me. I am the administrator at the Metro Society in Mt. View, California." Reach me at:
999 Horizon Avenue
Mountain View, CA 94045

'82 Barrow, Frank:
"Please call me in London. I am assigned to the British office of my company, and I miss my friends and classmates from Jeff."
09-21-5432

RETIRED PRINCIPAL ALLAN FERRIS SPEAKS AT '77 - '84 ALUMNI BREAKFAST

Dr. Allan Ferris, principal of Thomas Jefferson High School from 1976 to 1982, addressed over one hundred alumni representing the classes of '77 through '84. He recounted some of his experiences at the school and related some of the accomplishments of alumni from those years. He introduced Dr. Carolyn Cruz, the current principal. She invited all alumni to visit the school and to keep in touch through her office.

Class of '75 Reunion Planned

All '75 grads will be contacted this year with respect to the planned reunion. It will be held at LaMour Country Club and tickets will be $42 per person. Special honorees will be married couples who met at Jeff. Contact '75 alumni association president Joan Frye at 514-909-5555.

> **Jefferson Apparel**
>
> **Jefferson navy long sleeve sweater (L,XL), $17**
>
> **Jefferson "Alumni Assn" fisherman's knit natural-color 100% cotton sweater (M, L, XL), $30**
>
> **Jefferson navy sweatpants, (L, XL), $17**
>
> *Make checks payable to "Jefferson Alumni Assoc."*

CHAPTER 3

LESSON 1

CREATING, SAVING, AND EXITING A WORKSHEET

Exercises 1-4

- Explore the Worksheet Using the Mouse and Keyboard

- Enter Labels

- Make Simple Corrections

- Save a Workbook

- Close a Workbook

- Exit Excel

- Numeric Labels and Values

- Label Alignment

- Make Simple Corrections

EXERCISE

EXPLORE THE WORKSHEET USING THE MOUSE AND KEYBOARD

NOTES:

- The **active cell** is the cell that is ready to receive data or a command.

- When you change the active cell, the **name box** located on the left side of the formula bar shows the new **cell reference**.

- The cell reference identifies the location of the active cell in the worksheet by the column and row headings.

- You can change the active cell in a worksheet using the mouse or keyboard.

- The workbook window displays a limited portion of the worksheet. It is possible to view other portions of the worksheet by **scrolling** to the desired location.

- You can scroll to different areas in a worksheet using the mouse or keyboard. Scrolling does not change the active cell.

- There are 256 columns and 16,384 rows in a worksheet.

  ✓ *Note the illustrations of the outer edges of a worksheet:*

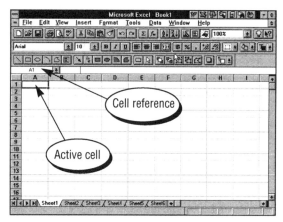

TOP LEFT OF WORKSHEET

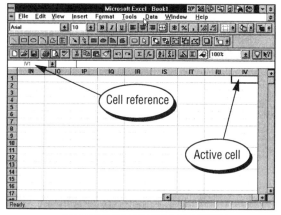

TOP RIGHT OF WORKSHEET

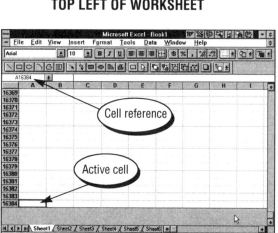

BOTTOM LEFT OF WORKSHEET

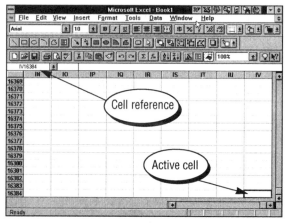

BOTTOM RIGHT OF WORKSHEET

- You can also change the active cell in a worksheet by selecting the **Go To** command on the **Edit** menu or by pressing F5.

    ✓ *Note the Go To dialog box that appears when **Go To** is selected or F5 is pressed:*

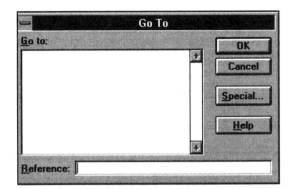

- You can also change the active cell in a worksheet by typing or selecting a reference in the **name box** ⬚.

✓ *Note the location of the name box with an active reference displayed.*

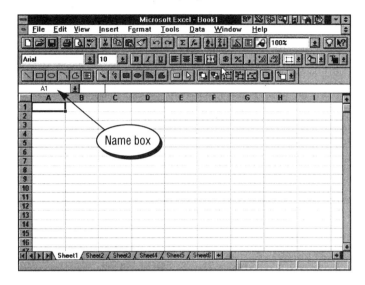

EXERCISE DIRECTIONS:

1. Click cell E5 to make it active.

   ✓ *Note the cell reference in the name box.*

2. Press the left arrow key until cell C5 is selected.

   ✓ *Note the cell reference in the name box.*

3. Select cell C9.

   ✓ *Note the cell reference in the name box.*

4. Use the arrow keys to select the following cells:
   - A6
   - R19
   - B14
   - AA45
   - G2
   - J33
   - H20
   - A1

5. Click the down scroll arrow on the vertical scroll bar.

   ✓ *Note the worksheet moves down by one row.*

6. Click the right scroll arrow on the horizontal scroll bar.

   ✓ *Note the worksheet moves right by one column.*

7. Click the scroll bar below the scroll box on the vertical scroll bar.

   ✓ *Note the worksheet moves down by one screen.*

8. Click the scroll bar to the right of the scroll box on the horizontal scroll bar.

   ✓ *Note the worksheet moves right by one screen.*

9. Drag the horizontal scroll box all the way to the right on the scroll bar.

   ✓ *Note how the view of the worksheet has changed.*

10. Drag the vertical scroll box all the way down on the scroll bar.

    ✓ *Note how the view of the worksheet has changed.*

11. Use the scroll bars to move to the following parts of the worksheet:
    - Down one screen
    - Up one screen
    - Right one screen
    - Left one screen
    - Lower left of worksheet
    - Top right of worksheet
    - Bottom right of worksheet

12. Select Edit on the menu bar.

13. Select Go To.

14. Type A10 in the Reference text box.

15. Click OK.

    Note the active cell is A10.

16. Using the Go To command, change the active cell to the following:
    - AB105
    - BG200
    - K965
    - A1 (Home)

    ✓ *Note the Go to list box displays the last four references you chose to go to.*

17. Click in the name box on the left side of the formula bar.

    ✓ *Note A1 becomes highlighted.*

18. Type C6 and press Enter.

    ✓ *Note C6 is now the active cell.*

19. Using the name box, change the active cell to the following:
    - P365
    - IV56
    - Lower left of worksheet (A16384)
    - Top right of worksheet (IV1)
    - Bottom right of worksheet (IV1684)
    - Top of worksheet (A1)

CHANGE ACTIVE CELL USING THE KEYBOARD

One cell right................................. ▶
One cell left.................................... ◀
One cell down .... ▼
One cell up.................................... ▲
One screen up .... `PgUp`
One screen down.............................. `PgDn`
One screen right.................... `Alt` + `PgDn`
One screen left .... `Alt` + `PgUp`
First cell in current row.................. `Home`
Last cell in current row............. `Ctrl` + ▶
First cell in worksheet......... `Ctrl` + `Home`
Last occupied cell .... `Ctrl` + `End`
in worksheet

CHANGE ACTIVE CELL USING THE MOUSE

Click desired cell.

✓ *If desired cell is not in view, use the scroll bars to move area of worksheet containing cell into view, then click the cell.*

SCROLL USING THE MOUSE

*The **vertical scroll bar** is located on the right side of the workbook window. The **horizontal scroll bar** (illustrated below) is located on the bottom of the workbook window.*

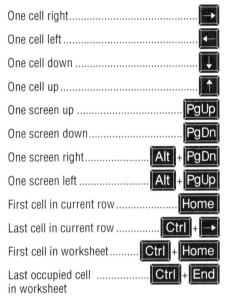

Scroll box

Scroll arrow

Scroll arrow

To scroll one column left or right:
Click left or right scroll arrow.

To scroll one row up or down:
Click up or down scroll arrow.

To scroll one screen up or down:
Click vertical scroll bar above or below the scroll box.

To scroll one screen right or left:
Click horizontal scroll bar to right or left of the scroll box.

To scroll to the beginning columns:
Drag horizontal scroll box to the extreme left of the scroll bar.

To scroll to the beginning rows:
Drag vertical scroll box to the top of the scroll bar.

To scroll quickly to an area in worksheet:
Drag scroll box to desired position on the scroll bar.

✓ *The limits of the scrolling area will depend on the location of data in the worksheet.*

To scroll quickly to the last row where data was entered:
Press **Ctrl** and drag vertical scroll box to the bottom of the scroll bar.

SCROLL USING THE KEYBOARD

One screen up .... `PgUp`
One screen down.............................. `PgDn`
One screen right.................... `Alt` + `PgDn`
One screen left .... `Alt` + `PgUp`
To active cell .... `Ctrl` + `Backspace`

CHANGE ACTIVE CELL USING GO TO

1. Press **F5** .... `F5`

   OR

   a. Click **Edit** .... `Alt` + `E`

   b. Click **Go To** .... `G`

2. Type cell reference...............*cellreference* in **Reference** text box.

   ✓ *The **Go** to list box displays the last four references you chose to go to.*

3. Click `OK` .... ◀┘

CHANGE ACTIVE CELL USING THE NAME BOX

1. Click in name box .... ⬇️ on left side of formula bar.

2. Type cell reference...............*cellreference*

3. Press **Enter**.................................... ◀┘

EXERCISE

2

■ ENTER LABELS ■ MAKE SIMPLE CORRECTIONS ■ SAVE A WORKBOOK ■ CLOSE A WORKBOOK ■ EXIT EXCEL

NOTES:

Enter Labels

■ The **status** of a cell is determined by the first character entered.

■ When an alphabetical character or a symbol (` ~ ! # % ^ & * ( ) _ \ | [ ] { } ; : ' " < > , ?) is entered as the first character in a cell, the cell contains a **label**.

■ By default, each cell is approximately nine (9) characters wide; however, it is possible to view an entered label that is longer than the cell width if the cell to the right is blank.

■ A label is entered in the cell after you do one of the following:

  • Press the Enter key, or

  • Press an arrow key, or

  • Click another cell, or

  • Click the Enter box ✓ on the formula bar.

■ The contents in a label will automatically align to the left of the cell, making it a left-justified entry.

Make Simple Corrections

■ Before data is entered, the Backspace key may be used to correct an error. To delete the entire entry, press the Escape key or click the Cancel

box ☒ on the formula bar. After text is entered, a correction may be typed directly over the existing text. This is referred to as the **strikeover** method of correction.

Save a Workbook

■ Each workbook is saved on a data disk or hard drive for future recall and must be given a name for identification. A saved workbook is called a **file**.

■ The **filename** may not exceed eight (8) characters. When you save a file, Excel automatically adds a period and a **filename extension** (usually.XLS) to the end of the filename. Because Excel identifies file types by their extension, you should not type the filename extension.

Close a Workbook

■ A workbook must be saved before closing it or all current or updated entries will be lost. If you attempt to close a workbook or exit Excel before saving, you will be asked if you want to save the changes.

  ✓ *Note: If you make a mistake and want to begin again, you may choose to close the workbook without saving it.*

In this exercise, you will begin to create a worksheet for the Family Pharmacy by entering labels. Numeric data will be entered in a later exercise.

EXERCISE DIRECTIONS:

1. Go to cell B2.

2. Type your name and look at the formula bar.

   ✓ *Note the Cancel and Enter boxes to the left of the formula bar.*

3. Cancel the entry by pressing the Escape key or by clicking the Cancel box ☒.

4. Create the worksheet to the right.

5. Enter the labels in the exact cell locations shown in the illustration.

6. Correct errors using the Backspace or strikeover method.

7. Save the workbook; name it **DAILY**.

8. Close the workbook.

	A	B	C	D	E	F	G	H
1				FAMILY PHARMACY				
2				DAILY SALES REPORT				
3	DATE:							
4								
5	CODE	DEPARTMENT		SALES	TAX	TOTAL	% OF TOTAL	
6								
7	A	BEAUTY AIDS						
8	B	CANDY						
9	C	CARDS						
10	D	MEDICINE(OTC)						
11	E	TOILETRIES						
12	F	VITAMINS						
13	G	PRESCRIPTIONS						
14								
15								
16								

ENTER A LABEL

✓ *Labels are right aligned and cannot be calculated.*

1. Click cell .... to receive label.

2. Type label text ....*labeltext*

3. Press Enter................................

   OR

   Click Enter box................................. on the formula bar.

   OR

   Press any arrow key .... to enter label and move to next cell.

SAVE A NEW WORKBOOK

1. Click **File** .... Alt + F

2. Click **Save As**.................................... A

   To select a drive:

   a. Click **Drives:** ..... Alt + V

   b. Select desired drive letter... ,

   To select a directory:

   • Double-click directory name in **Directories** list .... Alt + D , ,

3. Double-click in **File Name:**........................... Alt + N

4. Type filename ....*filename*

5. Click OK ....

   ✓ *If the Summary Info dialog box appears,fill in summary information as desired.*

CLOSE A WORKBOOK

1. Click **File** menu .... Alt + F

2. Click **Close**... C

If a save changes in workbook message appears:

Click Yes .... Y
to save changes to the workbook.

   ✓ *If you have not previously saved the workbook, the **Save As** dialog box appears. (See **SAVE A NEW WORKBOOK**, left.)*

   OR

Click No .... N
to close without saving the changes.

EXIT EXCEL

Press **Alt + F4** .... Alt + F4

   OR

1. Click **File** .... Alt + F

2. Click **Exit**.................................... X

If a save changes in workbook message appears:

Click Yes .... Y
to save changes to the workbook.

   ✓ *If you have not previously saved the workbook, the **Save As** dialog box appears. (See **SAVE A NEW WORKBOOK**, left.)*

   OR

Click No .... N
to close without saving the changes.

EXERCISE

- **ENTER LABELS** - **NUMERIC LABELS AND VALUES** - **SAVE A WORKBOOK**
- **LABEL ALIGNMENT** - **CLOSE A WORKBOOK**
- **MAKE SIMPLE CORRECTIONS**

NOTES:

Numeric Labels and Values

- When a number or a symbol (+-.=$) is entered as the first character in a cell, the cell contains a **value**.

- A value is entered after you do one of the following:
  - Press the Enter key, or
  - Press an arrow key, or
  - Click another cell, or
  - Click the Enter box on the formula bar.

- If a value is longer than the cell, Excel displays the number in scientific notation or number signs (######) appear in the cell. In this case, the column width must be reset. (*Setting column width will be covered in Exercise 11, page 230.*)

- A **numeric label** is a number that will not be used in calculation. Examples of numeric labels are social security numbers or identification numbers. To indicate that such numbers are to be treated as labels and not values, it is necessary to begin the entry with a **label prefix**, an apostrophe (').

- The label prefix is not displayed on the worksheet but is shown on the formula bar.

Label Alignment

- A value automatically aligns to the right of the cell, making it a right-justified entry.

- Since labels are left-justified and values are right-justified in a cell, column titles (which are labels) will not appear centered over numeric data. Column title labels above numeric data may be centered or right-aligned to improve the appearance of the worksheet.

  ✓ Note: The illustration of how data is aligned in cells.

TEXT	◄ ————	left justified label
123	◄ ————	right justified value
123	◄ ————	left justified numeric label

- You can align a label by using the alignment **buttons** on the Formatting toolbar. (See illustration below.)

- Labels may also be aligned by selecting the cells containing the label(s) to align and choosing an alignment through the menu system.

align left   align right

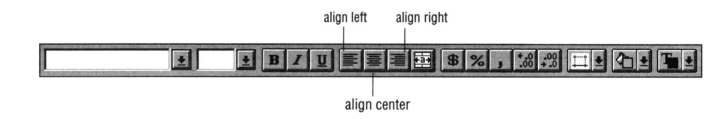

align center

In this exercise, you will create a payroll for employees of the Burlington National Bank. GROSS PAY refers to total salary earned before taxes; NET PAY refers to salary received after taxes are deducted; F.I.C.A. (Federal Insurance Contributions Act) is a designation for social security tax; and F.W.T. refers to Federal Withholding Tax.

EXERCISE DIRECTIONS:

1. Create the worksheet below.

2. Enter the labels in the exact cell locations shown in the illustration.

3. Correct any errors.

4. Right-align the HOURLY RATE and HOURS WORKED column heading.

5. Save the workbook; name it **SALARY**.

6. Close the workbook.

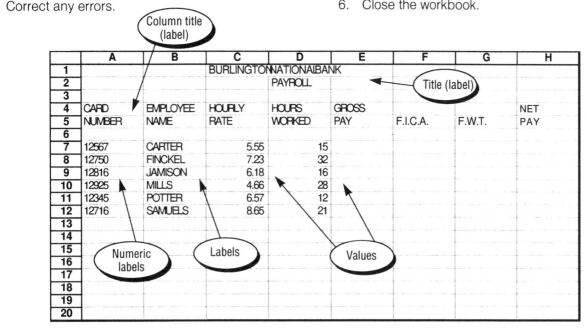

	A	B	C	D	E	F	G	H
1			BURLINGTON NATIONAL BANK					
2			PAYROLL					
3								
4	CARD	EMPLOYEE	HOURLY	HOURS	GROSS			NET
5	NUMBER	NAME	RATE	WORKED	PAY	F.I.C.A.	F.W.T.	PAY
6								
7	12567	CARTER	5.55	15				
8	12750	FINCKEL	7.23	32				
9	12816	JAMISON	6.18	16				
10	12925	MILLS	4.66	28				
11	12345	POTTER	6.57	12				
12	12716	SAMUELS	8.65	21				
13								
14								
15								
16								
17								
18								
19								
20								

ENTER A NUMERIC LABEL

✓ *Numbers, entered as numeric labels, are left-aligned and cannot be calculated.*

1. Click cell ....
   to receive numeric label.

2. Press ' (label prefix) ....

3. Type number ....*number*

4. Press **Enter**.....................................

ENTER A VALUE

✓ *Numbers, entered as values, are right-aligned and can be calculated.*

1. Click cell ....
   to receive value.

2. Type number ....*number*

   ✓ *Begin entry with a number from zero to nine or a decimal point. Precede a negative number with a minus sign (-) or enclose it within parentheses().*

3. Press **Enter**.................................

   ✓ *If Excel displays number signs (######) or the number in scientific notation, the column is not wide enough to display the value. Excel stores the value in the cell but cannot display it. To see the entry, double-click the right border of the column heading. If the value has more than eight decimal places, Excel automatically rounds it to eight places.*

SELECT (HIGHLIGHT) A RANGE OF CELLS USING THE MOUSE

1. Point to interior of first cell to select.
   Pointer becomes a ⊹

2. Drag through adjacent cells until desired cells are highlighted.

SELECT (HIGHLIGHT) A RANGE OF CELLS USING THE KEYBOARD

1. Press **arrow keys** ....

2. Press **Shift + arrow keys**...
   until adjacent cells to select are highlighted.

ALIGN LABELS USING THE TOOLBAR

1. Select cell(s) containing label(s).

   —FROM THE FORMATTING TOOLBAR—

2. Click **Align Left** button.......................

   OR

   Click **Center** button...........................

   OR

   Click **Align Right** button ....

LESSON 1
SUMMARY EXERCISE 4

Mr. Wiggins, the owner of the Hometown Gasoline and Auto Repair Shop, has asked you to prepare an inventory listing the items he stocks in his repair shop with the item numbers, unit cost, and selling price of each item.

Using the data below, create the worksheet. Include an appropriate two line worksheet title. Leave a blank column (column C) between ITEM and UNIT COST. Enter item numbers as numeric labels. Right-align column labels where appropriate.

ITEM NUMBER	ITEM	UNIT COST	SELLING PRICE
142	carburetor	120	168
321	spark plugs	2	3
093	tires	55	77
393	brakes	60	84
659	alarm	125	195
572	mats	45	63
175	battery	45	70
421	radio	185	265
932	fan belt	15	28

Save the workbook; name it **PARTS**.

LESSON 2

USING FORMULAS; FORMATTING; COPYING; PRINTING

Exercises 5-9

- Use Formulas

- File Functions (Open, Resave, Save As, Backup)

- Format Data (Fonts and Font Size)

- Use Ranges

- Copy Data

- Print a Worksheet

- Copy a Formula

EXERCISE

USE FORMULAS

5

NOTES:

- A **formula** is an instruction to calculate a number.

- A formula is entered in the cell where the answer should appear. As you type the formula, it appears in the **cell** and in the **formula bar**. After a formula is entered, the answer is displayed in the cell, and the formula is displayed in the formula bar.

- **Cell references** and **mathematical operators** are used to develop formulas. The cell reference can be typed or inserted into a formula. An equal sign (=) must precede a formula. For example, the formula =C3+C5+C7 results in the addition of the values in these cell locations. Therefore, any change to a value made in these cell locations causes the answer to change automatically.

  - ✓ Note: If you are using the number pad and enter the formula using a plus sign (+C3+C5+C7) as the first character, Excel will substitute the equal sign.

- The standard mathematical operators used in formulas are:

+	Addition	-	Subtraction
*	Multiplication	/	Division
^	Exponentiation		

- It is important to consider the **order of mathematical operations** when preparing formulas. Operations enclosed in parentheses have the highest priority and are executed first; exponential calculations are executed second. Multiplication and division operations have the next priority and are completed before any addition and subtraction operations.

- All operations are executed from left to right in the order of appearance. For example, in the formula =A1*(B1+C1), B1+C1 will be calculated before the multiplication is performed. If the parentheses were omitted, A1*B1 would be calculated first and C1 would be added to that answer. This would result in a different outcome.

- Multiplication and division formulas may result in answers with multiple decimal places. These numbers can be rounded off using a formatting feature. (See Format Data, *Exercise 6, page 216.*)

- When using a **percentage** as a numeric factor in a formula, you can enter it with a decimal or with the percent symbol. For example, you may enter either .45 or 45% to include 45 percent in a formula.

In this exercise, LIST PRICE refers to the manufacturer's suggested retail price; DISCOUNT refers to a reduction from the list price. The SALES TAX percentage for this exercise will be 8%. Note the formula used to calculate SALES TAX: 8% has been changed to .08.

EXERCISE DIRECTIONS:

1. Create the worksheet below.

2. Enter the labels and values in the exact cell locations shown in the illustration.

3. Enter the formulas, as shown in the indicated cells.

4. Enter the appropriate formulas to complete the problem.

5. Save the workbook; name it **PRICE**.

6. Close the workbook.

	A	B	C	D	E	F	G	H
1			LIST	DISCOUNT	SALE	SALES	TOTAL	
2	PRODUCT		PRICE		PRICE	TAX	PRICE	
3								
4	RED GOWN		745	185	=C4-D4	=E4*.08	=E4+F4	
5	BLUE JACKET		985	265				
6	BROWN SLACKS		395	98				
7								
8								
9								
10								
11								
12								
13								
14								
15								
16								
17								
18								
19								
20								

ENTER A FORMULA USING MATHEMATICAL OPERATORS

1. Click cell .... 🔲
   to receive formula.

2. Press **Equal** .... 🔳

3. Type formula .... *formula*
   using cell references and mathematical operators.

   Example: =A1(B2+B10)/2*

✓ You can select cells instead of typing references to tell Excel which cells you wish the formula to reference.

To insert cell references by selecting cells:

a. Click formula where cell reference will be inserted.

✓ If necessary, type preceding operator or parenthesis.

b. Select cell(s) you want formula to reference.
   Reference appears in formula.

c. Type desired operator or parenthesis.

d. Repeat steps a-c as needed.

4. Press **Enter** .... ◀

EXERCISE

- **USE FORMULAS** - **FILE FUNCTIONS (OPEN, RESAVE, SAVE AS, BACKUP)**
- **OPEN AND RESAVE A WORKBOOK FILE**
- **FORMAT DATA** - **USE RANGES**

NOTES:

Open Files

- Workbooks that have been saved and closed must be opened using the same drive designation and filename used during the saving process.

- When the **File** menu is accessed, a list of the last four files used is provided. One of these files may be opened by clicking the filename.

- A newly opened workbook becomes the **active workbook** and hides any other open workbook. A previously opened workbook will *not* be closed automatically and can be made the active workbook.

Save Files

- When resaving a workbook, the **Save** option overwrites the previous version.

- The **Save As** option allows for the changing of the filename as well as other save conditions. A new version of a previously saved workbook may be saved under a new name in order to keep both files.

- It is also possible to backup all workbooks as they are being saved. This option will create backup files with a .BAK extension.

Format Data

- You can change the appearance of data to make it more attractive and readable by **formatting** it. Some available number formats are currency, percent, date, time, and scientific notation.

- The following formats may be used for formatting money values:

  Number   Displays number with or without decimal places and commas.

  Currency Displays number with currency symbols: dollar signs, commas, and decimals.

  ✓ Note: *Other formats will be introduced in future exercises.*

Use Ranges

- A **range** is a defined area of a worksheet. For example, if you select the cells F4, F5, and F6, this range of cells can be indicated as F4:F6. You can format data in a column or row by selecting the range of cells containing the data to format.

- A **block of cells** may be defined as a range. For example, A1:G2 includes all the cells in columns A through G in rows one and two.

SAVE AS A DIALOG BOX

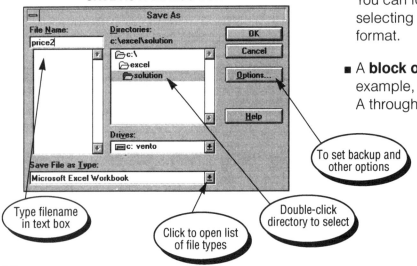

- As noted in Exercise 3, label text is left-aligned while values are right-aligned in a cell. The alignment buttons on the Formatting toolbar, or the alignment settings through the menu system, may be used to align a column title in a single cell or all the column titles in a selected range.

- Cell contents may be formatted or aligned before or after data is entered.

In this exercise, you will format money columns and column titles for the PRICE worksheet. In addition, the file will be saved using the save, backup and save as options.

EXERCISE DIRECTIONS:

1. Open **PRICE**.

2. Using the Number formatting option, format the data in columns C, D, E, and F for two decimal places.

3. Format column G data for Currency.

4. Center all column titles.

5. Resave/overwrite the workbook file.

6. Create a backup file by saving as **PRICE.BAK**.

7. Save the workbook as **PRICE2**.

8. Close the workbook.

	A	B	C	D	E	F	G	H
1			LIST	DISCOUNT	SALE	SALES	TOTAL	
2	PRODUCT		PRICE		PRICE	TAX	PRICE	Range C1:G2
3								
4	RED GOWN		745	185	560	44.8	604.8	
5	BLUE JACKET		985	265	720	57.6	777.6	
6	BROWN SLACKS		395	98	297	23.76	320.76	Range C4:G6
7								
8								
9								
10								
11								
12								
13								
14								
15								
16								
17								
18								
19								
20								

OPEN A WORKBOOK FILE

1. Click **Open** button.............................📂
   on the Standard toolbar.

   OR

   a. Click **File** ....[Alt]+[F]

   b. Click **Open**... ....[O]

   To select a drive:

   a. Click **Drive**.......................[Alt]+[V]

   b. Select desired drive letter..[↑↓],[←]

   *Files in current directory of selected drive appear in **File Name** list box.*

   To select a directory:

   Double-click directory name
   in **Directories**
   list box..............[Alt]+[D],[↑↓],[←]

   *Files in selected directory appear in **File Name** list box.*

   To list files of a different type:

   a. Click **List Files of Type**: ....[Alt]+[T]

   b. Click file type....................[↑↓],[←]
   to list.

   *Only files of specified type appear in **File Name** list box.*

   ✓ *Use this option to change the kinds of files displayed in the **File Name** list box. For example, if you want to open a Lotus file into Excel, you would select the **Lotus 1-2-3 Files (*.wk*)** item in the drop-down list.*

2. Click file to open in **File Name** list box.

   OR

   a. Select **File Name** list box.......[Alt]+[N],[Tab]

   b. Select file.................................[↑↓]
   to open.

3. Click [OK] ....[←]

RESAVE/OVERWRITE A WORKBOOK FILE

Click **Save File** button ....💾
on Standard toolbar.

   OR

1. Click **File** menu.................[Alt]+[F]

2. Click **Save**...............................[S]

SAVE AS

Saves and names the active workbook.

1. Click **File** ....[Alt]+[F]

2. Click **Save As**...................................[A]

   To select a drive:

   a. Click **Drives:** ....[Alt]+[V]

   b. Select desired drive letter..[↑↓],[←]

   To select a directory:

   Double-click directory name
   in **Directories**
   list box ....[Alt]+[D],[↑↓],[←]

3. Double-click
   in **File Name**: ....[Alt]+[N]

4. Type filename ....*filename*

   To set Excel to always create a backup of previous version when saving:

   a. Click [Options...] ....[Alt]+[O]

   b. Select **Always Create Backup** ....[Alt]+[B]

   c. Click [OK] ....[←]

5. Click [OK] ....[←]

   ✓ *If the **Summary Info** dialog box appears, enter summary information as desired.*

SELECT (HIGHLIGHT) A RANGE OF CELLS USING THE MOUSE

✓ *A range of cells is two or more cells. Cells in a selected range are highlighted and the active cell within the selection is white.*

To select a range of adjacent cells:

1. Point to interior of first cell to select.
   Pointer becomes a ⊹.

2. Drag through adjacent cells until desired cells are highlighted.

To select entire row or column:

Click row heading or column heading to select.

To select adjacent rows or columns:

1. Point to first row heading or column heading to select.
   Pointer becomes a ⊹.

2. Drag through adjacent headings until desired rows or columns are highlighted.

SELECT (HIGHLIGHT) A RANGE OF CELLS USING THE KEYBOARD

✓ *A range of cells is two or more cells. Cells in a selected range are highlighted and the active cell within the selection is white.*

To select a range of adjacent cells:

1. Press **arrow keys** ....
   until first cell to select
   is highlighted.

2. Press **Shift + arrow keys**...[Shift]+

To select entire row containing active cell:

Press **Shift + Space**............[Shift]+[Space]

To select entire column containing active cell:

Press **Ctrl + Space** ....[Ctrl]+[Space]

To select adjacent rows:

1. Press **arrow keys** ....[↑↓]
   until a cell in first row to select is outlined.

2. Press and hold **Shift** ....[Shift]
   then press
   Space.......................................[Space]
   to highlight first row to select.

3. Still pressing **Shift**, press
   up or down key ....
   to highlight adjacent rows to select.

Continued..

FORMAT NUMBERS USING THE MENU

1. Select cell(s) to format.

2. a. Click **Format**.................... `Alt` + `O`

   b. Click **Cells**.................................. `E`

   OR

   a. Right-click a selected cell.

   b. Click **Format Cells**.

3. Click **Number**.................. `Ctrl` + `Tab`

4. Click desired
   category...................... `Alt` + `C` , `↑↓`
   in **Category** list.

   Category list items include: All, Custom, Number, Accounting, Date, Time, Percentage, Fraction, Scientific, Text, and Currency.

5. Click desired format... `Alt` + `F` , `↑↓`
   in **Format Codes** list.

6. Click ☐ OK ☐ .... `↵`

FORMAT NUMBERS USING THE TOOLBAR

Applies commonly used number formats.

Select cell(s) to format.

—FROM FORMATTING THE TOOLBAR—

To apply currency style:

Click **Currency Style** button............... `$`

To apply percent style:

Click **Percent Style** button................. `%`

To apply the comma style:

Click **Comma Style** button................. `,`

To increase or decrease decimal places:

Click **Increase Decimal** button.......... `.0↑.00`

   OR

   Click **Decrease Decimal** button..... `.00↓.0`

EXERCISE

7

- OPEN AND RESAVE - WORKBOOK FILE - USE FORMULAS
- COPY DATA - FORMAT DATA - PRINT A WORKSHEET

NOTES:

Copy Data

- Formulas may be **copied**:
  - Horizontally or vertically, or
  - To another cell or range of cells, or
  - To another worksheet or workbook.

- When a formula is copied, the cell references change relative to their new location.

Print a Worksheet

- The workbook, the selected worksheet(s), or the selected range of data may be printed using the Print command. When the Print command is accessed, Excel allows you to select various print options. One way you can preview the print output is by selecting the Print Preview button in the Print dialog box (see below).

PRINT DIALOG BOX

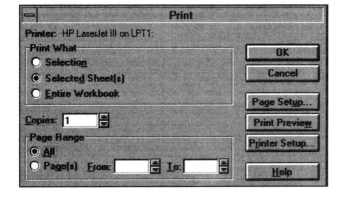

- Excel uses the default page size (usually 8 1/2" x 11") of the installed printer. The page size settings can be accessed by selecting the Page tab from the Page Setup option found on the File menu. The top and bottom default page margins are set at 1" and the right and left default page margins are set at 0.75". The

margin page settings can be accessed by selecting the Margins tab from the Page Setup option on the File menu.

PAGE SETUP DIALOG BOX WITH THE PAGE AND MARGINS TABS SELECTED

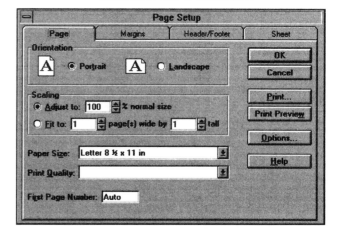

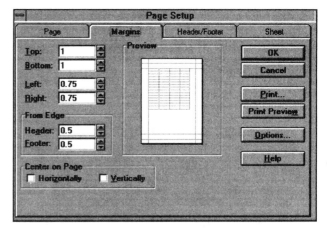

In this exercise, you will prepare and print a payroll where Federal Withholding Tax is calculated using a fixed percentage.

NOTE: F.W.T. is actually determined using a table where the tax varies according to your salary and number of exemptions.

EXERCISE DIRECTIONS:

1. Open ⌨ **SALARY** or 💾 **ESALARY.7**.

    ✓ Note: If you are using the data disk, the files should be opened using the Read Only feature. See Word Chapter 2, Exercise 7.

2. Enter a formula to calculate GROSS PAY for the first employee.

3. Copy the GROSS PAY formula for each employee.

4. Enter a formula to compute F.I.C.A. at 7.65%.

5. Copy the F.I.C.A. formula for each employee.

6. Enter a formula to calculate F.W.T. at 20%.

7. Copy the F.W.T. formula for each employee.

8. Enter a formula to calculate NET PAY.

9. Copy the NET PAY formula for each employee.

10. Format columns E, F, G, and H for two decimal places using the Number format option.

11. Center all column labels.

12. Print one copy of the worksheet.

13. Close and save the workbook, or *save as* **SALARY**.

    ✓ Note: If your file is SALARY, when you close the workbook you are asked to save changes to update the file. If you are using the data disk, you must use the save as command to create a SALARY file.

	A	B	C	D	E	F	G	H
1		BURLINGTON NATIONAL BANK						
2			PAYROLL					
3								
4	CARD	EMPLOYEE	HOURLY	HOURS	GROSS			NET
5	NUMBER	NAME	RATE	WORKED	PAY	F.I.C.A.	F.W.T.	PAY
6								
7	12567	CARTER	5.55	15				
8	12750	FINCKEL	7.23	32				
9	12816	JAMISON	6.18	16				
10	12925	MILLS	4.66	28				
11	12345	POTTER	6.57	12				
12	12716	SAMUELS	8.65	21				
13								

COPY USING THE MENU

Copies the data once and overwrites existing data in the destination cells.

1. Select cell(s) to copy.

2. Click **Edit** .... **Alt** + **E**

3. Click **Copy** .... **C**
   A flashing outline surrounds selection.

4. Select destination cell(s).

    ✓ Select an area the same size as the area to copy, or select the upper left cell in the destination cell range. The destination can be in the same worksheet, another sheet, or another workbook.

5. Press **Enter** .... ⏎

PRINT A WORKSHEET

Prints worksheet data using the current page settings.

    ✓ When printing a worksheet, Excel will only print the print area, if you defined one.

Click **Print** button .... 🖨
on Standard toolbar.

OR

1. Click **File** .... **Alt** + **F**

2. Click **Print** .... **P**

3. Select **Selected Sheet(s)** ... **Alt** + **D**

4. Click OK .... ⏎

EXERCISE 8

- **COPY A FORMULA (ABSOLUTE REFERENCE)**
- **FORMAT DATA (FONTS AND FONT SIZE)**
- **OPEN AND RESAVE A WORKBOOK FILE ▪ PRINT A WORKSHEET**

NOTES:

Copy Formulas (Absolute and Relative Reference)

- In some cases, a value in a formula must remain constant when copied to other locations. This is referred to as an **absolute reference.**

- To identify a cell as an absolute value, a dollar sign ($) must precede the column and row references for that cell.

- In this exercise, we must divide each department's sales by the total to find each department's percentage of total sales. Therefore, the total sales amount is a constant value in each line's formula. Note the formula indicated in the exercise. When this formula is copied, the total sales remains as a constant in every formula.

- If a formula with relative references is copied, a zero (0) appears if the formula is referring to empty cells.

Format Data

- Formatting may be used to change decimal answers into a percentage format.

- Excel lets you apply desktop publishing features to create a more attractive screen view and printout. Your monitor and printer, however, must be able to support these features.

- Worksheet enhancements such as changing the font and font size can be accomplished using the toolbar.

- A font is a set of characters that share a design and name. Since Windows TrueType fonts are scalable, a single TrueType font can be set to a variety of sizes. The current font name (usually Arial) is displayed in the Font box, and the current font size is displayed in the Font Size box.

- You can change the default or standard font Excel uses. To do this, select Options from the Tools menu. Then, from the General tab in the Options dialog box, set the Standard Font and font Size.

- The **font size** is an attribute that sets the height of characters in a scalable font. This size is measured in **points**. A point is 1/72 of an inch. When the size of a font is changed, Excel automatically adjusts the row height but does not adjust the column width.

- The easiest way to apply a new font or font size is to select the cells to format then select the font or font size in the **Font** or **Font Size box** on the Formatting toolbar.

- When a font and font size are selected, Excel immediately formats the text in the selected cells.

- You can change the font or font size for only those characters you select while editing a cell.

EXAMPLE SHOWING USE OF THE TOOLBAR TO CHANGE FONT AND FONT SIZE

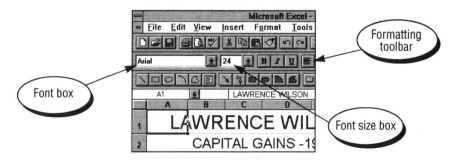

In this exercise, you will complete the Family Pharmacy daily sales report by calculating sales, tax, and total sales. To analyze departmental sales, the owner requests an analysis showing the percent each department's sales is of the total sales.

EXERCISE DIRECTIONS:

1. Open 📠 **DAILY** or 💾 **EDAILY.8**.

2. Enter sales data, as shown.

3. Enter a formula to calculate a 5% TAX on Beauty Aids.

4. Copy the TAX formula for each department *except* PRESCRIPTIONS.

5. Enter a formula to determine TOTAL for Beauty Aids.

6. Copy the TOTAL formula for each department.

7. Enter the label TOTAL SALES in cell B15.

8. Enter a formula in cell D15 to calculate TOTAL SALES.

9. Copy the TOTAL SALES formula to cells E15 and F15.

10. Enter the indicated formula using an absolute reference in the % OF TOTAL column.

11. Copy the % OF TOTAL formula for each department.

12. Copy the TOTAL SALES formula to find the total of the % OF TOTAL column.

13. Using the Number formatting option, format the money columns (E and F) for two decimal places.

14. Using the Percentage formatting option, format the % OF TOTAL column for two decimal places.

15. Center column A, D, E, and F labels.

16. Make the font changes indicated below:
    - Main title: Arial 24 point
    - Secondary title: Arial 18 point
    - Column titles: Arial 12 point
    - Data in rows: MS Serif 10 point
    - TOTALS row: Arial 10 point

    ✓ Note: If your system does not have these fonts, choose a font that best matches the illustration.

17. Print one copy of the worksheet.

18. Close and save the workbook, or *save as* **DAILY**.

	A	B	C	D	E	F	G	H
1				FAMILY PHARMACY				
2				DAILY SALES REPORT				
3	DATE:							
4								
5	CODE	DEPARTMENT		SALES	TAX	TOTAL	% OF TOTAL	
6								
7	A	BEAUTY AIDS		2238.02			=F7/$F$15	
8	B	CANDY		543.98				
9	C	CARDS		326.85				
10	D	MEDICINE(OTC)		1654.83				
11	E	TOILETRIES		196.37				
12	F	VITAMINS		413.29	▼	▼	▼	
13	G	PRESCRIPTIONS		1245.65				
14								
15		*TOTAL SALES*		▶	▶	▶	▶	
16								
17								
18								

ENTER FORMULAS FOR ABSOLUTE CONDITIONS

1. Select cell to receive formula.

2. Press **Equal** ....

3. Type formula .... *formula*
   using absolute references and
   mathematical operators.

   *Example of a formula using absolute
   references:* =$A$1*($B$2+$B$10)/2

   ✓ *You can select cells instead of typing
   absolute references to tell Excel
   which cells you wish the formula
   to reference.*

To insert cell references by selecting cells:

a. Click formula where cell reference will
   be inserted.

   ✓ *If necessary, type preceding operator
   or parenthesis.*

b. Select cell(s) you want formula to
   reference.
   Reference appears in formula.

c. Press **F4**.................................... F4
   until absolute reference appears.

d. Type desired operator or parenthesis.

e. Repeat steps a-d as needed.

4. Press **Enter**....................................

🌐 CHANGE FONT USING THE FONT BOX

1. Select cells or characters in cells to
   format.

2. Click **Font box** ....| Arial |▾|
   drop-down
   arrow on Formatting toolbar.

3. Select desired font ....

🌐 CHANGE FONT SIZE USING THE FONT SIZE BOX

1. Select cells or characters in cells to
   format.

2. a. Click **Font Size** box...........| 10 |▾|
      drop-down arrow
      on Formatting toolbar.

   b. Select a number in list.......

   OR

   a. Click **Font Size** box ....| 10 |▾|
      on Formatting toolbar.

   b. Enter
      desired number .... *number,*

3. Press **Enter**....................................

NEXT EXERCISE

LESSON 2
SUMMARY EXERCISE 9

You are applying for employment in the Registrar's Office at Grande University under the work-study program. As part of the employment test, you are asked to prepare a summary of the student enrollment in each major the college offers.

EXERCISE DIRECTIONS:

1. Create an appropriate title for your worksheet.

2. Enter a listing of each MAJOR and the NUMBER of students ENROLLED.

   BUSINESS, 8,700;
   COMMUNICATION ARTS, 2,267;
   COMPUTER SCIENCE, 3,000;
   ENGINEERING, 1,460;
   MICROBIOLOGY, 120;
   ZOOLOGY, 900

3. Find:
   • TOTAL ENROLLMENT
   • What PERCENT each major is of the total ENROLLMENT.

4. Format values in NUMBER ENROLLED column for commas with no decimal places.

5. Format PERCENT OF ENROLLMENT column for two-place percents.

6. Right-align all column titles over numeric data.

7. Use font and font size changes to enhance the spreadsheet.

8. Print one copy of the worksheet.

9. Save the workbook; name it **UNIV**.

LESSON 3

USING FORMULAS AND FUNCTIONS; EDITING; PRINTING OPTIONS

Exercises 10-16

- Use Formulas and Functions

- Change Column Width

- Create a Series

- Comma Format

- Print Options

- Print Preview

- Edit

- Page Breaks

- Page Setup

EXERCISE

USE FUNCTIONS **10**

NOTES:

Use Functions

- A **function** is a built-in formula that performs a special calculation automatically. For example, the SUM function can be used with a range of cells to add all values in the range specified. To add the values in A4, A5, and A6, the function appears in the formula as follows: =SUM(A4:A6).

- Functions appear in formulas in the following order: first the *function name* (in either uppercase or lowercase); followed by an *open parenthesis*; then the *number, cell, or range* of cells to be affected; followed by a *closed parenthesis*.

- A function may be used by itself, or it may be combined with other functions.

- Excel provides functions that are used for statistical and financial analysis or for database operations:

  AVERAGE() Averages values in a range of cells.

  COUNT() Counts all the non-blank cells in a range. Cells containing values as well as labels are counted.

MAX() Indicates the highest value in a range of cells.

MIN() Indicates the lowest value in a range of cells.

SUM() Adds all values in a range of cells.

- The data the functions require you to supply are called **arguments**. For example, in =MAX(A1:A5) the range of cells is the argument.

- You can type or insert functions into formulas. If you are typing a function and you wish to start the formula with a function, first type an equal sign (=). When you use the **Function Wizard** to insert a function at the beginning of a formula, however, do not type an equal sign; the Function Wizard enters one for you.

Function Wizard

- The **Function Wizard button** , located on the Standard toolbar or active formula bar, lets you insert functions into formulas by selecting the function from a list. It provides steps that prompt for required and optional arguments.

In this exercise, you will enter summary labels and find summary data using the AVERAGE, COUNT, MAX, and MIN functions to complete the PRICE worksheet.

EXERCISE DIRECTIONS:

1. Open **PRICE** or **EPRICE.10**.

2. Enter new labels in column A, as indicated.

3. Using the SUM function, total the LIST PRICE column and copy the formula to the remaining columns.

4. Using the AVERAGE function, average the LIST PRICE column. Copy the formula to the remaining columns.

5. Repeat this process using COUNT, MAX, and MIN functions. Copy formulas to the remaining columns.

6. Format summary data money amounts for two decimal places.

7. Close the workbook, or *save as* **PRICE**.

	A	B	C	D	E	F	G	H
1			LIST	DISCOUNT	SALE	SALES	TOTAL	
2	PRODUCT		PRICE		PRICE	TAX	PRICE	
3								
4	RED GOWN		745.00	185.00	560.00	44.80	604.80	
5	BLUE JACKET		985.00	265.00	720.00	57.60	777.60	
6	BROWN SLACKS		395.00	98.00	297.00	23.76	320.76	
7								
8	TOTAL						▶	
9	AVERAGE						▶	
10	COUNT						▶	
11	MAXIMUM						▶	
12	MINIMUM						▶	
13								
14								
15								
16								

INSERT A FUNCTION USING FUNCTION WIZARD

1. Click cell.................................... [⬚]
   to contain formula.

   OR

   a. Double-click cell
      containing formula..................... [F2]

   b. Click formula where function
      will be inserted. .... [⬚]

2. Click **Function Wizard** button .... [f∞]
   on Standard toolbar or formula bar.

   OR

   a. Click **Insert** menu .... [Alt]+[I]

   b. Click **Function**............................. [F]

   – FUNCTION WIZARD – STEP 1 OF 2 –

3. Select a category........ [Alt]+[C], [⬚]
   in **Function Category**
   list.

4. Select a function........ [Alt]+[N], [⬚]
   in **Function Name**
   list.

5. Click [Next >] .... [⬚]

– FUNCTION WIZARD – STEP 2 OF 2 –

6. Click desired argument box .... [Tab]

7. Type data ....data

   Depending on the function, enter the
   following kinds of data:

   • **numbers (constants)** – type
     numbers (integers, fractions, mixed
     numbers, negative numbers) as you
     would in a cell.

   • **references** – type or insert cell
     references.

   • **named references or formulas** –
     type or insert named references or
     formulas.

   • **functions** – type a function or click
     Function Wizard button [f∞] (to left
     of argument box)to insert a function
     into an argument (nest functions).

The Function Wizard describes the current
argument, indicates if the argument is
required, and shows you the result of the
values you have supplied.

8. Repeat steps 6 and 7, as needed.

9. Click [Finish] .... [⬚]

10. Type or insert remaining parts of formula.

   OR

   Press **Enter**...................................... [⬚]

EXERCISE

■ USE FUNCTIONS ■ CHANGE COLUMN WIDTH
■ CREATE A SERIES ■ COMMA FORMAT

NOTES:

Change Column Width

■ All worksheets in a workbook are set for a **standard column width** (default setting). This number represents the number of characters displayed in a cell using the standard font.

■ It is sometimes desirable to change (widen or narrow) the column widths so text or values can fit or have a better appearance. Only the width of an entire column or a group of columns may be changed, not the width of a single cell. You can use the Column, AutoFit Selection command on the Format menu, or the mouse to set the column width to fit the longest entry.

■ When you enter long labels, the text flows into the next column if the cell to the right is empty. If the next cell is not empty, text that exceeds the column width is covered by the data in the cell to the right.

■ Unlike label text, numeric data that exceeds the column width does not flow into the next column. If the column is not wide enough to display a numeric value, Excel fills the cell with number signs (######) or displays the number in scientific notation to indicate a need to widen the column.

Create a Series

■ You can use the Fill, Series command on the Edit menu to quickly enter sequential values in a range of cells. You can enter sequential numbers, dates or times in any increment (e.g., 2, 4, 6, 8 or 5, 10, 15, 20 or January, February, March, April).

■ Another way to fill a range with a series is to drag the **fill handle** of a selection containing the first or first and second series values over a range into which you want the series to be entered. Excel completes the series based on the value(s) in the selected cell(s).

Comma Format

■ To make large numbers more readable, **formatting** may be used to include commas. When formatting for commas, the number of decimal places to display may also be set.

In this exercise, you will create a worksheet for the Woodworks Furniture Company showing employees' quarterly SALES and COMMISSION earned. Each employee receives a 5% commission on sales.

EXERCISE DIRECTIONS:

1. Create the worksheet on page 233, or open 💾 **EWOOD.11**.

2. Set column widths as follows:
   Column A: 4   Column B: 15   Column C: 8
   Column E: 12   Column F: 12   Column G: 12

3. Using the Fill, Series option on the Edit menu, enter employee numbers starting with 110 and stopping at 115.

4. Delete the employee numbers.

5. Enter 1 and 2 as employee numbers for the first two employees. Select the numbers and use the fill handle to extend the series.

6. Copy BASE SALARY to the remaining employees.

   ✓ Note: All employees have the same base salary.

7. Enter a formula to find COMMISSION for the first employee. The commission rate is 5% of sales. Copy the formula to the remaining employees.

8. Enter a formula to find QUARTERLY SALARY for the first employee by adding BASE SALARY and COMMISSION for the quarter. Copy the formula to the remaining employees.

9. Enter formulas to find TOTALS, AVERAGES, HIGHEST, and LOWEST values. Copy the formulas to each column.

10. Center column title labels.

11. Format numeric data to include commas and two decimal places.

12. Save the workbook; name it **WOOD**.

13. Print one copy.

14. Close the workbook.

CHANGE COLUMN WIDTHS USING THE MENU

1. Select any cell(s) in column(s) to change.
2. Click **F**ormat .... 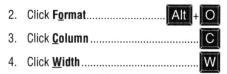 **Alt** + **O**
3. Click **C**olumn .... **C**
4. Click **W**idth .... **W**
5. Type number (0-255) ....*number* in **C**olumn Width text box.

   ✓ *Number represents number of characters that can be displayed in cell using the standard font.*

6. Click [OK] .... ⏎

CHANGE COLUMN WIDTHS USING THE MOUSE

Change One Column Width

1. Point to right border of column heading to size.

   Pointer becomes a ↔.

2. Drag ↔ left or right.

   Excel displays width on left side of formula bar.

Change Several Column Widths

1. Select columns to size.
2. Point to right border of any selected column heading.

   Pointer becomes a ↔.

3. Drag ↔ left or right.

   Excel displays width on left side of formula bar.

SET COLUMN WIDTH TO FIT LONGEST ENTRY

Double-click right border of column heading.

   OR

1. Select column. , **Ctrl** + **Space** to size.
2. Click **F**ormat menu .... **Alt** + **O**
3. Click **C**olumn .... **C**
4. Click **A**utoFit Selection .... **A**

SET STANDARD COLUMN WIDTH

Changes column widths that have not been previously adjusted in a worksheet.

1. Click **F**ormat .... **Alt** + **O**
2. Click **C**olumn .... **C**
3. Click **S**tandard Width .... **S**
4. Type new number (0-255) ....*number* in **S**tandard Column Width text box.

   ✓ *Number represents number of characters that can be displayed in cell using the standard font.*

5. Click [OK] .... ⏎

RESET COLUMNS TO STANDARD COLUMN WIDTH

1. Select column(s) to format.
2. Click **F**ormat .... **Alt** + **O**
3. Click **C**olumn .... **C**
4. Click **S**tandard Width... .... **S**
5. Click [OK] .... ⏎

CREATE A SERIES OF NUMBERS, DATES, OR TIMES USING THE MENU

1. Enter first series value in a cell to create a series from a *single value*.

   OR

   Enter first and second series values in consecutive cells to create a series from multiple values.

2. Select cell(s) containing series value(s) *and* cells to fill.

   ✓ *Select adjacent cells in rows or columns to fill.*

3. Click **E**dit .... **Alt** + **E**
4. Click **F**ill .... **I**
5. Click **S**eries .... **S**

   To change proposed step value:

   Type step value ....*number* in **S**tep Value text box.

   To change proposed direction of series:

   Select desired **Series in** option:

   - **R**ows .... **Alt** + **R**
   - **C**olumns .... **Alt** + **C**

   To change proposed series type:

   Select desired **Type** option:

   - **L**inear .... **Alt** + **L**
     to increase/decrease each value in series by number in **S**tep Value text box.

   - **G**rowth .... **Alt** + **G**
     to multiply each value in series by number in **S**tep Value text box.

   - **D**ate .... **Alt** + **D**
     to set increment by days, weekdays, months, or years.

   - Auto**F**ill .... **Alt** + **F**
     to fill cells based on values in selection.

Continued...

	A	B	C	D	E	F	G
1		WOODWORKS FURNITURE COMPANY					
2		QUARTERLY SALES AND SALARY REPORT - JANUARY-MARCH					
3							
4	EMP.			BASE		5%	QUARTERLY
5	NO.	NAME		SALARY	SALES	COMMISSION	SALARY
6							
7		ABRAMS, JUDY		1,500.00	113,456.67		
8		CHANG, PETER			150,654.87		
9		LINSEY, KELLY			234,765.36		
10		JOHNSON, LETOYA			89,765.43		
11		RIVERA, TONY			287,987.76		
12							
13		TOTALS					
14		AVERAGES					
15		HIGHEST					
16		LOWEST					

If Date was selected:

Select desired **Date Unit** option:

- **D**ay .... Alt + A
- **W**eekday .... Alt + W
- **M**onth .... Alt + M
- **Y**ear .... Alt + Y

To set stop value for series:

✓ Type a stop value if you want series to end at a specific number.

a. Click **Sto**p Value: .... Alt + O

b. Type stop value .... *number*

6. Click [OK] .... ↵

CREATE A SERIES OF NUMBERS, DATES, OR TIMES USING THE MOUSE

Creates a series by dragging the fill handle of a cell selection containing the first or first and second series value(s).

✓ The fill handle is a small square in the lower right corner of a selection.

Create a Series from a Single Value:

1. Enter first series value in a cell.

2. Select cell containing the first series value.

3. Point to fill handle.

   Pointer becomes a + *when positioned correctly.*

4. Press **Ctrl** and drag + over adjacent cells to extend border in rows or column to fill.

   ✓ Drag border down or to the right to create an ascending series. Drag border up or to the left to create a series decreasing in value.

Create a Series from Multiple Values:

1. Enter first and second series values in consecutive cells.

2. Select cells containing series values.

3. Point to fill handle.

   Pointer becomes a + *when positioned correctly.*

4. Drag + over adjacent cells to extend border in rows or columns to fill.

   ✓ Drag border down or to the right to create an ascending series. Drag border up or to the left to create a series decreasing in value.

EXERCISE

■ USE FUNCTIONS ■ EDIT
■ PAGE SETUP ■ PRINT PREVIEW

NOTES:

Print Options

■ When the **Print** command is accessed, Excel allows you to set various print options. You can choose to print a range of cells, use the Page Setup button to access page setting options for printing, and use the Print Preview button to preview, on screen, the output your settings will yield.

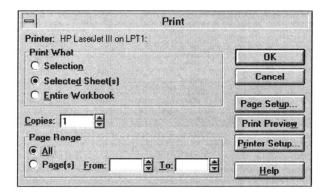

■ When you select the Page Setup button, and then select the Sheet tab, you can set various print options for the sheet, such as gridlines and row and column headings.

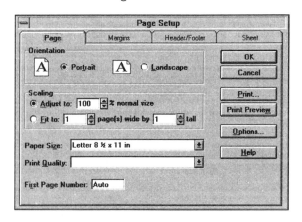

■ In the dialog boxes you can also select the Print Preview button to review, on screen, the output your settings will yield.

Edit Data

■ Data may be changed either before or after it has been entered in a cell.

■ Before data is entered, the Backspace key may be used to correct a keystroke.

■ To clear a cell's content before it is entered:
  • Press the Escape key, or
  • Click the Cancel box on the formula bar.

■ After data is entered, there are several methods of correction:
  • Replace the entire entry with new data, or
  • Edit part of an entry by **enabling cell editing**,
  • Erase a single cell entry, or
  • Erase a range of cell entries.

In this exercise, you will complete the payroll for the Burlington National Bank for the week ending May 15, 199-. You will then copy the entire worksheet to a new location and edit entries to create another payroll for the week ending May 22, 199-.

EXERCISE DIRECTIONS:

1. Open ⌨ **SALARY** or 💾 **ESALARY.12**.

2. Edit the first line of the title, as illustrated.

3. Erase the second line of the title. Replace it, as indicated.

4. Enter the new row labels, as indicated.

5. Find TOTALS and AVERAGES for GROSS PAY, F.I.C.A., F.W.T. and NET PAY columns.

6. Format TOTALS and AVERAGES for two decimal places.

7. Copy the range of data shown to a new location on the worksheet.

✓ Note: When copying a range, it is only necessary to specify the first position in the destination range.

– ON THE BOTTOM PAYROLL –

8. Edit the title to read:

FOR THE WEEK ENDING MAY 22, 199-

9. Edit the HOURS WORKED as follows:
CARTER, 20   FINCKEL, 31   JAMISON, 23
MILLS, 22   POTTER, 15   SAMUELS, 25

10. Preview the printout of this file.

11. Print one copy of the MAY 22nd payroll.

12. Close and save the workbook, or *save as* **SALARY**.

	A	B	C	D	E	F	G	H	I
1			BURLINGTON NATIONAL BANK			*PAYROLL*			
2			*FOR THE WEEK ENDING MAY 15, 199-*						
3									
4	CARD		HOURLY	HOURS	GROSS			NET	
5	NUMBER	NAME	RATE	WORKED	PAY	F.I.C.A.	F.W.T.	PAY	
6									
7	12567	CARTER	5.55	15	83.25	6.37	16.65	60.23	
8	12750	FINCKEL	7.23	32	231.36	17.70	46.27	167.39	
9	12816	JAMISON	6.18	16	98.88	7.56	19.78	71.54	
10	12925	MILLS	4.66	28	130.48	9.98	26.10	94.40	
11	12345	POTTER	6.57	12	78.84	6.03	15.77	57.04	
12	12716	SAMUELS	8.65	21	181.65	13.90	36.33	131.42	
13									
14	*TOTALS*								
15	*AVERAGES*								
16									
17									
18	COPY TO								
19	A17								
20									
21									
22									
23									
24									
25									
26									
27									
28									
29									
30									
31									
32									

EDIT CELL CONTENTS AFTER IT IS ENTERED (ENABLE CELL EDITING)

1. Double-click cell to edit.

   OR

   a. Select cell to edit. .... [↕↔]
   b. Press **F2** ....
      [F2]

   An insertion point appears in the active cell and these buttons appear on the formula bar:

   [X] *Cancel button – cancels changes made in cell.*

   [✓] *Enter button – accepts changes made in cell.*

2. Click desired data position .... [↩] in cell or in formula bar.

3. Type new data .... *data*

   OR

   Press **Backspace** .... [Backspace] to delete character to left of insertion point.

   OR

   Press **Delete** .... [Del] to delete character to right of insertion point.

   To accept changes:

   Press **Enter** .... [←]

   OR

   Click **Enter** button .... [✓] on the formula bar.

   To cancel changes:

   Press **Escape** .... [Esc]

   OR

   Click **Cancel** button .... [X] on the formula bar.

EDIT CELL CONTENTS WHILE TYPING

To delete character to the left of insertion point:

Press **Backspace** .... [Backspace]

To cancel all characters:

Press **Escape** .... [Esc]

ERASE CONTENTS OF CELL OR RANGE

1. Select cell or range containing contents to erase.

2. Press **Delete** .... [Del]

🌐 PRINT PREVIEW

1. Click **Print Preview** button .... [🔍] on Standard toolbar.

   OR

   a. Click **File** .... [Alt]+[F]
   b. Click **Print Preview** .... [V]

   – *FROM PREVIEW WINDOW* –

   To view next page:

   Click [Next] .... [Alt]+[N]

   To view previous page:

   Click [Previous] .... [Alt]+[P]

   To view a magnified portion of the page:

   a. Click area of page .... [Alt]+[Z] to magnify.

   b. Click any area of page .... [Alt]+[Z] to return to full page view.

2. Click [Close] .... [Alt]+[C] to exit Print Preview.

🌐 PRINT RANGE OF CELLS

Prints data in range using the current page settings.

✓ *When printing a range, this procedure will override a print area, if you defined one.*

1. Select range of cells to print.

2. Click **File** menu .... [Alt]+[F]

3. Click **Print** .... [P]

4. Click **Selection** .... [N]

5. Click [OK] .... [←]

🌐 SET PRINT OPTIONS FOR WORKSHEET

Sets a print area and shows or hides gridlines on printed sheet.

1. Click **File** menu .... [Alt]+[F]

2. Click **Page Setup**... .... [U]

3. Click **Sheet** .... [Ctrl]+[Tab]

   To set a print area:

   ✓ *Use this option to print a specific area of a worksheet each time you print.*

   a. Click in **Print Area**: .... [Alt]+[A]

   b. Select range of cells in worksheet to print.

      OR

      Type cell reference(s) .... *references* of area to print.

      NOTE: To remove a print area, delete the reference.

   To show or hide gridlines:

   Select or deselect **Gridlines** ...

4. Click [OK] ....

NEXT EXERCISE

EXERCISE

13

▪ USE FUNCTIONS ▪ CHANGE COLUMN WIDTH
▪ EDIT ▪ PRINT OPTIONS (PAGE SETUP, SCALE)

NOTES:

Page Setup

▪ Excel 5 uses the default page size (usually 8 1/2"x11") of the installed printer. To change the page size, use the **Page Setup** option on the File menu, then select the Page tab.

▪ Use the Page Setup option to control the print output for the selected page size. The Page Setup dialog box (*see below*) may be accessed directly from the File menu or from the Print or Print Preview options. The Page Setup dialog box has several tabs. Each tab contains options that control the print output.

PAGE SETUP DIALOG BOX WITH PAGE TAB SELECTED

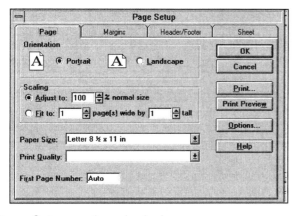

▪ Page Setup options include:

Page Tab

• **Orientation** The worksheet data may be printed in either **Portrait** (vertical) or **Landscape** (horizontal) paper orientation.

• **Scaling** The printed worksheet can be enlarged or reduced. The scaling options are: **Adjust to** % of normal size or **Fit to** pages wide by pages tall. Both scaling options proportionally scale the worksheet.

> ✓ Note: Scaling is often needed when you want a printed worksheet to fit on a page. You can use the Print Preview option to check how it will fit before printing.

• **Paper Size** The paper size options include: letter, legal, and other size options.

• **First Page Number** The starting page number for the pages on the current sheet.

Margins Tab

• **Margins** The page margins, the distance of the worksheet data to the **Top, Bottom, Left,** or **Right** edge of the page, may be set in inches. The **Header** and **Footer** margins, the distance of the header and footer data from the top and bottom edges of the worksheet, can be set in inches.

• **Center on Page** The worksheet data can be **Horizontally** and/or **Vertically** centered within the page margins.

Header/Footer Tab

• **Header/Footer** A line of text may be included above or below the worksheet. This may be used to include a title, a date, or a page number. *(See Exercise 14, page 240.)*

Sheet Tab

• **Print Area** Only define this area if you always want to print the same range of cells when printing a worksheet.

• **Print Titles** Descriptive information from designated **Rows** that will print on the top of each page and/or **Columns** that will print on the left of each page. *(See Exercise 15, page 244.)*

• **Print** Includes the following print options: **Gridlines, Notes, Draft Quality, Black and White, and Row and Column Headings.**

• **Page Order** The setting that determines the printed page order: **Down, then Across** or **Across, then Down.**

In this exercise, you will open the quarterly sales worksheet for the Woodworks Furniture Company, and expand the worksheet to include quarterly data.

EXERCISE DIRECTIONS:

1. Open ⌨ **WOOD** or 💾 **EWOOD.13**.

2. Edit the second line of the title. Replace MARCH with JUNE.

3. Replace QUARTERLY with JAN-MAR.

4. Change column widths as follows:
   Column C: 3
   Columns H, I, J: 12

5. Copy column titles SALES, COMMISSION, and SALARY to columns H, I, and J. Insert the label APR-JUN over SALARY in column J.

6. Center all new labels where necessary.

7. Enter new sales data in column H.

8. Copy the COMMISSION formula for the first employee in column F to column I.

9. Copy the COMMISSION formula down for each employee.

10. Enter the label APR-JUN in Column J in the location indicated.

11. Enter a formula in column J to compute BASE SALARY + COMMISSION for the second quarter.

12. Copy the BASE SALARY + COMMISSION formula down for each employee.

13. Find TOTALS, AVERAGES, HIGHEST, and LOWEST for the second quarter. (Copy formulas using one copy command.)

14. Format numeric data for commas and two decimal places.

15. Change the scale setting to fit worksheet on one page.

16. Check your scale setting, using Print Preview.

17. Print one copy.

18. Close and save the workbook, or *save as* **WOOD**.

	WOODWORKS FURNITURE COMPANY					←―12―→	←―12―→	←―12―→
	QUARTERLY SALES AND SALARY REPORT - JANUARY-~~MARCH~~				*JUNE*			
						JAN-MARCH		*APR-JUN*
EMP.			BASE		5%	~~QUARTERLY~~		
NO.	NAME		SALARY	SALES	COMMISSION	SALARY		
1	ABRAMS, JUDY		1,500.00	113,456.67	5,672.83	7,172.83	*114342.9*	
2	CHANG, PETER		1,500.00	150,654.87	7,532.74	9,032.74	*143276.7*	
3	LINSEY, KELLY		1,500.00	234,765.36	11,738.27	13,238.27	*187956.76*	
4	JOHNSON, LETOYA		1,500.00	89,765.43	4,488.27	5,988.27	*93984.69*	
5	RIVERA, TONY		1,500.00	287,987.76	14,399.39	15,899.39	*254768.6*	
	TOTALS		7,500.00	876,630.09	43,831.50	51,331.50		
	AVERAGES		1,500.00	175,326.02	8,766.30	10,266.30		
	HIGHEST		1,500.00	287,987.76	14,399.39	15,899.39		
	LOWEST		1,500.00	89,765.43	4,488.27	5,988.27		

CHANGE SCALE OF PRINTED DATA

1. Click **File** .... `Alt` + `F`
2. Click **Page Setup** .... `U`
3. Select **Page** .... `Ctrl` + `Tab`

To reduce or enlarge data on printed sheet:

a. Click **Adjust to:** .... `Alt` + `A`
b. Type percentage *(10-400)* ....*number*

✓ *You can also click the increment box arrows to select a percentage.*

4. Click `OK` .... `←┘`

EXERCISE

- **USE FUNCTIONS** - **CHANGE COLUMN WIDTHS** - **EDIT**
- **PRINT OPTIONS (HEADERS/FOOTERS)** - **PAGE BREAKS**

NOTES:

Page Breaks

- Before printing, you may set page breaks and add headers and footers.

- When the **Page Break** option is set, Excel stops printing on the current page and starts printing on the top of a new page.

- Excel inserts **automatic page breaks** based on the current paper size, scaling, and margin settings. Automatic page breaks appear as dashed lines on the worksheet. To view automatic page breaks, the **Automatic Page Breaks** check box must be selected on the View tab in the Options dialog box. You can override the automatic page breaks by inserting **manual page breaks** in your worksheet. Manual page breaks appear as bold dashed lines.

Headers and Footers

- **Headers** and **footers** are used when you want to repeat the same information at the top (header) or bottom (footer) of every page.

With Excel, you can select from built-in headers and footers, or you can customize one. These print enhancements can be set in the Page Setup dialog box from the Header/Footer tab.

- Headers/footers are limited to a single line of text. Header/footer text may, however, be separated into segments. Selected header/footer text can be formatted.

- When you create a custom header, text entered in the left-most section will be left-justified. Text entered in the middle section will be centered, and text entered in the right-most section will be right-justified.

- You may insert **codes** to print the current date, current time, page number, and/or workbook filename as part of the header/footer text by clicking a code button representing the desired item.

✓ *Note the illustration on the next page.*

CODE BUTTONS IN THE HEADER DIALOG BOX WITH SAMPLE PAGE RESULT BELOW IT

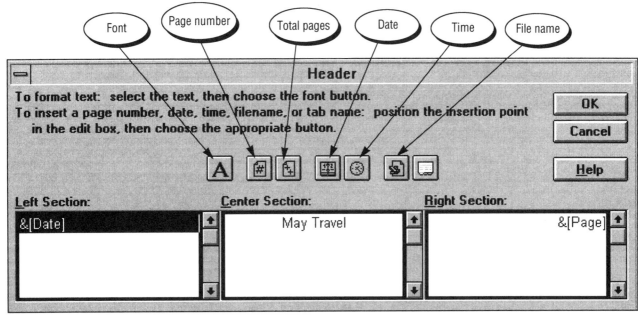

In this exercise, you will create a travel expense report for one of the salespeople at the Quick-Print Publishing Company. The May travel report will include two trips, each printed on a separate page with a header.

EXERCISE DIRECTIONS

1. Create the top worksheet shown on the next page, or open 💾 **ETRIPS.14**.

   ✓ Note: Enter the days of the month as numeric labels.

2. Set column widths as follows:
   Column A: 15
   Column B: 3

3. Find for Car(miles):
   • Total Miles
   • Total Travel Expense

   ✓ Note: Car mileage is computed at twenty-eight cents per mile.

4. Find for daily expenses:
   • Total Travel Expenses for the first item. Copy the formula to each item.
   • TOTALS for each day (which include the rows in the TRANSPORTATION [EXPENSES] section).
   • Total of Total Travel Expenses column (which includes the DAILY EXPENSES and the TRANSPORTATION costs).

5. Format all money columns for two decimal places.

6. Center all column titles.

7. Copy the entire top worksheet to cell A34.

8. Create a page break at cell A33.

9. Edit the DATES, PURPOSE, and DAILY EXPENSES to display the data for the next trip, as indicated.

   ✓ Note: Be sure the TOTALS for each day include the TRANSPORTATION expenses.

10. Print the file to fit columns to the page with a custom header that includes a left-justified date, a centered title that reads MAY TRAVEL, and a right-justified page number.

11. Save the workbook file; name it **TRIPS**.

12. Close the workbook.

	QUICK-PRINT PUBLISHING COMPANY					
	TRAVEL EXPENSE REPORT					
NAME: John Mc Carthy						
DATES: 5/3-5/6/9-		PURPOSE: School visits Chicago				
			Enter as numeric labels		Total	Total
					Miles	Travel
	May 3	May 4	May 5	May 6	@ $.28	Expenses
TRANSPORTATION						
Car (miles)	185	55	43	175		
Car Rental						
Plane						
Train						
DAILY EXPENSES						
Hotal	125.65	125.65	125.65	125.65		
Breakfast	0.00	5.59	15.95	7.55		
Lunch	15.60	12.95	45.95	43.55		
Dinner	39.35	95.86	135.85	0.00		
Tolls	0.00	1.50	2.00	0.00		
Parking	0.00	15.00	12.00	7.00		
Tips	6.00	18.00	22.00	11.00		
Phone	3.25	7.53	8.52	4.76		
Misc.	0.00	12.00	15.00	3.00		
TOTALS						

Include all in Total in this column only

Copy

	QUICK-PRINT PUBLISHING COMPANY					
	TRAVEL EXPENSE REPORT					
NAME: John Mc Carthy						
DATES: 5/14-5/16/9-		PURPOSE: School visits Los Angeles				
					Total	Total
					Miles	Travel
	May 14	May 15	May 16		@ $.28	Expenses
TRANSPORTATION						
Car (miles)						
Car Rental	65.00	65.00	65.00			
Plane	375.89					
Train						
DAILY EXPENSES						
Hotal	135.65	135.65	135.65			
Breakfast	0.00	6.68	5.76			
Lunch	35.55	13.64	43.32			
Dinner	88.75	145.76	0.00			
Tolls	3.50	4.50	4.00			
Parking	18.50	22.15	16.75			
Tips	10.00	25.00	15.00			
Phone	8.95	9.95	6.25			
Misc.	0.00	16.50	0.00			
TOTALS						

Enter page break

Include all in Total in all columns

INSERT MANUAL PAGE BREAKS

✓ *After you insert a manual page break, Excel adjusts the automatic page breaks that follow it. To display automatic page breaks see **SHOW AUTOMATIC PAGE BREAKS**, right.*

Insert a Horizontal Page Break:

1. Select row where new page will start.
2. Click **Insert** ....`Alt`+`I`
3. Click **Page Break** ....`B`

Insert a Vertical Page Break:

1. Select column where new page will start.
2. Click **Insert** ....`Alt`+`I`
3. Click **Page Break** ....`B`

Insert a Horizontal and Vertical Page Break:

1. Click cell ....`↕↔`
   where new pages will start
2. Click **Insert** ....`Alt`+`I`
3. Click **Page Break** ....`B`

REMOVE MANUAL PAGE BREAKS

✓ *After you remove a manual page break, Excel adjusts the automatic page breaks that follow it. To display automatic page breaks see **SHOW AUTOMATIC PAGE BREAKS**, right.*

Remove a Horizontal Page Break:

1. Select a cell immediately below page break.
2. Click **Insert** ....`Alt`+`I`
3. Click **Remove Page Break** ....`B`

Remove a Vertical Page Break:

1. Select a cell immediately to the right of page break.
2. Click **Insert** ....`Alt`+`I`
3. Click **Remove Page Break** ....`B`

Remove All Manual Page Breaks:

1. Click blank button at top left corner of worksheet grid.
2. Click **Insert** ....`Alt`+`I`
3. Click **Remove Page Break** ....`B`

SHOW AUTOMATIC PAGE BREAKS

1. Click **Tools** ....`Alt`+`T`
2. Click **Options**................................`O`
3. Select **View** tab ....`Ctrl`+`Tab`
4. Click **Automatic Page Breaks** ....`Alt`+`U`
5. Click `OK` ....`↵`

🌐 SET HEADER AND FOOTER OPTIONS

Adds text or special codes to top or bottom of each page.

1. Click **File** ....`Alt`+`F`
2. Click **Page Setup** ....`U`
3. Select **Header/Footer** tab..`Ctrl`+`Tab`

To select a built-in header:

a. Click **Header** ....`Alt`+`A`
   drop-down list.
b. Select desired..............................`↑↓`
   header type.

To select a built-in footer

a. Click **Footer**......................`Alt`+`F`
   drop-down list.
b. Select desired..............................`↑↓`
   footer type.

To customize selected header or footer:

a. Click `Custom Header...` .....`Alt`+`C`

   OR

   Click `Custom Footer...` .....`Alt`+`U`

b. Click in section to change:

   • **Left**.........................`Alt`+`L`
   • **Center** ....`Alt`+`C`
   • **Right** ....`Alt`+`R`

c. Type or edit text ....*text*
   to appear in header or footer section.

   To change font of header or footer text:

   i. Select text to format.

   ii. Click
      Font button `A`.......`Tab`+`↵`

✓ *Press **Tab** until **Font** button is highlighted.*

iii. Select desired font options.

iv. Click `OK` ....`↵`

To insert a header or footer code:

i. Place insertion point where code will appear.

ii. Click desired ....`Tab`+`↵`
   code button from
   the following choices:

   ✓ *Press **Tab** until desired code button is high-lighted.*

   `#` **Page Number** Inserts page number code.

   `📄` **Total Pages** Inserts total pages code.

   `📅` **Date** Inserts current date code.

   `🕐` **Time** Inserts current time code.

   `🖼` **Filename** Inserts filename code.

   `🗔` **Sheet Name** Inserts active sheet name code.

d. Repeat steps b and c for each section of custom header or footer to change.

e. Click `OK` ....`↵`

4. Click `OK` ....`↵`

EXERCISE

■ PRINT PREVIEW ■ USE FUNCTIONS ■ CHANGE COLUMN WIDTH
■ PRINT OPTIONS (SCALE, PRINT TITLES) ■ CREATE A SERIES

NOTES:

Print Titles

■ As a print option, you may print **column and row titles**. Titles may be useful when:

  • printing a range that is too wide or too long to fit on one page which then needs titles on the second page to clarify the data, or

  • printing part of a columnar series of data that does not have column or row titles adjacent to the number values.

■ The columns or rows titles you select:

  • will repeat only on the pages that follow the page containing the title data when an extra wide or extra long worksheet is set up as the print range.

  • should not be included in the print range when printing part of a columnar series of data that needs the column or row titles that have been set.

✓ *Note the example below. They show the first and second pages of a worksheet that was too wide for one page, (using 100% sizing). Since column titles were set for column A, both pages show the labels contained in column A.*

Page 2

	JUNE	TOTALS	AVERAGES
INCOME			
Service Fees	10359.45		
Consultations	1287.49		
Total Income			
EXPENSES:			
Advertising	165.00		
Salaries	1255.55		
Supplies	1276.54		
Truck Maint	324.65		
Other	798.43		
Total Expenses			

Column titles

Column titles

	COMPARATIVE INCOME STATEMENT				
	GREEN THUMB LANDSCAPE SERVICE				
	JANUARY	FEBRUARY	MARCH	APRIL	MAY
INCOME					
Service Fees	5342.87	5543.65	6165.87	8343.84	9862.89
Consultations	1564.98	1654.76	1689.76	1893.65	1498.62
Total Income					
EXPENSES					
Advertising	55.00	65.00	150.00	150.00	165.00
Salaries	754.65	754.65	1255.55	1255.55	1255.55
Supplies	154.76	245.65	589.53	769.54	965.62
Truck Maint	95.00	125.54	243.98	185.87	543.51
Other	143.43	43.54	231.65	326.43	654.65
Total Expenses					
NET INCOME					

Page 1

In this exercise, you will create a comparative income statement for the Green Thumb Landscape Service. To print data for only the last three months, it is necessary to set repeating print titles for the labels in the first column.

EXERCISE DIRECTIONS:

1. Create the worksheet below, and enter the months by dragging the fill handle to create the series, or open 💾 **EIS.15**.

2. Set column widths as follows:

Column A:	15
Column B:	3
Column C-J:	12

3. Find for each month:
   - Total Income
   - Total Expenses
   - NET INCOME

4. Find for each item in the income statement:
   - TOTALS
   - AVERAGE

5. Format all money columns for two decimal places.

6. Center all column titles.

7. Set column A as a repeating print title.

8. Create a header that includes the page number and total pages centered on the page.

9. Set the print range for the entire worksheet and be sure that scaling is set to 100% of normal size. Preview both pages of the worksheet.
   - ✓ Note: Page one will show column A with JANUARY through MAY data. Page two will show column A with JUNE through AVERAGES data.

10. Print one copy of the two-page report.

11. Change columns C-J back to the standard width.

12. Print one copy of the April-June data with column titles:
    - Highlight the April-June columns. Enter commands to print the selection.
    - Preview the print selection. (The column border was set previously.)
    - ✓ Note: The April-June data will be shown with the column titles in column A.
    - Print the selection.

13. Save the workbook file; name it **IS**.

14. Close the workbook.

		JANUARY	FEBRUARY	MARCH	APRIL	MAY	JUNE	TOTALS	AVERAGES
COMPARATIVE INCOME STATEMENT									
GREEN THUMB LANDSCAPE SERVICE									
INCOME									
Service Fees		5342.87	5543.65	6165.87	8343.84	9862.89	10359.45		
Consultations		1564.98	1654.76	1689.76	1893.65	1498.62	1287.49		
Total Income									
EXPENSES:									
Advertising		55.00	65.00	150.00	150.00	165.00	165.00		
Salaries		754.65	754.65	1255.55	1255.55	1255.55	1255.55		
Supplies		154.76	245.65	589.53	769.54	965.62	1276.54		
Truck Maint		95.00	125.54	243.98	185.87	543.51	324.65		
Other		143.43	43.54	231.65	326.43	654.65	798.43		
Total Expenses									
NET INCOME									

SET REPEATING PRINT TITLES FOR WORKSHEET

Sets titles to print on current and subsequent pages.

1. Click **File** .... `Alt` + `F`

2. Click Page Set**u**p... .... `U`

3. Select **Sheet** .... `Ctrl` + `Tab`

   To set columns as repeating print titles:

   a. Click **Columns** to Repeat at Left: .... `Alt` + `C`

   b. Select columns in worksheet.

   OR

Type column reference .... *columnreference*

   EXAMPLE: The cell reference $A:$A indicates column A.

   ✓ Columns must be adjacent. To remove print titles, delete the reference.

To set rows as repeating print titles:

   a. Click **Rows** to Repeat at Top: .... `Alt` + `R`

   b. Select rows in worksheet.

   OR

Type row reference .... *row reference*

   EXAMPLE: The cell reference $1:$4 indicates rows 1 through 4.

   ✓ Rows must be adjacent. To remove print titles, delete the reference.

4. Click `OK` .... `↵` to return to the worksheet.

   OR

   Click `Print...` .... `Alt` + `P` to print worksheet using current settings.

LESSON 3
SUMMARY EXERCISE 16

Your teacher, Ms. Roberta Eastman, has asked you to help her set up a worksheet to organize her grades. She plans to administer three major examinations this term for her Business Management 101 class.

EXERCISE DIRECTIONS:

1. Create a worksheet file that summarizes student exam grades. Create an appropriate title for your worksheet. Provide each student with a consecutive ID number. Begin with the number 200 for Aaronson.

   The students and their exam grades for Test 1, 2 and 3 are:

   ✓ *Note:* *Some of the students were absent for some of the exams. Leave the cell blank for absent grades. Line spacing was created to make it easier to copy data.*

   Aaronson: 78, 96, 80

   Barnett: 71, 89, 80

   Costello: 67, 79, 80

   Dionesios: 88, absent, 80

   Ellenberg: 90, 70, 73

   Falstaff: 76, 90, 90

   Garcia: 84, 91, 76

   Hamway: 87, 68, 80

   Ianelli: 98, absent, 70

   Jae Woo: absent, 80, 70

   Kelly: 75, 90, 93

2. Change column width of the name column to fit the widest entry.

3. Find for each student:
   - NUMBER OF TESTS TAKEN
   - TEST AVERAGE

4. Find for each test:
   - NO. OF PAPERS
   - CLASS AVERAGE
   - HIGHEST GRADE
   - LOWEST GRADE

5. Format all averages to one decimal place.

6. Center all column titles.

7. Print one copy that is 75% of the actual worksheet size. (Your teacher wants to insert the printout into a notebook.)

8. Edit the names to include a first initial for each student as follows:

   Aaronson, M.

   Barnett, F.

   Costello, A.

   Dionesios, A.

   Ellenberg, S.

   Falstaff, L.

   Garcia, H.

   Hamway, R.

   Ianelli, J.

   Jae Woo, K.

   Kelly, G.

9. Save the file; name it **TEST**.

LESSON 4

ADDITIONAL FORMATTING AND EDITING; WORKING WITH WORKBOOKS

Exercises 17-26

- Insert and Delete Columns and Rows

- Move (Cut/Paste)

- Copy (Drag and Drop)

- Transpose Data

- Freeze Titles

- Split Worksheet

- Create New Workbook

- Select Workbook

- Copy and Paste Special (Extract and Combine Data)

- Print Worksheet on Specified Number of Pages

- Named Ranges

- Arrange Workbooks

- Link Workbooks

- Print Workbook

- 3-D Formulas

- Duplicate Workbook Window

EXERCISE

■ INSERT AND DELETE COLUMNS AND ROWS ■ MOVE (CUT/PASTE) ■ COPY (DRAG AND DROP)

NOTES:

Insert and Delete Columns and Rows

- It is recommended that you save the workbook *before* you insert, delete, move, or copy data so you can retrieve the original worksheet in the event of an error.

- Columns and/or rows may be inserted or deleted to change the structure of a worksheet.

- When a column or row is **inserted,** a blank area is created. Existing columns or rows shift to allow for the newly created space.

- When a column or row is **deleted,** all data in that column or row is eliminated. Existing columns or rows shift to fill in the space left by the deletion.

Move (Cut/Paste)

- When **moving** data, the data is removed from one location and reinserted into another location. You may choose to overwrite existing data or insert the data and shift existing data in the way you specify.

Copy (Drag and Drop)

- Moving data can be accomplished using a combination of cutting and pasting to the paste location or selecting the range and dragging it to the paste location (known as **drag and drop**).

- Inserting, deleting, moving, or copying data can affect formulas. Be sure formulas are correct after an insert, delete, move, or copy operation.

- The format of the data will be moved or copied along with the data.

In this exercise, you will insert, delete, and move columns and rows to include additional information in the Burlington National Bank payroll worksheet. In addition, a new payroll worksheet will be created below the existing one for the new pay period.

EXERCISE DIRECTIONS:

. Open 🖹 **SALARY** or 💾 **ESALARY.17**.

. Make the following changes on the *top* payroll as shown in the illustration on the following page:
   - Insert a new column A.
   - Move the data in the EMPLOYEE NAME column to column A.
   - Set column width for column C to 11 and enter the label S.S. NO. as the column title.
   - Enter social security numbers as follows:

CARTER	069-65-4532
FINCKEL	123-75-7623
JAMISON	107-53-6754
MILLS	103-87-5698
POTTER	127-78-0045
SAMUELS	043-67-7600

   - Copy the social security number column title and data from the May 15 to the May 22 payroll.
   - Copy the entire May 22 payroll, including the title, to a new location below the existing worksheet.

. Make the following changes on the bottom payroll:
   - Edit the title to read:
     FOR THE WEEK ENDING MAY 29, 199-
   - Delete the row containing data for FINCKEL.
   - Insert a row where necessary to maintain alphabetical order for a new employee named NELSON.

   - Enter the following information for NELSON:

Card Number:	12967
S.S. No.:	146-93-0069
Hourly Rate:	$6.25

   - Edit the HOURS WORKED as follows:

CARTER	22
JAMISON	33
MILLS	21
NELSON	16
POTTER	18
SAMUELS	28

   - Copy payroll formulas to complete NELSON's data.

4. Format where necessary.

5. Print one copy to fit on a page.

6. Close and save the workbook file, or *save as* **SALARY**.

Move (cut/paste)

Insert new column A

CARD NUMBER	NAME	HOURLY RATE	HOURS WORKED	GROSS PAY	F.I.C.A.	F.W.T.	NET PAY	
BURLINGTON NATIONAL BANK PAYROLL								
FOR THE WEEK ENDING MAY 15, 199-								
12567	CARTER	5.55	15	83.25	6.37	16.65	60.23	
12750	FINCKEL	7.23	32	231.36	17.70	46.27	167.39	
12816	JAMISON	6.18	16	98.88	7.56	19.78	71.54	
12925	MILLS	4.66	28	130.48	9.98	26.10	94.40	
12345	POTTER	6.57	12	78.84	6.03	15.77	57.04	
12716	SAMUELS	8.65	21	181.65	13.90	36.33	131.42	
TOTALS				804.46	61.54	160.89	582.03	
AVERAGES				134.08	10.26	26.82	97.00	
FOR THE WEEK ENDING MAY 22, 199-								
CARD NUMBER	NAME	HOURLY RATE	HOURS WORKED	GROSS PAY	F.I.C.A.	F.W.T.	NET PAY	
12567	CARTER	5.55	20	111.00	8.49	22.20	80.31	
12750	FINCKEL	7.23	31	224.13	17.15	44.83	162.16	
12816	JAMISON	6.18	23	142.14	10.87	28.43	102.84	
12925	MILLS	4.66	22	102.52	7.84	20.50	74.17	
12345	POTTER	6.57	15	98.55	7.54	19.71	71.30	
12716	SAMUELS	8.65	25	216.25	16.54	43.25	156.46	
TOTALS				894.59	68.44	178.92	647.24	
AVERAGES				149.10	11.41	29.82	107.87	

Copy/Paste

INSERT COLUMNS/ROWS

Inserts blank columns or rows and shifts existing columns or rows to make room for the insertion.

1. Select as many adjacent columns or rows as you want to add to worksheet.

   ✓ *Be sure to select the entire column or row. New columns will be placed to the left of the highlighted columns. New rows will be placed above the highlighted rows.*

2. Click **Insert** .... `Alt` + `I`

3. Click **Columns** .... `C`

   OR

   Click **Rows** .... `R`

DELETE COLUMNS/ROWS

Deletes columns or rows and the data they contain. Existing columns or rows shift to fill in the space left by the deletion.

1. Select column(s) or row(s) to delete.

   ✓ *Be sure to select the entire column or row. When deleting more than one row or column, select adjacent columns or rows.*

2. Click **Edit** .... `Alt` + `E`

3. Click **Delete** .... `D`

🌐 MOVE (CUT/PASTE) USING THE MENU

Moves data in a cell or a range of cells to another area.

1. Select cell or range to move.

2. Click **Edit** menu .... `Alt` + `E`

3. Click **Cut** .... `T`

---

4. Select cell or range to receive data.

   ✓ *You only have to specify the top left cell. The destination range can be in another workbook or worksheet.*

To move and <u>overwrite</u> existing data in destination cells:

Press **Enter** .... `←`

To move and <u>insert</u> between existing cells:

a. Click **Insert** .... `Alt` + `I`

b. Click **Cut Cells** .... `E`

c. If prompted, select **Insert Paste** option:

   • **Shift Cells Right** .... `R`

   • **Shift Cells Down** .... `D`

🌐 MOVE (DRAG AND DROP)

Moves data in a cell or range of cells to another area.

1. Select cell or range to cut.

2. Move mouse pointer to edge of range. *Pointer becomes a ⬉.*

To move and <u>overwrite</u> existing data in destination cells:

a. Drag border outline to new location.

b. Click `OK` .... `←`

To move and <u>insert</u> between existing cells:

a. Press **Shift** and drag .... `Shift` +*drag* insertion outline onto row or column gridline.

   ✓ *If you drag the insertion outline onto a column gridline, cells are shifted right; if dragged onto a row gridline, cells are shifted down.*

b. Release mouse button, then the key.

🌐 COPY (DRAG AND DROP)

Copies data in a cell or range of cells to another area.

1. Select cell or range to copy.

2. Move mouse pointer to edge of range. *Pointer becomes a ⬉.*

To copy and <u>overwrite</u> existing data in destination cells:

a. Press **Ctrl** and drag .... `Ctrl` + *drag* border outline to new location.

b. Release the key, then mouse button.

c. Click `OK` .... `←`

To copy and <u>insert</u> between existing cells:

a. Press **Ctrl + Shift** and drag insertion outline .... `Ctrl` + `Shift` +*drag* onto row or column gridline.

   ✓ *If you drag the insertion outline onto a column gridline, cells are shifted right; if dragged onto a row gridline, cells are shifted down.*

b. Release mouse button, then the key.

EXERCISE

18

■ TRANSPOSE DATA ■ INSERT AND DELETE COLUMNS AND ROWS
■ MOVE (CUT/PASTE)

NOTES:

- To **Transpose data** is to copy and rearrange data so data in rows can be copied to columns and vice versa.

    ✓ *Note the example below. The labels in column B, when transposed, are copied to row 3.*

	A	B	C	D	E	F
1		JAN				
2		FEB				
3		MAR	→	JAN	FEB	MAR

- When transposing formulas, select the **Paste Values** option in the Paste Special dialog box. This selection ensures that only the values are copied to the new location, not the formulas. If you do not select the Paste Values option, the formulas will produce unwanted results.

In this exercise, you will insert a new expense item in the worksheet of the Green Thumb Landscape Service. In addition, you will use transposed data from the income statement to prepare an income statement analysis.

EXERCISE DIRECTIONS:

1. Open ⌨ **IS** or 💾 **EIS.18**.

2. Delete column B.

3. Set column widths for column B through column H to 10.

    To include a monthly interest expense of $25:
    - Insert a row between Truck Expenses and Other.
    - Enter the label: Interest.
    - Enter $25 for each month.
    - Copy the TOTALS and AVERAGES formulas to the interest line.
    - Format the interest line for two decimal places.

4. Enter new title and column labels below the existing worksheet, as illustrated.

5. Center column labels.

6. Transpose the column titles JANUARY through JUNE, including TOTALS, and excluding AVERAGES, to become row titles in column A in the range A30:A36.

7. Transpose Total Income data for JANUARY through JUNE, including TOTALS and excluding AVERAGES, to become row data for column B in the range B30:B36.

    ✓ *Note: Be sure to select the **Paste Values** option when transposing.*

8. Transpose Total Expenses data for JANUARY through JUNE, including TOTALS, and excluding AVERAGES, to become row data for column D in the range D30:D36.

    ✓ *Note: Be sure to select the **Paste Values** option when transposing.*

9. Transpose NET INCOME data for JANUARY through JUNE, including TOTALS, and excluding AVERAGES, to become row data for column F in the range F30:F36.

    ✓ *Note: Be sure to select the **Paste Values** option when transposing.*

10. Enter formulas in the % OF TOTAL columns to find what percent each item is of the six month total.

    Hint: Use absolute reference in the formula.

11. Format % OF TOTAL columns for percentage with one decimal place.

12. Print one copy to fit on a page.

13. Close and save the workbook file, or *save as* **IS**.

	A	B	C	D	E	F	G	H	I	J	K
1			COMPARATIVE INCOME STATEMENT								
2			GREEN THUMB LANDSCAPE SERVICE								
3											
4											
5			JANUARY	FEBRUARY	MARCH	APRIL	MAY	JUNE	TOTALS	AVERAGES	
6											
7	INCOME										
8	Service Fees		5342.87	5543.65	6165.87	8343.84	9862.89	10359.45	45618.57	7603.09	
9	Consultations		1564.98	1654.76	1689.76	1893.65	1498.62	1287.49	9589.26	1598.21	
10	Total Income		6907.85	7198.41	7855.63	10237.49	11361.51	11646.94	55207.83	9201.31	
11											
12	EXPENSES:										
13	Advertising		55.00	65.00	150.00	150.00	165.00	165.00	750.00	125.00	
14	Salaries		754.65	754.65	1255.55	1255.55	1255.55	1255.55	6531.50	1088.58	
15	Supplies		154.76	245.65	589.53	769.54	965.62	1276.54	4001.64	666.94	
16	Truck Maint		95.00	125.54	243.98	185.87	543.51	324.65	1518.55	253.09	
17	Interest		25.00	25.00	25.00	25.00	25.00	25.00	150.00	25.00	
18	Other		143.43	43.54	231.65	326.43	654.65	798.43	2198.13	366.36	
19	Total Expenses		1227.84	1259.38	2495.71	2712.39	3609.33	3845.17	15149.82	2524.97	
20											
21	NET INCOME		5680.01	5939.03	5359.92	7525.10	7752.18	7801.77	40058.01	6676.34	
22											
23											
24			*INCOME STATEMENT ANALYSIS*								
25			*GREEN THUMB LANDSCAPING SERVICE*								
26											
27	*MONTH*		*TOTAL*	*% OF*	*TOTAL*	*% OF*	*NET*	*% OF*			
28			*INCOME*	*TOTAL*	*EXPENSES*	*TOTAL*	*INCOME*	*TOTAL*			
29											
30											
31											
32											
33											
34											
35											
36											
37											
38											

Delete column B

Transpose

Insert row

TRANSPOSE DATA

Copies and transposes data from horizontal to vertical arrangement and vice versa.

1. Select range to transpose.

2. a. Click **Edit** .... `Alt` + `E`

   b. Click **Copy** .... `C`

   OR

   a. Right-click a cell in selection to open shortcut menu.

   b. Click **Copy.**

3. Click upper-left cell ....
   to receive transposed data.

4. a. Click **Edit** .... `Alt` + `E`

   b. Click **Paste Special** .... `S`

   OR

   a. Right-click destination cell to open shortcut menu.

   b. Click **Paste Special**.

5. Click **Transpose** .... `E`

   To paste transposed data as values, not formulas:

   Click **Values** .... `V`

6. Click `OK` .... `↵`

7. Press **Escape** .... `Esc`
   to end copying.

EXERCISE

- **INSERT AND DELETE COLUMNS ▪ FREEZE TITLES**
- **CREATE NEW WORKBOOK ▪ SELECT WORKBOOK**
- **COPY AND PASTE SPECIAL (EXTRACT DATA)**

NOTES:

- Excel provides two methods for working with large worksheets: freezing titles to keep titles in view and splitting the window into two panes or four panes.

Freeze Titles

- To keep headings or titles in view at the left or top edge of the worksheet when scrolling, it is necessary to hold, or **freeze**, them in place.

- To view different parts of a large worksheet at one time, the worksheet may be **split** horizontally or vertically so data may be viewed through each of the windows at the same time.

  When you split a window *vertically* the panes scroll together when you scroll up or down, but they scroll independently when you scroll left and right.

  When you split a window *horizontally* the panes scroll together when you scroll left or right, but they scroll independently when you scroll up and down.

- When you freeze a split worksheet, the top and/or left pane locks when you scroll through the worksheet.

Copy and Paste Special

- Use the **Copy** and **Paste Special** commands to copy part of a worksheet into another workbook.

- In the Paste Special dialog box, the **Formulas** and **Values** paste options affect the paste result. Select **Formulas** to extract values, labels and formulas *exactly as they exist.* Select **Values** to extract labels, values, *and the results of the formulas.* You should select **Values** if the range to be extracted contains formulas with reference to cells that do not contain the values to be calculated.

- New workbooks can be created to store new or extracted data.

- When working with more than one workbook at a time, you can use the **Window** menu to select the name of the workbook you want to work with.

In this exercise, you will divide the data into quarterly information. To do this, you must insert and delete columns. However, because inserting or deleting columns from the top portion of the worksheet will affect the bottom portion, you will extract the bottom portion of the worksheet, save it to another file, and delete it from the original. The top portion of the worksheet will then be expanded and edited.

EXERCISE DIRECTIONS

Open ▓ **IS** or 💾 **EIS.19**.

Use the Copy and Paste Special commands to extract the Income Statement Analysis portion of the worksheet to a new workbook; name the new workbook file **ANA**.

✓ Note: Select the **Values** option in the Paste Special dialog box to ensure that the results of the formulas are copied, and not the formulas themselves.

Delete the Income Statement Analysis portion from the **IS** worksheet.

Insert a column between MARCH and APRIL and enter the column titles:

1ST QTR.

TOTALS

Format the new column for two decimal places.

Insert a column between JUNE and TOTALS and enter the column titles:

2ND QTR.

TOTALS

Format the new column for two decimal places.

Edit column title TOTALS to read:

COMBINED

TOTALS

Delete the AVERAGES column.

. Find 1ST QTR. TOTALS.

. Copy the formula to the remaining items.

. Copy the formulas for 1ST QTR. TOTALS to the column for 2ND QTR. TOTALS.

. Edit the formula in the COMBINED TOTALS column to add 1ST QTR. TOTALS and 2ND QTR. TOTALS.

14. Freeze titles in column A.

15. Enter third quarter data indicated below beginning in the next available column of your worksheet.

	A	K	L	M
1				
2				
3				
4				
5		JULY	AUGUST	SEPT.
6				
7	INCOME			
8	Service Fees	11986.45	11050.65	10573.87
9	Consultations	1343.27	1186.87	965.78
10	Total Income			
11				
12	EXPENSES:			
13	Advertising	165.00	165.00	150.00
14	Salaries	1255.55	1255.55	1255.00
15	Supplies	1887.98	1667.09	1654.98
16	Truck Maint	486.98	245.90	327.65
17	Interest	25.00	25.00	25.00
18	Other	674.79	543.87	476.98
19	Total Expenses			
20				
21	NET INCOME			
22				
23				

16. Copy and edit formulas, where necessary, to complete the worksheet.

17. Find 3RD QTR. TOTALS.

18. Copy the formula to the remaining items.

19. Center column title labels.

20. Format numeric data for two decimal places.

21. Save the file, or *save as* **IS**.

22. Print one copy of IS to fit on a page.

23. Open **ANA**.

24. Format and align data as needed.

25. Resave **ANA**, then print one copy.

26. Close both workbook files.

	A	B	C	D	E	F	G	H	I	J
1		COMPARATIVE INCOME STATEMENT			*Insert column 1ST QTR. TOTALS*				*Insert column 2ND QTR. TOTALS*	
2		GREEN THUMB LANDSCAPE SERVICE								
3										
4										
5		JANUARY	FEBRUARY	MARCH	APRIL	MAY	JUNE	TOTALS	AVERAGES	
6										
7	INCOME									
8	Service Fees	5342.87	5543.65	6165.87	8343.84	9862.89	10359.45	45618.57	7603.09	
9	Consultations	1564.98	1654.76	1689.76	1893.65	1498.62	1287.49	9589.26	1598.21	
10	Total Income	6907.85	7198.41	7855.63	10237.49	11361.51	11646.94	55207.83	9201.31	
11										
12	EXPENSES:								*Delete column*	
13	Advertising	55.00	65.00	150.00	150.00	165.00	165.00	750.00		
14	Salaries	754.65	754.65	1255.55	1255.55	1255.55	1255.55	6531.50	1088.58	
15	Supplies	154.76	245.65	589.53	769.54	965.62	1276.54	4001.64	666.94	
16	Truck Maint	95.00	125.54	243.98	185.87	543.51	324.65	1518.55	253.09	
17	Interest	25.00	25.00	25.00	25.00	25.00	25.00	150.00	25.00	
18	Other	143.43	43.54	231.65	326.43	654.65	798.43	2198.13	366.36	
19	Total Expenses	1227.84	1259.38	2495.71	2712.39	3609.33	3845.17	15149.82	2524.97	
20										
21	NET INCOME	5680.01	5939.03	5359.92	7525.10	7752.18	7801.77	40058.01	6676.34	
22										
23										
24				INCOME STATEMENT ANALYSIS						
25				GREEN THUMB LANDSCAPING SERVICE						
26										
27	MONTH	TOTAL	% OF	TOTAL	% OF	NET	% OF			
28		INCOME	TOTAL	EXPENSES	TOTAL	INCOME	TOTAL		*Extract to new workbook and save new workbook as ANA*	
29										
30	JANUARY	6907.85	12.5%	1227.84	8.1%	5680.01	14.2%			
31	FEBRUARY	7198.41	13.0%	1259.38	8.3%	5939.03	14.8%			
32	MARCH	7855.63	14.2%	2495.71	16.5%	5359.92	13.4%			
33	APRIL	10237.49	18.5%	2712.39	17.9%	7525.1	18.8%			
34	MAY	11361.51	20.6%	3609.33	23.8%	7752.18	19.4%			
35	JUNE	11646.94	21.1%	3845.17	25.4%	7801.77	19.5%			
36	TOTALS	55207.83		15149.82		40058.01				
37										
38										
39										
40										

COPY AND PASTE SPECIAL (EXTRACT DATA)

Copies a portion of the current worksheet to a new workbook.

1. Copy range to extract to the clipboard:

   a. Select range of worksheet to extract.

   b. Click **Edit** .... Alt + E

   c. Click **Copy** C

2. Open a new workbook:

   a. Click **File** .... Alt + F

   b. Click **New** .... N

   – FROM NEW WORKBOOK –

3. Use Paste Special command:

a. Click **Edit** .... Alt + E

b. Click **Paste Special** .... S

c. Click **Values** V
   to copy data as it appears in cells
   (results of formulas).

OR

Click **Formulas** .... F
to copy data as it exists in
formula bar (formulas)

✓ *Only relative cell references in
formulas will adjust.*

d. Click [OK] .... ⏎

4. Save and name the new workbook.

a. Click **File** .... Alt + F

b. Click **Save As** .... A

c. Type new filename .... *filenam*

✓ *The filename you type replaces
default name of the workbook.*

d. Click [OK] .... ◄

CREATE NEW WORKBOOK

*Opens a new workbook based on the defaul
template.*

Click **New Workbook** button ....
on the Standard toolbar.

OR

Continued

1. Click **File** .... `Alt`+`F`
2. Click **New** .... `N`

SELECT WORKBOOK

✓ *When more than one workbook is open, the workbook you want may be hidden or reduced to an icon. In order to use the workbook, you need to select the workbook window or open the workbook icon.*

To select a workbook window:

Click anywhere on workbook window.

OR

1. Click **Window** menu .... `Alt`+`W`
2. Select name of workbook... `↑↓`, `←` near bottom of the menu.

To open a workbook icon:

Double-click workbook icon.

OR

1. Click **Window** .... `Alt`+`W`
2. Select name of workbook... `↑↓`, `←` near bottom of the menu.

SPLIT WORKSHEET INTO PANES USING SPLIT BOXES

Provides simultaneous scrolling of up to four panes. You can freeze panes (see right) to prevent top, left, or both panes from scrolling.

1. Point to horizontal split box ▬ or vertical split box ▮ on scroll bar.
   Pointer becomes a ╪ or ╫.
2. Drag ╪ or ╫ along scroll bar until split bar is in desired position.

SPLIT WORKSHEET INTO PANES USING THE MENU

Provides simultaneous scrolling of up to four panes. You can freeze panes (see right) to prevent top, left ,or both panes from scrolling.

1. Select row below which horizontal split will occur.

   OR

   Select column to right of which vertical split will occur.

   OR

   Select cell below and to the right of which horizontal and vertical split will occur.

2. Click **Window** .... `Alt`+`W`
3. Click **Split** .... `S`

REMOVE SPLIT BARS

Double-click any part of split bar.

OR

1. Click **Window** .... `Alt`+`W`
2. Click **Remove Split** .... `S`

ADJUST WORKSHEET PANES

1. Point to horizontal split box ▬ or vertical split box ▮ on scroll bar.
   Pointer becomes a ╪ or ╫.
2. Drag ╪ or ╫ along scroll bar until split bar is in desired position.

MOVE BETWEEN WORKSHEET PANES

Click desired pane.

OR

Press **F6** .... `F6` until active cell is in desired pane.

FREEZE PANES ON A SPLIT WORKSHEET

Locks top and/or left pane when scrolling.

1. Click **Window** .... `Alt`+`W`
2. Click **Freeze Panes** .... `F`

UNFREEZE PANES

1. Click **Window** .... `Alt`+`W`
2. Click **Unfreeze Panes** .... `F`

FREEZE TITLES

Locks display of title row and/or title column on the screen. This procedure is for a worksheet that has not been split into panes.

1. Select row below horizontal titles to freeze.

   OR

   Select column to right of vertical titles to freeze.

   OR

   Select cell below and to the right of horizontal and vertical titles to freeze.

2. Click **Window** .... `Alt`+`W`
3. Click **Freeze Panes** .... `F`

UNFREEZE TITLES

1. Click **Window** .... `Alt`+`W`
2. Click **Unfreeze Panes** .... `F`

EXERCISE

20

- **INSERT AND DELETE COLUMNS AND ROWS**
- **WORKBOOK SHEETS** ▪ **PRINT WORKBOOK**
- **PRINT WORKSHEET ON SPECIFIED NUMBER OF PAGES**

NOTES:

Workbook Sheets

- By default, each new workbook contains sixteen worksheets labeled Sheet1 through Sheet16. **Sheet tabs** show the names of the sheets *(see illustration below).*

- You can select multiple sheets (grouping) to work on several sheets simultaneously. In a group selection **selected sheet tabs** are white, and the **active sheet tab** is bold.

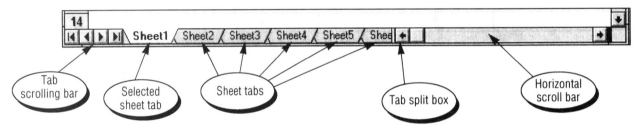

- Excel lets you work with sheets in many ways. For example, you can delete, insert, rename, move, copy, and hide sheets. These features let you arrange your workbook to fit your work objectives.

- Excel provides a **tab split box** between the sheet tabs and the horizontal scroll bar. You can drag this split box left or right to show more or fewer sheet tabs.

- You can use the **tab scrolling buttons** to scroll a hidden sheet tab into view. If no sheet tabs are visible, you can tell Excel to show them by selecting **Sheet Ta_b_s** from the Options dialog box.

Print Workbook

- You can tell Excel on how many pages you want a worksheet to print. Then, Excel will automatically scale the worksheet to fit on the specified number of pages.

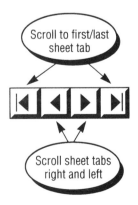

In this exercise, you will create a payroll template for future use. To do this you will delete unnecessary sheet tabs, insert and rename sheet tabs, and work with grouped sheets to quickly edit data on more than one worksheet at a time.

EXERCISE DIRECTIONS:

. Open ⌨ **SALARY** or 💾 **ESALARY.20**.

. Resave the workbook file as **SALNEW.**

. Click sheet tab named Sheet2 to select it.

   ✓ Note that Sheet2 is empty.

. Select Sheet1.

. Use tab scrolling buttons to scroll to last sheet.

. Use tab split box to increase, then decrease, the amount of visible sheet tabs.

. Select Sheet16 and delete it.

. Select Sheet2 through Sheet15.

   ✓ Note selected sheet tabs are white and [Group] appears on the title bar.

. Delete the grouped worksheets.

   ✓ Note only Sheet1 remains.

0. Rename Sheet1 to May.

1. Insert a new worksheet; name it June.

2. Move the June sheet to the right of May.

3. Insert a new worksheet; name it July.

4. Move the July sheet to the right of June.

5. To make payrolls uniform:
   • Finckel has left our employment; delete the Finckel rows in the top two payrolls.
   • Copy the Nelson information from the last payroll to the first two payrolls in the correct order.

6. Select the May sheet and edit the titles in each week's payroll to read:

   FOR THE WEEK ENDING

   ✓ Note: Delete the dates.

17. Select all the data in the May sheet and copy it to the clipboard.

   HINT: You can click the Select All button to select the entire worksheet.

18. Group the June and July sheets.

19. Select the June sheet and select cell A1.

20. Use the Paste command to copy the May worksheet data to the active cell in the grouped sheets (June and July).

21. Click cell A1 to deselect the range.

22. Select the May sheet.

23. Click cell A1 to deselect the range.

24. Select all the sheets in the workbook (May through July).

   – WHILE ALL SHEETS ARE GROUPED –

25. Clear the data in the cells containing the hours worked for each employee in each payroll week. (Do not delete the column.)

26. Mills has left our employment; delete the Mills row in each payroll week.

27. Deselect grouped sheets and check that each sheet contains identical data.

28. Set each worksheet to fit on one page when printed.

   ✓ Note: You can not set print page options for a group.

29. Print the entire workbook.

30. Close and save the workbook file.

	A	B	C	D	E	F	G	H	I
1			BURLINGTON NATIONAL BANK PAYROLL						
2			FOR THE WEEK ENDING MAY 15, 1994						
3									
4	EMPLOYEE	CARD		HOURLY	HOURS	GROSS			NET
5	NAME	NUMBER	S.S.NO.	RATE	WORKED	PAY	F.I.C.A.	F.W.T.	PAY
6									
7	CARTER	12567	069-65-4532	5.55	15	83.25	6.37	16.65	60.23
8	FINCKEL	12750	123-75-7623	7.23	32	231.36	17.70	46.27	167.39
9	JAMISON	12816	107-53-6754	6.18	16	98.88	7.56	19.78	71.54
10	MILLS	12925	103-87-5698	4.66	28	130.48	9.98	26.10	94.40
11	POTTER	12345	127-78-0045	6.57	12	78.84	6.03	15.77	57.04
12	SAMUELS	12716	043-67-7600	8.65	21	181.65	13.90	36.33	131.42
13									
14		TOTALS				804.46	61.54	160.89	582.03
15		AVERAGES				134.08	10.26	26.82	97.00
16									
17			FOR THE WEEK ENDING MAY 22, 1994						
18									
19	EMPLOYEE	CARD		HOURLY	HOURS	GROSS			NET
20	NAME	NUMBER	S.S.NO.	RATE	WORKED	PAY	F.I.C.A.	F.W.T.	PAY
21									
22	CARTER	12567	069-65-4532	5.55	20	111.00	8.49	22.20	80.31
23	FINCKEL	12750	123-75-7623	7.23	31	224.13	17.15	44.83	162.16
24	JAMISON	12816	107-53-6754	6.18	23	142.14	10.87	28.43	102.84
25	MILLS	12925	103-87-5698	4.66	22	102.52	7.84	20.50	74.17
26	POTTER	12345	127-78-0045	6.57	15	98.55	7.54	19.71	71.30
27	SAMUELS	12716	043-67-7600	8.65	25	216.25	16.54	43.25	156.46
28									
29		TOTALS				894.59	68.44	178.92	647.24
30		AVERAGES				149.10	11.41	29.82	107.87
31									
32			FOR THE WEEK ENDING MAY 29, 1994						
33									
34	EMPLOYEE	CARD		HOURLY	HOURS	GROSS			NET
35	NAME	NUMBER	S.S.NO.	RATE	WORKED	PAY	F.I.C.A.	F.W.T.	PAY
36									
37	CARTER	12567	069-65-4532	5.55	22	122.10	9.34	24.42	88.34
38	JAMISON	12816	107-53-6754	6.18	33	203.94	15.60	40.79	147.55
39	MILLS	12925	103-87-5698	4.66	21	97.86	7.49	19.57	70.80
40	NELSON	12967	146-93-0069	6.25	16	100.00	7.65	20.00	72.35
41	POTTER	12345	127-78-0045	6.57	18	118.26	9.05	23.65	85.56
42	SAMUELS	12716	043-67-7600	8.65	28	242.20	18.53	48.44	175.23
43									
44		TOTALS				884.36	67.65	176.87	639.83
45		AVERAGES				147.39	11.28	29.48	106.64
46									

Copy A1:I46 to June and July sheets

Delete row

Delete row

Delete row

USE TAB SPLIT BOX

Lets you show more or fewer tabs.

1. Point to tab split box.
   Pointer becomes a ↔.

2. Drag split box left or right.

SELECT SHEETS

Select One Sheet:

1. If necessary, click tab .... scrolling buttons to scroll a hidden sheet tab into view.

2. Click desired sheet tab .... \ Sheet # /

Select All Sheets:

1. Right-click any sheet tab.. \ Sheet # /

2. Select **Select All Sheets** ....

Select (Group) Consecutive Sheets

IMPORTANT: When you group sheets, entries and formatting applied to one sheet are duplicated on all sheets in the group.

1. If necessary, click tab .... scrolling buttons to scroll hidden sheet tabs into view.

2. Click first sheet .... \ Sheet # / tab to select

3. If necessary, click tab .... scrolling buttons to scroll hidden sheet tabs into view.

4. Press **Shift** and click........ \ Sheet # / last sheet tab to select
   [Group] appears in title bar.

Select (Group) Non-Consecutive Sheets

IMPORTANT: When you group sheets, entries and formatting applied to one sheet are duplicated on all sheets in the group.

1. If necessary, click .... tab scrolling buttons to scroll hidden sheet tabs into view.

2. Click .... \ Sheet # / first sheet tab to select

3. If necessary, click .... tab scrolling buttons to scroll hidden sheet tabs into view.

Continued.

4. Press **Ctrl** and click .... `\ Sheet # /`
   each sheet tab to select
   [Group] appears in title bar.

DESELECT GROUPED SHEETS

Click .... `\ Sheet # /`
any sheet tab that is not
in the group.

OR

1. Right-click .... `\ Sheet # /`
   any sheet tab in group.

2. Click **Ungroup Sheets** .... `[↑/↓]`,`[←]`

DELETE SHEETS

Delete One Sheet:

1. Right-click .... `\ Sheet # /`
   sheet tab to delete.

2. Click **Delete** .... `[↑/↓]`,`[←]`

3. Click `[ OK ]` .... `[←]`

Delete Multiple Sheets:

1. Select sheet tabs to delete.

2. Right-click any .... `\ Sheet # /`
   selected sheet tab.

3. Click **Delete** .... `[↑/↓]`,`[←]`

4. Click `[ OK ]` .... `[←]`

RENAME A SHEET

1. Double-click .... `\ Sheet # /`
   sheet tab to rename.

OR

a. Right-click................. `\ Sheet # /`
   sheet tab.

b. Select **Rename** .... `[↑/↓]`,`[←]`

2. Type new name ....*name*

3. Click `[ OK ]` .... `[←]`

INSERT SHEETS

Insert One Worksheet:

1. Right click sheet tab .... `\ Sheet # /`
   before which new sheet
   will be inserted.

2. Click **Insert**... .... `[↑/↓]`,`[←]`

3. Select **Worksheet**........................`[↑/↓]`
   in **New** list box.

4. Click `[ OK ]` .... `[←]`

*Excel inserts sheet and makes the new
sheet active.*

Insert Multiple Worksheets:

1. Highlight as many sheets as you wish to
   insert.

2. Right-click
   sheet tab........................ `\ Sheet # /`
   before which new
   sheets will be inserted.

3. Click **Insert**... .... `[↑/↓]`,`[←]`

4. Select **Worksheet** .... `[↑/↓]`
   in **New** list box.

5. Click `[ OK ]` .... `[←]`

*Excel inserts sheets and makes the first
new sheet active.*

MOVE SHEETS WITHIN A WORKBOOK

Move One Sheet:

1. If necessary, click .... `|◄ ◄ ► ►|`
   tab scrolling buttons
   to scroll a hidden sheet tab into view.

2. Drag sheet tab to
   desired sheet tab position.

   *Pointer becomes a ⬚, and black triangle
   indicates point of insertion.*

Move Multiple Sheets:

1. If necessary, click tab .... `|◄ ◄ ► ►|`
   scrolling buttons to scroll
   a hidden sheet tab into view.

2. Select sheets to move.

3. Drag selected sheet tabs to desired sheet
   tab position.

   *Pointer becomes a ⬚, and black triangle
   indicates point of insertion.*

🌐 PRINT WORKBOOK

*Prints worksheet data using the current page
settings.*

1. Click **File** menu .... `[Alt]`+`[F]`

2. Click **Print**.......................................`[P]`

3. Click **Entire Workbook** ....`[Alt]`+`[E]`

4. Click `[ OK ]` .... `[←]`

SET WORKSHEET TO PRINT ON SPECIFIED NUMBER OF PAGES

*Determines how much to scale printed data to
fit on a specified number of pages.*

✓ *Excel ignores manual page breaks when
   this setting is selected.*

1. Click **File** menu .... `[Alt]`+`[F]`

2. Click **Page Setup**............................`[U]`

3. Select **Page** tab................`[Ctrl]`+`[Tab]`

4. Select **Fit to:**..........................`[Alt]`+`[F]`

   To change settings for number of pages:

   a. Type number of pages.............*number*
      in **page(s) wide**.

   b. Select **by tall**............................`[Tab]`

   c. Type number of pages.............*number*

5. Click `[ OK ]` .... `[←]`

EXERCISE

■ INSERT AND DELETE ROWS ■ FREEZE TITLES ■ NAMED RANGES

21

NOTES:

Named Ranges

- Excel allows you to assign a **name** to a cell or range of cells rather than use the cell reference for identification.

- Naming ranges makes formulas easy to read and understand and makes printing and combining ranges easier to accomplish. For example, when you define a print area you can type the name of a range (such as EMPS), rather than typing the cell reference (such as A1:D17). You should keep range names short and descriptive. Since spaces are not allowed, use an underscore to simulate a space character. Do not use range names that could be interpreted as a number or a cell reference.

- Range names may contain up to 255 characters and may consist of letters, numbers, underscores (_), backslashes (\), periods (.), and question marks (?).

- You can insert in your worksheet a list of named ranges you created and their corresponding cell references by selecting the **Paste List** button in the Paste Name dialog box.

- The name box [⬇] provides a way to view a list of named ranges you have created and is an easy way to name or select a range.

- It is possible to modify a named range by changing the range or the name.

In this exercise, you will include third-quarter sales commission data and name ranges in the report for printing and for later use in combining files.

EXERCISE DIRECTIONS

1. Open ⌨ **WOOD** or 💾 **EWOOD.21**.

2. Edit the title to read:
   QUARTERLY SALES AND SALARY REPORT – JANUARY– SEPTEMBER

3. Insert a row to include a new employee hired on July 1. Employee Number, 6; Name, THOMPSON, JIM; Base Salary, $1500.

   ✓ Note: Format base salary to be consistent with other formatting.

4. Freeze columns A-D for vertical titles.

5. Change column widths to 12 for columns K, L, and M.

6. Enter the following data in columns K, L, and M:

	K	L	M
1			
2			
3			
4			JULY-SEPT
5	SALES	COMMISSION	SALARY
6			
7	112469.32		
8	152643.36		
9	215050.16		
10	98463.14		
11	246315.19		
12	76451.13		
13			
14			
15			

7. Format all data to be consistent with other formatting.

8. Copy the COMMISSION formulas to the new column.

9. Find JULY-SEPT SALARY using the BASE SALARY + COMMISSION.

10. Copy the formula to the remaining employees.

11. Copy the formulas for TOTALS, AVERAGES, HIGHEST, and LOWEST to the new columns.

12. Clear the freeze.

13. Edit the formulas for TOTALS, AVERAGES, HIGHEST, and LOWEST in the BASE SALARY column to include the new employee data.

14. Copy the edited formulas to all columns.

15. Create the following named ranges:
EMPS	A1:D17
JAN_MAR	G1:G17
APR_JUNE	J1:J17
JUL_SEPT	M1:M17

16. Print one copy of the range EMPS.

17. In range beginning at cell B19, insert list of named ranges.

18. Close and save the workbook file, or *save as* **WOOD**.

	A	B	C	D	E	F	G	H	I	J	K	L	M
1		WOODWORKS FURNITURE COMPANY											
2		QUARTERLY SALES AND SALARY REPORT - JANUARY-SEPTEMBER									←12→	←12→	←12→
3													
4	EMP.			BASE			JAN-MAR			APR-JUN			JULY-SEPT
5	NO.	NAME		SALARY	SALES	COMMISSION	SALARY	SALES	COMMISSION	SALARY	SALES	COMMISSION	SALARY
6													
7	1	ABRAMS, JUDY		1,500.00	113,456.67	5,672.83	7,172.83	114,342.90	5,717.15	7,217.15			
8	2	CHANG, PETER		1,500.00	150,654.87	7,532.74	9,032.74	143,276.70	7,163.84	8,663.84			
9	3	LINSEY, KELLY		1,500.00	234,765.36	11,738.27	13,238.27	187,956.76	9,397.84	10,897.84			
10	4	JOHNSON, LETOYA		1,500.00	89,765.43	4,488.27	5,988.27	93,984.69	4,699.23	6,199.23			
11	5	RIVERA, TONY		1,500.00	287,987.76	14,399.39	15,899.39	254,768.60	12,738.43	14,238.43			
12													
13		TOTALS		7,500.00	876,630.09	43,831.50	51,331.50	794,329.65	39,716.48	47,216.48			
14		AVERAGES		1,500.00	175,326.02	8,766.30	10,266.30	158,865.93	7,943.30	9,443.30			
15		HIGHEST		1,500.00	287,987.76	14,399.39	15,899.39	254,768.60	12,738.43	14,238.43			
16		LOWEST		1,500.00	89,765.43	4,488.27	5,988.27	93,984.69	4,699.23	6,199.23			
17													

insert row

NAME/MODIFY A RANGE USING THE MENU

1. Click **Insert** .... Alt + I
2. Click **Name** .... N
3. Click **Define** .... D

   *Active cell reference appears in **Refers to** text box.*

   To name a range:

   a. Type name for range .... *name* in **Names in Workbook** text box.
   b. Click [Add] .... Alt + A
   c. Drag through existing reference .... Alt + R in **Refers to** text box.
   d. Select cells in worksheet to name.

      OR

      Type reference of cells .... *reference* to name.

   To delete a name:

   a. Click name .... Tab , ↑↓ to delete in list box.
   b. Click [Delete] .... Alt + D

   To change a name:

   a. Click name .... Tab , ↑↓ to change in list box.
   b. Double-click in **Names in Workbook** .... Alt + W
   c. Type new name .... *name* for range.
   d. Click [Add] .... Alt + A
   e. Click old name .... Tab , ↑↓ to delete in list box.
   f. Click [Delete] .... Alt + D

To change reference a name refers to:

a. Click name .... Tab , ↑↓ to edit in list box.
b. Drag through existing reference .... Alt + R in **Refers to** text box.
c. Select cells in worksheet to reference.

   OR

   Type new reference .... *reference*

4. Click [OK] .... ↵

NAME A RANGE USING THE NAME BOX

1. Select range to name.
2. Click in name box on left side of formula bar.
3. Type name of range .... *name* to create.
4. Press **Enter** .... ↵

SELECT A NAMED RANGE

Select a Named Range Using the Name Box:

1. Click drop-down arrow in name box on left side of formula bar.
2. Click desired named range.

Select a Named Range Using Go To:

1. Press **F5** F5
2. Type name .... *name* to select in **Reference** text box.
3. Click [OK] .... ↵

INSERT LIST OF NAMED RANGES

Inserts a list of named ranges and their corresponding references in current worksheet.

1. Select upper-left cell in range to receive list.
2. Click **Insert** .... Alt + I
3. Click **Name** .... N
4. Click **Paste** .... P
5. Click [Paste List] .... Alt + L

   ✓ *Excel includes sheet names in references.*

6. Press any **arrow key** .... ↑↓

SET PRINT AREA FOR A NAMED RANGE

✓ *Use this option only when you want to print a specific area of a worksheet each time you print.*

1. Follow steps to **SET PRINT OPTIONS FOR WORKSHEET,** page 236.
2. When you set the print area, type named range *name* in **Print Area** text box.
3. Follow steps to **PRINT A WORKSHEET,** page 221.

PRINT A NAMED RANGE

1. Follow steps to **SELECT A NAMED RANGE,** left.
2. Follow steps to **PRINT RANGE OF CELLS**, page 236.

NEXT EXERCISE

EXERCISE

■ CREATE NEW WORKBOOK ■ SELECT WORKBOOK
■ COPY AND PASTE SPECIAL (EXTRACT AND COMBINE DATA)

NOTES:

Copy and Paste Special

■ The **Paste Special** command gives you added controls on how data is pasted when copied. With the Paste Special command you can:

- Indicate which attributes of the selection will be copied.
- Indicate how to combine data when the paste area contains data.
- Tell Excel to skip blanks.
- Tell Excel to transpose data in the paste area.

■ Paste options in the Paste Special dialog box include:

All	Replaces paste area cells with all formulas, formats, and notes contained in copied cells.
Formulas	Copies data that exists in formula bar of copied cells (the formulas).
	✓ Note: Relative cell references in formulas will adjust.
Values	Copies data as it appears in copied cells (results of formulas).
Formats	Copies only the formats of cells.
Notes	Copies notes cells may contain.

■ The Paste Special command also gives you control on how the data is pasted when copied. The Operation options in the Past Special dialog box provide a variety of ways to combine data.

■ In this lesson you will use the **Add** operation option in the Paste Special dialog box to extract and combine data to the same range in another workbook.

■ Operation options in the Paste Special dialog box include:

None	Replaces paste cells with copied cells (default setting).
Add	Adds numeric data in copied cells to values in paste cells.
Subtract	Subtracts numeric data in copied cells from values in paste cells.
Multiply	Multiplies numeric data in copied cells by values in paste cells.
Divide	Divides numeric data in copied cells by values in paste cells.

In this exercise, you will extract data in a named range to a new file. Then you will use the Paste Special command to combine (add) the quarterly totals (as values) in the new workbook file, thus, creating a summary workbook.

REMINDER:

*When you paste data using the **Add** and **Values** options in the **Paste Special** dialog box, the new combined data will not include formulas. Therefore, averages, highest, and lowest results will be incorrect and will require that a new formula be entered to obtain the correct answers.*

EXERCISE DIRECTIONS:

1. Open ⌨ **WOOD** or 💾 **EWOOD.22**.

2. Use the Copy and Paste Special commands to extract the named range EMPS to a cell A1 in a new workbook file using the Formulas option; save and name the new workbook **WOODSUM**.

3. Edit the second line of the **WOODSUM** workbook title to read:

   COMPENSATION SUMMARY - JANUARY-SEPTEMBER

4. Select the ⌨ **WOOD** or 💾 **EWOOD.22** workbook.

5. Use the Copy and Paste Special commands to extract and combine the following named ranges into cell F1 of **WOODSUM** workbook.
   JAN_MAR
   APR_JUNE
   JUL_SEPT

   IMPORTANT: Each time you paste data to cell F1 using **Paste Special,** set the Paste option to **Values** and the Operation option to **Add.**

– IN COLUMN F OF WOODSUM WORKBOOK –

6. Enter the column title:
   TOTAL
   COMPENSATION

7. The combined summary data for AVERAGES, HIGHEST, and LOWEST is now incorrect. To correct this information, copy the formulas for TOTALS, AVERAGES, HIGHEST, and LOWEST, from the BASE SALARY column to the TOTAL COMPENSATION column.

8. Format column F to show two decimal places.

9. Adjust the column width to show all values.

10. Save **WOODSUM** and print one copy.

11. Close both workbook files.

	A	B	C	D	E	F	G	H	I	J	K	L	M
1		WOODWORKS FURNITURE COMPANY											
2		QUARTERLY SALES AND SALARY REPORT - JANUARY-SEPTEMBER											
3													
4	EMP.			BASE			JAN-MAR			APR-JUN			JULY-SEPT
5	NO.	NAME		SALARY	SALES	COMMISSION	SALARY	SALES	COMMISSION	SALARY	SALES	COMMISSION	SALARY
6													
7	1	ABRAMS, JUDY		1,500.00	113,456.67	5,672.83	7,172.83	114,342.90	5,717.15	7,217.15	112469.32	5,623.47	7,123.47
8	2	CHANG, PETER		1,500.00	150,654.87	7,532.74	9,032.74	143,276.70	7,163.84	8,663.84	152643.36	7,632.17	9,132.17
9	3	LINSEY, KELLY		1,500.00	234,765.36	11,738.27	13,238.27	187,956.76	9,397.84	10,897.84	215050.16	10,752.51	12,252.51
10	4	JOHNSON, LETOYA		1,500.00	89,765.43	4,488.27	5,988.27	93,984.69	4,699.23	6,199.23	98463.14	4,923.16	6,423.16
11	5	RIVERA, TONY		1,500.00	287,987.76	14,399.39	15,899.39	254,768.60	12,738.43	14,238.43	246315.19	12,315.76	13,815.76
12	6	THOMPSON, JIM		1,500.00							76451.13	3,822.56	5,322.56
13													
14		TOTALS		9,000.00	876,630.09	43,831.50	51,331.50	794,329.65	39,716.48	47,216.48	901,392.30	45,069.62	54,069.62
15		AVERAGES		1,500.00	175,326.02	8,766.30	10,266.30	158,865.93	7,943.30	9,443.30	150,232.05	7,511.60	9,011.60
16		HIGHEST		1,500.00	287,987.76	14,399.39	15,899.39	254,768.60	12,738.43	14,238.43	246,315.19	12,315.76	13,815.76
17		LOWEST		1,500.00	89,765.43	4,488.27	5,988.27	93,984.69	4,699.23	6,199.23	76,451.13	3,822.56	5,322.56

Range A1:D17 named EMPS

COPY AND PASTE SPECIAL (COMBINE DATA)

Combines data copied to the paste area in the way you specify.

- Select range of worksheet to extract.

- Click **Edit** .... Alt + E

- Click **Copy** C

To change destination workbook or worksheet:

Select workbook and/or sheet to receive data.

- Select upper-left cell in destination area.

- Click **Edit** .... Alt + E

- Click **Paste Special**.......................... S

7. Select **Paste** option:

   - **All** .... A
   - **Formulas** .... F
   - **Values** V
   - **Formats** .... T
   - **Notes** .... N

   To combine copied data with paste area data:

   Select **Operation** option:

   - **None** .... O
   - **Add** .... D
   - **Subtract** .... S
   - **Multiply** .... M
   - **Divide** I

To prevent overwriting existing data with blank cells:

Click **Skip Blanks**.................... B

To change orientation of data in paste area:

Click **Transpose**........................ E

8. Click OK .... ↵

EXERCISE

23

- COPY AND PASTE SPECIAL (EXTRACT AND COMBINE DATA)
- CREATE NEW WORKBOOK ■ SELECT WORKBOOK
- DELETE COLUMNS AND ROWS ■ NAMED RANGES

NOTES:

In this exercise, you will update the Green Thumb Landscape Service worksheet to include fourth-quarter data. In addition, you will create a new worksheet comparing quarterly data using Copy and Paste Special to extract and combine file data.

EXERCISE DIRECTIONS:

1. Open ⌨ **IS** or 💾 **EIS.23**.

2. Delete the COMBINED TOTALS column.

3. Enter fourth-quarter data indicated below, beginning in the next available column of your worksheet.

	N	O	P	Q
1				
2				
3				
4				4TH QTR.
5	OCT	NOV	DEC	TOTALS
6				
7				
8	9968.54	6235.87	5256.78	
9	1065.93	968.54	1054.32	
10				
11				
12				
13	150.00	55.00	55.00	
14	1255.00	754.65	754.65	
15	1435.62	567.87	102.54	
16	95.87	325.65	627.89	
17	25.00	25.00	25.00	
18	546.87	325.87	95.87	
19				

4. Copy formulas, where necessary, to complete the worksheet.

5. Find 4TH QTR. TOTALS.

6. Copy the formula to the remaining items.

7. Center column title labels.

8. Format numeric data for two decimal places.

9. Create the following named ranges (notice underscores) for each quarterly total column:
   _1ST_QTR
   _2ND_QTR
   _3RD_QTR
   _4TH_QTR

   ✓ *Note: Include blank cells in column, for example E1:E21 for _1ST_QTR.*

10. Clear the freeze on Column A titles.

11. Save the file, or *save as* **IS**.

12. Use the Copy and Paste Special commands to extract column A data, rows 1 through 21, to cell A1 in a new workbook file; save and name the new workbook **ISQTRS.**

    HINT: Use the name box to select the named references quickly.

13. In ISQTRS workbook, enter a worksheet title beginning in cell C1 that reads:
    GREENTHUMB LANDSCAPE SERVICE
    QUARTERLY INCOME STATEMENT COMPARISON

14. Select the IS workbook.

15. Use the Copy and Paste Special commands to copy the named range _1ST_QTR to the range beginning in C1 in the ISQTRS workbook.

    *IMPORTANT: Set the Paste option to **Values**, Operation option to **None**, and select **Skip Blanks**.*

Continued..

6. Repeat step 15 for the _2ND_QTR, _3RD_QTR, and _4TH_QTR named ranges. Paste ranges in ISQTRS workbook in columns D1, E1, and F1, respectively.

– FROM ISQTRS WORKBOOK –

7. Enter title in column G:

COMBINED

TOTALS

18. Find the combined total for Service Fees INCOME.

19. Copy the formula to the remaining items.

20. Format all numeric values for two decimal places.

21. Adjust column widths as needed.

22. Save the **ISQTRS** workbook and print one copy.

23. Close the workbook files.

Insert 4TH QTR data

	A	B	C	D	E	F	G	H	I	J	K	L	M	N	O
1		COMPARATIVE INCOME STATEMENT													
2		GREEN THUMB LANDSCAPE SERVICE													
3															
4					1ST QTR.				2ND QTR.	COMBINED				3RD QTR.	
5		JANUARY	FEBRUARY	MARCH	TOTALS	APRIL	MAY	JUNE	TOTALS	TOTALS	JULY	AUGUST	SEPT.	TOTALS	
6															
7	INCOME														
8	Service Fees	5342.87	5543.65	6165.87	17052.39	8343.84	9862.89	10359.45	28566.18	4561 8.57	11986.45	11050.65	10573.87	33610.97	
9	Consultations	1564.98	1654.76	1689.76	4909.50	1893.65	1498.62	1287.49	4679.76	9589.26	1343.27	1186.87	965.78	3495.92	
10	Total Income	6907.85	7198.41	7855.63	21961.89	10237.49	11361.51	11646.94	33245.94	55207.83	13329.72	12237.52	11539.65	37106.89	
11															
12	EXPENSES:														
13	Advertising	55.00	65.00	150.00	270.00	150.00	165.00	165.00	480.00	750.00	165.00	165.00	150.00	480	
14	Salaries	754.65	754.65	1255.55	2764.85	1255.55	1255.55	1255.55	3766.65	6531.50	1255.55	1255.55	1255.00	3766.1	
15	Supplies	154.76	245.65	589.53	989.94	769.54	965.62	1276.54	3011.70	4001.64	1887.98	1667.09	1654.98	5210.05	
16	Truck Maint	95.00	125.54	243.98	464.52	185.87	543.51	324.65	1054.03	1518.55	486.98	245.90	327.65	1060.53	
17	Interest	25.00	25.00	25.00	75.00	25.00	25.00	25.00	75.00	150.00	25.00	25.00	25.00	75	
18	Other	143.43	43.54	231.65	418.62	326.43	654.65	798.43	1779.51	2198.13	674.79	543.87	476.98	1695.64	
19	Total Expenses	1227.84	1259.38	2495.71	4982.93	2712.39	3609.33	3845.17	10166.89	15149.82	4495.30	3902.41	3889.61	12287.32	
20															
21	NET INCOME	5680.01	5939.03	5359.92	16978.96	7525.10	7752.18	7801.77	23079.05	40058.01	8834.42	8335.11	7650.04	24819.57	
22															
23															
24															

Extract to new file, ISQTRS

EXERCISE

24

■ TEMPLATES ■ ARRANGE WORKBOOKS ■ LINK WORKBOOKS

NOTES:

Templates

■ When you need to create multiple workbooks containing similar data and formulas, you can save a model workbook as a **template**. When you open a template file, Excel opens a copy of it and leaves the original file as it was so you can use it again.

> ✓ Note: Template files have .XLT filename extensions.

Arrange Workbooks

■ When working with a number of open files, you may want to use the **Arrange** command on the Window menu to position the workbook windows automatically so you can easily select one or the other workbook.

Link Workbooks

■ **Linking workbooks** allows you to consolidate and merge data from several workbooks into one summary workbook. Linking allows the summary workbook to be automatically or manually updated when the linked data changes.

■ The workbooks that provide the data are referred to as **source workbooks**; the workbook that references the data is referred to as the **dependent workbook**. References to cells in other workbooks are called **external references**.

■ By default, links are set to automatic updating. Excel updates links when you open the dependent workbook and when the source workbook data is changed when the dependent workbook is open.

■ Linking differs from combining data (Copy and Paste Special) in that the combining

of data merely copies, adds, or subtracts data to the dependent file. A change in the source workbook can not be made to update the dependent workbook except by repeating the combining procedure.

■ There are three ways to link a file:

• The copied data from the source workbook may be pasted into the dependent workbook as a **pasted link** which automatically creates an external reference that links the workbooks.

> ✓ Note: In this exercise, we will use the Paste Link method.

• An external reference may be typed in a formula using the following format:
drive:\path\[file.xls]sheetname!reference
EXAMPLES:
=c:\excel\[SAM.xls]Sheet1!A1 creates a link to A1 in SAM workbook.

=sum([sam.xls]Sheet1!A1:D1) + B3 finds sum of A1:D1 in SAM workbook and adds it to contents of B3 in current workbook.

> ✓ Note: If the source file is in the same directory you can omit the path.

• An external reference may be added to a formula by selecting cells in the source workbook while editing or creating a formula in the dependent workbook.

■ If the external reference includes a formula, only the formula result will be brought forward.

■ When possible, follow these guidelines for saving linked workbooks:

• Save linked workbooks in the same directory.

• Save the source workbooks before the dependent workbook.

■ An illustration of the linking process appears on the right.

	KITCHEN KING			
	SALES CONSULTANT:		SAM JIN	
	MONTHLY SALES AND SALARY STATEMENT			
PRODUCTS				
	Cabinets		42067.00	
	Appliances		18956.00	
	Installations		22954.00	
	TOTAL SALES			83977.00
COMMISSION @ 3%				2519.31
BASE SALARY			550.00	
Taxes Withheld			135.75	
NET PAY				414.25
TOTAL COMPENSATION				2933.56

	KITCHEN KING			
	SALES CONSULTANT:		CAROL MANNING	
	MONTHLY SALES AND SALARY STATEMENT			
PRODUCTS				
	Cabinets		37549.00	
	Appliances		13598.00	
	Installations		19567.00	
	TOTAL SALES			70714.00
COMMISSION @ 3%				2121.42
BASE SALARY			550.00	
Taxes Withheld			135.75	
NET PAY				414.25
TOTAL COMPENSATION				2535.67

	KITCHEN KING				
	MONTHLY SALES COMMISSION AND SALARY SUMMARY				
SALES CONSULTANT		SAM	CAROL	JOHN	TOTALS
SALES		83977.00	70714.00	67189.00	221880.00
COMMISSION		2519.31	2121.42	2015.67	6656.40
NET PAY		414.25	414.25	374.25	1202.75
TOTAL PAYMENT		2933.56	2535.67	2389.92	7859.15

	KITCHEN KING			
	SALES CONSULTANT:		JOHN WILLIAMS	
	MONTHLY SALES AND SALARY STATEMENT			
PRODUCTS				
	Cabinets		32987.00	
	Appliances		16549.00	
	Installations		17653.00	
	TOTAL SALES			67189.00
COMMISSION @ 3%				2015.67
BASE SALARY			500.00	
Taxes Withheld			125.75	
NET PAY				374.25
TOTAL COMPENSATION				2389.92

In this exercise, the Kitchen King Company creates a monthly sales and salary statement for each sales consultant. They would like a summary workbook consolidating the information about the consultants' sales performance. Using the Linking feature, the data on the consolidated workbook will automatically update monthly as the consultant data changes.

EXERCISE DIRECTIONS:

1. Create template workbook A, as indicated on the right, or open 💾 **ESALETMP.24**.

2. Add formulas to template to find:
   - TOTAL SALES
   - COMMISSION at 3%
   - NET PAY
   - TOTAL COMPENSATION

   ✓ *Note: Formulas will result in zero values.*

3. Format all money columns for two decimal places.

4. Save the file as a template; name it **SALETMP.**

5. Close **SALETMP.**

6. Reopen **SALETMP.**

   HINT: *Since you just saved the file, you can select it from near the bottom of the **File** menu.*

   ✓ *Note: Excel opens a copy of the template file and renames it **SALETMP1**.*

7. Use the template to create a workbook for each sales consultant using the data below. After each workbook is completed, save and name each workbook file SAM, CAROL, and JOHN, respectively.

   ✓ *Note: Do not close these files after saving.*

8. Open a new workbook and create workbook B (dependent), as indicated on the right; save the workbook; name it **SUMM** or open 💾 **ESUMM.24**.

9. Minimize all workbook windows except **SAM** and **SUMM;** arrange the open workbooks so data in both can be seen.

10. Link TOTAL SALES, COMMISSION, and NET PAY in SAM workbook to the cells D6, D7, and D8 in SUMM workbook.

    ✓ *Note: ·You can use a multiple selection to do this in one step or link each reference one at a time.*

11. Minimize SAM workbook.

12. Open CAROL workbook icon; arrange open workbooks.

13. Link TOTAL SALES, COMMISSION, smf NET PAY in CAROL workbook to the cells E6, E7, and E8 in SUMM workbook.

14. Minimize CAROL workbook.

15. Open JOHN workbook icon; arrange open workbooks.

16. Link TOTAL SALES, COMMISSION, and NET PAY in JOHN workbook to the cells G6, G7, and G8 in SUMM workbook.

CONSULTANT:	SAM JIN	CAROL MANNING	JOHN WILLIAMS
Cabinets	42067.00	37549.00	32987.00
Appliances	18956.00	13598.00	16549.00
Installations	22954.00	19567.00	17653.00
BASE SALARY	550.00	550.00	500.00
Taxes Withheld	135.75	135.75	125.75

Continued..

17. Find all totals in SUMM workbook.

18. Save the SUMM workbook.

19. Print one copy of SUMM workbook.

20. Minimize all windows except SAM and SUMM; arrange open workbooks 8. Open a new workbook and create workbook B (dependent), as indicated on the right; save the workbook; name it SUMM.

21. Select SAM workbook and change his cabinet sales to $42067.

22. Note the updated values in the SAM column of the SUMM workbook and the updated totals.

23. Close all workbook files, *without* resaving.

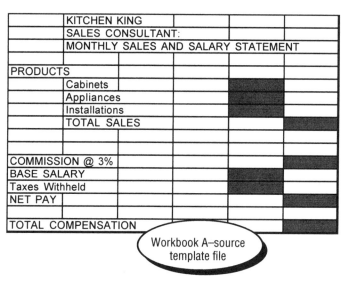

Workbook A–source template file

Workbook B dependent file

CREATE A TEMPLATE WORKBOOK

Saves and names the active workbook as a template file.

1. Click **File** .... `Alt`+`F`
2. Click **Save As** .... `A`
3. Click **Save File as Type** .... `Alt`+`T`
4. Select **Template** file type .... `↑/↓`, `↵`
5. Double-click in **File Name** ..... `Alt`+`N`
6. Type filename ....*filename*
7. Click `OK` .... `↵`

   ✓ *If the Summary Info dialog box appears, enter summary information as desired.*

ARRANGE WORKBOOK WINDOWS

1. Click **Window** .... `Alt`+`W`
2. Click **Arrange** .... `A`

3. Select desired **Arrange** option:

   • **Tiled** .... `T`
   • **Horizontal** .... `O`
   • **Vertical** .... `V`
   • **Cascade** .... `C`
4. Click `OK` .... `↵`

ORIGINAL TEMPLATE FILE

Normally, Excel opens a copy of a template file. Use this procedure to open the original template file.

1. Follows steps 1 and 2 to **OPEN A WORKBOOK FILE**, page 218.

2. Press **Shift** and
   click `OK` .... `Shift`+`↵`

LINK WORKBOOKS USING PASTE LINK

1. Open workbooks to link.

2. Arrange workspace so both workbooks are in view.

3. Select cell(s) to reference in source workbook.

4. Click **Edit** .... `Alt`+`E`
5. Click **Copy** .... `C`
6. Select cell(s) to receive reference(s) in dependent workbook.

   ✓ *If referencing more than one cell, select upper-left cell in paste cell range.*

7. Click **Edit** .... `Alt`+`E`
8. Click **Paste Special** .... `S`
9. Click `Paste Link` .... `Alt`+`L`
10. Press **Escape** .... `Esc`
    to end procedure.

EXERCISE

■ **WORKBOOK SHEETS** ■ **3-D FORMULAS** ■ **DUPLICATE WORKBOOK WINDOW**
■ **SELECT WORKBOOK** ■ **PRINT WORKSHEET ON SPECIFIED NUMBER**
OF PAGES ■ **ARRANGE WORKBOOKS**

NOTES:

3-D Formulas

■ You can use references to values that exist in any sheet or range of sheets in a workbook. These references are often called **3-D references**.

■ In a 3-D reference, exclamation points (!) separate the sheet name from the cell reference. Colons (:) between the worksheet names indicate a range of worksheets. Use quotation marks if the worksheet name contains a space.

To refer to:	3D reference examples:
Cells in a **different worksheet** (Sales 96)	"Sales 96"!A1:D1
Cells in r**ange of worksheets** (ranges A1:D4 on Sheet3 through Sheet5)	Sheet3:Sheet5!A1:D4

■ You can type a 3-D reference in a formula, or you can insert it by selecting the cells in the worksheet you wish to reference while typing or editing a formula.

   ✓ *Note the illustration of a 3-D reference on the following page.*

Workbook Sheets

■ You can use the sheet tabs or the menu to **copy sheets** and the data they contain. You should consider copying a sheet when you need to create multiple sheets that contain similar or identical data arrangements.

Duplicate Workbook Window

■ You can create **duplicate workbook windows** of the active workbook to view more than one worksheet at a time.

Consider the following when working with duplicate workbook windows:

• Excel places the new workbook window in front of the active workbook window.
   ✓ *Note:*   *If the active workbook is maximized, you will not be able to see the new workbook.*

• Duplicate workbook windows are indicated in the title bar which shows the workbook name followed by a colon and a number. For example, BOOK1:1

• Your system memory determines the amount of duplicate windows you can open.

• Closing a duplicate window will not close the workbook.

• You can add or edit data in the original or duplicate window.

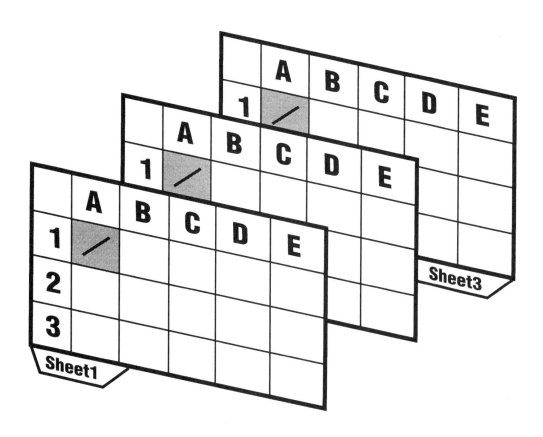

EXAMPLE: Using 3-D references to add the
            values in A1 in a range of sheets.

            =SUM(Sheet1:Sheet3!A1) or
            =Sheet1!A1+Sheet2!A1+Sheet 3!A1

In this exercise, you will recall the SALNEW payroll file and add a new worksheet (Totals) to it. In the new worksheet you will enter formulas containing 3-D references to the May, June, and July worksheets. Finally, you will open a duplicate workbook window so you can view the Totals worksheet while you change test values in the May worksheet.

EXERCISE DIRECTIONS:

1. Open ⌨ **SALNEW** or 💾 **ESALNEW.25**.

2. Copy the July sheet.

3. Rename July (2) sheet; name it **Totals**.

4. Move the Totals tab to the right of July.

5. Group the May, June, and July worksheets.

6. Select May and while worksheets are grouped enter test values in the HOURS WORKED columns for each employee as shown:

   10   for first payroll week

   20   for second payroll week

   30   for third payroll week

7. Deselect grouped sheets and check that test values have been entered on each month's worksheet.

8. Select cell E7 in the TOTALS worksheet and enter a 3-D formula that adds the values in cell E7 in the May, June, and July worksheet.

   HINT: The completed formula should read: =May!E7+June!E7+July!E7 and the 30 (the sum of the test values) should appear in the cell.

9. Repeat step 8 for each employee in each payroll week.

10. Open a duplicate workbook window and select the Totals worksheet in the duplicate window.

11. Arrange workbook windows so data in both workbook windows is in view.

12. Select the May worksheet in the original window and change the HOURS WORKED test values in the first payroll week to 50 for each employee.

    ✓ *Note that the Totals worksheet in the duplicate window shows updated values.*

13. Change the HOURS WORKED test values back to 10.

14. Close the duplicate workbook window.

15. Select the Totals worksheet and set it to fit on one page when printed.

16. Print the Totals worksheet.

17. Group the May, June, and July worksheets.

18. Select the May worksheet and delete all test values in HOURS WORKED.

19. Deselect grouped sheets and check that test values have been deleted on each month's worksheet.

20. Save **SALNEW** as a template file.

21. Close the workbook file.

COPY SHEETS WITHIN A WORKBOOK

✓ *Excel will rename sheets that you copy.*

Copy One Sheet by Dragging

Press **Ctrl** and ....  Sheet #
Drag sheet tab to copy to
desired sheet tab position.

Pointer becomes a 🖑, *and black triangle
indicates point of insertion.*

Copy Multiple Sheets by Dragging

. Select sheets to copy.

. Press **Ctrl** and drag selected sheet tabs to
desired sheet tab position.

Pointer becomes a 🖑, *and black triangle
indicates point of insertion.*

Copy Sheets Using the Menu

. Select sheets to copy.

. Click **Edit** .... `Alt`+`E`

. Click **Move or Copy Sheet** ...... `Alt`+`M`

. Select location in **Before Sheet** ...... `↑↓`
list to insert copied sheet.

. Click **Create a Copy** .... `Alt`+`C`

. Click `  OK  ` .... `⏎`

INSERT 3-D REFERENCE IN FORMULA

1. If necessary, type or edit formula.

2. Place insertion point in formula where
reference will be inserted.

3. Select sheet containing cell(s) to
reference.

   ✓ *When you click a sheet tab, its name
   appears in the formula bar.*

4. Select cell(s) to reference.

   ✓ *When you select the cell(s), the
   complete 3-D reference appears in
   the formula bar.*

   **To enter a 3-D reference for a range of
   worksheets:**

   Press **Shift** and click last worksheet tab to
   reference.

5. Type or insert remaining parts of formula.

6. Press **Enter** .... `⏎`

   ✓ *When you press Enter, Excel returns
   to the starting worksheet*

TYPE A 3-D REFERENCE IN FORMULA

1. If necessary, type or edit formula.

2. Place insertion point in formula where
reference will be typed.

3. Type the sheet name ....*sheetname*

   ✓ *If the sheet name contains a space,
   type single or double quotes before
   and after the sheet name.*

**To type a 3-D reference for a range of
worksheets:**

a. Press **colon** (:) .... `:`

b. Type last sheet name ....*sheet name*
   in range

4. Press **exclamation** (!) .... `!`

5. Type cell reference or range ....*reference*

   EXAMPLES: *Sheet1:Sheet5!A1:A5*
   'Total Sales'!A1:A5

OPEN A DUPLICATE WORKBOOK WINDOW

*Creates a new window for active workbook
window.*

1. Click **Window** .... `Alt`+`W`

2. Click **New Window** .... `N`

CLOSE A DUPLICATE WORKBOOK WINDOW

Double-click workbook window
control menu box .... `▭`

   OR

1. Select duplicate........... `Ctrl`+`Tab`
   workbook

2. Press **Alt + F4**................ `Alt`+`F4`

LESSON 4
SUMMARY EXERCISE 26

Ms. Eastman administered three additional exams plus a final examination to her class. She needs to revise the worksheet she prepared earlier to include new test data and two new students. In addition, Ms. Eastman's supervisor has requested a separate worksheet showing student names and final exam averages.

EXERCISE DIRECTIONS:

✓ Note: *Freeze row labels to facilitate data entry.*

1. Open ⌨ **TEST** or 💾 **ETEST.26**.

2. Insert rows in alphabetical sequence for the following two new students: Einhorn, J., ID# 211 and Hawthorne, M., ID# 212.

3. Insert the columns of data, as shown on the right, for TESTS 4, 5, and 6 after the TEST 3 column.

4. Edit the NO. TESTS TAKEN and TEST AVERAGE columns to include the new test data.

5. Enter the FINAL EXAM grades after the TEST AVERAGE column:

    Aaronson, 72; Barnett, 85; Costello, 86; Dionesios, 70; Einhorn, 69; Ellenberg, 65; Fallstaff, 91; Garcia, 71; Hamway, 89; Hawthorne, 71; Ianelli, 61; Jae Woo, 80; Kelly, 96

6. Find the FINAL AVERAGE for each student. The final exam is worth 1/3 of the final average, while the tests are worth 2/3 of the final average.

    HINT: (FINAL EXAM + TEST AVERAGE + TEST AVERAGE)/3

7. Format test averages to one decimal place and center new titles.

8. Complete the worksheet.

9. Save the workbook file, or *save as* **TEST**.

10. Print one copy to fit on a page.

11. Using the Copy and Paste Special feature, create separate workbook showing student names and final averages.

12. Create an appropriate title.

13. Save the new file; name it **TESTSUM**.

14. Print one copy of TESTSUM.

15. Close the workbook files.

	A	F	G	H
1				
2				
3				
4				
5	STUDENT	TEST 4	TEST 5	TEST 6
6	Aaronson, M.	75		69
7	Barnett, F.	85	79	82
8	Costello, A.	83	84	76
9	Dionesios, A.	76	74	78
10	Einhorn, J.	52	61	70
11	Ellenberg, S.		69	52
12	Falstaff, L.	84	88	
13	Garcia, H.	72		80
14	Hamway, R.	82	85	81
15	Hawthorne, M.	41	59	57
16	Ianelli, J.	72	76	79
17	Jae Woo, K.		84	73
18	Kelly,G.	91	94	84
19				
20	NO. OF PAPEI			
21	CLASS AVERA			
22	HIGHEST GRA			
23	LOWEST GRA			
24				

LESSON 5

LOGICAL FUNCTIONS; AUTOFORMAT; PROTECTING AND HIDING DATA

Exercises 27-34

- Insert IF Functions

- Enter a Date as Numerical Data

- Format Numerical Dates

- AutoFormat

- Color Buttons

- What-if Data Tables

- Insert Lookup Functions

- Protect a Sheet

- Lock Cells in a Worksheet

EXERCISE

▪ INSERT AN IF FUNCTION

NOTES:

▪ An **IF statement** is a logical function which sets up a conditional statement to test data. The truth or falsity of the condition will determine the results of the statement.

▪ The format for an IF statement is:
=IF(CONDITION,X,Y)

▪ Note that if the condition is true, the function results in X; if the condition is false, the function results in Y.

▪ In this exercise, the teacher uses an IF statement to determine the final grade based on the final average. The passing grade is 71. Therefore, an IF statement can be used to test whether the final average is greater than 70.9, then the student passes and the word PASS is entered in the function location. If the condition is false, the word FAIL is entered in the function location.

✓ Note the breakdown of one of the IF statement formulas used in this problem:

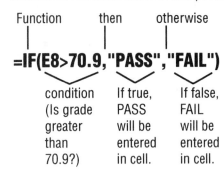

✓ Note: Since PASS and FAIL are labels, you must enclose them in quotation marks (").

▪ IF statements may use conditional operators of:

=	Equals	<=	Less than or equal to
>	Greater than	>=	Greater than or equal to
<	Less than	&	Used for text concatenation
<>	Not equal to		

✓ Note: IF statements may be used in combination with OR, AND, and NOT statements to evaluate complex conditions.

In this exercise, you will calculate the FINAL GRADE and CREDITS GRANTED for Roberta Eastman's class based on a 71% passing grade by using IF statements.

EXERCISE DIRECTIONS:

1. Open 🖳 **TESTSUM** or 🖫 **ETESTSUM.27**.

2. Insert the following columns after FINAL AVERAGES:

   FINAL   CREDITS

   GRADE   GRANTED

3. Enter an IF statement for the first student in the FINAL GRADE column that will produce the word PASS if the final average is greater than 70.9 and FAIL if it is not.

4. Copy the formula to the other students.

Continued..

5. Enter an IF statement for the first student in the CREDITS GRANTED column that will produce the number three if the final average is greater than 70.9 and zero if it is not.

6. Copy the formula to the other students.

7. Center all new entries.

8. Delete the row containing Number of Papers.

9. Print one copy of the worksheet.

11. Close and save the workbook file, or *save as* **TESTSUM**.

FINAL AVERAGES			
BUSINESS MANAGEMENT 101			
MS. ROBERTA EASTMAN			
STUDENT	FINAL AVERAGE	*FINAL GRADE*	*CREDITS GRANTED*
Aaronson, M.	77.1		
Barnett, F.	82.3		
Costello, A.	80.8		
Dionesios, A.	76.1		
Einhorn, J.	63.7		
Ellenberg, L.	68.9		
Falstaff, S.	87.4		
Garcia, H.	77.4		
Hamway, R.	83.3		
Hawthorne, M.	58.6		
Ianelli, J.	73.0		
Jae Woo, K.	77.8		
Kelly, G.	90.6		
NO. OF PAPERS			
CLASS AVERAGE	76.7		
HIGHEST GRADE	91		
LOWEST GRADE	59		

INSERT AN IF FUNCTION USING FUNCTION WIZARD

✓ *You can also type a function to insert it.*

1. Click cell .... [image]

2. Click **Function Wizard** button .... [*f*∞] on Standard toolbar.

3. Select **Logical** .... [image] in **Function Category** list.

4. Select **IF** function .... **Function Name** list.

5. Click [Next >] .... [↵]

6. Type condition .... *condition* in **logical_test** box.

✓ *You can click cells in worksheet to insert cell references.*

7. Click **value_if_true** box .... [Tab]

8. Type the argument .... *argument* if condition is true.

9. Click **value_if_false** box .... [Tab]

10. Type the argument .... *argument* if condition is false.

11. Click [Finish] .... [↵]

EXERCISE

IF FUNCTION | 28

NOTES:

- An IF statement may be created to perform one calculation if the condition is true and perform another calculation if the condition is false.

- When creating a condition using the **greater than** operator (>), care must be taken to use the correct value. In this problem, when testing if the years of seniority are more than 5, it is necessary to use >5 or >=6 in the formula so that a value of 5 is interpreted as a false condition.

The Killington Manufacturing Company has decided to change its policy and give salary increases based on seniority. Employees who have more than five years of service will receive a 7.25% raise; otherwise, they will receive a 4.5% raise.

You will do a salary analysis by comparing the amount of SALARY and % INCREASE each employee received this year over last year. In addition, you will show the effects of the new policy by showing the amount of the raise, percent of increase, and the new salary each employee will receive for the next year.

EXERCISE DIRECTIONS:

1. Create the worksheet on the right exactly as shown or open ⌷ **EINCR.28**.

2. Freeze titles vertically at column E.

3. Find:
   - AMOUNT OF RAISE (from 1993 to 1994)
   - % INCREASE (based on 1993 salary)

4. Copy the formula to the remaining employees.

5. Using YEARS OF SENIORITY as a condition, create an IF statement to enter the AMOUNT OF RAISE for 1995.

   HINT: If YEARS OF SENIORITY is greater than five (>5 or >=6), compute a 7.25% raise; otherwise, compute a 4.5% raise.

6. Using YEARS OF SENIORITY as a condition, create an IF statement to enter the percent of the raise (7.25% or 4.5%) in the % INCREASE column.

   HINT: If YEARS OF SENIORITY is greater than five, .0725; otherwise, .045.

7. Format all money columns for two decimal places and all percent columns for two-place percents.

8. Find SALARY 1995.

9. Copy the formula to the remaining employees.

10. Total all money columns.

11. Set column widths, as necessary.

12. Clear the freeze.

13. Save the file; name it **INCR**.

14. Print one copy to fit on a page.

15. Close the file.

EMPLOYEE		YEARS OF SENIORITY	SALARY 1993	SALARY 1994	AMOUNT OF RAISE	% INCREASE		1995 SALARY DATA AMOUNT OF RAISE	% INCREASE	SALARY 1995
		KILLINGTON MANUFACTURING COMPANY								
		ANALYSIS OF SALARY INCREASES								
Miller, John		15	45500.00	49000.00						
Vantnor, Link		11	32300.00	35000.00						
Barrow, Wilson		5	16500.00	17500.00						
Abrahams, Larry		3	18500.00	20000.00						
Nunex, Maria		7	21000.00	23000.00						
Tse, Sandra		4	25600.00	27000.00						
D"Agostino, Joe		8	28500.00	30000.00						
Harrison, Reggie		9	33000.00	35000.00						
Wingate, George		6	25400.00	27000.00						
Ingold, Terry		10	38000.00	41500.00						
TOTALS										

EXERCISE

■ ENTER A DATE AS NUMERICAL DATA ■ FORMAT NUMERICAL DATES

NOTES:

Enter Date as Numerical Data

■ As previously noted, dates can be entered as label data, but when there is a need to add or subtract dates, they must be entered as numerical data.

■ Excel recognizes the number format you desire based on your data entry. For example, if you enter 25%, the entry is recognized as a value with the percent format.

■ Excel also provides a handy shortcut for entering the current date. Pressing the Ctrl key and the semicolon (;) inserts the date automatically.

Format Numerical Dates

■ If you enter a date in one of the standard formats Excel automatically recognizes the entry as a numerical date value or **serial value**.

> ✓ Note: To view a serial value for a date, format the date as a number.

■ Illustrated below are a number of **standard date formats** Excel recognizes as numerical date values. Notice the serial value for a date and time is expressed as a decimal number. When you subtract one date value from another, Excel subtracts the serial values of the numbers and displays the result. In the Excel date system, the date January 1, 1900 is represented by the serial value 1.

Formats:	Example Entries	Formula Bar:	Serial values:
mm/d/yy	12/24/00	12/24/1900	359
d-mmm-yy	12/24/00	12/24/2000	36884
d-mmm	25-Jul	07/25/95	34905
mmm-yy	Jul-95	07/25/95	34905
mm/d/yy hh:mm	12/24/00 6:30	12/24/2000 6:30 AM	36884

In this exercise, you will make modifications to a stock analysis worksheet to find how many days each stock was held. You will then be able to determine the annual rate of return on each stock. In addition, you will modify the range named PRINTALL to include the larger worksheet.

EXERCISE DIRECTIONS:

1. Create the Worksheet as shown on the next page, or open 🖫 **EMARKET.29**.

    REMINDER: Columns A and B were frozen when this file was previously saved.

2. Edit the title to include the current year.

3. Set column width to 10 for DATE BOUGHT and DATE SOLD columns.

Continued..

4. Insert dates, using the year provided, as numerical data.

5. Format the dates to D-MMM-Y format.

6. Find DAYS HELD.
   Hint: DATE SOLD-DATE BOUGHT

7. Find the ANNUAL YIELD based on a 365 day year.
   Hint: (DIVIDENDS EARNED/COST)/DAYS HELD*365

8. FIND the GAIN OR LOSS.
   Hint: SELLING PRICE-COST.

9. Find the % GAIN OR LOSS.
   Hint: GAIN OR LOSS/COST

10. Copy the formulas to the remaining stocks.

11. Center all column titles.

12. Format the ANNUAL YIELD and % GAIN OR LOSS columns for two-place percents.

13. Format GAIN OR LOSS for two-place decimals.

14. Find the totals for the SELLING PRICE, COST, DIVIDENDS EARNED, and GAIN OR LOSS columns.

15. Copy the formula from the % GAIN OR LOSS column to the totals line to find the % gain or loss on the portfolio.

16. Create a range named PRINTALL to include the entire worksheet.

17. Print one copy to fit on a page using the range PRINTALL.

18. Save and close the workbook file as **MARKET**.

			LAWRENCE WILSON							
			STOCK ANALYSIS - TRANSACTIONS FOR 1994							
NO. OF	COMPANY		DATE	DATE		SELLING		DIVIDENDS		GAIN OR	% GAIN OR
SHARES	NAME	SYMBOL	BOUGHT	SOLD		PRICE	COST	EARNED		LOSS	LOSS
200	General Auto	GNA	15-Jan-94	5-Nov-94		6548.95	7453.76	585.50		-319.31	-4.28%
100	Paul Moggis	PM	31-Jan-94	30-Jun-94		9057.43	6923.12	325.40		2459.71	35.53%
50	IGM	IGM	17-Feb-94	25-Apr-94		3248.95	2576.98	0.00		671.97	26.08%
300	Unigen	UNI	17-Feb-94	5-Dec-94		3954.69	5391.23	0.00		-1436.54	-26.65%
500	Hewett Gas	HG	28-Mar-94	20-Dec-94		15487.54	14326.54	1054.50		2215.5	15.46%
	TOTALS					38297.56	36671.63	1965.40		3591.33	9.79%

Edit dates so they are formatted as numerical data as shown

ENTER DATE AS NUMERICAL DATA

✓ *Dates, entered as numerical data, are right-aligned and can be calculated.*

1. Select cell to receive date.

   To enter current date:

   Press **Ctrl + ;** (semicolon) .... [Ctrl]+[;]

   To enter a specific date:

   Type date ....*date*
   in valid format.

   You may use the following formats:

   - **m/d/yy** (e.g. 6/24/94)
   - **d-mmm** (e.g. 24-Jun)
   - **d-mmm-yy** (e.g. 24-Jun-94)
   - **mmm-yy** (e.g. Jun-94)

2. Press **Enter** .... [←]

   ✓ *If Excel displays number signs (######), the column is not wide enough to display the date. To see the entry, double-click the right border of the column heading.*

FORMAT NUMERICAL DATES

1. Select cells containing numerical dates to format.

2. a. Click **Format** .... [Alt]+[O]
   b. Click **Cells** .... [E]

   OR

   a. Right-click any selected cell.
   b. Click **Format Cells.**

3. Select **Number** tab .... [Ctrl]+[Tab]

4. Select **Date** .... [Alt]+[C], [↕]
   in **Category** list.

5. Select desired format.. [Alt]+[F], [↕]
   in **Format Codes** list:
   - m/d/yy
   - d-mmm-yy
   - d-mmm
   - mmm-yy
   - mm/d/yy h:mm

6. Click [OK] .... [←]

Excel

Lesson 5: Logical Functions; AutoFormat; Protecting and Hiding Data

EXERCISE

30

■ IF FUNCTION ■ NUMERICAL DATE FORMATS ■ NUMERICAL DATES
■ AUTOFORMAT ■ COLOR BUTTONS

NOTES:

AutoFormat

■ Excel provides built-in formats which can be applied to a range of data. These formats, **AutoFormats**, include number formats, fonts, borders, patterns, colors, alignments, row heights, and column widths. They give the worksheet a professional, organized appearance.

■ The AutoFormat dialog box provides a selection of table formats that may be applied to a range of data. (See the illustration below.) Any of the AutoFormats may be customized through the Options dialog box.

Color Buttons

■ The Color buttons on the Formatting Toolbar provide a palette of colors that can be used to color the foreground area or the text in a selected cell. (See the illustration below.)

■ Accounts Receivable are records for customers who owe money to a company. Aging of accounts receivable is done to determine how many days the customers' payments are overdue.

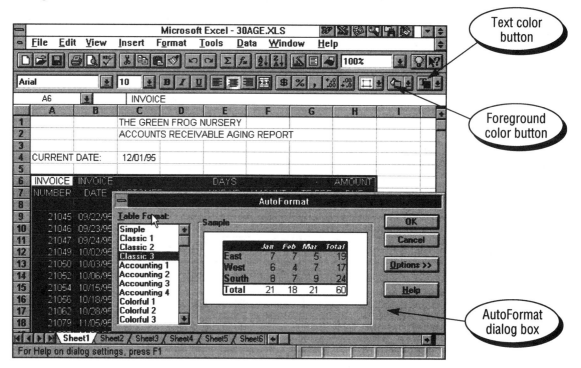

In this exercise, your supervisor has asked you to determine how many days, as of today (December 1, 1995), the accounts receivable invoices have been unpaid. In addition, she wants you to calculate a late fee of 1% on unpaid amounts that are outstanding for more than 30 days.

EXERCISE DIRECTIONS:

1. Create the worksheet below, or open 💾 **EAGE.30**.

2. Find the DAYS UNPAID.

   HINT: DAYS UNPAID = CURRENT DATE-
   INVOICE DATE

   ✓ Note: The reference to the current date
   should be an absolute reference.

3. Use an IF statement to find a 1% LATE FEE *only* if
   the days unpaid are greater than 30.

4. Copy the formula to the remaining invoices.

5. Find AMOUNT DUE and copy to all invoices.

6. Total all money columns.

7. Select the range A6 to H21 and choose the Classic
   3 table format in the AutoFormat dialog box.

   ✓ Note: As you highlight each table format, an
   example of the style appears in the
   Sample box.

8. Select the heading range A1 to H4 and do the
   following:

   • Format the text for bold type.

   • Change the foreground color to dark navy.

   • Change the text color to white.

9. Save the file; name it **AGE**.

10. Print one copy so that it all fits on one page.

11. Close the workbook file.

		THE GREEN FROG NURSERY					
		ACCOUNTS RECEIVABLE AGING REPORT					
CURRENT DATE:	12/01/95						
INVOICE	INVOICE			DAYS			AMOUNT
NUMBER	DATE	CUSTOMER		UNPAID	AMOUNT	LATE FEE	DUE
21045	09/22/95	BROWN BROTHERS			475.43		
21046	09/23/95	REDLY FARMS			321.43		
21047	09/24/95	BROWN BROTHERS			543.98		
21049	10/02/95	PINKSTON CORP.			32.45		
21050	10/03/95	J.J. BURGUNDY			1324.32		
21052	10/06/95	REDLY FARMS			124.98		
21054	10/15/95	BLUETOWN CO.			564.12		
21056	10/18/95	PINKSTON CORP.			187.65		
21062	10/28/95	J.J. BURGUNDY			454.56		
21079	11/05/95	M. MAROON			308.21		
21087	11/20/95	REDLY FARMS			163.28		
TOTALS							

APPLY AUTOFORMAT

1. Select range of data to be formatted.

2. Click **Format**............................ `Alt` + `O`

3. Click **AutoFormat**.............................. `A`

4. Select desired format.

5. Click `OK` .... `◄`

APPLY COLOR TO CELL FOREGROUND

1. Select object or range of cells.

2. Click on Foreground Color Button arrows.

3. Select color

OR

1. Select object or range of cells.

2. Click **Format** .... `Alt` + `O`

3. Click **Cells**...... .... `E`

4. Select **Patterns** tab .... `Ctrl` + `Tab`

5. Click **Color...** .... `Alt` + `C`

6. Select color.

7. Click **OK** `OK` .... `◄`

APPLY COLOR TO TEXT

1. Select range of data.

2. Click on Text Color Button arrows.

3. Select color.

OR

1. Select object or range of cells.

2. Click **Format** .... `Alt` + `O`

3. Click **Cells** .... `E`

4. Select **Font**......................... `►` `◄`

5. Click **Color** .... `Alt` + `C`

6. Select color.

7. Click **OK** `OK` .... `◄`

EXERCISE

■ WHAT-IF DATA TABLES ■ PAYMENT FUNCTION

NOTES:

What-If Data Tables

■ A **What-if worksheet** is used to answer a question based on one or more factors that might influence the outcome.

■ You can create a **data table** (what-if table) to evaluate a series of possible answers for values you supply in the first row and left-most column of the table. These values are called **substitution values.**

■ The data table created in a what-if problem may be used to evaluate different situations based on certain variables and enables you to find the best solution. For example, if you wanted to

purchase a home and can only afford to spend $1,000 per month on your mortgage payment, you might want to determine the maximum mortgage amount you can afford to borrow and the number of years for which you should apply. A data table should be created showing the mortgage payments for various loan amounts and loan payment periods. Then you can determine what you can afford.

When you use the data table command, Excel uses the formula in the upper-left corner of the table to calculate the substitution values. Data tables that require two sets of substitution values (a row and a column) are called **two-input data tables.** Note the illustration below:

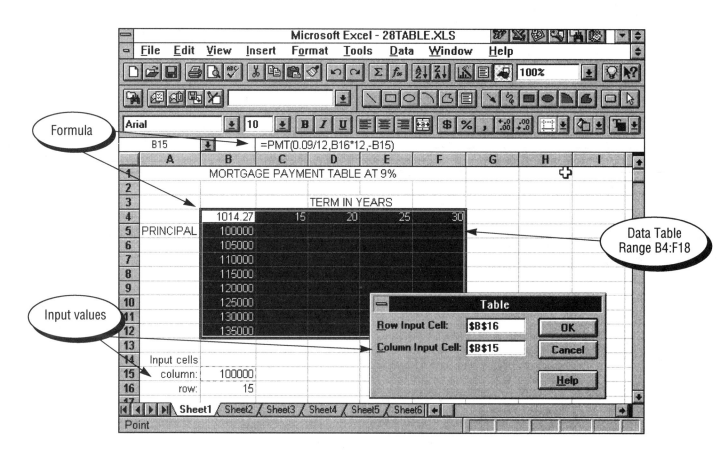

The format of a two-input data table must meet the following criteria:

- The **column and row input values** that the formula will refer to must be outside the table.
- The **formula** must be in the top-left cell of the table range and must refer to the column and row input values.
- The **substitution values** for the table must be arranged in the first row and column of the table as shown in illustration A.

To create the table values, you will select the data table range (which includes the formula), then indicate the row and column input cells (the cells that contain the column and row input values) from the Table dialog box.

Payment Function

The **PMT** (payment) **function** can be applied to calculate a loan payment amount using principal, interest rate, and number of payment periods. The PMT function uses the following format and contains three parts, which are defined on the right.

The arguments for the PMT function are:

=PMT *(rate,nper,pv)*

rate   Interest rate per period (for example, interest/12).

nper   Number of payment periods (for example, term*12).

pv   Present value – total amount that a series of future payments is worth now (for example, the principal).

✓ *Note:*   *The rate and the number of payment periods (nper) must be expressed in the same manner. For example, if you are calculating a <u>monthly</u> payment at a 9% rate of interest for 25 years and the interest is expressed as an annual rate, you must enter .09/12 as the rate; and if the term is expressed in years, you must enter 25*12 to get the number of monthly payment periods (nper).*

In this exercise, you will create a mortgage payment table to determine payment amounts at 9% for various principal amounts and for various numbers of years.

EXERCISE DIRECTIONS:

1. Create the worksheet below, or open 💾 **ETABLE.31**.

2a. Find in B4 the monthly mortgage payment for $100,000 at 9% for 15 years using the input cell data for principal and term.

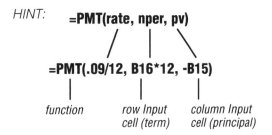

HINT: **=PMT(rate, nper, pv)**

=PMT(.09/12, B16*12, -B15)

function / row Input cell (term) / column Input cell (principal)

HINT: =PMT (rate, nper, pv)

✓ Note: If you type a minus sign before the principal, Excel finds a positive number as the monthly mortgage payment; otherwise, the result will be a negative number.

2b. The formula must reference the input values in cells B15 and B16. These input values will not affect the computed values in the table when it s generated.

3. Format answer for two decimal places.

4. Create a two variable data table by completing the Table dialog box.

5. Save the file; name it **TABLE**.

6. Print one copy.

❓ Based on the data in the table, what would be the highest principal you can borrow with a payment of approximately $1000 a month?

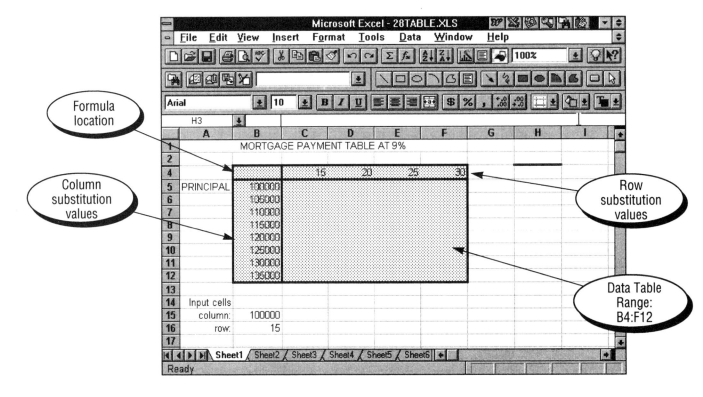

TWO-INPUT DATA TABLES (WHAT-IF TABLES)

Data tables generate values that change from one or two values in a formula. For example, a two-input table displays results of changing two values in a formula.

*The **row input cell** is used to indicate an initial input value that the formula will reference.*

*The **column input cell** is used to indicate an initial input value that the formula will also reference.*

✓ *Because Excel uses a table function to generate answers for each pair of substitution values, you cannot edit or delete any single value in the answer set. You can, however, delete **all the answers** in the generated data table.*

Although instructions listed below are for a two-input data table, you could also create a one-input data table that would find answers for a single row or column of substitution values.

CREATE A TWO-INPUT DATA TABLE

1. Enter initial value ....*number* in row input cell.

2. Enter initial value ....*number* in column input cell.

3. Enter series of substitution ....*numbers* values in a column.

4. Enter series of substitution ....*numbers* values in a row.

   ✓ *The first value in row and column will contain a single formula.*

5. Click upper-left cell .... 🔢 in table.

6. Type formula ....*formula*

   ✓ *Formula must refer to row and column input cells.*

7. Select all cells in data table range.

   ✓ *Select cells containing formula, substitution values and cells where results will be displayed.*

8. Click **Data** .... Alt + D

9. Click **Table** .... T

10. Click row input cell in worksheet.

    OR

    Type reference ....*reference* of input cell in **Row Input Cell** text box.

11. Click **Column Input Cell:** .... Alt + C

12. Click column input cell in worksheet.

    OR

    Type reference ....*reference* of column input cell.

13. Click [OK] .... ⏎

USE THE PMT FUNCTION

Applies the PMT function to find the monthly payment for a principal for a specific number of years.

1. Click cell .... 🔢 where answer should appear.

2. Press **Equal** .... =

3. Type *PMT* .... P M T

4. Press **(** (open parenthesis) .... (

5. Type rate /12 ....*rate* / 1 2

   ✓ *The **rate** is a percentage. You can type the percentage or type the cell reference containing the percentage.*

6. Press **,** (comma) .... ,

7. Type term *12 ....*term* * 1 2

   ✓ *The **term** is the number of years. You can type the number or type the cell reference containing the number.*

8. Press **,** (comma) .... ,

9. Type principal ....*principal*

   ✓ *The **principal** is the amount of the loan. You can type the amount or type the cell reference containing the amount. If you want the answer expressed as a positive number, type a minus sign before the principal.*

10. Press **)** (close parenthesis) ....)

    EXAMPLES
    *=PMT(.06/12,20*12,-100000)*
    *=PMT(A1/12,A2*12,-A3)*

11. Press **Enter** .... ⏎

EXERCISE 32

▪ INSERT LOOKUP FUNCTIONS

NOTES:

▪ The **lookup functions** (VLOOKUP and HLOOKUP) select a value from a table and enter it into a location on the worksheet. For example, the VLOOKUP function may be used to look up taxes on a tax table to create a payroll or to look up postage rates to complete a bill of sale.

▪ The table containing the data to be looked up must be created in a blank or empty location on the worksheet. The mortgage payment table below, created in Exercise 31 may be used for a lookup function.

	A	B	C	D	E	F
1		MORTGAGE PAYMENT TABLE AT 9%				
2						
3				TERM IN YEARS		
4		1014.27	15	20	25	30
5	PRINCIPAL	100000	1014.27	899.73	839.20	804.62
6		105000	1064.98	944.71	881.16	844.85
7		110000	1115.69	989.70	923.12	885.08
8		115000	1166.41	1034.68	965.08	925.32
9		120000	1217.12	1079.67	1007.04	965.55
10		125000	1267.83	1124.66	1049.00	1005.78
11		130000	1318.55	1169.64	1090.96	1046.01
12		135000	1369.26	1214.63	1132.92	1086.24
13		1	2	3	4	5
14	Input cells					
15	column:	100000				
16	row:	15				

(table range B5:F12)

(column positions)

▪ The lookup function is entered in the location on the worksheet that requires data from a table.

▪ There are two ways to look up data, depending on the way the data is arranged: **vertically** or **horizontally.**

  • **VLOOKUP** (vertical lookup) looks up data in a particular *column* in the table, while

  • **HLOOKUP** (horizontal lookup) looks up data in a particular *row* in the table.

▪ The VLOOKUP function uses the following format and contains three arguments (parts), defined below and right:

=VLOOKUP(item,table-range,column-position)

  • **ITEM** is text, a value, or a cell reference of the item you are looking for (search item) and should be in the first column of the VLOOKUP table. Numerical search items should be listed in ascending order.

  • **TABLE-RANGE** is the range reference or range name of the lookup table in which the search is to be made. If the lookup function is to be copied, the range should be expressed as an absolute reference.

  • **COLUMN-POSITION** is the column number in the table from which the matching value should be returned. The far left column has a position number of one; the second column has a position number of two, etc.

    ✓ *Note: Column positions are counted from the left column in the range, not from the left column of the worksheet.*

▪ For example, note the outlined lookup table on the left. To look up the mortgage payment for a mortgage amount of $105,000 for 25 years at 9%, a lookup formula would be created as follows:

=VLOOKUP(105000,B5:F12,4)

▪ In looking up numeric data, the lookup function returns to the formula location:

The value from the table (in this case 881.16) or the largest value that is less than or equal to the search item.

▪ If you need to look up more than one item and copy the lookup formula, the formula should use the cell reference (not the value) as the search item. In addition, the range should be absolute so the table range remains constant.

EXAMPLE:

=VLOOKUP(E6,$B$5:$F$12,4)

In this exercise, you will retrieve the mortgage table created earlier and create a worksheet for the Home Money Depot to calculate the mortgage amount and the customer's monthly mortgage payment for 25 or 30 years. Use the VLOOKUP function to enter mortgage payments depending upon the mortgage amount.

EXERCISE DIRECTIONS:

1. Open ⌨ **TABLE** or 💾 **ETABLE.32**.

   REMINDER: The values in cells B4, B15, and B16 are needed to compute the values in the table. Do not delete or change these values.

2. Create the HOME MONEY DEPOT worksheet below MORTGAGE PAYMENT TABLE, as indicated.

3. Center all column titles.

4. Find MORTGAGE AMOUNT by subtracting the DOWN PAYMENT from the CONTRACT PRICE.

5. Copy the formula to the remaining customers.

6. Using the VLOOKUP function, find the monthly payment for the first customer (for 25 years) based on the amount to be mortgaged.

   ✓ Note the outlined range and column position which have been illustrated.

7. Format the result for two decimal places.

8. Copy the formula to the remaining customers.

9. Using the VLOOKUP function, find the monthly payment for the first customer (for 30 years) based on the amount to be mortgaged.

   ✓ Note the range and column position illustrated.

10. Format the result for two decimal places.

11. Copy the formula to the remaining customers.

12. Save the workbook file; name it **HOME**.

13. Print one copy of the bottom portion of the worksheet to fit on one page.

14. Close the workbook file.

	A	B	C	D	E	F	G	H	I
1		MORTGAGE PAYMENT TABLE AT 9%							
2									
3				TERM IN YEARS					
4		1014.27	15	20	25	30			
5	PRINCIPAL	100000	1014.27	899.73	839.20	804.62			
6		105000	1064.98	944.71	881.16	844.85			
7		110000	1115.69	989.70	923.12	885.08			
8		115000	1166.41	1034.68	965.08	925.32			
9		120000	1217.12	1079.67	1007.04	965.55			
10		125000	1267.83	1124.66	1049.00	1005.78			
11		130000	1318.55	1169.64	1090.96	1046.01			
12		135000	1369.26	1214.63	1132.92	1086.24			
13		1	2	3	4	5			
14	Input cells								
15	column:	100000							
16	row:	15							
17									
18		HOME MONEY DEPOT							
19							MONTHLY	MONTHLY	
20			CONTRACT	DOWN	MORTGAGE		PAYMENT	PAYMENT	
21	CUSTOMER		PRICE	PAYMENT	AMOUNT		25 YEARS	30 YEARS	
22									
23	LOGENBERRY, L.		185000	80000					
24	MARTINS, D.		255000	120000					
25	POTTER, C.		320000	200000					
26	SANCHEZ, J.		195000	80000					
27	THOMPSON, I.		215000	105000					

table range B5:F12

column positions

VLOOKUP functions

INSERT A VLOOKUP OR HLOOKUP FUNCTION USING FUNCTION WIZARD

✓ You can also type a function to insert it.

1. Click cell 🔲 to receive function.

2. Click **Function Wizard** button .... 𝑓ₓ on Standard toolbar.

3. Select **Lookup & Reference** .... 🔲 in **Function Category** list.

4. Select **VLOOKUP** or **HLOOKUP** .... Alt + N, ⇅ in **Function Name** list.

5. Click ⌊ Next > ⌋ .... ↵

6. Type item .... *item* in **lookup_value** box.

   ✓ Item can be an actual column item or a reference to a cell containing the column item. You can click cell in worksheet to insert cell reference.

7. Click **table_array** box .... Tab

8. Type reference .... *reference* to table range.

   ✓ You can select range in worksheet to insert cell references.

9. Click **col_index_num** box .... Tab

10. Type the column position .... *number*

11. Click ⌊ Finish ⌋ .... ↵

EXERCISE

▪ LOOKUP FUNCTIONS ▪ PROTECT A SHEET ▪ LOCK CELLS IN A WORKSHEET

NOTES:

Lookup Functions

▪ In Exercise 32, you created lookup formulas using the cell references of the table range. It is possible to use a named range rather than the cell reference of the table. When you copy a formula containing a named range, the reference will not change (that is, it will always refer to the original table location).

Protect a Sheet

▪ It is possible to **protect**, or **lock**, an entire worksheet, individual cells, or a range of cells from accidental changes or unauthorized use.

▪ To keep certain cells accessible in a protected worksheet, these cells must be unlocked before the worksheet is protected.

▪ When a worksheet is protected, the message "Locked cells cannot be changed" will appear when you try to change the contents of a locked cell.

> IMPORTANT: If you set a password when protecting a worksheet and you forget the password, you will not be able to make changes to the worksheet.

The Green Frog Nursery is updating its accounts receivable aging report as of 2/1/96. Paid invoices will be deleted from this new report, while new outstanding invoices will be added.

In addition, Green Frog has changed its late fee policy. It will now determine late fees based on the number of days the account is unpaid. Using Lookup, you will determine the late fee to charge.

EXERCISE DIRECTIONS:

1. Open ⌨ **AGE** or 💾 **EAGE.33**.

2. Delete rows for invoices marked on the right.

3. Insert rows below remaining invoices and enter the following new invoices.

21093	12/10/95	YELLOW BROS.	169.42
21106	12/16/95	PINKSTON CORP	396.16
21142	12/29/95	REDLY FARMS	84.96
21179	01/04/96	GREENBERG BROS.	1490.14
21205	01/10/96	BLUETOWN CO	354.75
21246	01/25/96	PINKSTON CORP.	742.15

4. Change the CURRENT DATE to 2/1/96.

5. Copy the Days Unpaid formula for the new invoices.

6. Create the LATE FEE TABLE below the worksheet.

7. Name the range in the LATE FEE TABLE containing days and interest values LATETABLE.

8. Insert a column between AMOUNT and LATE FEE, and enter the label INTEREST RATE.

9. Delete values in the LATE FEE and AMOUNT DUE columns.

10. Format INTEREST RATE column for three decimal places.

11. Protect the LATE FEE TABLE:
    - Unlock all cells in entire worksheet.
    - Select cells in LATE FEE TABLE and lock them.
    - Turn worksheet protection on.

12. Using VLOOKUP, find INTEREST RATE (based on the days unpaid).

13. Copy the function to the remaining items.
    > ✓ Note: If you did not use the LATETABLE range name in the function, you must set the table range to absolute before copying.

14. Find:
    - LATE FEE
    - AMOUNT DUE

15. Copy formulas to the remaining items.

Continued..

16. Format all remaining money columns for two decimal places.
17. Center column titles.
18. Edit the TOTAL formulas.
19. Disable worksheet protection.
20. Change the interest rate for one unpaid day to be 0.005.
21. Protect the worksheet.
22. Print one copy of the top portion of the worksheet.
23. Close and save the workbook file, or *save as* **AGE**.

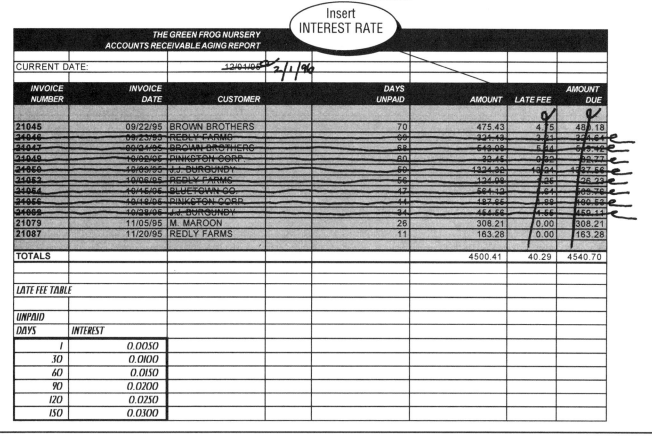

Insert INTEREST RATE

THE GREEN FROG NURSERY
ACCOUNTS RECEIVABLE AGING REPORT

CURRENT DATE: 12/01/95 2/1/96

INVOICE NUMBER	INVOICE DATE	CUSTOMER	DAYS UNPAID	AMOUNT	LATE FEE	AMOUNT DUE
21045	09/22/95	BROWN BROTHERS	70	475.43	4.75	480.18
21046	09/23/95	REDLY FARMS	69	321.13	3.21	324.64
21047	09/24/95	BROWN BROTHERS	68	543.09	5.44	548.42
21049	10/02/95	PINKSTON CORP.	60	33.45	0.33	33.77
21050	10/03/95	J.J. BURGUNDY	59	1324.32	13.24	1337.56
21052	10/06/95	REDLY FARMS	56	124.98	1.25	126.23
21054	10/15/95	BLUETOWN CO.	47	564.13	5.64	569.76
21055	10/18/95	PINKSTON CORP.	44	187.65	1.88	189.53
21062	10/28/95	J.J. BURGUNDY	34	454.56	4.55	459.11
21079	11/05/95	M. MAROON	26	308.21	0.00	308.21
21087	11/20/95	REDLY FARMS	11	163.28	0.00	163.28
TOTALS				4500.41	40.29	4540.70

LATE FEE TABLE

UNPAID DAYS	INTEREST
1	0.0050
30	0.0100
60	0.0150
90	0.0200
120	0.0250
150	0.0300

PROTECT A SHEET

Prevents changes to locked cells, graphic objects, embedded charts in a worksheet or chart items in a chart sheet.

1. Lock or unlock cells as desired.

   ✓ *By default, all cells and objects in a worksheet are locked.*

2. Click **Tools** .... Alt + T
3. Click **Protection** .... P
4. Click **Protect Sheet** .... P

To password protect sheet:

Type password .... *password* in **Password (optional)** text box.

To protect cell contents and chart items:

Click **Contents** .... Alt + C

To protect graphic objects:

Click **Objects** .... Alt + O

To protect scenarios:

Click **Scenarios** .... Alt + S

5. Click [OK] .... Alt

If a password was typed:

a. Retype password .... *password* in text box.
b. Click [OK] .... ↵

UNPROTECT A SHEET

1. Click **Tools** .... Alt + T
2. Click **Protection** .... P
3. Click **Unprotect** Sheet........................ P

If sheet is password protected:

a. Type password .... *password* in **Password** text box.
b. Click [OK] .... ↵

LOCK/UNLOCK CELLS IN A WORKSHEET

Locks or unlocks specific cells. By default, all cells in a worksheet are locked. Locking takes effect when a worksheet is protected.

1. If necessary, unprotect worksheet.

   ✓ *You cannot lock or unlock cells if the worksheet is protected.*

2. Select cell(s) to unlock or lock.
3. Click **Format**.......................... Alt + O
4. Click **Cells**... .... E

   ✓ *Press **Ctrl + 1** to access Format options quickly.*

5. Select **Protection** tab .... Ctrl + Tab
6. Deselect or select **Locked** ...... Alt + L

   ✓ *A gray check box indicates the current cell selection contains mixed (locked/unlocked) settings.*

7. Click [OK] .... ↵
8. Repeat steps for each cell or object to lock or unlock.
9. Protect worksheet to enable locking.

LESSON 5
SUMMARY EXERCISE 34

A national distributor of paper goods pays its sales personnel a commission on their total sales. To provide an extra incentive for the sales staff to be more productive, the company has adopted a graduated commission scale. The more a person sells, the higher the commission percentage. Note the table below. Only those salespeople in Category 2 receive a flat salary of $200 per week in addition to their commissions.

EXERCISE DIRECTIONS:

1. Create the worksheet and table as shown below, or open 💾 **EREWARD.34**. Be sure to enter CATEGORY numbers as labels.

2. Compute each salesperson's earnings for the week and complete the worksheet.

3. Find:
   - COMMISSION RATE
     ✓ Note: Use a Lookup function.
   - COMMISSION
   - SALARY
     ✓ Note: Use an IF statement.
   - TOTAL EARNINGS.

✓ Note: Only Category 2 salespeople receive a flat salary of $200 per week in addition to their commission. Use quotation marks for the category number in your formula, since it is entered as a label.

4. Set column width, as necessary.

5. Format appropriately.

6. Find TOTALS for each column, as indicated.

7. Unlock all cells except the RATE OF COMMISSION table, then turn worksheet protection on.

8. Print one copy of the top portion of the worksheet.

9. Save the workbook file; name it **REWARD**.

10. Close the workbook file.

	A	B	C	D	E	F	G	H
1			SALES STAFF EARNINGS REPORT					
2			MONTH ENDED WEDNESDAY, MARCH 31, 199-					
3								
4	CATE-		TOTAL	COMMISSION			TOTAL	
5	GORY	NAME	SALES	RATE	COMMISSION	SALARY	EARNINGS	
6								
7	1	Sullivin	11,000.00					
8	3	Tran	26,000.00					
9	4	Ulster	31,000.00					
10	2	Velez	28,000.00					
11	4	Washington	26,000.00					
12	2	Yurokoff	34,000.00					
13	6	Zeflowitz	22,000.00					
14								
15	TOTALS							
16								
17	RATE OF COMMISSION TABLE							
18			RATE OF					
19		SALES	COMMISSION					
20								
21		10,000.00	7.00%					
22		11,000.00	7.25%					
23		12,000.00	7.50%					
24		13,000.00	7.75%					
25		14,000.00	8.00%					
26		15,000.00	8.25%					
27		16,000.00	8.50%					
28		17,000.00	8.75%					
29		18,000.00	9.00%					
30		19,000.00	9.25%					
31		20,000.00	9.50%					
32		21,000.00	9.75%					
33		22,000.00	10.00%					
34		23,000.00	10.25%					
35	.	24,000.00	10.50%					
36		25,000.00	10.75%					
37		26,000.00	11.00%					
38		27,000.00	11.25%					
39		28,000.00	11.50%					
40		29,000.00	11.75%					
41		30,000.00	12.00%					
42		31,000.00	12.25%					
43		32,000.00	12.50%					
44		33,000.00	12.75%					
45		34,000.00	13.00%					

LESSON 6

CHARTING

Exercises 35-38

- Create and Edit Charts

- Print Charts

EXERCISE

35

- ■ **CREATE COLUMN, LINE AND PIE CHARTS** ■ **CHANGE CHART TYPE**
- ■ **SELECT AND SIZE EMBEDDED CHART** ■ **SELECT CELLS TO CHART**
- ■ **ENABLE CHART EDITING** ■ **EDIT CHART TEXT**

NOTES:

Create Charts

- ■ **Charts** are a way of presenting and comparing data in a graphic format.

- ■ You can create **embedded charts** or **chart sheets.**

  - When you create an embedded chart, the chart exists as an *object* in the worksheet along side the data.

  - When you create a chart sheet, the chart exists on a separate sheet in the workbook. Excel names chart sheets Chart1, Chart2, etc. You can change these sheet names to better describe the chart.

- ■ All charts are linked to the data they plot. When you change data in the plotted area of the worksheet, the chart also changes.

- ■ To create a chart, you must first select the data to plot. Here are some guidelines for selecting data to chart:

  - The selection should be rectangular.

  - The selection should not contain blank columns or rows.

  - Non-adjacent selection is used to plot data separated by other data or blank columns or rows.

- Hide columns you do not wish to plot.

- The blank cell in the upper-left corner of a selection tells Excel the data below and to the right of the blank cell contains labels for the values to plot.

- The selection determines the orientation (in columns or rows) of the data series. However, orientation may be changed as desired.

- ■ Typically the selection of worksheet data will include these parts of a chart:

  Data series   Values the chart represents.

  Series labels   Labels identifying the charted values. These labels appear in the chart **legend** which identifies each data series in the chart.

  Category labels Labels identifying each data series shown on the horizontal or x-axis.

The illustration below shows two selections that would result in the same displayed chart. Both selections are rectangular and contain a blank cell (outlined) in the upper-left corner. The second selection (B) contains non-adjacent ranges required because of the blank column between the data.

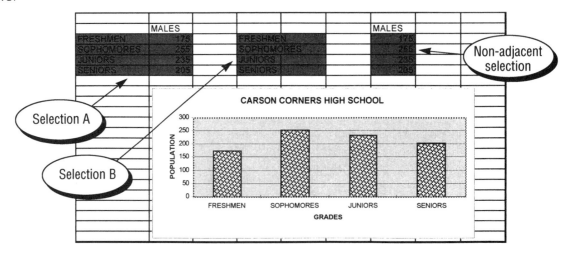

- For charts which use axes (except pie charts):

  - The **y-axis** typically represents the vertical scale. The scale values are entered automatically, based on the values being charted.

  - The **x-axis** is the horizontal scale and typically represents the data series categories.

  - The **x-axis title** describes the x-axis (horizontal) data. (GRADES in the illustration on the previous page.)

  - The **y-axis title** describes the y-axis (vertical) data. (POPULATION in the illustration on previous page.)

- The basic steps to creating a chart are:

  1. Select the worksheet data to chart.

  2. Select Chart from the Insert menu, then select On This Sheet (for an embedded chart) or As New Sheet.

✓ *Note:* *You can also create an embedded chart by clicking the **ChartWizard** button.*

3. If creating an embedded chart, indicate desired size and position in the worksheet.

4. Follow the ChartWizard prompts to select desired chart type and other chart characteristics.

Change Chart Types

- Excel provides many chart types. In this exercise we will discuss and explore three of them (illustrated below and on the following page):

  - **Column charts** compare individual or sets of values. The height of each bar is proportional to its corresponding value in the worksheet.

  - **Pie charts** are circular graphs used to show the relationship of each value in a data range to the entire data range. The size of each wedge represents the percentage each value contributes to the total.

    Only one numerical data range may be used in a pie chart to indicate the values to be represented as pie slices.

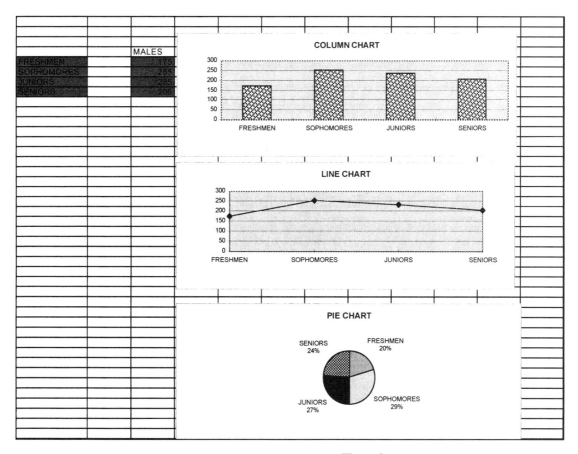

Pie charts may be formatted to indicate the percentage each piece of the pie represents of the whole.

- **Line charts** are another way of presenting data graphically. Line charts are especially useful when plotting trends since lines connect points of data and show changes over time effectively.

■ Charts can be copied and then edited to produce a different chart that uses the same worksheet data.

> ✓ *Note:* *The contents of the clipboard remain unchanged until another item is copied. Therefore, you can paste a copied object more than once.*

Select and Size Embedded Charts

■ Two ways of working with embedded charts are:

- You can click an embedded chart once to format it as an *object*. When you click it, **handles** (small squares) appear around its

border. When selected in this way, you can size, move, and copy it, for example.

- You can double-click an embedded chart to edit it as a *chart*. When you double-click it, a thick border with handles appears or, if the entire chart was not displayed on the sheet, the chart appears in a window.

Enable Chart Editing

■ To edit a chart sheet, just click the sheet tab of the chart you want to change.

■ All chart items, such as the **legend** and **data markers** *(illustrated below)*, can be changed and enhanced. Chart items may be changed by clicking them and making changes. Double-clicking some chart items opens a dialog box for entry changes. When you right-click chart items, Excel displays a shortcut menu containing relevant commands.

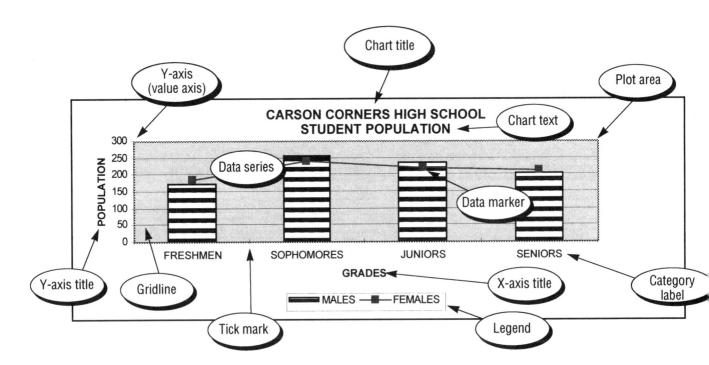

- ■ To edit a chart, Excel provides the following features:
  - **Menu bar options**

    Excel modifies the menu bar so options specific to the chart type and selected chart item are available. For example:

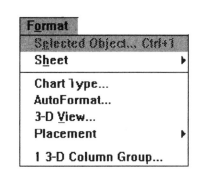

- **Shortcut menu options**

  Excel displays the following shortcut menu items appropriate to the part of the chart you right-click:

  Clear

  Insert: Axes, Data Labels, Error Bars, Gridlines, Titles, Trendline

  Format: Axis, Axis Title, Chart Area , Chart Title, Data Labels, Data Point, Data Series, Error Bars, Gridlines, Legend, Legend Entry, Legend Key, Trendline

  Chart Type

  Autoformat

  3-D View

  Format Chart Type Group

- **Name box**

  Displays the selected chart item.

In this exercise, you will create a column chart, a line chart, and a pie chart with labels showing student population data for the Carson Corners High School.

EXERCISE DIRECTIONS:

1. Create the worksheet as shown on the next page, or open 💾 **EHS.35**.

2. Create an embedded chart to show the male population by grade:
   - Select the non-adjacent ranges indicated by the shaded cells in the worksheet.
   - Insert the chart on the worksheet and place it in the range B10:G24.
   - Follow the ChartWizard steps and make the following selections:

     Step 1: Note the reference to the range of data to chart in the worksheet. Do not change it.

     Step 2: Note the default chart type (Column). Do not change it.

     Step 3: Note the default format (6) for the column chart type. Do not change it.

   Step 4: Note the orientation of the data series is set to Columns. Do not change it.

   Step 5: • Remove the legend.

   ✓ *Note the changes in the sample chart.*

   - Add the legend.
   - Add the chart title:

     CARSON CORNERS HIGH SCHOOL
   - Add the following axis titles:

     Category (X): GRADES

     Value (Y): POPULATION

3. Size the chart so that the category labels (GRADES) fit on one line.

4. Copy the embedded chart to the worksheet range beginning at B26.

5. Enable chart editing for the copied chart and change the chart type to a line chart.

Continued...

Excel

Lesson 6: Charting

6. Reselect the worksheet data and insert a pie chart as a new sheet:
   - Follow the ChartWizard steps and make the following selections:

   Step 1: Note the reference to the range of data to chart in the worksheet. Do not change it.

   Step 2: Select the Pie chart type.

   Step 3: Select the default format (7) for the pie chart type.

   Step 4: Note, but do not change, the settings for ChartWizard step 4.

   Step 5:
   - Add a legend.
   - Add the chart title:

   CARSON CORNERS HIGH SCHOOL

7. With the chart sheet selected, edit the chart title to add the second line:

   MALE POPULATION

8. Preview the pie chart on the chart sheet.
   - ✓ *Note the chart will print on its own sheet.*

9. Select Sheet1 and deselect the worksheet data.

10. Preview Sheet1.
    - ✓ *Note the column and line charts will print with the worksheet data.*

11. Save the workbook file; name it **HS.**

12. Close the workbook file.

	A	B	C	D	E
1		CARSON CORNERS HIGH SCHOOL			
2		STUDENT POPULATION			
3					
4				MALES	
5	FRESHMEN			175	
6	SOPHOMORES			255	
7	JUNIORS			235	
8	SENIORS			205	
9					

SELECT NON-ADJACENT CELLS USING THE MOUSE

1. Click first cell.

2. Press **Ctrl** and click each additional cell.

   AND/OR

   Press **Ctrl** and drag through cells until desired cell ranges are highlighted.

SELECT NON-ADJACENT CELLS USING THE KEYBOARD

1. Select first cell in range .... 🔲

2. Select first range of cells.. Shift + 🔲

3. Press **Shift + F8** .... Shift + F8
   to begin ADD mode.

4. Move active cell .... 🔲
   to first cell in next range to select.

5. Select cells in range .... Shift + 🔲

6. Repeat steps 2-4 for each additional range to select.

CREATE A CHART FROM WORKSHEET DATA

1. Select cells containing data to plot.

2. a. Click **Insert** .... Alt + I

   b. Click **Chart** .... H

   c. Click **On This Sheet** .... O

   OR

   Click **As New Sheet** .... A

   - ✓ *You can click the **ChartWizard** button on the Standard toolbar to create an embedded chart on the worksheet.*

   If On This Sheet was selected:

   Pointer becomes a +⊞ .

   Drag chart outline to desired size.

   - ✓ *To create a square chart, press **Shift** while dragging chart outline. To align chart with cell structure, press **Alt** while dragging chart outline.*

– CHARTWIZARD – STEP 1 OF 5 –

3. If necessary, select cells in worksheet to plot.

   OR

   Type reference ....*reference* to cells to plot in **Range** text box.

4. Click Next > .... ◄

   – CHARTWIZARD – STEP 2 OF 5 –

5. Select desired chart type .... 📊

   Chart types include: *Area, Bar, Column, Line, Pie, Doughnut, Radar, XY [Scatter], Combination, 3-D Area, 3-D Bar, 3-D Column, 3-D Line, 3-D Pie, 3-D Surface*

6. Click Next > .... ◄

   – CHARTWIZARD – STEP 3 OF 5 –

7. Select desired chart format.

   - ✓ *Available formats depend upon the selected chart type.*

Continued.

3. Select desired chart options:

To change orientation of data series:

Click **Rows** .... `Alt`+`R`

OR

Click **Columns** .... `Alt`+`C`

Excel shows the result of your selections in a sample chart.

To specify rows or columns to use for axis labels, legend text, or chart title:

Select number of .... `Alt`+`U`,
rows/columns in
increment box **Use First**.

✓ *Options depend upon the selected chart type. To plot values in first row or column (not use them as labels) select 0 (zero).*

4. Click `Next >` .... `←`

10. Select desired chart options:

To add or remove legend:

Click **Yes** .... `Alt`+`E`

OR

Click **No** .... `Alt`+`N`

To add a chart title:

a. Click **Chart Title** .... `Alt`+`C`

b. Type desired chart title .... *charttitle*

To add axis titles:

Type titles in provided **Axis Titles** text boxes.

✓ *Options depend upon the selected chart type.*

11. Click `Finish` .... `←`

ENABLE CHART EDITING

Embedded Chart:

Double-click embedded chart.

The chart is surrounded by a thick border with handles or, if the entire chart was not displayed on the sheet, the chart appears in a window.

Chart Sheet:

Select chart sheet.

A Chart toolbar may appear with these chart buttons:

📊	**Chart Type**	
📈	**Default Chart**	
📉	**ChartWizard**	
☰	**Horizontal Gridlines**	
☰	**Legend**	

DISABLE CHART EDITING

Embedded Chart:

Click any cell in worksheet.

✓ *The chart remains selected as an object. Click any cell again to deselect the chart object.*

Chart Sheet:

Click another sheet tab.

SELECT EMBEDDED CHART AS AN OBJECT

If chart editing is enabled, click any cell in worksheet.

OR

Click anywhere on embedded chart.

Handles *(black squares) appear on chart border.*

SIZE EMBEDDED CHARTS

1. Select chart.

2. Point to handle on side of border to size.

Pointer becomes a ↖ ↔ ↗ ↕ when positioned correctly.

✓ *To size object proportionally, point to corner handle.*

To size object without constraints:

Drag border outline until desired size is obtained.

To size object and align to gridlines:

Press **Alt** and drag border outline until desired size is obtained.

CHANGE CHART TYPE FOR ENTIRE CHART

1. Enable chart editing.

2. Click **Format** .... `Alt`+`O`

3. Click **Chart Type** .... `T`

4. Click **Entire Chart** .... `Alt`+`E`

5. Click **2-D** .... `Alt`+`2`

OR

Click **3-D** .... `Alt`+`3`

6. Select desired chart type ..... `Tab`, ⤢

7. Click `OK` .... `←`

EDIT CHART TEXT IN CHART

Edits unlinked chart text (such as axis and chart titles, text boxes, and trendline labels) and some linked text (data labels and tick mark labels).

✓ *When you edit linked text in a chart, Excel removes the link to the worksheet data.*

1. Enable chart editing.

2. Click chart item containing text.

To replace existing text with new text:

a. Type desired text .... *text*
Text appears in formula bar.

b. Press **Enter** .... `←`

To edit existing text:

a. Click desired character position in chart text.

b. Insert and delete characters as desired.

✓ *To insert a line break, press **Enter**.*

c. Click anywhere outside of chart text.

EXERCISE

36

- **CREATE A COMBINATION CHART** - **CHANGE CHART SUBTYPE**
- **DELETE AN EMBEDDED CHART** - **SELECT CHART ITEMS**
- **CHANGE LEGEND POSITION**

NOTES:

Change Chart Subtype

- When you create a chart, you will want to select a chart type and format that best presents the worksheet data. Worksheet data may be charted using one of fifteen chart types: Area, Bar, Column, Line, Pie, Doughnut, Radar, XY (Scatter), Combination, 3-D Area, 3-D Bar, 3-D Column, 3-D Line, 3-D Pie, and 3-D Surface.

- Excel also provides **chart subtypes** which are variations on the selected chart type. Each chart type has at least one chart subtype.

- The **stacked column chart** is an example of a chart subtype. This chart is often used to show the total effect of several sets of data. Each bar consists of sections representing values in a range. For example, in the illustration below each bar has two sections representing male and female population values.

STACKED COLUMN CHART

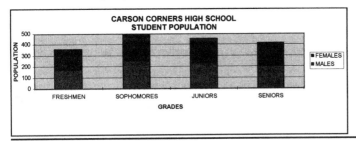

- The **combination chart** is a special chart type that lets you plot each data series as a different chart type. For example, in the illustration below the line chart type is used to plot the female population and the column chart type to plot the male population.

COMBINATION CHART

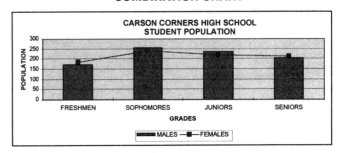

Change Legend Position

- A chart **legend** is usually created automatically when the data is charted. Legend placement and labels may be changed or edited.

In this exercise, you will retrieve the Carson Corners High School population statistics, include additional data, and prepare several graphs. The principal wants to compare the number of males and females

EXERCISE DIRECTIONS:

1. Open 📠 **HS** or 💾 **EHS.36**.
2. Enter new data in column E, as shown below.

	A	B	C	D	E
1		CARSON CORNERS HIGH SCHOOL			
2		STUDENT POPULATION			
3					
4				MALES	FEMALES
5	FRESHMEN			175	185
6	SOPHOMORES			255	240
7	JUNIORS			235	220
8	SENIORS			205	215
9					

3. Delete all embedded charts in Sheet1.
4. Rename Sheet1; name it **DATA**.

5. To create an embedded column chart showing male and female student population in the DATA sheet:
   - Select the non-adjacent ranges indicated by the shaded cells in the worksheet.
   - Place the chart in the range B10:G24.
     – FROM CHARTWIZARD –
   - Select the default chart type (Column) and format (6).
   - Add the chart title:
     CARSON CORNERS HIGH SCHOOL

304

Continued..

- Create axis titles as follows:

  Category (X):   GRADES

  Value (Y):   POPULATION

6. Size the chart as needed.

7. Change legend position to bottom of the chart.

8. Edit the chart and add a second line to the chart title:

   STUDENT POPULATION

9. Select the chart as an object and cut it to the clipboard.

10. In Sheet2, select cell A1 and paste the chart stored in the clipboard.

11. Select cell A17 and paste the chart stored in the clipboard again.

12. Edit the chart pasted to cell A17 and change it to a line chart.

13. In Sheet2, select cell A33 and paste the chart stored in the clipboard.

14. Change the subtype of this chart to stacked column

(second chart pictured in the Subtype group).

15. Place legend on right side of chart.

16. Select the column chart (first chart in Sheet2) as an object and copy it to the clipboard.

17. In Sheet2, select cell A49 and paste the column chart stored in the clipboard.

18. Change the new chart to a combination chart:
    - Select the female data series.
    - Change the chart type for the selected female data series to line.

19. Rename Sheet2; name it **EMBEDDED CHARTS**.

20. Rename Chart1; name it **PIE CHART**.

   To preview the embedded charts:
    - Select EMBEDDED CHARTS sheet.
    - Set it to print on one page.
    - Preview the worksheet.

21. Select the DATA sheet.

22. Close and save the workbook file, or *save as* **HS**.

DELETE AN EMBEDDED CHART

1. Select embedded chart as an object.

2. Press **Delete** .... Del

CHANGE CHART SUBTYPE

1. Enable chart editing.

2. Click **Format** .... Alt + O

3. Click **Chart Type** .... T

4. Select **Entire Chart** .... Alt + E

5. Click Options... .... Alt + O

6. Select **Subtype** .... Ctrl + Tab

7. Select desired style .... Alt + S , 🔲
   in **Subtype** group.

8. Click OK .... ↵

CREATE A COMBINATION CHART

Change chart type for specified data series.

1. Enable chart editing.

2. Select data series for which a new chart type will be selected.

3. Click **Format** .... Alt + O

4. Click **Chart Type** .... T

5. Click **Selected Series** .... Alt + S

6. Click **2-D** .... Alt + 2

OR

   Click **3-D** .... Alt + 3

7. Select desired chart type .... Tab , 🔲

8. Click OK .... ↵

POSITION LEGEND IN CHART

1. Enable chart editing.

2. Right-click legend.

3. Select **Format Legend** .... ↓ , ↵

4. Select **Placement** .... Ctrl + Tab

5. Select desired position:
    - **Bottom** .... Alt + B
    - **Corner** .... Alt + C
    - **Top** .... Alt + T
    - **Right** .... Alt + R
    - **Left** .... Alt + L

6. Click OK .... ↵

SELECT CHART ITEMS

Select chart items (such as the legend or a data series) prior to selecting commands to change the item in some way.

  ✓ Excel marks the currently selected chart item with squares, and displays its name in the name box.

Enable chart editing.

To select next or previous class of chart items:

Press **up** or **down** .... 🔲

To select next or previous item for selected chart class:

Press **left** or **right** .... 🔲

To select a specific item with the mouse:

Click chart item.

To select a data series:

Click any data marker in data series.

To select a data marker:

a. Click any data marker in data series.

b. Click data marker in selected series.

To select the chart area:

Click any blank area outside plot area.

To select the plot area:

Click any blank area inside plot area.

To select the legend or legend items:

  ✓ Legend items are the legend entry and key.

a. Click legend.

b. Click item in legend.

To deselect a selected chart item:

Press **Escape** .... Esc

EXERCISE

37

■ **PRINT CHARTS** ■ **PRINT EMBEDDED CHART SEPARATELY**
■ **SET CHART PRINT OPTIONS**
■ **SET PAGE ORIENTATION OF PRINTED PAGE**

NOTES:

Print Charts

■ Charts can be printed with the worksheet or as separate sheets. You can select an embedded chart to print it apart from the worksheet.

■ You can use Print Preview to see how a worksheet or chart will print.

From Print Preview, you can also:

• View the Previous or Next page when more than one page will be printed.

• Change the page margins by dragging handles that appear when you select the Margins Button.

• Click the Setup button to access the Page Setup dialog box from which you can change many page print settings such as scaling.

• Print the chart or worksheet.

Print Embedded Chart

■ When printing a selected embedded chart or a chart sheet:

• Excel selects the page orientation (**Portrait or Landscape**) that best matches the shape of the chart. You can change the page orientation from the Page tab in the Page Setup dialog box.

• The Sheet tab becomes a Chart tab in the Page Setup dialog box. You can set the chart print options such as **Printing Quality** and the **Printed Chart Size** from the Chart tab.

■ If your computer equipment includes a color monitor, the chart components will be shown in different colors. When you print these charts on a black and white printer, the colored text and lines are printed in black; the colored areas are printed in shades of gray; and the background color is ignored.

In this exercise, you will print the charts you created for the principal of Carson Corners High School.

EXERCISE DIRECTIONS:

1. Open 🖾 **HS** or 🖫 **EHS.37**.

2. Select the PIE CHART sheet.

3. Preview the chart sheet and note the orientation of page.

4. Click the Setup button and change the orientation of the page (Landscape or Portrait).

5. Close the dialog box and preview the chart sheet.

6. If the page orientation is set to portrait, change it back to landscape.

7. Print the chart sheet from the Print Preview window.

8. Select EMBEDDED CHARTS sheet and preview the worksheet.

9. From the print preview window, select the Setup button.

– FROM PAGE SETUP DIALOG BOX –

10. Click on the Sheet tab and turn printing of gridlines off.

11. Click on the Page tab and set worksheet scale to one page wide by one page tall.

12. Return to the Preview screen and print the worksheet.

13. In the worksheet, edit the line chart, then select Print Preview.

✓ *Note that only the line chart appears.*

14. Select the Setup button.

15. From the Chart tab, set the Printed Chart Size to scale to fit the page; set print quality to draft.

16. Return to Print Preview and print the chart.

17. Close and save the workbook file, or *save as* **HS**.

PRINT CHARTS

Print chart sheet or embedded chart as part of the worksheet.

1. Select worksheet or chart sheet containing chart to print.

2. Follow steps to **PRINT A WORKSHEET**, page 221.

PRINT EMBEDDED CHART SEPARATELY

1. Enable chart editing for chart to print.

2. Follow steps to **PRINT A WORKSHEET**, page 221.

SET CHART PRINT OPTIONS

1. Double-click on chart to be printed.

   – FROM PRINT PREVIEW –

2. Click `Setup...` .... `Alt` + `S`

   OR

   – FROM WORKSHEET OR CHART SHEET –

   a. Click **File** .... `Alt` + `F`

   b. Click **Page Setup** .... `U`

3. Select **Chart** tab .... `Ctrl` + `Tab`

   ✓ *Available options depend upon the currently selected printer.*

To set printed chart size:

Select desired fit:

- **Use Full Page** .... `Alt` + `U`

- **Scale to Fit Page** .... `Alt` + `F`

- **Custom** .... `Alt` + `C`

   ✓ *With **Custom** selected, you can center the chart on the page form the **Margins** tab.*

To set print quality of chart:

Click **Draft Quality** .... `Alt` + `Q`

To print chart in black and white:

Click **Print in Black and White** .... `Alt` + `B`

4. Click `OK` .... `↵`
   to return to sheet or Print Preview.

SET PAGE ORIENTATION OF PRINTED PAGE

   – FROM PRINT PREVIEW –

1. Click **Page Setup** .... `Alt` + `U`

2. Select **Page** tab .... `Ctrl` + `Tab`

   OR

   – FROM WORKSHEET OR CHART SHEET –

   a. Click **File** .... `Alt` + `F`

   b. Click **Page Setup** .... `U`

3. Click **Portrait** .... `Alt` + `T`

   OR

   Click **Landscape** .... `Alt` + `L`

4. Click `OK` .... `↵`
   to return to sheet or Print Preview.

LESSON 6
SUMMARY EXERCISE 38

As an employee of the United States Labor Department, you have been asked to analyze employment trends in the state of New Jersey using data from the 1980 and 1990 censuses.

You will create a worksheet using the data below and create several graphs as directed.

Employment in Selected Industries

	1980	1990	Change
Agriculture, etc.	24,447	40,161	64.3%
Mfg., nondurable	414,416	347,224	-16.2%
Mfg., durable	405,728	306,212	-24.5%
Finance, real estate	231,953	346,037	49.2%

EXERCISE DIRECTIONS:

1. Create a worksheet using the data above or open **ENJDATA.38**.

2. Format appropriately and set column widths where needed.

3. Create an embedded column graph comparing 1980 and 1990 trends.

4. Include appropriate titles and legends, as well as horizontal gridlines.

5. Using the same data and titles above, create line and combination charts.

6. Create an embedded pie chart of 1990 data. Use varied hatch patterns, and explode a section of the pie representing the largest employment area in the state.

7. Include appropriate titles and data labels.

8. Use Edit, Cut and Edit, Paste to move each chart to a separate worksheet.

9. Rename each sheet containing a chart as follows:
   COLUMN CHART
   LINE CHART
   COMBINATION CHART
   3-D COLUMN CHART
   PIE CHART

10. Rename Sheet1; name it DATA.

11. Save the workbook file, name it **NJDATA**

12. Close the workbook.

CHAPTER 4

LESSON 1

CREATING A DATABASE FORM

Exercises 1-5

- Database Basics

- Creating Database Datasheets and Forms

- Entering Data

- Enhancing Datasheets and Forms

EXERCISE

- DATABASE BASICS ▪ PLANNING A DATABASE
- CREATING AND SAVING A DATABASE TABLE

NOTES:

- Access is a **Relational Database Management System**. A **database** is a collection of related information which is organized into separate tables (listings) within the file. This allows you to store related information in one place (the database). Each table is created to contain data pertaining to a specific aspect of the database. For example: A company that has many stores can create one table that contains generalized information for each store and a second table that contains a listing of computer equipment in each store. These tables would be stored in the Company Database. Information can be organized and accessed from each table in a database file.

- An Access database file is like a filing cabinet of **related** information in which each drawer contains a specific aspect of that information.

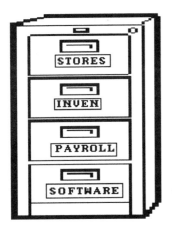

Each drawer in the filing cabinet contains individual "index cards" called **records**. A record contains information about one item of the database. Therefore, a collection of related items or records would be stored together in an Access datasheet or table.

- All the records in a cabinet drawer have data stored using the same category names. Each category is referred to as a **field**. There are two parts to a field: the **field name** and the **field contents**. See a typical computer inventory record below.

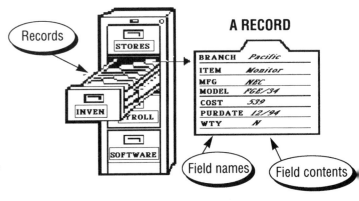

Planning the database

- Before creating a database, you should plan the fields you want to include in each datasheet–that is, what type of information the database should contain and how you wish it organized. Plan your database on paper first by writing the field names that would best identify the information entered as field contents. If you want to access information simultaneously from two or more datasheets, you should have these datasheets share common field names and contents. When your plan is complete, you are ready to enter your field names and data into the computer.

- It is often advisable to organize data into its smallest unit for greatest flexibility. For example: Using field names of FIRST and LAST gives you more options than using NAME for the entire name.

Creating a Database File

- At the opening Access window (see below), choose the File menu and New Database option.

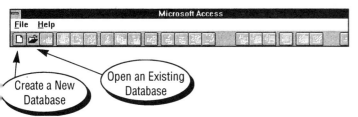

- The default database name of DB1 should be changed to a name that is more appropriate for your database. The file will be stored in the main Access directory unless you choose to change its destination. Access adds a **.MDB** extension to a database file.

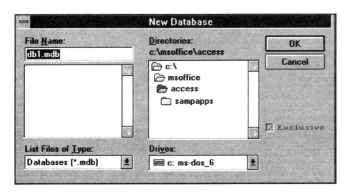

- After naming your database file, an object creation window appears with the file name on the title bar. The relational database objects are summarized in this window and accessed by using the object tabs. Database object categories are Table, Query, Form, Report, Macro, and Module.

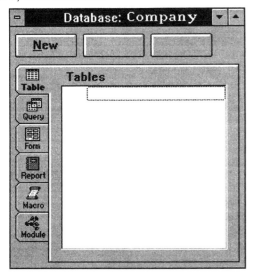

OBJECT CREATION WINDOW OF A NEW DATABASE

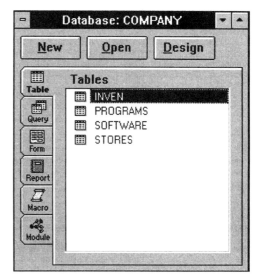

OBJECT CREATION WINDOW FOR A DATABASE WITH EXISTING TABLES

The best way to begin creating database objects is to create tables (the default option).

Creating a Table (Datasheet) Design

- From the object creation window, select the New option to create a table. You will be presented with a Design view screen for entering Field Names, Data Types, and item Description in the top pane and Field Properties in the bottom pane (see below).

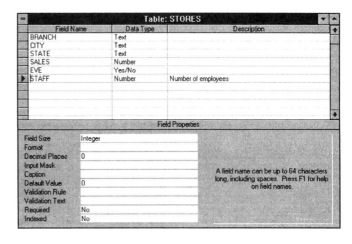

- A field name can contain a maximum of 64 characters. These characters can include letters, numbers, spaces (except leading spaces), and special characters except the period (.), exclamation mark (!), backquote ('), either the left or right brackets ([]), or printer control codes.

■ The default data type is text with a default field size set at 50 characters. You can reset all default settings to reflect the field contents. If your selection of a data type or any of its related properties do not agree with the entered data, Access will not accept that entry.

Available:

Data Types	Supports
Text	A maximum of 255 characters
Memo	Like text, but can have a maximum of 64,000 characters
Number	Various forms of numerical data
Date/Time	Date and time entries in various formats
Currency	Currency values expressed in various formats
Counter	A value that will automatically be incremented at each successive entry
Yes/No	A check box with an X for Yes or blank for No
OLE Object	If item is linked to an object in another file

■ To efficiently select information from different tables within the database, Access uses a primary key field. The field used as a **primary key field** must have unique field values. Therefore, do not use a field such as LAST NAME as a primary field since more than one person in a datasheet may have the same last name. An employee ID number would be an appropriate choice for a primary key field. If you do not set a primary key field when you create your table, Access will ask if one should be created before saving the file. Access will insert a primary key field Record ID, whose data type is Counter, if a key field is not specified.

Saving a Datasheet Design

■ After a database object has been designed, it must be named and saved using the Save or Save As option in the File menu.

Bit-Byte Computer Stores, Inc. has opened numerous branches throughout the United States during the last several months. In order to keep track of the branches and the cities in which the branches are located, you have been asked to create a database file to organize information relating to these stores.

EXERCISE DIRECTIONS:

1. Select New Database from the File menu.

2. Replace the default file name of DB1 with **COMPANY**.

3. Select OK.

4. Select New.

5. Select New Table (not Table Wizards).

6. Create a table design using the data listed below:

7. Save the table design; name it STORES. (Do not add a primary key.)

8. Switch to Datasheet view from the View menu.

9. Close the STORES datasheet.

10. Close the **COMPANY** database.

FIELD NAMES	DATA TYPE	SIZE	DESCRIPTION
STORE NUMBER	Number	Integer	
BRANCH	Text	16	
CITY	Text	13	
ST	Text	2	
STAFF	Number	Integer	Number of employees

🌐 OPEN AND RENAME A NEW FILE

1. Click **File** .... `Alt` + `F`

2. Click **New Database** .... `N`

3. Replace file name......................*filename*

4. Click **OK**................................... `Enter`

CREATE A TABLE DESIGN

1. Open a new file (see above) or open existing file.

2. Click **New** .... `Alt` + `N`

3. Click **New Table** .... `N`

4. Type field name ....*filename*

5. Press TAB .... `Tab`

6. Use pull down list to select data type (default type is text).

7. Press F6 .... `F6`
   to switch to field properties.

8. Enter properties ....*properties*

9. Press F6 to switch to table .... `F6`

10. Press TAB .... `Tab`

11. Enter description, if desired.

12. Press Enter............................... `Enter`

13. Repeat steps 4-9 until table is complete.

14. Save table design (see below).

TO SAVE TABLE DESIGN

1. Click **File**............................. `Alt` + `F`

2. Click **Save As**................................... `A`

3. Type table name.......................*tablename*

4. Click **OK**................................... `Enter`

5. Click **No**............................... `N`
   to bypass creation of primary key.

CHANGE FROM TABLE DESIGN TO DATASHEET VIEW

When in Table Design view:

1. Click **View** .... `Alt` + `V`

2. Click **Datasheet** .... `S`

EXERCISE

CREATING AND SAVING A DATABASE TABLE DESIGN

2

NOTES:

- A database may contain all the related data for a company. For example: In the COMPANY database, created in Exercise 1, you saved a datasheet for STORES for information about each branch. You will now create a datasheet for INVENTORY, listing equipment purchased for each store.

In order to keep track of equipment purchased by the Bit-Byte Computer Stores, Inc., your employer has asked you to create an inventory table for your COMPANY database.

EXERCISE DIRECTIONS:

1. Open the 🖮 **COMPANY** database or 💾 **ACOMPANY.2**.

2. Create a new table using the field data listed below:

NAME	DATA TYPE	SIZE	FORMAT
BRANCH	Text	16	
ITEM	Text	15	
MFG	Text	8	
MODEL	Text	15	
COST	Currency		Standard
PURDATE	Date/Time		Short Date
WTY	Yes/No (default value Yes)		

3. Save and Close the table design; name it HARDWARE. (Do not set a primary key.)

4. Switch to HARDWARE datasheet.

5. Close the HARDWARE datasheet and COMPANY database or save as **COMPANY**.

🌐 **OPEN A FILE**

1. Click **File** .... Alt + F
2. Click **Open Database**....................... O
3. Select file in proper directory.
4. Click **OK**.................................... Enter

NEXT EXERCISE

EXERCISE

■ **OPENING A DATASHEET** ■ **ENTERING RECORDS** ■ **CHANGING DATASHEET COLUMN WIDTH**

NOTES:

Opening a Datasheet (Table)

■ When you create or open a database file, a window appears listing all previously created tables.

■ A saved **table** (datasheet) **design** can be opened for the purpose of entering records by highlighting the desired table name and selecting the Open option. A row and column format, similar to a spreadsheet, is displayed with the previously entered field names as the column headings. This **Datasheet view** gives you an efficient way to work with more than one record on the same screen. In this view, each row will contain the data of a single record.

DATASHEET VIEW

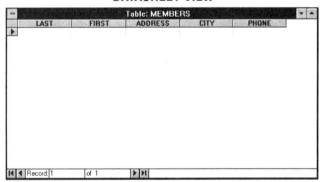

■ Once records have been added to a Datasheet, you can use the arrow-head buttons on the Status bar to scroll through the records.

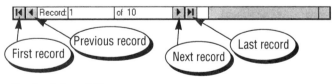

Switching Views

■ You can switch between Table Design view and Datasheet view by using the appropriate option on the View menu. Table Design view displays the format of the table while Datasheet view

shows the records entered into the table. Data is entered or edited in Datasheet view.

Change Datasheet Column Width

■ You may find that the default column width on your table is not appropriate for your entries, and/or the table is too wide to fit on one screen. Column size can be changed at any time. The previously set field size is NOT affected by the column display.

Entering Records; Correcting a Field Entry

■ To enter records in a Datasheet, type the data below each field name as you would in a spreadsheet. Use the Tab key to advance from column to column. To advance to the next row, click in the first column of the new row. Use the Tab key or the direction-arrow keys. When you leave a record row, your data will automatically be saved in the table.

■ It is recommended that field data be entered in upper and lower case so that it may be used in word processed files. Field headings may be entered in upper case to distinguish them from field data.

■ Use the Backspace key to correct an error made while keyboarding an entry. If you have already advanced to another field, you can return to the field that needs correction by clicking in the field and pressing Shift+Tab or by using the direction arrow keys. Retype the entry, or press F2, to access edit mode, make the correction, and then move to another field.

■ You may use the Copy or Cut and Paste options to quickly enter repetitive data. You can copy either one cell entry or an entire record. To select an entire row, click the shaded area to the left of the first field in the row.

316

You are the president of HUG, a computer users' group. One of your responsibilities is to send announcements and annual reports to the members. To make your mailings easier, you have decided to create a name and address file for your computer users' group. In this exercise, you will create a database file which will contain a table of data and a Form view for this data.

EXERCISE DIRECTIONS:

1. Create a new database file; name it **HUGCLUB**.

2. Create a table using the field names and field widths indicated below:

   All fields have a text data type.
LAST	10
FIRST	8
ADDRESS	20
CITY	15
PHONE	13

3. Save the table design;
   name it MEMBERS.
   (Do not set a primary key.)

4. Switch to the MEMBERS datasheet.

5. From the notebook page illustrated below, enter the information for each person into your table.

HUG MEMBERSHIP LIST
California Members

Leanne Barnes	808 Summer Street	Anaheim	(213)555-4987
Miles Brown	154 Newburg Road	Anaheim	(213)555-4837
Stuart Griffith	1551 Dean Street	Beverly Hills	(213)555-3010
Michael Moon	17 Pine Street	Beverly Hills	(213)555-9275
Trina Smith	3954 Wood Avenue	Anaheim	(213)555-7283
Sheila Smith	417 Specific Court	Anaheim	(213)555-7284
Bette Walker	1584 F. Street	North Hollywood	(213)555-9174
Carl Castillo	1956 Park Avenue	North Hollywood	(213)555-5192
John Davis	P.O. Box 2333	North Hollywood	(213)555-8129
Amy Dixon	237 Albee Street	North Hollywood	(213)555-8917

6. Adjust column widths to accommodate the longest entry in each field.

7. Correct errors.

8. Save and Close the MEMBERS table.

9. Close the **HUGCLUB** database.

CHANGE FROM DATASHEET TO TABLE DESIGN VIEW

In Datasheet view:

1. Click **View** .... `Alt`+`V`
2. Click **Table Design** .... `D`

CHANGE DATASHEET COLUMN WIDTH

Keyboard:

1. Click field selector for desired column.
2. Click **Format** .... `Alt`+`O`
3. Click **Column Width** .... `C`
4. Click **Best Fit** .... `B`

   OR

   Type column width ....*number*
5. Click OK .... `Enter`

Mouse:

1. Click right edge of the field name cell.
2. Click and drag border to desired size.

🌐 EDITING DATA

Before data is entered, data may be edited by backspacing and correcting the entry.

After data is entered:

1. Press Shift+Tab .... `Shift`+`Tab`
   to return to a field.
2. Press **F2** .... `F2`
3. Make corrections.

EXERCISE

4

▪ OPENING AN EXISTING DATASHEET ▪ ENTERING RECORDS ▪ ENHANCING A DATASHEET ▪ CHANGING DATASHEET COLUMN WIDTHS

NOTES:

Enhancing a Datasheet

▪ Access has established default settings for a datasheet. The default settings for items such as format and gridlines affect the entire datasheet and can be changed.

▪ When you are in Datasheet view, a Format menu option is available.

DATASHEET VIEW MENU

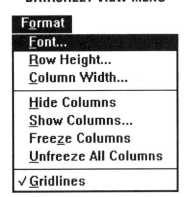

The Font option gives you a list of all available fonts, their size, and style options. A sample box allows you to preview your choices before making changes. The other items on the Format menu are self-explanatory.

The √, to the left of the Gridlines option, indicates that the datasheet will be displayed with a grid. This is a toggle option that is clicked off or on, as desired.

> ✓ Note: All the format selections will affect the entire datasheet display. Enhancement changes to a datasheet are NOT reflected in its Form view.

Your manager at Bit-Byte has just given you a list of the new branches and their locations. She has asked you to enter this information into your database table STORES. The datasheet will be enhanced using font and gridline options.

EXERCISE DIRECTIONS:

1. Open the ⌨ **COMPANY** database or 💾 **ACOMPANY.4**.

2. Open the STORES table and enter the data listed below.

STORE NUMBER	BRANCH	CITY	ST	STAFF
1	Big Apple	New York	NY	15
2	Pacific	Los Angeles	CA	14
3	Sunset	San Francisco	CA	21
4	Lakeview	Chicago	IL	15
5	Peach Tree	Atlanta	GA	9
6	Bean Town	Boston	MA	16
7	Astro Center	Houston	TX	8
8	Twin Cities	San Diego	CA	7
9	Wheatland	Topeka	KS	12
10	Oceanview	Providence	RI	6

3. Change the font size to 10 point.

4. Adjust column widths to accommodate the longest entry.

5. Remove datasheet gridlines.

6. Save and Close the datasheet.

7. Open the STORES table again.

8. Change the font size to 8.

9. Add datasheet gridlines.

10. Adjust column widths, if necessary.

11. Save and Close the datasheet.

12. Close the **COMPANY** database.

SET FONT FORMAT OPTIONS

1. Click **Format** .... Alt + O

2. Click **Font** .... F

To select font:

a. Click **Font** .... Alt + F

b. Select desired font .... ↑ ↓

To select font style:

a. Click **Font Style** .... Alt + Y

b. Select desired style .... ↑ ↓

To select font size:

a. Click **Size** .... Alt + S

b. Select desired size .... ↑ ↓

To underline text:

a. Click **Underline** .... Alt + U

3. Click **OK** .... Enter

EXERCISE

■ CREATING A FORM FROM AN EXISTING DATASHEET ■ ENTERING RECORDS ■ ENHANCING FORM DESIGN ■ CHANGING A FORM'S DATA AREA WIDTH

NOTES:

- You may view a table in either Datasheet or Form view. **Datasheet view** displays the table in a column and row format, similar to a spreadsheet grid.

DATASHEET VIEW

	LAST	FIRST	ADDRESS	ZIP	M/F	GRAD YR	COUNSELER	ID NO
▶	Johnson	Marie	108 Wilder Street	11554	F	1997	Litt	4535
	Harris	Richard	34 Desmond Avenu	11554	M	1997	Litt	7654
	Russo	Ron	22 Hapins Lane	11554	M	1996	Lifton	5467
	Lakhani	Deepa	87 Pine Street	11554	F	1996	Lifton	8765
	Lopez	Maria	987 Stiles Street	11590	F	1998	Cohen	9999
	Freeman	Keisha	5 Winding Way	11554	F	1998	Cohen	6776
	Yu	Vicki	888 Martin Court	11554	F	1998	Cohen	2323
	Rifsky	Vlad	109 Maple Lane	11554	M	1996	Scalisi	3213
	Craig	David	23 Oak Lane	11590	M	1996	Scalisi	9898
	Kim	Phil	11 Oak Lane	11590	M	1997	Cohen	5533
▶	Wasif	Ahman	1234 Woodrow St.	11590	M	1997	Litt	5543

Table: STUDENTS

Form view displays your records one at a time.

FORM VIEW

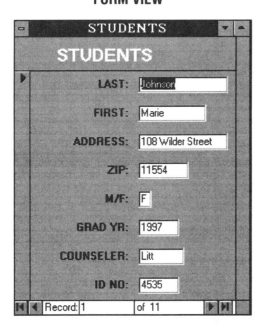

- The **AutoForm** button on the toolbar automatically creates a Form view of the fields and data listed in an open table.

- Once records have been added to either a Datasheet or a Form, you can use the arrow-head buttons on the Status bar to scroll through the records.

- To quickly switch between Form Design, Form, and Datasheet views, when using forms, use the appropriate option on the View menu.

Entering Records; Correcting a Field Entry

- It is easier to enter records in Datasheet view. Records added in either view will automatically be entered in the other. You enter data in Form view in the same manner as in Datasheet view. Pressing the Tab key after the last field brings up the next record form, and data is automatically saved as entered.

Changing Width of Form Item Areas

- If you discover that the Form view data areas need adjusting, you must return to Design view to make desired changes. To resize a field item area, first click on the item, click and hold down the left mouse button on one of the handles, and move in the desired direction.

Enhancing A Form Design

■ You can only make enhancement changes to a form in its Design view. The enhancement options become available on an added Form Design Toolbar that appears when a form item is selected. By clicking on the appropriate Form Design toolbar button, you can change the selected item's font type, size, and style or the alignment for the selected item.

Making font changes may result in a need to reset the item's allotted area (see right).

✓ Note: Access refers to form items as Controls. Enhancement changes to Form items DO NOT affect the related datasheet.

Undoing Item Adjustments

■ You can undo all enhancement changes by selecting the item to be reset and using the Apply Default option from the Format menu.

✓ Note: For enhancements to permanently affect the Form view you must save the revised design.

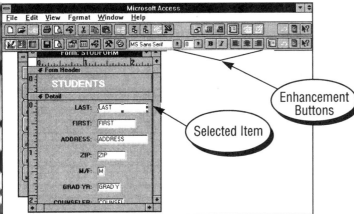

DESIGN VIEW

> *Your school wants to create a database file that will keep track of students who apply for school activities and clubs. You will create the form for this database.*

EXERCISE DIRECTIONS:

1. Create a new database file; name it **CLUBS**.

2. Design a table in the **CLUBS** file using the field information listed below:
   All fields will be Text fields.
   No primary key field is to be set for this table.

FIELD NAME	FIELD SIZE
LAST	20
FIRST	15
ADDRESS	20
ZIP	5
M/F	1
GRAD YR	4
COUNSELOR	10
ID NO	4

3. Save the table; name it STUDENTS.

4. Close the datasheet design window.

5. Open the STUDENTS datasheet; click the AutoForm button on the toolbar.

6. Save the created form; name it STFORM.

7. Select FORM from the database objects window.

   STFORM name will be highlighted.

8. Select Open to view the created form.

9. Close STFORM.

10. Open the STUDENTS table.

11. From the information listed below that was taken from the applications for membership in the NHS (National Honor Society) Club, enter the first three records using the STUDENTS table.

12. Adjust column widths to accommodate the longest column entry.

13. Save and close the STUDENTS datasheet.

14. Open the STFORM.

15. Scroll through all the records for this form.

16. Add the fourth, fifth, and sixth records from the listing below in either Datasheet or Form view.

17. Open STFORM in Design view.

18. Select the LAST field name item; change the font size to 12 point.

19. Select the LAST data area and make the following changes:

    Font size - 10 point; style - bold; alignment - centered.

20. Adjust item widths, if necessary.

21. Save the new Form design.

22. Using the View menu, switch to Form view.

23. View the results of your enhancements.

24. Return to the Form design.

25. Select each item that was changed; apply default settings.

26. Save this form design.

27. Close the database file **CLUBS**.

	Name	Address	Zip	M/F	Grad Yr	Counselor	ID #
1	Marie Johnson	108 Wilder St.	11554	F	1997	Litt	4535
2	Richard Harris	34 Desmond Ave.	11554	M	1997	Litt	7654
3	Ron Russo	22 Hapins Lane	11554	M	1996	Lifton	5467
4	Deepa Lakhani	87 Pine St.	11554	F	1996	Lifton	8765
5	Maria Lopez	987 Stiles St.	11590	F	1998	Cohen	9999
6	Keisha Freeman	5 Winding Way	11554	F	1998	Cohen	6776

CREATE FORM VIEW FOR TABLE

. Open file and table.

. Press **AutoForm** button..................

ENTER DATA IN FORM VIEW

. Type data in first field ....*data*

. Press **Tab**.................................... `Tab`

. Repeat steps 1 and 2 until complete.

. Press **Enter**.............................. `Enter`

CHANGE WIDTH OF FORM ITEM

. Change to Form Design view (see above).

. Click on the item to be sized.

. Using right handle, drag to size.

CHANGE FROM FORM TO FORM DESIGN VIEW

1. Click **View**............................. `Alt`+`V`
2. Click **Form Design**............................ `D`

DISPLAY FORM DESIGN TOOLBAR

1. Click **View**............................. `Alt`+`V`
2. Click **Toolbars**................................. `B`
3. Select **Form Design**........................ `↓`
4. Click **Show**....................................... `S`

FORMAT FORM DESIGN

1. Select item to be formatted.
2. Click button that applies from the Form Design Toolbar.

RETURN TO DEFAULT SETTINGS

1. Click **Format**........................`Alt`+`O`
2. Click **Apply Default**.......................... `D`

LESSON 1
SUMMARY EXERCISE 6

Your department is responsible for ordering and evaluating software products used at company stores. To keep track of the types of software you order, their price, and where they are stored, you have been asked to set up a company database table.

EXERCISE DIRECTIONS:

1. Open the ⌨ **COMPANY** database or 💾 **ACOMPANY.6**.

2. Create a new table using the field data listed below:

NAME	DATA TYPE	SIZE	DESCRIPTION
BRANCH	Text	16	Where currently in use.
TITLE	Text	11	
TYPE	Text	17	
PRICE	Currency	(Use Fixed Format)	
PURDATE	Date/Time	(Use Short Date Format)	
STORED	Text	4	Storage Drawer #

3. Save and Close the table design; name it SOFTWARE.

4. Open the SOFTWARE table.

5. Click the AutoForm button on the toolbar.

6. Save the created form; name it SOFTFORM.

7. Switch to Form view.

8. Enter the software data listed below in either Form or Datasheet view:

9. In Form view, scroll through all the records to verify data.

10. Switch to the Form Design.

11. Select the BRANCH field name; change font size to 12.

12. Enlarge the BRANCH field name area to accommodate the larger font size.

13. Select the BRANCH data area; make the following changes: font size - 10 point; style - bold; alignment - center.

14. Save this design.

15. Change to Form view. Note the results of your enhancements.

16. Check for the necessity for design adjustments; make these adjustments.

17. Switch to Datasheet view.

18. Change font size to 10 point; adjust column widths as necessary.

19. Save and Close the datasheet.

20. Close the **COMPANY** database.

Branch	Software Title	Type	Price	Purchase Date	Stored
Sunset	Word-O	Word Processing	499.85	8/17/94	D230
Big Apple	Micro Words	Word Processing	459.80	6/14/94	D230
Pacific	Word-O-D	Word Processing	499.85	5/18/94	D235
Lakeview	Word-O-2	Word Processing	499.85	2/20/94	D235
Lakeview	Tulip5	Spreadsheet	594.20	3/21/94	D238
Big Apple	Exceller	Spreadsheet	475.50	3/21/94	D238
Pacific	Accessor	Database	550.50	12/15/94	A114
Big Apple	InfoBase	Database	488.88	1/20/95	A114
Bean Town	BBS	Communications	111.50	3/15/95	D230
Wheatland	Officemate	Integrated	479.95	3/15/95	D238
Sunset	Harwood	Graphics	299.95	1/30/95	D230
Lakeview	Pagemaker	Desktop	399.40	2/15/95	A114

LESSON 2

EDITING AND PRINTING A DATABASE

Exercises 7-12

- Modifying Datasheets and Forms

- Editing Data

- Printing Datasheets and Forms

EXERCISE

MODIFYING A DATASHEET DESIGN

7

NOTES:

- Fields may be added, moved, or deleted in a table or a form. All structural changes must be made in Design view.

- When a field is changed in a datasheet it DOES NOT automatically transfer to related forms. Since modifying a Form design is a multi-step process, it is much easier to recreate the related form after changing a datasheet.

Adding a Field to a Datasheet

- You can create space for a new field by clicking on the field selector, the gray area to the left of the row, where the new field is to be added, or you can add a new field to a datasheet after the last existing field and then move it to a more desirable location.

Deleting a Field in a Datasheet

- The field to be deleted is selected using the field selector and then deleted. The data will reposition itself.

Moving a Field in Design View

- A field may be moved most efficiently by dragging it to a new position in Design view. If you wish to move a field in a datasheet, it must be done by inserting a row, reentering the field name, deleting the original row, and then pasting the data into the new column. Copy and paste operations should not be used for the field name or the data will be lost.

You have been given student applications for the NHS Club. You can now enter the information in your Clubs' database Students table. You will want to add a new first field into this table to keep track of which club is being applied for.

EXERCISE DIRECTIONS:

1. Open the ▦ **CLUBS** database or 🖫 **ACLUBS.7**.

2. Open the **STUDENTS** table Design view.

3. Open a new first row.

4. Add the new field CLUB (Data type - text; Field size - 5).

5. Save and close Design view.

6. Switch to the STUDENTS table.

7. Enter the data taken from the membership applications to the NHS Club into the appropriate fields.

8. Adjust column widths to accommodate the longest column entry.

9. Save and close the STUDENTS datasheet.

10. Open the Design view for this table.

11. Move the CLUB field so that it is positioned after the ZIP column.

12. Using AutoForm, create a Form view of this datasheet; name it **CLUBFORM**.

13. Scroll through the records in the created form.

14. Save and Close the form and the database CLUBS.

Name	Address	Zip	Club	M/F	Grad. Yr.	Counselor	ID #
Marie Johnson	108 Wilder St.	11554	NHS	F	1997	Litt	4535
Richard Harris	34 Desmond Ave.	11554	NHS	M	1997	Litt	7654
Ron Russo	22 Hapins Lane	11554	NHS	M	1996	Lifton	5467
Deepa Lakhani	87 Pine St.	11554	NHS	F	1996	Lifton	8765
Maria Lopez	987 Stiles St.	11590	NHS	F	1998	Cohen	9999
Keisha Freeman	5 Winding Way	11554	NHS	F	1998	Cohen	6776
Vicki Yu	888 Martin Court	11554	NHS	F	1998	Cohen	2323
Vlad Rifsky	109 Maple Lane	11554	NHS	M	1996	Scalisi	3213
David Craig	23 Oak Lane	11590	NHS	M	1996	Scalisi	9898
Phil Kim	11 Oak Lane	11590	NHS	M	1997	Cohen	5533
Wasif Ahman	1234 Woodrow St.	11590	NHS	M	1997	Litt	5543

ADD FIELDS

1. Click in top available Field Name area, if necessary.

2. Type new field name .... *fieldname*

   ✓ *Field names may be up to 64 characters long.*

3. Press **Tab** .... `Tab`

4. Click drop-down arrow .... `Alt` + `↓` to reveal data type list.

5. Select **data type** .... `↓`

6. Press **Tab** .... `Tab`

7. Type description, if desired.

8. Press **Tab** .... `Tab`

DELETE A FIELD

In Design view:

1. Click the field selector (left of field name).

2. Press **Delete** .... `Del`

MOVE A FIELD

1. Click the field selector (left of field name).

2. Click and drag field selector to new location.

EXERCISE

8

▪ OPENING AN EXISTING DATASHEET ▪ MODIFYING THE DATASHEET ▪ ENTERING RECORDS ▪ CHANGING DATASHEET COLUMN WIDTHS ▪ SIMPLE PRINTING ▪ HIDING DATASHEET FIELDS

NOTES:

Changing a Datasheet

▪ To open an existing table, you must first open the database file which contains that table. A listing of all the tables currently existing in this database file appears when the file is opened.

Simple Printing

▪ You can get a printout of current screen data in either Datasheet view or Form view. To print the current screen data, either choose the Print option from the File menu or click on the print icon. The dialog box that appears gives you the ability to choose the print range, quality, number of copies, and setup options. Note the Print dialog box below:

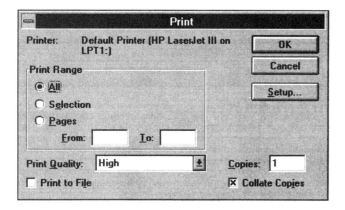

Hiding Datasheet Fields

▪ You may display and/or print selected fields in a datasheet by hiding unwanted fields. Hiding columns DOES NOT affect either the table's design definition or any form that was created for the datasheet. Columns may be redisplayed by using the Show option.

Your manager at Bit-Byte has just asked you to add two more fields to your STORES table. She realized that sales information and whether or not a branch has evening hours should have been included.

EXERCISE DIRECTIONS:

1. Open the ⌨ **COMPANY** database or 💾 **ACOMPANY.8**.

2. Select the STORES table.

3. Open the STORES Design view.

4. Insert two blank rows above the STAFF field row.

5. Add two new fields:

   SALES
   (Data type - number; Field size - long integer; Format - standard; Decimal places - 0)

   EVE
   (Data type - text; Field size - 3)

6. Delete the STORE NUMBER field.

7. Save and Close the new design.

8. Open the STORES table.

9. From the list below, enter the information for each branch.

BRANCH	SALES	EVE
Big Apple	789,300	YES
Pacific	685,400	NO
Sunset	876,988	NO
Lakeview	755,420	NO
Peach Tree	457,800	YES
Bean Town	682,450	YES
Astro Center	541,000	NO
Twin Cities	235,420	YES
Wheatland	352,415	YES
Oceanview	433,443	YES

10. Adjust column widths to accommodate the longest entry.

11. Print Preview the datasheet.

12. Hide SALES field.

13. Print Preview the datasheet.

14. Print this datasheet display.

15. Show SALES field.

16. Save the datasheet.

17. Use AutoForm to create a related Form view of this datasheet; name it STFORM.

18. Scroll through STFORM to locate the Lakeview form.

19. Print this form.

20. Close the database **COMPANY**.

🌐 PREVIEW FORM/TABLE

Click **Print Preview** button .... 🖺

OR

a. Click **File** menu .... `Alt`+`F`

b. Click **Print Preview** .... `V`

PRINT DATA IN A FORM

1. View form to print.

   OR

   Select form in Database window.

2. Click **File** menu .... `Alt`+`F`

3. Click **Print** .... `P`

4. Click a Print Range option to select:

- **All** .... `Alt`+`A`

- **Selection** .... `Alt`+`E`

- **Pages** .... `Alt`+`P`

5. Select a **Print Quality** .... `Alt`+`Q`
   option, if desired.

6. Type number .... `Alt`+`C`
   in **Copies** text box, if desired.

7. Click **OK** .... `⏎`

PRINT DATA IN A TABLE

1. Click **File** menu .... `Alt`+`F`

2. Click **Print** .... `P`

3. Click **OK** .... `⏎`

HIDE A COLUMN

1. Click in column you would like to hide.

2. Click **Format** menu .... `Alt`+`O`

3. Click **Hide Columns** .... `H`

SHOW A COLUMN

1. Click **Format** menu .... `Alt`+`O`

2. Click **Show Columns** .... `S`

3. Highlight column you would like to show.

4. Click **Show** .... `Alt`+`S`

5. Click **Close** .... `Alt`+`C`

EXERCISE

■ **MODIFYING A DATASHEET** ■ **PRINTING** ■ **PRINTING WITH HEADERS AND FOOTERS**

9

NOTES:

Print Setup

■ Before actually printing a Datasheet or Form records, you can use the File menu's Print Setup to choose various print options. You can change:

- Printer
- Print Orientation (Portrait - the default, Landscape - to print sideways)
- Paper Size (Letter - the default, Legal, Envelope, User Defined Size)
- Margins
- Data Only (Default - unselected, when selected - datasheet gridlines will not print)
- Options: Gray Scale, Paper Source, Duplex Printing, etc.

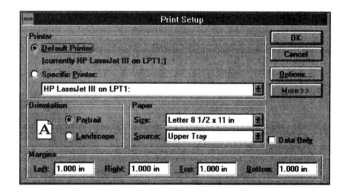

■ In Form view there are additional printing options that can be accessed by the More button in Print Setup. You can set the number of items to print across the page; the layout, the row, and column spacing; and the width and height of the items. The Print Preview option allows you to check the layout before printing. Note the illustrations of the Print Preview screens for one column and two column printouts:

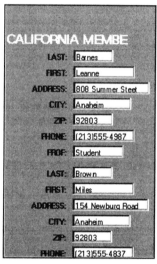

PRINT PREVIEW WITH 1 ITEM ACROSS

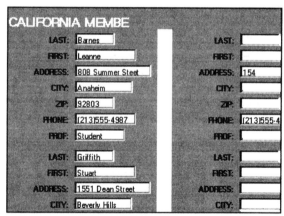

PRINT PREVIEW WITH 2 ITEMS ACROSS

Add Header and/or Footer

■ Headers or footers CANNOT be included directly in a datasheet printout. Headers and footers can only be included when a report is created. (*The procedures necessary to create a report for a datasheet will be discussed in Lesson 5.*)

Form Headers and Footers

- In form design view an upper section titled Form Header and a lower section titled Form Footer appears when Form Headers/Footers is selected from the Format menu. A form header or footer may be added using the text tool. If you double-click on the gray area in this section, an All Properties window will appear. To control when the Form Header section will appear, select the Display When option, the default setting is Always, and other options are Print Only or Screen Only.

Page Headers/Footers

- If you wish the printout heading to be different from the header on each form, you may set a page header or footer using the Format, Page Header/Footer options. You can control when the page header will appear in the same way as for a form header.

In order to use the HUG membership list for mailings, it is necessary to include a zip code for each member. Since certain mailings apply only to a particular professional group, it would be helpful to include a field that will identify a person's profession. This will enable us to send information to one particular group rather than to everyone on our list. In this exercise, you will add two new fields (ZIP and PROF) and print selected records.

EXERCISE DIRECTIONS:

1. Open the ⌨ **HUGCLUB** database or 💾 **AHUGCLUB.9**.

2. Open the **MEMBERS** table design view.

3. Add two new fields, ZIP and PROF, in the locations noted below; set an appropriate field size.

4. Add the data indicated for these new fields.

5. Change the table font size to 10 point.

6. Adjust column widths, as necessary.

7. Save the MEMBERS datasheet.

8. Use Print Setup to change:

   The orientation to Landscape and margins to .5 ".

9. Preview the printout.

10. Print the datasheet.

11. Create a form for the updated datasheet; name it MEMFORM.

12. Open the MEMFORM Design view.

13. If the form header section is not displayed, use the Format, Form Header/Footer option. Enter California Member as the form header.

14. Open the Properties window for the Form Header section; set Display When to Screen Only.

15. From the Format menu, select Page Header/Footer.

16. In the new Page Header section that appears, enter the heading **CALIFORNIA MEMBERS**.

17. Open the Properties window for the Page Header section; set Display When to Print Only.

18. Close Design view.

19. Open MEMFORM.

20. Set up for two column printing.

21. Print Preview.

22. Print the records.

23. Save and Close MEMFORM.

24. Close the database.

California Members

LAST	FIRST	ADDRESS	CITY	ZIP	PHONE	PROF
Barnes	Leanne	808 Summer Street	Anaheim	92803	(213)555-4987	Student
Brown	Miles	154 Newburg Road	Anaheim	92803	(213)555-4837	Accountant
Griffith	Stuart	1551 Dean Street	Beverly Hills	90210	(213)555-3010	Lawyer
Moon	Michael	17 Pine Street	Beverly Hills	90210	(213)555-9275	Teacher
Smith	Trina	3954 Wood Avenue	Anaheim	92803	(213)555-7283	Student
Smith	Sheila	417 Specific Court	Anaheim	92803	(213)555-7284	Chiropractor
Walker	Bette	1584 F. Street	North Hollywood	91615	(213)555-9174	Lawyer
Castillo	Carl	1956 Park Avenue	North Hollywood	91615	(213)555-5192	Banker
Davis	John	P.O. Box 2333	North Hollywood	91615	(213)555-8129	Student
Dixon	Amy	237 Albee Street	North Hollywood	91615	(213)555-8917	Orthopedist

ADD HEADER TO FORM

1. View form design.

2. Click **Format** menu................ `Alt`+`O`

3. Click desired option to select:

   • **Form Header/Footer**................. `H`

   • **Page Header/Footer**................. `P`

DELETE HEADER

1. View form design.

2. Click **Format** menu................ `Alt`+`O`

3. Click desired option to clear:

   • **Form Header/Footer**................. `H`

   • **Page Header/Footer**................. `P`

DISPLAY SECTION PROPERTY SHEET

   ✓ *The contents of the property sheet will vary depending on the section selected.*

1. Double-click section or section header.

   OR

   Place pointer on section or section header and click to select.

2. Click **Properties** button................... 🗐

   OR

   a. Click **View** menu............... `Alt`+`V`

   b. Click **Properties**.......................... `P`

DISPLAY FORM PROPERTY SHEET

1. Double-click gray area to the right of any section.

   OR

   Click gray area to the right of any section.

2. Click **Properties** button................... 🗐

   OR

   a. Click **Edit** menu............... `Alt`+`E`

   b. Click **Select Form**....................... `R`

   c. Click **View** menu............... `Alt`+`V`

   d. Click **Properties**.......................... `P`

CHANGE FORM OR SECTION PROPERTIES

1. Select form or section.

2. Display property sheet.

3. Choose desired property category.

4. Click desired property..................... `↓`

5. Type desired value ....*value*

   ✓ *Options will vary depending on form, section, or property chosen.*

   OR

   Click drop-down arrow........... `Alt`+`↓`

6. Repeat steps 4 and 5 for each change.

7. Click **Properties** button to close....... 🗐

   OR

   Double-click property........... `Alt`+`F4`
   sheet's control menu box
   to close.

   OR

   a. Click **View** menu............... `Alt`+`V`

   b. Click **Properties**.......................... `P`

PRINT SETUP

1. Click **File** menu...................... `Alt`+`F`

2. Click **Print Setup** .... `R`

3. Select an Orientation:

   Portrait... `R`

   OR

   Landscape...................................... `L`

4. Click **OK**.. `↵`

EXERCISE

▪ EDITING A RECORD ▪ ADDING AND DELETING A RECORD

NOTES:

Editing a Record

- To change the data that has already been entered in a field: highlight the existing data and retype the new data. This may be done in either Datasheet or Form views. You may also click on the section of data that needs revising and make the needed changes.

- To delete the contents of a field: select the data, then press the Delete key or select the Delete option from the Edit menu.

Adding a Record

- Records may be added in either Datasheet or Form views but only at the end of the existing records.

Deleting a Record

- Records may be deleted in either Datasheet or Form views by using the Select Record option from the Edit menu and the Delete key. Access will renumber the records when a new record is added or when a record is deleted.

  NOTE: You can undo the last action performed by selecting the Undo option from the Edit menu.

Several students are no longer being considered for membership in the National Honor Society (NHS), and several new students have just submitted applications. You have also discovered several errors in the records. You will need to edit your datasheet to reflect these changes. Applications have just been received for the Academy of Finance Program (AFP). You will need to add these to your datasheet.

EXERCISE DIRECTIONS:

1. Open the ⌨ **CLUBS** database or 💾 **ACLUBS.10**.

2. Open the STUDENTS table.

3. The students listed below have applied for admission to the Academy of Finance Program (AFP). Add their records to the database.

NAME	ADDRESS	ZIP	M/F	GRAD YR	COUNSELOR	ID #
Kristin DeLorenzo	871 River Road	11554	F	1997	Litt	6661
Matthew Chasin	99 Bridle Lane	11554	M	1996	Lifton	9976
Chad Wilkinson	2 Token Court	11554	M	1996	Lifton	1212
Ebony Rivers	33 Pine St.	11554	F	1997	Litt	5555
Jennifer Juliana	78 Token Court	11554	F	1997	Litt	8888

4. Ron Russo is no longer being considered for membership in the NHS; delete his record.

5. The students listed below have applied for admission to the NHS; add their records to the datasheet.

NAME	ADDRESS	ZIP	M/F	GRAD YR	COUNSELOR	ID #
Wendy Chou	9012 Hylan Blvd.	11554	F	1997	Cohen	5536
Rick Smith	9012 Hylan Blvd.	11554	M	1997	Cohen	2234

6. Adjust column widths to accommodate the longest entry.

7. Save the datasheet.

8. Hide the ADDRESS and ZIP columns.

9. Preview your page.

10. Print the datasheet.

11. Display the hidden fields.

12. Save and Close the datasheet.

13. Open the STFORM design view.

14. Open the Properties window for the Form Header section; set Display When to Screen Only.

15. From the Format menu, select Page Header/Footer.

16. In the new Page Header section that appears, enter the heading APPLICANTS.

17. Open the Properties window for the Page Header section; set Display When to Print Only.

18. Close form Design view.

19. Open the STFORM.

20. Set the Print Setup for two column printing.

21. Print Preview.

22. Print the records.

23. Close the **CLUBS** database file.

EDIT DATA

Replace Data in a Field:

✓ *Access automatically saves changes to fields when you move to the next record. A pencil icon appears at left of record in Datasheet view and at the top left of the window in Form view to indicate that the changes have not yet been saved.*

1. Place insertion point .... `Tab` in field to change.

OR

Press the **Down-Arrow** key .... `↓`

OR

Click and drag to select field contents.

2. Type desired new value ....*value*

DELETE A RECORD

In Form View:

1. Scroll to the record to be deleted.

2. Click **Edit** .... `Alt`+`E`

3. Click **Select record** .... `L`

4. Press **Delete** .... `Del`

OR

a. Click **Edit**............................ `Alt`+`E`

b. Click **Delete** .... `E`

5. Click **OK** .... `↵`

EXERCISE

■ EDITING RECORDS ■ INSERTING AND DELETING RECORDS
■ PRINTING RECORDS

Bit-Byte has opened several new branches. In some branches there have been personnel changes. The datasheet STORES, therefore, will need to be updated.

EXERCISE DIRECTIONS:

1. Open the 🖮 **COMPANY** database or
   💾**ACOMPANY.11**.

2. Open the **STORES** datasheet.

3. Add the following new branches to the datasheet.

8. Use Print Setup to print in Landscape orientation.

9. Print the datasheet.

10. Reset the datasheet's gridlines.

11. Save and Close the datasheet.

BRANCH	CITY	ST	STAFF	SALES	EVE
Liberty	Philadelphia	PA	19	423,150	YES
Seal City Center	Anchorage	AL	6	185,420	NO
Central States	San Diego	CA	14	144,524	NO
Federal Plaza	Washington	DC	11	245,860	NO
Desert View Mall	Phoenix	AZ	8	189,252	YES
Rocky Mountain	Denver	CO	9	102,563	YES
Southland	Mobile	AL	7	104,566	NO
River View Plaza	Atlanta	GA	6	215,400	NO
Dixieland	Atlanta	GA	14	352,622	YES
Iron City Plaza	Cleveland	OH	13	543,233	NO

4. Adjust column widths to accommodate the longest entry.

5. There have been changes in the number of employees in the following branches.

   Make these changes in the datasheet:

Big Apple	20
Wheatland	11
Astro Center	12
Peach Tree	16
Sunset	13

6. The Twin Cities branch closed; delete the record.

7. Remove the datasheet's gridlines.

✓ *Note:* *It is possible to remove the gridlines from a datasheet before printing or as a view preference. Use the Format, Gridlines commands to turn the gridlines on or off as desired.*

LESSON 2
SUMMARY EXERCISE 12 PART I

In the past, computer equipment inventory records for your company were kept on "inventory cards." In an earlier exercise, you created an inventory datasheet design, HARDWARE. In this exercise, you will enter information from those cards into the database.

EXERCISE DIRECTIONS:

1. Open the 🖮 **COMPANY** database or 💾 **ACOMPANY.12**.

2. Open the HARDWARE table design.

3. Add two fields to the end of the existing design:

   ASSIGNED TO (Field size - 15);
   SERIAL # (Field size - 7).

4. Save the new design; do not create a primary key.

5. Change to Datasheet view.

6. The listing below represents "inventory card" data. Enter the field data in upper and lower case, except where names are represented by initials (NEC, IBM, etc.). Change the default WTY setting, where needed.

7. Adjust column widths.

8. Print the datasheet.

9. Save the datasheet; do not close the datasheet.

10. Create a Form view of this datasheet.

11. Save Form view; name it HARDFORM.

12. Use Print Setup from the File menu to make the following changes: Landscape orientation; all print margins to .5 ".

13. Use the Print Setup More window to set for 3 Items Across.

14. Print the form records.

15. Save and close Form view.

BRANCH	ITEM	MFG	MODEL	COST	PUR-DATE	WTY	ASSIGNED TO	SERIAL #
Big Apple	Computer	IBM	PS2	$1248.50	6/94	Yes	Accounting	651198
Big Apple	Printer	IBM	ExecJet II	$335.00	6/94	Yes	Accounting	55211
Sunset	Computer	IBM	Thinkpad 350C	$2199.00	6/94	Yes	Accounting	AB2059
Pacific	Computer	IBM	Thinkpad 500	$1399.00	6/94	Yes	Accounting	671150
Pacific	Hard Drive	Quantum	LPS40 170MB	$199.00	6/94	Yes	Accounting	54219
Sunset	Hard Drive	Conner	CFS4 210MB	$200.00	6/94	No	Purchasing	12345
Pacific	Printer	HP	Laserjet	$1479.00	7/94	No	Accounting	88842
Bean Town	Computer	Canon	Notebook 486	$1889.00	1/94	Yes	Shipping	1445A

LESSON 2
SUMMARY EXERCISE 12 PART II

Your company has acquired new equipment. These new purchases must be added to the inventory. When checking the datasheet, you find several errors which need to be corrected.

EXERCISE DIRECTIONS:

1. Open the HARDWARE table.

2. From the information below, add the new equipment purchases.

BRANCH	ITEM	MFG	MODEL	COST	PUR-DATE	WTY	ASSIGNED TO	SERIAL #
Wheatland	Printer	NEC	FGE/3V	539	8/94	No	Purchasing	87098
Lakeview	Printer	NEC	FGE/4V	589	12/94	No	Shipping	11112
Bean Town	Modem	Intel	PCMCIA	115	9/94	No	Accounting	098A
Bean Town	Printer	Okidata	ML320	295	8/94	Yes	Shipping	98983
Sunset	Printer	HP	Deskjet	429	11/94	Yes	Accounting	99911
Pacific	Printer	HP	Deskjet	429	11/94	Yes	Purchasing	22230
Wheatland	Computer	Canon	Notebook	2436	8/94	Yes	Purchasing	98763
Lakeview	Computer	Canon	Notebook	2436	8/94	Yes	Shipping	76666

3. Adjust column widths, if necessary.

4. The correct cost of the IBM PS2, purchased on 6/94, was $1348.50; make the correction.

5. The Quantum hard drive is not under warranty; make the correction.

6. The HP Laserjet printer, purchased on 7/94, is no longer in use; delete the record from the datasheet.

7. Change the datasheet Font to Times New Roman, size 12 point.

8. Change the datasheet Row Height to 14.

9. Print Preview your datasheet. (The preview will have 2 pages.)

10. Change the print orientation to Landscape.

11. Preview this setup.

12. Return to the datasheet; adjust column widths, as desired.

13. Print one copy of the datasheet.

14. Reset the font to the default setting (MS Sans Serif, 8 point).

15. Reset the Row Height setting to Standard Height.

16. Save and Close the database.

LESSON 3

SEARCHING AND SORTING A DATABASE

Exercises 13-17

- Searching Datasheets and Forms

- Sorting Data

- Creating Subsets from Datasheets and Forms

EXERCISE

■ **FINDING RECORDS** ■ **USING WILDCARDS** ■ **FINDING RECORDS AND REPLACING DATA**

NOTES:

Finding Records

- The Edit menu contains options which assist in the finding and replacing of data. These options are available in both Datasheet and Form views.

- You may wish to find a specific record to edit or get information from. Access will search below or above a selected record. Therefore, to search the entire set of records, select the first record and choose the down direction or select the last record and choose the up direction. After opening either Datasheet or Form view of the records to be searched, select Find from the Edit menu and the Find dialog box will appear:

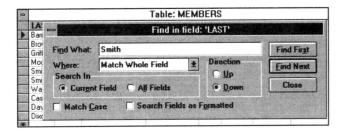

- After making the appropriate entry in the Find What box, set the Find window conditions:

  Where option - Match Whole Field or Any Part of Field

  Search in - Current Field - cursor's field location or All Fields

  Match Case - select to match exactly upper and lower case entries or, if not selected, search will ignore case of entry

  Search Fields as Formatted (if data format in view is different from defined format) - selected or not selected

  Direction of search (Up or Down)

- When all the appropriate conditions have been set, select Find First to begin the search. The first record, containing the search data, is presented with the search data highlighted. You can now view or edit the located record. To edit a record, close the Find window, make the needed changes, and reopen the Find window to continue.

- To search for another record that contains the same data, select Find Next. The next record containing the search data or a message that no more records were found (click OK to remove this message) is presented.

  ✓ *Note: The Find box may overlap the records. You can move this window (click and drag the Title bar of the window) to another screen location. The Find box can be removed from the screen only by selecting the Close option. To speed up the find process, select the field to be searched, in either Datasheet or Form view, and select the Current Field option in the Find window.*

Searching Using Wildcards

- A wildcard is a symbol used in a search value to substitute for unknown characters. There are two wildcard symbols that broaden the find command: the asterisk (*) and the question mark (?).

  The asterisk (*) is used to indicate an unknown group of characters. For example: If you were searching for a particular name but were certain of only the first two letters, you would indicate the search value as Br*. This will find all records in which the last name begins with Br.

The question mark (?) is used to substitute for an unknown single character. If you were searching for a particular name but were uncertain of some characters in the spelling, the search value could be entered as, for example, Br?wn or Br?w? or B??wn. This would find records with any letter in the question mark location.

Finding and Replacing

If you know that all records with the same field data should be replaced, you can use a find and replace option. After you select Replace from the Edit menu a Replace window will appear.

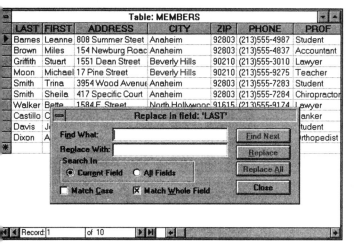

The Replace window has many of the same options as the Find window. In the Replace window, make the appropriate entries in the Find What and Replace With boxes. When all the appropriate conditions have been set, select:

Find Next - to find the first occurrence of your search entry. You may choose to make the replacement or find the next occurrence.

OR

Replace All - to automatically change all occurrences. Access will NOT ask you to confirm replacements.

✓ Note: The Replace box may overlap the records. You can move this window to another screen location. The Replace box can be removed from the screen only by selecting the Close option.

To speed up the search and replace process, select the field to be searched, in either Datasheet or Form view, and select the Current Field option in the Replace window.

> *Several new members have joined HUG, your computer users' group. In addition, you have been notified that several members' records need to be updated. After updating your records, you will be in a better position to generate membership information.*

EXERCISE DIRECTIONS:

1. Open the ⌨ **HUGCLUB** database or 💾 **AHUGCLUB.13**.

2. From the information below, add the new members to your current datasheet.

LAST	FIRST	ADDRESS	CITY	ZIP	PHONE	PROF
Kendall	Gale	15 Imperial Way	Beverly Hills	90210	(213)555-9888	Teacher
Dagger	Janice	27 Ocean Avenue	Anaheim	92804	(213)555-7777	Orthopedist
Chow	Michae	l88 Riverside Drive	Culver City	90311	(213)555-7655	Accountant
Wagner	David	879 Beverly Drive	Beverly Hills	90210	(213)555-6676	Banker
Smith	Cleo	90 Rodeo Drive	Beverly Hills	90210	(213)555-2222	Student
Anderson	Carolyn	666 Santa Ana Drive	Culver City	90312	(213)555-9988	Lawyer
Ramaz	Nadine	9012 Wilshire Blvd.	Beverly Hills	90210	(213)555-2211	Teacher
Yakar	Winston	776 Prince Lane	North Hollywood	91615	(213)555-1584	Student
Mancuso	Mary	12 Pacific Court	North Hollywood	91615	(213)555-7773	Banker

3. Using Edit, Find search the database for the answers to the following questions. Make note of the answers.

   a. Which members live in Anaheim?

   b. Which members live in Beverly Hills?

   c. Which members are Lawyers?

   d. How many members are Students?

   e. What is Trina Smith's profession?

4. Locate the record for Michael Moon.

   Make the following changes on his record:

   His new address is 32 Oak Street.

   His new phone number is (213)555-8750.

5. Locate the record for Bette Walker.

   Make the following changes on her record:

   Her new name is Bette Walker-Sim.

   Her new address is 1745 River Street, located in North Hollywood, 91615.

   Her new phone number is (213)555-8520.

6. Locate the record for Sheila Smith. Change her phone number to (213)555-7284.

7. Find and replace all occurrences of Avenue with Ave.

8. Adjust column widths, as necessary.

9. Save and Close the datasheet.

10. Close the **HUGCLUB** database.

FIND AND REPLACE DATA

1. Click field to match or, in Datasheet view, click field selector or any field in column.

2. Click **Edit** menu .... `Alt`+`E`

3. Click **Replace** .... `R`

4. Type data to replace ....*data* in **Find What** text box.

5. Type replacement data .... `Alt`+`P` in **Replace With** text box.

6. Click search range to select desired option:

   • **Current Field** .... `Alt`+`E`

   • **All Fields**.......................... `Alt`+`L`

7. Click **Match Case** .... `Alt`+`C` to restrict search.

8. Click **Match Whole Field** .... `Alt`+`W` to restrict search.

   To replace text in next matching field only:

   Click **Replace**........................ `Alt`+`R`

   To replace text in all matching fields at once:

   Click **Replace All** .... `Alt`+`A`

To view next matching field only:

Click **Find Next**...................... `Alt`+`F`

9. Click **Close** when finished.

10. Click **OK**............................. `Close` to confirm changes.

FIND RECORDS USING FIND OPTIONS

1. Click field to match or, in Datasheet view, click field selector or any field in column.

2. Click **Find** button. .... 🔍

   OR

   a. Click **Edit** menu .... `Alt`+`E`

   b. Click **Find** .... `F`

3. Type value in **Find What** text box......*value*

4. Select .... `Alt`+`H` , `Alt`+`▼` desired part of field to match in **Where** list:

   • **Any Part of Field**

   • **Match Whole Field**

   • **Start of Field**

---

5. Set search range by clicking desired option to select:

   • **Current Field** .... `Alt`+`E`

   • **All Fields**........................... `Alt`+`L`

6. Choose direction of search by clicking option to select:

   • **Up**...................................... `Alt`+`U`

   • **Down** .... `Alt`+`D`

7. Click **Match Case**, ... `Alt`+`C` if desired.

8. Click **Search Fields**............... `Alt`+`O` as F**o**rmatted.

   ✓ *Matches formatting of number, date, currency, and yes/no field rather than data actually stored in table.*

9. Click **Find Next**...................... `Alt`+`F`

   OR

   Click **Find First**...................... `Alt`+`S`

EXERCISE

■ SORTING RECORDS ■ MULTIPLE SORTS

NOTES:

Sorting Records

■ The order in which records are entered is frequently not appropriate to locate and update records. Sorting allows you to rearrange the information so that you can look at it in different ways.

■ Sorting a collection of records can provide the following:

Data arranged in alphabetical or numerical order

Data arranged to see the largest or smallest number in a numerical field

Data arranged into groups (example: all people who live in Washington)

A method to find duplicate entries

■ Database records can be sorted in either Form or Datasheet views. However, it is easier to see the rearranged records in Datasheet view.

■ Sorting is accomplished in either ascending or descending order. Ascending order goes in alphabetical order from A to Z or in numerical order. Dates are sorted from the oldest to the most recent date and time from the earliest to the latest. Descending order is the opposite.

Sorting Records Using Quick Sort

■ A quick sort option is available on the records menu in either the Datasheet or Form view. When Records, Quick Sort is selected, the choice of ascending or descending is provided. Quick sort may also be accomplished using the ascending or descending sort buttons illustrated below.

✓ Note: *The selected column(s) will be **temporarily sorted**. The sorted records can be printed at this time. This version can become permanent only by saving the table or form.*

Multiple Sorts

■ Several columns of data may be sorted at one time, and each column's sort order can be determined independently to provide a sort on multiple criteria. A datasheet or form may be sorted on multiple criteria by using Edit Filter/Sort from the Records menu. When the Filter window appears, the fields to be sorted should be dragged to the lower section grid in the sort order desired.

■ To undo the sort, select Show All Records from the Records menu.

Your company manager has requested the STORES datasheet records to be sorted. This way it would be easier to find information. In this exercise, you will sort records on one or more fields.

EXERCISE DIRECTIONS:

1. Open the 📇 **COMPANY** database or 💾 **ACOMPANY.14**.

2. Open the HARDWARE table.

3. Sort the datasheet in each of the following ways:

   a. in ascending (alphabetical) order by ITEM

   b. in ascending order by ASSIGNED TO

   c. in descending order by COST

   d. in alphabetical order by MFG and alphabetical order by ITEM

   e. in alphabetical order by ITEM, alphabetical order by MFG, and descending order by COST Print one copy of this sort.

4. Change to Form view.

5. Sort the forms into descending (reverse-alphabetical) order.

6. Print the forms.

7. Close the database.

USE QUICK SORT

1. Open the datasheet or form.

2. Select the column(s) to be sorted in Datasheet view or one field in Form view.

3. Click **Records**........................ Alt + R

4. Click **Quick Sort**.............................. Q

5. Select Ascending or Descending.

   OR

   Click on appropriate button,...... sheet or form.

FILTER AND SORT RECORDS

Sorts and displays specified records in Form or Datasheet view. Filters are similar to queries but are not usually saved with the form.

1. View desired form or datasheet.

2. Click **Edit Filter/Sort** .... button.

   OR

   a. Click **Records** menu .... Alt + R

   b. Click **Edit Filter/Sort**.................... F

3. Drag desired field from field list to field cell in lower part of window.

4. Click **Sort**.

5. Place pointer in Criteria cell............*criteria*

6. Repeat steps 3-5 for each additional field to search or sort.

7. Click **Apply Filter/Sort** .... button.

   OR

   a. Click **Records** menu .... Alt + R

   b. Click **Apply Filter/Sort**.................

REMOVE SORT

Click **Show All Records** button ....

   OR

   a. Click **Records** menu .... Alt + R

   b. Click **Show All Records**............... S

EXERCISE

- ISOLATING A RECORD SUBSET ▪ SORTING A RECORD SUBSET ▪ EDITING A RECORD SUBSET

NOTES:

- There are times when the most efficient way to get information from datasheet or form records is to isolate (filter out) only those records that satisfy a specific set of conditions. Access refers to the filtered subsets as dynasets.

- The Records menu contains two options, Edit Filter/Sort and Apply Filter/Sort, that will perform the actions needed to filter out a set of records based on entries for selected fields. As stated in Exercise 14, records are selected for the Edit Filter/Sort window by dragging the required field(s) to the lower pane's table and the selected records sorted. If you include added criteria for this field, the filter can extract a more specific subset of records. Note the illustration of the Filter Box.

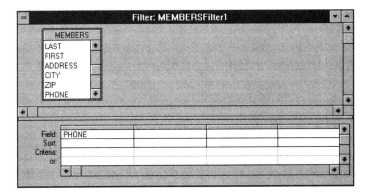

- You can further define those records that you wish to filter out of the complete set of records. In the Criteria area of the Filter Box, you can use any one of a number of **relational operators**:

Use:	For Criteria:
=	is equal to (the default symbol can be left out)
<	is less than
<=	is less than or equal to
>	is greater than
>=	is greater than or equal to
<>	is not equal to
Like	to match a pattern of characters
And	to select records that satisfy 2 or more conditions
Or	to select records that satisfy any of the listed conditions
Between...And	to select a value in a given range
In	to select a value from a list of values
Is	to determine if a value is null

For example: To sort out branches with more than 50 employees, you would use the appropriate field and a criteria setting of >50 (greater than 50) to select those branches.

- If you want to perform a number of tasks which all involve using filters, you can return to the Filter screen to change the entries in order to create successive subsets by once again selecting the Edit Filter/Sort option from the Records menu.

The MEMBERS datasheet of the HUGCLUB needs revision. Due to increasing population, the phone company has decided to revise the telephone exchanges. Each city will now have a different exchange. You will use a filter to isolate the members in each city and make the needed correction. You will then print a sorted listing of the membership list.

EXERCISE DIRECTIONS:

1. Open the ⌨ **HUGCLUB** database or 💾 **AHUGCLUB.15**.

2. Open the MEMBERS table.

3. Select the Edit Filter/Sort option from the Records menu.

4. Drag the CITY field name to the first field box in the lower pane.

5. To select the records from Anaheim, enter A* in the criteria box for this field.

6. Select Apply Filter from the Records menu.

7. Highlight the PHONE field.

8. Select Replace from the Edit menu.

9. Make the following entries:

   Find What   213
   Replace With   818
   Deselect, if necessary, Match Whole Field.

10. Make the replacements.

11. Close the Replace window.

12. Select the Edit Filter /Sort option from the Records menu.

13. Repeat steps 2 - 11 to change the telephone area code:

    817 for North Hollywood; 214 for Culver City.

14. Create an alphabetical listing of members who live in Anaheim.

15. Print these records.

16. Close the HUGCLUB database.

FILTER AND SORT RECORDS
(See Exercise 14)

REMOVE A FILTER

Click **Show All Records** button...............

   OR

   a. Choose **Records** menu...... Alt + R

   b. Choose **Show All Records**...........

EXERCISE

■ ISOLATING A FORM SUBSET ■ SORTING A FORM SUBSET

NOTES:

■ The techniques applied for creating a subset
(dynaset) of records are the same when working
in Form view as they were in Datasheet view.

*You need to create subsets of records from the STUDENTS record collection. You decide to use
student records in form view for your searches.*

EXERCISE DIRECTIONS:

1. Open the ⌨ **CLUBS** database or 💾 **ACLUBS.16**.

2. Open STFORM.

3. Select Edit Filter/Sort option from the Records menu.

4. Drag the COUNSELOR field name to the first field
box in the lower pane.

5. Set criteria to select the records for Mr. Litt.

6. Select Apply Filter from the Records menu.

7. Scroll through the presented record forms.

8. Create a dynaset of records for Mr. Litt that will
contain an alphabetical collection of all his male
students.

9. Select Apply Filter from the Records menu.

10. Create a dynaset that will include the above
information for Mr. Lifton as well as for Mr. Litt.

    (*Hint: Use the COUNSELOR criteria or box.*)

11. Switch to Datasheet view.

12. Select Edit Filter/Sort and create a record subset
for:

    Counselor - Mr. Litt
    Students in M/F order
    Students in alphabetical order by LAST name
    ID numbers greater than 6000

13. Print these records.

14. Create a dynaset for students not counseled by
Mrs. Scalesi.

15. Close the **CLUBS** database.

LESSON 3
SUMMARY EXERCISE 17 PART I

The owner of Jane's Boutique, a local clothing store, has hired you to create an inventory system for her store. The clothing is arranged by style number, type of garment, color, and size. This store specializes in junior sizes from 5 to 13. In this exercise, you will create a database to keep track of inventory and the number of garments on hand. You will then search it when customers call about availability of stock or when information is needed for reordering merchandise.

EXERCISE DIRECTIONS:

1. Create a new database file; name it **JANESHOP**.

2. From the information listed below, create a datasheet design for your database.
   Use the column headings as field names.
   Determine the appropriate field properties from the information shown in the fields.

STYLE	TYPE	COLOR	J5	J7	J9	J11	J13	DATEMFG
J8510	SKIRT	BLACK	4	4	2	4	2	10/18/95
J5540	BLOUSE	WHITE	5	6	6	4	3	11/12/95
J4309	PANTS	TAN	2	12	12	4	4	11/17/95
J3254	DRESS	BLUE	4	15	16	3	14	7/16/95
J7654	SUIT	GREEN	12	17	34	12	12	9/18/95
J7455	BLAZER	BLACK	23	32	21	32	32	9/23/95
J3280	DRESS	YELLOW	5	7	4	34	12	11/17/95
J5532	SKIRT	PURPLE	12	21	32	5	21	10/19/95
J4230	PANTS	GRAY	24	4	6	12	13	12/12/95
J5550	BLOUSE	ORANGE	12	24	43	7	4	8/21/95
J7676	SUIT	WHITE	9	6	5	25	7	8/21/95
J7405	BLAZER	YELLOW	12	32	32	3	21	10/8/95
J5555	BLOUSE	GREEN	13	32	45	6	9	6/19/95
J3290	DRESS	BLUE	23	32	33	23	12	11/17/95
J3317	DRESS	WHITE	3	6	7	3	4	1/7/95
J2222	PANTS	BLACK	32	23	32	54	16	2/2/96
J3290	DRESS	RED	17	21	35	32	18	10/8/95

3. Enter the data for each item.

4. Adjust column widths to accommodate the longest field entry, where necessary.

5. Change the field name DATEMFG to DATEORD and save the design change.

6. Search the datasheet for answers to the following questions:

   a. What color is style number J7654?
   b. Which item is orange?
   c. What are the style numbers for black items?

7. Replace the type description of BLAZER with JACKET.

8. Save the datasheet; name it **STOCK**.

LESSON 3
SUMMARY EXERCISE 17 PART II

Jane Blackwell, your boss at Jane's Boutique, has asked you to enter new purchases into the computer inventory you created earlier, (STOCK). In addition, she would like you to enter three new fields and then provide lists arranged in various orders.

EXERCISE DIRECTIONS:

1. Open the STOCK table, if necessary.
2. Add the highlighted information to your datasheet, in the positions indicated.

f. Which items are black or white? List these items in alphabetical order by color.
g. Which items were ordered after 10/31/95 and have 13 or more J7 items in stock?

STYLE	TYPE	COLOR	J5	J7	J9	J11	J13	PRICE	DATEORD
J8510	SKIRT	BLACK	4	4	2	4	2	26.00	10/18/95
J5540	BLOUSE	WHITE	5	6	6	4	3	18.59	11/12/95
J4309	PANTS	TAN	2	12	12	4	4	44.50	11/17/95
J3254	DRESS	BLUE	4	15	16	3	14	61.99	7/16/95
J7654	SUIT	GREEN	12	17	34	12	12	85.50	9/18/95
J7455	JACKET	BLACK	23	32	21	32	32	50.99	9/23/95
J3280	DRESS	YELLOW	5	7	4	34	12	59.44	11/17/95
J5532	SKIRT	PURPLE	12	21	32	5	21	23.67	10/19/95
J4230	PANTS	GRAY	24	4	6	12	13	49.99	12/12/95
J5550	BLOUSE	ORANGE	12	24	43	7	4	23.99	8/21/95
J7676	SUIT	WHITE	9	6	5	25	7	106.99	8/21/95
J7405	JACKET	YELLOW	12	32	32	3	21	48.50	10/8/95
J5555	BLOUSE	GREEN	13	32	45	6	9	19.99	6/19/95
J3290	DRESS	BLUE	23	32	33	23	12	56.88	11/17/95
J3317	DRESS	WHITE	3	6	7	3	4	62.65	1/7/95
J2222	PANTS	BLACK	32	23	32	54	16	39.99	2/2/96
J3290	DRESS	RED	17	21	35	32	18	48.25	10/8/95
J2121	SWEATER	BROWN	40	4	6	6	7	29.99	2/7/95
J2123	SWEATER	OLIVE	5	5	6	7	9	35.75	2/7/96
J7699	SUIT	NAVY	12	10	10	8	7	110.10	2/7/96
J9090	VEST	RED	23	22	22	25	25	20.00	2/7/96
P214	BLOUSE	RED	5	6	8	9	9	25.50	2/10/96
P232	SKIRT	BLACK	5	5	5	5	7	29.50	2/10/96
P287	JACKET	NAVY	7	9	11	14	14	75.50	2/10/96
P987	SKIRT	BLACK	3	4	5	6	7	30.75	2/10/96
P998	SKIRT	NAVY	2	4	4	5	7	35.40	2/10/96
P999	VEST	NAVY	6	6	7	7	7	25.50	2/10/96
P765	JACKET	RED	7	9	11	11	11	60.99	2/10/96

3. The following items are no longer in stock. Delete the records:
   J3280
   J7405
   J2222
4. Format the price so that the $ sign is included.
5. Search the datasheet for answers to the following questions:
   (*HINT: Use filters.*)
   a. Which item costs $19.99?
   b. Which items cost more than $50?
   c. What are the style numbers for black jackets?
   d. Which skirts cost less than $40?
   e. How many items have more than 15 pieces on hand in size J13? List these items so that the number of pieces are in descending order.

6. Sort the selected datasheet records in each of the following ways:
   a. in alphabetical order by COLOR and ascending order by PRICE within each color
   b. skirts by COLOR and descending order by PRICE
   c. for size 5 items, alphabetical order by TYPE and ascending order by PRICE
   d. in alphabetical order by COLOR, in alphabetical order by TYPE, and ascending order by STYLE
7. Use Print Setup, set the left and right margins to .5" and the top margin to 2.5"; set print orientation to Landscape.
8. Print one copy of the 6d (above) subset of records.
9. Close the database file.

LESSON 4

QUERIES

Exercises 18-22

- Query Basics

- Enhancing and Printing a Query

- Creating a Query Using Data from Multiple Tables

EXERCISE 18

■ CREATING A QUERY ■ SAVING A QUERY ■ USING A QUERY

NOTES:

- As seen in Lesson 3, Access allows us to find specific records, replace data, get a subset of records, and print this subset in the original datasheet order with all fields included. Access also provides us with a more powerful searching tool called a **Query**. A query can isolate a group of records, determine which fields to include and in what order, and be created using data from more than one table of a database. Queries can be saved and used as a basis for a report.

Creating a Query:

- Access provides Wizards to help you develop queries. In these lessons you will create queries without using a Query Wizard. After you open the database file to be queried and select Query, New, New Query, two windows appear.

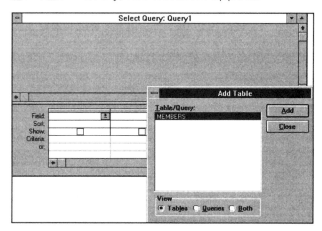

The Add Table window lists the database tables that may be used for the query. The tables to be included may be highlighted and added to the query before closing the window.

- After the Add Table window is closed, the Query Design window appears and looks very much like the Filter window, except for an added row option, Show. The Show box will be turned on, by default, whenever a field name is inserted into a column. You can click on this box if you want a field to be involved in your query but do not want this field to be included in the resulting datasheet layout.

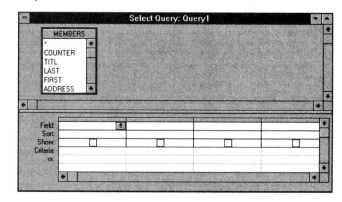

The fields may be selected in any order and will determine the column order of the resulting datasheet. The field's criteria or sorting condition should be entered.

> ✓ Note: The fields that are listed in the first row of the query design are joined using an implicit "AND". When you want to use multiple criteria for a field ("OR"), use the field's criteria row and those below it. The data will be sorted by City "AND" Last name in alphabetical order and will select those names with a title of Mr. and print only the city and first and last names.

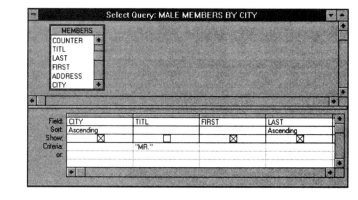

To see the results of your Query Design use the View menu Datasheet option or the Run option from the Query menu.

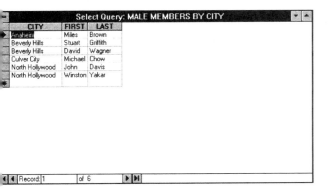

CITY	FIRST	LAST
Anaheim	Miles	Brown
Beverly Hills	Stuart	Griffith
Beverly Hills	David	Wagner
Culver City	Michael	Chow
North Hollywood	John	Davis
North Hollywood	Winston	Yakar

✓ Note: If you make changes to the data in a Query Datasheet they will automatically be transferred to the related datasheet.

To return to the Query Design window from the Datasheet view, use the View menu Query Design option.

Changing a Query Design

Field entries or their order in a Query design can be changed in a number of different ways.

To add a field to the design:

Drag a field name from the table window to the desired column. The fields to the right of this position will automatically be moved to the right to make room for this insertion.

OR

Place the cursor into the column that is to receive the new field and select the Insert Column option from the Edit menu. A blank column will be inserted, and the existing fields to the right of this position will automatically be moved to the right. You can now either drag a new field name into the blank column or use the Copy or Cut and Paste options of the Edit menu to move an existing entry.

- If two columns have the same field listed, you will have duplicate entries in your datasheet. Duplicate field columns should be deleted.

To delete a field from the design:

Select the entire field column and press the Del key.

OR

Place the cursor into the column that is to be deleted and select the Delete Column option from the Edit menu.

Saving a Query

- Save the query from the File menu by either selecting Save Query, Save Query As, or Close without saving. Query names can contain a maximum of 64 characters including spaces. Access supplies a numbered default name for queries (Query1, Query2, etc.).

As the secretary of the HUG Club, you have been asked to insert a title field in the MEMBERS datasheet. This field will be used for future mailings. You also have been asked to search the datasheet to find records that meet various criteria. To save time and effort, you will save some of the search conditions for later use.

EXERCISE DIRECTIONS:

1. Open the ⌨ **HUGCLUB** database or 💾 **AHUGCLUB.18**.

2. Open the MEMBERS datasheet.

3. Add the title field and the information, as listed below.

4. Close the datasheet.

5. Select Query.

6. Select New.

7. Select New Query.

8. With the MEMBERS table highlighted, select Add on the Add Table.

9. Select Close on the Add Table window.

	TITLE	LAST	FIRST	ADDRESS	CITY	ZIP	PHONE	PROF
1	Ms.	Barnes	Leanne	808 Summer Street	Anaheim	92803	(818)555-4987	Student
2	Mr.	Brown	Miles	154 Newburg Road	Anaheim	92804	(818)555-4837	Accountant
3	Mr.	Griffith	Stuart	1551 Dean Street	Beverly Hills	90210	(213)555-3010	Lawyer
4	Mr.	Moon	Michael	32 Oak Street	Beverly Hills	90210	(213)555-8750	Teacher
5	Ms.	Smith	Trina	3954 Wood Ave.	Anaheim	92803	(818)555-7283	Student
6	Ms.	Smith	Sheila	417 Specific Court	Anaheim	92803	(818)555-7284	Chiropractor
7	Ms.	Walker-Sim	Bette	1745 River Street	North Hollywood	91615	(817)555-8520	Lawyer
8	Mr.	Castillo	Carl	1956 Park Ave.	North Hollywood	91615	(817)555-5192	Banker
9	Mr.	Davis	John	P.O. Box 2333	North Hollywood	91615	(817)555-8129	Student
10	Ms.	Dixon	Amy	237 Albee Street	North Hollywood	91615	(817)555-8917	Orthopedist
11	Ms.	Kendall	Gale	15 Imperial Way	Beverly Hills	90210	(213)555-9888	Teacher
12	Ms.	Dagger	Janice	27 Ocean Ave.	Anaheim	92804	(818)555-7777	Orthopedist
13	Mr.	Chow	Michael	88 Riverside Drive	Culver City	90312	(214)555-7655	Accountant
14	Mr.	Wagner	David	879 Beverly Drive	Beverly Hills	90210	(213)555-6676	Banker
15	Ms.	Smith	Cleo	90 Rodeo Drive	Beverly Hills	90210	(213)555-2222	Student
16	Ms.	Anderson	Carolyn	666 Santa Ana Drive	Culver City	90312	(214)555-9988	Lawyer
17	Ms.	Ramaz	Nadine	9012 Wilshire Blvd.	Beverly Hills	90210	(213)555-2211	Teacher
18	Mr.	Yakar	Winston	776 Prince Lane	North Hollywood	91615	(817)555-1584	Student
19	Ms.	Mancuso	Mary	12 Pacific Court	North Hollywood	91615	(817)555-7773	Banker

0. Create a query to get a listing of all members in the club in city order.

   Select the fields listed below and add the indicated conditions:

   CITY Sort - Ascending

   LAST Sort - Ascending

   FIRST Sort - Ascending

   PROF

1. Switch to Datasheet view.

2. Select a Save option from the File menu; name the query **MEMBERS BY CITY**.

3. Switch to Design view.

4. Insert PROF into column 2 and sort in alphabetical order.

   Remember to delete any duplicate fields.

5. Add PHONE as the last field of the query.

6. Switch to Datasheet view.

7. Save the query as **MEMBERS PROFESSION BY CITY** and close the query.

8. Create a new query to list female members by profession.

   Include the fields: PROF, TITLE, FIRST, LAST, and PHONE.

   Sort Prof and LAST in alphabetical order.

   Set Criteria to select female members.

9. Switch to Datasheet view.

0. Switch to Design view.

20. Make the following changes:

    Show off for the TITLE field.

    Add CITY between LAST and PHONE.

21. Switch to Datasheet view.

22. Save and Close; name it **FEMALE MEMBERS BY PROFESSION**.

23. Create new or use existing queries to answer each of the following questions. After determining the needed information, close the query without saving.

    a. Which members live in Beverly Hills and are Teachers?

    b. Which members live in North Hollywood and are Bankers?

    c. Which members have a last name beginning with "D" and live in North Hollywood? Change John Davis' phone number to (817)-555-8563.

    d. Which members have a last name beginning with "D" or "M" and live in North Hollywood?

24. Close the HUGCLUB database.

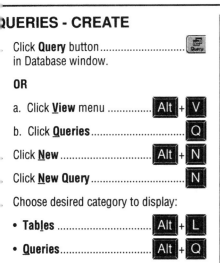

QUERIES - CREATE

Click **Query** button............................
in Database window.

OR

a. Click **View** menu .... Alt + V

b. Click **Queries**.............................. Q

Click **New**.............................. Alt + N

Click **New Query**.............................. N

Choose desired category to display:

• **Tables** .... Alt + L

• **Queries**............................ Alt + Q

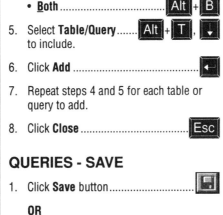

• **Both**.................................. Alt + B

5. Select **Table/Query**....... Alt + T , ↓
   to include.

6. Click **Add** .... ←

7. Repeat steps 4 and 5 for each table or query to add.

8. Click **Close** .... Esc

QUERIES - SAVE

1. Click **Save** button............................

   OR

a. Click **File** menu .... Alt + F

b. Click **Save**.................................... S

2. Type query name............................*name*
   if saving query for the first time.

   ✓ *Don't give a query the same name as an existing table unless you want to replace the existing table.*

3. Click **OK**... ←

EXERCISE 19

■ CREATING QUERIES ■ RENAMING A QUERY ■ ENHANCING AND PRINTING A QUERY

NOTES:

Using All Fields of a Table for a Query

■ When a selected table appears in the top pane of a query design window, the first field option is an asterisk (*), which represents **all fields** of the selected table. If this is selected, only the table name shows in the lower pane.

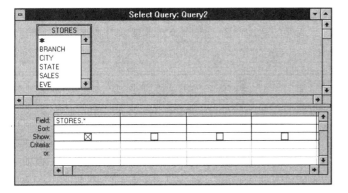

To sort or set criteria for any field in this mode, you can add that field and set the desired conditions, but you must turn the Show condition off, or you will have duplicate entries.

Repositioning a Datasheet Column

■ In Datasheet view, columns can be repositioned by selecting the column by clicking on the field name. The selected column will be represented in reverse video, i.e., with light text on a dark background. When the field name is clicked again and the mouse button is held down, the column will be represented by a thick line in reverse video. By clicking on the thick line without releasing the mouse button, you can drag the line to the vertical grid line that will become the new left boundary of the moved column. Release the mouse button.

✓ Note: Adjacent columns can be moved together. When moving datasheet columns, the Design view positions will not be changed nor will the

source Table. When the query is saved, its Query Datasheet view will be saved as well.

Renaming a Query

■ If you mistype or want to change an existing query name, you may highlight the name to be edited and use the Rena_me_ option from the _F_ile menu.

Enhancing a Query Datasheet

■ Query datasheets can be changed and enhanced like other datasheets. Use the Fo_r_mat menu options of _F_ont, _R_ow Height, _C_olumn Width, _H_ide Columns, _S_how Columns, and _G_ridlines to customize the datasheet.

Printing a Query Datasheet

■ A query datasheet can be printed in the same manner as was used to print other database objects.

The printout will include:
• A header that contains the query name and the current date, and
• A footer that contains the current page number on each page.

> *Your manager at Bit-Byte Computer Stores has many questions about the branch stores. You can provide the answers by searching the company database you have developed.*

EXERCISE DIRECTIONS:

1. Open the 📠 **COMPANY** database or 💾 **ACOMPANY.19**.

2. Open the STORES datasheet.

3. Create a New Query for all stores in the company.

   All fields of the STORES table will be used.

   STATE, CITY, and BRANCH fields are to be sorted in alphabetical order.

4. View the resulting datasheet.

5. Move the columns into the following order:

   STATE, CITY, BRANCH, SALES, STAFF, EVE

6. *Save As* **Bit-Byte Stores in State Order**.

7. Change the Query Design to select only stores with evening hours.

   ✓ Note: *The datasheet shows the EVE data as Yes or No but the field data type has been as Yes/No and not Text. Therefore, internally the settings are **-1 for Yes** and **0 for No**. These MUST be the numbers used to set Yes/No criteria.*

8. View the resulting datasheet.

9. Switch to Design view and turn EVE Show condition off .

10. Save this design as **Has Evening Hours**.

11. Change the Query Design to select stores that do not have evening hours.

12. Switch to Datasheet view.

13. Save and Close the query; name it **Stores WITHOUT evening hours**.

14. Select the Rename option from the File menu; rename Has Evening Hours to read **Stores WITH evening hours**.

15. Create a new Query to locate stores that have sales of less than $400,000.

Do not use dollar ($) or comma (,) symbols in the Criteria setting.

The Query should include the BRANCH names (in alphabetical order), CITY, STAFF, and SALES.

Save the query; name it **POOR PERFORMERS**.

16. Make the following changes in Datasheet view:

   Font size to 10 point
   Column widths to improve the general appearance
   BRANCH column to the right of the CITY column

17. Print Preview the Datasheet view.

   Return to the Datasheet if adjustments have to be made.

18. Print the Query Datasheet.

19. Save and Close the Query.

20. Open the appropriate Query or create a new one to answer each of the following questions.

   ✓ Note: *A Query Design may be temporarily changed to aid in a search. DO NOT SAVE THE REVISIONS.*

   a. What stores are located in Atlanta?

   b. In what city is the Federal Plaza Store located?

   c. Which store has sold exactly $245,860 worth of merchandise?

   d. Which stores have sold more than $400,000 worth of merchandise?

   e. Which stores have sold more than $400,000 worth of merchandise and are open evenings?

   f. Which stores have sold more than $400,000 worth of merchandise and have more than 10 employees?

   g. Which stores are in CA (California) or GA (Georgia)?

21. Return to the COMPANY database window.

MOVING A COLUMN IN A QUERY

1. Click on the header bar of the column to move.

   The entire column will be highlighted.

2. Drag the header bar to the desired location.

   The column will be represented by a thick vertical line.

3. Release the mouse button.

RENAMING A QUERY

1. View Database window.

2. Click **Query**.

   OR

   a. Click **View** menu. .... `Alt`+`V`

   b. Choose **Queries**.......................... `Q`

3. Select query to rename.

4. Click **File**.............................. `Alt`+`F`

5. Click **Rename** .... `M`

6. Type new query name ....*name*

7. Click **OK**.. `⏎`

USING ALL FIELDS OF A QUERY

1. Double-click title bar of field list.

   OR

   Click asterisk (*) at top of table field list.

   ✓ *If asterisk is used, all fields in table will always be used in query even if table is later modified.*

2. Drag group to QBE grid.

EXERCISE

20

■ CREATING A QUERY ■ APPLYING A QUERY ■ CHANGE FIELD FORMATS AND NAMES ■ PRINTING A QUERY TABLE

NOTES:

Changing Field Format in Query Design

■ When a query is created from a Table, all the table properties are transferred with it, as you experienced with the Yes/No data type. However, some properties can be changed for the purposes of the query. For example: If a currency data type was set for a format that did not include the dollar ($) or comma (,) symbols, you could change your query datasheet to include them. To change a field format in Design view:

Move the pointer (I) into the Field name box of field that is to be revised. Select the Table Properties option from the View menu. In the Format row enter the desired format name. The change can be seen in Datasheet view.

Changing Field Names in a Query Design

■ A field name may be changed in Design view by clicking to the left of the first letter of the field name to be replaced in the lower pane of Design view. Then, type a new name followed by a colon (:). Your replacement will appear in the query's datasheet and may require a column width adjustment.

Your company is preparing to purchase new computer equipment. Before doing so, management needs to know information about the current inventory. Your supervisor has asked you to respond to a survey by searching the hardware table.

EXERCISE DIRECTIONS:

1. Open the 🖳 **COMPANY** database or 💾 **ACOMPANY.20**.

2. Create a new query for the HARDWARE table:

   Include the BRANCH, ITEM, MFG, MODEL, COST, WTY, and PURDATE fields.

   The first two fields are to be sorted in alphabetical order.

   View the Datasheet.

   Save the query; name it **All Hardware**.

3. Using this query datasheet, make the following changes:

   a. The Quantum hard drive is under warranty.

   b. The correct model number for the Okidata printer is ML330RR.

4. Return to Design view and make the following changes:

   a. Change the field name PURDATE to DATE OF PURCHASE.

   b. Change the format of the COST field to include dollar signs ($) and commas (,).

5. View the results of your changes in Datasheet view.

6. Save the new layout.

7. Print the ALL HARDWARE datasheet.

8. Create a new query for the HARDWARE table.

   Include the ASSIGNED TO, BRANCH, ITEM, MFG, MODEL, and COST fields.

   The first three fields are to be sorted in alphabetical order.

   View the Datasheet.

   Save and Close the query; name it **Department Hardware Assignments**.

9. Open the All Hardware query.

10. Make the following change to the Query Design to create a new query to isolate records that are under warranty:

    Criteria for **WTY** set to **Yes** and **Show** set for **off**.
    ✓ Note: The WTY field was set as Data Type - Yes/No (-1,0).

11. View the datasheet.

12. *Save As* **Hardware Under Warranty**.

13. Return to Design view; change criteria for WTY to No.

14. Close and *Save As* **Hardware Not Under Warranty**.

15. Open the appropriate query to determine the purchase dates of computers which are under warranty and cost less than $2,000. How many are there?

16. Close the query.

17. Close and save the database.

EDIT FIELD NAMES

1. Highlight the field name to change.

2. Click **View** menu .... `Alt`+`V`

3. Click **Properties**............................. `P`

4. Click in caption box.

5. Type new field name .... *fieldname*

6. Close Properties window ...... `Alt`+`F4`

CHANGE FIELD FORMAT

1. Highlight the field name to change.

2. Click **View** menu .... `Alt`+`V`

3. Click **Properties**............................. `P`

4. Click in format box.

5. Type new format name .... *formatname*

6. Close Properties window ...... `Alt`+`F4`

EXERCISE
21

- CREATING A QUERY USING DATA FROM MULTIPLE TABLES
- PRINTING A QUERY TABLE

NOTES:

Creating a Query Using Data from Multiple Table

- You can create a query that contains field data from various datasheets or queries. This allows you to find data using information from the entire database.

  - From the database window select Query.

  - Select New Query from the New Query window.

  - Select from the Add Table, accessing a list of database Tables, Queries, or Both.

  - Add each of the tables or queries you need before closing the Add Table window.

  - Select the field names, from the field listings available, and drag them to the desired query design location.

  - Draw a Join Line between the selected database objects to indicate the relationship between them.
    - ✓ Note: To draw a join line, drag a field name in one listing on top of its related field in the other.

  - Proceed, as previously discussed, naming, saving, and viewing the resulting datasheet.

Your manager at Bit-Byte Computer Stores has many questions about branch stores. You can provide the answers by searching the company database objects that you have developed.

EXERCISE DIRECTIONS:

1. Open the **COMPANY** database or
   🖫 **ACOMPANY.21**.

2. Select the Query object screen.

3. Create a New Query.

4. From the Add Table select the STORES and HARDWARE tables.

5. Join the BRANCH fields.

6. Create a query using the following fields:

   BRANCH, CITY, STATE, ITEM, MODEL, and COST.

7. Sort the BRANCH, STATE, and ITEM fields in alphabetical order.

8. View the query's datasheet.

9. Return to Design view and save this query; name it **Hardware Store Assignments**.

10. Change the format of COST field to Currency.

    (Hint: See NOTES - Exercise 20.)

11. View the query's datasheet.

12. Save this new layout.

13. Close the query.

14. Create a new query that will list the branches that have equipment not under warranty.

    Use the STORES table and Hardware Not Under Warranty query.

    The query should contain BRANCH, CITY, ITEM, MODEL, COST, and PURDATE.

    BRANCH and ITEM are to be sorted in alphabetical order.

15. Save this query as **Stores with Hardware Not Under Warranty**.

16. Change the field name PRUDATE to PURCHASE DATE.

17. View the datasheet; adjust columns as necessary.

18. Print this datasheet, adding enhancements.

19. Save the query enhancements.

20. Close the query.

21. Close and save the database.

QUERY MULTIPLE DATASHEETS OR QUERIES

1. View Database window.

2. Click **Query**.

   OR

   a. Click **View** menu .... `Alt`+`V`

   b. Click **Queries** .... `Q`

3. Click **New** .... `Alt`+`N`

4. Click **New Query** .... `N`

5. Click **Both** .... `Alt`+`B`

6. Highlight Table/Query to add.

7. Click **Add** .... `Alt`+`A`

8. Repeat steps 6 and 7 until all desired Tables/Queries are added.

9. Click **Close** .... `Alt`+`C`

You are being asked to collate information relating to all computer supplies. You will have to pull information from the various tables that were created in the company database.

EXERCISE DIRECTIONS:

1. Open the ⌨ **COMPANY** database or 💾 **ACOMPANY.22**.

2. Create a New Query using SOFTWARE table fields:

   TYPE (in alphabetical order), TITLE (in alphabetical order), PRICE, BRANCH, and PURDATE; name it **Software by Type**.

3. Change:

   PURDATE to PURCHASED

   Format PURCHASED to Medium Date and PRICE to Currency

4. View the datasheet; adjust and enhance columns.

5. Print the query.

6. *Save As* **Software by Type**.

7. Create a New Query using STORES and SOFTWARE.

   Draw a join line between BRANCH fields.

   Use fields: BRANCH (in alphabetical order), CITY, TYPE (in alphabetical order), and TITLE.
   Name it **Software used in Cities**.

8. Create a New Query using information from HARDWARE, Software by Type, and STORES.

   Draw a join line between BRANCH fields.

   Use fields: BRANCH (in alphabetical order), ST, TYPE (in alphabetical order), TITLE, PRICE, ITEM, MFG, and COST.

   Name it **Branch Software**.

9. Change the field names: TYPE to SOFTWARE and ITEM to HARDWARE.

10. Change format of money columns to Currency, if necessary.

11. View the datasheet; adjust columns as necessary.

12. Change:

    Font (your choice) - 10 point

    Row height to 11

    Print orientation to Landscape

    All print margins to .5"

13. Preview the printout; make changes as necessary.

14. Print the datasheet.

15. Save and Close the query.

16. Select a query from the above to answer each of the following questions in the most efficient manner:

    a. How many word processing programs are in use?

    b. How many word processing and spreadsheet programs are in use?

    c. How much was paid for Tulip5 software?

    d. Which software costs less than $300 and is a word processor?

    e. Which database programs cost less than $500?

17. Close and save the database.

LESSON 5

REPORTS

Exercises 23-28

- Using a Wizard to Create a Report

- Changing and Enhancing a Report

- Changing Item Properties

- Adding New Fields to a Report

EXERCISE
USING A WIZARD TO CREATE A REPORT
23

NOTES:

- Reports allow you to present data in a customized way.

- Reports can be presented in a number of ways by using the fields of a table:

  Single column - records are presented with selected fields listed below each other (like a form)

  Tabular form - records are presented with fields in a grid (like a datasheet)

  Group/Totals - field data is grouped with totals entered for each group

  Mailing label form

  Summary

  AutoReport - all records and their fields are presented in a single column

  Ms Word Mail Merge

- Reports can include:

  Report headers and footers

  Page headers and footers

  Summary statistics

  Objects imported from other sources (such as graphics)

- You can design a report from scratch using a Report Design window (see below), which looks and behaves very much like the Form Design view, or you can let Access design a report for you by using a Report Wizard.

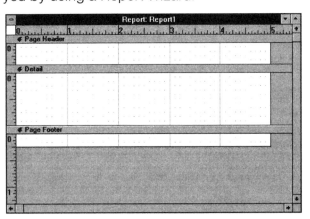

Creating Reports with a Wizard

- A Report Wizard will ask you to respond to some questions, create the report, and present you with a Sample Report screen. You can redesign the resulting report. To begin creating a report with a Report Wizard:

  - Open the database that contains the table or query from which to select the report data.

  - Select the Report section of the database window.

  - In the Report window, select New.

  - Enter the data source, either table or query name.

  - Select Report Wizard.

  - Respond to a series of questions to select:

  - Type of report you want created

  - Fields from the selected data source, in the order of desired presentation

  - Sort order, if any

  - Style for the report

  - Report title and print options

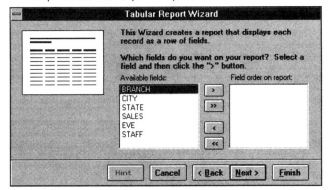

- A report will be created, and you will be presented with a zoomed-in version of the Print Preview screen.

  There are two preview options:

  - Print Preview lets you preview the entire report as it will be printed.

- Sample Preview only includes a sample of the report's data. This is faster to construct and is therefore useful for large reports.

Press the Esc key to return to the report's Design view from any preview screen.

> ✓ Note: All aspects of a report are controlled from the Design view. Note the illustration below of Report Design view.

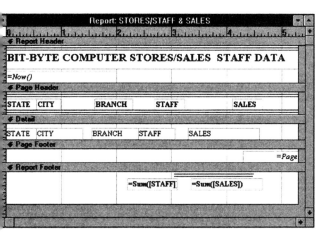

The manner in which page numbers, totals, counts, etc. are included in a report will be discussed in another lesson.

Moving the Design View Items

- By default, numbers are right justified, and text is left justified. This often causes the need to adjust the spacing and alignment in a report. To move a report detail item, click and hold down the mouse button within the item's boundary. The appearance of a hand indicates that the item can be moved. Drag the box to the desired position. The rulers at the top and left side of the screen should be used to help position the item.

- To change the size of a boundary box, click on the item and release the mouse button. Move the mouse until you see a double-headed arrow, click on the handles surrounding the box, and drag into position. Print Preview from the File menu may be used to see the results of your adjustments, and then you can press the Esc key to return to Design view. You may have to repeat the adjustment routine a number of times.

- To change the size of the design sections, click on the bar of the section heading, release the mouse button, and then drag the design section title bar with the double-headed arrow that appears.

Saving a New Report

- Reports are saved and named by using the Save As option of the File menu. The name you choose will appear in the Database Report section.

Your manager at Bit-Byte must submit reports to the president of the company. You have been asked to create these reports from your available records.

EXERCISE DIRECTIONS:

1. Open the 🖫 **COMPANY** database or 🖫 **ACOMPANY.23**.

2. Select Report section of the database.

3. Select New.

4. Enter STORES for the selected table.

5. Select Report Wizards.

6. Select Tabular.

7. Select the fields in the order listed below:

   ST, CITY, BRANCH, STAFF, SALES.

8. Choose to sort by ST and then by CITY.

9. Change the print orientation to Portrait.

10. For the report title use **BIT-BYTE COMPUTER STORES - SALES & STAFF DATA**.

    Select to see all fields on one page.

    Choose Finish.

11. Make note from the Print Preview screen what spacing, alignment, and size adjustments are necessary.

12. Press Esc key to return to the Design window.

13. Make any desired adjustments.

14. Select Print Preview from the File menu.

15. If necessary, repeat steps 12 and 13.

16. Select Save As from the File menu; name the report **SALES & STAFF**.

17. Print the report.

18. Close the report.

19. Close and save the database.

CREATE NEW REPORT USING REPORT WIZARDS

1. Click **Report** button ....
   in Database window

   OR

   a. Click **View** menu .... Alt + V
   b. Click **Reports**.............................. R

2. Click **New** button................... Alt + N

3. Click drop-down arrow.......... Alt + ↓
   to select a table or query.

4. Click **Report Wizards** button.. Alt + W

5. Select a report style.......................... ↓
   from the following:

Single Column	Each value on a separate line, one record on a screen
Groups/Totals	Row and column format, with data sorted into groups which can contain subtotals
Mailing label	Many formats available
Summary	Contains totals
Tabular	In table form
AutoReport	Creates a report immediately, without further user input
MS Word Mail Merge	Creates report based partly on a Microsoft Word word processing document

6. Click **OK** .... Ins

7. Follow screen instructions for specific form type.

CREATE REPORT

1. Click **Report** button ....
   in Database window.

   OR

   a. Click **View** menu .... Alt + V
   b. Click **Report**.............................. R

2. Click **New** .... Alt + N

   OR

   a. Click **File** menu .... Alt + F
   b. Click **New** .... W
   c. Click **Report**............................ R

3. Select table or query......................... ↓

4. Click **Blank Report** .... Alt + B

OPEN REPORT

1. View Database window.

2. Click Report button ....
   in Database window.

   OR

   a. Click **View** menu .... Alt + V
   b. Click **Report**.............................. R

3. Select report .... ↓

4. Click **Design** to view.............. Alt + D
   report Design view.

   OR

   Click **Preview** to view............. Alt + P
   report as it will appear
   when printed.

SAVE REPORT

1. Click **File** menu .... Alt + F
   in Report window.

2. Click **Save**.. S

3. Type name in text box,............*reportname*
   if saving for first time.

4. Click **OK** .... ↵

PREVIEW REPORT

✓ *Sample Preview displays font, font size, and layout features with a few records, while Print Preview displays the report exactly as it will be printed. Both are close-up views.*

SAMPLE PREVIEW

1. View report Design view.

2. Click **Sample Preview** button...........

   OR

   a. Click **File** menu .... Alt + F
   b. Click **Sample Preview**.................. M

RETURN TO DESIGN VIEW

Press **Esc**... Esc

SELECT CONTROLS

Click control or attached label to select both.

To select more than one control:

Press **Shift** and click desired controls .. Shift

   OR

   Click and drag rectangle to touch desired . controls to select.

MOVE CONTROLS

1. Select control or controls to move.

2. Place pointer on control border to move control and attached label.

   Pointer will appear as a five-fingered hand.

   OR

   Place pointer on upper left corner to move label or control only.

   Pointer will appear as a pointing hand.

3. Click and drag to new location.

   ✓ *A label or control alone cannot be dragged to a different report section.*

CHANGE CONTROL SIZE

1. Select control to change.

   ✓ *Only one control can be sized at a time.*

2. Place pointer on any of the three small corner handles.

   Pointer will become a diagonal, two-headed arrow.

3. Click and drag border to new size.

CHANGE SECTION SIZE

1. Place pointer at bottom edge of section to change.

   Pointer will become a line with a black, two-headed arrow.

2. Click and drag to new size.

EXERCISE

CHANGING AND ENHANCING A REPORT

24

NOTES:

Changing A Report

- Creating a report using a Report Wizard simplifies creating a basic report structure. However, the result may include unwanted items and exclude desired items. Also, the general alignment and positioning of a column heading and its related data, its font, and style may not yield an attractive report.

Editing Report Sections and Items

- To edit items, click on the specific item until the insertion pointer is visible (I) and make changes.
- To delete an item, click on the item, and when the box handles appear, press the Del key.

Changing Item Order

- To change the order of report items usually requires that you move some existing items to a temporary location. You can move items to the right edge of the report, and the report will expand to accommodate the moved item. After you have repositioned items, move the right edge of the report to the last item entry or you may get blank page(s) inserted into the report.

Enhancing A Report

- To change an item's font, font size, alignment, or palette enhancement (color, border, or shading), you need to use the Report Design Toolbar. Note the illustration of the toolbar below:

- To show the Report Design Toolbar:
  - Select the Toolbar option from the View menu.
  - Highlight Report Design option.
  - Click the Show button.
  - Click OK.
- To make a change or enhancement:
  - Select an item.
  - Choose the appropriate icon on the Report Design toolbar.
    - ✓ Note: When a toolbar icon has been selected, it will be highlighted. When changing fonts or font sizes you often have to change an item's boundary box to accommodate the change and all items that have previously been lined up with it. To center the Report Heading, extend the heading's right boundary to the extent of the report width. Click on the center icon on the Report Design toolbar.

- If you wish to select a group of items upon which the same condition is to apply:
  Select the first item.
  Hold down the Shift key when selecting the others.

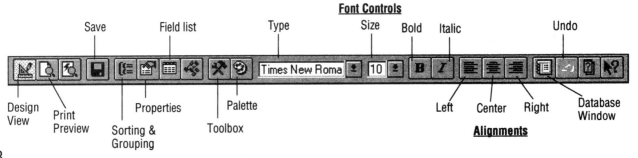

368

In order to prepare for a computer equipment inventory audit, you have been asked to prepare a report that will list specific information about this hardware.

EXERCISE DIRECTIONS:

1. Open the ⌨ **COMPANY** database or 💾 **ACOMPANY.24**.

2. Open the Report section of the COMPANY database.

3. Create a New report for the data from the HARDWARE table.

    Respond to the Tabular Report Wizard as follows:

    List Fields in given order: ITEM, MFG, MODEL, PURDATE, COST.

    Sort by ITEM and MFG.

    Select Presentation style, Portrait print orientation, and Line spacing 0".

    Title the report: **BIT-BYTE COMPUTER STORES, INC**.

    See all fields on one page.

4. Return to Design view.

5. Change Page Headers:

    MFG to MANUFACTURER

    PURDATE to PURCHASED

6. Move the =Now() item to the left edge of the Page Footer section.

7. Show the Report Design Toolbar.

8. Change both the Date and Page footers to bold, without italics.

9. Change the report title to **COMPUTER EQUIPMENT INVENTORY**.

10. Change the title font size to 18 point.

11. Use the Palette to shade the title (back color) light gray.

12. Change all page headings to 12 point.

13. Adjust report items to accommodate the increases in font size.

14. Center the Report header.

15. Print Preview your adjustments.

16. Print the report.

17. Save the report; name it **COMPUTER EQUIPMENT**.

18. Interchange the ITEM and MFG fields and headers.

19. Change the title to **COMPUTER EQUIPMENT by MANUFACTURER**.

20. Print Preview.

21. Adjust spacing and alignment.

22. Save this version as **COMPEQUIP by MFG**.

23. Close and save the database.

EXERCISE 25

CHANGING ITEM PROPERTIES

NOTES:

Changing Item Properties

- Each item, in every section of a report, has properties that can be changed. To open the Properties window for an item requires that you should first select the item and either select the Properties option on the View menu or click on the Properties icon on the Report Design toolbar.

- The Properties window remains on the screen until you close it, which allows you to preview changes and return to make further changes without having to reopen this window. In addition, the Properties window will be updated for each new selected item. Note the illustration of the Properties window below.

- An alternate method to dragging items to align them in Design view, is to use the boundary positions of a selected item (Left, Top, Width, and Height) as shown in the properties window. You can align items by setting all the boundary positions to the same setting so that the control boxes are aligned.

Changing Displayed Data Formats

- To change the format of field data for display purposes:

  Select the Detail Item, whose format is to be changed.

  Open its Property box.

  Click on the Format option.

  Click on the down arrow.

  Select the display format desired.

  Close the Property window.

Hiding Duplicate Entries

- If you have duplicate column entries and would like to display only the first one, you can suppress the others by using the Properties window for that detail element. For example: If you are listing your friends in order of their state of residence in a tabular listing, you can suppress all but the first state entry in each group.

  To hide duplicate entries:

  - Select the item for which duplicates should be suppressed.
  - Open the Properties window for that item (View menu).
  - Change the Hide Duplicates entry to Yes and Close the Properties box.

After taking inventory at Jane's Boutique, your manager wants you to create a report that will list the type of items that the store has in stock.

EXERCISE DIRECTIONS:

1. Open the 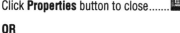 **JANESHOP** database or 🖫 **AJANSHOP.25**.

2. Create a New Report for the JANESHOP database using the STOCK table.

3. Create a Tabular report using the STOCK table:

   Include the fields TYPE, COLOR, PRICE, and STYLE, in the order listed.

   Sort by TYPE, COLOR, and PRICE.

   Select Ledger style, Portrait orientation, Line spacing set to 0".

   Name the report **STOCK ITEMS**.

4. In Design view, delete the Sum function item in the Report Footer.

5. Set the following items to Bold:

   Date function in the Report Header section

   Page function in the Page Footer section

6. Select the detail item TYPE and open its Properties window.

7. Change the Hide Duplicates option to Yes.

8. Print Preview the report and return to Design view.

9. Select the detail item COLOR and open, if necessary, its Properties window.

10. Change the Hide Duplicates option to Yes.

11. Print Preview the report and return to Design view.

12. Change the format of the PRICE detail item to fixed, with two decimals.

13. Center the Report Headers.

14. Change the font size of the subtitle to 10 point.

15. Print Preview and adjust the report layout, as necessary.

16. Print the report.

17. Save and Close the report; name it **STOCK.ITEMS**.

18. Close the database.

CHANGE REPORT PROPERTIES

1. Select Control.

2. Click Properties button .... 🖼

   OR

   a. Click **View** menu .... `Alt` + `V`

   b. Click **Properties** .... `P`

3. Click desired property text box.

4. Click drop-down arrow .... `Alt` + `▼`

5. Select desired option.

6. Click **Properties** button to close .... 🖼

   OR

   Double-click .... `Alt` + `F4`
   control menu box to close.

SET REPORT TO HIDE DUPLICATES

Hide Duplicates stops a text box which contains the same value as the text box in the previous record from being printed.

1. Select control.

2. Display property sheet.

3. Click drop-down button to choose Layout Properties.

4. Click Hide Duplicates text box.

5. Click drop-down arrow .... `Alt` + `▼`

6. Select **Yes** .... `▼`

7. Click **Properties** button to close .... 🖼

   OR

   Double-click .... `Alt` + `F4`
   control menu box to close.

SET DATA FORMAT IN REPORT

1. Select Control.

2. Click **Properties** button .... 🖼

   OR

   a. Click **View** menu .... `Alt` + `V`

   b. Click **Properties** .... `P`

3. Click **Format** text box.

4. Click drop-down arrow .... `Alt` + `▼`

5. Select desired format.

6. Click **Properties** button to close .... 🖼

   OR

   Double-click .... `Alt` + `F4`
   control menu box to close.

EXERCISE

■ CREATING A REPORT FROM A QUERY ■ ADDING REPORT SECTIONS AND ITEMS ■ ADDING REPORT STATISTICS

NOTES:

Creating a Report from a Query

■ You can select a previously created query as a report reference. A query that includes all the data necessary for a needed report has already isolated the data necessary and is easier to work with than the source table. Only those fields and records that belong to the query will be included in the report.

Adding Report Sections and Items

■ If you wish to add an item to a report design section, you need to open the Toolbox. This is done by selecting the Toolbox option from the View menu or from the Report Design toolbar. The Toolbox window will appear and remain visible until you close it. The various toolbox options are described in the Status bar when the mouse pointer is resting on them. Note the illustration of the toolbox below.

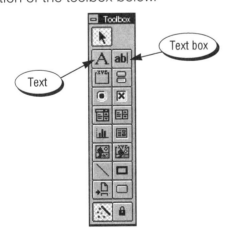

■ The toolbar **A** icon is used to add a label and the **ab|** icon is used to add a text box for most other items. Click the appropriate icon and then move the mouse pointer to the proper location and draw a box to receive the data. Once the item box (control) has been created, you can enter the appropriate item identifier.

Grouping Items and Adding Item Headers and Footers

■ Items can be sorted and grouped in report design view to improve the readability of the report. Grouped items can be given a group header and/or footer. To group data, open the Sorting and Grouping window from the View menu. The current settings are reflected in the upper pane. You can control all the report's group settings from this window, but groupings can only be applied to sorted fields. In the uppe pane you can add or change field entries and sort settings. Note the illustration of the window below:

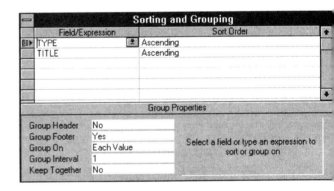

■ The lower pane options are:

Group Header and/or Footer - Yes will open a header or footer section for the selected item.

Group On - yields an option list related to the selected field's data type that is to be grouped.

Kept Together options:

No - page breaks may split the group

Whole group - group must be printed on the same page

With first detail - group header and at least the first record on the same page

✓ Note: *The Groups/Totals Report Wizard completes most of the above.*

dding Report Statistics

The Report Wizard adds two entries to its preformatted report form:

=Now() - enters the date the report is printed.

=Page - enters the printed page number.

You can also add text boxes to the report design which, with the appropriate entry, can calculate:

Count of field data items **=Count**([field detail name])

For numerical field data:

Sums	**=Sum**([field detail name])
Averages	**=Avg**([field detail name)])
Maximum values	**=Max**([field detail name)])
Minimum values	**=Min**([field detail name)])

(For other options, see Access Help topic "functions".)

> *Before your company orders more software, they want to determine which products have been assigned to each department, the cost of the package they have purchased, etc. You have been asked to prepare a report so that your manager can make an analysis.*

EXERCISE DIRECTIONS:

1. Open the 🖮 **COMPANY** database or 💾 **ACOMPANY.26**.

2. Create a New Report for the COMPANY database.

3. Use the Branch Software query to create a Tabular report.

   Include the fields, in the order listed: BRANCH, TYPE, TITLE, and PRICE.

   Sort by BRANCH and TYPE.

   Report should be set for Portrait orientation with Line spacing set to 0".

   Title report: BRANCH SOFTWARE.

4. In Design view delete the two lines under the Page Header.

5. Increase the Detail section height by moving the Page Footer title bar down .5".

6. Increase the size of the framing boxes to accept two lines of text for the four field headings.

7. Change the column headings to read:

BRANCH OFFICE	PROGRAM TYPE	PROGRAM TITLE	PROGRAM PRICE

8. Change the detail BRANCH to hide Duplicate entries.

9. Select detail BRANCH; open Sorting and Grouping window from the View menu.

10. Change the Group Footer entry to Yes and close the window.

11. Print Preview the report; return to Design view.

12. Open the Toolbox from the View menu.

13. Click on the abl icon; draw a text box in the Branch Footer under the BRANCH detail entry.

14. Enter =Count([BRANCH]).

    > ✓ *Note: This entry will yield a count of entries in each group.*

15. Create another text box in the Report Footer area under the CITY detail entry.

16. Enter: =Count([BRANCH]).

17. Open the Properties window for this item and change Running Sum entry to Over All and close the window.

    > ✓ *Note: This entry will yield the total count of entries in the field.*

18. Print Preview the report; return to Design view.

19. Add a text box below the Sum function, in the Report Footer, and enter =Avg([PRICE]).

20. Print Preview the report; return to Design view.

21. Change the format for the Sum and Average to Currency.

22. Create labels, in the appropriate positions, for each of the Report Footer entries:

    > *Hint: Use the **A** toolbox icon to draw a label box. Label boxes can overlap text boxes without hiding the report data.*

23. Print Preview the report and return to Design view.

24. Make adjustments, where necessary, to the report layout.

25. Center the report headings.

26. Add other report enhancements, as desired.

27. Print Preview the report; return to Design view.

28. Print the report.

29. Save and Close the report; name it **BRANCH SOFTWARE**.

30. Close and save the database.

USE QUERY TO CREATE A REPORT

✓ *Queries control data that can be viewed in a form or report. Queries may also be used as the basis for a form to enter or edit data, but some values may not be able to be edited.*

QUERY/FIELD TYPE	CHANGEABLE?
Query - one table	Yes
Query - two tables, one-to-one	Yes
Query - two tables, one-to-many	Usually
Query with totals	No
Query - one-to-one self join	No
Query with unique values set to yes	No
Query - crosstab	No
Field - calculated	No
Query - union	No
Query - pass through	No
Read - only field	No
Query with attached table with no unique index or primary key	No

CHANGE HEIGHT IN REPORT

1. Place pointer at bottom edge of section to change.

   Pointer will appear as a horizontal line with two arrows.

2. Click and drag edge to desired new location.

CHANGE SIZE IN REPORT

1. Place pointer at bottom edge of section to change.

   Pointer will become a line with a black, two-headed arrow.

2. Click and drag to new size.

GROUP REPORT DATA

1. View report in Design view.

2. Click **Sorting and Grouping** button ..

   OR

   a. Click **View** menu ....

   b. Click **Sorting and Grouping** ....

3. Set sort order.

4. Select desired field in Field/Expression column to group on.

5. Click in Group Header ....

6. Click drop-down arrow........... 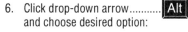 and choose desired option:

   Yes - to add a group header for this field to the report

   No - remove group header for field from report

7. Click in Group Footer text box. ....

8. Click drop-down arrow........... and choose desired option.

9. Repeat steps 4-8 for each field to group on.

10. Double-click .... control menu box to close.

11. Add desired controls to new group header or group footer sections.

DEFINE AN EXPRESSION FOR A REPORT

✓ *An expression in a text box on a report is not stored in the database but calculated each time the report is displayed or printed.*

ENTER EXPRESSION IN TEXT BOX

1. View report in Design view.

2. Select text box to contain expression.

   OR

   a. Click **Text Box** tool in the toolbox.

   b. Click form at desired location of default sized text box.

   OR

   Click and drag pointer at desired location on report.

4. Click inside text box.

5. Press the **Equal Sign key (=)**............

6. Type desired expression ....*expression*

EXERCISE

ADDING NEW FIELDS TO A REPORT

27

NOTES:

- A saved report can be used to create a new report. Open the previously saved report design, make changes, such as adding new fields, and save the new design using a new report name.

- To add a new field to a report, use the Field List option in the View menu in report design view to

open a window that will list all fields in the source table or query. To add a field, select a field and drag it to the desired detail position on the Design view screen. You can then add a label to the Page Header section and proceed was discussed in previous lessons.

You have been asked to create another report relating to your company's hardware inventory. You decide to use a previously created report as a basis for this new report since it contains only one additional field.

EXERCISE DIRECTIONS:

1. Open the 🖾 **COMPANY** database or 🖫 **ACOMPANY.27**.

2. Select the REPORT section.

3. Open the Design of the COMPUTER EQUIPMENT report.

4. Select the Field List option in the View menu.

5. Add the ASSIGNED TO field to the end of the detail section items.

6. Add a label item to the Page Header section; enter DEPT.

7. Adjust the size and position of DEPT. label and ASSIGNED TO detail item.

8. Extend existing lines to include the new entries.

9. Delete the report's subtitle and replace with the label **In Item Order**.

10. Change the font size to 12 point.

11. Extend Page Header boundaries to the new report width.

12. Center the new subtitle.

13. For an ascending sort add PURDATE to the Sorting and Grouping window.

14. Create a Group Footer for ITEM.

15. Remove duplicate entries from the ITEM and MFG. columns.

16. Set ITEM and MFG. detail items to print in Bold.

17. Change the Sum footer format to Currency.

18. Add the label TOTAL COST = to the Sum footer

19. Print Preview; make any needed adjustments.

20. Change print orientation to Landscape, with all margins set for .5 ".

21. Print the report.

22. Save report as **HARDWARE INVENTORY WITH ASSIGNED DEPT**.

23. Close and save the database.

LESSON 5
SUMMARY EXERCISE 28

This summary exercise will review and apply all database concepts learned.

> *You have been hired by the Human Resources Department of Boynton College. One of your first jobs is to help organize information about the faculty. Once a database is created, you will be asked to update and modify the database, as well as create several reports requested by the President.*

EXERCISE DIRECTIONS:

Creating and Saving a Database Table:

Create a new database file; name it **COLLEGE**.

2. Create a table using the field names and properties indicated below.

6. Adjust column widths to accommodate the longest entry in each field.

7. Print one copy.

8. Close the COLLEGE database.

continued...

Field Name	Type	Size	Description
TITLE	Text	3	
LAST	Text	10	
FIRST	Text	8	
DEPT	Text	4	
BUDGET	Number	Integer	For Supplies
BLDG	Text	1	M=Main, A=Annex
NO OF CLASSES	Number	Integer	
START	Date/Time	Short Date	When Hired
TENURE	Text	1	

3. Save the table; name it **TEACHERS**.

4. Create a Datasheet view of this table.

Entering Records:

Enter the records below into the table.

TITLE	LAST	FIRST	DEPT	BUDGET	BLDG	NO OF CLASSES	START	TENURE
Dr.	Fernandez	Jose	Eng	200	M	5	9/16/85	Y
Ms.	Marcus	Diana	Eng	250	M	4	9/16/85	Y
Ms.	Hargrave	Sally	Eng	250	M	5	9/16/84	Y
Mr.	Bergman	Paul	Math	150	A	3	9/16/83	N
Mr.	Pax	Robert	Sci	200	A	3	9/16/85	N
Mr.	Chassin	Matthew	Math	120	A	2	1/10/87	N
Ms.	Blane	Jaime	PE	120	M	3	9/16/87	N
Ms.	Chen	Julie	Sci	160	M	4	9/16/85	Y
Ms.	Brown	Donna	Hist	200	A	5	2/1/88	Y
Mr.	Anderson	Harvey	Hist	200	A	5	1/10/86	N
Dr.	Brown	Donald	Lang	140	M	3	2/1/86	Y
Mr.	Mastresi	William	Sci	120	A	2	9/16/87	N
Mr.	Zhan	Rafu	Sci	200	M	5	9/9/83	Y
Ms.	Browning	Paula	Eng	150	A	4	9/9/82	Y
Dr.	Ng	Tom	Lang	180	M	3	9/9/87	N
Mr.	Greene	Ralph	Math	140	A	5	2/20/89	N
Ms.	Linn	Sarah	Bus	180	A	4	2/10/88	N
Ms.	Fernandez	Ricardo	Bus	180	A	3	1/20/88	N
Dr.	Keltz	Mel	Bus	200	A	5	2/10/90	N
Mr.	Grosso	Lenny	PE	140	M	2	9/16/85	Y

DIRECTIONS CONTINUED:

Modifying the Datasheet/Adding Records:

9. Open the **COLLEGE** database table **TEACHERS**.

10. To keep track of faculty members' years of teaching experience, add one new number field (Field size - integer) to the table, EXP.

11. From the list below, enter the experience information into the table.

12. Adjust column widths to accommodate the longest entry.

Searching the Database Table:

15. Using the Edit menu Find option, search the database for the answers to the following questions:

    a. Which teachers work in the English Department?

    b. In what building does Ralph Green work?

16. Using the Edit menu Replace option, search the database for all Hist Dept entries and change to S.S.

TITLE	LAST	FIRST	DEPT	BUDGET	BLDG	NO OF CLASSES	START	TENURE	EXP
Dr.	Fernandez	Jose	Eng	200	M	5	9/16/85	Y	15
Ms.	Marcus	Diana	Eng	250	M	4	9/16/85	Y	12
Ms.	Hargrave	Sally	Eng	250	M	5	9/16/84	Y	13
Mr.	Bergman	Paul	Math	150	A	3	9/16/83	N	14
Mr.	Pax	Robert	Sci	200	A	3	9/16/85	N	18
Mr.	Chassin	Matthew	Math	120	A	2	1/10/87	N	10
Ms.	Blane	Jaime	PE	120	M	3	9/16/87	N	9
Ms.	Chen	Julie	Sci	160	M	4	9/16/85	Y	13
Ms.	Brown	Donna	Hist	200	A	5	2/1/88	Y	8
Mr.	Anderson	Harvey	Hist	200	A	5	1/10/86	N	12
Dr.	Brown	Donald	Lang	140	M	3	2/1/86	Y	10
Mr.	Mastresi	William	Sci	120	A	2	9/16/87	N	16
Mr.	Zhan	Rafu	Sci	200	M	5	9/9/83	Y	15
Ms.	Browning	Paula	Eng	150	A	4	9/9/82	Y	15
Dr.	Ng	Tom	Lang	180	M	3	9/9/87	N	10
Mr.	Greene	Ralph	Math	140	A	5	2/20/89	N	8
Ms.	Linn	Sarah	Bus	180	A	4	2/10/88	N	9
Ms.	Fernandez	Ricardo	Bus	180	A	3	1/20/88	N	9
Dr.	Keltz	Mel	Bus	200	A	5	2/10/90	N	7
Mr.	Grosso	Lenny	PE	140	M	2	9/16/85	Y	11

13. Several teachers' records were omitted from the table. Add the following records.

17. Using a Filter search, find the answers to each of the following questions:

    a. Which teachers work in the main building and have more than 10 years experience?

TITLE	LAST	FIRST	DEPT	BUDGET	BLDG	NO OF CLASSES	START	TENURE	EXP
Dr.	Blanc	Pamela	Sci	200	M	5	9/9/80	Y	17
Mr.	Talley	Charles	Sci	140	A	3	2/10/84	N	13
Ms.	Goodcoff	Kayli	PE	160	A	4	2/10/81	Y	16
Mr.	Bergman	Thomas	Lang	150	A	3	9/10/89	N	8
Dr.	Knossos	Joyce	Math	200	A	5	2/10/82	Y	16

b. Which English teachers hold a doctoral degree?

Doing a Quick Sort of the Datasheet:

14. Sort the datasheet in ascending order by LAST NAME.

c. Which Math teachers work in the Annex and have a supply budget of at least $140?

18. Create a Query of those teachers who work in the Main Building by Dept:

   Include the fields: DEPT (alphabetically), TITLE (alphabetically), LAST (alphabetically), FIRST, TENURE, and BLDG.

DIRECTIONS CONTINUED:

9. Save the query; name it **MAIN BUILDING STAFF**.

0. Print the query.

Preparing Reports:

Report I:

1. Create a Tabular report.

   Respond to the Report Wizard as follows:

   List fields in given order: START, TITLE, FIRST, LAST, and EXP.

   Sort by START date.

   Set Portrait orientation, Line spacing 0".

   Title report: BOYNTON COLLEGE.

   See All fields on one page.

2. Delete the Report Footer.

3. Add the subtitle **Faculty List**.

4. Center the first two Report Headers.

5. Bold all headers and footers, without italics.

6. Change detail data:

   START DATE to a descending sort

   TITLE to alphabetical sort

   START DATE with duplicate entries hidden

7. Change the Page Headers to read:

START DATE	TITLE	FIRST NAME	LAST NAME	EXPER- IENCE

8. Print Preview.

9. Make any adjustments necessary to make the report more attractive.

0. Add labels:

   Page to the page function

   Seniority Order as of: to the current date function

1. Adjust the date line to conform with the other two headers.

2. Print one copy.

3. Save and Close the report.

Report II:

4. Create a Tabular report.
   Respond to the Report Wizard as follows:

   List fields in given order: DEPT, BUDGET, and BLDG.

   Sort by DEPT and BUDGET.

   Set presentation style, Portrait orientation, Line spacing 0 ".

Title report: DEPARTMENT BUDGETS.

   See All fields on one page.

35. Delete the Date Report Header.

36. Add a Report Header subtitle: **1996**.

37. Center report headers and building column data.

38. Add, below the Sum function, a function to determine the Average of the budget figures.

39. Shade the Sum and Average values in light gray.

40. Add appropriate labels to the Sum and Average amounts.

41. Change the properties of the following:

   Format all money amounts to currency.

   Remove DEPT duplicates.

   For DEPT set Group footer to Yes.

42. Add a Sum function in the Group footer to total the budget of each department.

43. Shade all sums and the average values.

44. Change format of BUDGET to currency.

45. Print Preview.

46. Make adjustments as necessary.

47. Print Preview.

48. Print one copy.

49. Save and Close the report.

Report III:

50. Create and Save a query to list those teaching in the Annex who have four or more classes.

   List fields in given order: TITLE, FIRST, LAST, BLDG, NO OF CLASSES, and DEPT.

   Set criteria to select Annex teachers who only teach four or more classes.

   Save and Close the query.

51. Create a Tabular report using this query.

   Respond to the Report Wizard as follows:

   List fields in given order: TITLE, FIRST, LAST, NO OF CLASSES, and DEPT.

   Sort by NO OF CLASSES.

   Title report: BOYNTON COLLEGE - ANNEX.

   See All fields on one page.

52. Move the current date function to the Page Footer section.

DIRECTIONS CONTINUED:

53. Add a subtitle: **Teachers with Four or More Classes**

54. Change the column heading NO OF CLASSES to CLASSES.

55. Center the Report Headers and detail data for CLASSES.

56. Set main Page Header to italics.

57. Add the label **Total # of Classes:** for the Sum function value.

58. Add a Count of teachers' functions to the Report Footer with a label of **Total # of Teachers**.

59. Change font style to Bold for all labels.

60. Change Page Footer items to Bold, without italics.

61. Print Preview.

62. Make adjustments, as necessary.

63. Print one copy.

64. Save and Close the report and database.

CHAPTER 5

LESSON 1

CREATING, SAVING, AND PRINTING A PRESENTATION

Exercises 1-5

- About PowerPoint
- Starting PowerPoint
- Using the Blank Presentation Option
- Using the Template Option
- Adding Text to Placeholders
- Adding Slides to Presentations
- Saving a Presentation
- Exiting PowerPoint
- Opening a Presentation
- Adding a Slide to a Presentation
- Slide Views
- Printing
- Working with Object Slides
- Using Undo
- Changing a Slide's Layout and Template
- Moving, Copying, and Deleting Slides
- Using Slide Sorter View
- Using Outline View

PowerPoint
Lesson 1: Creating, Saving, and Printing a Presentation

EXERCISE 1

- ABOUT POWERPOINT - STARTING POWERPOINT - USING THE BLANK PRESENTATION OPTION - USING THE TEMPLATE OPTION - ADDING TEXT TO PLACEHOLDERS - ADDING SLIDES TO A PRESENTATION - SAVING A PRESENTATION - EXITING POWERPOINT

NOTES:

About PowerPoint

- PowerPoint is the presentation graphics component of Microsoft Office that lets you create and save presentations.

- A presentation is a collection of slides relating to the same topic which may be shown while an oral report is given to help summarize data and emphasize report highlights. From the presentation slides, you can prepare handouts for the audience, speaker notes to use during the presentation, or outlines to provide an overview of the presentation. In addition, you can use slides as a table of contents and overhead transparencies. You can also create 35 mm slides of your presentation.

- PowerPoint slides may include text, drawings, charts, outlines, and/or graphics.

- Outlines created in Word or data created in Access or Excel may be imported into a PowerPoint slide. A PowerPoint slide may be imported into a Word document. (*See Integration Chapter, Exercise 8.*)

Starting PowerPoint

- To start PowerPoint, click on the PowerPoint application icon in the MOM toolbar 📇.

- After launching PowerPoint, the following PowerPoint dialog box appears which presents options to create a new presentation or to open an existing presentation. Two of the options use Wizards. As noted in the other applications, Wizards walk you through the presentation development process. Using PowerPoint Wizards will not be covered in this book.

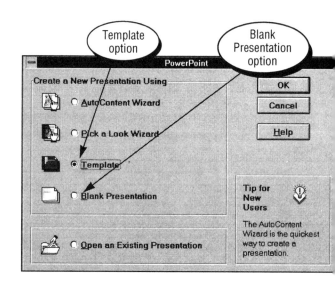

Creating a Presentation Using the Blank Presentation Option

- The **Blank Presentation** option allows you to build your own unique presentation from blank slides which contain standard default formats and layouts.

- After selecting Blank Presentation and clicking OK, the New Slide dialog box appears.

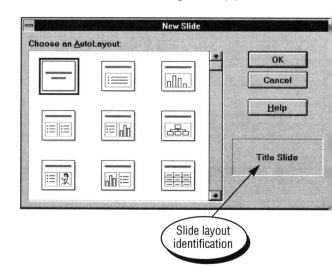

The New Slide dialog box includes a set of 21 different AutoLayout formats that arrange various types of objects on slides. Objects include such things as titles, charts, graphics, or bulleted lists—standard objects that you might want to place on the slide.

AutoLayout formats follow the natural progression of your presentation. They start with a Title Slide format and move to more complex layouts.

✓ Note: In later exercises, you will learn to rearrange objects and design your own layouts so that the slides become more suitable for your needs.

Each layout is identified in the box at the lower right corner of the New Slide layout window. Select a slide layout which is appropriate to the data you are presenting. The Title Slide is the default setting for the first slide in every presentation.

■ After selecting the Title Slide layout and clicking OK, the PowerPoint screen appears.

Creating a Presentation Using the Template Option

The **Template** option allows you to create slides with a predesigned format. PowerPoint provides over 100 professionally designed formats with colorful backgrounds and text from which you can choose.

■ After selecting Template and clicking OK, a Presentation Template dialog box appears which lists the available templates. As you click on each template name, a sample of it appears in the preview window.

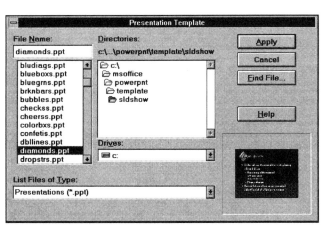

■ After selecting the template design you desire and clicking OK, then selecting a layout from the AutoLayout screen and clicking OK, the PowerPoint screen appears.

The PowerPoint Screen

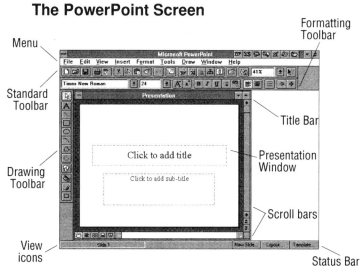

- PowerPoint places the generic title *Presentation* in the **Title Bar** of each presentation you create.

- The **Drawing Toolbar**, located down the left side of the screen, contains some of the most common tools used to add drawings to slides.

- **View icons**, located at the bottom of the Presentation window, control the number of slides PowerPoint displays and the display layout. (*Views will be covered in Exercise 2.*)

- The **Status Bar**, located at the bottom of the PowerPoint window, contains information and buttons which make performing the most common tasks more efficient:

Slide number   Identifies the slide currently displayed.

New Slide   Creates a new slide and displays the New Slide window to allow you to select a layout.

Save   New Slide   **STANDARD TOOLBAR**

Layout   Displays the New Slide dialog box and allows you to change the layout of the active slide.

Template   Displays the Presentation Template dialog box and allows you to select a design for your presentation.

Adding Text to Placeholders

- PowerPoint displays a slide containing **placeholders** (an empty box or boxes) which identify the placement and location of the objects on the slide. Each placeholder contains directions to help you complete the slide.

- Whether you select the Blank Presentation or Template option, **Title placeholders** contain the format for title text while **body text placeholders** include format and design for subtitles or bulleted lists.

- To type text into a placeholder, click inside the placeholder and note the handles that appear. Enter the text as prompted.

- If you start typing without selecting the text placeholder, PowerPoint automatically places the text in the first text placeholder.

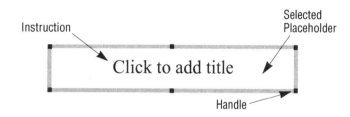

Instruction   Selected Placeholder

Click to add title

Handle

Adding Slides to a Presentation

- To add a new slide to the presentation, click the New Slide button on the Status Bar or click the Insert New Slide icon on the Standard Toolbar. The AutoLayout dialog box appears for you to select a layout for the new slide.

- The Bulleted List format is automatically selected when you add a second slide to a presentation.

- Five different bulleted sublevels are available. Pressing Tab indents text and produces sublevels of bulleted items. Different bullet shapes identify the tab levels, and the text size gets smaller with each sublevel. Pressing Shift+Tab returns you to the previous bullet level.

> - Level 1
>   - Sub-Level 2
>   - Sub-Level 3
>   - Sub-Level 4
>   - Sub-Level 5

- PowerPoint places the new slide immediately after the slide that is displayed or selected at the time you create the new slide.

Saving Presentations

- Presentations are saved using the same procedures used to save Word documents and Excel spreadsheets.

- The Summary Information window allows you to add key words, a presentation title, comments, and other information you want to save with the file.

- PowerPoint automatically adds a .PPT extension to presentations.

Closing a Presentation File/Exiting PowerPoint

- PowerPoint follows the same procedures for closing a presentation file and exiting as in the Word and Excel application tools.

- If the presentation you are working on has been modified or has not yet been saved, you will be prompted to save it.

EXERCISE DIRECTIONS:

1. Start PowerPoint and create a NEW Blank Presentation.

2. Accept the default Title Slide layout for the first slide.

3. Type the title as shown in Illustration A.

4. Select New Slide and accept the default bulleted list slide for the second slide.

5. Type the bulleted list as shown in Illustration A.

6. Save the presentation; name it **KIT**. Fill in the summary information as follows:

   Title: (Accept the default)

   Subject: Sales Presentation

   Author: Your name

7. Close the presentation window.

8. Create a NEW Template presentation using the DIAMONDS.PPT template.

9. Accept the default Title Slide layout for the first slide and the bulleted list slide for the second slide.

10. Type the title and bulleted list slides shown in Illustration B on page 386.

11. Save the presentation; name it **FLAGSHIP**. Fill in the summary information as follows:

    Title: (Accept the default)

    Subject: Company Introduction

    Author: Your name

12. Close the presentation window.

ILLUSTRATION A

CREATIVE SALES

Sales Meeting
January 8, 1996

TITLE SLIDE

SALES KITS

- Tool for making initial client contact
- A support system for sales rep
- Way to provide clients with materials to make an informed decision about buying your product

BULLETED LIST SLIDE

ILLUSTRATION B

FLAGSHIP REALTY

Jawanza Hughes, President

TITLE SLIDE

QUALIFIED LEADER IN PROPERTIES OF DISTINCTION

- ◆ Unparalleled knowledge of and commitment to high-end properties on the North Fork
- ◆ Demonstrated track record
- ◆ Unique ability to match client needs and inventory
- ◆ Broad international client base

BULLETED LIST SLIDE

TART POWERPOINT 4.0

Open Microsoft Office group on Windows
Program Manager.

Double-click Microsoft PowerPoint
program icon.

OR

Click PowerPoint icon on .... 🖼️
on MOM Toolbar.

DD NEW SLIDE

TRL + M

Click 🖼️ .... `Alt` + `I` , `N`

OR

Click **New Slide** .... `New Slide...`
on status bar.

Select an AutoLayout format.

Click **OK** .... `Enter`

CREATE NEW PRESENTATION USING A TEMPLATE

Click 🗋 .... `Alt` + `F` , `N`

2. Click **Template** .... `T`

3. Click **OK** .... `Enter`

4. Select desired template in **File Name** text
box.

   ✓ *As a template is selected, a preview of
   the format is presented in the lower
   right-hand corner of the window.*

5. Click **Apply** .... `Enter`

   ✓ *All slides in the active presentation are
   formatted using the selected template.*

ADD TEXT TO PLACEHOLDERS

1. Click desired placeholder.

2. Type the text; press Enter to move to a
new line.

CLOSE MENU

Click off the menu .... `Esc` or `Alt`

🌐 SAVE PRESENTATION

Ctrl + S

1. Click 🖼️ .... `Alt` + `F` , `S`

2. Type the presentation name ....*name*
in the **File Name** text box.

3. Select alternate drive and directory, if
desired.

4. Click **OK** .... `Enter`

5. Type the desired summary information.

6. Click **OK** .... `Enter`

🌐 EXIT POWERPOINT 4.0

Alt + F4

Double-click 🖼️ .... `Alt` + `F` , `X`

EXERCISE

■ OPENING A PRESENTATION ■ SLIDE VIEWS ■ PRINTING

2

NOTES:

Opening a Presentation

■ Presentations may be opened by selecting <u>O</u>pen an Existing Presentation from the PowerPoint dialog box or by using the procedures used to open documents in other Microsoft Office applications.

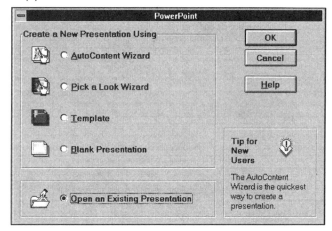

Slide Views

■ PowerPoint allows you to view your presentation in five different ways.

- **Slide view**, the default, allows you to see a single slide on screen. You may edit or modify a slide in this view.

SLIDE VIEW

- **Outline view** displays slide text on a notebook page layout to give an overview of the content of a presentation. Use this view to organize a presentation. *(This view will be detailed in a later exercise.)*

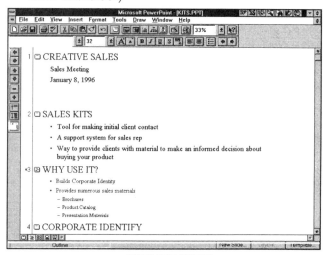

OUTLINE VIEW

- **Slide Sorter view** allows you to see miniature copies of your slides on screen so that you can see the flow of the presentation. Use this view to move, copy, and delete slides. *(Moving, copying, and deleting slides will be detailed in the next exercise.)*

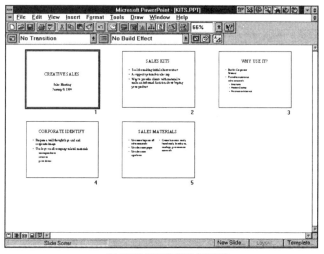

SLIDE SORTER VIEW

- **Notes Page view** allows you to display speaker's note pages for each slide. *(This view will be detailed in a later exercise.)*

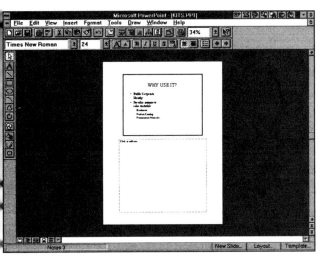

NOTES PAGE VIEW

- **Slide Show view** allows you see your slides as an on-screen presentation. *(This view will be detailed in a later exercise.)*

Views may be changed by clicking the appropriate view icon on the bottom left of the presentation window or by selecting the desired view from the View main menu.

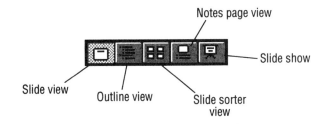

Notes page view

Slide show

Slide view

Outline view

Slide sorter view

Displaying Slides

When there are a number of slides included in a presentation, you will find it necessary to move from slide to slide to edit, enhance, or view the slide information. PowerPoint offers a variety of ways to select and display slides in Slide View:

- Press PgDn to display the next slide or PgUp to display the previous slide.

- Click the **Next Slide** or **Previous Slide** button on the vertical slide scroll bar.

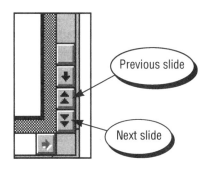

Previous slide

Next slide

- Drag the vertical slide scroll box up or down until the desired slide number is displayed.

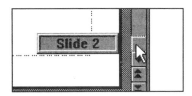

Spell Checking

- The spelling feature may be used in PowerPoint as it was used in the other Office tools.

- After creating your presentation, click the spelling icon on the Toolbar ⬛ or select Spelling from the Tools main menu.

Printing a Presentation

- Slides in your presentation may be used as an on-screen show, transparencies, 35mm slides, notes pages, handouts, or as an outline. Therefore, you must specify certain setup information, depending on how you wish to use the slides or printouts. Select Slide Setup from the File main menu, and indicate your print specifications in the Slide Setup dialog box which follows.

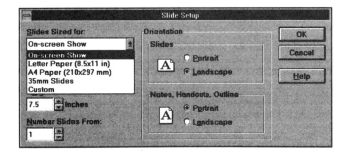

PowerPoint

Lesson 1: Creating, Saving, and Printing a Presentation

■ Printing PowerPoint slides is similar to printing pages in a Word document and worksheets in an Excel workbook. To print PowerPoint slides, select Print from the File main menu, or press Ctrl+ P. In the Print dialog box which follows, you may print the active slide, a selected slide range, or all slides in a presentation. When you print all slides of a presentation, each slide prints on a separate page. The **Print What** feature allows you to indicate whether you want your presentation printed as slides, notes pages, handouts with 2, 3 or 6 slides per page, or as an outline. (*Notes pages and handouts will be detailed in Exercise 15.*)

■ You can also click the **Print** icon 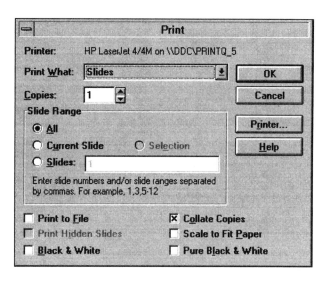 on the Standard Toolbar. When you use this technique, you bypass the Print window and send the print command directly to the printer. PowerPoint automatically prints information using the settings last selected in the Print window.

■ The default selection in the Print window prints All slides. Other options include:

Option	Description
Print to File	Print the presentation to a disk file so that it may be sent to a service bureau for printing in alternate format such as 35 mm slides.
Print Hidden Slides	Print slides that had been hidden.
Black & White	Turn all color fills to white and add a thin black frame to all unbordered objects without text. *Use this option if you plan to use your slides as overhead transparencies or if you have a printer that only prints black and white.*
Collate Copies	Print multiple copies as collated sets.
Scale to Fit Paper	Scale presentation slides to fit a custom or different sized paper.
Pure Black & White	Turn all color fills to white, text and lines to black, add outlines or borders to filled objects, and print objects in grayscale. *Use this option if you plan to use your slides as overhead transparencies or if you have a printer that only prints black and white.*

In this exercise, you will add new slides to a previously created presentation. You will then use different slide views to see flow of your presentation.

EXERCISE DIRECTIONS:

1. Start PowerPoint and select <u>O</u>pen an Existing Presentation from the PowerPoint dialog box.

   ✓ *Note:* *If PowerPoint is already running, select <u>F</u>ile, <u>O</u>pen to open a presentation.*

2. Open **FLAGSHIP**.

3. Display slide two by clicking the Next Slide button.

4. Display slide one by dragging the scroll box.

5. Create a new bulleted list slide using the following information:

   ✓ *Note:* *The slide will be inserted after slide one. You will move it into a desired order in a later exercise.*

   ┌───┐
   │ SERVICES INCLUDE   │
   │ • Private financial evaluation   │
   │ • Mortgage payment table constructed for each│
   │   buyer   │
   │ • Property tour videos   │
   │ • Internet access for international sales and listings │
   └───┘

6. Switch to Slide Sorter view.

7. Switch back to Slide view.

8. In the Print dialog box, select Handouts with three slides per page as the Print <u>W</u>hat option. Print one copy in Black and White.

9. Close the file; save the changes.

10. Open **KIT**.

11. Display slide two using the PgDn key.

12. Display slide one using the PgUp key.

13. Create a new bulleted list slide using the following information:

    ┌───┐
    │ CORPORATE IDENTITY   │
    │ • Prepare a well-thought logo and corporate image │
    │ • Use logo on all company-related materials │
    │   -correspondence   │
    │   -invoices   │
    │   -price sheets   │
    └───┘

14. Switch to Slide Sorter view.

15. Switch to Slide view.

16. Spell check.

17. Use the default print slide setup.

18. In the Print dialog box, select Handouts with three slides per page as the Print <u>W</u>hat option. Print one copy in Black and White.

19. Close the file; save the changes.

OPEN A PRESENTATION

CTRL + O

1. Click  .... `Alt`+`F`, `O`

2. Type presentation name ....*name* in **File <u>N</u>ame** text box, or select presentation in list.

3. Click **OK**.................................... `Enter`

   ✓ *You can also double-click a presentation name in the list and skip step 3.*

SWITCH VIEWS

Select desired view button option:

• ▭ **<u>S</u>lides**.................... `Alt`+`V`, `S`

• ▤ **<u>O</u>utline**................. `Alt`+`V`, `O`

• ▢ **<u>N</u>otes Pages**.......... `Alt`+`V`, `N`

• ▦ **Sli<u>d</u>e Sorter**........... `Alt`+`V`, `D`

ADD SUBLEVELS

1. Press **Tab**...................................... `Tab` to move to indent text to next level.

   ✓ *Five different bulleted sublevels are available. Different bullet shapes identify the tab levels. Text size gets smaller with each sublevel.*

   OR

   Press **Shift+Tab**............... `Shift`+`Tab` to return to previous level.

DISPLAY SLIDES

Press **PgUp** .... `PgUp` to display previous slide

   OR

   Press **PgDn** .... `PgDn` to display next slide

   OR

   Click **Next Slide** ▼ or **Previous Slide** ▲ button on scroll bar.

   OR

   Drag scroll box until desired slide is identified.

PRINT A PRESENTATION

Ctrl + P

1. Click  .... `Alt`+`F`, `P`

2. Select desired options.

3. Click **OK**.................................... `Enter`

PowerPoint

EXERCISE 3

■ WORKING WITH OBJECT SLIDES ■ USING UNDO ■ CHANGING A SLIDE'S LAYOUT OR TEMPLATE

Insert Clip Art

STANDARD TOOLBAR

NOTES:

Working with Object Slides

■ In Exercise 1, you learned that a placeholder is an empty box which identifies the placement of objects on a slide. You entered text into placeholders for a title and a bulleted slide. Some slides, however, contain special placeholders to hold a particular type of item, like clip art, a graph, or a chart. Some slides contain an *object* placeholder which holds any type of object—text, clip art, or a chart.

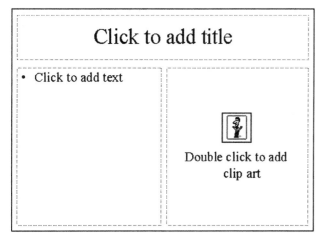

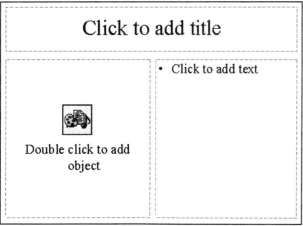

■ When you select a slide layout containing a special placeholder, the placeholder asks that you double-click within the placeholder to add the object. If you are adding clip art, for example, double-clicking will open the Microsoft ClipArt Gallery so you can insert a clip art image in a clip art placeholder.

■ You can also insert clip art by clicking on the Insert Clip Art button 🖻 on the Standard Toolbar. In later exercises, you will learn how to add a graph and/or a chart into placeholders as well as move and resize the objects inserted.

Using Undo

■ Like the other Microsoft Office applications, the Undo feature reverses the most recent action. Note the keystrokes on page 395 to review Undo procedures.

Changing a Slide's Layout

■ The layout or template of a slide may be changed at any time. If you have objects on the slide when changing the layout, they will not be lost; they will be rearranged.

■ Use Slide View when changing a Slide's layout or template.

- To change the layout, click the Layout button on the Status bar or select Slide Layout from the Format main menu. The AutoLayout dialog box appears, allowing you to make another layout selection.

Changing a Slide's Template

- Templates are organized by type and saved in three subdirectories (folders) within the template subdirectory of the PowerPoint directory. Each category of templates contains designs and layouts which are effective for the media to which they might be applied:

  - **blwovrhd** folder contains templates for black and white overheads.
  - **clrovrhd** folder contains templates for color overheads.
  - **sldshow** folder contains templates for slide shows.

- As you select a template from the File Name list, an example of the template design appears in the lower right corner of the window.

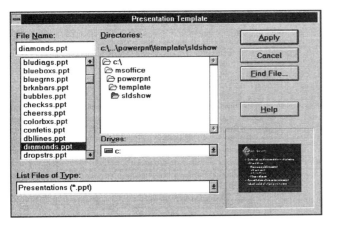

- All exercises in this chapter use the templates contained in the *sldshow* folder.

- To change the template, click the Template button on the Status bar, or select Presentation Template from the Format main menu, or select Template from the PowerPoint dialog box when you create a new presentation. The Presentation Template dialog box appears, allowing you to make another template selection.

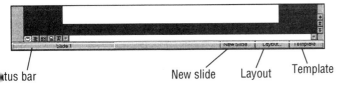

tus bar   New slide   Layout   Template

In this exercise, you will add a slide to each of the presentations you created in previous exercises. You will also change the layout and template in each presentation.

EXERCISE DIRECTIONS:

1. Open **FLAGSHIP**.

2. Create a new slide using the Text & Clip Art layout.
   - ✓ Note: This slide will be inserted after slide one. You will move the slides into a desired order in the next exercise.

3. Enter the bulleted information shown in Illustration A of the exercise. Insert any relevant clip art graphic.

4. Create another new slide using the Clip Art & Text Layout.

5. Enter the bulleted information shown in Illustration B of the exercise. Insert any relevant clip art graphic.

6. Switch to Slide Sorter view.

7. Switch back to Slide view.

8. Use the default print slide setup.

9. Spell check.

10. In the Print dialog box, select Handouts with six slides per page as the Print What option.

11. Print one copy in Black and White.

12. Close the file; save the changes.

13. Open **KIT**.

14. Create a new slide using the Text & Clip Art layout.
    - ✓ Note: This slide will be inserted after slide one. You will move the slides into a desired order in the next exercise.

15. Enter the bulleted information shown in Illustration C of the exercise. Insert any relevant clip art graphic.

16. Create another new slide using the Clip Art and text layout.

17. Enter the bulleted information shown in Illustration D on page 395; insert any relevant clip art graphic.

18. Switch to Slide Sorter view.

19. Switch back to Slide view.

20. Change the template to the SPLATS.PPT design.

21. Use the default print slide setup.

22. In the Print dialog box, select Handouts with six slides per page as the Print What option.

23. Print one copy in Black and White.

24. Close the file; save the changes.

ILLUSTRATION A

PERTY TYPES

- ❖ Homes of Distinction
- ❖ Commercial Properties
- ❖ Residential Townhouses
- ❖ Exclusive Agent for Pineview Estates

ILLUSTRATION B

R SALES FORCE

- ❖ 85 Professional Salespeople
- ❖ 50% are members of Flagship's Private Brokerage Council
  - – Designation awarded to sales agents who handled sales over $1 million

ILLUSTRATION C

WHY USE IT?

- • Builds corporate identity
- • Provides numerous sales materials
  - – Brochures
  - – Product Catalog
  - – Presentation Materials

SALES MATERIALS

- the same logo on all materials
- the same paper
- the same typefaces
- business cards, letterheads, brochures, catalogs, presentation materials

---

CHANGE LAYOUT

Display Slide view:

. Click 🖃 .... Alt + V , S

. Click **Layout** .... Layout...
   on Status bar.

OR

1. Click **F_ormat**................... Alt + O
2. Click **Slide F_ormat**..................... O

CHANGE TEMPLATE

Display Slide view:

1. Click 🖃 .... Alt + V , S

2. Click **Template** .... Template...
   on Status bar.

OR

1. Click **F_ormat**................... Alt + O
2. Click **P_resentation Template** ...... P

UNDO

Ctrl + Z

Click  .... Alt + E , U

USE AUTOLAYOUT TO INSERT CLIP ART

1. Select a layout that has Clip Art option available.

2. Double-click 🖼 .... Alt + I , E
   in template or on toolbar.

3. Double-click desired Clip Art graphic.

4. Select desired Clip Art.

5. Click **OK**................................... Enter

EXERCISE

4

■ MOVING, COPYING, AND DELETING SLIDES ■ USING SLIDE SORTER VIEW

NOTES:

Moving, Copying, and Deleting Slides

■ Each slide in a presentation is part of the entire presentation. Slides may be moved, copied, or deleted within the presentation.

■ You should save a presentation before moving, copying, or deleting slides to prevent loss of data. If you move, copy, or delete a slide and change your mind, use the Undo feature to reverse the action. Remember, however, that PowerPoint allows the reversal of only the last action and does not save multiple actions for reversal.

Using Slide Sorter View

■ You may move, copy, or delete slides from all views using menu commands or cut/copy and paste procedures. However, it is easiest and more efficient to perform these tasks in **Slide Sorter view** since all slides are displayed in miniature, and you can easily see the flow of the presentation in this view.

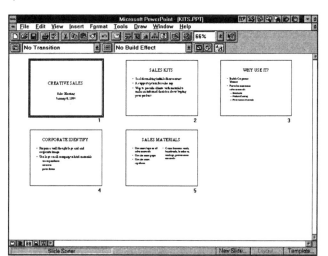

■ To move, copy, or delete a slide in Slide Sorter view, click the Slide Sorter view icon ▦ on the Status bar or select Slide Sorter from the View menu.

■ Select the slide to be moved, copied, or deleted. (Selected slides are outlined by a darker border). You can select slides using a number of different techniques:

  • Click the desired slide.

  • Press the insertion point arrow keys until a dark border outlines the desired slide.

  • Press Shift and click each slide when you want to select multiple slides. Selecting multiple slides allows you to move, copy, or delete them as a group.

■ The easiest way to move a slide in Slide Sorter view is to select it and drag it to a new location. When the slide is being moved, the mouse pointer becomes a slide icon carrying a **+** sign, 🔲⁺ and a vertical dotted bar with arrows on each end identifies the new position of the slide. When the bar appears in the position where you want to place the slide, release the mouse button.

■ To copy a slide, press Ctrl and drag the slide you want to copy to a new location.

■ To delete a slide, select the slide and press Delete.

Returning to Slide View

■ Since you cannot edit slide contents in Slide Sorter view, you will need to return to Slide view to make changes and adjust text. You can return to Slide view using one of the following techniques:

  • Double-click a slide.

  • Select the slide and click the Slide view icon ▢ on the Status bar.

  • Select the desired slide and select Slides from the View menu.

EXERCISE DIRECTIONS:

1. Open **KIT**.

2. Create a new slide using a Bulleted List layout.

3. Enter the information shown in Illustration A.

4. Create a new slide using a Two-Column text layout.

5. Enter the information shown in Illustration B.

6. Create a new slide using a Text & Clip Art layout.

7. Enter the information shown in Illustration C. Insert a relevant graphic.

8. Switch to Slide Sorter view.

9. Move the slides into the order shown in Illustration D on page 399.

10. Delete the slide entitled, CORPORATE IDENTITY.

11. Switch to Slide view.

12. Change the template to MOVNGLNS.PPT.

13. Spell check.

14. Print one copy of the presentation as Handouts with six slides per page in Pure Black and White.

15. Close the file; save the changes.

ILLUSTRATION A

THE SALES BROCHURE

◆ Similar to marketing brochure
  ◆ contain creative headlines
  ◆ contain attractive graphics
◆ Should possess the same visual elements of your corporate identity
◆ Should motivate the reader to learn more about your company
◆ Result should be company and product exposure

ILLUSTRATION B

THE PRODUCT CATALOG

- ◆ Contains more specific information about company products
- ◆ May include prices and discount offers
- ◆ May be sent through mail to prospective clients

- ◆ More effective when handed out personally on a sales call or visit to set up a sales call
- ◆ Use simple drawings or photos to show product line

ILLUSTRATION C

PRESENTATON MATERIALS

- ◆ The flip chart
  - ◆ visuals are printed on sheets of paper and inserted into flip chart carrier
- ◆ Refrigerator magnet
  - ◆ leave-behind gift upon completion of sales call

MOVE SLIDES

1. Select slide to move.
2. Drag slide to new location.

COPY SLIDES

1. Select slide to copy.
2. Press Ctrl and drag slide to new location.

DELETE SLIDES

1. Select slide to delete.
2. Press **Delete** .... Del

SPELL CHECK

F7

1. Click **Spelling** button .... on Toolbar.

   OR

   Click **Tools** .... Alt + T

   Click **Spelling** .... S

CREATIVE SALES

Sales Meeting
January 8, 1996

1

WHY USE IT?

- Builds corporate identity
- Provides numerous sales materials
  - Brochures
  - Product Catalog
  - Presentation Materials

2

SALES KITS

- Used for making initial client contact
- A support system for sales rep
- Way to provide clients with material to make an informed decision about buying your product

3

SALES MATERIALS include...

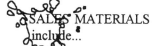

- the same logo on all materials
- the same paper
- the same typefaces
- business cards, letterheads, brochures, catalogs, presentation materials

4

THE SALES BROCHURE

- Similar to marketing brochure
  - contain creative headlines
  - contain attractive graphics
- Should possess the same visual elements of your corporate identity
- Should motivate the reader to learn more about your company
- Result should be company and product exposure

5

THE PRODUCT CATALOG

- Contains more specific information about company products
- May include prices and discount offers
- May be sent through mail to prospective clients
- More effective when handed out personally on a sales call or visit to set up a sales call\
- Use simple drawings or photos to show product line

6

PRESENTATON MATERIALS

- The flip chart
  - visuals are printed on sheets of paper and inserted into flip chart carrier
- Refrigerator magnet
  - leave-behind gift upon completion of sales call

7

CORPORATE IDENTITY

- Create a well-thought logo and corporate image
- Use logo on all company-related materials
  - correspondence
  - invoices
  - price sheets

8

EXERCISE

USING OUTLINE VIEW **5**

NOTES:

Outline View

- **Outline** view displays slide text as titles and subtitles in an outline format to give an overview of the content of a presentation. This view is used to organize a presentation.

- Outline view may be used before creating text on slides to organize your thoughts in an outline format. Or, you may create your presentation on slides first, then switch to Outline view to see the flow of your presentation in an outline format. It can also serve as a Table of Contents to distribute to your audience.

- Note the illustration below of the KIT presentation displayed in Outline view. Slides are numbered down the left side of the screen and slide icons identify the start of each new slide.

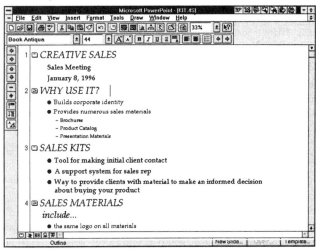

- Graphics and objects do not appear in Outline view. However, a slide which contains such items will be identified by shapes in the miniature slide icon which appears to the right of the slide numbers.

- To display Outline view, click the Outline view icon on the bottom left of the presentation window or select Outline from the View menu.

- The Outlining toolbar replaces the Drawing toolbar in the presentation window. The Outlining toolbar contains tools for making some of the more common tasks associated with outlines

more efficient. Many of these tasks are not available on the menus.

OUTLINING TOOLBAR

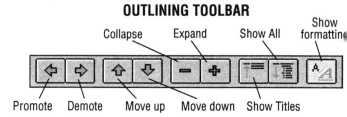

- **Promote/Demote** icons allow you to quickly reformat bulleted text to title text (promote) and title text to subitem text (demote).

- **Move up/Move down** icons allow you to select text from one slide and move the text to a new location. This procedure can be used effectively to move or rearrange individual text items or complete slides.

- **Expand Selection** icon allows you to display all title text as well as subitem text for selected slides and/or items containing multiple levels and subitems.

- **Collapse Selection** icon allows you to remove subitems from display for individual items or for groups of selected items.

- **Show Titles** icon allows you to display only the title text for all slides in a presentation.

- **Show All** icon allows you to display all levels of text for every slide in a presentation.

- **Show Formatting** icon allows you to display text formatted and enhanced as it appears on the slide. When this feature is inactive, text for all slides appears as plain text in the default font.

Adding Slides in Outline View

- The same four procedures may be used to add slides in Outline view that you used to add slides in Slide view:

- Click Insert New Slide icon on the Standard Toolbar.

- Click New Slide button [New Slide...] on the Status bar .
- Press Ctrl+M.
- Select Insert, New Slide from the menus.

■ In addition, you may add a slide by pressing Enter after typing the slide title. When bulleted items or subtitles are included on a slide, you can create a new slide by pressing Shift+Tab

until both a new slide number and a new slide icon appear.

Printing an Outline

■ You print an outline using the same basic procedures you used to print copies of your slides. You must, however, select Outline View from the **Print What** drop-down list.

In this exercise, you will create a presentation in Outline view. After creating the presentation, you will move slides, add a new slide, and print the presentation.

EXERCISE DIRECTIONS:

1. Create a NEW Blank presentation.
2. Switch to Outline view.
3. Enter the following titles and subtitles to create your outline.
   1. Smartfood, Inc.
      "Eat Well and Stay Trim"
   2. Smartfood Products
      - Frozen dinners
      - Cakes and cookies
      - Crackers
      - Ice cream
      - Soft drinks
   3. Smartfood's Success...
      - People are eating healthier to reduce body fat.
      - People want low-fat, low-calorie foods that taste great!
   4. International Expansion--Where and When?
      - Paris, 6 months
      - Milan, 8 months
      - London, 12 months
      - Madrid, 18 months
      - Sydney, 20 months
      - Hong Kong, 24 months
4. Switch to Slide View.
5. Display slide1.
   - ✓ Note: PowerPoint selected the slide layouts for you. You may, however, change them.

6. Switch to Slide Sorter view.
7. Move slide 4 to become slide 3.
8. Switch to Slide view and display slide 2.
9. Change the layout to Clip Art & Text. Insert a relevant graphic.
10. Change the template to TROPICS.PPT.
11. Switch to Slide view.
12. Insert a new slide after slide 3 that reads,

US Markets
• East-New York
• North-Illinois
• West-California
• South-Florida

13. Switch to Slide view.
14. Change the layout to Clip Art & Text. Insert a relevant graphic.
15. Switch to Slide Sorter view, then to Outline view.
16. Spell check.
17. In the Slide Setup dialog box, change the orientation for Handouts to Landscape.
18. Print one copy as Handouts with six slides per page in Pure Black and White.
19. In the Slide Setup dialog box, change the orientation for Handouts to Portrait.
20. Print one copy as Handouts with six slides per page in Pure Black and White.
21. Save the file; name it **FOOD**. Fill in the appropriate Summary Information.
22. Close the presentation window.

SWITCH TO OUTLINE VIEW

Click [≣] .... [Alt]+[V], [O]

ADD SLIDES IN OUTLINE VIEW

Ctrl + M

Click [↖] .... [Alt]+[I], [S]
OR
Click .... [New Slide...]
OR

Press **Enter** after typing the title ...... [Enter]
for a slide which contains no subtitle or subitems.

OR

Press **Shift +Tab** until a .... [Shift]+[Tab]
new slide number and slide appear.

ADD TEXT IN OUTLINE VIEW

Click [→] .... [Tab]
to indent or add subitems.

- ✓ To add a bulleted item under the Title line, press **Enter** and then press **Tab**.

OR

Click [←] .... [Shift]+[Tab]
to go back one text or subitem level.

LESSON 1
SUMMARY EXERCISE

In this exercise, you will create a presentation in Outline View. You will move the slides, change the layouts of selected slides, and print the presentation.

EXERCISE DIRECTIONS:

1. Create a NEW Blank Presentation.
2. Switch to Outline view.
3. Create the outline shown below.
4. Print one copy of the outline (select Print What, Outline View from the Print menu).
5. Switch to Slide view.
6. Display slide 1.
7. Change the template to WORLDS.PPT.
8. Switch to Slide Sorter view.
9. Move slide 5 to become slide 4.
10. Delete slide 8 (Bonds).
11. Undo the last action.
12. Display slide 3 and change the layout to a Title slide.
13. Display slide 6 and change the layout to a Title slide.
14. Display slide 9 and change the layout to Text & Clip Art. Insert a relevant graphic.
15. Display slide 8 and change the layout to Clip Art and Text. Insert a relevant graphic.
16. Insert a new slide after Underevaluation that reads

    Political Stability
    - Current Leadership
    - Free Elections

    Use a layout which includes clip art. Insert a relevant graphic.
17. Spell check.
18. Switch to Slide Sorter view.
19. Print one copy as Handouts with six slide per page in Black and White.
20. Save the file; name it **BRAZIL**. Fill in the appropriate summary information.
21. Close the presentation window.

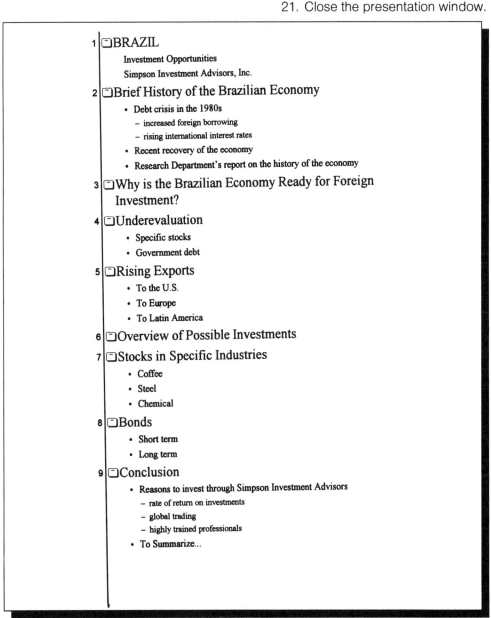

1. BRAZIL
   Investment Opportunities
   Simpson Investment Advisors, Inc.

2. Brief History of the Brazilian Economy
   - Debt crisis in the 1980s
     - increased foreign borrowing
     - rising international interest rates
   - Recent recovery of the economy
   - Research Department's report on the history of the economy

3. Why is the Brazilian Economy Ready for Foreign Investment?

4. Underevaluation
   - Specific stocks
   - Government debt

5. Rising Exports
   - To the U.S.
   - To Europe
   - To Latin America

6. Overview of Possible Investments

7. Stocks in Specific Industries
   - Coffee
   - Steel
   - Chemical

8. Bonds
   - Short term
   - Long term

9. Conclusion
   - Reasons to invest through Simpson Investment Advisors
     - rate of return on investments
     - global trading
     - highly trained professionals
   - To Summarize...

LESSON 2

ENHANCING SLIDES; WORKING WITH TEXT AND OBJECTS

Exercises 6-11

- Selecting, Aligning, and Changing the Appearance of Text

- Copy Text Formatting

- Moving and Copying Text

- Using Slide Master

- Inserting Page Numbers

- Formatting Bullets

- Drawing Graphic Objects

- Using Autoshapes

- Creating Text Objects

- Inserting a Graph and Table Slide

- Inserting an Organization Chart Slide

EXERCISE 6

SELECTING, ALIGNING, AND CHANGING THE APPEARANCE OF TEXT

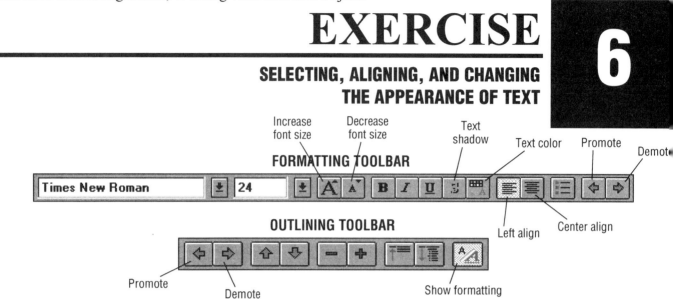

NOTES:

Selecting Text

■ When pointing to text with the mouse, the mouse pointer changes to an I-beam to signify that the text insertion mode is active, just as you found in word processing. Click the text you want to edit, and use the same techniques for selecting blocks of text in PowerPoint that you used to select text in Word:

- Double-click to select a word.

- Triple click to select a paragraph, complete title, or bulleted item including all subitems.

- Click the bullet to the left of bulleted item to select all text and subtext for that item. The mouse pointer changes to a four-headed black arrow ⊕ when you are in the correct position.

■ These techniques can be used to select and edit text in Slide or Outline view. Text may not be edited in Slide Sorter or Notes Pages views.

Aligning Text

■ PowerPoint allows you to align text left, center, or right of a placeholder or textbox, as well as to justify text in the placeholder or textbox. Because the most frequently used alignments in PowerPoint are left and center, icons for these two alignments are included on the Formatting Toolbar. Right and justified alignment options are available by selecting Alignment from the Format menu.

■ To change the alignment of title text or text for one bulleted item, position the I-beam in the title or bulleted item and click the desired alignment icon. To change the alignment for more than one bulleted item, select text for the bulleted items you want to change before clicking the alignment icon, or select the alignment option from the menu.

■ While you can set alignment in both Outline or Slide views, use Slide view to change text alignment because text formatting is displayed in this view.

■ When you want to change the alignment of title text, all text in the title placeholder for that slide is realigned. To align text on one line of a title differently from text of other lines, remove the lines you want to align differently from the title placeholder and include them in the body placeholder. Each line in the body placeholder can then be aligned separately.

Changing the Appearance of Text

■ PowerPoint controls font, size, alignment, emphasis (bold, italics, shadow, underline), and color on each slide layout. However, you can change these attributes using the same techniques described in Word and Excel.

■ Use the Formatting toolbar to apply one formatting change to text quickly; use the Font dialog box to apply more than one formatting change to text.

404

The Formatting toolbar in PowerPoint has several icons not included on the Formatting toolbars in Word and Excel. These icons perform tasks unique to PowerPoint:

- Use the **Increase/Decrease Font Size** icons  to incrementally increase or decrease the font size until it fits within the space you need.

- Use the **Text Shadow and Text Color** icons to enhance text and create special effects. Color may be added in Slide view only.

- Use the **Promote (Indent less)** and **Demote (Indent more)** icons to adjust the levels of bulleted items.

■ Format changes and enhancements affect the complete word in which the insertion point rests unless you have selected specific text.

■ The **Show Formatting** icon on the Outlining toolbar is defaulted to display font style, font size, bold, italics, and underline. When you turn off the Show Formatting feature, text appears in the default font with no enhancements. The Show Formatting icon is available in Outline and Slide Sorter views.

EXERCISE DIRECTIONS:

1. Open **KIT**.
2. Using Slide view, change titles in all slides to a sans serif green font.
3. Center align the titles in slides 2-7.
4. Reduce the font size of the bulleted text on slide 5 (THE SALES BROCHURE) using the Decrease Font Size icon on the Toolbar.
5. Italicize subheadings on all slides.
6. Switch to Outline view.
7. Use the Show Formatting icon on the Outlining Toolbar to turn the formatting on and off.

8. Insert a New Slide after slide 6 that reads,

   CREATIVE SALES KITS provide...
   - Sales Brochures
   - Business Cards
   - Letterheads
   - Brochures
   - Catalogs
   - Presentation Materials

9. Switch to Slide view.
10. Apply the same formatting changes to the new slide as you did to the other slides.
11. Switch to Slide Sorter view.
12. Print one copy as Handouts with six slides per page in Black and White.
13. Close the file; save the changes.

In this exercise, you will insert a new slide as well as align and change the appearance of text to selected slides in your previously created presentation.

CHANGE FONT

1. Position insertion point in word to format.

   OR

   Select text to format.

2. Select `Times New Roman` desired font from Formatting toolbar **Font** drop-down list.

   OR

   1. Click **Format, Font**.. `Alt` + `O`, `F`
   2. Select desired font and options.
   3. Click **OK**..............................`Enter`

CHANGE FONT SIZE

1. Position insertion point in word to format.

   OR

   Select text to change.

2. Select desired size ....`32` from Formatting toolbar **Font Size** drop-down list.

   OR

   1. Click **Format, Font**.. `Alt` + `O`, `F`
   2. Select desired font size.
   3. Click **OK**..............................`Enter`

   OR

   Click `A` `A` to increase/decrease font incrementally.

CHANGE EMPHASIS (BOLD, ITALICS, SHADOW, UNDERLINE, COLOR)

1. Position insertion point in word to change.

   OR

   Select text to change.

2. Click `B` `I` `U` `S` ` ` desired emphasis icon on Formatting toolbar.

   OR

   a. Click **Format, Font** ... `Alt` + `O`, `F`
   b. Select desired options.

   c. Click **OK**..............................`Enter`

ALIGN TEXT

1. Position insertion point in text to align.

2. Click ` ` **Left Alignment** icon on Toolbar.

   OR

   Click ` ` **Center Alignment** icon on Toolbar.

   OR

   1. Click........................`Alt` + `O`, `A` **Format, Alignment**.

   2. Select desired alignment:

      - **Left**..`L`
      - **Center**......................................`C`
      - **Right**..`R`
      - **Justify**......................................`J`

EXERCISE

▪ COPY TEXT FORMATTING ▪ MOVING AND COPYING TEXT ▪ MOVING AND SIZING PLACEHOLDERS

Cut   Copy   Paste   Format Painter

STANDARD TOOLBAR

NOTES:

Copy Text Formatting (Format Painter)

■ As in Word, The Format Painter feature may be used in PowerPoint to copy formatting, such as font face, style, size, and color, from one part of text to another.

■ To copy formatting from one location to another, select the text that contains the format you wish to copy. Then click the Format Painter icon on the Standard Toolbar (the I-beam displays a paintbrush) and select the text to receive the format. To copy formatting from one location to several locations, select the text that contains the format you wish to copy, then double-click the Format Painter icon. Select the text to receive the format, release the mouse button and select additional text anywhere in the document. To turn off this feature and return the mouse pointer to an I-beam, click the Format Painter icon or press Escape. Or, you may pick up and apply text formatting by selecting Pick Up Text Style and Apply Style from the Format main menu.

■ When you use the Format Painter in Outline view, some formatting will not appear until you return to Slide view.

Copying and Moving Text on a Slide

■ You can use the same methods to cut, copy, paste, and drag and drop text in PowerPoint that you used in Word and Excel. In addition, you may use the **Move Up** or **Move Down** icons on the Outlining Toolbar to reposition text up or down one line at a time.

■ You can move text only in Slide or Outline views. However, it is more efficient to use Outline view to move or copy text on a slide.

■ Use cut/copy and paste techniques to copy text to more than one new location or to copy text to different presentation. Use the drag and drop technique in Outline view to move or copy text to a new location or to rearrange bulleted items. Use the drag and drop feature in Slide view to move text on one slide.

■ To move or copy bulleted items in Outline or Slide views, position the mouse pointer on the bullet until it turns to a four-headed arrow and click once. The bulleted item as well as the subitems will highlight. Place the mouse pointer in the selection, hold and drag it until you see a horizontal line positioned where you want to insert the text. Release the mouse button and your text will drop into place.

Moving and Sizing Placeholders

■ Text, clip art, and object placeholders can be moved, copied, sized, and deleted.

■ To move, copy, size, or delete a placeholder, you must first display handles to put the placeholder into an edit mode. Click on the text to display the placeholder, then click on the placeholder border to display the handles. Click on the clip art or object to display the handles.

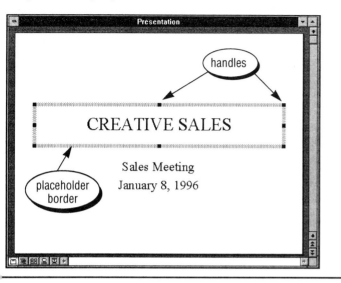

- When handles appear, you can **size** the placeholder as you did when working with graphics (drag a top or bottom middle handle to change the vertical size (height); drag a left or right middle handle to change the horizontal size (width); drag a corner handle to size the placeholder proportionally). When you size a text placeholder, the text within it will adjust to the new borders.

- You can **move** the placeholder and its contents by displaying the handles, then placing the pointer on the border (not a handle), clicking and holding the left mouse button while dragging the placeholder to a desired location.

In this exercise, you will manipulate placeholders and change the size and color of text on slides. Check your changes with the Desired Result shown on the next page.

EXERCISE DIRECTIONS:

1. Open **BRAZIL**.
2. Switch to Slide view.
3. Change the template to BANNERS.PPT.
4. Change the first slide title to a sans serif font.
5. Using Format Painter, change all slide titles to a sans serif font.
6. Display slide 1.
7. Move BRAZIL to the top part of the slide (in the banner area).
8. Display slide 2 and change to Outline view.
9. Move the second bulleted item down to become the last bulleted item.
10. Switch to Slide view.
11. Change the color of the first bulleted item (not the subitems) to light yellow.
12. Using Format Painter, change the remaining bulleted items to light yellow.
13. Display slide 3.
    - Change the layout to Clip Art and Text.
    - Reduce the size of the title text to 32 point and move it into the banner.
    - Delete the text placeholder.
    - Insert a relevant graphic into the clip art placeholder. Move it into the center of the slide and size it proportionally so it fills the center of the slide.
14. Display slide 7.
    - Change the layout to Clip Art and Text.
    - Delete the text placeholder.

- Insert a relevant graphic into the clip art placeholder. Move it into the center of the slide and size it proportionally so it fills the center of the slide.
15. Display slide 8.
    - Increase the bulleted text size to 48 point. Highlight the text and click Format Painter.
16. Display slide 6.
    - Use Format Painter to increase the bulleted text size to 48 point.
    - Stretch the graphic to fill the right side of the slide.
17. Display slide 9.
    - Increase the bulleted text size to 48 point.
    - Reduce the size of the placeholder.
    - Move the placeholder to the middle right of the graphic.
18. Display slide 5.
    - Increase the bulleted text size to 48 point.
    - Reduce the size of the placeholder.
    - Move the placeholder to the center of the slide.
19. Display slide 4.
    - Increase the bulleted text size to 48 point.
    - Reduce the size of the placeholder.
    - Move the placeholder to the center of the slide.
20. Switch to Slide Sorter view.
21. Print one copy as Handouts with six slides per page in Pure Black and White.
22. Close the file; save the changes.

BRAZIL

Investment Opportunities
Simpson Investment Advisors,
Inc.

1

Brief History of the Brazilian
Economy

- Debt crisis in the 1980s
  - increased foreign borrowing
  - rising international interest rates
- Research Department's report on the
  history of the economy
- Recent recovery of the economy

2

Why is the Brazilian Economy Ready for
Foreign Investment?

3

Rising Exports

- To the U.S.
- To Europe
- To Latin America

4

Underevaluation

- Specific stocks
- Government debt

5

Political Stability

- Current
  Leadership
- Free
  Elections

6

Overview of Possible
Investments

7

Stocks in Specific Industries

- Coffee
- Steel
- Chemical

8

Bonds

- Short term
- Long term

9

Conclusion

- Reasons to invest through Simpson
  Investment Advisors
  - rate of return on investments
  - global trading
  - highly trained professionals
- To Summarize...

10

COPY TEXT FORMATTING

1. Position insertion point in text containing format to copy.

2. Click 🔷 .... **Alt** + **O**, **K**

   ✓ *Double-click icon if format is to be applied to multiple selections of text. If no text is selected, this option on the menu will not be available.*

3. Select text.................... **Alt** + **O**, **Y**
   that you want to change
   or click to apply format to a word.

4. Press **Esc** to drop the .... **Esc**
   paint brush, if necessary.

COPY

Ctrl + C

1. Select the text to copy.

2. Click ▤ .... **Alt** + **E**, **C**

   OR

   Select **Copy** from the Shortcut menu.

MOVE (CUT)

Ctrl + X

1. Select the text to move (cut).

2. Click ✂ .... **Alt** + **E**, **T**

   OR

   Select **Cut** from the Shortcut menu.

PASTE

Ctrl + V

1. Position cursor where text is to be inserted.

2. Click ▤ .... **Alt** + **E**, **P**

   OR

   Select **Paste** from the Shortcut menu.

DRAG AND DROP

1. Select text or bulleted section to copy or move.

2. Position mouse pointer on selected text.

   ✓ *Mouse pointer must be a white pointer arrow ⟍ -not a four- headed black arrow.*

3. Click and drag text...........................
   until vertical bar appears
   in desired new text position.

   ✓ *To copy text using this process, **Ctrl** while dragging the text.*

4. Release mouse button.

EDITING PLACEHOLDERS

To display handles:

1. Click inside the text placeholder.

2. Click on placeholder border.

   OR

   Click the clip art graphic or object.

Move:

1. Display handles.

2. Position mouse pointer on border (not on a handle).

3. Hold down left mouse button and drag text to new location.

4. Release mouse button.

Copy:

1. Display handles.

2. Position mouse pointer on border (not on a handle).

3. Press **Ctrl** and position mouse pointer on border (not on a handle).

4. Hold down mouse button and drag text to new location.

5. Release mouse button.

Size:

1. Display handles.

2. Position mouse pointer on a top or bottom middle handle to change height, a left or right handle to change width, or a corner handle to change size proportionally.

3. Drag the handle until the placeholder is the desired size.

Delete:

1. Display handles.

2. Press **Delete**..................................

   ✓ *If you delete a title or text placeholder, an empty text placeholder appears. Press Delete again to delete the entire placeholder.*

EXERCISE

8

▪ USING SLIDE MASTER ▪ INSERTING PAGE NUMBERS ▪ FORMATTING BULLETS

Bullets

FORMATTING TOOLBAR

NOTES:

Using Slide Master

▪ The **Slide Master** contains the default settings for the format of a slide. By changing the formatting (font style, font size, color, and/or position) of text or object placeholders on Slide Masters, all slides are automatically reformatted uniformly throughout the presentation. If, for example, you wanted to include clip art as your company's logo or a saying or quote on all slides in your presentation, you would include it on the Slide Master, and it would appear on all slides of your presentation.

▪ Text formatted on separate slides override changes made on the Slide Master.

▪ Changes made on the Slide Master affect *all* slides in a presentation *except* Title Slide AutoLayout format. Changes to the Slide Master affect only the active presentation.

▪ Slide Master may be accessed by selecting Master from the View menu, and then selecting Slide Master.

▪ After making the desired changes on the Slide Master, click Slide view and display each slide in the presentation to see their effects. You may need to make adjustments to the Slide Master after seeing the effects on individual slides.

Inserting Page Numbers

▪ Page numbers may be inserted on all slides of your presentation using Slide Master.

▪ To insert page numbers, select Slide Master view, then select Page Number from the Insert main menu. A page number placeholder containing number signs (##) appears in the center of the slide. Move the page number placeholder into a desired position on the slide. You may format the page number as you did all other text within a text placeholder.

▪ The actual slide number will appear on your slides when you print and during a slide show. *(Presenting slide shows will be covered in Exercise 12.)*

Formatting Bullets

▪ Many AutoLayout formats include bulleted body text. The bullet styles and shapes are set in the Slide Master. You can change the bullet style, size, and shape individually for each bulleted item on each slide, or you can save time and keep the format consistent by using the Slide Master. Bullets formatted individually will override formatting set in the Slide Master.

```
┌─────────────────────────────────────┐
│  ╔═══════════════════════════════╗   │
│  ║            TITLE              ║   │
│  ╚═══════════════════════════════╝   │
│  ☎First Point                        │
│  ☎Second Point                       │
│     ➔subtext                         │
│     ➔subtext                         │
│  ☎Third Point                        │
│                                      │
│                                      │
│                                      │
└─────────────────────────────────────┘
```

- If you wish to include text below bulleted items but would prefer no bullet on the explanatory text, you can remove the bullets. Click the Bullet On/Off icon 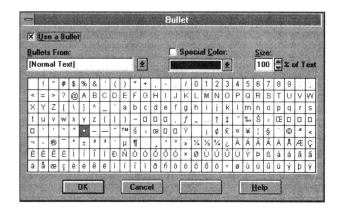 on the Formatting Toolbar to turn bullets on and off on individual items or on selected text. You can also turn the bullet feature on or off by selecting or deselecting Use a Bullet check box in the Bullet dialog box.

- To change the format and size of bullets, display the slide or Slide Master and position the insertion point on the bulleted item or bullet list level you want to change. Then select Bullet from the Format menu. If the insertion point is not positioned in bulleted text and no bulleted items are selected, the option will not be available. In the Bullet dialog box which appears, select a desired bullet, size, and color.

- You can select a bullet style from several character sets containing symbols and shapes (Wingdings, Monotype Sorts, etc).

In this exercise, you will use Slide Master to add a graphic, change the bullets, and insert page numbers, affecting all slides in the presentation. See Desired Result on the next page.

EXERCISE DIRECTIONS:

1. Open **FLAGSHIP**.
2. Switch to Slide Master view.
3. Format the Slide Master as shown below:
   - Decrease the width of the Master title style placeholder and move it slightly to the right.
   - To represent the company's logo, insert the clip art shown on top of the diamond shape.
   - Insert a page number in the lower right corner of the slide using the default font and size.
4. Change the format of the main bullet to a yellow flag (Wingdings character set) and the first subitem bullet to a pink flag.
5. Switch to Slide view.

6. Display slide 2.
   - Change the clip art to another appropriate graphic and size it to fill the right side of the slide.
   - Move the text placeholder down on the slide.
7. Display slide 5.
   - Use the decrease font size button on the Toolbar to incrementally decrease the font size of the title once.
   - Move the text placeholder down on the slide.
8. Print one copy as Handouts with six slides per page in Black and White.
9. Close the file; save the changes.

DESIRED RESULT

FLAGSHIP REALTY

Jawanza Hughes, President

PROPERTY TYPES

℞ Homes of
   Distinction
℞ Commercial
   Properties
℞ Residential
   Townhouses
℞ Exclusive Agent for
   Pineview Estates

OUR SALES FORCE

℞ 85 Professional
   Salespeople
℞ 50% are members of
   Flagship's Private
   Brokerage Council
   ℞ Designation
      awarded to sales
      agents who handled
      sales over $1 million.

SERVICES INCLUDE

℞ Private financial evaluation
℞ Mortgage payment table constructed
   for each buyer
℞ Property tour videos
℞ Internet access for international sales
   and listings

*QUALIFIED LEADER IN
PROPERTIES OF
DISTINCTION*

℞ Unparalleled knowledge of an
   commitment to high-end properties on
   the North Fork.
℞ Demonstrated track record.
℞ Unique ability to match client needs
   and inventory.
℞ Broad international client base.

FORMAT TEXT ON SLIDE MASTERS

1. Open the desired presentation or create a new presentation.

2. Click **View** .... `Alt`+`V`

3. Click **Master** .... `M`

4. Click **Slide Master** .... `S`

5. Select placeholder to change.

   OR

   Select text level to change.

6. Format text font, size, alignment, and enhancements as desired.

7. Click `⬚` .... `Alt`+`V`, `S`

DELETE PLACEHOLDER

1. Select placeholder to delete.

2. Press **Delete** .... `Del`

RESTORE PLACEHOLDER

1. Display slide to restore.

2. Click `Layout...` ...... `Alt`+`O`, `O`

3. Select desired AutoLayout format.

4. Select **Reapply** .... `Alt`+`A`
   to restore original layout.

   OR

Select **Apply** .... `Alt`+`A`
to apply different layout.

TURN BULLETS ON/OFF

1. Position insertion point in bulleted paragraph to change.

2. Click .... `Alt`+`O`, `B`, `U`, `Enter`
   `≡` .

   ✓ *An X in the box beside Use a Bullet indicates that the feature is active. An empty box means the feature is inactive and no bullet will appear.*

CHANGE BULLET CHARACTER

1. Position insertion point in desired bulleted item or select several bulleted items.

2. Click **Format** .... `Alt`+`O`

3. Click **Bullet** .... `B`

4. Select .... `Alt`+`B`, `↓`
   desired character set from **Bullets From** list.

5. Select desired bullet character.

6. Click **Use a Bullet**, ... `Alt`+`U`
   if necessary.

7. Click **OK** .... `Enter`

CHANGE BULLET SIZE

1. Position insertion point in bulleted item to change or select several bulleted items.

2. Click **Format** .... `Alt`+`O`

3. Click **Bullet** .... `Alt`+`B`

4. Select **Size** box .... `Alt`+`S`
   in upper right corner.

5. Type desired percentage size ....*number*

   OR

   Click `⬍` to increase or decrease bullet size.

6. Click **OK** .... `Enter`

INSERTING PAGE NUMBERS

1. Click **View** .... `Alt`+`V`

2. Click **Master** .... `M`

3. Click **Slide Master** .... `S`

4. Click **Insert** .... `Alt`+`I`

5. Click **Page Number** .... `U`

6. Move number place holder into a desired position on the slide.

   ✓ *Actual page numbers will display when printing or during a slide show.*

EXERCISE 9

■ DRAWING GRAPHIC OBJECTS ■ USING AUTOSHAPES ■ CREATING TEXT OBJECTS ■ GROUPING AND UNGROUPING OBJECTS ■ LAYERING OBJECTS

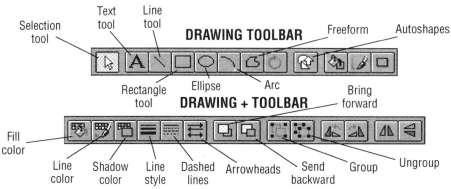

NOTES:

Drawing Graphic Objects

■ **Drawing tools** are used to create simple objects or designs on your slides. Drawing tools are found on the Drawing Toolbar, which displays by default. A second Drawing Toolbar may be displayed by selecting Toolbars, Drawing+ from the View main menu.

■ Drawings created using the Drawing Toolbar are considered graphic objects. Graphic objects include lines, shapes, and freehand designs. Closed shapes may be filled with a color or pattern.

■ Drawings may be added to slides in only Slide or Slide Master views.

■ To draw an object, click the desired object on the toolbar you wish to draw. The insertion point changes to a crosshair (+). Position the crosshair where you want to start the object; click and drag the crosshair to the point where you want to end the object. After the object is drawn, it will appear with handles. To remove the handles, click the Selection Tool ( ) or press Esc. To redisplay the handles, click the Selection tool and click the object.

■ The Drawing Tools and their uses are described below:

• Use the **line tool** to draw a straight line. The line style and color may be changed by selecting the line, then clicking the Line Style, Dashed Lines, Arrowheads or Line Color button on the Drawing+ Toolbar.

• Use the **ellipse tool** to draw circles or ovals. To draw a perfect circle, hold down the Shift key while dragging the mouse.

• Use the **rectangle tool** to draw squares or rectangles. To draw a perfect square, hold down the Shift key while dragging the mouse.

• Use the **arc tool** to draw an arc (a curved line segment).

• Use the **freeform tool** to draw a *freehand shape*. When drawing a freehand shape, using your mouse is like using a pencil.

• Use the **freeform tool** to draw a *polygon* (a closed or open object which consists of three or more points connected by a straight line). *Follow keystrokes on page 417 carefully to draw a polygon.*

Using AutoShapes

■ When you select the **AutoShapes Tool** from the Drawing or Drawing+ Toolbars, a palette of predefined shapes appears (arrows, stars, diamonds, triangles). The Rectangle and Ellipse

AutoShape tool buttons also appear as tools on the Drawing toolbar.

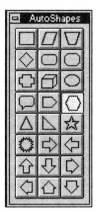

- To draw an AutoShape, click on the desired shape from the palette of shapes, then click and drag the mouse to expand the shape to the desired size. The color of the shape may be changed by selecting the shape with the selection tool, then clicking the Fill Color button on the Drawing+ Toolbar.

Creating Text Objects

- Text entered on slides thus far has been entered into placeholders. Text added using the Text Tool creates a separate object that can be moved, sized, deleted, etc., without affecting text in placeholders.

- Use the Text Tool on the Drawing Toolbar 🔤 to add text to pictures or other objects, including placeholders.

- After selecting the Text Tool, outline the area of the slide that the text should occupy using the procedures you used to draw a rectangle.

Grouping and Ungrouping Objects

- When a drawing is comprised of several basic shapes, it is difficult to move, copy, or duplicate all the shapes as a whole object. **Grouping** allows you to select all the shapes in the group and treat them as a whole object so that copying, duplicating, and moving the object becomes possible.

- To group an object comprised of individual shapes, select each shape (hold the Shift key down while you click each shape) and select Group from the Draw main menu, or click the Group icon 🔳 on the Drawing+ Toolbar. You can undo the grouped objects by selecting **Ungroup** from the Draw main menu, or select the Ungroup icon 🔳 on the Drawing+ Toolbar.

Layering Objects

- Shapes may be layered or stacked on top of each other to create interesting effects. You may adjust the layers by moving them back or bringing them forward in the stack. To adjust the layers of shapes or objects, click the shape or object and select Send to Back or Bring to Front from the Draw main menu, or click the Bring Forward or Send Backward icon on the Drawing+ Toolbar.

In this exercise, you will create a logo using the AutoShapes and Text buttons on the Drawing Toolbar and place them on the Slide Master. You will then view each slide in your presentation to see their effects.

EXERCISE DIRECTIONS:

1. Open **FOOD**.
2. Switch to Slide Master view.
3. Format the Slide Master as shown in Illustration A on the following page. Illustration B shows results of changes made on Slide Master.
   - Shorten the Master title style placeholder and move it slightly to the right.
   - Insert an AutoShape star in the upper left corner of the slide and fill it yellow.
   - Using the text tool, create a text object with the initials SF in sans serif 28 point bold italics. Center the initials in the text placeholder. Color the text blue and position it in the middle of the star as shown.
   - Group the star and the text. Move grouped

objects to the bottom left of the slide, then back to the top left of the slide.
   - Using the text tool, create a text object with the words, "Eat Well and Stay Trim" in sans serif 28 point. Color the text white and position it at the bottom center of the slide as shown.
4. Change the format of the main bullet to a yellow heart (Wingdings character set).
5. Switch to Slide view.
6. Display Slide 3.
   - Move the text placeholder down on the slide.
7. Display Slide 1.
   - Delete the subtitle placeholder.
8. Print one copy as Handouts with six slides per page in Black and White.
9. Close the file; save the changes.

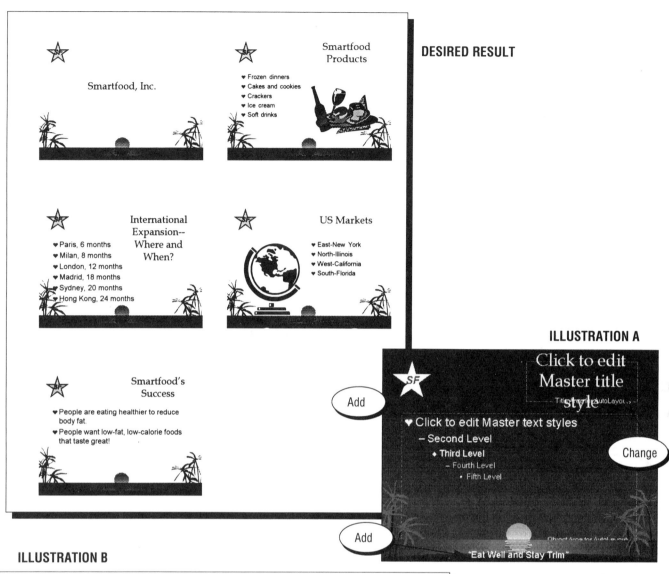

DESIRED RESULT

ILLUSTRATION A

Add

Change

Add

ILLUSTRATION B

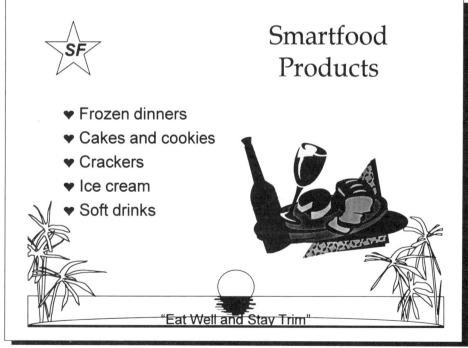

DRAW SHAPES

1. Select desired tool from **Drawing** toolbar.
2. Position crosshair (+) at point where shape will start.
3. Click and drag mouse diagonally to shape ending point.
4. Release mouse button.

DRAW A PERFECT CIRCLE/SQUARE

1. Click ⬚ on **Drawing** toolbar.
2. Position crosshair (+) at point where shape will start.
3. Press the **Shift** key while dragging mouse diagonally to ending point.
4. Release mouse button.

DRAW ARC

1. Click on **Drawing** toolbar.
2. Position crosshair (+) at arc start point.
3. Click and drag to arc end point.

   ✓ *The distance and drag direction determine size and shape of the arc. Experiment to determine how it will form.*

DRAW FREEHAND OR POLYGON

1. Click ⬠ on **Drawing** toolbar.
2. Position crosshair (+) at drawing start point.
3. Press and hold left mouse button until it becomes a pencil ✐.
4. Move pointer to draw shape, clicking to change direction or angle, if necessary.
5. Double-click to stop drawing.

CREATE TEXT OBJECTS

1. Click **A** on **Drawing** toolbar.
2. Position I-beam at text start point.
3. Click and drag to form confined text box.

   OR

   Click to type without outlining box.
4. Type desired text.
5. Press **Esc** when text is complete .... Esc

   OR

   Click ⬚ on **Drawing** toolbar.

GROUP OBJECTS

1. Hold down **Shift** while clicking objects to group.
2. Click .... Alt + D , G
   on **Drawing+** toolbar.

UNGROUP OBJECTS

1. Select desired grouped object.
2. Click .... Alt + D , U
   on **Drawing+** toolbar.

REGROUP OBJECTS

Regroups most recently ungrouped object. If slide containing ungrouped object becomes inactive, object cannot be regrouped using this procedure. It will have to be grouped.

Select **Draw, Regroup** .... Alt + D , R

   ✓ *The top three alignments apply to horizontal placement of objects. The bottom three alignments apply to vertical placement of objects.*

LAYER OBJECTS

1. Select desired object.
2. Click .... Alt + D , B
   on **Drawing+** toolbar
   to send object back one layer.

   OR

   Click .... Alt + D , F
   on **Drawing+** toolbar
   to bring object forward one layer.
3. Repeat step 2 until object is properly placed.

   OR

   1. Select desired object.
   2. Click **Draw** menu............ Alt + D
   3. Select desired option:

OPTION	MOVEMENT
Bring to Front	Places object on top of all other objects.
Send to Back	Places object beneath all other objects.
Bring Forward	Moves object one layer up on the stack.
Send Backward	Moves object one layer down on the stack.

CYCLE THROUGH OBJECTS

1. Press **Ctrl + A** to select.......... Alt + A
   all objects.
2. Press **Tab** until desired object........ Tab
   is selected.

EXERCISE

INSERTING A GRAPH AND TABLE SLIDE

GRAPHING TOOLBAR

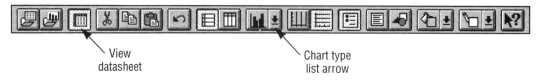

View datasheet

Chart type list arrow

NOTES:

Inserting a Graph Slide

■ A graph may be added to a PowerPoint slide by importing one that was already created in Excel, or by using the Graph slide in PowerPoint to create one. *(See Integration Chapter to import an Excel chart and workbook data.)*

■ To create a Graph on a slide, double-click a graph placeholder on an AutoLayout slide or select Microsoft Graph from the Insert main menu.

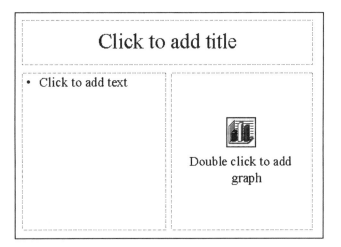

■ A datasheet window displays along with a Graphing Toolbar which replaces the Drawing Toolbar. Enter the data you wish to chart (and delete the sample data) as you did in Excel. The graph will reflect the new data. Click on the graph to hide the datasheet. If you wish to see

the datasheet again, click the View Datasheet button [▦] on the Graphing Toolbar.

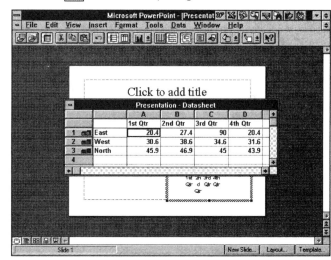

■ The default chart type is 3-D Column. However, you may change the graph type before or after you enter data in the datasheet by clicking the graph on the slide and selecting Chart Type from the Format main menu or clicking the list arrow next to the Chart Type button on the Graphic Toolbar. Select one of the chart types from the choices displayed.

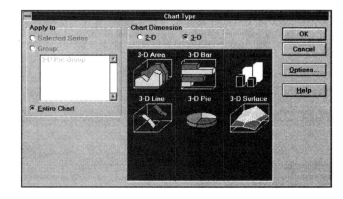

You may enhance your graph with a title and data labels. Data labels allow you to indicate the exact value of each data point. Follow keystrokes on page 421 to insert a graph title and data labels.

serting a Table Slide

A Table may be added to a PowerPoint slide by importing one that was already created in Word, or by using a Table slide in PowerPoint to create one.

To create a Table on a slide, double-click a table placeholder on an AutoLayout slide or select Word Table from the Insert main menu. PowerPoint offers one AutoLayout slide containing a table format.

After clicking the table placeholder, the Insert Word Table dialog box displays for you to indicate how many columns and rows you need for your table. You will note, too, that Table replaces Draw as a main menu selection.

- The columns and rows will be evenly spaced within the size of the slide—8" wide by 4.5" high. You can adjust the column widths and row heights as you did in Word.

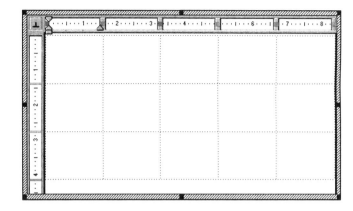

- Click in a cell and enter the desired text. Press Tab to move the insertion point from cell to cell. Use the same procedures to format and size your table in PowerPoint as you did in Word. (If you click on the Table main menu, you will note the same submenu items you found in Word.) After you have entered all table text, click the slide outside the table to return to PowerPoint, or press Escape.

In this exercise, you will insert a graph and table slides into a previously created presentation.

EXERCISE DIRECTIONS:

. Open **FLAGSHIP**.
. Insert a New Slide and select the Graph AutoLayout.
. Enter the slide title shown in Illustration A. Double-click graph icon, delete the data from the datasheet and enter the new data shown below:

	1993	1994	1995	1996
ownhouses	20	40	85	88
Comm. Prop.	8	12	24	31
Houses	45	44	87	91

. Insert a graph title that reads, Townhouse, Commercial Property and House Unit Sales over Four Years
. Include data labels in your chart.
. Switch to Slide Sorter view.
. Move this new slide to become Slide 4.
. Switch to Slide view.
. Switch to Slide 3 (OUR SALES FORCE).

10. Create a balloon AutoShape above the graphic and fill it pink. Using the text tool, insert the words, We care! into the balloon shape as shown in Illustration B.
11. Insert a New Slide after slide 4, and select the Table AutoLayout.
12. Enter the table data shown in Illustration C.
   - Create 5 columns and 4 rows.
   - Set column heading text to sans serif 24 point bold.
   - Set column text to sans serif 18 point.
   - Center column headings as well as column 2 and 3 text.
   - Adjust column widths and row heights so text appears like illustration.
   - Enter the slide title shown in the illustration.
13. Switch to Slide Sorter view.
14. Print one copy as Handouts with 6 slides per page in Black and White.
15. Close the file; save the changes.

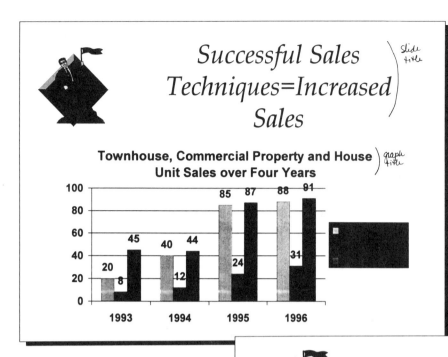

Successful Sales Techniques=Increased Sales ⟩ Slide title

ILLUSTRATION A

Townhouse, Commercial Property and House Unit Sales over Four Years ⟩ graph title

ILLUSTRATION B

OUR SALES FORCE

- 85 Professional Salespeople
- 50% are members of Flagship's Private Brokerage Council
  - Designation awarded to sales agents who handled sales over $1 million.

SAMPLE INVENTORY

ILLUSTRATION C

TYPE	RMS	BATHS	PRICE	UNIQUE FEATURES
Country Estate	7	4	$1,300,000	swimming pool, spa and exercise room
Townhouse	8	3	$500,000	formal dining room
Colonial Estate	10	5	$1,585,000	waterfront property w/400 ft. bulkhead

CREATE A GRAPH ON AN AUTOLAYOUT SLIDE

Select a slide from AutoLayout containing a Graph placeholder.

Double-click the graph placeholder.

Enter the data you wish to chart in the datasheet.

To delete Data in a Datasheet:

a. Press **Ctrl+A** .... `Ctrl` + `A`
   to select the data.

b. Press **Delete** .... `Del`

Click the graph to hide the datasheet or

Click View Graph button .... `🖑`

Insert a Title:

1. Select the graph.

2. Click **Insert** .... `Alt` + `I`

3. Click **Titles** .... `T`

4. Click **Chart Title** .... `Alt` + `T`

5. Type title..*title*

Insert Data Labels:

1. Select the graph.

2. Click **Insert** .... `Alt` + `I`

3. Click **Data Labels** .... `D`

4. Select desired label type.

5. Click **OK** .... `Enter`

CREATE A TABLE IN AN AUTOLAYOUT SLIDE

1. Select a slide from AutoLayout containing a Table placeholder.

2. Enter the title in the title placeholder.

3. Double-click the table placeholder.

4. Enter desired number of **Columns**.

5. Enter desired number of **Rows**.

6. Click **OK** .... `Enter`

7. Click the first cell and enter desired text.

8. Press **Tab** .... `Tab`
   to advance to the next cell.

   OR

   Press **Shift + Tab** .... `Shift` + `Tab`
   to move to the
   previous cell.

9. Click on slide to insert table and return to PowerPoint.

PowerPoint
Lesson 2: Enhancing Slides; Working with Text and Objects

EXERCISE

INSERTING AN ORGANIZATION CHART SLIDE

NOTES:

- An **Organization Chart** is used to illustrate a company's hierarchy or structure.

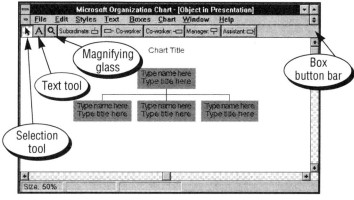

- Organization charts may also be used to show the flow of a project or a family tree.

- PowerPoint contains an organization chart AutoLayout *(org chart)*. To create an organization chart, select the org chart AutoLayout and double-click on the organization chart placeholder.

- By default, four boxes display. However, you can attach additional boxes to existing boxes, and rearrange boxes. In addition, you can format each box with different fonts, font sizes, fill colors and borders, as well as align text left, center, or right within the box.

- There are four types of boxes: Managers, Subordinates, Co-Workers and Assistants; each box type attaches to the existing boxes differently. Note the Box button bar.

- You can enter up to four lines of text in each box. As you type, the box will adjust its size to fit the text.

- After you have added the desired boxes and entered the desired text, select Exit and Return to Presentation from the File main menu.

In this exercise, you will insert an organization chart and a graph slide to a previously created presentation. See Desired Result on page 425.

EXERCISE DIRECTIONS:

1. Open **KIT**.

2. Switch to Slide view.

3. Insert a New Slide and select the Org Chart AutoLayout.

4. Enter the slide title chart information shown in Illustration A using a sans serif green font.

   ✓ Note: Add an Assistant box to include box 5 information.

5. Insert a New Slide and select the Graph AutoLayout.

6. Enter the slide title shown in Illustration B using a sans serif green font. Delete the data from the datasheet and enter the new data shown below:

   ✓ Note: Since you will not need all the columns and rows in the datasheet, highlight the row and/or column you do not need and select Exclude Rows/Columns from the Data main menu.

Sales Before and After Using Creative Kits			
	Great Foods	Harly Hotel	Venus Graphics
Before	100	485	195
After	200	555	305

7. Switch to Slide Sorter view.

Continued..

8. Move the graph slide to become slide 9 and the organization chart slide to become slide 10 (the last slide).

9. Switch to Slide Master view.

10. Using AutoShapes, create a yellow diamond shape and insert the initials CS vertically in 32-point bold as shown in Illustration C.

11. Insert a page number on the bottom middle of the slide.

12. Switch to Slide view and display Slide 1.

13. Create a red arrow as shown in Illustration C. (This arrow will appear on slide 1 only.)

14. Display Slide 7 (CREATIVE SALES KITS provide...)

15. Change the Layout to Text & Clip Art and insert the graphic shown in Illustration D. If this graphic is available to you, use AutoShapes to create a design on the chart which the man is holding.

16. Print one copy as Handouts with 6 slides per page in Black and White.

17. Close the file; save the changes.

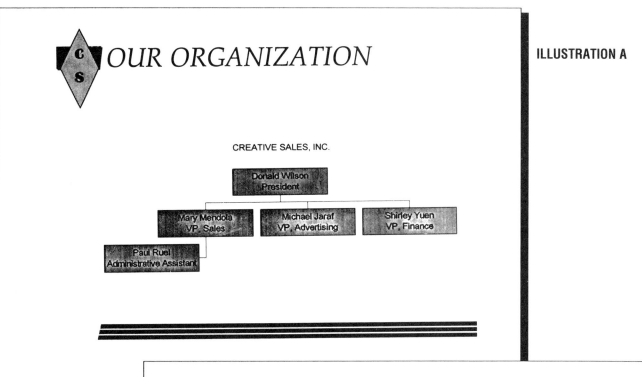

ILLUSTRATION A

ILLUSTRATION B

ILLUSTRATION C

CREATIVE SALES

Sales Meeting
January 8, 1996

ILLUSTRATION D

CREATIVE SALES KITS
provide...

- Sales Brochures
- Business Cards
- Letterheads
- Brochures
- Catalogs
- Presentation Materials

CREATE AN ORGANIZATION CHART IN AN AUTOLAYOUT SLIDE

1. Select a slide from AutoLayout containing an Organization Chart Layout.
2. Enter the title in the title placeholder.
3. Double-click the Organization Chart placeholder.
4. Select box to enter text.
5. Type name and press **Enter**.
6. Type title and press **Enter**.
7. Type comment (if desired) and press **Enter**.
8. Click another box and repeat steps 5-7

    OR

    Click outside the box to close box.
9. Click **File** .... Alt + F
10. Click **Exit and Return** X
    to Presentation.

Insert a Box:

1. Click the appropriate box tool you wish to attach.
2. Click existing box on which you wish to attach new one.

Rearrange Boxes:

1. Select the box to be moved.
2. Position mouse pointer on border of box to be moved.
3. Drag box to new location.
4. Release mouse button.

CREATIVE SALES

Sales Meeting
January 8, 1996

WHY USE IT?

- Builds corporate identity
- Provides numerous sales materials
  - *Brochures*
  - *Product Catalog*
  - *Presentation Materials*

SALES KITS

- Tool for making initial client contact
- A support system for sales rep
- Way to provide clients with material to make an informed decision about buying your product

SALES MATERIALS
include...

- the same logo on all materials
- the same paper
- the same typefaces
- business cards, letterheads, brochures, catalogs, presentation materials

THE SALES BROCHURE

- Similar to marketing brochure
  - *contain creative headlines*
  - *contain attractive graphics*
- Should possess the same visual elements of your corporate identity
- Should motivate the reader to learn more about your company
- Result should be company and product exposure

THE PRODUCT CATALOG

- Contains more specific information about company products
- May include prices and discount offers
- May be sent through mail to prospective clients
- More effective when handed out personally on a sales call or visit to set up a sales call
- Use simple drawings or photos to show product line

CREATIVE SALES KITS
provide...

- Sales Brochures
- Business Cards
- Letterheads
- Brochures
- Catalogs
- Presentation Materials

PRESENTATON MATERIALS

- The flip chart
  - *visuals are printed on sheets of paper and inserted into flip chart carrier*
- Refrigerator magnet
  - *leave-behind gift upon completion of sales call*

CREATIVE SALES KITS IMPROVE YOUR BUSINESS

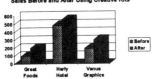

Sales Before and After Using Creative Kits

OUR ORGANIZATION

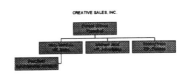

CREATIVE SALES, INC.

LESSON 2
SUMMARY EXERCISE

In this exercise, you will create a presentation for GreatGains Mutual Fund, a company that wants more investors to purchase their securities. This presentation will include a table, chart, and graph slides. You will use Slide Master to include information on all slides.

EXERCISE DIRECTIONS:

1. Create a NEW Template Presentation; use the DBLLINES.PPT template.
2. Switch to Slide Master view.
3. Create the logo shown on the top and bottom right corner of the presentation in Slide 1 of Illustration A.

   Hint :To create the double G logo on the top right, create two separate text boxes and enter the letter G in each. Size one of the letters to 54 point and the other to 28 point. Overlap the boxes, and draw and circle (using AutoShapes) around the boxes. Send to back the circle, and group the items. Then, adjust the size of the grouped items. You will need to use a similar procedure to create the text and AutoShapes balloon on the bottom right of the slide. Use a serif 16 point white font for the text and an aqua-blue fill for the balloon.

   - Insert page numbers where shown in 18 point using a pink font color.
   - Change the default first two bullet styles to another desired style.
   - Adjust the title placeholder so it does not interfere with the logo.

4. Switch to Slide view.
5. Create the presentation shown in Illustration B on pages 427 and 428 using the appropriate slide layouts.

- Enter the data below to create the graph:

Sales (in $ millions)			
	1994	**1995**	**1996**
GreatGains	200	325	420
FastMoney	156	173	165

6. Use the names and titles below for the organization chart:

Rachael Black: Head Fund Manager
John Chou: Vice President
Pamela Haupt: Vice President
Jaime Cohen: Vice President
Harry Smith: Associate
David Stuart: Associate
Chandra Rao: Associate

7. Display each slide. Adjust the placeholders and/or the font size of the titles so they do not interfere with the logos.
8. Spell check.
9. Save the file; name it **INVEST**. Accept the default summary information.
10. Print one copy of each slide in Black and White. Compare each slide with those in Illustration B.
11. Print one copy in Outline view.
12. Close the presentation window.

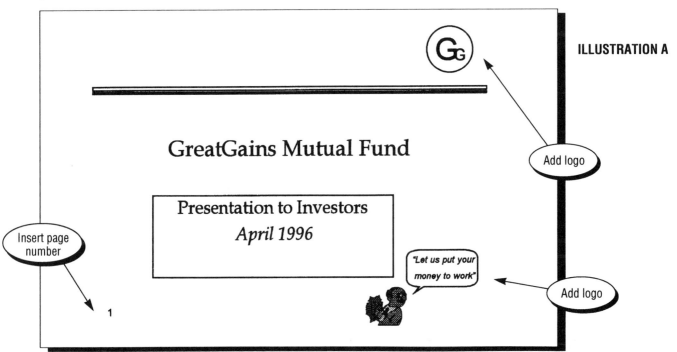

ILLUSTRATION A

GreatGains Mutual Fund

Presentation to Investors
April 1996

Add logo

Insert page number

"Let us put your money to work"

Add logo

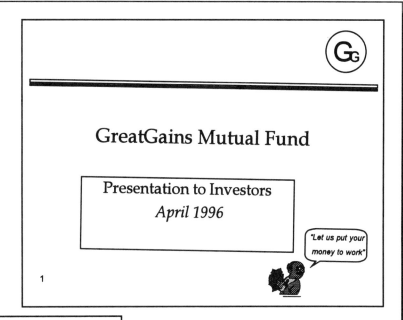

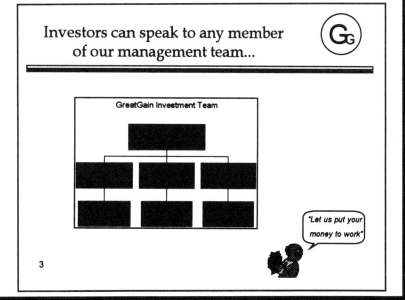

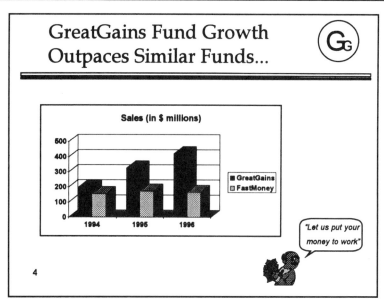

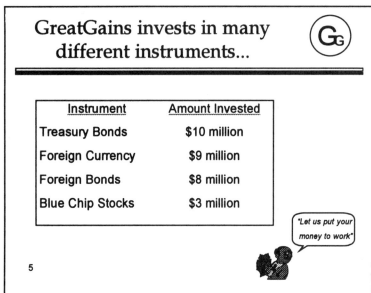

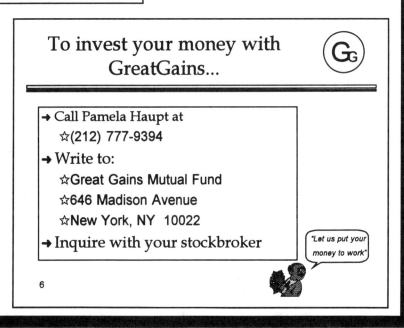

LESSON 3

WORKING WITH SLIDE SHOWS

Exercises 12-15

- Showing a Presentation

- Adding Transitions and Timings

- Creating Builds

- Using the Annotator

- Creating Continuously Running Presentations

- Creating Notes Pages and Handout Master

- Printing Notes Master and Handout Master

EXERCISE

12

■ SHOWING A PRESENTATION ■ ADDING TRANSITIONS AND TIMINGS

NOTES:

Showing a Presentation

■ PowerPoint enables you to show an on-screen presentation of your slides to an audience.

■ Slides may be shown one at a time as an oral report is given, or they may run continuously if used at a trade show or at a demonstration counter in a store.

■ When a slide show is presented, each slide displays on the entire screen without showing the PowerPoint program.

■ Changing slides may be activated by clicking the mouse or pressing a key.

> ✓ Note: If you plan to show your slide presentation to a large audience, you will need to project the computer image onto a large screen. This will require a projection device. See your local computer dealer for projection device information.

■ To activate a slide show, display the first slide to be shown, then click the Slide Show icon 🖳 on the lower left of the screen or select Slide Show from the View main menu.

Adding Transitions

■ **Transitions** control the way slides move on and off the screen.

■ Transitions may be added to slides in all views, but Slide Sorter view offers the quickest and easiest way to add transitions because the Slide Sorter toolbar contains tools for performing these tasks.

■ In Slide Sorter view, slides containing transitions are marked by a slide icon appearing below and to the left of the miniature slide image.

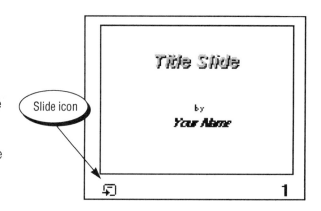

■ To add transitions to slides in views other than Slide Sorter, you *must* select Transition from the Tools main menu. In the Transitions dialog box which follows, you can select a transition effect, the speed of the transition, and whether you want to change the slides manually (by a mouse click) or automatically (after a specified number of seconds).

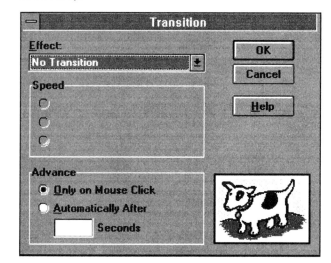

No Transition | No Build Effect

Rehearse Timings

- Transitions include a number of special effects. Select a transition type and note its effect in the window on the bottom right of the dialog box. A description of transition types and their effect appears below.

Random Assigns a random transition effect as you move from slide to slide. Assigning Random to numerous slides generates a random assortment of transitions.

Blinds Creates an effect of opening and closing venetian blinds and can be set for horizontal or vertical.

Box Forms a box and opens from the center outward or the edges inward.

Checkerboard Creates a checkerboard effect by placing small black squares randomly on the screen to reveal the new slide.

Cover Replaces the slide with the next slide from the specified direction.

Cut Replaces the slide with the next slide without directional motion.

Dissolve Sprinkles the slide on and off the screen.

Fade Gradually darkens the slide to black before revealing the next slide.

Random Bars Reveals the new slide gradually by placing horizontal or vertical bars on the screen.

Split Reveals and removes a slide from the center outward or inward, horizontally or vertically.

Strips Reveals and removes a slide from one corner of the screen to the other using a variety of directions.

Uncover Reveals a new slide as the active slide is removed.

Wipe Removes one slide from the screen in the specified direction, revealing the new slide.

Adding Timings

- **Timings** control the speed with which slides replace other slides. Setting a time tells PowerPoint how long the slide will remain on the screen.

- Timings may be included as part of the transition. Timings are set in seconds with .05 representing 5 seconds.

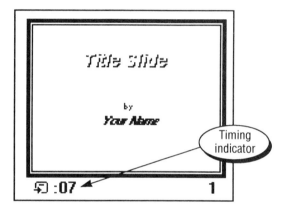

- Timings may be set individually for each slide or collectively for all slides. Slides containing timings may, however, be advanced manually when necessary. Timings may be set using the Transition window in Slide view, Outline view, or Slide Sorter view. Slide timings display to the right of the transition slide icon in Slide Sorter view.

- The **Rehearse Timings** feature allows you to rehearse your presentation and note how much time you would like each slide to remain on screen. To rehearse a presentation, click the Rehearse Timings button 🕮 on the Transition Toolbar. Each slide will appear on screen with a second counter clicking off time. Note how much time you wish each slide to remain on screen. Then, return to individual slides to reset their timing, or let PowerPoint assign the timings based on your rehearsal.

In this exercise, you will edit a previously created presentation by adding items to the Slide Master, inserting new slides, and adding transitions and timings to selected slides. You will also view your slide presentation. See Desired Result on page 434.

EXERCISE DIRECTIONS:

1. Open **BRAZIL.**

2. Switch to Slide Master view.

3. Insert the company name in the left corner of the slide in a serif 20 point orange font. Using AutoShapes, create a star following the company name as shown in Illustration A.

4. Insert a page number in the right corner of the slide in the default font and size.

5. Switch to Slide view.

6. Insert a New Slide and select the Org Chart AutoLayout.

7. Enter the chart information as shown in Illustration B. (Do not include a chart title.)

   Set the text in each box to a different color. Use bright colors for each industry name.

8. Switch to Slide Sorter view.

9. Move the new slide to become slide 10.

10. Select Slides 1 and 4 and select a transition effect from the **Effects** drop-down list on the Slide Sorter toolbar.

11. Switch to Outline view and set a transition effect for Slides 2 and 3 using the Transition dialog box.

12. Switch to Slide view and add a transition speed for each slide in the presentation using the Transition dialog box.

13. Save the changes to the presentation; do not close the file.

14. View the slide show.

15. Add slide timings to each slide as you desire.

16. Change the advance method to advance slides automatically.

17. View the slide show again.

18. Print one copy as Handouts with 6 slides per page in Black and White.

19. Close the file; save the changes.

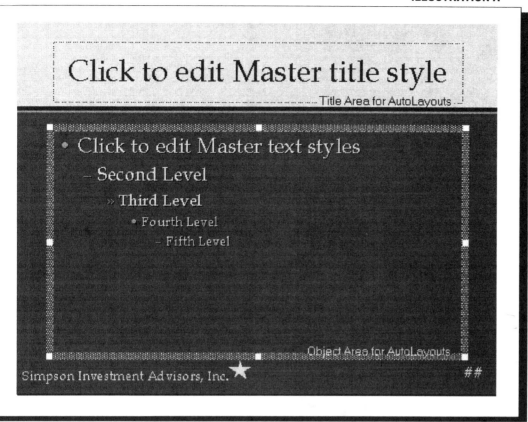

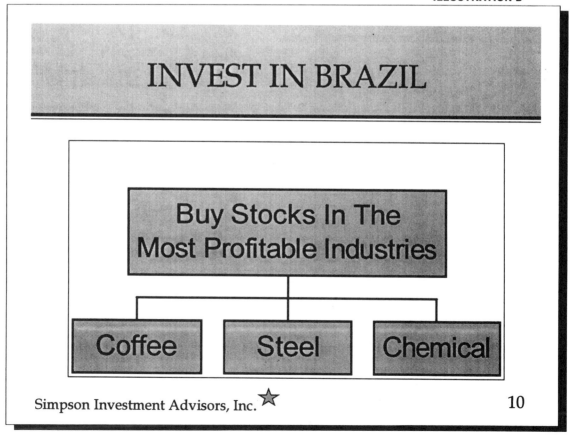

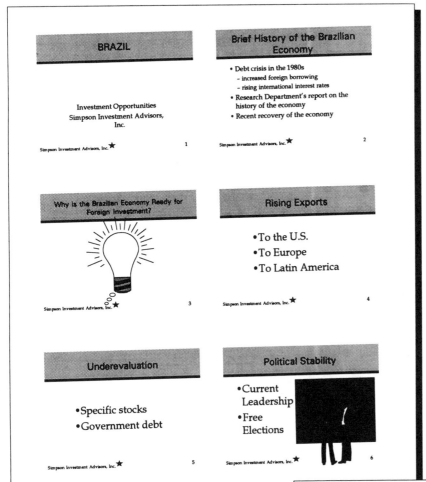

DESIRED RESULT

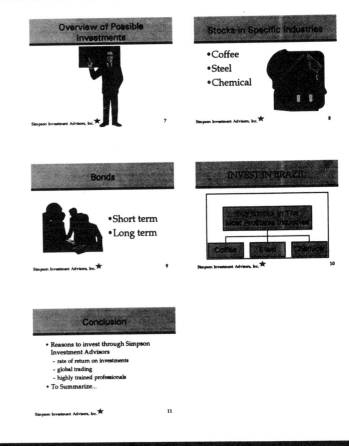

SHOW PRESENTATION

1. Open desired presentation.

2. Click 🖳 .... **Alt** + **V** , **W**

   ✓ *If you use the view icon approach for showing a slide show, you may skip the next two steps.*

3. Type slide numbers..................*numbers* if necessary.

4. Click **Show**, if necessarY........ **Alt** + **S**

ADVANCE SLIDES

1. Start presentation.

2. Click left mouse button.

   OR

   Press **Enter**............................... **Enter**

SHOW SELECTED SLIDES

1. Open presentation to show.

2. Click **View**, ... **Alt** + **V** , **W**
   Slide Show.

3. Type first slide .... **Alt** + **F** , *number* number to show in **From** box.

4. Type last slide .... **Alt** + **T** , *number* number to show in **To** box.

5. Click **Show** .... **Enter**

ADD TRANSITIONS IN SLIDE SORTER VIEW

1. Open desired presentation.

2. **Select Slide** Sorter view.

3. Click `No Transition ▣` on **Slide Sorter** toolbar to display a list of effects.

   OR

   Click ▣ .... **Alt** + **E** on Slide Sorter toolbar and click **Effect** drop-down list.

4. Select desired transition.

5. Click **OK**,................................... **Enter** if necessary.

ADD TRANSITION IN ANY VIEW

1. Open desired presentation.

2. Display desired view.

3. Click **Tools**,.............. **Alt** + **T** , **T**
   Transition

   ✓ *No transition options are available until a transition effect is selected.*

4. Select .... **Alt** + **↓** , *transition* desired transition from **Effect** drop-down list.

5. Select desired speed for transition:

   • **Slow** .... **Alt** + **S**

   • **Medium** .... **Alt** + **M**

   • **Fast** .... **Alt** + **F**

6. Select desired advance method:

   • **Only on Mouse Click** .... **Alt** + **O**

   • **Automatic**............ **Alt** + **A** , *number* After # Seconds

7. Click **OK**................................... **Enter**

SET SLIDE TIMINGS IN ALL VIEWS

1. Open desired presentation.

2. Select or display desired slide.

3. Click **Tools**,.............. **Alt** + **T** , **T**
   Transition

4. Click **Automatically After** .... **Alt** + **A** # Seconds.

5. Type number of seconds ....*number*

6. Click **OK**................................... **Enter**

EXERCISE

CREATING BUILDS

13

NOTES:

- A **build** is the style in which each bulleted item appears on a slide. PowerPoint allows you to specify whether you want a slide to contain builds and the build effect. A slide that *does not* contain a build will reveal all bulleted items during a slide show. A slide that *does* contain a build will reveal no bulleted items until you activate each one when you are ready to discuss that point.

- To create a build, select Slide Sorter view. Click the slide to receive the build, and select Build from the Tools main menu, or click the Build button ▦ next to the Build Effects text box on the Slide Sorter Toolbar.

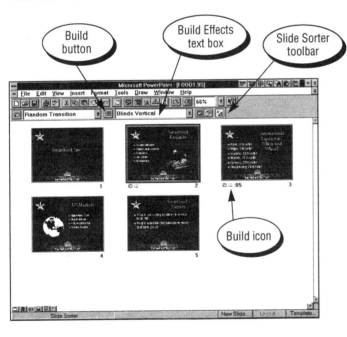

- In the Build dialog box which follows, you have several options for the way a bulleted item displays on a slide. Click the Build Body Text and Effect check boxes; then select an Effect from the drop down list.

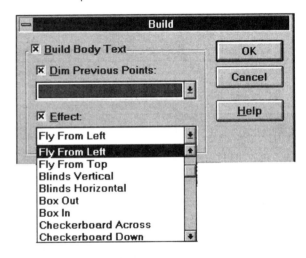

- To have previous text dim as new text appears, click the Dim Previous Points check box and select a color for the dimmed items from the drop down list.

- In Slide Sorter view, slides containing builds are marked by a build icon below and to the left of the miniature slide image.

In this exercise, you will edit a previously created presentation by adding page numbers, a graph slide, builds, and timings to selected slides. You will then view your slide show.

EXERCISE DIRECTIONS:

1. Open **FOOD**.
2. Switch to Slide Master view.
3. Insert a page number in the sun (bottom middle) of the slide using a blue serif font in 20 point.
4. Switch to Slide view.
5. Insert a New Slide and select the Graph AutoLayout.
6. Select Pie Chart as the graph type. Enter the slide title shown in Illustration A. Delete the data from the data sheet and enter the new data shown below.

Paris	Milan	London	Madrid	Sydney	Hong Kong
400	600	800	300	300	900

- Create the title and position it as shown in the illustration.
- Insert data labels and select Show Percent.

7. Switch to Slide Sorter view.
8. Move the new slide to become Slide 4.
9. Create a transition effect for each slide.
10. Add a 5-second slide timing for Slide 4.
11. Create a build on Slides 2, 3, 5, and 6 using any desired effect .
12. Save the changes to the presentation; do not close the file.
13. View the slide show.
14. Print one copy of Slide 4 (the pie chart) in Black and White.
15. Close the presentation window.

ILLUSTRATION A

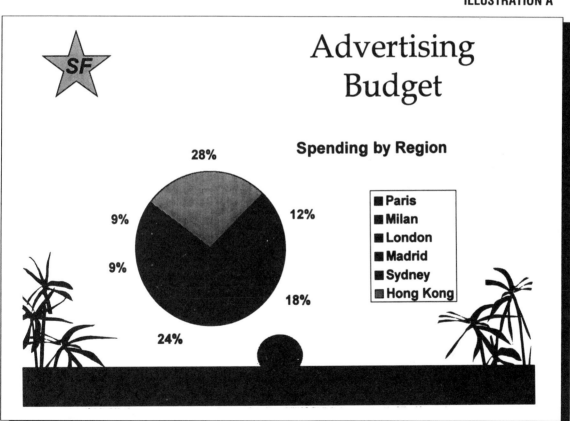

CREATE A BUILD

- Switch to .... Alt + T , D
  Slide Sorter View
- Click slide to receive a build.
- Click **Tools** .... Alt + T
- Click **Build** .... B

OR

- Click [ ] on **Slide Sorter** Toolbar.

5. Click **Build Body Text** .... Alt + B

AND/OR

1. Click .... Alt + D
   Dim Previous Points

2. Select Color to Dim Points.

6. Click **Effect** .... Alt + E

7. Click **Effect** list arrow and select desired effect.

8. Click **OK** .... Enter

EXERCISE

▪ USING THE ANNOTATOR ▪ CREATING CONTINUOUSLY RUNNING PRESENTATIONS

NOTES:

Using the Annotator

- The **Annotator** feature permits you to draw on the screen during a slide show. Annotations made on the screen during a slide show do not alter the slide in any way. Timings are suspended when you are annotating and begin again when you turn the Annotator off.

- Annotator may be accessed by clicking on the Freehand Annotation button ✏ which appears in the lower-right corner of the screen during a slide show. After clicking the Annotation button, your mouse becomes a pencil point so you can write on the slide. To turn Annotator off, click the button when you are finished.

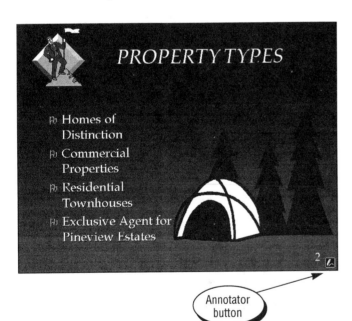

Annotator button

Creating Continuously Running Presentations

- Slide shows can be set to run continuously so you do not have to click the mouse or press a key to activate a slide. Self-advancing slide shows are particularly useful when displayed at trade shows or on a sales counter.

- Timings must be set for each slide in a continuously running presentation to tell PowerPoint how long to display each slide. It is important to allow enough time for people to review the information presented on each slide when you set timings for a continuously running presentation.

- To create a continuously running presentation, switch to Slide Sorter view, press Ctrl + A to select all slides. In the Transition dialog box, select Automatically and indicate the number of seconds you wish each slide to stay on screen.

- A continuously running slide show can be stopped by pressing Esc.

In this exercise, you will edit a previously created presentation by adding transitions, builds, and timings to selected slides. You will also use the Annotator during your slide presentation.

EXERCISE DIRECTIONS:

1. Open **FLAGSHIP**.

2. Switch to Slide Sorter view.

3. Assign a transition effect and a transition speed for each slide in the presentation.

4. Create a build on slides 2, 3, 6 and 7 using any desired effect.

5. Save the changes to the presentation.

6. View the slide show. Use the Annotator to circle Pineview Estates on Slide 2 and the Country Estates row on Slide 7.

7. Add slide timings to each slide and change the advance method to advance automatically.

8. Set the slide show to run continuously and view the slide show again.

9. After viewing the entire presentation, stop the presentation.

10. Close the file; save the changes.

ANNOTATE DURING SLIDE SHOWS

1. Open desired presentation and start slide show.

2. Click [✏] in lower right corner of screen to turn Annotator on.

3. Use left mouse button to position pencil and write/draw.

4. Click [↖] to turn Annotator off. .

RUN SLIDE SHOW CONTINUOUSLY

1. Open desired presentation.

2. Set timings for each slide.

3. Click **View** menu .... `Alt` + `V`

4. Click **Slide Show** .... `W`

5. Click **Run Continuously** .... `Alt` + `C`
   Until 'Esc'

Stop Continuous Run of Slide Show:

Press **Esc** ....

EXERCISE

15

▪ CREATING NOTES PAGES AND HANDOUTS ▪ NOTES MASTER AND HANDOUT MASTER ▪ PRINTING NOTES MASTER AND HANDOUT MASTER

NOTES:

Creating Notes Pages and Handouts

▪ In the previous exercises, you printed your presentation either as individual slides or as Handouts with six slides per page. PowerPoint provides other options for printing your presentation.

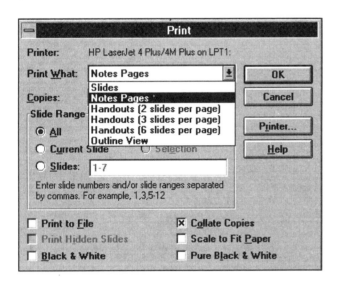

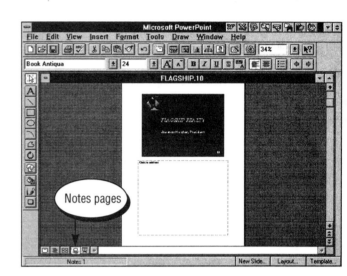

Notes pages

▪ In addition to printing **handouts** with six slides per page, handouts can also be printed with two or three slides per page. When handouts are printed with three slides on each page, they appear down the left side of the page with space on the right side for notetaking.

Notes Master and Handout Master

▪ In Exercise 8, you learned to use the Slide Master if you wanted to insert text or graphics on one slide and have it appear on all slides of your presentation.

▪ Using Notes Master and Handouts Master also allows you to insert text and/or graphics on one page of your notes or handouts and have it appear on all pages. Often, the time, date, and speaker's name are added to audience handouts.

▪ Notes Master and Handouts Master may be accessed by selecting Master, Notes Master or Handouts Master from the View main menu.

Printing Notes Pages and Handouts

▪ Use the same procedures to print notes pages and handouts that you used to print slides.

▪ The **Notes Pages** option prints your presentation showing a small image at the top of the page and a blank box (notes placeholder) below the image. You can enter reminders and/or additional information about the slide in the notes placeholder, or you can leave the box blank so that your audience can use it for notetaking.

▪ To add notes to your slides, click the Notes Pages view button on the bottom left of your screen or select Notes Pages from the View main menu. Then, enter the desired text in the notes placeholder.

In this exercise, you will create a table slide and add reminders on notes pages. You will also use Notes Pages master to insert text to appear on all notes pages.

EXERCISE DIRECTIONS:

1. Open **FOOD**.

2. Switch to Slide view.

3. Display Slide 4. Change the slide title to read, International Advertising Budget.

4. Display Slide 5.

5. Insert a New Slide and select the Table AutoLayout.

   ✓ Note: The new slide should be Slide 6.

   • Enter the slide title and table data shown in Illustration A.
   • Create 3 columns and 5 rows.
   • Set column heading text to sans serif 28 point italic bold. Use the default font size for column text.
   • Center column headings.
   • Adjust row heights so text fits attractively on the slide.

6. Switch to Notes Pages view. Add the following notes to the slides indicated (See example shown in Illustration B.):

   Slide 1:
   • **Introduce the purpose of the presentation.**
   • **Give a general overview of the items to be covered in the presentation.**

   Slide 2:
   • **Review the different Smartfood Products available and identify the features of each.**

   Slide 3:
   • **Explain new market expansion and why these markets were selected.**

   Slide 4:
   • **Explain domestic markets and reasons for success in each.**

7. Switch to Notes Master.

8. Using the text tool, enter the information on the notes page shown in Illustration B in 12 point.

9. Switch to Handout Master.

10. Using the text tool, enter the the same information in the same location and using the same font size on the handouts master as you did on the notes page master as shown in Illustration C, on pages 443 and 444.

11. Print one copy of each notes page.

12. Print one copy of the presentation as Handouts with three slides per page.

13. Close the file; save the changes.

ILLUSTRATION A

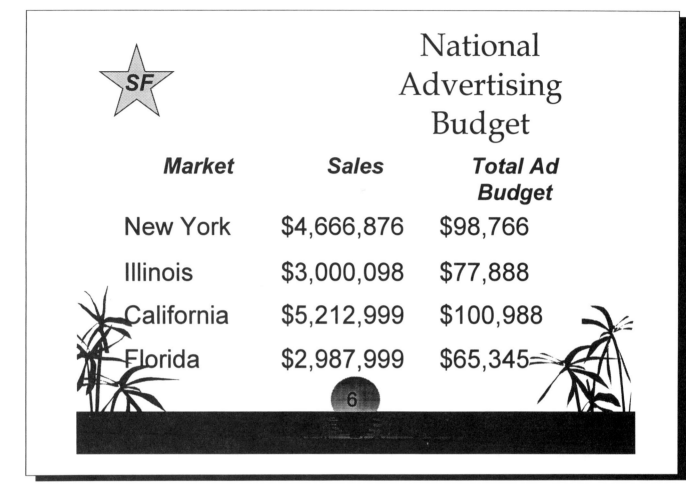

National Advertising Budget

Market	Sales	Total Ad Budget
New York	$4,666,876	$98,766
Illinois	$3,000,098	$77,888
California	$5,212,999	$100,988
Florida	$2,987,999	$65,345

CREATE NOTES PAGES

1. Open desired presentation.
2. Click 🖳 .... Alt + V , N
3. Click on notes placeholder at bottom of page.
4. Type notes.

PRINT NOTES PAGES AND HANDOUTS

1. Open desired presentation.
2. Prepare Notes Pages.
3. Click **File** .... Alt + F
4. Click **Print** .... P

5. Click **Print What** .... Alt + W , ↓
   list arrow
6. Select **Notes Pages** or **Handouts**.
7. Select desired options, if necessary.
8. Click **OK** .... Enter

FORMAT TEXT ON NOTES MASTER AND HANDOUT MASTER

1. Open a presentation or create a new presentation.
2. Click **View** .... Alt + V
3. Click **Master** .... M
4. Click **Notes Master** .... N
   OR

Handout Master .... D

5. Select placeholder to change formatting.

   OR

   Using the text, drawing, and/or formatting tools, create desired master information.
6. Click 🖳 .... Alt + V , N
7. Click **Notes Pages** or click **Notes Pages** view button.

   ✓ *To see effect of additions to Handout Master, print one copy of Handouts with any number of slides per page.*

•Introduce the purpose of the presentation.

•Give a general overview of the items to be covered in the presentation.

Your name

Presentation to Bd of Directors, June 1996

ILLUSTRATION C
Handout Master

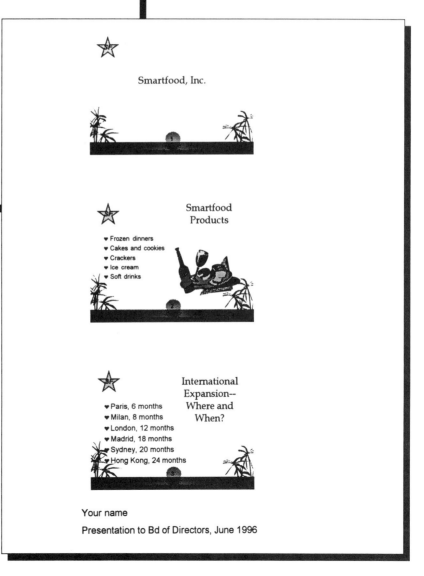

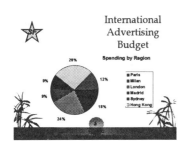

International
Advertising
Budget

Spending by Region

- Paris
- Milan
- London
- Madrid
- Sydney
- Hong Kong

US Markets

- East-New York
- North-Illinois
- West-California
- South-Florida

National
Advertising
Budget

Market	Sales	Total Ad Budget
New York	$4,666,876	$98,766
Illinois	$3,000,098	$77,888
California	$5,212,999	$100,988
Florida	$2,987,999	$65,345

Your name

Presentation to Bd of Directors, June 1996

ILLUSTRATION C
Handout Master

ILLUSTRATION C
Handout Master

Smartfood's
Success

- People are eating healthier to reduce body fat.
- People want low-fat, low-calorie foods that taste great!

Your name

Presentation to Bd of Directors, June 1996

LESSON 3
SUMMARY EXERCISE

In this exercise, you will get your presentation ready for a slide show. You will add transitions, builds and timings, prepare audience handouts and notes pages. You will use the Notes Page Master to add information to all notes pages.

EXERCISE DIRECTIONS:

1. Open **INVEST**.
2. Switch to Slide Sorter view.
3. Assign a transition effect and a transition speed to each slide in the presentation.
4. Create a build on slides 2 and 6 using any desired effect.
5. Save the changes to the presentation; do not close the file.
6. View the slide show.
7. Use the Annotator to circle the highest bar on the graph.
8. Switch to Notes Master view.
9. Using the text tool, create the company name and date as shown in Illustration A in sans serif 20 point. Use the line tool to create the horizontal line. Insert a page number on the top right corner of the page.
10. Using the copy feature, copy the bottom text to the clipboard.
11. Switch to Handout Master view.
12. Paste the company name text on the bottom of the page. Create a horizontal line below the name. Insert a page number on the top right of the page, as shown in Illustration B.
13. Print one copy of each notes page.
14. Print one copy of the presentation as Handouts with three slides per page.
15. Add slide timings to each slide and change the advance method to advance automatically.
16. Set the slide show to run continuously and view the slide show again.
17. After viewing the entire presentation, stop the presentation.
18. Close the file; save the changes.

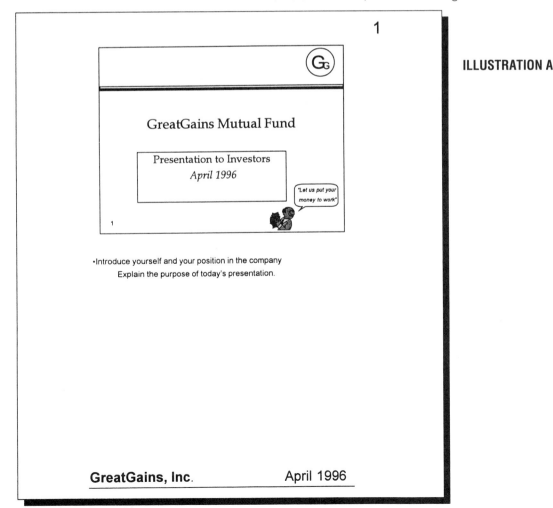

ILLUSTRATION A

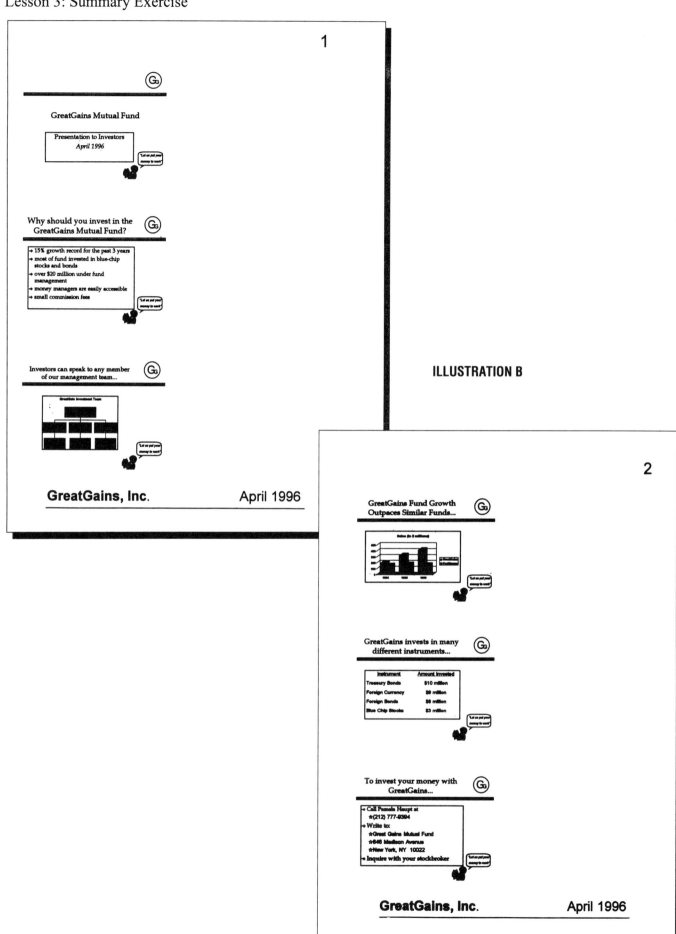

ILLUSTRATION B

CHAPTER 6

Exercises 1-9

- Windowing Files in One Application

- Windowing Files from Different Applications

- Integrating an Excel Worksheet and a Word Document

- Integrating an Excel Worksheet and a Word Document (Copy/ Paste, Drag/Drop)

- Integrating an Excel Worksheet and a Word Document (Linking, Embedding, Office Links)

- Integrating an Excel Chart and a Word Document

- Outputting an Access Database to an Excel File

- Merging an Access Table with a Word Main Document

- Exporting PowerPoint Slides into a Word Document

- Exporting a PowerPoint Presentation into a Word Document

EXERCISE

■ WINDOWING FILES IN ONE APPLICATION ■ WINDOWING FILES FROM DIFFERENT APPLICATIONS

NOTES:

Windowing Files in One Application

■ Microsoft Office allows you to work with several files simultaneously by displaying them in separate windows. The exact number of files that can be used at once depends on available memory. Windowing lets you view files as you work with them.

■ When you begin a new application, Office provides a full-screen or maximized window for your work. The controls on the title bar let you size and arrange Office within the Windows screen. (See Chapter I - Office Basics, Exercise 2.) The controls to the left and right of the menu bar allow you to size and arrange the current application window. See the illustration below:

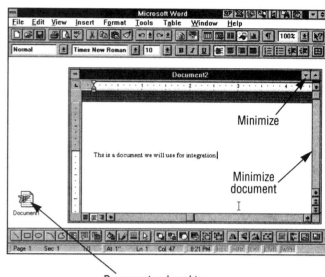

Document reduced to an icon. Double-click to view.

Document window control box

■ Minimizing a window, or reducing its size, allows you to view several files at once. To minimize a window, click the down arrow of the document restore button on the menu bar. The file will be reduced to a small rectangle. The file can be further reduced to an icon by clicking on the down arrow or minimize button ▣ on the file title bar. The icon can be restored or maximized by selecting the feature after clicking on the icon.

■ You can size the minimized window by dragging the frame of the window. Both the width and length can be changed by dragging the corner of the window.

■ If you are viewing multiple files created in the same application, you may view the open documents on the screen at once using the Arrange All command. The files will be arranged so that all can be viewed and highlighted in a tiled fashion.

In Excel, Access, and PowerPoint, a Cascade arrangement of files may be available. **Cascaded windows** allow you to view the title bar of each open document. The windows are overlapped so that the title bar of each file is displayed. Note the illustration of three PowerPoint files cascaded with the active presentation on top. To make a presentation active, click any visible portion of the desired window.

CASCADED FILE

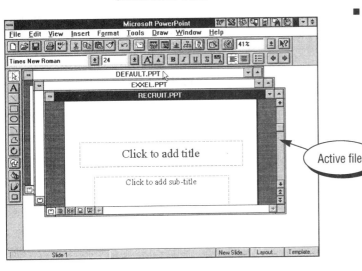

■ When files are arranged or tiled, every file is visible without overlapping . The active window is indicated by the shaded title bar. Any window can be clicked to be made active and the maximize button ▲ to the right of the title bar can be clicked to enlarge or maximize any file. (*See Exercise 32, Word.*)

ARRANGED OR TILED FILE

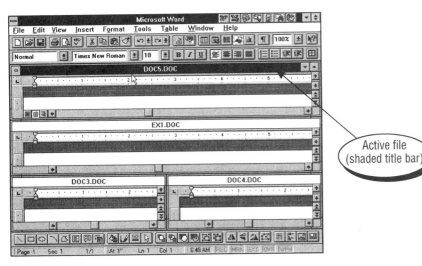

■ You can also switch between file windows whether they are currently displayed or not by selecting <u>W</u>indow from the menu and choosing the document from the open files listed.

■ A window can be closed by double-clicking the control menu, which is the box at the left on the title bar.

Windowing Files from Different Applications

■ If you wish to move between an opened Word document and Excel workbook file or between any Office applications, you click on the appropriate icon on the MOM toolbar at the top of the screen.

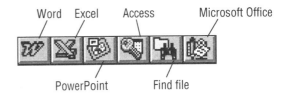

However, if you wish to see files from different applications on the screen at once, you can hold down the Shift key before clicking the application icon. This will arrange or tile windows for each file so that they can be viewed, selected, and managed.

In this exercise, you will work with four Excel workbooks and a Word document. You will arrange the workbooks so you can view each file and use windowing to view the worksheets and document at the same time.

EXERCISE DIRECTIONS:

1. Create a new workbook in EXCEL.

2. Open 💾 **DAILY** or 💾 **IDAILY.XLS**.

3. Open 💾 **UNIV** or 💾 **IUNIV.XLS**.

4. Open 💾 **INCR** or 💾 **IINCR.XLS**.

5. Open 💾 **REWARD** or 💾 **IREWARD.XLS**.

6. Arrange all the worksheets.

7. Make **DAILY(IDAILY)** the active workbook.

8. Make **INCR(IUNIV)** the active workbook.

9. Reduce **REWARD (IREWARD)** to an icon.

10. Restore **REWARD(IREWARD)**.

11. Click the WORD icon on the MOM bar to switch to the word processor.

12. Open 💾 **BULLETIN** or 💾 **IBULLETN.DOC**.

13. Switch back to the EXCEL screen by clicking the icon on the MOM bar.

14. View the document on the Excel screen by pressing the Word icon and holding down the Shift key.

15. Make **BULLETIN** or **IBULLETN.DOC** the active file.

16. Size the window so that it is larger.

17. Close each window.

ARRANGE (ALL)

Positions document windows next to each other as non-overlapping tiles.

- Click **Window** .... `Alt` + `W`
- Click **Arrange All** .... `A`

CLOSE WINDOW

Double Click Control menu .... `▭`
of active document window.

OR

a. Click Control menu .... `Alt` + `-`

b. Click **Close** .... `C`

OR

Press Ctrl+W (Word) .... `Ctrl` + `W`

OR

Press Ctrl+F4 .... `Ctrl` + `F4`
(Excel or Access)

MAXIMIZE WINDOW

Fills the application window with the active file.

Click Maximize box of .... `▲`
active file (not available if window
is already maximized.)

OR

a. Click Control menu .... `Alt` + `-`

b. Click **Maximize** .... `X`

OR

Press Ctrl+F10 .... `Ctrl` + `F10`
(Word or Excel)

MINIMIZE WINDOW

Reduces active file window to an icon..

Click Minimize box of .... `▼`
active file (only visible if window
has been changed to resizeable view
with Restore command.)

OR

a. Click Control menu .... `Alt` + `-`

b. Click **Minimize** .... `N`

OR

Press Ctrl +F9 .... `Ctrl` + `F9`
(Excel)

SWITCH AMONG OPEN DOCUMENTS

Click any visible portion of desired document.

OR

1. Click **Window** .... `Alt` + `W`

2. Click name of desired document.

OR

Type document number.

WINDOW FILES FROM DIFFERENT APPLICATIONS

1. Click first application icon.

2. Open desired file.

3. Click second application icon.

4. Open desired file.

5. Press Shift and first icon to tile files.

EXERCISE 2

INTEGRATING AN EXCEL WORKSHEET FILE AND A WORD DOCUMENT FILE (COPY AND PASTE, DRAG AND DROP)

NOTES:

- **Integration** is the sharing or combining of data between Microsoft Office tools. The **source** file is used to send data; the **destination** file is used to receive data. For example, an Excel chart or worksheet (the source file) can add supporting or visual documentation of material to a Word document (the destination file).

- The Microsoft Office Manager may be used to switch or transfer information between applications. To integrate an Excel table into a Word document, for example, you can copy and paste the data or use the drag and drop procedure. Both of these methods places the table into the document, which may be edited. However, the integrated table has no connection to the original worksheet and the formulas are not accessible. These methods should only be used when updated or linked data is not necessary and when formulas do not need editing.

- **Copying** places the data onto the clipboard where it can then be pasted to the desired location. Therefore, you open both the Word document and the Excel worksheet. Make the Excel worksheet active and copy the desired worksheet data. After you make the Word document active, you paste the worksheet to the specific location in the document.

- The **drag and drop** technique may also be used to copy and paste the data if both the source and destination documents are made visible using the windowing options discussed in Exercise 1. When using drag and drop, you bypass the clipboard and directly copy the data. However, you must hold down the Ctrl key to copy (rather than move) the data.

  ✓ Note: If you have difficulty placing the worksheet, drag it to any spot on the document, then maximize the document, and adjust the placement.

In this exercise, Harriet Cardoza's memorandum needs to be enhanced by adding a worksheet showing the salary summary for the Osford Branch of the Woodworks Furniture Company. You will save the newly integrated document under a new name.

EXERCISE DIRECTIONS:

1. Click on the Word icon on the Microsoft Office Manager bar.
2. Open 🖮 **BRANCH** or 💾 **IBRANCH.DOC**.
3. Click on the Excel icon on the Microsoft Office Manager bar.
4. Open 🖮 **WOODSUM** or 💾 **IWOODSUM.XLS**.
5. Copy the entire worksheet.
6. Switch to the Word document using the Word icon on the MOM toolbar.
7. Paste the worksheet after the first paragraph in the memorandum as indicated.
8. Use the mouse to widen the columns to fit the headings on one line
   ✓ Note: You can change data but cannot view or edit formulas. This is table mode.

9. Select and cut all the worksheet data in the document.
10. Switch to the Excel file and display it on the screen with the Word document.
    ✓ Note: Use the Shift key with the Excel icon to tile the applications.
11. Use the Ctrl key and the drag and drop method to select and copy the worksheet to the Word document.
12. Save the file as **BRSUM**.
13. Print one copy.
14. Close all files.

TO: Dennis Jones, Corporate Financial Manager

FROM: Harriet Cardoza

DATE: Today's

SUBJECT: Quarterly Salary Summary

I have arranged the quarterly salary summary for the first three quarters of this year for the Oxford branch. As you can see, last quarter we added a new employee, Jim Thompson.

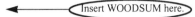 Insert WOODSUM here.

I know you are in the process of compiling expense data from all the Woodworks Furniture Company's stores to help you in long-term planning for our organization. The addition of our new employee increases our expenses at a difficult economic juncture for our company. However, Jim has indispensable community contacts that we expect will increase our level of sales.

Early indications show that we have made the right decision. Our sales have picked up and there is an increase in sales to corporate clients. We will be sending a point by point data analysis report next week.

hc/

copy to: Andrea Zoren

WOODWORKS FURNITURE COMPANY					
COMPENSATION SUMMARY - JANUARY-SEPTEMBER					
EMP.			BASE		TOTAL
NO.	NAME		SALARY		COMPENSATION
1	ABRAMS, JUDY		1500		21513.44
2	CHANG, PETER		1500		26828.75
3	LINSEY, KELLY		1500		36388.61
4	JOHNSON, LETOYA		1500		18610.66
5	RIVERA, TONY		1500		43953.58
6	THOMPSON, JIM		1500		5322.56
	TOTALS		9000		152617.60
	AVERAGES		1500		25436.27
	HIGHEST		1500		43953.58
	LOWEST		1500		5322.56

COPY AND PASTE DATA BETWEEN APPLICATIONS

. Open both applications and appropriate files.

. In the source file, highlight the data to be copied.

. Click **Edit** .... `Alt` + `E`

. Click **Copy** .... `C`

. Switch to the destination file.

6. Place cursor at the point of insertion.

7. Click **Edit** .... `Alt` + `E`

8. Click **Paste Cells** .... `P`

COPY DATA BETWEEN APPLICATIONS WITH DRAG AND DROP EDITING

1. Open and display both applications and files.

2. In the source file, highlight the data to be copied.

3. Move pointer to right edge of selection until arrow appears.

4. Hold Ctrl while dragging the data to the location in the destination file.

EXERCISE

- **INTEGRATING AN EXCEL WORKSHEET FILE AND A WORD DOCUMENT FILE (LINKING, EMBEDDING, OFFICE LINKS)** - **EDITING A LINKED FILE**

NOTES:

- **Object Linking and Embedding** or OLE is the system Microsoft uses to link or embed objects between applications.

Linking files

- As discussed in Excel, Exercise 24, linking files allows the data in the destination file to change if the source file is updated. For example, suppose you integrated an Excel worksheet (source file) into a Word document (destination file), but you need to update your worksheet data on a weekly basis. By linking the worksheet and document files, the Word document automatically updates with the most current data. In addition, the linking procedure saves disk space since the linked file is actually stored in the source location. Linking is accomplished by using the Copy, Paste Special commands on the Edit menu with the Paste Link option selected. To identify the object, the type of file, "Microsoft Excel 5.0 object," should be selected before choosing Paste Link.

Editing a Linked File

- When a linked file from one application is double-clicked within another application, the source application and file open for you to edit. For example, if you double-click on a linked Excel worksheet in a Word file, you are brought into Excel to do the edits. Therefore, changes are made to the source file which automatically appear on the linked file. Conversely, if you make changes directly into the source file and then open the destination file with the linked data, the updated worksheet will appear.

Embedding a File

- **Embedding** files enables you to edit data in the application but does not change or modify the source file. For example, double-clicking on an embedded worksheet in a Word document allows you to make edits in Excel which will not change the source file. This is preferable if you wish to make changes within Excel that are not reflected in the source file or if the source file is not always available. Unlike linking, embedding creates a larger destination file since it includes the embedded or integrated object. To embed a file, use the Insert, Object, Create from File options or the Copy, Paste Special commands or the Edit menu without selecting the Paste Link option.

Office Links

- **Office Links** may be used to create a new worksheet in a Word document by clicking the Insert Microsoft Excel Worksheet button on the Standard toolbar in Word. This worksheet may be sized using the handles on the worksheet and may be created by using the Excel menus that appear. To embed a new file, use the Insert, Object, Create New options. The workbook you create within a document gives you all the capabilities of Excel within the document.

In this exercise, the Greenthumb Landscape Service Operating Expense Analysis report needs to be enhanced by adding a worksheet showing the Income and Expense data for the year. You will integrate and edit the report in linked and embedded modes.

EXERCISE DIRECTIONS:

1. Click the Word icon on the Microsoft Office Manager bar.

2. Open ⌨ **SOD** or 🖫 **ISOD.DOC**.

3. Make the changes indicated on the document. as shown in Illustration A.

4. Click on the Excel icon on the Microsoft Office Manager bar.

5. Open ⌨ **ISQTRS** or 🖫 **IISQTRS.XLS**.

6. Copy the entire worksheet.

7. Switch to the Word document by clicking the Word icon on the Microsoft Manager bar.

8. Link the worksheet, using the Paste Special, Paste Link options to the location shown on the document.

   ✓ Note: This is a linked file that will reflect changes in the source file.

9. Double-click on the worksheet in the Word file. (This brings you into Excel.)

10. Insert two rows under the title and add the third heading shown in Illustration B on page 457.

11. Move the three-line header to Column C.

12. Click the Word icon to return to the document and note the updated worksheet.

13. Click the Excel icon and delete one row under the heading.

14. Return to Word and note the updated worksheet.

15. Insert the header;
    Greenthumb Landscape Service
    Operating Expense Analysis
    Page #

    Be sure to suppress the header on the first page.

16. Save the file as **SODQTR**.

17. Select and cut the worksheet from the document.

18. Use the Insert, Object, Create New from File options to embed the worksheet into the document.

    ✓ Note: This is an embedded file or part of the Word file and it may be edited without changing the source file.

19. Select the worksheet file and format the numbers for Total Income and Net Income to bold.

20. Click the Excel icon and note that the worksheet did not change.

21. Close and save the Excel file.

22. Print one copy of **SODQTR**. The printed report will include the first version of the worksheet.

23. Close the Word file without saving the changes.

ILLUSTRATION A

(Insert Text) Note The Quarterly Income Statement below:

Insert Worksheet

GREENTHUMB LANDSCAPE SERVICE
OPERATING EXPENSE ANALYSIS
199-

#

We have seen many changes at Greenthumb Landscape Services this year. An explanation of the Quarterly Income Statement for 199- is worthwhile. After much analysis, we have decided to place our advertising with our local radio station, WDOV. We have developed a comprehensive advertising program that runs year-round in an effort to develop business during our lighter winter months.

The lower expense and income figures for the first quarter reflect the closing of our service center during the month of February. The policy to close in February is under review for this winter, since we have developed and sold additional contracts for snow removal. The executive committee will be meeting to develop a vacation system for full-time employees so that the center is staffed at all times. For winter services, we are contemplating the purchase of another snow removal vehicle to increase our capability. We are aware that our snow handling equipment must be kept in good repair to avoid the breakdowns we experienced last winter. These factors will cause increases in repair and depreciation expenses for next year which should be offset by our increased revenues.

Our salaries expenses very with the seasons. We are continuing the practice of maintaining a core full-time staff while hiring additional part-time staff for the peak service periods of the year. This has worked well in the past; however, we are being pressured to increase benefits for our full-time employees. The high cost of health insurance and vacation days may result in the necessity to reduce our core staff and increase our part-time staff in order to reduce the expenses for employee benefits.

The high expenses for Supplies in the third quarter reflects the increase in our full landscaping service. We have become one of the primary landscaper for the new developments of single-family homes in our area. The sod, seed and plantings that we install have been produced by our supplier in Pennsylvania who gives us an excellent package price on our orders.

We are ever striving to improve our service to our customers and community and continue to monitor our expenditures while increasing our client base.

For the year ended December 31, 199-

Insert 2 rows

	A	B	C	D	E	F	G	H	I	J
1		GREENTHUMB LANDSCAPE SERVICE								
2		QUARTERLY INCOME STATEMENT COMPARISON								
3										
4			1ST QTR.	2ND QTR.	3RD QTR.	4TH QTR.	COMBINED			
5			TOTALS	TOTALS	TOTALS	TOTALS	TOTALS			
6										
7	INCOME									
8	Service Fees		17052.39	28566.18	33610.97	21461.19	100690.73			
9	Consultations		4909.50	4679.76	3495.92	3088.79	16173.97			
10	Total Income		21961.89	33245.94	37106.89	24549.98	116864.70			
11										
12	EXPENSES:									
13	Advertising		270.00	480.00	480.00	260.00	1490.00			
14	Salaries		2764.85	3766.65	3766.10	2764.30	13061.90			
15	Supplies		989.94	3011.70	5210.05	2106.03	11317.72			
16	Truck Maint		464.52	1054.03	1060.53	1049.41	3628.49			
17	Interest		75.00	75.00	75.00	75.00	300.00			
18	Other		418.62	1779.51	1695.64	968.61	4862.38			
19	Total Expenses		4982.93	10166.89	12287.32	7223.35	34660.49			
20										
21	NET INCOME		16978.96	23079.05	24819.57	17326.63	82204.21			
22										

LINK DATA BETWEEN APPLICATIONS

Open both applications and appropriate files.

In the source file, highlight the data to be copied.

Click **Edit** .... 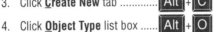 Alt + E

Click **Copy** C

Switch to the destination file.

Place cursor at the point of insertion.

Click **Edit** .... Alt + E

Click **Paste Special** .... S

Select **Paste Link** L

Select the Document Object linkage

Click **OK** .... Enter

MBEDDED OBJECTS

reate New:

Click **Insert** .... Alt + I

Click **Object** .... O

The Object dialog box will appear.

3. Click **Create New** tab .... Alt + C

4. Click **Object Type** list box ...... Alt + O

5. Select application .... ↑↓
   from which to create object.

6. Click **OK** to create .... Enter

   The selected application will open.

7. Create desired information.

8. Click outside the object to return to original application.

Create from File:

1. Click **Insert** menu .... Alt + I

2. Click **Object** .... O

   The Object dialog box will appear.

3. Click **Create from File** tab ...... Alt + F

4. Click **Drives** drop-down .... Alt + V
   list box.

5. Type or select drive letter or .... ↑↓
   drive containing file you want
   to insert.

6. Double click directory in Directories list box containing file you want to insert.*

7. Double-click file in.................. Alt + N
   File Name list box.

8. Click **OK** .... Enter

   * This method may be used to Link the file by selecting **L**ink to File check box at this point.

EMBED DATA USING PASTE SPECIAL

1. Open both applications and appropriate files.

2. In the source file, highlight the data to be copied.

3. Click **Edit** .... Alt + E

4. Click **Copy** C

5. Switch to the destination file.

6. Place cursor at the point of insertion.

7. Click **Edit** .... Alt + E

8. Click **Paste Special** .... S

9. Click **OK** .... Enter

EXERCISE

▪ INTEGRATING AN EXCEL CHART AND A WORD DOCUMENT FILE (LINKING AND EMBEDDING) ▪ EDITING

NOTES:

- You can insert an Excel chart into a Word document using Linking or Embedding commands. The OLE system and the consequences of using linking or embedding, as described in Exercise 3 for worksheets, apply to charts as well. If the chart is part of the worksheet, it is advisable to use the **Copy, Paste Special** procedure since the chart can be selected and isolated. If the chart is on a separate sheet, the **Insert, Object, Create from File** procedure may be used.

Embedding a Chart

- If you wish to edit a chart in Word without changing the source material, the chart should be embedded. When the chart is double-clicked, Excel menus and toolbars appear for editing purposes. You can return to the Word document by clicking outside the object or by clicking the Word icon.

Linking a Chart

- If a chart must be linked to data that is updated periodically, or you wish to minimize the size of the Word file, you should link the chart object. Edits made on the linked chart object affect the source file, or, if the source file is changed, the object in the destination file is automatically updated.

Editing a Chart

- A workbook may include multiple sheets and the chart may be on a separate sheet. The sheet that was active when the workbook was last saved will appear as the embedded object. By double-clicking on the object, you may adjust the sizing of the object, edit data, and switch to the proper sheet, if necessary.

EXERCISE DIRECTIONS:

Click the Word icon on the Microsoft Office Manager toolbar.

Open 📠 **SODQTR** or 💾 **ISODQTR.DOC**.

Make the changes indicated on page 2 of the document.

Click on the Excel icon on the Microsoft Office Manager toolbar.

Open 💾 **IISQTR3S.XLS**.

✓ Note: If you do not have the data disk, create a column chart of all the expenses for each quarter, with a legend and the following heading:

Greenthumb Landscape Service Expenses

Select and copy the Expenses Chart.

Switch to the Word document by clicking the Word icon on the Microsoft Manager toolbar.

Link the chart object, using the Paste Special, Paste Link options to the location shown on the document.

✓ Note: This is a linked file that will reflect changes in the source file.

Double-click the chart in the Word file. (This brings you into Excel.)

). Edit the second heading line to read: EXPENSES - 12-31-9-

1 Click outside the object to return to the document or click the Word icon and note the updated chart.

2. Switch to Excel and note the levels of the bars for Other Expenses.

13. Change the 4th Quarter Other Expenses number from 968.61 to 1968.61.

14. Note the changes on the chart.

15. Switch to the Word document and note the linked updated chart object.

16. Switch to the Excel worksheet and return Other Expenses to $968.61.

17. Switch to the Word document and size the chart to extend to the margins of the document.

18. Change the font size to 12 point.

19. Save the file as **SODQTR**.

20. Print one copy of **SODQTR**.

21. Close all files.

GREENTHUMB LANDSCAPE SERVICE
OPERATING EXPENSE ANALYSIS
199-

We have seen many changes at Greenthumb Landscape Services this year. Note the Quarterly Income Statement below:

GREENTHUMB LANDSCAPE SERVICE
QUARTERLY INCOME STATEMENT COMPARISON

	1ST QTR. TOTALS	2ND QTR. TOTALS	3RD QTR. TOTALS	4TH QTR. TOTALS	COMBINED TOTALS
INCOME					
Service Fees	17052.39	28566.18	33610.97	21461.19	100690.73
Consultations	4909.50	4679.76	3495.92	3088.79	16173.97
Total Income	21961.89	33245.94	37106.89	24549.98	116864.70
EXPENSES:					
Advertising	270.00	480.00	480.00	260.00	1490.00
Salaries	2764.85	3766.65	3766.10	2764.30	13061.90
Supplies	989.94	3011.70	5210.05	2106.03	11317.72
Truck Maint	464.52	1054.03	1060.53	1049.41	3628.49
Interest	75.00	75.00	75.00	75.00	300.00
Other	418.62	1779.51	1695.64	968.61	4862.38
Total Expenses	4982.93	10166.89	12287.32	7223.35	34660.49
NET INCOME	16978.96	23079.05	24819.57	17326.63	82204.21

An explanation of the Quarterly Income Statement for 199- is worthwhile. After much analysis, we have decided to place our advertising with our local radio station, WDOV. We have developed a comprehensive advertising program that runs year-round in an effort to develop business during our lighter winter months.

The lower expense and income figures for the first quarter reflect the closing of our service center during the month of February. The policy to close in February is under review for this winter, since we have developed and sold additional contracts for snow removal. The executive committee will be meeting to develop a vacation system for full-time employees so that the center is staffed at all times. For winter services, we are contemplating the purchase of another snow removal vehicle to increase our capability.

Greenthumb Landscape Service
Operating Expense Analysis
Page 2

(Insert Text) Note the illustration below comparing expenses for each quarter: (Insert chart here)

We are aware that our snow handling equipment must be kept in good repair to avoid the breakdowns we experienced last winter. These factors will cause increases in repair and depreciation expenses for next year which should be offset by our increased revenues.

Our salaries expenses very with the seasons. We are continuing the practice of maintaining a core full-time staff while hiring additional part-time staff for the peak service periods of the year. This has worked well in the past; however, we are being pressured to increase benefits for our full-time employees. The high cost of health insurance and vacation days may result in the necessity to reduce our core staff and increase our part-time staff in order to reduce the expenses for employee benefits.

The high expenses for Supplies in the third quarter reflects the increase in our full landscaping service. We have become one of the primary landscaper for the new developments of single-family homes in our area. The sod, seed and plantings that we install have been produced by our supplier in Pennsylvania who gives us an excellent package price on our orders.

We are ever striving to improve our service to our customers and community and continue to monitor our expenditures while increasing our client base.

EXERCISE

- **OUTPUT AN ACCESS DATABASE TO AN EXCEL FILE**
- **ANALYZE DATABASE DATA**

NOTES:

- You may wish to use an Excel workbook to summarize and analyze information saved in an Access database. One method of accomplishing this is to export, or send, data from Access to Excel. Exporting is used if you wish to create a new workbook file with the database data or with part of a database table.

- To export a table from Access, open the Access file and select the table, then select Ouput To or Export from the File menu. Switch to Excel and open the file. If you select Output To, the Excel data will format as it was in Access. If you select Export the text appears in the default Excel workbook format. The Export command can also be invoked from the Access Toolbar (*See illustration on the right.*)

- Part of the standard Access toolbar has the Import, Export, Merge It, and Analyze it With MS Excel buttons. The **Analyze It With MS Excel**

button combines the Output To command with the opening of the new file in Excel. It will output the table to an Excel file, open the new file, and provide you with the opportunity to convert the file to earlier versions of Excel. Note the partial toolbar illustration below:

STANDARD ACCESS TOOLBAR (PARTIAL VIEW)

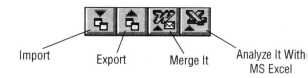

Import   Export   Merge It   Analyze It With MS Excel

- Once the file is exported or output to Excel, you can work with the file as an Excel file. The column headings are the field names you used in the database and may be edited or changed in the Excel format.

In this exercise, Jane's Boutique would like to analyze the data in the Stock table in its inventory database. You will output the database to an Excel file and change the format of the data for presentation and analysis purposes.

EXERCISE DIRECTIONS:

1. Click the Access icon on the Microsoft Office Manager bar.

2. Open ⌨ **JANESHOP** or 💾 **IJANSHOP.MDB**.

3. Select the STOCK table, but don't open it.

4. On the standard Access toolbar, click the Analyze It With MS Excel button.

   ✓ *Note: The table will be output to Excel and will be opened as an Excel file.*

5. Make the following changes to the file in Excel:

   a. Insert three rows above the table to create room for a heading.

   b. Enter a heading that reads:

      JANE'S BOUTIQUE
      INVENTORY - MARCH 31, 1996

   c. Retype the column headings in uppercase letters.

   d. Widen the columns to fit the widest entry.

   e. Insert a new column after the Color column.

   f. Cut and paste the Date Ordered column to the new column created after the Color column.

Continued...

g. Insert a new column after J13 and enter the title TOTAL.

h. Add a column after the Price column and title it VALUATION.

i. Format the column headers to be consistent in shading (use the Format Painter).

j. Find the total number of items in stock for each item in the TOTAL column.

k. Find the Valuation of the inventory for each item by multiplying the Total number of items by the unit price.

l. Format the Valuation figures for currency.

m. Skip one line under the table and enter the label TOTAL and find the total Valuation of the inventory.

7. Save the file as **STOCKE**.

   ✓ Note: You may be prompted to upgrade the Excel file. Do so if you use Excel 5.0.

8. Print one copy of the worksheet.

9. Close all files.

EXPORT A TABLE FROM ACCESS

Data will appear in default format of destination and will give you the opportunity to convert to earlier versions of destination software.

. Open the database.

. Select the table to be exported.

. Click **File** .... Alt + F

. Click **Export** .... Alt + E

. Select the data destination .... ⬆⬇

. Click **OK** .... Enter

7. Select the Access object .... ⬆⬇

8. Enter the filename to export to ..... *filename*

9. Click **OK** .... Enter

OUTPUT A TABLE FROM ACCESS

Data will be formatted as it was in Access.

1. Open the database.

2. Select the table to be exported.

3. Click **File** .... Alt + F

4. Click **Output To** .... Alt + T

5. Select the data destination .... ⬆⬇

6. Click **OK** .... Enter

7. Enter the filename to export to ..... *filename*

8. Click **OK** .... Enter

ANALYZE AN ACCESS TABLE WITH EXCEL

1. Open the database.

2. Select the table to be exported.

3. Click **Analyze It** ....
   With MS Excel button.

EXERCISE

MERGING AN ACCESS TABLE WITH A MAIN DOCUMENT - MAIL MERGE

6

NOTES:

■ Database information from Access can be merged with a main document created in Word. This process is automated with the mail merge feature as was discussed in Word, Exercise 43. Mail merge may also be accomplished using data from an Excel worksheet or a Word table.

■ The first step in the process is to set up the main document in Word to accept information from the Access database. Use the Tools menu in Word and select Mail Merge to access The Mail Merge Helper Dialog box as shown below:

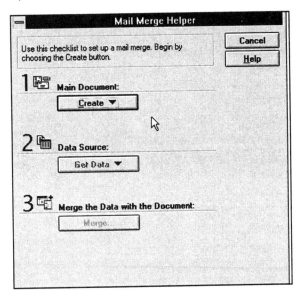

■ As you will note above, the three steps in the procedure are to create the main document, identify the source of the variable data, and merge the data and document files.

• First, create the main document in Word. An existing document may be used by selecting the Active Window option in the form letter dialog box. After creating a mail merge document, the Mail Merge toolbar displays.

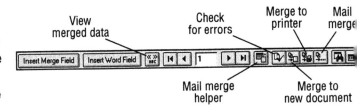

• Second, identify the source of the data as an Access table and select the specific table. The field names used in the Word main document must be the same as those used in the Access database. When the database is specified as the data source, the fields become available in a drop-down list as shown below by clicking the Insert Merge Field bar on the Mail Merge toolbar. Insert the field names from the drop-down list into your main document. Use Edit the Main Document if the field names do not agree. If possible, the database should be planned using the commonly used titles to expedite the merge feature.

List of field names that appears after the database is specified and the Insert Merge Field button is clicked.

- Third, after all the fields are entered into the letter, select Merge from the dialog box.

When a merge is complete, the information from the selected Access table merges into the form letter in the locations you specified for each field. A new document is created for each record in the database containing personal information in the field locations. Each letter should be separated by a section break, and the form letter is intact for future use.

- The merge operation may be started from Access using the **Merge It** button on the Standard toolbar. When the Merge It button is clicked, the Microsoft Mail Merge Wizard appears which will step you through the merge procedure, including transferring you to Word to complete the main document.

In this exercise, the Hug club would like to send a letter to its members in California using the information from its database and a letter previously created in Word You will edit the form letter and merge the database information to create a letter for each member.

EXERCISE DIRECTIONS:

. Click the Word icon on the Microsoft Office Manager bar.

. Open 🖬 **HUGMN** or 🖬 **IHUGMN.DOC**.

. Create a main document by selecting Tools, Mail Merge.

   ✓ *Note: Since **HUGMN** was saved as a main document, you do not have to indicate it now.*

. Select the data source by doing the following:

   a. In the Mail Merge Helper box, select the Get Data button, and then select Open Data Source.

   b. Select the correct directory to open 🖬 **HUGCLUB** or 🖬 **IHUGCLUB.MDB**.

   c. Click OK.

   d. Click on the Table tab and the Members Table, and click OK.

   e. Click the Edit Main Document Button.

       The Main Merge toolbar appears.

. Edit the main document to insert merge fields to match the database by doing the following:

   a. Place the cursor at the first position for variable data (the Title field).

   b. Select the first line of the address and click on the Insert Merge Field button.

   c. Choose Title, and enter a space.

   d. Repeat until all the fields are inserted for the first and second lines of the address.

   e. Since there is no State field in the database, enter the City field, a comma, CA (for California), and then the Zip field. Be sure to enter spaces and punctuation where necessary.

   f. Insert the fields into the proper locations in the salutation and the last paragraph of the letter.

6. Merge the files by doing the following:

   a. Select Tools, Mail Merge.

   b. In the Mail Merge Helper box, select the Merge button.

   c. In the Merge dialog box, select the Merge button.

       The default setting is to create a new document consisting of the merged letters.

7. Scroll down through the merged document and note the merged information and the separation of each letter by a page break.

8. Save the new document as **HUGLETS**.

9. Close all documents in Word.

10. To practice starting the merge from Access, switch to the database using the MOM bar.

11. Click the database table tab and Members table to make it active.

12. Click on Merge It on the Standard toolbar.

    The Microsoft Word Mail Merge Wizard appears.

13. Click on the Link data to an existing Word document selection and click OK.

14. Open 🖬 **HUGMN** or 🖬 **IHUGMN.DOC** and click OK.

    ✓ *Note: The documents merge automatically.*

15. Scroll down through the merged document and note the merged information and the separation of each letter by a page break.

16. Close all files without saving the data.

Today's Date

Title FirstName LastName
Address1
City, State PostalCode

Dear **Title LastName**:

The New York Chapter of the HUG Computer Users' Group cordially invites you to attend our first annual computer conference. The conference will take place at the Plaza Hotel in New York City on Thursday, June 22 at 8:30 a.m.

We are confident that this year's conference will be inspiring and informative. We have several leading representatives of the computer industry who will be conducting seminars at the conference. A conference program and registration form is enclosed.

Please let me know, **Title LastName**, if you plan to attend by returning the completed registration form no later than June 1.

Sincerely,

Thomas Mann
President
NY Chapter

tm/yo
enclosure

ee Word, Exercise 43, for additional Mail
Merge Keystrokes

TTACH DATA SOURCE

Follow procedures under Set Up Main Document

Click **Tools** ....**Alt** + **T**

3. Click **Mail Merge** ....**R**

   Mail Merge Dialog Box appears.

4. Click **Get Data** ....**Alt** + **G**

   This option is unavailable if active Word document has not been set up as a mail merge main document.

5. Click **Open Data Source**....................**O**

6. Follow procedures to Open a File.

EXERCISE

- **IMPORTING A WORD OUTLINE INTO A POWERPOINT PRESENTATION**
- **EXPORTING A WORD OUTLINE INTO A POWERPOINT PRESENTATION**
- **IMPORTING AN EXCEL WORKSHEET INTO A POWERPOINT PRESENTATION**

NOTES:

- An outline created in Word may be used as the text in a PowerPoint presentation. The outline is imported, or brought, into PowerPoint by converting the file format to create a presentation file. The Word outline must be closed before it can be imported. An outline can also be exported, or sent, out from Word by saving the file in RTF (Rich Text Format) which is used by PowerPoint.

- In a Word outline, heading levels, which can be viewed using Outline View, provide the structure for the data. When the outline is imported into PowerPoint, each Heading 1 level becomes a separate slide. The other levels are shown as subtopics on the slide. The formatting or styles in the Word outline will be imported into PowerPoint. See the illustration below:

- The imported outline can be edited and enhanced within PowerPoint. A template can be applied to the outline to give it a professional appearance.

- Data from Word or another application can be linked to PowerPoint so that the PowerPoint slide will update if the linked file is changed. As previously discussed, when linking Word and Excel files, the Copy, Paste Special, Paste Link options are selected to link application files in PowerPoint.

- An Excel chart or worksheet can be linked or embedded into a PowerPoint slide. To link a chart, the chart should be selected in Excel, copied, and linked using the Paste Special, Paste Link options.

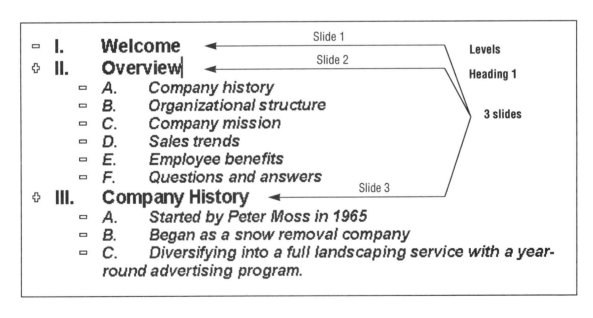

In this exercise, an outline created in Word for the Greenthumb Landscape Service will be imported into a PowerPoint presentation. The slides will be enhanced and a template style will be applied to the presentation.

EXERCISE DIRECTIONS:

. To import an outline:

a. Click the PowerPoint icon on the Microsoft Office Manager toolbar.

b. Click the Open button on the Standard toolbar.

c. Click Outlines from the List Files of Types list in the Open dialog box.

Files with a .DOC extension may be opened using the Outline type.

d. Open ⌨ **GREEN** or 🖫 **IGREEN.DOC**.

The outline is converted and imported into the PowerPoint format in outline view.

e. Click Slide view to see the outline as slides.

f. Use the navigation buttons to move through and check the slides.

g. Close the file without saving.

. To export an outline:

a. Click the Word icon on the Microsoft Office Manager toolbar.

b. Click the Open button on the Standard Toolbar.

c. Open ⌨ **GREEN** or 🖫 **IGREEN.DOC**.

d. Save the file as **GREEN** in Rich Text Format (RTF).

e. Switch to PowerPoint using the icon on the MOM toolbar.

f. Open **GREEN**.

g. Click the Slide view to see the outline as slides.

h. Use the navigation buttons to move through and check the slides.

. To apply a template design to the slides:

a. Click Format, Presentation Template.

b. Open the MSOFFICE\POWERPNT\TEMPLATE\CLROVRHD directory to view the templates available for overhead presentations in color.

c. Select CONFETIC.PPT.

d. Click Apply.

. Edit the Welcome slide; add the following text:

> ★ *Panel Members:*
> – *John Moss, President*
> – *Pamela Leigh, Finance*
> ★ *Presenter*
> – *Wendy Hynes, Vice President*

5. Edit the Employee Benefits slide:

Change the font size of the text to 24 point.

6. Edit the Questions and Answers slide; add the following text:

> ★ *Members of the panel and several architects from our landscaping department are available for questions.*
> ★ *Brochures*
> ★ *Portfolio of Elegant Gardens*

7. Save the file as **GREENPP**.

8. Link an Excel chart to the Sales Trends slide:

a. Switch to Excel by clicking the icon on the MOM toolbar.

b. Open 🖫 **ISQTRCHT.XLS**.

✓ *Note: If you do not have the data disk, use the ISQTRS file to create a column chart of the quarterly service fees, consultations, and total income figures with a legend and the following heading: Greenthumb Landscape Service Quarterly Income – 199-*

c. Select and copy the chart showing income trends.

d. Switch to PowerPoint by clicking the icon on the MOM toolbar.

e. Change to Slide view.

f. Paste Special, Paste Link the chart in the text box on the Sales Trend chart.

g. Adjust the size of the chart to fit the slide.

9. Return to the first slide and view the slides using the Slide Show view.

10. Switch to Slide Sorter view and add desired Build and Transition effects.

11. Check the presentation using the Slide Show view.

12. Save and close the file.

EXERCISE

8

■ EXPORT A POWERPOINT SLIDE INTO A WORD DOCUMENT ■ EXPORT A POWERPOINT PRESENTATION INTO A WORD DOCUMENT ■ EMBED A POWERPOINT PRESENTATION INTO A WORD DOCUMENT

NOTES:

■ You can bring a presentation or a slide into Word to create a handout or report that includes the slides and any additional text. Or, you can include a complete PowerPoint presentation in a Word document so that the slides may be viewed one at a time.

Export a PowerPoint Slide

■ If you wish to send one slide into a Word document, you can use the Copy, Paste method or the Copy, Paste Special, Paste Link procedure if the data should be linked.

Export a PowerPoint Presentation

■ Data from a PowerPoint presentation may be sent into a Word document using the Report It button on the Standard Toolbar in PowerPoint. If the Convert File dialog box appears, you must select the RTF (Rich Text Format) file type so that the file is saved in a format that Word can read. Normally, however, the file is automatically converted and you are switched to Word so that you can edit and save the document as a Word file. You can also export a presentation by using the Save As dialog box to save the presentation as an Outline (RTF) file, and then switch to Word and open the outline file.

Embed a PowerPoint Presentation

■ When you embed a PowerPoint presentation into a Word document, you are including it as an object which can be viewed using the PowerPoint Viewer. The PowerPoint Viewer becomes part of the presentation in Word and allows you to view the presentation, even if PowerPoint is not installed. The PowerPoint Viewer is a separate application that is included in PowerPoint that must be installed using the Office Setup program.

■ The PowerPoint presentation is embedded using the Insert, Object, Create from File tab selection in the Word document at the point where the presentation should appear. The first slide of the presentation will appear in the document at the point of insertion. The object can be clicked to size it to fit better in the document. To view the presentation, the embedded object should be double-clicked. A full-screen view of the first slide will appear. When the slide is clicked, the next slide appears. When the last slide is clicked, you will be returned to the Word document. Note the illustration of an embedded presentation.

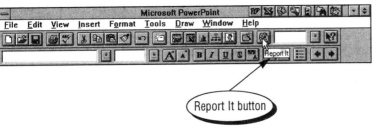

Report It button

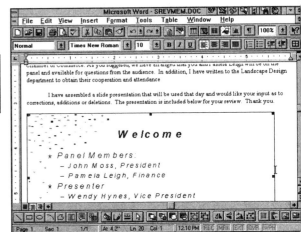

In this exercise, Wendy Hynes uses PowerPoint slides and presentations in three memoranda regarding the Greenthumb Landscaping Service presentation. The presentation will be embedded in one memorandum, a slide will be used in another, and the presentation outline will be edited in Word to create another document.

EXERCISE DIRECTIONS:

Export a Slide:

1. Click the Word icon on the Microsoft Office Manager bar.

2. Open 🖫 **ILANMEM.DOC,** or create the memo as indicated in Illustration A.

3. Add the additional text in the first paragraph.

4. Switch to PowerPoint using the icon on the MOM bar.

5. Open 🖾 **GREENPP** or 🖫 **IGREENPP.PPT**.

6. In Slide or Slide Sorter view, select the entire Question and Answer slide.

7. Using the Copy command, switch to the memorandum in Word, and paste the slide to the location indicated.

8. Click on the slide to select it and size it appropriately for the memorandum.

9. Save the file as **LANDMEM** and print one copy.

Export a Presentation Outline:

10. Switch to PowerPoint using the icon on the MOM bar.

11. Press the Report It button on the Standard Toolbar to open the outline in Word as a RTF file.

12. Make the insertions and deletions as indicated in Illustration B.

13. Add a line below the outline and the text indicated below:

What are your landscaping needs?

Total Redesign	_____
Total Landscape Care Program	_____
Seasonal Maintenance	_____
Winter only Maintenance	_____
Summer only Maintenance	_____
Feed and Weed Program	_____
Customized Program	_____
Consultation Only	_____

Name	_____
Firm	_____
Address	_____
City, State, Zip	_____
Telephone, extension	_____
Contact Person	_____

14. Save the file as **CONTACT.DOC**.

(Be sure to save the file as a Word document file. If it is saved as is, it will remain in RTF format.)

15. Print one copy of the document.

Embed a PowerPoint Presentation:

16. Open 🖫 **IREVMEM.DOC,** or create the memo as indicated in Illustration C.

17. At the insertion point specified, use the Insert, Object, Create from File tab procedures to insert the **GREENPP.PPT** file as an embedded object in the memorandum.

18. Find the edge of the presentation slide, click on it, and size the slide to fit appropriately into the memorandum.

The first slide of the presentation will appear on the memorandum.

19. Double-click the slide to view it on a full screen. Click to change and review each slide.

20. Save the memorandum as **REVMEM**.

21. Print one copy.

22. Close all files in all applications.

ILLUSTRATION A

M E M O R A N D U M

TO: Landscape Design Department

FROM: Wendy Hynes, Vice President

RE: March 15 Presentation

DATE: February 15, 199-

On Friday, March 15, we will be giving a presentation about our firm and our capabilities to the Chamber of Commerce. In our presentation, we will be discussing the growth of our landscape design and consultation divisions and will provide time for questions from the audience.

In addition, we expect to show the pictures and renderings in our Portfolio of Elegant Gardens. Please update the portfolio so that we can bring the latest pictures to the meeting.

Thank you for your assistance with this important project.

(Insert Text) Note the presentation slide below:

Insert Questions & Answers slide here

ILLUSTRATION B

Greenthumb Landscaping Service Presentation March 15, 199-

Welcome

★ Panel Members:
  – John Moss, President
  – Pamela Leigh, Finance
★ Presenter
  – Wendy Hynes, Vice President

Overview

★ Company history
★ Organizational structure
★ Company mission
★ Sales trends
★ Employee benefits
★ Questions and answers

Company History

★ Started by Peter Moss in 1965
★ Began as a snow removal company
★ Diversifying into a full landscaping service with a year-round advertising program.

Greenthumb Landscaping Service

★ John Moss, President
★ Wendy Hynes, Vice President
★ Pamela Leigh, Finance
★ Matt Chasin, Customer Service

Company Mission

★ To design quality landscapes in this city.
★ To maintain quality landscapes of all customers

~~Sales Trends~~
Employee Benefits

★ Health Benefits
  – Life Insurance
  – Medical, dental, optical
    › GHI
    › Major Medical
★ Commissions and Bonus
★ Vacation and Sick Leave
  – Vacation: 2 weeks after 12 months
  – Sick leave: 2.5 days earned each month
  – Extra provisions for employees who work winters

Questions and Answers

★ Members of the panel and several architects from our landscaping department are available for questions.
★ Brochures
★ Portfolio of Elegant Gardens

Insert new data here.

ILLUSTRATION C

MEMORANDUM

TO: John Moss, President

FROM: Wendy Hynes, Vice President

RE: March 15 Presentation

DATE: February 15, 199-

On Friday, March 15, I will be giving a presentation about our firm and our capabilities to the Chamber of Commerce. As you suggested, we have arranged that you and Pamela Leigh will be on the panel and available for questions from the audience.

I have assembled a slide presentation that will be used that day and would like your input as to corrections, additions or deletions from the data presented. The presentation is included below for your review. I have written to the Landscape Design department to obtain their cooperation and attendance. Thank you.

Insert presentation here.

XPORT A POWERPOINT RESENTATION INTO A WORD OCUMENT

Open the PowerPoint presentation to be exported.

Click **Report It** button on the standard toolbar.

The presentation will be converted to RTF file format and you are switched to Word with the document opened. It should be resaved as a Word document. If the Convert file dialog box opens, specify RTF format.

EMBED A POWERPOINT PRESENTATION INTO A WORD DOCUMENT

1. Open the Word document to receive the presentation.

2. Click **Insert**............................ Alt + I

3. Click **Object**.................................... O

4. Select **Create from File** tab.... Alt + F

5. Select directory and....................... ↑↓
    PowerPoint file to be embedded.

6. Click the edge of the file to size.

    The first slide of the presentation will appear on the memorandum.

VIEW AN EMBEDDED PRESENTATION

The PowerPoint Viewer, a separate application in PowerPoint, must be loaded into PowerPoint so that the presentation may be viewed in Word without having PowerPoint loaded.

1. Double-click on the first slide of the embedded presentation.

2. Click slide to change to the next slide.

3. After the last slide, you are returned to the document.

CHAPTER 6
SUMMARY EXERCISE 9
▪ Importing a PowerPoint Outline into Word ▪ Importing an Excel Worksheet into Word ▪ Importing an Excel Worksheet Object into PowerPoint ▪ Exporting a PowerPoint Slide into Word ▪ Mail Merge a Word Document ▪ Using an Access Database

In this exercise, Michael Miller, of the Finance department at the College, is making a presentation about investing in Brazil to his fellow college professors. He would like to obtain input from Ms Washington, his investment advisor affiliate, who will assist him at the meeting. Once her suggestions are incorporated into the presentation, a memo will be sent to the college professors that will be attending the meeting using the Mail Merge procedure. A slide will be incorporated into the memorandum.

EXERCISE DIRECTIONS:

1. Click the Word icon on the Microsoft Office Manager toolbar.
2. Open **IPRESENT.DOC** or create the letter as indicated in Illustration A.
3. Click the PowerPoint icon on the MOM toolbar
4. Open **IBRAZIL.PPT** and switch to outline view.
5. Copy the outline from PowerPoint into the Word document in the location indicated in the letter.
6. Since this is now a two page letter, place an appropriate header on the second page of the letter.
7. Save the file as **PRESENT** and print one copy.
8. Open **IREPLY.DOC** or create the response as indicated in Illustration B.
9. Switch to Excel using the icon on the MOM toolbar.
10. Open **IINFLAT.XLS** or create the worksheet and chart in Illustration C.
11. Select the chart and use the Copy, Paste Special procedure to embed the chart into the Word letter where indicated in the text.
12. Save the file as **REPLY** and print one copy.
13. Close the Excel file.
14. Switch to PowerPoint and modify the presentation as follows:
    Insert a new slide as Slide 7 with the heading, "Low Inflation"
15. Switch to Word and select the Excel chart object in the letter and copy it below the Low Inflation heading on Slide 7 in the PowerPoint presentation.

16. Continue to modify the presentation as follows.
    Edit Slide 1 which should read:
    Economic and Historical Prospectives on Brazilian Investment
    Presenter: Michael Miller
    Finance Department
    Assistant: Jennifer Washington
    Simpson Investment Advisors
    Use slide sorter to add builds and transitions for Slide 7.
17. Use slide show to view the presentation.
18. Save the presentation.
19. Click the Word icon on the Microsoft Office Manager toolbar.
20. Open **IINVITE.DOC** or create the memorandum as indicated in Illustration D.
21 Switch to PowerPoint and select the first slide in Slide or Slide Sorter view. Copy it to the memorandum below the text.
22. Create a main document (form letter) using the memorandum.
23. Select the data source to open **COLLEGE.MDB** or **ICOLLEGE.MDB**.
24. Edit the main document to insert merge fields to match the database.
25. Merge the files into a new document.
26. Scroll through the newly merged document to check the merge.
27. Save the file as **INVITMER**.
28. Close and save all files.

Today's date

Ms. Jennifer Washington
Simpson Investment Advisors
777 Madison Avenue
New York, NY 10022

Dear Ms. Washington:

I am writing regarding the upcoming presentation we will be making to the staff at the college on the topic of investments in Brazil. I will be using the historical and economic background of the country to interest the group in Brazilian investment. It is my position that the Brazilian economy has substantially recovered since the Brazilian debt crisis in the 1980s and that this may be a good time to invest profitably in specific situations in Brazil.

Find below a preliminary outline which I have drafted for the presentation:

Insert PowerPoint outline

If you have any suggestions or anything to add to this outline, please contact me as soon as possible. Otherwise, I will be in touch with you the week prior to the meeting to confirm hotel arrangements.

Sincerely yours,

Michael Miller
Finance Department

Today's date

Mr. Michael Miller
Boynton College
342 Palm Boulevard
Ocean City, VA 05555

Dear Mr. Miller:

Thank you for your letter regarding our presentation at the college on Brazilian investments. I trust that you will be filling in the historical and economic background from your extensive knowledge of the country.

In addition to setting up an introductory heading in the outline, I would suggest that you include some data on the vast changes in the inflation rate. I am including below a chart showing the trend of the inflation rate over the last 15 years. This is a clear indication of the changes that have taken place and it should be included in the section where you discuss the current low inflation rate.

Insert chart

I look forward to seeing you in two weeks and will call to confirm my arrangements for the visit. Thank you.

Sincerely yours,

Jennifer Washington
Investment Advisor

ILLUSTRATION C

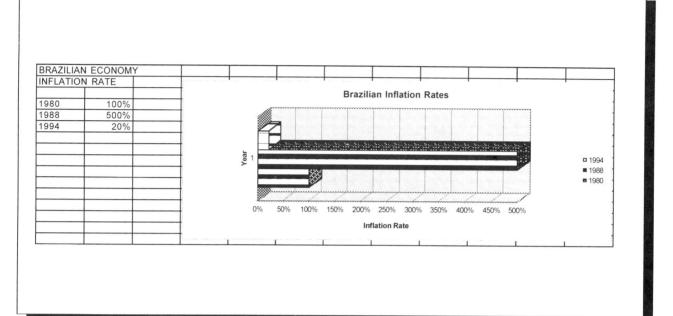

BRAZILIAN ECONOMY	
INFLATION RATE	
1980	100%
1988	500%
1994	20%

ILLUSTRATION D

MEMORANDUM

TO:	Title FirstName LastName
DEPARTMENT:	Department
BUILDING:	Building
FROM:	Michael Miller
	Finance Department
RE:	Monthly Investment Seminar
DATE:	Today's date

This month our meeting will focus on Brazil. We will be joined by Ms. Jennifer Washington of the Simpson Investment Advisors group. The meeting will be held in the Faculty Lounge in Beaver Hall at 8:00 p.m. on the last Tuesday evening of the month.

As in the past, please note below the introductory slide of our presentation and post this notice in your department office. Thank you.

INDEX

477

INDEX

Transparencies For Training

Talk to your students with the screen illustration in front of you, and they will see what you are explaining. Every word has double impact when you point to the screen element you are discussing. Nothing beats the visual it all boils down to this: Do you want to teach quickly, or do you want to teach slowly? What's your teaching time worth?

If this screen was sitting on your projector, large as life, and you had your pointer, how would you go about explaining spreadsheets?

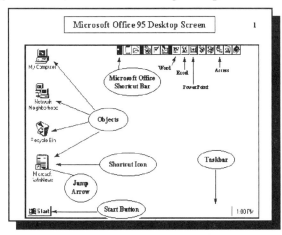 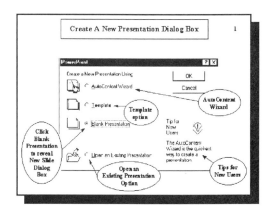

Price $50 ea. Each set contains 20 transparencies, index sheet, & album.

F-44	Access 7	F-45	PowerPoint 7 for Windows 95
F-36	DOS 5-6.22	F-35	Windows 3.1 & 3.1
F-37	Excel 5	F-41	Windows 95
F-43	Excel 7 for Windows 95	F-38	Word 6
F-33	Lotus 1-2-3 DOS	F-47	Word 7 for Windows 95
F-46	Lotus 1-2-3 Windows Rel. 5	F-39	WordPerfect 5.1 DOS
F-34	Lotus 1-2-3 Windows	F-31	WordPerfect 6.0 DOS
F-40	MS Office 4.3	F-32	WordPerfect 6.0 Win
F-48	MS Office Windows 95	F-42	WordPerfect 6.1 Win
		F-49	Works 4 Windows 95

275 Madison Avenue, New York, NY 10016
Ph.: 800-528-3897, Fax: 800-528-3862

MATERIALS

Vocabulary   **Points to Emphasize**

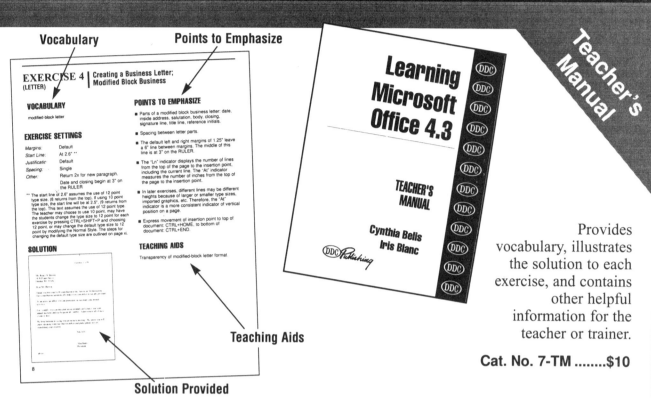

Teaching Aids

Solution Provided

Provides vocabulary, illustrates the solution to each exercise, and contains other helpful information for the teacher or trainer.

Cat. No. 7-TM $10

3 1/2" Disks

Selected transparencies of screens, menus, and dialog boxes. Call outs define and explain as you teach.

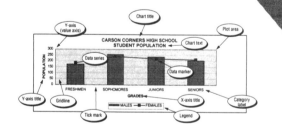

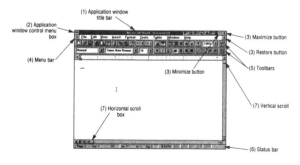

Data Disks provide the data for each exercise. They reduce keyboarding which enables the trainer to skip exercises.

Solution Disks provide the solution to each exercise as it should appear on your screen. They also check the accuracy of your work.

Data Disks Cat. No. DDZ-6 (4 disks) $15

Data Disks Site License Cat. No. DDZ-6SL $65

Solutions Disks Cat. No. SLZ-6 (5 disks)...........$17.50

Solutions Disks Site License   Cat. No. SLZ-6SL $65

Microsoft® Office 4.3
20 Transparencies Cat. No. F40 ....$50

We just put a teacher in your computer...

"Did I hear that right? I always have trouble learning computer software."

Yes, and DDC Publishing's new **CD-ROM Interactive training method** makes it that way and much more.

"Are you sure? All the other teaching methods that I have tried bored me."

LESSON OBJECTIVES

HINT BUTTON FOR HELP

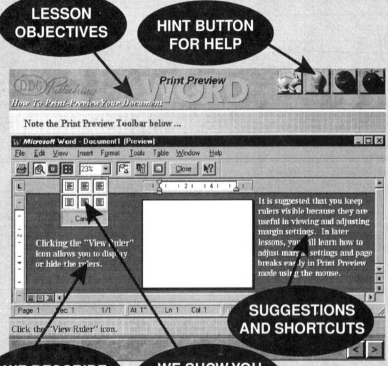

WE DESCRIBE THE FEATURE

WE SHOW YOU THE MENUS AND DIALOG BOXES

SUGGESTIONS AND SHORTCUTS

Computer based training for Introductory Microsoft® Office Windows® 95 to teach Word 7, Excel 7, Access 7, and PowerPoint 7

Our computer scientists present their instructions orally and visually, live and on screen. Their CD ROM takes the written word off the page, talks to the learner, explains the concept, and tells you what to do.
You hear and see the instructions along with a demonstration on how to perform the function.

You hear, you see, you do, you learn.
Our computer teacher has been programmed to advise you when a mistake is made, and to ask you to try again, until you get it correct. Our CD ROM also gives a quiz. It is programmed to score and record your performance so that you can see your progress.
You can skip around and work on only those functions needed. We also made a correlated workbook with reinforcement exercises, optional.

Talk about motivation!
If you have our computer based trainer in your computers you have a personal instructor at your command. This teacher sits right at their elbow, sight unseen, ready to correct your errors and tell you how to do it. Until you get it correct.
Our CBT provides the additional learning you need to achieve passing grades.

DDC® Quick Reference Guides
find software answers faster
because you read less

FREE TEMPLATE ON BACK COVER

What took you five minutes now takes one minute.

The illustrated instructions put your fingers on the correct keys – fast. We tell you what to do in five or six words. Sometimes only two.

No narration or exposition. Just "press this – type that" illustrated commands.

Spiral binding keeps pages flat so you can type what you read.

The time you save will pay for the book the first day. Free template on back cover.

Office Managers

Look at the production time you can gain when these quick-find, low-cost guides go to work for you. It will pay for the guides the first day you use them.

ORDER FORM

QTY.	GUIDE	CAT. NO.
__	Access 2 for Win	O-AX2
__	Access 7 for Win 95	AX95
__	Computer Terms	D-18
__	Corel WordPerfect Suite Win 95	G-11
__	Corel WordPerfect 7 for Win 95	G-12
__	DOS 6.0 - 6.22	O-DS62
__	Excel 5 for Win	F-18
__	Excel 7 for Win 95	XL7
__	Internet	I-17
__	Laptops & Notebooks	LM-18
__	Lotus 1-2-3 Rel. 3.1 DOS	J-18
__	Lotus 1-2-3 Rel. 3.4 DOS	L3-17
__	Lotus 1-2-3 Rel. 4.0 DOS	G-4
__	Lotus 1-2-3 Rel. 4.0 Win	O-301-3
__	Lotus 1-2-3 Rel. 5.0 Win	L-19
__	Lotus 1-2-3 Rel. 6 Win	G-13
__	Lotus Notes 3	O-LN3
__	Lotus Notes 4	G-15
__	Lotus Smartsuite	SS-17
__	Microsoft Office	MO-17
__	Microsoft Office for Win 95	MO-95
__	MS Project for Win 3.1&95	MP-17
__	Mosaic/World Wide Web	WW-17
__	MS Works 3 for Win	O-WKW3
__	PageMaker 5 Win & Mac	PM-18

QTY.	GUIDE	CAT. NO.
__	Paradox 4.5 for Win	PW-18
__	PerfectOffice	PO-17
__	PowerPoint 4.0 for Win	O-PPW4
__	PowerPoint 7 for Win 95	PPW7
__	Quattro Pro 6 for Win	QPW6
__	Quicken 8 for DOS	QKD8
__	Windows 3.1 & 3.11	N3-17
__	Windows 95	G-6
__	Word 6.0 for Win	O-WDW6
__	Word 7 for Win 95	WDW7
__	WordPerfect 5.1+ DOS	W-5.1
__	WordPerfect 5.1/5.2 Win	Z-17
__	WordPerfect 6.0 for DOS	W-18
__	WordPerfect 6.1 for DOS	G-10
__	WordPerfect 6.0 for Win	O-WPW6
__	WordPerfect 6.1 for Win	W-19
__	Works 4 for Win 95	WKW4

Desktop Publishing

QTY.	GUIDE	CAT. NO.
__	Word 6.0 for Win	G-3
__	WordPerfect 5.1 for DOS	R-5

SEE OUR COMPLETE CATALOG ON THE INTERNET
@:http://www.ddcpub.com

DDC Publishing
275 Madison Avenue,
New York, NY 10016

$12 each **$15** hardcover edition

BUY 3 GUIDES GET ONE FREE

Phone: 800-528-3897
Fax: 800-528-3862

☐ Visa ☐ MasterCard

No._____ Exp._____

☐ Check enclosed. Add $2 for postage & handling & $1 postage for ea. add. guide. NY State res. add local sales tax.

Name _____

Firm _____

Address _____

City, State, Zip _____

Telephone No. _____

Short Course Learning Books
Approximately 25 hours of instruction per book

We sliced our learning books into short courses, *introductory* & *intermediate*.

- We extracted pages from our Fast-teach Learning books and created shortened versions.
- Each book comes with a data disk to eliminate typing the exercise.

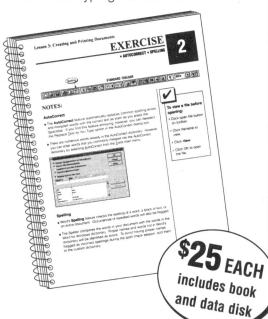

$25 EACH includes book and data disk

Title	Cat. No.	Title	Cat. No.	Title	Cat. No.
Access 2 Introductory	AB-10	Microsoft Office 4.3 Introductory	AB-14	WordPerfect 6.1 Win Introductory	AB-1
Access 7 Introductory	AB-23	Microsoft Office Win 95 Introductory	AB-15	WordPerfect 6.1 Win Intermediate	AB-2
DOS Introductory	AB-13	PowerPoint 4 Introductory	AB-11	Word 6 Windows Introductory	AB-4
Excel 5 Windows Introductory	AB-7	PowerPoint 7 Introductory	AB-24	Word 6 Windows Intermediate	AB-5
Excel 5 Windows Intermediate	AB-8	Windows 3.1 Introductory	AB-12	Word 7 Windows 95 Introductory	AB-17
Excel 7 Windows 95 Introductory	AB-20				

New Short Courses (College Level)....$25ea.
Teacher Manual and Exercise
Solutions on Diskette ....$12ea.
Files saved in Word 7

Title	Cat No.
Microsoft Office Windows 95	AB-15
Pagemaker 6 Intro	AB-16
No Teacher Manual	
Word 7 Intro	AB-17
Word 7 Intermed (OCTOBER)	AB-18
Word 7 Advanced (OCTOBER)	AB-19
Excel 7 Intro	AB-20
Excel 7 Intermed (OCTOBER)	AB-21
PowerPoint 7 Intro	AB-15
Access 7 Intro	AB-23

ORDER FORM

DDC Publishing 275 Madison Avenue, New York, NY 10016

QTY.	CAT. NO.	DESCRIPTION

☐ Check enclosed. Add $2.50 for postage & handling & $1 postage for each additional guide. NY State residents add local sales tax.

☐ Visa ☐ Mastercard   ***100% Refund Guarantee***

No._____ Exp._____

Name_____

Firm _____

Address_____

City, State, Zip _____

Phone (800) 528-3897   Fax (800) 528-3862